MICROECONOMICS

177.17

MICROECONOMICS

Roger A. Arnold
University of Nevada, Las Vegas

West Publishing Company

St. Paul ■ New York ■ Los Angeles ■ San Francisco

COPY EDITING: Pat Lewis
COMPOSITION: Parkwood Composition Service
ARTWORK: John and Jean Foster and Rolin Graphics
PROOFREADING: Elaine Levin
COVER: *Centrion* by Brian Halsey, copyright 1980

COPYRIGHT ©1989 **By WEST PUBLISHING COMPANY**
50 W. Kellogg Boulevard
P.O. Box 64526
St. Paul, MN 55164-1003

Printed in the United States of America

96 95 94 93 92 91 90 89   8 7 6 5 4 3 2 1

Library of Congress Cataloging-in-Publication Data

Arnold, Roger A.
  Microeconomics / Roger A. Arnold.
    p.   cm.
  Includes index.
  ISBN 0-314-47687-3
  1. Microeconomics.   I. Title.
HB172.A675   1989   88-37295
338.5--dc19   CIP

Photo Credits

34 The Granger Collection; **37** Gary S. Becker; **66** Historical Pictures Service, Inc., Chicago; **103** Historical Pictures Service, Inc., Chicago; **196** Historical Pictures Service, Inc., Chicago; **198** George J. Stigler; **219** Gordon Tullock; **228** Arthur Grace, The New York Times; **242** Cynthia Larson; **354** Jane Reed, Harvard University; **385** Harold Demsetz; **388** Washington University in St. Louis Photographic Services; **411** Carl Zitzmann; **427** The Granger Collection; **435** Michael J. Lutch; **487** Marnie Crawford Samuelson; **501** Murray Rothbard; **506** The Granger Collection; **521** Robert Lekachman.

Acknowledgments

4 Buchanan, James. *What Should Economists Do?* (Indianapolis: Liberty Press, 1979), p. 120. Reprinted with permission. **9** Reprinted by permission of The Putnam Publishing Group from *On the Road with Charles Kuralt* by Charles Kuralt. Copyright © 1985 by Charles Kuralt. **14** Friedman, Milton. "The Methodology of Positive Economics," *Essays in Positive Economics* (Chicago: The University of Chicago Press, 1953), p. 15. Reprinted with permission. **77** Radford, R. A. "The Economic Organization of a P.O.W. Camp," *Economica* (November 1945), p. 189–201. Reprinted with permission. **138** From TWO CHEERS FOR CAPITALISM, by Irving Kristol. Copyright © 1978 by Basic Books, Inc. Reprinted by permission of Basic Books, Inc., Publishers. **149** Samuelson, Paul. "Proof That Properly Discounted Present Values of Assets Vibrate Randomly." Copyright 1973. Reprinted from *The Bell Journal of Economics* with permission of the RAND Corporation. **161** Friedman, David. *Price Theory: An Intermediate Text.* (Cincinnati: South-Western Publishing Company, 1986), p. 280. Reprinted with permission. **238** Posner, Richard A. "Theories of Regulation." Copyright 1974. Reprinted from *The Bell Journal of Economics* with permission of the RAND Corporation. **356** Friedman, Milton. *Capitalism and Freedom.* (Chicago: The University of Chicago Press, 1952), p. 191. Reprinted with permission. **401 , top:** Buchanan, James. *The Limits of Liberty, between Anarchy and Leviathan.* (Chicago: The University of Chicago Press, 1975), p. 149. Reprinted with permission. **Middle:** From the song *Elected* by Alice Cooper. Reprinted with permission. **403** Cartoon from *The Wall Street Journal*—Permission, Cartoon Features Syndicate. **510** Smith, Adam. *The Theory of Moral Sentiments.* (Oxford: Oxford University Press, 1976), p. 234. Reprinted with permission.
Material from *The New Palgrave: A Dictionary of Economics* reprinted with permission from Macmillan Press Ltd.

To
Sheila and Daniel

Contents in Brief

AN INTRODUCTION TO ECONOMICS — 1

Part 1 The Essentials of Economic Thinking 3

MICROECONOMICS — 91

Part 2 Microeconomic Fundamentals 93

Part 3 Microeconomic Theories (Product Markets) 177

Contents

Chapter 3 Supply, Demand, and Price: Theory 49

Chapter 4 Supply, Demand, and Price: Applications 74

MICROECONOMICS   91

Part 2   Microeconomic Fundamentals   93

Chapter 5   The Logic of Consumer Choice   94

Appendix B   Budget Constraint and Indifference Curve Analysis

Chapter 6 Elasticity

Chapter 7 The Firm   137

Part 3 Microeconomic Theories (Product Markets) 177

Chapter 11   Monopolistic Competition and Oligopoly   224

Part 4   Microeconomic Theories (Factor Markets)   251

Part 5   Microeconomic Problems and Public Policy   313

Chapter 15   Agriculture: Problems and Policies   314

Chapter 16   The Distribution of Income and Poverty   332

THE WORLD ECONOMY   415

Part 6 International Economics: Theory and Policy 417

Chapter 20   International Trade   418

Preface

The stature of economics has grown in the recent past. There are, I believe, two major reasons for this. First, people have come to realize that economics plays an important role in their lives. Recession, inflation, the exchange value of the dollar, the savings rate, taxes, mergers, business starts, the budget and trade deficits, all matter. They touch lives, they affect dreams.

Second, economists have developed better tools and more refined methods of analysis; they have extended their analytical apparatus beyond the traditional confines of the science into such areas as sociology, law, political science, biology, and more. There have been peaks and valleys along the way, but mostly economics has performed well.

The challenge for the economics textbook writer today is to convey to the student all that has occurred and is occurring in economics in a way that is understandable, exciting, and meaningful. Specifically, I believe the principles book should accomplish three goals: (1) Introduce the student to the facts, concepts, and analytic methods of economics. (2) Use the tools of economics to give the students a better handle on their world. (3) Push the frontier of the students' world outward. I have tried my best to meet all three goals in this book in a way that allows students to experience some of the richness, subtlety, and power of economics.

ORGANIZATION

This book is organized into three sections. Section I discusses the key concepts and tools in economics. Two of the four chapters are devoted to supply-and-demand analysis. On completion of this section, the student should have a solid understanding of the economic way of thinking.

Section II focuses on the theoretical underpinnings of economics, microeconomic theory. I have tried to be rigorous in developing microeconomic tools and generous with applications, knowing that it is the constant back and forth between theory and applications that gives the student an appreciation of the explanatory and predictive power of economics.

Section III contains generous quantities of microeconomic analysis applied to the world economy. Here I have used economic analysis to try to unravel the mysteries of international economic events, and to show students how these events, far removed in space from their home, city, state, or nation, can nevertheless sharply affect their world.

PEDAGOGY AND SPECIAL FEATURES

To motivate the student and make the learning experience more interesting and fulfilling, this book contains the following pedagogical features:

Introduction. The chapter introduction was designed to capture the student's attention and to pique his or her curiosity.

What This Chapter Is About. This feature serves as a road map for the chapter, noting the topics that will be discussed and in what order.

Key Questions to Keep in Mind as You Read. Each chapter begins with key questions that focus the student's attention on what is important in the chapter.

Interspersed Questions and Answers. Throughout each chapter are questions that students may ask as they are reading. Each question is then answered by the author. The question-answer format allows the student to have their questions answered as they arise and to play a more active role in the learning process. This is a unique feature of this book.

Margin Definitions. Key words are printed in boldface and defined in the margins as well as in the text.

Glossary. All margin definitions are listed alphabetically in the glossary at the end of the book.

Economics In Our Times. This is one of the two applications features in the book. Economics In Our Times applications focus on current, exciting topics that are of particular interest to students.

Theory in Practice. Theory in Practice applications go beyond the student's world and immediate interests and apply economic theory in areas of special importance to professional economists. The mix of Theory and Practice and Economics In Our Times is designed to both deal with and extend the student's interests.

Interviews. Twelve well-known economists were interviewed expressly for this book on topics that the student will be familiar with, having read the material in the chapter in which an interview appears. Not only do the interviews provide the student with insights into the thinking of some of our most respected contemporary economists but also in many cases they give a glimpse of these persons' experiences and personalities. The economists interviewed include George Stigler, Robert Solow, James Buchanan, Lester Thurow, Murray Rothbard, John Kenneth Galbraith, Gary Becker, William Baumol, Harold Demsetz, Robert Lekachman, Gordon Tullock, and Murray Weidenbaum.

Biographies. Biographical sketches of famous economists are used in this book to convey to the student some of the rich history of economics in more personal terms.

Summary. Summary points at the end of each chapter are categorized according to topic heading.

Questions to Answer and Discuss. End-of-chapter questions are based on the material discussed in the chapter and are answered in the instructor's manual.

DIAGRAMS

Diagrams are an integral part of the economic way of thinking, and as all economics instructors know, the sooner and more comfortably students begin to "think diagrammatically," the better. A personal objective has been to write a book that contains clear, colorful, complete-captioned diagrams that draw the student into them. To this end, each diagram in this book has been carefully crafted to mix color, content, and substance in a way that conveys the central message of the piece at a glance, while subtly informing the student "why" and "how" economists use diagrams.

SUPPLEMENTS

This book is accompanied by a complete teaching and learning package. The *Study Guide* was principally written by Thomas Wyrick (Southwest Missouri State University). Each chapter explains, reviews, and tests the student on important facts, concepts, and diagrams found in corresponding chapters in this book. Chapter parts include an introduction to and purpose of the chapter, a review of concepts from earlier chapters, a fill-in-the-blank review of concepts to be learned, and problems and exercises. I wrote the self-test that ends each chapter.

The *Instructor's Manual* was written by Keith A. Rowley (Baylor University) and offers detailed lecture assistance for this book. Chapter parts include an overview of each text chapter, a list of chapter objectives, a list of key terms, a detailed chapter outline with lecture notes, and answers to end-of-chapter questions.

Twenty *Enrichment Lectures* with accompanying transparencies are included in the supplement package. The lectures are on current topics of high interest to instructors and students alike. The lectures were prepared by Keith A. Rowley (Baylor University) and Thomas Wyrick (Southwest Missouri State University).

Dale Boisso (Southwest Missouri State University), Terry Ridgway (University of Nevada, Las Vegas) and I prepared the *Test Bank*. There are an average of 90 questions per chapter, 75 multiple-choice and 15 true-false. Each set of chapter questions tests the student's knowledge of definitions, facts, diagrams, concepts, theory, policy, and applications. The test bank is available on *Westest Microcomputer Testing Service*, which allows instructors to select or randomly generate test questions.

Audio Cassette Tapes provide students with a chapter by chapter review of major economic concepts. The tape scripts were written by Keith A. Rowley (Baylor University).

Software Tutorials for both macroeconomics and microeconomics are available. Each tutorial contains 10 modules that explain and test a student on the key theory issues discussed in this book.

Transparencies. The supplement package includes transparencies of key exhibits featured in the text and in the 20 enrichment lectures. There are 100 transparencies in total.

IN APPRECIATION

This book could not have been written and published without the generous and expert assistance of many people. A deep debt of gratitude is owed to the 76 reviewers of this book, who offered their detailed comments, suggestions, and ideas. I am indebted to:

Jack Adams
University of Arkansas, Little Rock

William Askwig
University of Southern Colorado

Michael Babcock
Kansas State University

Dan Barszcz
College of DuPage, Illinois

Robert Berry
Miami University, Ohio

George Bohler
Florida Junior College

Tom Bonsor
Eastern Washington University

Michael D. Brendler
Louisiana State University

Baird Brock
Central Missouri State University

Kathleen Bromley
Monroe Community College, New York

Kathleen Brook
New Mexico State University

Douglas Brown
Georgetown University

Ernest Buchholz
*Santa Monica Community College,
    California*

Gary Burbridge
Grand Rapids Junior College, Michigan

Maureen Burton
*California State Polytechnic University,
    Pomona*

Carol Carnes
Kansas State University

Paul Coomes
University of Louisville, Kentucky

Eleanor Craig
University of Delaware

Diane Cunningham
Glendale Community College, California

Wilford Cummings
Grossmont College, California

Douglas C. Darran
University of South Carolina

Edward Day
University of Central Florida

Johan Deprez
University of Tennessee

James Dietz
California State University, Fullerton

Stuart Dorsey
University of West Virginia

Richard Douglas
Bowling Green State University, Ohio

Natalia Drury
Northern Virginia Community College

Lu Ann Duffus
California State University, Hayward

John Eckalbar
California State University, Chico

John Elliott
University of Southern California

Charles Fischer
Pittsburg State University, Kansas

John Gemello
San Francisco State University

Carl Guelzo
Catonsville Community College, Maryland

Jan Hansen
University of Wisconsin, Eau Claire

John Henderson
Georgia State University

Ken Howard
East Texas Baptist University

Mark Karscig
Central Missouri State University

Stanley Keil
Ball State University, Indiana

Richard Kieffer
State University of New York, Buffalo

Gene Kimmett
William Rainey Harper College, Illinois

Luther Lawson
University of North Carolina

Frank Leori
College of San Mateo, California

Kenneth Long
New River Community College, Virginia

Michael Magura
University of Toledo, Ohio

Bruce McCrea
Lansing Community College, Michigan

Gerald McDougall
Wichita State University, Kansas

Kevin McGee
University of Wisconsin, Oshkosh

Francois Melese
Auburn University, Alabama

Herbert Miliken
American River College, California

Richard Miller
Pennsylvania State University

Ernest Moser
Northeast Louisiana University

Farhang Niroomand
University of Southern Mississippi

Eliot Orton
New Mexico State University

Marty Perline
Wichita State University, Kansas

Harold Petersen
Boston College

Douglas Poe
University of Texas, Austin

Joseph Rezny
St. Louis Community College, Missouri

Terry Ridgway
University of Nevada, Las Vegas

Thomas Romans
State University of New York, Buffalo

Robert Ross
Bloomsburg State College, Pennsylvania

Keith A. Rowley
Baylor University, Texas

Anandi Sahu
Oakland University, Michigan

Richard Scoggins
California State University, Long Beach

Alan Sleeman
Western Washington University

John Sondey
University of Idaho

Shahram Shafiee
North Harris County College, Texas

Paul Seidenstat
Temple University, Pennsylvania

Robert W. Thomas
Iowa State University

Roger Trenary
Kansas State University

Richard L. Tontz
California State University, Northridge

Bruce Vanderporten
Loyola University, Illinois

Richard O. Welch
University of Texas at San Antonio

Thomas Weiss
University of Kansas

Donald A. Wells
University of Arizona

John Wight
University of Richmond, Virginia

Thomas Wyrick
Southwest Missouri State University

I offer my sincerest thanks to the twelve economists who appear in the interviews in this book. Each was generous with his or her time, genuinely interested in reaching students, and always gracious. Their contributions have greatly added to the range and richness of views found in this book.

My deep appreciation goes to Thomas Wyrick, who besides writing the study guide and five enrichment lectures, read the entire manuscript and provided detailed comments and invaluable suggestions. Only a good and true friend would be so generous with his time and care so much that the finished product be as good as it could be. I had numerous long and detailed conversations with Terry Ridgway during the writing of this book, and for his patience and helpfulness in this regard, as well as for his work on the test bank, I will always be grateful. I am also thankful to Keith Rowley, who had his capable hands in three supplement projects (instructor's manual, enrichment lectures, scripts for the audio cassette tapes), but still had time to advise and guide. My thanks also to Dale Boisso (Southwest Missouri State University) for his work on the test bank, and to Larry Cox (Southwest Missouri State University) for the price index data.

The person who is most directly responsible for the finished product you have in your hands, and to whom I owe the deepest debt of gratitude, is Clyde Perlee, Jr., editor-in-chief of West's college division. He saw this book in me even before I did. Whatever it is that makes an extraordinary editor, he has it in abundance. I am in awe of his creativity, his editor's sixth sense, and I deeply value his friendship. My heartfelt thanks go to Bill Stryker, who, as production editor, skillfully handled the myriad tasks to bring this book into the world. He deserves special credit for the book's appearance. He is simply the best at what he does. I am also grateful to Theresa O'Dell, developmental editor for this book. She worked hard and capably communicating with reviewers and arranging and supervising the details of the supplement package. She also made working on this project fun.

Others who worked on this project and whose efforts I appreciate include: Pat Lewis, copy editor; Elaine Levin, proofreader; Kristin McCarthy, coordinator for the marketing program; Jeff King of Rolin Graphics and John and Jean Foster for their art work; and Lucinda Gatch for her work on the software tutorials.

On a more personal level, it means much to be able to thank my mother and father, who indirectly are responsible for this book by emphasizing, throughout my life, the importance of an education, and for giving me the means and desire to acquire it. I am also thankful to my sister, Elizabeth, who has always offered her friendship and support.

I owe the deepest personal debt to Sheila, my wife. She has provided me with the encouragement, time, and inspiration to do what needed to be done, day after day, to write a book like this. Without her, accomplishment would mean little. To Daniel, my son, who will be one-year old when this book is published, I thank for daily crawling down the hallway of our home, pushing open my office door, and giving me a big smile as I was writing. No joy could be greater.

RAA

MICROECONOMICS

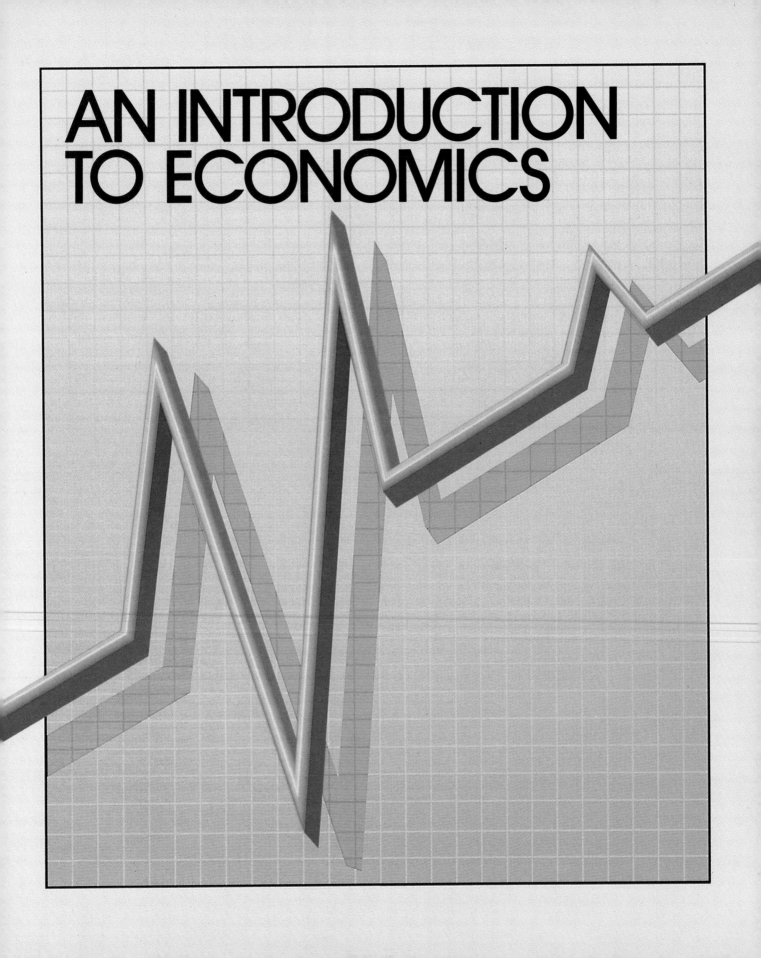

AN INTRODUCTION TO ECONOMICS

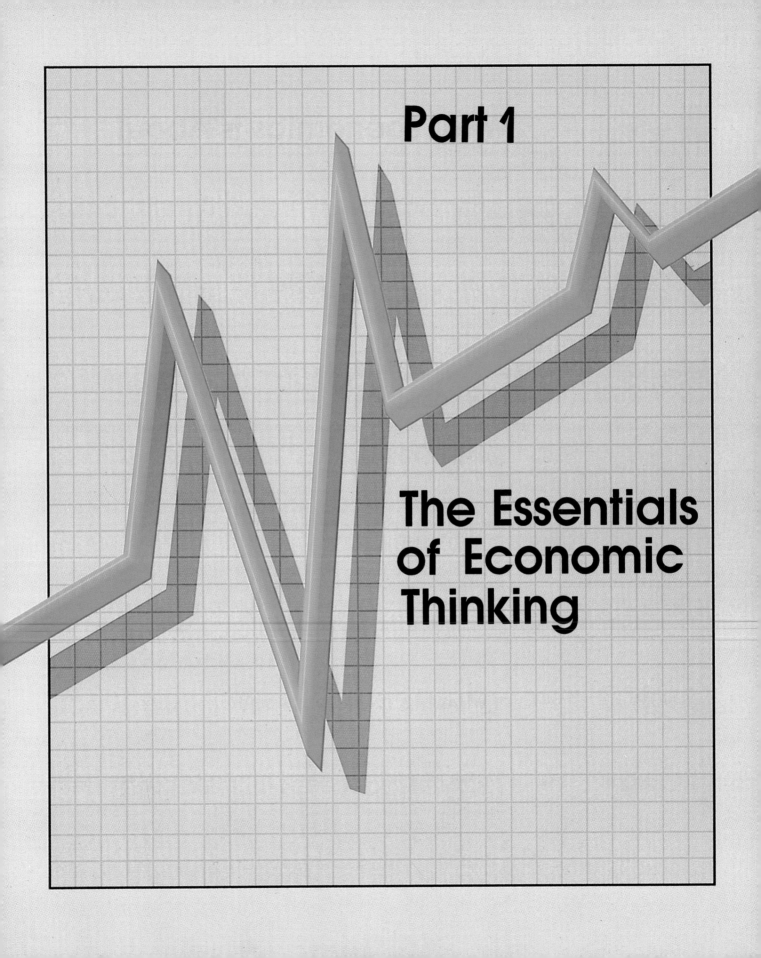

Part 1

The Essentials of Economic Thinking

Chapter 1

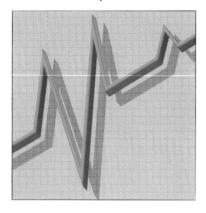

What Economics Is About

■ INTRODUCTION

Think of how the world looks to a person without perfect eyesight. Without eyeglasses, everything looks fuzzy and unclear. Some things only 10 to 20 feet away are, for all practical purposes, invisible. Now slip on the glasses. Ahhh, how comforting. The world is in focus. Things that once were invisible are now visible.

Economics is a lot like eyeglasses. It turns a fuzzy picture into a clear one and often makes the invisible visible. James Buchanan, a Nobel Prize winner in economics, said that "what a science [for example, economics] does, or should do, is simply to allow the average man . . . to command the heights of genius. The basic tools are the simple principles, and these are chained forever to the properly disciplined professional. Without them, he is a jibbering idiot, who makes only noise under an illusion of speech."[1]

Think about it. Economics makes it possible for the average person to command the heights of genius. Keep that in mind as you approach the study of economics. It tells you something of the power of economics . . . and of what it can do for you.

■ WHAT THIS CHAPTER IS ABOUT

Economics professors are quick to point out to their students that there is an *economic way of thinking*, and that the faster it is mastered, the more they will enjoy studying economics, the better they will understand the world they live in, and the higher their exam grades will be. At which point the student may say, "Tell me what the economic way of thinking is so that all these good things will be mine."

It would be nice if it were that easy. Some argue that the economic way of thinking is not something one can teach the way one teaches facts. A fact—Thomas Jefferson was born in 1743, for example—can be taught and learned easily: It requires only

[1]James Buchanan, *What Should Economists Do?* (Indianapolis: Liberty Press, 1979) p. 120. Reprinted with permission.

that one person make a statement and another person hear that statement. Message delivered, message received.

The economic way of thinking is not a fact. Dictionaries and encyclopedias do not define it; even economics textbooks do not define it in a strict and formal way (you won't find a definition in a textbook glossary, for example). Do not blame the authors of the textbooks, for even if they attempted a definition, it would be incomplete, unsatisfactory, and subject to misinterpretation.

How then do people learn about this important but mysterious concept, the economic way of thinking? They learn by *watching* economists do economics, by *thinking* about what the economists are doing and how they are doing it, and by *identifying* the essence of economic problem solving. *Watch, think, identify.* The economic way of thinking takes time and effort, but it is worth both. In this chapter we begin the journey with a discussion of the basics of economics: scarcity, choice, and opportunity cost. The chapter concludes with a discussion of the nature and role of theory in economics.

Key Questions To Keep In Mind As You Read

1. What is economics?
2. What is scarcity?
3. What is the relationship between scarcity and choice?
4. What is opportunity cost?
5. Why do economists construct theories?
6. What are some of the errors in economic thinking?
7. What is positive economics? Normative economics? Microeconomics? Macroeconomics?

THE BASICS OF ECONOMICS: SCARCITY, CHOICE, OPPORTUNITY COST

In this section we start with a definition of economics. Next we discuss the basics of economics, which include scarcity, choice, and opportunity cost. Here are a few of the questions we shall ask and answer. What is scarcity? What are the consequences of scarcity? What is the relationship between scarcity and choice? What is the relationship between choice and opportunity cost?

What Is Economics?

Consider the definitions of economics put forth by three economists:

■ Alfred Marshall defined economics as "a study of mankind in the ordinary business of life . . ."
■ Milton Friedman said that economics "is the science of how a particular society solves its economic problems."
■ Lionel Robbins, whose definition of economics is widely cited, said that economics is "the science which studies human behavior as a relationship between ends and scarce means which have alternative uses."

Do these different definitions of economics have anything in common? We think they do. Two of the definitions refer to economics as a *science* (Friedman and Robbins). One refers explicitly to *means* and *ends* (Robbins), and one implicitly to *ends* (Friedman). One refers explicitly to the *alternative uses of the means* (Robbins). All three economists, Marshall, Friedman, and Robbins, refer either explicitly or

Economics

The science that deals with the actions of individuals and societies directed toward meeting certain ends in a world where the means necessary to meet those ends have alternative uses.

Scarcity

The condition where our wants outstrip the limited resources available to satisfy those wants.

Good

Anything from which individuals receive utility or happiness.

Bad

Anything from which individuals receive disutility.

Utility

The satisfaction or happiness one receives from the consumption of a good.

implicitly to individual or societal *actions*. Distilling the essence of these definitions of economics, we define **economics** as

1. the science, that
2. deals with the actions of individuals and societies, whereby
3. those actions are directed toward meeting certain ends, in
4. a world where the means necessary to meet those ends have alternative uses.

Scarcity

Some things have always been and always will be. For example, gravity has always existed and always will exist; the earth has always been round and always will be round. There has always been scarcity, and there always will be scarcity.

What is scarcity? **Scarcity** is the condition where our wants outstrip the limited resources available to satisfy those wants. Scarcity is the basic economic problem facing all individuals and all societies. Bluntly put, given the wants of people, there is never enough.

We need to be careful, however. When we say "there is never enough," someone might retort "never enough of *what?*" Do we mean that there is never enough of everything in the world—from apples to pollution? Might there be too much of some things—pollution, for example? Economists break down "things" in the world into two categories: **goods** and **bads.** A good is anything from which individuals receive **utility** or happiness. A bad is anything from which individuals receive disutility. Goods are such things as clothing, education, leisure time, food, television sets, and houses. Bads are such things as pollution and garbage.

The category *goods* is broken down further into *economic goods* and *free goods*. A free good is a good sufficiently available from nature to satisfy all possible desires. More formally, a free good is a good where the amount available is greater than the amount people want at zero price. An example would be clean air before the days of air pollution.

An economic good is scarce: It is a good for which the quantity available is less than people would want if it were given away at zero price. All the goods we listed above (clothing, houses, television sets), and many more are economic goods.

So when we ask, Never enough of *what?* we are referring to *economic goods*. There are never enough economic goods to satisfy all human wants. This is the case whether people live in the United States, the Soviet Union, France, Brazil, or anyplace else in the world.

Question:

It was stated that "clean air before air pollution" is an example of a free good. Does this mean that clean air today is not a free good? People don't pay for the air they breathe today; doesn't it follow that it must be a free good?

Answer:

The answer is twofold: (1) A free good at one time may be an economic good at another. (2) People may pay for something even if there is no explicit charge. Consider the air in Los Angeles County today. Some of the air is dirty, some is very dirty, some is clean. For example, the air in Malibu is relatively clean compared to the air in Pasadena or Riverside. The people who live in Malibu may be implicitly buying clean air by paying a higher price for Malibu property. Before pollution, when all air was equally clean, individuals would not have paid for clean air either explicitly or implicitly. But now that Malibu has an environmental advantage, property values have risen there relative to Pasadena and Riverside. Residents who pay more to live in Malibu certainly don't consider the clean air free.

Follow-up Question:

In Manhattan the air is dirtier and real estate prices higher than in the suburbs of Connecticut. Doesn't this prove that people do not pay for clean air? After all, if they did pay for clean air wouldn't real estate prices be higher in the Connecticut suburbs than in Manhattan?

Answer:

First, we must ask if real estate prices in Manhattan would be higher or lower (than they are currently) if Manhattan air were clean instead of dirty? If people continued to value clean air, Manhattan real estate prices would be higher. This implies that Manhattan real estate prices *today* are lower *than they would be* if the air in Manhattan were clean.

Still, when comparing the two places, real estates prices are higher in Manhattan than in the suburbs where the air is cleaner. This does not mean that people do not value clean air. The point is that air quality is *not the only difference* between living in Manhattan and living in the suburbs. Manhattan has some things the suburbs do not have—things that people are willing to pay to live near. And the suburbs have some advantages that Manhattan does not have—like clean air—for which individuals are willing to pay. We would predict that if the suburbs had everything they now have (room to move around, clean air, and so forth) *plus* everything that Manhattan has (theaters, well-known restaurants, and the like), real estate prices would be higher in the suburbs.

To summarize: We know that real estate prices would be higher in Manhattan if it had everything it now has *plus* clean air. We know that real estate prices would be higher in the suburbs if they had everything they now have *plus* everything that Manhattan has. We conclude that people pay for such things as room to move around, theaters, well-known restaurants, and clean air.

Our short discussion here is related to economists' use of the **ceteris paribus** condition (*ceteris paribus* is a Latin phrase meaning "all other things held constant"), which we discuss more fully later in this chapter.

Ceteris Paribus
Latin phrase meaning "all other things held constant."

Scarcity Implies Choice

Choice is the act of selecting among restricted alternatives. Scarcity implies choice; choice is a consequence of scarcity. In other words, if scarcity did not exist, there would be no need to make choices.

The logic is straightforward: Because of scarcity, because our wants hit up against limited resources, some wants must go unsatisfied. We must therefore choose which wants we will satisfy and which we will not. For example, John Heckerson wants a one-month vacation in Hawaii, many new clothes, and a down payment for a car. He cannot satisfy all his wants; he chooses the down payment for a car.

We are always either making choices or living the consequences of choices we have made. At this moment you are living the consequence of a choice made earlier. That choice was to read this chapter (you could have been doing something else). Daily you make choices about what to buy, how much to buy, what to do, and so on. There is no way to get around making choices because (can you guess why?) . . . there is no way to get around scarcity.

Choice
The act of selecting among restricted alternatives.

Theory in Practice

Breakfast at Café du Monde, Lunch at the Acme Oyster Bar, and Dinner at La Provençe

Charles Kuralt, the author and journalist, once told a story about what he would do if he could do anything. It is a story about traveling, eating, fishing, sightseeing, and generally enjoying life. But it is also an economics story, a story about scarcity, a story of unlimited wants and limited resources. It goes like this.

"If I were able to work things out just right, I'd spend every January in New Orleans getting myself up to fighting weight for the year to come. I'd have beignets and strong coffee for breakfast every morning at the Café du Monde, oysters for lunch every noon at the Acme Oyster Bar, and whatever they are serving at night at Le Ruth's, La Provence, or La Riviera.

"By February, I'd have to leave because Mardi Gras arrives in February and I don't like big parties. So every February I'd wander slowly along the coast through Mobile and Pensacola and Tampa until I got to Sanibel Island and spend the rest of the month there reading under a palm tree, with special attention to the page one stories in the *St. Petersburg Times* about the snow and slush in Chicago and New York.

"In March, I'd mosey along up to the Okefenokee to give my regards to the 'gators and the iris and the ibis and then settle down in Savannah to watch the azaleas bloom in the Bonaventure Cemetery.

"April, certainly, I'd spend in Chapel Hill, North Carolina. I am a Tar Heel born and a Tar Heel bred and when I die I'm a Tar Heel dead, as we say in Chapel Hill, and April is North Carolina's glory, the month of daffodils and dogwood blossoms and soft breezes from the south. I'd go to Chapel Hill in April and imagine myself young again.

"I'd give my May to the Bay and the foghorns. San Francisco is our most beautiful city, no doubt, and May is the month the fog rolls in under the Golden Gate and pours down the hills into the city streets and swirls inland, making ghostly the cedars of Point Lobos and the wind-bent pines of Point Reyes. I love that coast in May.

"By June, I'd be ready to see blue sky again, and I'd go to Oregon to find it, around Newport where in June the wild

Consider how choice operates in the following scenario: Three U.S. senators are having a discussion. "We need more schools," says the senator from Florida.

"Indeed we do," says the senator from South Carolina, "but not at the expense of a stronger national defense. First we must rebuild our defenses, and then later we will build more schools."

"You are both misguided," says the senator from Virginia. "What we need to do first is to take better care of the unfortunate among us: the old, the sick, and poor."

Sound familiar? It should. Words to this effect are spoken daily in the U.S. Congress, on college campuses, in state legislatures, in homes, and on news programs. Probably, you did not pay much attention to such talk and viewed it as simply part of life. People disagree; so what?

Notice, though, that the disagreements concern choices. The senator from Florida chooses education over national defense and other options. The senator from South Carolina chooses national defense over education and other things. The senator from Virginia chooses helping the poor over education, defense, and other things. They are involved in a political tug-of-war because not all the senators can get what they want. More resources for education mean fewer resources for defense. Why? The answer can be put in one word: scarcity.

roses grow at the edge of the fir forests and the meadows are filled with daisies.

"In July, I'd go straight to Ely, Minnesota. There, I'd rent a canoe and paddle it slowly north into the boundary waters, away from all pavement and neon. They don't allow motorboats there; they don't even allow planes to fly over. So the loons make the loudest sound.

"I'd spend August in Rockport, Maine. One day I'd give to the annual antique show, one day to a sail on a schooner, and one day to the Shakespeare play up the road at Camden. The other twenty-eight days of August, I'd sit still, contemplating the perfect harbor of Rockport, Maine.

"Right after Labor Day, I'd go to West Yellowstone, Montana. There, on every remaining day of September, I'd stand in a different trout river—the Firehole, the Yellowstone, the Madison, the Henrys Fork—trying to learn how to fool a trout with a little bit of floating fur and feather. (I have been trying to master this deception on these rivers for many years and may never become good at it. But September in Yellowstone country is a glorious time and place to try.)

"Spring starts at the Okenfenokee Swamp and moves north: fall starts at Derby Line, Vermont, and moves south. So I'd come south with the fall, right down Vermont Route 100 through Westfield, Waterbury, Warrens, Weston, Wards-boro, Wilmington. The crimson and gold of October in Vermont is so stunning that you can't remember from one year to the next how beautiful it is, which makes Vermont a shock to the senses every fall.

"November I'd spend in San Antonio walking along the river and soaking up sun and sangria in the sidewalk cafes. A hundred other cities could have made their riverbanks as joyful as this, but only San Antonio did it.

"I'd want to be in New York City for December. The great old lady looks a little shabby the rest of the year, but in December she dresses up and puts a garland of white lights in her hair. One year, somehow, I missed seeing the ice skaters gliding round and round at the base of New York's Christmas tree and felt I had missed Christmas.

"That's my year. You'll notice I haven't done any work at all. I've never spent a year anything like this one, of course; these are bits of many years pieced together. I realize it's a year that wouldn't suit everybody; some North Dakotans find February appealing right there at home. But if there are any idle rich among us who can spend twelve months as they choose, and choose to try this itinerary, I say to them: Damn you for your good luck. And send me a postcard once in a while."

Source: Charles Kuralt, *On the Road with Charles Kuralt* (New York: Ballantine Books, 1985), pps. 335–337. Reprinted by permission of the Putnam Publishing Group from On the Road with Charles Kuralt by Charles Kuralt Copyright© 1985 by Charles Kuralt.

Choice and Opportunity Cost

Opportunity Cost
The most highly valued opportunity or alternative forfeited when a choice is made.

Choices imply opportunities or alternatives forfeited. For example, when you chose to read this chapter, you forfeited the opportunity to do something else—watch television, talk on the telephone, or sleep, for example. The most highly valued opportunity or alternative forfeited when a choice is made is known as **opportunity cost.** If watching television is what you would have done had you not chosen to read this chapter, if it was your *next best alternative*, then the opportunity cost of reading this chapter is watching television.

Can you make a choice without incurring a cost? (Economists often leave off the word "opportunity" before the word "cost." We occasionally follow this accepted practice.) Can you choose to attend class tomorrow without giving something up? Can you choose to buy a Toyota without giving up the opportunity to buy a Ford? Can the United States choose to build more roads without giving up the opportunity to build more schools? The answer to all these questions is no. Choice naturally implies cost. And because scarcity implies choice, we conclude that scarcity indirectly (or one step removed) implies cost. Thus the concepts scarcity, choice, and cost are linked.

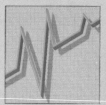

Economics in Our Times

Why Rock Stars and Fashion Models Rarely Go to College

Look around your class. Are there any rock stars between the ages of 18 and 25 in the class? Any movie stars? Any fashion models? Probably not. The reason is that for these people the opportunity cost of attending college is much higher than it is for most 18-to-25-year-olds.

What do you give up to go to college? Most people say the tuition money. If you pay $1,000 a semester for eight semesters, this is $8,000. But, of course, as long as you could be earning income working at a job, this $8,000 is not the full cost of attending college. For example, if you weren't in college you might be working at a full-time job earning $25,000 annually. Certainly this $25,000, or at least a part of it if you are currently working part-time, is forfeited because you attend college. It is part of the cost of your attending college.

Even if the tuition cost is the same or nearly the same for everyone who attends your college, the opportunity cost of attending is not the same or nearly the same for everyone. What would an 18-year-old rock star be forfeiting in unearned income if he decided to attend your college? What would a 17-year-old top fashion model be giving up in income? Such persons rarely attend college—although the tuition cost would be easy for them to pay—because of their relatively high opportunity costs. They might say that they "can't afford to attend college." This doesn't mean that they can't afford the tuition, but that they don't want to do without the large income they would earn if they do not attend college. An economist would put it this way: The opportunity costs are sufficiently high for the individual that the benefits of attending college are outweighed by the costs.*

*There are some exceptions. For example, model–actress Brooke Shields attended Princeton University.

Question:

A person who reads or hears the word "cost" naturally thinks of money. Someone who asks "How much did the car cost?" is really asking how many dollars were paid for the car. But the word "cost" seems to be used in a different way in this text. If Carol is reading this book right now, according to the text, there is a cost to her reading. This cost occurs even though she is not currently paying any money to anyone (she bought the book a few days ago). Can there be a cost without money changing hands?

Answer:

Yes. Think what *cost* implies. It implies sacrifice. To pay the cost is to incur a sacrifice; that is, to give something up. Is it possible to give something up without taking dollars out of your pocket? Certainly, it is. Suppose someone gives you a free ticket to the ballet. Is there a cost to attending the ballet? You paid no money for the ticket, but still there is a cost: The time spent at the ballet could have been devoted to alternative uses. Also, the ballet ticket could have been traded or sold for something else of value—a pair of shoes, for example. Thus choices involve costs when money changes hands, and also when it does not. For example, when money changes hands—say, you buy a television set for $500—what you would have purchased with the $500 had you not used it to buy the television set is the opportunity cost of the television set.

THE NATURE AND ROLE OF THEORY

There is no getting around the fact that there are numerous theories and much theorizing in economics. Occasionally this is a source of frustration for the economics student. A common complaint goes something like this: "Why don't economists say things simply, in everyday terms, and why aren't they content to describe the real world as it is, instead of abstracting from it and coming up with all those unrealistic assumptions?"

This is a natural response from someone who doesn't know the role theories and theorizing perform in economics or in any science, for that matter. So before we present theories and begin to theorize, let's discuss the major role both play in economics.

The Uses of Theory

Everyone uses theories or models to explain and predict.[2] Facts and events are the matter of theories and theorizing. Because facts often do not "speak for themselves," theories are built to explain them. For example, suppose it is a fact that a friend or relative has been acting oddly. You want to understand *why*—that is, you want to be able to explain this fact to yourself. As a first step in finding an explanation, you build a **theory.** You are not doing anything different from the economist who wants to explain the behavior of, say, prices. You are not doing anything different from the sociologist who wants to explain the behavior of adult males reared in slums.

Theory

A simplified abstract representation of the real world used to better understand the real world.

A theory is a construction built on the critical factors or variables that (the theorist believes) explain some event. The essence of theory building is separating the wheat from the chaff. For example, suppose a criminologist's objective is to explain why some people turn to crime. She considers a number of variables: the ease or difficulty of getting a gun, parental childrearing practices, the neighborhood a person grew up in, whether a person was abused as a child, family education, the type of friends a person has, a person's IQ, the weather, and a person's diet.

You may think that some of these variables greatly affect the chance that a person will become a criminal, while some affect it only slightly, and others do not affect it at all. A theory emphasizes only those variables that (the theorist believes) are the main or critical variables that explain an event. Thus, if the criminologist in our example thinks that parental childrearing practices and family education are more likely to explain criminal behavior than the other variables, her theory will emphasize these variables.

Abstraction in Theory: Getting More with Less

The process of focusing on a limited number of variables or factors to explain an event is called *abstraction*. Theories are necessarily abstractions from the real world. If they were descriptions of the real world (which newcomers to the scientific method think they ought to be), they would not be theories.

Albert Einstein said, "Everything should be made as simple as possible, but not more so." Building theories is a way to make things simple and manageable; after all, this is a natural consequence of focusing on key variables *only*.

A simple example illustrates how abstraction can be helpful, how "leaving certain variables out" is sometimes the best thing to do. Suppose you are walking across campus and someone asks you how to get to the president's office. How much detail would you give? We expect that it would be just enough (and no more) to get the person from where he or she is to where he or she wants to go. You might say, "Go

[2]For most purposes, the words "model" and "theory" are interchangeable.

straight until you come to the big red building, turn right, walk about 100 yards, and then turn left. The president's office is in the circular building.''

You would probably not say, ''Go straight for 556 yards, during which time you will pass the English building, in which Dr. Quirk teaches English 101 in Room 156, and the music building, which, by the way, was constructed in 1899. When you get to the John Vernon Building (Vernon gave $10 million to the college in 1961), turn right and walk by the tulips and daffodils. When you are about 10 feet away from the white wall, turn left. Walk past the sign that says, 'Keep off the grass.' Once past the sign, look to the northeast. The president's office is in the circular building called the Y. L. Kidderbody Administrative Building.''

The simple, direct set of instructions leaves out certain information such as where Dr. Quirk teaches English and when the music building was constructed. But if the objective is to get the person to the president's office rather than to give a tour of the campus, this information is unnecessary and is better left out. Too much information simply clutters and makes accomplishing the objective at hand more difficult.

Question:

Suppose a person criticizes theory X because it doesn't consider all the variables or factors that might explain the phenomenon it seeks to explain. Is this a weak or strong criticism of theory X?

Answer:

It is a weak criticism. The reason is that *no* theory considers all the variables or factors that might explain a given phenomenon. *All* theories are abstractions from reality. But it doesn't follow that (abstract) theories cannot *explain* reality. The real trick in theory or model building is to ignore those variables that are essentially irrelevant to the case at hand, so that it becomes easier to isolate the important variables that the untrained observer would probably miss.

The Parts of a Theory

A theory consists of (1) variables, (2) assumptions, (3) hypotheses, and (4) predictions. We discuss each in turn.

Variables.   Words cannot be composed without the letters of the alphabet, and theories cannot be composed without variables, which are magnitudes that can take on different values. Variables are the most basic elements of theories. For example, suppose we want to explain the buying behavior of consumers. Our ''theory of buying behavior'' may be built upon the variable, price. We use it to explain and predict the buying behavior of consumers.

Assumptions.   An economist, trying to explain and predict how firms operate, might make the assumption that firms seek to maximize profits. This is a claim about the motivation of the owners of firms. It is also an abstraction from reality because owners surely care for more than just profits. But possibly a theory built upon this assumption may explain and predict the behavior of firms better than a theory built upon any other assumption. We shall say more on this shortly.

Hypotheses.   A hypothesis is a conditional statement about how two or more variables are related. Typically, hypotheses follow the ''if-then'' form: For example, *if* you smoke cigarettes, *then* you will increase the probability of getting lung cancer. Hypotheses are tested to see whether they are true. An untested hypothesis is much closer to an assumption (a claim) than to a fact.

Predictions.   Predictions are statements that logically follow from the assumptions and hypotheses of the theory. For example, based on the assumption that *individuals are mean when the sun is shining and nice when it is not,* and the hypothesis that *the sun shines as long as the witch doctor is awake,* we deduce that *individuals will be mean when the witch doctor is awake.* This is a prediction.

Question:

Since logic was used to deduce the prediction, does it follow that the prediction must be true?

Answer:

No. A logically deduced statement and a true statement need not be the same. (In fact, we used a rather bizarre example to make this point implicitly.) Usually a prediction is subjected to testing to determine whether it is consistent with actual events. More formally, a theory is tested to see if the evidence can reject it. We deliberately use the word "reject" instead of "prove" because it is widely accepted that evidence cannot prove a theory, it can only *fail to reject it.*

To illustrate, suppose a theory says that all swans are white. Researchers go out into the field and record the color of all the swans they see. Every swan they see is white. The evidence does not prove the theory (is correct) because there may be swans that are not white that the researchers did not see. How can the researchers be certain they saw all the swans? It is more nearly correct to say that the evidence fails to reject the theory.

How Do We Judge Theories?

Many people think the assumptions in many theories are unrealistic. In fact, countless jokes have been made about economists theorizing on the basis of unrealistic assumptions.

In one of the more popular jokes, a physicist, a chemist, and an economist are shipwrecked on a desert island. A few days pass and a can of beans is washed up on the shore.

The physicist, explaining to the others how the can may be opened, says, "I've calculated that the terminal velocity of this can thrown to a height of 27 feet is 204 feet per second. If we place a rock under the can, the impact will burst the seams without splattering the beans."

The chemist says, "That's risky since we can't be sure we will throw the rock to exactly 27 feet high. Here's a better idea. We can start a fire and heat the can over it for 88 seconds. According to my calculations, the heat should just burst the seams.

The economist thinks about it a minute and then says, "Both of your methods for opening the can may work, but they are too complicated. My approach is much simpler. Assume a can opener."

Are there unrealistic assumptions in economics? We have already partly answered this question by saying that making assumptions is part of the abstraction process implicit in theorizing. But perhaps the question is out of place. Many economists maintain that arguing about assumptions is a waste of time ("My assumptions are more nearly realistic than yours") because a theory is better judged by its results than by the degree of realism of its assumptions. This is the approach taken by economist Milton Friedman. He argues that

> . . . the relevant question to ask about the "assumptions" of a theory is not whether they are descriptively "realistic," for they never are, but whether they are sufficiently good approximations for the purpose in hand. And this question can be answered only by seeing whether the theory works, which means whether it yields sufficiently accurate predictions.[3]

Thus, according to Friedman, a theory should be judged by how well it predicts, not the degree of realism of its assumptions. To illustrate, Friedman cites Newton's law of falling bodies, which assumes, unrealistically, that bodies fall in a vacuum. Specifically, the Newtonian theory predicts that the distance traveled by a falling body is equal to $1/2gt^2$ where g is some constant, or approximately 32 feet per second on earth, and t is time in seconds. Does the theory predict well even though it is based on an unrealistic assumption? For many falling bodies, such as a rubber ball dropped off a roof, it does. Friedman would argue that the theory is useful because is predicts well for numerous falling bodies, even though in the real world bodies do not always fall in a vacuum. We could say that for many falling bodies it is *as if* they were falling in a vacuum. Friedman would say that the assumption of a vacuum is a "sufficiently good approximation for the purpose in hand."

The Friedman position might be summarized as follows: If the theory works, if the evidence fails to reject the theory, then it is a good and useful theory, and the assumptions of the theory, no matter what anyone might think of them, are a sufficiently good approximation for the purpose in hand. Some economists accept Friedman's position, along with all its implications.[4] Other economists, many of them well respected, do not. As you will soon find out, there are not only numerous theories in economics, there are also numerous debates.

The Scientific Approach

In Exhibit 1-1 we have outlined the scientific approach typically used in economics. First, variables are noted and defined, assumptions are made, and hypotheses are formulated. Second, predictions (or implications) are deduced. Third, the predictions are stated. These three steps constitute "building the theory." Fourth, the predictions of the theory are tested. At this point, the evidence either fails to reject the theory or rejects it.[5] If it fails to reject the theory, no further action is necessary, although most economists will continue to examine the theory closely. If the evidence rejects the theory, one of two things is done: Either a new theory is formulated, or the old theory is amended and the process repeats itself. The failure of "old" theories to explain and predict events is sometimes the immediate cause of "economic revolutions," some of which we discuss in later chapters.

---

[3]Milton Friedman, "The Methodology of Positive Economics" in *Essays in Positive Economics* (Chicago: The University of Chicago Press, 1953), p. 15. Reprinted with permission.

[4]All parts of this position are not original with Friedman. However, he is given credit for refining the position and arguing its merits.

[5]Instead of saying that the evidence "fails to reject" the theory, economists sometimes say the evidence "confirms" or "fails to disprove" the theory. All three terms are used to express the same basic idea. On this issue, Friedman says that "factual evidence can never 'prove' a hypothesis; it can only fail to disprove it, which is what we generally mean when we say, somewhat inexactly, that the hypothesis has been 'confirmed' by experience." See Friedman, "The Methodology of Positive Economics," p. 9.

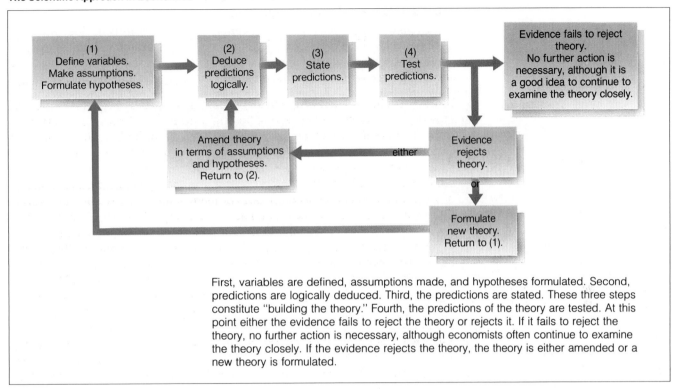

First, variables are defined, assumptions made, and hypotheses formulated. Second, predictions are logically deduced. Third, the predictions are stated. These three steps constitute "building the theory." Fourth, the predictions of the theory are tested. At this point either the evidence fails to reject the theory or rejects it. If it fails to reject the theory, no further action is necessary, although economists often continue to examine the theory closely. If the evidence rejects the theory, the theory is either amended or a new theory is formulated.

Question:

The way the scientific approach is laid out in Exhibit 1-1 suggests that economic theories improve over time, so that if a theory has problems, it is amended until it has fewer or no problems. Does it follow that the economic theories widely accepted today are necessarily better, say, in terms of explaining and predicting events, than the theories of years past?

Answer:

No, they are not *necessarily* better. Errors in the scientific approach can be made. For example, a "true" theory might be discarded and a "false" theory accepted because the predictions of each were incorrectly tested.

Association Is Not Causation and the Fallacy of Composition

The economic way of thinking involves seeing through fallacies and mistakes in reasoning. One common error in reasoning is believing that association is causation. We emphatically state that *association is not causation.* A fallacy to be aware of is the *fallacy of composition*.

Association Is Not Causation.   Consider the following scenario: X occurs at 10:10, and at 10:14 Y occurs. Did X cause Y? Is X the cause, Y the effect? Before answering, suppose X = swallow poison and Y = get sick. Defined this way, we would say that X is the cause of Y. But now suppose X = a heavy rain and Y = you win the lottery. Is the heavy rain the cause of your winning the lottery? Obviously it is not. Although two events may occur close to each other in time and may be associated with each other, the association does not imply causation. This is obvious when we are dealing with examples as extreme as the rain–lottery example. But less extreme examples are not so simple. Suppose interest rates increased two weeks ago and today it is announced that the inflation rate has increased. Do you think the higher interest rates caused the higher inflation rate? (We hope not.) Does it necessarily follow that what came first (higher interest rates) caused what came afterward (the higher inflation rate)? (No.) Could it be that both the higher interest rates and the higher inflation rate are effects of some yet unidentified or undetermined cause? (Yes.)

The Fallacy of Composition.   The fallacy of composition is the erroneous view that what is good (true) for the individual (or a part of the whole) is necessarily good (true) for the group (or the whole). In fact, what is good for the individual may be good for the group, but not necessarily. For example, John stands up at a soccer game and sees the game better. Does it follow that if everyone stands up at the soccer game everyone will see better? No. Mary moves to the suburbs because she dislikes the crowds in the city. Does it follow that if everyone moves from the city to the suburbs for the same reason as Mary everyone will be better off? No.

The *Ceteris Paribus* Condition: Taking One Thing at a Time

As we mentioned earlier, the Latin term *ceteris paribus* means "all other things held constant." It is a widely used term in economics where it is used to separate out effects. To illustrate, assume that both good nutrition and moderate exercise increase the number of years people live, and that bad nutrition and little-to-no exercise decrease the number of years people live. Suppose now that a person eats well. Will he or she live longer or not? Economists would answer, "If a person eats well, that person will live longer, *ceteris paribus*." But why do the economists say *ceteris paribus*? Why do they add the condition that all other things are held constant? The reason is that, as we have already pointed out, another factor, little-to-no exercise, can decrease the number of years a person lives. Thus a person who eats well but doesn't exercise may end up living a shorter life. If this were the case, would it mean that good nutrition does not increase the number of years a person lives? Not at all. It only means that the lack of exercise reduced the person's life by more than the good nutrition added to it, *making it appear as if* good nutrition does not increase the number of years a person lives. In order for economists to convey the correct relationship between good nutrition and years lived, they must use the *ceteris paribus* condition.

Positive and Normative Economics

Positive economics attempts to determine *what is*. **Normative economics** addresses *what should be*. Many topics in economics can be discussed within both a positive and a normative framework. For example, consider the minimum wage. An economist practicing positive economics would want to know the effects of the minimum wage. Does the unemployment rate go up or down if the minimum wage increases? Is the minimum wage tied to a higher teenage unemployment rate? In short, positive economics focuses on cause-effect relationships. An economist practicing normative economics would address issues that directly or indirectly relate to whether the

Positive Economics
The study of "what is" in economic matters.

Normative Economics
The study of "what should be" in economic matters.

minimum wage should exist. In normative economics, value judgments and opinions are present.

This book deals mainly with positive economics. For the most part, we discuss not the way things should be but the economic world and the way it works. Nonetheless, there are two points to keep in mind. First, although we have taken pains to keep our discussions within the boundaries of positive economics, at times we may operate perilously close to the normative border. If, here and there, we drop a value judgment into the discussion, recognize it for what it is. It would be wrong for you to accept as true something that cannot be proved. Second, keep in mind that no matter what your normative objectives, positive economics can shed some light on how they might be accomplished.

For example, suppose you believe that absolute poverty *should be* eliminated, the unemployment rate *should be* lowered, the economy *should be* stabilized, and so forth. No doubt you have "ideas" as to how these goals can be accomplished. But are they correct? Will doing *X*, for example, actually eliminate absolute poverty? Will doing *Y* actually lower the unemployment rate? Will doing *Z* actually stabilize the economy? In short, there is no guarantee that the means you *think* will bring about certain ends will do so. This is where sound positive economics can help. It helps us see *what is*. As someone once said, It is not enough to want to do good, it is important also to know how to do good.

Question:

It is easy to see how economists might disagree about what should be, but do they also disagree over *what is* (when it comes to economic matters)?

Answer:

Yes. In fact, many of the debates in economics are over what is. This is especially true in macroeconomics (see the next section for the difference between microeconomics and macroeconomics). Furthermore, simply because an economist is doing positive economics, it does not necessarily follow that he or she will not make mistakes. Biologists make mistakes trying to find out *what is* in the biological world, and economists make mistakes trying to find out *what is* in the economic world. A science does not move forward every minute of every day.

Macroeconomics and Microeconomics

Microeconomics
The branch of economics that deals with human behavior and choices as they relate to relatively small units— the individual, the firm, the industry, the single market.

Macroeconomics
The branch of economics that deals with human behavior and choices as they relate to either highly aggregated markets or the entire economy.

It has been said that the tools of microeconomics are microscopes, the tools of macroeconomics telescopes. Macroeconomics stands back from the trees in order to see the forest. Microeconomics gets up close and examines the tree itself, its bark, its limbs, and the soil in which it stands. **Microeconomics** is the branch of economics that deals with human behavior and choices as they relate to relatively small units— the individual, the firm, the industry, a single market. **Macroeconomics** is the branch of economics that deals with human behavior and choices as they relate to either highly aggregated markets or the entire economy. In microeconomics economists discuss a single price, in macroeconomics they discuss the price level. Microeconomics deals with the demand for a particular good (say, apples); macroeconomics deals with aggregate or total demand. Microeconomics examines how a tax change affects a single firm's output; macroeconomics looks at how the tax change affects the entire economy's output. As we said, the perspective is one of microscopes and telescopes.

Why Learn Economics?

Why learn economics? An economist might answer that economics is an interesting subject, a rewarding subject, a subject that provides insights into the way the world works.

All this is correct, but it could also be said about many subjects. Furthermore, it is a cliché, and the tone is reminiscent of your mother telling you to eat your peas when you were a child: "They are good for you . . . they will make you strong . . . you'll like them."

Forget the words of the economist. Just look around you, and you'll see why it is important to learn economics:

- Economics is regularly the subject of reports on the nightly news shows.
- Economists are regularly interviewed on news programs.
- Economics is on the mind of the president of the United States.
- Economics is on the minds of the U.S. senators.
- Economics is on the minds of the members of the House of Representatives.
- Economics is on the minds of the nation's business leaders.
- Economics is on the minds of the nation's labor leaders.
- Economics is on the mind of the person buying a house, the person buying a car, the person starting a business.
- Economics is on the mind of the person buying stock in the stock market.

Doesn't it make sense to want to learn about something that is so important to so many people, including yourself?

And there is more. Paul Samuelson, a Nobel Prize winner in economics, once said that he envies the person who is "setting out to explore the exciting world of economics for the first time. That is a thrill which, alas, no one can experience twice." Those people who teach, research, and write economics know exactly what Samuelson is talking about, and he put it perfectly. In a way, understanding economics for the first time is like driving your first car, tasting the first bite of your favorite ice cream, or enjoying the first day of spring. The first experience is sometimes the best. No matter how hard you try to relive that first experience, it can't be done. We are not saying that your second car, your second bite of ice cream, or the second day of spring are miserable experiences. That wouldn't even be close to the truth. What we're saying is that sometimes there is something special, something magical, about the first experience. So it is with the first time you understand what economics is about, the first time you understand the richness of economic analysis, and the first time you come to know what it means to think like an economist. You are in for a treat.

Now that we've raised your expectations about economics (I didn't know economics could be like ice cream, you say), we should say something about the reality of learning economics. The "economic high" usually does not come ten minutes, or even ten weeks, after you have "tasted" economics. For most people, the gratification is far from instant. It would be nice if it were otherwise, because if instant gratification came from studying economics, more people would study it (by the way, it is economics that teaches us this), and more people would be economically literate. This is not the way things work, however, and if we were to tell you differently, we could justly be accused of painting an unrealistic picture of what the study of economics entails.

So, there are thrills associated with exploring the world of economics, especially on the first go-around, but you shouldn't expect a thrill a minute, because there are some rough spots, too, and sometimes the rough spots must be traversed before the thrills can be experienced. As someone once put it, The gold is there, but it doesn't jump into your pocket.

CHAPTER SUMMARY

Scarcity, Choice, Opportunity Cost

- Scarcity is the condition where our wants outstrip the limited resources available to satisfy those wants. It is the basic problem that every society faces.
- Scarcity implies choice. In a world of limited resources, we must choose which wants will be satisfied and which will go unsatisfied.
- Choice implies opportunity cost. Opportunity cost is the most highly valued opportunity or alternative forfeited when a choice is made. Cost implies sacrifice and can involve both a money and a nonmoney dimension. Cost affects behavior, as "Why Rock Stars and Fashion Models Rarely Go To College" illustrated. The higher the opportunity cost of going to college, the lower the likelihood that an individual will go to college; the lower the opportunity cost of going to college, the higher the likelihood of going to college, *ceteris paribus*.

Goods and Bads

- A good is anything from which individuals receive utility or happiness. A bad is anything from which individuals receive disutility.
- Economists usually speak of two types of goods: economic goods and free goods. A free good is a good where the amount available is greater than the amount people want at zero price. An economic good is scarce: It is a good where the quantity available is less than people would want if it were given away at zero price.

Theory and Errors in Thinking

- Economists construct theories in order to explain and predict real-world events. Theories are necessarily abstractions from, as opposed to descriptions of, the real world.
- The four parts of a theory are variables, assumptions, hypotheses, and predictions. Logical deduction is the process by which the theorist moves from the variables, assumptions, and hypotheses to the predictions.
- A widely held (but not the only) view in economics is that theories are best judged by their predictive power and not by the degree of realism of their assumptions. For Milton Friedman, for example, the assumptions of a theory need only be "sufficiently good approximations for the purpose in hand."
- Association is not causation. For example, the dog's wagging its tail may be associated with lightning in the sky (suppose the dog wags its tail at 2:01:43 P.M., and the lightning flashes at 2:01:45), but the wagging did not cause the lightning.
- The fallacy of composition is the erroneous view that what is true for the individual (or part of the whole) is necessarily true for the group (or the whole).

QUESTIONS TO ANSWER AND DISCUSS

1. Explain the link between scarcity, choice, and opportunity cost.

2. If someone were to say that there is zero opportunity cost to your doing homework, what would this mean?

3. Give an example that illustrates that a person can incur a cost without spending dollars.

4. A city has not had any rain for three months. The people of the city hire someone to do a rain dance. Twenty-four hours after the rain dance, it begins to rain, leading some citizens to remark on how successful the rain dance was. What might the comment of a scientist be?

5. Which of the following statements would Milton Friedman agree with and why?
Statement 1: The theory does not work because its assumptions are false.
Statement 2: The assumptions are false because the theory does not work.

6. Undertake a short experiment that will help you understand the concept of opportunity cost. On one side of a sheet of paper, list all the goods you buy and the activities you undertake in a single day. On the other side, note the opportunity cost of each purchase or activity. Are any of the opportunity costs different from what you thought they might be?

7. Write a one-page paper on what you think the "economic way of thinking" is.

8. Discuss the opportunity costs of attending college for four years. Is college more or less costly than you thought it was? Explain.

9. Think of a few everyday examples that illustrate that association is not causation.

10. How would your life be different if you didn't live in a world characterized by scarcity?

Chapter 2

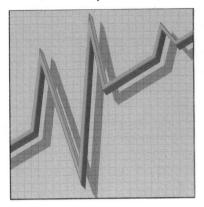

Fundamentals of Economic Thinking

■ INTRODUCTION

Once upon a time there was an old man who knew everything there was to know about precious gems. One day a young boy, an ambitious boy, went to the old man and asked to be taught all that he knew. The old man consented to teach the boy.

The first thing the old man did was to give the boy an emerald. He said, "This is an emerald, look at it carefully, study it, feel it, smell it, get to know everything about it." The young boy, thinking that this was an odd way to learn about precious gems, nevertheless did as he was told.

The next day the old man told the boy to do what he had done the day before. "But what about my lessons?" the boy asked. "When will you teach me about precious gems?" The old man simply repeated his instructions. The boy complied.

This continued for weeks. Every day the young boy spent hours looking at the emerald and feeling it, and the old man never spoke to the boy except to tell him to continue to study the emerald.

Then one day the old man brought a fake emerald to the young boy. It was the best fake emerald that he had ever come across. He gave it to the boy and said, "Here, take this emerald." The boy took it in his hand. He looked at it, he smelled it, he rubbed it over and over, and then he said, "This is not an emerald, this is a fake."

The old man smiled. He knew that he had taught the young boy well. And the boy smiled, too, for now he realized that he had been taught well.

We try to teach economics in this chapter in much the same way that the old man taught the young boy about precious gems. We try to do it without being too obvious, without overwhelming you with tiny details. We try to present you with the flavor of economics, with something of how economics "hangs together," with the knowledge of how economists approach problems and how they think. At the end of the chapter if you say that you can almost sense what economics is about, then our objective will have been accomplished, and you will be ready to learn specific things about specific economic subjects.

■ WHAT THIS CHAPTER IS ABOUT

In Maine in the spring it is common to see buckets attached to maple trees and hear the drip, drip, drip of maple sap into the buckets. The maple sap is collected and put into a boiler, where the water in the sap is separated from what turns out to be maple syrup. Suppose we did to economics what is done to the maple sap? Suppose we put all of economics into a boiler and separated the heavy from the light; the syrup, so to speak, from the water. What would be left? Many economists think we'd be left with the key principles in this chapter. We agree.

You will encounter the principles in this chapter again in other chapters. We discuss them here, as a group, for two reasons. First, by discussing them together, we think you will more likely and more quickly understand what we mean by the *economic way of thinking*. Second, sometimes key principles have to be encountered more than once before they are fully understood. Those discussed in this chapter include rational self-interest; there is no such thing as a free lunch; decision making at the margin; efficiency; and exchange.

Key Questions To Keep In Mind As You Read

1. What is rational self-interest? Is it the same as selfishness?
2. What does "There is no such thing as a free lunch" mean?
3. How do economists believe decisions are made?
4. What is efficiency? What is inefficiency?
5. What is the difference between exchange and the terms of exchange?
6. What are some of the economic facts faced by all societies?

RATIONAL SELF-INTEREST

Rational Self-Interest
When used to describe human behavior, it means to act to maximize the difference between benefits and costs.

A key principle in economics is that individuals behave according to **rational self-interest.** What does behaving according to rational self-interest mean? Simply put, it means to act to maximize the difference between (subjectively evaluated) benefits and costs. It means to maximize utility, or satisfaction.

Does describing individuals' behavior in terms of rational self-interest give too narrow a picture of men and women? Is the picture too unrealistic to use when constructing economic theories? Some people think so. At times this is because they mistakenly believe rational self-interest means something it does not.

What Rational Self-Interest Is Not

The term *self-interest* raises red flags for some people. They think a rational self-interested person is a selfish person, a person who cares only for himself or herself—an Ebenezer Scrooge, for example. True, Ebenezer Scrooge was a rational self-interested person, but before you jump to any conclusions, so were Albert Schweitzer, the physician and scholar who won the 1952 Nobel Peace Prize for his humanitarian work; Jonas Salk, the virologist who invented the first polio vaccine; Ludwig van Beethoven, the great composer; Thomas Jefferson, the third president of the United States and author of the Declaration of Independence; Martin Luther King, the civil rights leader; and Saint Francis of Assisi, who renounced riches and turned to a life of poverty and service to the poor.

Rational self-interested behavior and selfish behavior are not the same. All persons exhibit rational self-interest; all persons seek to maximize their utility. This is true for the volunteer medical worker in Ethiopia as much as for the political dictator of a country. These persons simply maximize their utility *in different ways*. The volunteer sees benefits from helping people get well, the dictator sees benefits from throwing his political enemies into jail. The volunteer receives utility (personal satisfaction) by helping others, the tyrant receives utility by helping himself at the expense of others.

Question:

This seems to be saying that both the saint and the sinner exhibit rational self-interested behavior. Everybody does. But this is like saying that everybody breathes air, or that everybody has two eyes. Such facts are of little use in explaining how the world works. What is the significance of knowing that everybody exhibits rational self-interested behavior?

Answer:

Knowing that everybody exhibits rational self-interested behavior is not as important as knowing what rational self-interested behavior implies: that an individual's behavior changes as his or her perception of benefits and costs changes. For example, ask yourself if your behavior would be different if someone offered you $5,000 as opposed to $5 to walk 10 miles. For $5, the benefits to you of walking 10 miles would probably be less than the costs of walking 10 miles, and you would not make the walk. For $5,000, however, the benefits would probably be greater than the costs, and you would make the walk. If you decide to walk 10 miles for $5,000 but not for $5, are you rational (self-interested) in the one instance and irrational in the other? Or are you rational in both? We believe you are rational in both because in both instances you decide what to do based on your evaluation of the benefits and costs. We learn from this that *rational self-interested men and women change their behavior when their perceptions of benefits and costs change*. This is an important economic principle.

THERE IS NO SUCH THING AS A FREE LUNCH

Economists are fond of saying that *there is no such thing as a free lunch*. This is a catchy phrase that expresses a fundamental principle of economics, namely, that because of scarcity, choices need to be made, and thus opportunity costs are incurred (see Chapter 1). To say "there is no such thing as a free lunch" is to say that there are always opportunity costs to making choices.

Perhaps this is an obvious point. But consider how often people mistakenly assume that there *is* such a thing as a free lunch: for example, the couple who, because they do not pay tuition for their children to attend elementary school, think education is free. Sorry, but there is no such thing as a free lunch. Free implies no sacrifice, no opportunities forfeited, and this is not the case with elementary education. Resources that could be used for other things are used to provide elementary education.

Consider, too, the people who speak about free medical care, free housing, free bridges ("there is no charge to cross it"), and free parks. None are free. Some people may think otherwise because someone else is bearing the cost of providing these goods. But something is free only if *no one* forfeits anything to bring it about. In summary, zero price does not mean something is free, only zero opportunity cost does. And zero opportunity cost is not likely.

A Way to Make the Invisible Visible: Say "No Free Lunch"

In Chapter 1 we stated that economics has the ability to make the invisible visible. Consider how the three words, *no free lunch* (the shortened version of "there is no such thing as a free lunch"), which express the principle of opportunity cost, can do this.

Suppose the federal government builds a new interstate highway system. It hires thousands of people to work on the project. The newspapers in the towns the interstate highway passes through report on all the increased job activity. It looks as if there are more people working on road construction and no fewer people working at anything else; it looks as if there are more highways and nothing less of anything else (no fewer cameras, cars, computers, and so on). But say the words "no free lunch" and see if the picture changes.

"No free lunch" reminds us that something must have been given up to build the new interstate highway system. The taxpayers gave up dollars, so we add taxpayers to our picture.

But what specifically did the taxpayers give up by paying taxes? They gave up the opportunity to buy more clothes, cars, books, and so on. So we add to our picture all the goods and services that would have been produced and consumed had the highway not been built. And if, say, more clothes would have been produced had the highway not been built, it follows that more people would have worked in the clothing industry than worked in it when the highway system was built. We add them to our picture. When we remind ourselves that there is no such thing as a free lunch, we begin to see things that *might have been*. And that, we think, is something worth seeing.

DECISION MAKING AT THE MARGIN

Deciding at the Margin
Decision making characterized by weighing additional benefits of a change against the additional costs of a change with respect to current conditions.

What does a student ask herself when she decides whether to study for one more hour? What does an employee ask himself when he decides whether to work overtime? What does the president of the United States ask when deciding whether to take 30 minutes to meet with the speaker of the House of Representatives?

In each case, the person asks (sometimes without even knowing it) if the *additional benefits* from doing something outweigh the *additional costs*. For example, the student asks herself if the additional benefits of studying one more hour outweigh the additional costs. If the answer is yes, she studies one more hour; if the answer is no, she does not. Economists refer to choices made on the basis of this type of question—where the additional benefits of an incremental change are measured against the additional costs—as *marginal choices*.[1] Individuals are said to be **deciding at the margin.**

Decision making at the margin has two implicit characteristics that we shall make explicit. First, the unit of change under consideration is usually (but not always) relatively small: say, one more hour of study instead of one thousand more. Second, the changes are evaluated with *current conditions* in mind. For example, a firm deciding whether to produce 100 more computers considers the additional benefits and additional costs of the 100 computers with the number it *currently* produces, say, 100,000 (not some number unrelated to its operation). In short, the status quo is the take-off point for decision making at the margin.

Consider the implications of decision-making at the margin. First, the focus of choice is on additional or marginal benefits and costs, not on *total* benefits and

[1]In economics, the word *marginal* is often used as a synonym for *additional*. For example, an economist usually speaks of marginal benefits and marginal costs instead of additional benefits and additional costs.

Theory in Practice

How Much for that Soda?

Economist Tom Wyrick wrote a piece for the *Wall Street Journal* that illustrates the concepts of marginal decision making and opportunity cost. We will tell the story that Wyrick told and then make some necessary points.

Suppose you are in a supermarket buying your groceries. Suddenly, the manager announces that for the next five minutes you can buy two bottles of your favorite soft drink for the price of one. Let's say your favorite soft drink sells for $1 a bottle. With the manager's special, you can buy two bottles for $1. You decide to take part in the special offer.

At home, later that day, there is a knock at your door. It is a neighbor who has unexpected company and asks to buy one bottle of soda from you. What price do you charge the neighbor?

Here are three options:

1. You charge zero price, thinking to yourself that the bottle you give to the neighbor is the "free" bottle you picked up earlier at the grocery store. (If there is no free lunch, can there be a free bottle?)

2. You charge 50 cents, which is the average price of the bottle of soda ($1/2 bottles = 50 cents per bottle).
3. You charge $1, because when you buy the next bottle of soda you will have to pay $1 (the two-for-one sale has expired).

An economically rational person, who is not interested in giving someone a gift, would charge $1. To do otherwise would decrease your *wealth,* since if you charge zero price and replace the bottle of soda for $1, your wealth falls by $1. (Wealth is the value of your assets minus the value of your liabilities; both money and the bottle of soda are assets. If you give away a bottle of soda, you give away one asset and do not get another asset like money in return. As a result, your wealth declines.) If you charge 50 cents and replace the bottle of soda for $1, your wealth falls by 50 cents. But if you charge $1 and replace the bottle of soda for $1, your wealth stays constant.

Notice how the concepts of marginal decision making and opportunity cost are at work here. Specifically, by charging a $1 price, thus maintaining your wealth, you charge the price that is consistent with the *opportunity cost* of the *additional* bottle of soda. To an economist, this is the *marginal opportunity cost.* In short, if maintaining wealth is important to people (and we reasonably assume it is), then people will naturally make *decisions at the margin,* in full consideration of *opportunity cost.*

Source: Thomas Wyrick, "Marginal-Cost Policy Making and the Guy Next Door," *Wall Street Journal,* April 12, 1984.

costs. For example, when deciding whether to buy a bottle of water at the grocery store, what matters is the additional benefits and costs to you of that single additional bottle of water. You do not think about the total benefits and costs of water. You are not deciding between water and no water—an all-or-nothing decision. You are deciding between the status quo and one more bottle of water at this time.

Second, marginal choices necessarily ignore past choices, and therefore *sunk costs* (sometimes called *past costs* or *historical costs*) associated with past choices. A shopowner pondering whether to stay open until midnight tonight instead of closing at 10:00 P.M. focuses on the additional (marginal) benefits and costs of staying open two more hours. She will ask herself: What are the additional benefits of staying open two more hours? What are the additional costs? It is unlikely that she will concern herself with the benefits and costs of anything else—in particular, past benefits and costs. For her the past is irrelevant. What does it matter what the costs were of staying open from 6:00 P.M. to 10:00 P.M.? What does it matter what the costs were of staying open to 11:00 P.M. two weeks ago? All this is in the past; bygones are bygones, as economists are quick to point out.

Question:

Does the preceding discussion mean that people do *employ marginal decision making or that they* should *employ marginal decision making?*

Answer:

They *do* employ it. Choices are made at the margin.

Follow-up Question:

Suppose a person says he is not aware that his choices are marginal choices. Is it possible for him to be doing something that he does not think he is doing?

Answer:

Yes it is. For example, suppose Bob thinks he is *not* a **utility maximizer.** He thinks this because he does things daily he would rather not do: He gets up early in the morning to go to work, he works at a job he doesn't particularly enjoy, he spends two hours in bumper-to-bumper traffic commuting to and from work. Do we conclude that Bob is not a utility maximizer, that he does not attempt to make himself better off, or do we conclude that he is a utility maximizer but doesn't realize that maximizing utility and a smile on one's face do not always go together (think of the pain on the face of the athlete training for the Olympics)? A stronger case can be made for the latter. Bob is trying to make himself better off, not simply at one instant in time (if it were this, he would probably stay home and read a good novel by the pool), but over time. Even if he says he is not a utility maximizer, it does not necessarily follow that he is not. Words do not make it so.

Utility Maximizer

One who strives to maximize utility or satisfaction.

Efficiency

In terms of production, efficiency refers to the condition where the maximum output is produced with given resources and technology. Efficiency implies the impossibility of gains in one area without losses in another.

EFFICIENCY

Efficiency is one of those words that means different things to different people. Economists speak about different types of efficiency. Here we discuss *efficiency in production* (productive efficiency). We say that the economy is **efficient** if it is producing the maximum output with given resources and technology. A useful way to view efficiency is to look at it within the framework of the *production possibilities frontier (PPF)*. We do that in this section. Beforehand, though, we develop the PPF framework and illustrate a few other economic concepts within it.

Land

All natural resources, such as minerals, forests, water, and unimproved land.

Labor

The physical and mental talents people contribute to the production process.

Capital

Capital consists of produced goods that can be used as inputs for further production, such things as machinery, tools, computers, trucks, buildings, and factories.

Resources

Goods are produced with *resources*. Sometimes resources are referred to as *inputs* or *factors of production. Economists usually divide resources into four categories:* **land, labor, capital,** and **entrepreneurship.** Land includes all natural resources, such as minerals, forests, water, and unimproved land. Labor refers to the physical and mental talents that people contribute to the production process. Capital consists of produced goods that can be used as inputs for further production, such things as machinery, tools, computers, trucks, buildings, and factories. Entrepreneurship refers to the particular talent that some people have for organizing the resources of land, labor, and capital into the production of goods and to the search for new business opportunities and the development of new ways of doing things.

Entrepreneurship
The particular talent that some people have for organizing the resources of land, labor, and capital into the production of goods, and seeking new business opportunities and developing new ways of doing things.

Production Possibilities Frontier
Represents the possible combinations of two goods that an economy can produce in a certain period of time, given available resources and existing technology.

Technology
Refers to the body of skills and knowledge concerning the use of inputs or resources in production. An advance in technology commonly refers to the ability to generate more output with a fixed amount of inputs, or the ability to generate the same output with fewer inputs.

The Production Possibilities Frontier

We deal here with the production possibilities frontier for a nation's economy. Within this context, we discuss two production possibilities frontiers: (1) one in which there is a constant trade-off between two goods and (2) one in which there is a changing trade-off between two goods.

Constant Trade-off between Goods: The Case of the Straight-Line Production Possibilities Frontier.   Consider an economy in which only two goods can be produced: red cars and white cars. In order to understand what a production possibilities frontier is, do the following: First, assume that all the economy's resources are used to produce red cars. The total number of red cars that can be produced in a year is, say, 50,000.

Second, assume that instead of all the economy's resources being used to produce red cars, they are used to produce white cars. The total number of white cars that can be produced in a year is, say, 50,000.

Third, plot these two points, one point representing 50,000 red cars and 0 white cars and the other point representing 50,000 white cars and 0 red cars, and then draw a line between the two points as in Exhibit 2-1. This is a **production possibilities frontier;** it represents the possible combinations of two goods that an economy can produce in a certain period of time, given available resources and existing **technology.**

Changing Trade-off between Goods: The Case of the Curved (Bowed Outward) Production Possibilities Frontier.   There is not always a constant trade-off between goods, one for one, or two for one, and so on. Sometimes the trade-off changes as more of one good is produced. If this is the case, the production possibilities frontier will not be a straight line (as in Exhibit 2-1) but instead will be curved (bowed outward). To illustrate, let's look at the case for two goods: guns (usually used to represent military goods) and butter (used to represent civilian goods).

■ **EXHIBIT 2-1**
Production Possibilities Frontier (Constant Trade-off between Goods)

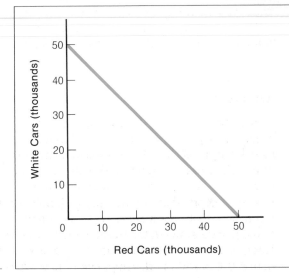

The trade-off between red cars and white cars is assumed constant at one for one. If all the economy's resources are used to produce red cars, 50,000 are produced. If all the economy's resources are used to produce white cars, 50,000 are produced. If we plot two points (one representing 50,000 red cars and 0 white cars and the other representing 50,000 white cars and 0 red cars) and then connect them, we have a production possibilities frontier.

If all the resources of the economy are put into production of guns, 80,000 can be produced in a year. If all the resources of the economy are put into producing butter, 130,000 units can be produced in a year. Besides these two maximum amounts of guns and butter, the following combinations of the two goods can be produced in a year: 72,000 units of butter and 60,000 guns; 104,000 units of butter and 40,000 guns; 120,000 units of butter and 20,000 guns. Plotting the different combinations of the two goods and connecting the points, we obtain the production possibilities frontier in Exhibit 2-2.

Economic Concepts within a Production Possibilities Frontier Framework

Numerous economic concepts can be illustrated and explained within a production possibilities frontier (*PPF*) framework: for example, scarcity, choice, and opportunity cost; the link between more (fewer) resources and output and between greater (lesser) productivity and output; the law of increasing opportunity costs; and efficiency. All but efficiency are discussed in this section. Exhibit 2-3 illustrates the discussion.

Scarcity. Recall that scarcity is the condition where wants are greater than resources. The finiteness of resources is graphically portrayed by the production possibilities frontier in Exhibit 2-3a. The frontier tells us, ''At this point in time, that's as far as you can go. You cannot go any farther. You are limited to choosing any combination of the two goods on the frontier or below it.''

The frontier separates two regions: (1) an *attainable region,* which consists of the points on the PPF itself and all points below it and (2) an *unattainable region,* which consists of the points above the PPF. Scarcity implies that some things are attainable and some things are unattainable.

■ **EXHIBIT 2-2**
Production Possibilities Frontier (Changing Trade-off between Goods)

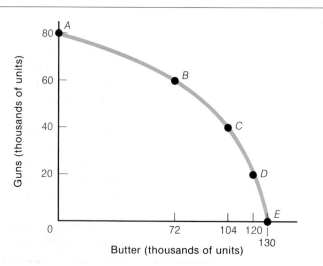

POINT	BUTTER (number of units)	GUNS (number of units)
A	0	80,000
B	72,000	60,000
C	104,000	40,000
D	120,000	20,000
E	130,000	0

The trade-off between the two goods is assumed to change as more of one good is produced. The five points, *A–E,* represent the different combinations of guns and butter the economy can produce. Plotting and connecting the data points gives a production possibilities frontier.

Economic Concepts within a Production Possibilities Frontier (*PPF*) Framework

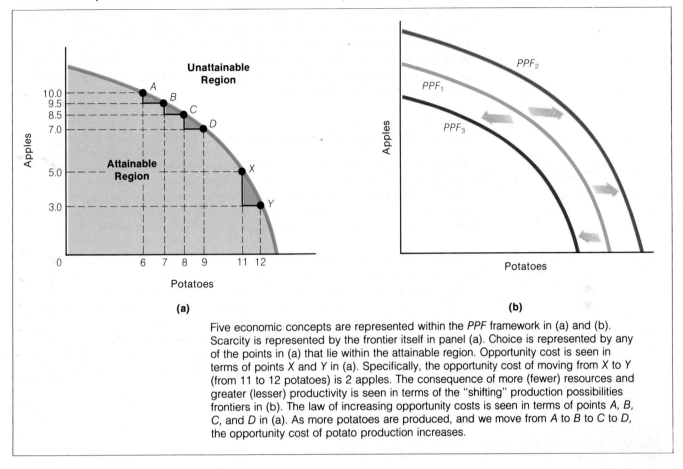

Five economic concepts are represented within the *PPF* framework in (a) and (b). Scarcity is represented by the frontier itself in panel (a). Choice is represented by any of the points in (a) that lie within the attainable region. Opportunity cost is seen in terms of points *X* and *Y* in (a). Specifically, the opportunity cost of moving from *X* to *Y* (from 11 to 12 potatoes) is 2 apples. The consequence of more (fewer) resources and greater (lesser) productivity is seen in terms of the "shifting" production possibilities frontiers in (b). The law of increasing opportunity costs is seen in terms of points *A*, *B*, *C*, and *D* in (a). As more potatoes are produced, and we move from *A* to *B* to *C* to *D*, the opportunity cost of potato production increases.

Choice and Opportunity Cost. Choice and opportunity cost are also visible in Exhibit 2-3a. Note that within the attainable region individuals must choose the combination of the two goods they want to produce. Obviously there are hundreds of different combinations. Consider only two: *X* and *Y*. It is impossible to be at more than one point at the same time. One must be chosen.

Opportunity cost becomes visible as we move from one point to another. Suppose we are at point *X* and choose to move to point *Y*. At *X* we have 11 potatoes and 5 apples. At *Y* we have 12 potatoes and 3 apples. In moving from *X* to *Y*, what is the opportunity cost of the additional potato? Obviously it is what must be forfeited to obtain the additional potato—that is, 2 apples.

The resources-output, productivity-output links. The United States does not have the same production possibilities frontier today that it had in 1945, 1960, or 1988. PPFs change; they may shift inward or outward for a number of reasons. Two of the main reasons are changes in supplies of resources and changes in productivity. An increase in resources shifts the *PPF* outward, since with more resources, more output can be produced. In Exhibit 2-3b this is a shift from *PPF*$_1$ to *PPF*$_2$. A decrease in resources shifts the *PPF* inward from *PPF*$_1$ to *PPF*$_3$. An increase in productivity, which implies that more output can be produced with the same quantity of resources, shifts

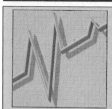

Economics in Our Times

Economic Growth: An Expanding *PPF* Ends the Political Tug-of-War, for a While

Liberals and conservatives of both political parties often pull in different directions. To illustrate, suppose we are currently at point *A* in Exhibit 2-4 with X_2 of good *X* and Y_2 of good *Y*. Conservatives prefer *C* to *A* and thus try to convince the liberals and the rest of the nation to move to *C*. The liberals, however, prefer *B* to *A* and try to convince the conservatives and the rest of the nation to move to *B*. Thus we have a political tug-of-war.

Is there a way that both groups can get what they want? There is, but the production possibilities frontier must shift outward from PPF_1 to PPF_2. This can occur if there is economic growth. With a new production possibilities frontier, *D* represents the quantity of *X* that the conservatives want and the quantity of *Y* that the liberals want. At point *D*, conservatives have X_3 units of good *X*, which is what they would have had at *C*; and liberals have Y_3 units of good *Y*, which

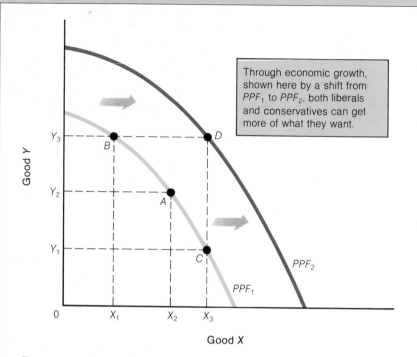

Through economic growth, shown here by a shift from PPF_1 to PPF_2, both liberals and conservatives can get more of what they want.

The economy is at point *A*, but conservatives want to be at *C* and liberals want to be at *B*. As a result, there is a political tug-of-war. Both conservatives and liberals can get the quantity of the good they want through economic growth. This is represented by point *D* on PPF_2.

is what they would have had at *B*. Through economic growth, both conservatives and liberals can get what they want; the political tug-of-war will cease, at least for a while.

We say "for a while" because even at point *D* there is scarcity: The wants of liberals and conservatives are both greater than the resources available to satisfy those wants. Starting at

point *D*, liberals might push for a movement up the production possibilities frontier and conservatives for a movement down it.

A question to think about: Would you expect to see more intense political battles in a growing economy or in a stagnant economy, *ceteris paribus*? Why?

the *PPF* outward from PPF_1 to PPF_2. A decrease in productivity shifts the *PPF* inward from PPF_1 to PPF_3.

Law of Increasing Opportunity Costs. When resources are specialized (to any degree), increased production of one good comes at increased opportunity costs.[2]

[2]A resource is *specialized* if it is better suited to the production of one good than others. A resource is *nonspecialized* if it is equally suited to the production of all goods.

This is the law of increasing opportunity costs, which is illustrated in Exhibit 2-3a. Notice that moving from point A to point B (an increase of one unit of potatoes) requires giving up fewer apples than moving from B to C (an increase of one unit of potatoes) and that moving from B to C requires giving up fewer apples than moving from C to D, and so on. We conclude that as more potatoes are produced, the opportunity cost of each additional potato is greater than for the preceding unit. This is a special application of the law of increasing opportunity costs.

It is easy to see that increasing costs give the production possibilities frontier its curvature. But since a production possibilities frontier need not be curved, but can be a straight line, increasing costs need not occur.

But we wonder, are most production possibilities frontiers curved? Do increasing costs occur often? The answer is yes. The reason is that most resources are simply better suited for the production of some goods than others. For example, some land is better suited for the production of wheat than corn. Some individuals are better suited for producing cars than tomatoes. Also, in the early stages of the production of a good, it is likely that the resources most suited to its production are used and that as production increases more and more less-well-suited resources are used.

Consider the production of houses. In the early stages of house production, no doubt the persons most skilled at house building are employed. If house production increases, though, less skilled individuals will enter the house-building industry. Where three skilled house builders could build a house in a week, as many as seven unskilled builders may be required to build it in the same time.

Efficiency

Like other economic concepts, efficiency can be illustrated within a production possibilities frontier framework. In Exhibit 2-5, points A, B, C, D, and E are all efficient points. Notice that each point lies *on* the production possibilities frontier

■ **EXHIBIT 2-5**
Efficiency and Inefficiency within a PPF Framework

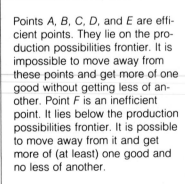

Points A, B, C, D, and E are efficient points. They lie on the production possibilities frontier. It is impossible to move away from these points and get more of one good without getting less of another. Point F is an inefficient point. It lies below the production possibilities frontier. It is possible to move away from it and get more of (at least) one good and no less of another.

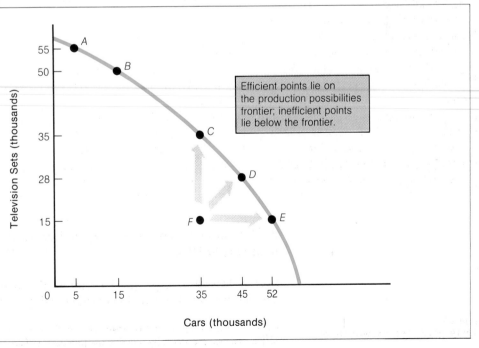

Efficient points lie on the production possibilities frontier; inefficient points lie below the frontier.

instead of below it. Each point represents a maximum combination of the two goods, cars and television sets. Since each point is on the production possibilities frontier, each point represents the outer limit of the attainable region. As we noted earlier, we conclude that the economy exhibits *efficiency* if it is producing the maximum output with given resources and technology. A layperson might put it this way: We are getting the most out of what we have.

Consider another way of viewing efficiency. Start at point A and move to B. We go from a position of more television sets (55,000) and fewer cars (5,000) to a position of fewer television sets (50,000) and more cars (15,000). Move now from point B to A. We go from a position of fewer television sets (50,000) and more cars (15,000) to a position of more television sets (55,000) and fewer cars (5,000). Notice that if we start at an efficient point, it is impossible to get more of one good without getting less of another good. Once again, we can move from A to B and get more cars, but not without getting fewer television sets. Consider point F, which is an **inefficient** point, because it does not lie on the production possibilities frontier. At F the economy is not producing the maximum output with given resources and technology. A layperson might put it this way: We could do better with what we have.

Now let's move from F to C. We get more television sets and no fewer cars. What if we move from F to D? We get more television sets and more cars. Finally, move from F to E. We get more cars and no fewer television sets. We can only conclude that movement from F can give us more of at least one good and no less of another good. (Moving from F to D, we got more of *both* goods.)

Efficiency implies that gains are impossible in one area without losses in another. Inefficiency implies that gains are possible in one area without losses in another.

Think of the common sense of this. If efficiency exists, we already are getting the most we can out of what we have; therefore we *cannot* do better in one area (getting more of one good) without necessarily doing worse in another (getting less of another good). But if inefficiency exists, we are not getting the most out of what we have; therefore we *can* do better in one area without necessarily doing worse in another.

Inefficiency

In terms of production, inefficiency refers to the condition where less than the maximum output is produced with given resources and technology. Inefficiency implies the possibility of gains in one area without losses in another.

Question:

Suppose we move from point F to B. More television sets are produced but fewer cars—in other words, more of one good but less of another. Doesn't this mean F is an efficient point although it was labeled an inefficient point?

Answer:

Efficiency implies that gains are *impossible* in one area without losses in another. Point F does not fit this definition, since from F we could move to C, D, or E—all these moves are *possible*—and get gains in one area without getting losses in another. It follows that F is an inefficient point. Simply because a move from F to B brings gains in one area and losses in another, it does not necessarily follow that a move from F to some other point would always bring the same results. In short, as long as it is *possible* to move from F to some point and get gains in one area without getting losses in another, then F is an inefficient point.

EXCHANGE

Exchange—trading one thing for another, usually money for goods and services—is all around us; we are involved with it every day. Few of us, however, have considered the full dimensions of exchange. We do so here, looking first at the

Theory in Practice

The Efficiency Criterion: Economists Rarely Leave Home Without It

Besides production, economists also evaluate policies, programs and institutions in terms of efficiency. Here they employ the *efficiency criterion*, which, broadly speaking, addresses the question of whether an alternative arrangement exists that can make one person better off without making anyone else worse off.

For example, suppose the U.S. government has placed a tariff on imported shoes. An economist might ask if this is an efficient or inefficient policy. Obviously it is an efficient policy if it is *impossible* to move away from it and make at least one person better off without making someone else worse off. It is an inefficient policy if it is *possible* to move away from it (say, to a nontariff policy) and make at least one person better off and no one worse off.

What are other areas in which the efficiency criterion might be applied? We could ask if the tax code is efficient (can we change it and make at least one person better off and no other person worse off?). What about rent controls, government spending on education, and the 55 mph speed limit? Are these efficient or inefficient?

Suppose it is wartime and the government rations gaso-line. Each person is given 10 ration tickets per week, each ticket permits the holder to buy one gallon of gasoline, and people are prohibited from selling their ration tickets. Is this gasoline rationing system efficient or inefficient?

Consider John and Barbara. John is a traveling salesman who usually buys 50 gallons of gasoline a week. Barbara is a writer, who usually works at home and buys 3 gallons of gasoline a week. Suppose Barbara agrees to illegally sell John a few ration tickets. They agree to a price of $1 per ticket. At this price John buys seven tickets from Barbara. Who is better off? Who is worse off? Both John and Barbara expect to be better off (they wouldn't have traded otherwise), and it appears, that no one is worse off. We conclude that the specific gasoline rationing system, where rationing tickets are not bought and sold, is an inefficient system. An alternative system used by John and Barbara, in which ration tickets are bought and sold, helps at least one person (in this example it helped two) and makes no one worse off.

Question:

A legal gasoline rationing system has been labeled inefficient, *and it is strongly implied that an illegal gasoline rationing system is preferable to it. Is this the type of conclusion that we want?*

Answer:

We don't look for specific types of conclusions. We want only to do positive economic analysis. We see the point, however. In rough terms, it appears as if that which is legal is "not so good" and that which is illegal is "not so bad." This appears to be the way things are *sometimes*. We must realize, however, that what is illegal in one instance may not be in another. For example, it is illegal to buy and sell certain books in some countries, but not in others.

---

periods relevant to exchange and then at the difference between exchange and the terms of exchange.

Periods Relevant to Exchange

Here we discuss three periods relevant to the exchange process: the period before the exchange, the point of exchange, and the period after the exchange.

Before the Exchange. Before an exchange is made, a person is said to be in the **ex ante** position. For example, suppose Ramona has the opportunity to exchange what she has, $500, for something she does not have, a color television set. She could be thinking either (1) that she will be better off with the television set than

Ex Ante
Before, as in "before" the exchange.

Biography
Adam Smith
(1723–1790)

Brief biography

Adam Smith, the father of modern economics, was born in Kircaldy, on the east coast of Scotland on June 5, 1723, and died on July 17, 1790. He was the son of Adam Smith, who died before his son was born, and Margaret Douglas. Smith studied at both Glasgow University and Balliol College, Oxford University. He was greatly disappointed with the teaching at Oxford. He wrote, "In the university of Oxford, the greater part of the public professors have, for these many years, given up altogether even the pretense of teaching."* Smith was a bachelor and lived during much of his lifetime with his mother.

1776

In 1776, the year the Declaration of Independence was signed, Smith

*Adam Smith, *An Inquiry into the Nature and Causes of The Wealth of Nations*, vol. 2 (Chicago: University of Chicago Press, 1976), p. 284.

published his famous work, *An Inquiry into the Nature and Causes of The Wealth of Nations*. Many of this country's founding fathers were familiar with Smith's work. For example, Thomas Jefferson, in a letter dated June 14, 1807, recommended it highly.

Self-Interest

Smith believed that self-interest could produce great and unexpected things. The idea was expressed in his famous passage:

> It is not from the benevolence of the butcher, the brewer, or the baker, that we expect our dinner, but from their regard to their own interest.**

In other words, the butcher, the brewer, and the baker are interested in making themselves better off; they want to earn more income, which they can then use to buy what they want. But to obtain the income, they must first provide something of worth to others.

Voluntary Exchange

Smith argued that both parties to a voluntary exchange must benefit, or they would not enter into the exchange. In similar fashion, he waged an intellectual war against the mercantilist philosophy of the day, which said a country's wealth depends on how much gold and silver it possesses. Mercantilists urged their country to export goods, for which it received gold and silver in return, and to curb or eliminate imports, for which it had to pay gold and silver. Smith argued that it was not the amount of gold and silver that made a nation wealthy, but the amount of goods and

**Smith, The Wealth of Nations, vol. 1, p. 18.

services available to its people— whether these goods and services were produced at home or abroad.

Minimal Government

Smith was an advocate of minimal government. In his view, government existed to provide goods that the free market did not provide or did not provide in the quantities desired by the populace, such as national defense, a court system, roads, and education. Beyond this, Smith believed that there was not much government should or could do without creating problems. Smith was aware that government often stifled trade (between domestic consumers and foreign manufacturers); that its law-making powers could be used by one group of persons to take advantage of another group; and that its regulations could be used to prevent citizens from pursuing their occupations of choice. Smith argued that such government policies decreased the wealth of the nation below the level it could potentially attain.

A Personal Note

Smith was said to be extremely shy in the company of ladies. He was also perhaps the quintessential absent-minded scholar. Fond of walking along the country roads near his home, he nevertheless would sometimes concentrate so intensely on his thoughts that he would lose his way or fall into a hole.

with $500 worth of other goods or (2) that she will be better off with $500 worth of other goods than with the television set. For example, if she believes that she will be better off with the television set than with $500 worth of other goods, she will make the exchange. In fact, everyone who makes an exchange has believed ex ante (before the exchange) that the exchange will make him or her better off.

At the Point of Exchange. Ramona now gives $500 to the person in possession of the television set. Does Ramona still believe she will be better off with the television set than with the $500? Of course she does. Her action gives witness to this.

Ex Post
After, as in "after" the exchange.

After the Exchange. After the exchange is made, a person is said to be in the **ex post** position. Suppose two days have passed. Does Ramona still feel the same way about the exchange as she did before the exchange and at the point of exchange? Maybe, maybe not. Ramona may look back on the exchange and be happy that she made it. Or she may look back on the exchange and regret it. She may say that if she had it to do over again, she would not trade the $500 for the television set. In general, though, people expect to be made better off by an exchange, and in most cases probably are made better off. But there is no guarantee that any one exchange a person makes will turn out as expected. This is not a fault of the exchange process, however; it is a consequence of living in the real world where no one has a crystal ball.

Exchange and the Terms of Exchange

Emilio walks into a bookstore and browses through a few of the best sellers. Minutes later he walks up to the cashier with a book in hand, takes $20 out of his wallet (the price of the book), gives it to the cashier, and walks out. Away from the store, he thinks, they charged too much for the book; I've been taken.

Given Emilio's thoughts, and accepting that he is currently in the ex post position, is it correct to assume that he now regrets the exchange he made only a few seconds earlier? Perhaps the answer is yes, but probably it is no. It is likely that Emilio is expressing his discontent over paying as much for the book as he paid. Perhaps he would rather have paid $15 for the book. Would any buyer be different?

Exchange
The process where one thing is traded for another.

Terms of Exchange
Descriptive of how much of one thing is traded for how much of another.

This brings us to the difference between **exchange** and the **terms of exchange.** Exchange simply refers to the process whereby "things" (money, goods, services, and so on) are traded or swapped. The terms of exchange refer to *how much* of one thing is traded for *how much* of something else. For example, if $20 is traded for a best-selling book, the terms of exchange are 1 best-selling book for $20. If the price of a loaf of bread is $1.50, the terms of exchange are 1 loaf of bread for $1.50. Buyers and sellers can always think of "better" terms of exchange than the terms they exchange at. Buyers prefer lower prices, sellers prefer higher prices, *ceteris paribus*.

Knowing that there is a difference between exchange and the terms of exchange prevents us from slipping into the trap of believing that anytime someone says he or she has been taken, or "ripped off," that this is evidence that the person has been harmed by the exchange. Many times it is no more than the person expressing his or her desire to have paid less (if a buyer) or to have been paid more (if a seller) for the good or service that was exchanged. As the French say, "C'est naturelle" (it's natural).

ECONOMIC FACTS OF LIFE—NO MATTER WHERE YOU LIVE

No matter where a person lives—the United States, the Soviet Union, the People's Republic of China, Poland, Brazil, or anywhere in between—he or she is affected by some fundamental economic facts of life. We discuss a few such economic facts in this chapter. In the last chapter of this text, we discuss how different *economic systems* deal with them.

Economic Facts of Life

Here we discuss four of the numerous facts of economic life that you are already familiar with.

Scarcity. Americans have to deal with scarcity, and so do Canadians, Mexicans, and Belgians. But what about Russians, or Chinese, or people who live on some tropical island in the South Pacific? Do they have to deal with scarcity too? Most assuredly, they do. If you live on the planet Earth, you have to deal with scarcity, in much the same way that you have to deal with gravity. What distinguishes economic systems is *not* that some have to deal with scarcity and others do not, but rather *how* different systems deal with scarcity.

Opportunity Cost, or No Free Lunch. We have learned that opportunity cost is a consequence of scarcity, so wherever scarcity exists, so will opportunity cost. In short, there is no such thing as a free lunch in any society. There are no free lunches in New York City or Moscow. There are no free lunches in Rio de Janeiro or Zurich.

Rational Self-Interested Behavior. Would you expect people in the United States to exhibit rational self-interested behavior and people in some other country not to? We think not. Rational self-interested behavior means to act in such a way as to maximize the difference between the benefits and costs as perceived by the individual. Key words here are "as perceived by the individual." Not everyone will see the benefits and costs of a given action in the same way, but everyone can still behave in such a way as to maximize the difference between the benefits and costs he or she sees. Simply stated, it is widely accepted that all people, no matter where they live, act so as to maximize utility, which is different from saying that all people maximize utility in the same way or gain utility by doing the same things.

What to produce? How to produce it? Who produces it? For whom is it produced? All societies must answer four questions: What goods are to be produced? How are these good to be produced? Who is going to produce these goods? For whom are these goods produced?

First consider what goods are to be produced. We know that in a world of efficiently utilized scarce resources, more of one good necessarily means less of something else. Should we have more cars and fewer subways or more subways and fewer cars? More generally, should we have more military goods and fewer civilian goods? Implicit here is the question of who decides what the economy produces. For example, will it be the marketplace, composed of millions of buyers and sellers (see Chapter 3), or a central government committee (see Chapter 23)? In short, there has to be some way of deciding where a society will be on the production possibilities frontier.

Once the goods to be produced have been determined the society must decide how these goods are to be produced. For example, will farmers with primitive tools or farmers with modern tractors produce food? Will the food be produced on private farms, as in the United States, or on collective farms, as in the Soviet Union?

Economics in Our Times

Interview: Gary Becker

Gary Becker has been described as "one of the most original minds in modern economics" and as an "economic imperialist" because of his work in extending the economic way of thinking into traditionally non-economic areas, such as sociology, political science, social biology, law, and anthropology. He is currently at the University of Chicago. We conducted the following interview with Professor Becker on February 19, 1988.

Professor Becker, economists are quick to point out that there is an "economic way of thinking." Moreover, few economists would doubt that you are a master of it. How would you describe your economic way of thinking?

The economic way of thinking attributes certain types or kinds of behavior to participants, namely, that they

are rational, in the sense that they are forward-looking and try to maximize their welfare as measured by utility or profits. So the economic way of thinking posits forward looking and maximizing individuals. These individuals interact in formal or informal markets where their behavior must be harmonized to varying degrees and made consistent with the total constraint on resources. That, in a nutshell, is what I think the economic way of thinking consists of.

Do you find it is very difficult to get people to understand the economic way of thinking?

After you give lots of examples and show how this way of looking at things leads to results and interpretations that are insightful, people begin to see its usefulness. But it takes a while. It is a foreign way of thinking and hard to get across in a short period of time. Usually, at the end of a course students will begin to get a feel for this way of thinking, although it will take longer than just one course before they can do it well on their own.

How and when did you first come to the realization that economic theory could be used to analyze behavior outside the marketplace? And was it a gradual realization, or did it occur suddenly?

It was gradual on my part. A couple of things I did early in my career involved applications outside the traditional areas. One was on racial discrimination. No economist had been looking at that problem although it had been a major social problem. About the same time I did a shorter piece on the application to political behavior. Then I worked on such topics as human capital, population, allocation of time, and so forth. Only

gradually did I begin to see that the economic way of thinking provided a way to approach many subjects in the social sciences.

How was your work initially received by economists at the University of Chicago and other economists who came across your work?

With some exceptions, my work on discrimination was not initially well received by the economics profession. But some of my teachers at the University of Chicago encouraged me, which was important to me. So did some economists and sociologists who reviewed my book. But on the whole it was neglected and ignored by economists until the mid-1960s (it came out in 1957). Most economists thought it really wasn't economics.

The same happened to my work on population. A paper I gave at a conference was not well received by some economists there. So on the whole I would say that the economics profession was very hostile at first.

Do you think it was simply a matter of time before the new ideas you were presenting could sink in?

That was partly it, and partly people seeing that some of this could be useful. A lot of people still don't accept these applications, but of course fewer than when they first came out. Many excellent economists now work on these and other problems outside conventional economics.

Economics sometimes has a way of showing us that what we think is true is not. Is there anything that stands out in your mind that you believed was true, but later, because of your study of, or work in, economics, found out wasn't true?

Economics opened my mind to a lot of things that I had not thought true.

Let me give one example from the family, the effect of divorce laws. It seems plausible that the change in the divorce laws in the United States from requiring consent of both husband and wife to unilateral divorce will lead to an increase in the divorce rate. But a very simple model of economic bargaining suggests this isn't true. In fact the data show that it hasn't had much of an effect on the divorce rate, even though it seems like such a radical change in access to divorce.

Similarly, in more conventional areas of economics, my assessment of rent control, minimum wages, and many other policies was greatly affected by economic analysis. And that's why economists take such different views from other social scientists on some of these policies. Others usually deny that rent control leads to the deterioration of housing and to shortages. But very simple economic analysis shows that these effects do happen. Apparently this is hard to see if you are not an economist.

You have argued that people's behavior can best be analyzed by as-suming they have a stable set of preferences. Some people might question this assumption. Is there a simple way of convincing people that when it comes to analyzing human behavior it is better to assume "stable preferences" than "changing preferences"?

It is a question largely of seeing how well one does with the assumption of stable preferences. The great advantage of assuming stable preferences is a methodological one: namely, you are constrained from assuming ad hoc changes in preferences. Economists are very prone to do that. When one can't explain something, it is very tempting to say that preferences changed or are different between groups.

Do you see it as a cop-out?

Yes, I do think it is a cop-out. The assumption of stability may have problems, but it prevents such ad hoc assumptions about preferences. You see how far you can go with the tools that you have. Maybe you can't go far, but at least you reach that conclusion more honestly.

You have been both a graduate student and a professor at the University of Chicago. Since the "Chicago School of Economics" figures so prominently in economics, I wonder if you might give us some of the reasons why you think the University of Chicago is a special place at which to learn and teach economics?

I was always happy I went to Chicago. I found it one of the most stimulating experiences of my life. The reason I think it is stimulating to both students and faculty is that ideas are taken seriously at Chicago. There is less reliance on authority, and there is a lot of fairly open give-and-take in an intellectually good-natured way (although it may at times seem a little harsh), but the idea is to try to get more at the truth and understand what's going on. Chicago is a very exciting place, it has been a very innovative place, it has been a controversial place. If you are serious about your economics you will learn an awful lot here. I continue to learn much from the students and my colleagues.

Next, the society must decide who is going to do the producing. Will it be anyone who wants to do the producing or some select group of people (and if it is the latter, who or what does the selecting)?

Finally, the society must determine for whom the goods are produced. One possible answer is anyone who pays the price for the goods; another possible answer is that government decides who will have the goods.

At this level of analysis, you should not be concerned with exactly how these questions are answered. You should simply be aware that there are different ways of answering them and that no society can get around having to answer them.

The Scales of Economics

The eight-year-old girl or boy who takes piano lessons usually spends months practicing scales over and over again. The piano teacher says a good piano player must first learn the basics. And the scales are the basics.

Economics is not much different. Students must first learn the basics as you have been doing in this chapter and the last. Scarcity, choice, opportunity cost, the *ceteris paribus* condition, rational self-interest, there is no such thing as a free lunch, the production possibilities frontier, the law of increasing opportunity costs, decision making at the margin, efficiency, and exchange are some of the key notes the economist regularly plays. Listen as you read the rest of this text, and see if you can hear them under some of the more popular tunes that are played.

■ CHAPTER SUMMARY

Rational Self-Interest

■ A person who behaves according to rational self-interest acts to maximize the difference between (subjectively evaluated) benefits and costs.

■ Rational self-interest and selfishness are not synonyms. A rationally self-interested person is not necessarily a selfish person.

■ Rational self-interest implies that an individual's behavior changes as benefits and costs change.

There Is No Such Thing as A Free Lunch

■ There is no such thing as a free lunch is a shorthand way of reminding ourselves that making choices always involves opportunity costs.

Decision Making at the Margin

■ Economists refer to choices based on the additional benefits and costs of an incremental change as *marginal choices*. Individuals are said to be *deciding at the margin*.

■ Decision making at the margin is characterized by evaluating (usually small) changes in reference to current conditions. It implies the consideration of additional (marginal) benefits and costs instead of total benefits and costs and ignores sunk costs.

Economic Concepts in the *PPF* Framework

■ Whether the production possibilities frontier is a straight line (Exhibit 2-1) or curved (Exhibit 2-2) depends on whether there is a constant trade-off between goods. For example, if the trade-off between X and Y is always two for one, the production possibilities frontier is a straight line. If the trade-off between X and Y changes, the production possibilities frontier is curved.

■ All points on and below the production possibilities frontier are in the attainable region: They represent combinations of goods that can be produced. All points that lie above the frontier are in the unattainable region: They represent combinations of goods that cannot be produced.

■ Scarcity, which implies that some things are unattainable, is represented by the frontier itself. Choice is represented by the fact that from all the attainable combinations of goods that exist, one combination must be selected. Opportunity cost is represented by the fact that to be at one point is not to be at another. It is most visible when moving from one point to another on the production possibilities frontier.

■ An increase in resources shifts the production possibilities frontier outward; a decrease in resources shifts it inward. An increase in productivity shifts the production possibilities frontier outward; a decrease in productivity shifts it inward.

Efficiency

■ All points on the production possibilities frontier are efficient points; all points below it are inefficient.

■ Efficiency implies that gains are impossible in one area without losses in another. Inefficiency implies that gains are possible in one area without losses in another. Economists regularly use the efficiency criterion to evaluate policies, programs, and institutions.

Exchange

■ Ex ante (before the exchange), individuals expect to be made better off by the exchange. At the point of exchange they also expect to be made better by the exchange. Ex post (after the exchange), they may believe they have been made better or worse off by the exchange. In general, though, individuals look on exchange as a way of making themselves better off.

■ Exchange refers to the process whereby "things" are traded or swapped. The terms of exchange refer to how much of one thing is traded for how much of something else. A person may be dissatisfied with the terms of exchange (buyers always prefer lower prices and sellers higher prices, *ceteris paribus*) but not with the exchange itself. For example, Taylor may be happy she bought the house, but dissatisfied that she could not have bought it for $2,000 less.

■ QUESTIONS TO ANSWER AND DISCUSS

1. True or false? If Clarkson smokes two packs of cigarettes a day and Rhodes does not smoke, it follows that both Clarson and Rhodes cannot be exhibiting rational self-interested behavior.

2. Some employees remark that they receive free health insurance from their employers. Is this truly free health insurance?

3. Give two examples of marginal decision making.

4. What might cause a country's production possibilities frontier to shift outward? Inward?

5. Explain how scarcity, choice, and opportunity cost can be illustrated within a production possibilities frontier framework.

6. What condition must hold before the production possibilities frontier is curved, specifically, bowed outward?

7. The chapter gave a few examples of statements and arguments that implicitly assumed there is such a thing as a free lunch, such as the couple who assumed their daughter's education was free because they paid no tuition for her elementary school. Give examples of other statements or arguments that make the mistake of implicitly assuming there is such a thing as a free lunch.

8. At any one time, the U.S. economy has a production possibilities frontier. What effect would a war be likely to have on the production possibilities frontier? What effect would a discovery of resources be likely to have?

9. Even at this early stage, it is important that you begin to think in terms of frameworks. Making use of the production possibilities frontier framework, explain each of the following: (1) a disagreement between a person who advocates more domestic welfare spending and one who advocates more national defense spending; (2) an increase in the population; (3) a technological change that makes resources less specialized; (4) an increase in the productivity of some resource.

Appendix A   **Working with Graphs**

A picture is worth a thousand words. It is with this familiar saying in mind that economists construct their graphs. A few lines, some curves, a few points, and much can be said. Consider, for example, the graph of the production possibilities frontier. With that one graph we explained five concepts: scarcity, choice, opportunity cost, the law of increasing costs, and efficiency. Who said economists don't know how to economize?

HOW TO READ GRAPHS

Most graphs look like one-half of a picture frame with something inside. For example, take a look at Exhibit 2A-1. It has two axes: the vertical axis and the horizontal axis. On the vertical axis we have written "Y" and on the horizontal axis "X." As we

■ **EXHIBIT 2A-1**
A Downward-Sloping Line: What It Says, How to Calculate Its Slope

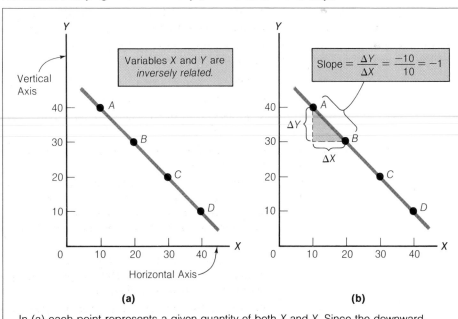

In (a) each point represents a given quantity of both X and Y. Since the downward-sloping line indicates that as X rises (falls), Y falls (rises), the two variables are inversely related. In (b) the slope is calculated as $\Delta Y/\Delta X$.

Inversely Related

Two variables are inversely related if they move in opposite directions.

Directly Related

Two variables are directly related if they move in the same direction.

Independent

Two variables are independent if as one changes, the other does not.

move up the vertical axis and to the right on the horizontal axis, the numbers become larger.

Inside the area marked off by the two axes is a downward-sloping line with four points, *A, B, C,* and *D.* Each point corresponds to so much *X* and so much *Y.* For example, point *A* corresponds to *10X* and *40Y* and *B* corresponds to *20X* and *30Y.* The downward-sloping line indicates the relationship between the two variables. It tells us that as *X* rises, *Y* falls; and as *X* falls, *Y* rises. If one variable goes up as the other goes down, the two variables are **inversely related**.

Consider now the lines in Exhibit 2A-2. In (a) *X* and *Y* move in the same direction: As *X* rises, *Y* rises; as *X* falls, *Y* falls. The two variables are **directly related**. In (b)

■ **EXHIBIT 2A-2**
Different Relationships

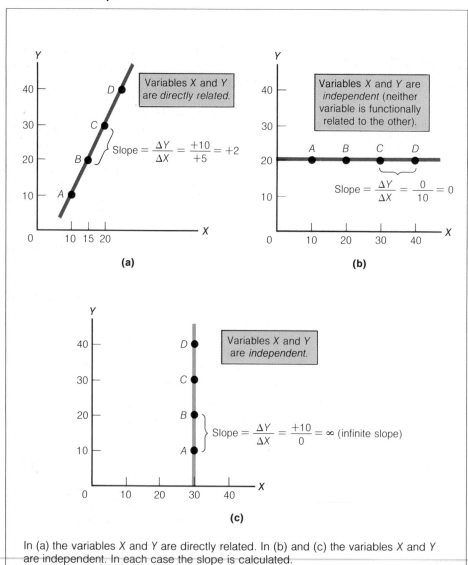

In (a) the variables *X* and *Y* are directly related. In (b) and (c) the variables *X* and *Y* are independent. In each case the slope is calculated.

as X increases, Y does not change. The two variables are **independent.** In (c) as Y increases, X does not change. Again the two variables are *independent.*[1]

SLOPE OF THE LINE

Slope
The ratio of the change in the variable on the vertical axis to the change in the variable on the horizontal axis.

It is often not only important to know *how* two variables are related but also to know *how much* one variable changes as the other variable changes. To find out, we need only calculate the **slope** of the line. The slope is the ratio of the change in the variable on the vertical axis to the change in the variable on the horizontal axis. For example, if Y is on the vertical axis and X on the horizontal axis, the slope is equal to $\Delta Y/\Delta X$. (The symbol "Δ" means "change in.")

$$\text{Slope} = \frac{\Delta Y}{\Delta X}$$

Suppose we calculate the slope between point A and B in Exhibit 2A-1b. The change in Y is equal to -10 (from 40 down to 30); the change in X is equal to $+10$ (from 10 up to 20). The slope therefore is $-10/+10 = -1$.[2] We have also calculated the slopes of the lines in Exhibit 2A-2.

THE SLOPE OF A CURVE

Economic graphs use both lines and curves. The slope of a curve is not constant throughout as it is for a straight line. The slope of a curve varies from one point to another.

Calculating the slope of a curve at a given point requires two steps as illustrated for point A in Exhibit 2A-3. First, draw a line tangent to the point (a tangent line is one that just touches the curve but does not cross it). Second, pick any two points on the tangent line and determine the slope. In Exhibit 2A-3 the slope of the line

[1]Instead of the term *inversely related,* some economists speak of two variables that move in opposite directions as being *negatively related.* Inversely related = negatively related. Similarly, instead of the term *directly related,* some economists speak of two variables that move in the same direction as being *positively related.* Directly related = positively related.

[2]The minus sign before the number 1 signifies that the two variables, X and Y, are inversely related. A plus sign signifies that the two variables are directly related.

■ **EXHIBIT 2A-3**
Calculating the Slope of a Curve (at a Particular Point)

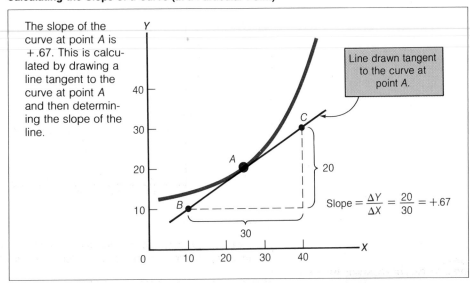

between points *B* and *C* is + .67. It follows that the slope of the curve at point *A* (and only at point *A*) is + .67.

THE 45° LINE

Economists sometimes make use of the *45° line*. This is a straight line that bisects the right angle formed by the intersection of the vertical and horizontal axes. (See Exhibit 2A-4.) As a result, the 45° line divides the space enclosed by the two axes into *two equal parts*. We have illustrated this by shading the two equal parts in different colors. The major characteristic of the 45° line is that any point that lies on it is equidistant from both the horizontal and vertical axes. For example, point *A* is exactly as far from the horizontal axis as it is from the vertical axis. It follows that point *A* represents as much *X* as it does *Y*. Specifically, in the exhibit we see that point *A* represents 20 units of *X* and 20 units of *Y*.

PIE CHARTS

In numerous places in this text you will come across a *pie chart*. A pie chart is a convenient way to represent the different parts of something which when added together equal the whole. Suppose we consider a typical 24-hour weekday for Charles Myers. On a typical weekday, Charles spends 8 hours sleeping, 4 hours taking classes at the university, 4 hours working at his parttime job, 2 hours doing homework, 1 hour eating, 2 hours watching television, and 3 hours doing really nothing (we'll call it "hanging around"). It is easy to represent the breakdown of a typical weekday for Charles in pie chart form. We have done this in Exhibit 2A-5. As you will notice, pie charts give you a quick visual message as to rough percentage breakdowns and relative relationships. For example, in Exhibit 2A-5 it is easy to see that Charles spends most of his time sleeping, and twice as much time working as doing homework.

BAR GRAPHS

Gross National Product
The total market value of all final goods and services produced annually in an economy.

The bar graph is another visual aid that economists use to convey relative relationships. For example, suppose we wanted to represent the **gross national product** (GNP) for different countries in a single year, say 1986. Gross national product is the total market value of all final goods and services produced annually in an economy. In a bar chart we not only can note the actual GNP for each country but

■ **EXHIBIT 2A-4**
The 45° Line

Any point on the 45° line is equidistant from both axes.

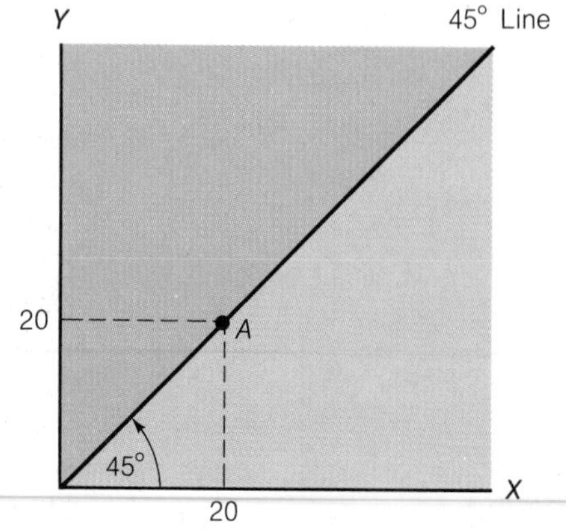

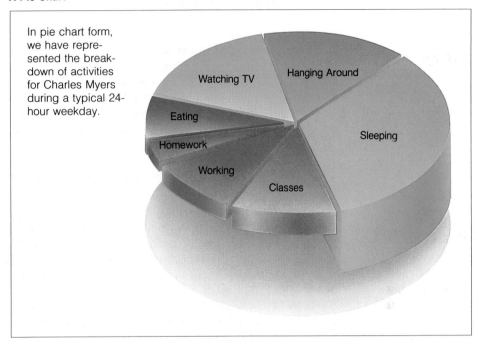

In pie chart form, we have represented the breakdown of activities for Charles Myers during a typical 24-hour weekday.

Watching TV Hanging Around Eating Sleeping Homework Working Classes

also provide a quick picture of the relative relationships between the GNPs of different countries. For instance, in Exhibit 2A-6 it is easy to see that the U.S. GNP was slightly over two times the GNP of Japan in 1986.

LINE GRAPHS

Sometimes information is best and most easily displayed in a line graph. Line graphs are particularly useful when illustrating changes in a variable over some time period. For example, suppose we want to illustrate the variations in "average points per game" for a college basketball team in different years. As you can see from Exhibit 2A-7, the basketball team has been on a roller coaster during the years 1975–88. Perhaps the message that is transmitted here is that there is a lack of consistency in the performance of the team from one year to the next.

Suppose now we were to plot the data presented in (a) of Exhibit 2A-7 in (b) of the exhibit, except this time we use a different measurement scale on the vertical axis. As you can see, there appears much less variation in the performance of the basketball team than appeared in (a). In fact, we could choose some scale such that if we were to plot the data we would end up with close to a straight line. Our point is a simple one: Data plotted in line graph form may convey different messages depending upon the measurement scale used.

Sometimes economists will present two line graphs in one exhibit. This is usually done when someone either (1) wants to draw attention to the relationship between the two variables, or (2) the difference between the two variables is noteworthy. In Exhibit 2A-8, we use line graphs to note the variation and trend in federal government expenditures and tax receipts for the years 1975–1987 and to draw attention to what has been happening to the "gap" between the two. Since for the years noted, expenditures were greater than receipts, the "gap" is the **budget deficit.** (If expenditures are greater than receipts, there is a budget deficit; if expenditures are less than receipts, there is a budget surplus.)

Budget Deficit
Occurs when government expenditures outstrip tax receipts.

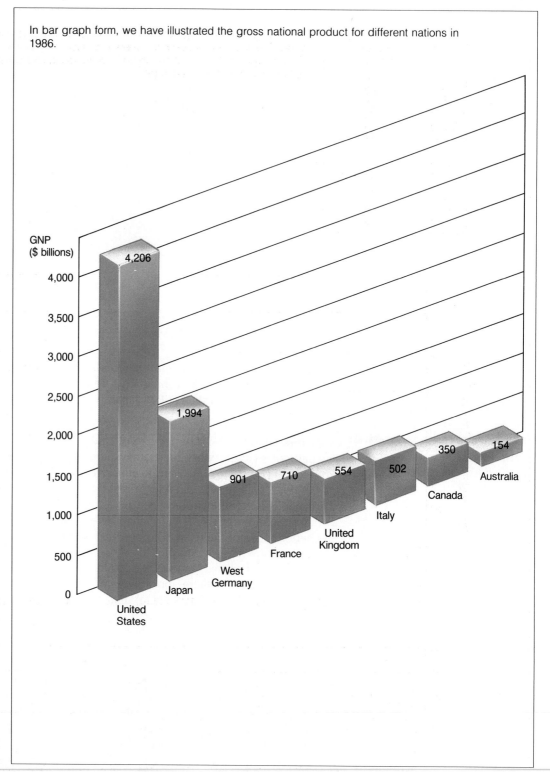

In bar graph form, we have illustrated the gross national product for different nations in 1986.

GNP ($ billions)

United States 4,206
Japan 1,994
West Germany 901
France 710
United Kingdom 554
Italy 502
Canada 350
Australia 154

SOURCE: U.S. Bureau of the Census, Statistical Abstract of the United States, 1988 (Washington, D.C.: U.S. Government Printing Office, 1988).

Year	Average Points per Game
1975	50
1976	40
1977	59
1978	51
1979	60
1980	50
1981	75
1982	63
1983	60
1984	71
1985	61
1986	55
1987	70
1988	64

In (a) we plot the average points per game for a college basketball team in different years. The variation between the years is pronounced. In panel (b) we plot the same data as were plotted in (a) and there appears much less variation in the performance of the team than appeared in (a).

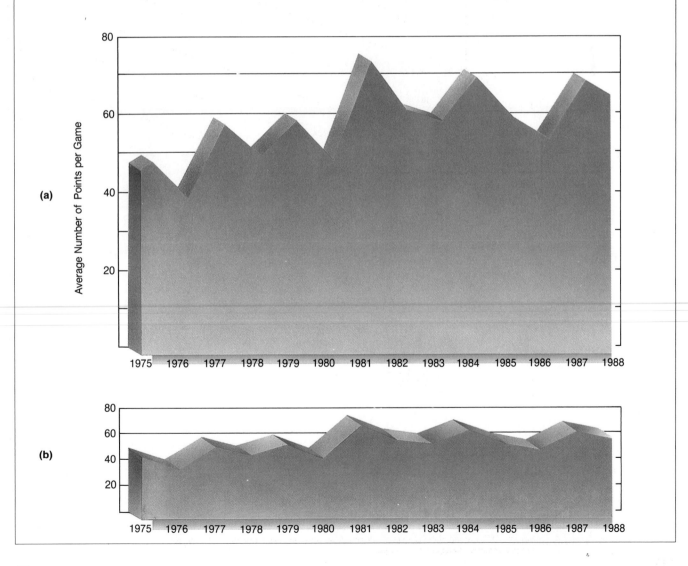

(a)

(b)

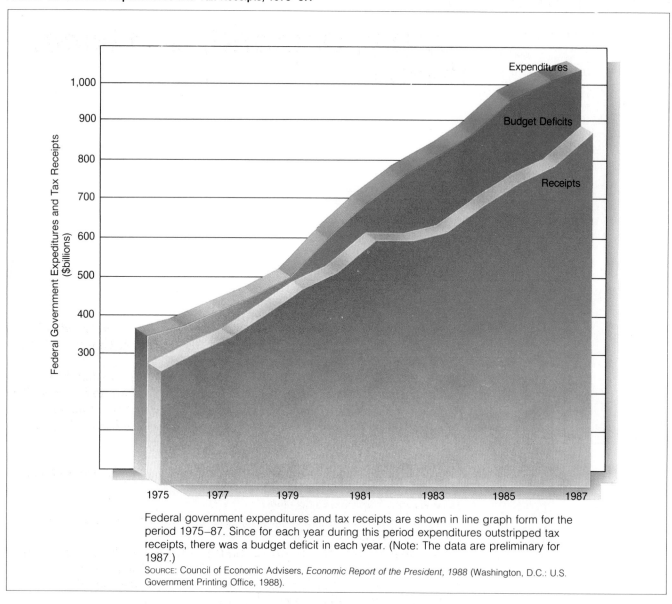

Federal government expenditures and tax receipts are shown in line graph form for the period 1975–87. Since for each year during this period expenditures outstripped tax receipts, there was a budget deficit in each year. (Note: The data are preliminary for 1987.)

SOURCE: Council of Economic Advisers, *Economic Report of the President, 1988* (Washington, D.C.: U.S. Government Printing Office, 1988).

Chapter 3

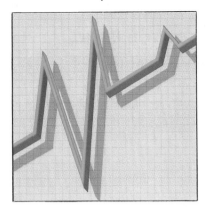

Supply, Demand, and Price: Theory

■ INTRODUCTION

The Russian government official boarded the plane in Moscow and headed for Washington, D.C. His objective? To buy American brainpower from the U.S. Department of Brains.

His plane was met by a U.S. government official. After the two men had greeted each other, the Russian expressed his desire to get down to business. The American complied. He took the Russian to the U.S. Department of Brains.

"In this case," said the American, "we have the brains of a judge. The price is $1,000 per ounce."

"Interesting," said the Russian.

"And in this case over here," said the American, "we have the brains of a nuclear physicist. The price is $2,000 per ounce."

The Russian listened and nodded.

"And in this case," said the American, "we have the brains of an economist. The price is $50,000 per ounce."

"Fifty thousand dollars!" the Russian gasped. "That is ridiculous. I don't understand your capitalist system. The brains of a judge are $1,000 per ounce, the brains of a nuclear physicist are $2,000, but the brains of an economist are $50,000 per ounce. This is simply ridiculous."

The American, startled by the Russian's reaction, replied, "Yes, but do you have any idea how many economists it takes to get an ounce of brains?"

■ WHAT THIS CHAPTER IS ABOUT

Psychologists play a game called *word association* to learn more about their patients. The psychologist says a word, and the patient says the first word that comes into his or her head. Morning, night. Girl, boy. Sunrise, sunset. If an economist were to play this game and the psychologist said "supply," the economist would undoubtedly answer "demand." To economists, supply and demand go together. (Thomas Carlyle, the historian and philosopher, said that "it is easy to train economists. Just teach a parrot to say 'Supply and Demand.'" Not funny, Carlyle.) Supply and demand have been called the "bread and butter" of economics. In this chapter we discuss them, first separately and then together.

Key Questions to Keep in Mind as You Read

1. What is the difference between absolute price and relative price?
2. What is the law of demand?
3. What is the difference between a change in quantity demanded and a change in demand?
5. What is the law of supply?
6. Why do most supply curves slope upward?
7. What is the difference between a change in quantity supplied and a change in supply?
8. How are equilibrium prices and quantities arrived at?

DEMAND

Market
Any arrangement by which people exchange goods and services.

Law of Demand
As the price of a good rises, the quantity demanded of the good falls, and as the price of a good falls, the quantity demanded of the good rises, ceteris paribus.

A **market** is any arrangement by which people exchange goods and services. There are two sides to a market: a buying side and a selling side. (Can there be an exchange without both a buyer and a seller? No.) *Demand* is relevant to the buying side, *supply* is relevant to the selling side. In this section we discuss the buying side of the market.

The Law of Demand

Suppose the airline fare from New York to London falls from $800 to $450, *ceteris paribus*. Will individuals want to buy more or fewer airline tickets on this route? Most people would say, more. Now suppose the airline fare from New York to London rises from $800 to $1,200, *ceteris paribus*. Will individuals want to buy more or fewer airline tickets on this route? Most people would say, fewer. If you answered the questions the way most people would, you instinctively understand the **law of demand,** which holds that *as the price of a good rises, the quantity demanded of the good falls, and as the price of a good falls, the quantity demanded of the good rises, ceteris paribus*. Simply put, the law of demand states that the price of a good and the quantity demanded of the good are inversely related, *ceteris paribus*:[1]

$$P \uparrow \quad Q_d \downarrow$$
$$P \downarrow \quad Q_d \uparrow \quad \textit{ceteris paribus}$$

where P = price, and Q_d = quantity demanded.

What Is Quantity Demanded? *Quantity demanded* is the amount of a good that individuals are *willing to buy* at a particular price during some time period (per day, week, month, and so forth). For example, suppose individuals are willing to buy 100 units of X per week at the price of $4 per unit. One hundred units of X is therefore the quantity demanded of good X at $4.

---

[1]The law of demand holds for *services* as well as *goods*. Goods are tangible and include such things as shirts, books, and television sets. Services are intangible and include such things as dental care, medical care, and an economics lecture. To simplify the discussion, however, we refer to only *goods*.

Absolute Prices and Relative Prices

Absolute Price

The price of a good in money terms.

Relative Price

The price of a good in terms of another good.

The **absolute price** of a good is its price in money terms. For example, the absolute price of a car might be $12,000. The **relative price** of a good is its price in terms of another good (not in terms of money). Suppose the absolute price of a car is $12,000 and the absolute price of a computer is $2,000. The relative price of the car (in terms of computers) is 6 *computers*. A person necessarily gives up the opportunity to buy 6 computers when he or she buys a car.

What happens to the relative price of a good as its absolute price increases (decreases), *ceteris paribus?* For example, suppose the absolute price of the car rises to $20,000. The relative price of the car (in terms of computers) rises to 10 computers. If the absolute price of the car falls to $8,000, the relative price of the car falls to 4 computers. We conclude that as the absolute price of a good rises, the relative price of the good rises; as the absolute price of a good falls, the relative price of a good falls, *ceteris paribus*. (If we had omitted "*ceteris paribus*," the statement would not necessarily be true.)

Question:

Is it possible for the absolute price of a good to rise while its relative price falls?

Answer:

Yes. To illustrate, suppose there are two goods, A and B, whose absolute prices are $10 and $5, respectively. The relative price of 1 unit of A is 2 units of B. Now suppose the absolute price of A rises to $15 and the absolute price of B rises to $10. This is a 50 percent increase in the absolute price of A and a 100 percent increase in the absolute price of B. The relative price of A is 1.5 units of B. We conclude that even though the absolute price of A has increased (from $10 to $15), its relative price has decreased (from 2 to 1.5 units of B). The relative price of A decreased as its absolute price increased (A is more expensive in dollar terms but cheaper in relative terms) because the absolute price of B increased by a greater percentage.

Consider a real-world example. The *Economic Report of the President* shows that between 1967 and 1987, apparel prices increased 116.9 percent while medical care prices increased 362.2 percent. Obviously both apparel prices and medical care prices increased in absolute terms during this period, but since medical care prices increased more (in percentage terms), the relative price of apparel fell.

From the Law of Demand to a Demand Schedule to a Demand Curve

Demand Schedule

The numerical tabulation of the quantity demanded of a good at different prices.

Demand Curve

The graphical representation of the law of demand.

A **demand schedule** is one way of representing the inverse relationship between price and quantity demanded specified by the law of demand. It is the numerical tabulation of the quantity demanded of a good at different prices. A demand schedule for good X is illustrated in Exhibit 3-1a.

In Exhibit 3-1b the four price-quantity combinations are plotted and the points connected, giving us a **demand curve**.[2] A demand curve is the graphical represen-

[2]Although the points A, B, C, and D lie along a *line*, many economists loosely refer to it as a demand *curve*. Don't let this confuse you. The standard practice in economics is to call the graphical representation of the inverse relationship between price and quantity demanded a demand *curve* whether it is a curve or a line. Strictly speaking, though, Exhibit 3-1b depicts a *straight-line demand curve*. Of course, another way to look at this is to say that economists often use a downward-sloping line to *approximate* a downward-sloping demand curve.

Theory in Practice

Apples in the Big Apple

It is time to think through a problem the way an economist would. Suppose that both high-quality and medium-quality apples are grown in the state of Washington. Their absolute prices are 10 cents and 5 cents, respectively. It follows that the relative price of a high-quality apple is 2 medium-quality apples. Now suppose the cost of transportation to New York City per apple, irrespective of quality, is 5 cents. In New York, therefore, a high-quality apple is 15 cents and a medium-quality apple is 10 cents. It follows that the relative price of a high-quality apple is 1.5 medium-quality apples. In short, although the absolute price of both types of apples is higher in New York than in Washington, the relative price of high-quality apples is lower in New York than in Washington.

Washington

1 high-quality apple = 10 cents
1 medium-quality apple = 5 cents
1 high-quality apple = 2 medium-quality apples

New York

1 high-quality apple = 15 cents
1 medium-quality apple = 10 cents
1 high-quality apple = 1.5 medium-quality apples

In which place, Washington or New York, would you predict *relatively more* high-quality apples are consumed, *ceteris paribus*? The answer is New York. The reason is that we would expect *relatively more* high-quality apples to be consumed where high-quality apples are *relatively cheaper*. And this is in New York.

Question:

Is there a difference between New Yorkers buying relatively more *high-quality apples and New Yorkers buying* more *high-quality apples?*

Answer:

Yes. *More* indicates a larger absolute number; *relatively more* indicates a greater percentage. For example, New Yorkers may be buying relatively more high-quality apples than Washingtonians, but they are still buying fewer high-quality apples.

Let's say that Washingtonians buy 10,000 high-quality apples and 30,000 medium-quality apples, and New Yorkers buy 5,000 high-quality apples and 7,500 medium-quality apples. Washingtonians buy *more* high-quality apples. But New Yorkers buy *relatively more* high-quality apples. Of all the apples New Yorkers buy, 40 percent are high-quality apples (5,000 is 40 percent of 12,500). Of all the apples Washingtonians buy, 25 percent are high-quality apples (10,000 is 25 percent of 40,000).

---

tation of the demand schedule, which is the numerical representation of the inverse relationship between price and quantity demanded specified by the law of demand. In short, the demand curve is a picture of the law of demand.

How Much of a Good
Buyers Are Willing to Buy Depends on Price, Among Other Things

How many car stereos are people willing to buy? How many 16-year-olds on summer vacation are local businesses willing to hire? For example, are people willing to buy 5,000 car stereos and hire 3,300 16-year-olds? Is there one specific number in each case? No. People might be willing to buy anywhere from 0 to 50,000 car stereos. It depends on the price of car stereos. At $50 they will probably buy more car stereos than at $200.

Demand Schedule for Good X

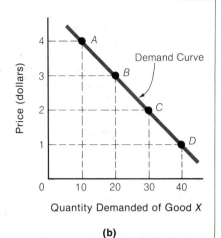

PRICE (dollars)	QUANTITY DEMANDED	POINT IN PANEL (b)
4	10	A
3	20	B
2	30	C
1	40	D

(a) **(b)**

(a) A demand schedule for good X. (b) A demand curve, obtained by plotting the different price-quantity combinations and connecting the points. On a demand curve the price (in dollars) represents price per unit of the good; and the quantity demanded, on the horizontal axis, is always relevant for a specific time period (a week, a month, and so on).

This is an obvious point, perhaps. But think of how often we mistakenly believe that the quantity demanded of a good is independent of the price of the good. For example, some people often speak as if there are a fixed number of jobs in the United States. You might have heard someone say, "We've got to protect U.S. jobs from foreign competition, because if foreign firms outcompete U.S. firms, U.S. workers will lose their jobs, and it is unlikely they will find work elsewhere because there are *only so many jobs.*"

But it is not true that there are only so many jobs. There are only so many jobs at a *particular wage rate* (just as people are willing to buy only so many car stereos at a particular price). The lower the wage rate, the greater the quantity demanded of labor, and the more jobs there are, *ceteris paribus.*

Question:

The economics department at the university has hired additional economics professors during the past five years even though salaries have stayed constant. The additional professors were hired because of a rise in student enrollment. Doesn't this indicate that the number of jobs in the economics department depends on how many students want to take economics classes, not on the salaries of economics professors?

Answer:

Recall that how much of a good people are willing to buy depends on price, *among other things.* Student enrollment is one of the *other things.* But simply because student enrollment affects the number of job openings for economics professors, it does not follow that professors' salaries do not.

Look at it this way. Suppose *all other things* (student enrollment and so forth) are held constant while professors' salaries go down. What would the university do? It might hire more economics professors and have smaller classes (classes averaging 30 students instead of 40 students, for example). Now suppose salaries rise. What would the university do? It might not be as willing to grant permanent positions to its faculty, and it probably will have bigger classes.

Factors That Can Cause the Demand Curve to Shift

We constructed the demand schedule in Exhibit 3-1a and plotted the demand curve in (b) with the condition that all other things are held constant. But what if any of those other things change? Obviously the demand schedule will change, and the demand curve will shift. Here we discuss what these other things are and how changes in them can affect (shift) the demand curve.

Income.   As a person's income rises, he or she *can* buy more of any particular good (say, blue jeans) at given prices. But the ability to buy more blue jeans does not necessarily imply the willingness to do so.

Let's consider two cases. First, suppose a person's income increases and her willingness to buy blue jeans increases too. In this case the demand curve for blue jeans shifts rightward, or, as economists also say, the demand for blue jeans has increased. In this case blue jeans are a **normal good.** The demand for a normal good rises as income rises and falls as income falls. The demand for a normal good and income are directly related.

Now suppose a person's income increases and her willingness to buy blue jeans decreases. In this case, the demand curve for blue jeans shifts leftward, or demand decreases; this time blue jeans are an **inferior good.** The demand for an inferior good falls as income rises and rises as income falls. The demand for an inferior good and income are inversely related. Hotdogs and used cars might be inferior goods because many people usually buy less of these goods as their incomes rise.

Exhibit 3-2a illustrates a rightward shift in the demand curve (implying that people are willing to buy larger quantities of the good at each price), and Exhibit 3-2b illustrates a leftward shift in the demand curve (implying that people are willing to buy smaller quantities of the good at each price).

Preferences.   Peoples' preferences affect the amount of a good they are willing to buy at a particular price. A change in preferences in favor of a good shifts the demand curve rightward. A change in preferences away from the good shifts the demand curve leftward. For example, if people begin to favor spy novels to a greater degree than previously, the demand for spy novels increases, and the demand curve shifts rightward.

Prices of Related Goods.   There are two types of related goods: **substitutes** and **complements.** Two goods are substitutes if they satisfy similar needs or desires. With substitutes, the demand for one rises as the price of the other rises, and the demand for one falls as the price of the other falls. For example, for many people Coca-Cola is a substitute for Pepsi-Cola; thus higher Coca-Cola prices will increase the demand for Pepsi-Cola as people substitute Pepsi for the higher priced Coke (Exhibit 3-3a). Other examples of substitutes include coffee and tea, corn chips and potato chips, two brands of margarine, and foreign and domestic cars.

Two goods are complements if they are consumed jointly. For example, tennis rackets and tennis balls are used together to play tennis. With complements, the demand for one rises when the price of the other falls and the demand for one falls as the price of the other rises. For example, as the price of tennis rackets rises, the

Normal Good

A good the demand for which rises (falls) as income rises (falls).

Inferior Good

A good the demand for which falls (rises) as income rises (falls).

Substitutes

Two goods that satisfy similar needs or desires. With substitutes, the demand for one rises as the price of the other rises (or the demand for one falls as the price of the other falls).

Complements

Two goods that are used jointly in consumption. With complements, the demand for one rises as the price of the other falls (or the demand for one falls as the price of the other rises).

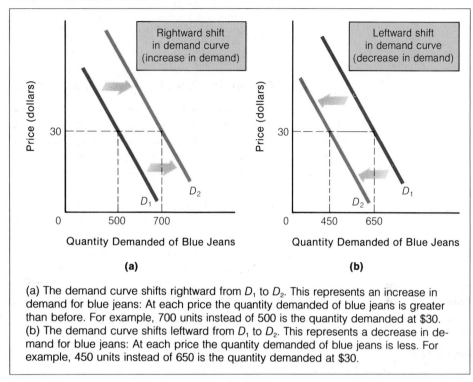

(a) The demand curve shifts rightward from D_1 to D_2. This represents an increase in demand for blue jeans: At each price the quantity demanded of blue jeans is greater than before. For example, 700 units instead of 500 is the quantity demanded at $30.
(b) The demand curve shifts leftward from D_1 to D_2. This represents a decrease in demand for blue jeans: At each price the quantity demanded of blue jeans is less. For example, 450 units instead of 650 is the quantity demanded at $30.

demand for tennis balls falls, as Exhibit 3-3b shows. Other examples of complements include cars and tires, shirts and trousers, lightbulbs and lamps, and golf clubs and golf balls.

Number of Buyers.   The demand for a good in a particular area is related to the number of buyers in the area. The more buyers, the higher the demand; the fewer buyers, the lower the demand. The number of buyers may increase owing to a higher birth rate, increased immigration, the migration of people from one region of the country to another, and so on. The number of buyers may decrease owing to a higher death rate, war, the migration of people from one region of the country to another, and so on.

Expectations of Future Price.   Buyers who expect the price of cars to be higher next month may buy cars now, increasing the current demand for cars. Buyers who expect the price of cars to be lower next month may put off buying cars now, decreasing the current demand for cars and increasing the future demand for cars.

A Change in Quantity Demanded versus a Change in Demand

A *change in demand* refers to a shift in the demand curve as illustrated in Exhibit 3-4a. For example, saying that the demand for apples has increased is the same as saying that the demand curve for apples has shifted rightward. As we have seen, the factors that can change demand (shift the demand curve) include income, preferences, prices of related goods, number of buyers, and expectations of (future) price.

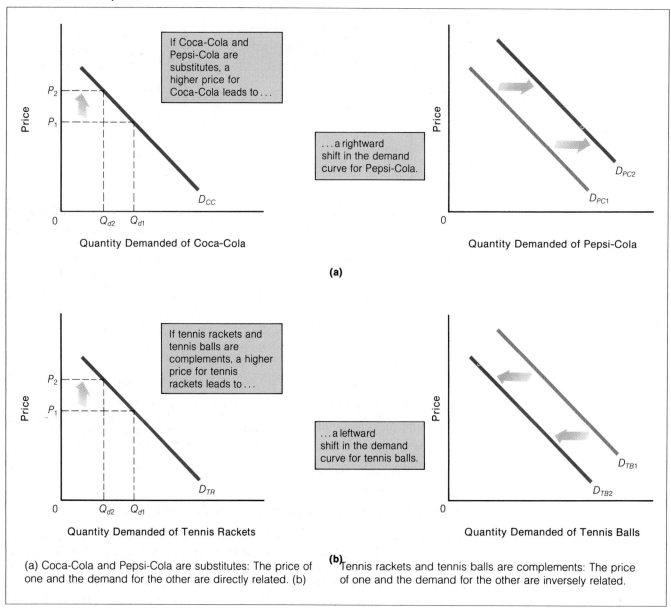

If Coca-Cola and Pepsi-Cola are substitutes, a higher price for Coca-Cola leads to ...

...a rightward shift in the demand curve for Pepsi-Cola.

If tennis rackets and tennis balls are complements, a higher price for tennis rackets leads to ...

...a leftward shift in the demand curve for tennis balls.

(a)

(b)

(a) Coca-Cola and Pepsi-Cola are substitutes: The price of one and the demand for the other are directly related. (b) Tennis rackets and tennis balls are complements: The price of one and the demand for the other are inversely related.

A *change in quantity demanded* refers to a movement along a demand curve as in Exhibit 3-4b. What can cause a change in the quantity demanded of a good? A change in the price of the good, or (its) **own price.**

It is important to distinguish between a *change in demand* (shift in the demand curve) and a *change in quantity demanded* (movement along a demand curve) as the following exercise illustrates.[3]

Own Price

The price of a good. For example, if the price of oranges is $1, this is (its) own price.

[3]Note to students: Economics professors are sticklers when it comes to your knowing the difference between a change in demand and a change in quantity demanded. Consequently, you can expect a question or two that relate to the difference on the next test. A typical true-or-false question might be ''A rise in the price of oranges will lead to a fall in the demand for oranges, *ceteris paribus.*'' The correct answer is False. A rise in the price of oranges will lead to a fall in the *quantity demanded* of oranges, *ceteris paribus.* Remember, own price directly changes quantity demanded.

EXHIBIT 3-4
A Change in Demand versus a Change in Quantity Demanded

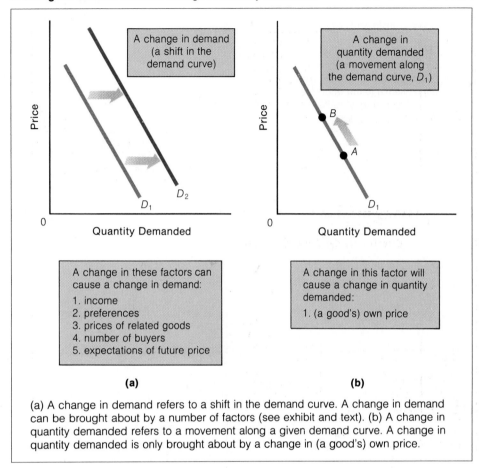

(a) A change in demand refers to a shift in the demand curve. A change in demand can be brought about by a number of factors (see exhibit and text). (b) A change in quantity demanded refers to a movement along a given demand curve. A change in quantity demanded is only brought about by a change in (a good's) own price.

An Exercise: Learning to Keep the Law of Demand Straight

Your friend says, "I've noticed that the price of eating out at restaurants has gone up. I've also noticed that more people are eating out at restaurants. But the law of demand predicts the opposite. It holds that if the price of a good rises, less of that good will be consumed. Obviously, the law of demand must be wrong."

Suppose we accept as truth that the price of eating out at restaurants has gone up and that more people are eating out at restaurants. Does it follow that the law of demand does not hold? Not at all. The inverse relationship between price and quantity demanded holds if *all other things are held constant*. What your friend has observed is a case where all other things were not constant.

To illustrate, consider Exhibit 3-5a. Your friend may initially have observed two points, *A* and *B*, where *B* represents a higher price and a greater consumption of meals than *A*. From this he concluded that people buy more restaurant meals at higher prices than lower prices. In short, your friend sees the demand curve as upward sloping as in Exhibit 3-5b.

But the important point is that the 14 millions meals consumed at point *B is not the result of a higher price but the result of a higher demand curve* as in Exhibit 3-5c. In short, the consumption of meals has increased from 10 million to 14 million because the demand curve has shifted rightward from D_1 to D_2 (owing perhaps to

■ **EXHIBIT 3-5 Keeping the Law of Demand Straight**

Your friend initially observes the equivalent of points *A* and *B* in (a). He believes that higher restaurant prices cause people to buy more restaurant meals. That is, he thinks (b) is the accurate representation of buying behavior. He is mistaken, however. People buy more restaurant meals because the demand curve for restaurant meals has shifted rightward as in (c).

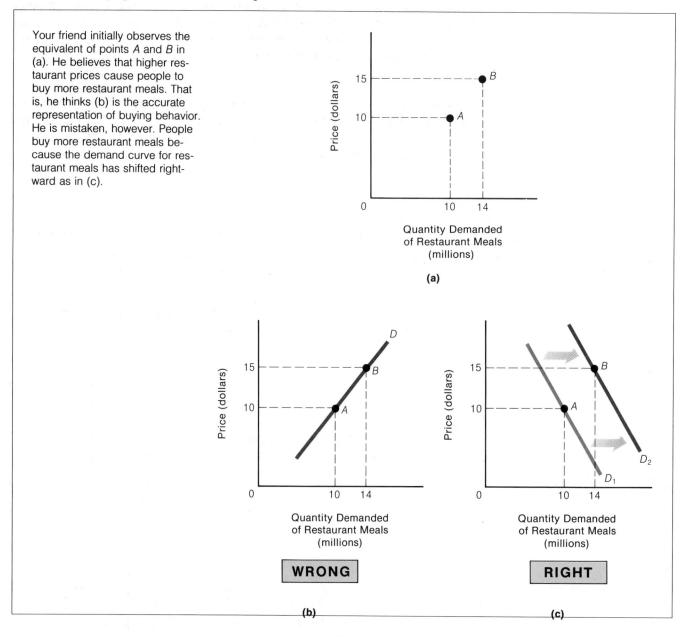

a rise in incomes or a change in preferences), not because price has increased from $10 to $15 (as your friend mistakenly thought was the case).

The Market Demand Curve

An *individual demand curve* represents the price-quantity combinations for a single buyer. A *market demand curve* represents the price-quantity combinations for all buyers of a particular good. For example, we could speak about Jones's demand for honey. Here an individual demand curve would be relevant. Or we could speak about (all) buyers' demand for honey. Here a market demand curve would be relevant.

In Exhibit 3-6 we have derived a market demand curve by "summing up" the individual demand curves. A demand schedule for Jones, Smith, and "all other buyers" is shown in (a). The market demand schedule is then obtained by adding up the quantity demanded by each party at each price. In (b) the data points are plotted, giving us a market demand curve.

SUPPLY

We turn now to the other side of the market: supply. Using a format similar to our discussion of demand, we first define the law of supply, then discuss the factors that can cause the supply curve to shift. Finally, we distinguish between a change in quantity supplied and a change in supply.

■ **EXHIBIT 3-6**
Deriving a Market Demand Schedule and Market Demand Curve

In (a) the market demand schedule is derived by adding up the quantity demanded by each party at each price. In (b) the data points are plotted, giving us a market demand curve. Only two points on the market demand curve are noted.

Quantity Demanded

PRICE	JONES	SMITH	OTHER BUYERS	ALL BUYERS
$15	1	2	20	23
14	2	3	45	50
13	3	4	70	77
12	4	5	100	109
11	5	6	130	141
10	6	7	160	173

(a)

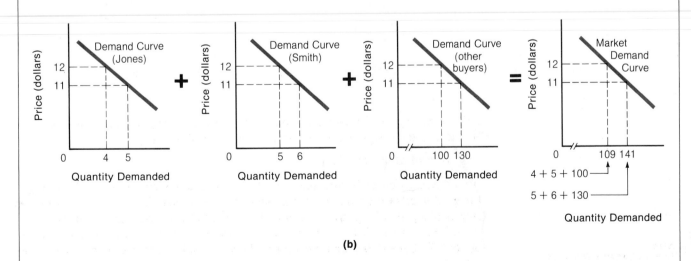

(b)

The Law of Supply

Law of Supply

As the price of a good rises, the quantity supplied of the good rises, and as the price of a good falls, the quantity supplied of the good falls, *ceteris paribus*.

(Upward-Sloping) Supply Curve

The graphical representation of the law of supply.

The **law of supply** states that *as the price of a good rises, the quantity supplied of the good rises, and as the price of a good falls, the quantity supplied of the good falls, ceteris paribus*. Simply put, the price of a good and the quantity supplied of the good are directly related, *ceteris paribus*.[4] (*Quantity supplied* is the amount of a good sellers are willing to sell at a particular price.) The *upward-sloping* **supply curve** is the graphical representation of the law of supply[5] (Exhibit 3-7).

The law of supply can be summarized as

$$P \uparrow \qquad Q_s \uparrow$$
$$P \downarrow \qquad Q_s \downarrow \quad \textit{ceteris paribus}$$

where P = price and Q_s = quantity supplied.

The law of supply holds for the production of most goods. It does not hold when *there is no time to produce more units of a good*. For example, a theater in Atlanta is sold out for tonight's play. Even if ticket prices were to increase from $30 to $40, there would be no additional seats in the theater. There is no time to produce more seats. The supply curve for theater seats is illustrated in Exhibit 3-8a. It is fixed at the number of seats in the theater, 500.[6]

The law of supply also **does not hold** *for goods that cannot be produced* (over any period of time). For example, since the violin maker Antonio Stradivari died in 1737, a rise in the price of Stradivarius violins does not affect the number of Stradivarius violins supplied, as Exhibit 3-8b illustrates.

---

[4]The law of supply, like the law of demand, holds for *services* as well as *goods*.

[5]As with the demand curve, we use the word supply *curve* even if the curve is a line. Strictly speaking, the picture in Exhibit 3-7 is of a *straight-line supply curve*.

[6]The vertical supply curve is said to be *perfectly inelastic*. This term is defined in Chapter 6.

■ **EXHIBIT 3-7**
A Supply Curve

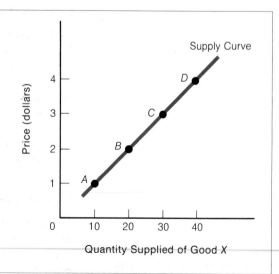

The upward-sloping supply curve is the graphical representation of the law of supply, which holds that price and quantity supplied are directly related, *ceteris paribus*. On a supply curve the price (in dollars) represents price per unit of the good; and the quantity supplied, on the horizontal axis, is always relevant for a specific time period (a week, a month, and so on).

Supply Curves When There Is No Time To Produce More or No More Can Be Produced

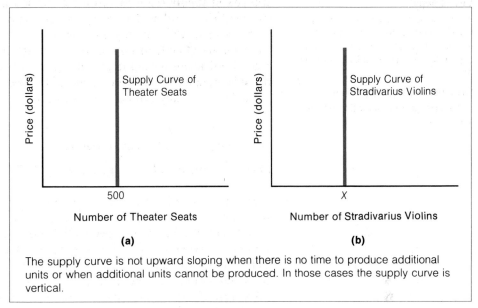

The supply curve is not upward sloping when there is no time to produce additional units or when additional units cannot be produced. In those cases the supply curve is vertical.

Question:

The law of supply holds that price and quantity supplied are directly related. The upward-sloping supply curve is the graphical representation of this law. But then what do the vertical supply curves in panels (a) and (b) of Exhibit 3-8 represent? It can't be the law of supply.

Answer:

They represent an independent relationship between price and quantity supplied.

Why Most Supply Curves Are Upward Sloping

Most supply curves are upward sloping. The fundamental reason for this involves the *law of diminishing marginal returns*, which we discuss at length in Chapter 8. Here, it suffices to say that an upward-sloping supply curve reflects the fact that under certain conditions a higher price is an incentive to producers to produce more of a good. For example, if the price of watermelons rises, farmers have an added incentive to grow and sell more watermelons, all other things held constant. More important, though, an upward-sloping supply curve reflects the fact that generally per-unit production costs rise when more units of a good are produced, so a higher price is necessary to elicit more output.

Factors That Can Cause the Supply Curve to Shift

The supply curve in Exhibit 3-7 is based on the condition that all other things are held constant. But what if any of these other things change? Obviously, the supply curve will shift rightward or leftward as in Exhibit 3-9. Here we discuss what these other things are and how changes in them can affect (shift) the supply curve.

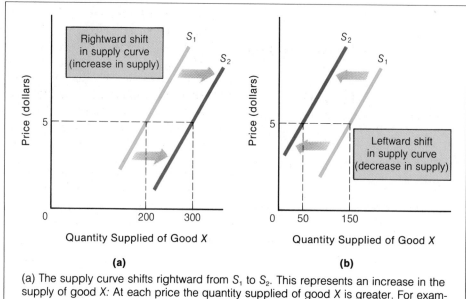

(a) The supply curve shifts rightward from S_1 to S_2. This represents an increase in the supply of good X: At each price the quantity supplied of good X is greater. For example, 300 units instead of 200 is the quantity supplied at $5. (b) The supply curve shifts leftward from S_1 to S_2. This represents a decrease in the supply of good X: At each price the quantity supplied of good X is less. For example, 50 units instead of 150 is the quantity supplied at $5.

Prices of Relevant Resources.   Resources are necessary to produce goods. For example, resource X may be necessary to the production of good Y. If the price of resource X falls, the supply curve of Y shifts rightward; if the price of resource X rises, the supply curve of Y shifts leftward. For example, a fall in the price of farmland, fertilizer, and tractors decreases the per-unit cost of producing corn, and therefore increases the amount of corn that farmers will want to sell at each price. In short, it shifts the supply curve of corn rightward.

Technology.   In Chapter 2 we defined *technology* as the body of skills and knowledge relevant to the use of inputs or resources in production. We also said that an advance in technology refers to the ability to generate more output with a fixed amount of resources, thus reducing per-unit production costs. If this occurs, the quantity supplied of a good at each price increases. Why? The reason is that lower costs increase profitability and therefore provide producers with an incentive to produce more. For example, if corn growers develop a way to grow more corn using the same amount of water (and other resources), it follows that per-unit production costs fall, profitability increases, and growers will want to grow and sell more corn at each price. The supply curve of corn shifts rightward.

Number of Sellers.   If more sellers begin producing a particular good, perhaps because of high profits, the supply curve shifts rightward. If some sellers stop producing a particular good, perhaps because of losses, the supply curve shifts leftward.

Expectations of Future Price.   If the price of a good is expected to be higher in the future, producers may hold back some of the product today (if possible—for example,

Economics in Our Times

Getting Taken for a Ride in a New York Taxi

Ask yourself what requirements a person who wants to operate a taxi business should meet. You may say that the person should prove that he or she is a good driver, has auto insurance, is familiar with the city, is not a criminal, and is in possession of a car or cars that is (are) mechanically safe. Would you think that this person should also have to pay approximately $65,000 for a taxi license? If this seems excessive, you may be surprised to hear that this is the case in New York City. Before a person can operate a taxi business, he or she must be licensed, which entails purchasing a taxi medallion, which are in limited number. In the mid-1980s the price of a medallion was approximately $65,000.

There is little doubt that licensing leads to fewer taxis on the streets of New York City than there would be without it. And, as we shall learn when we put supply and demand together, because there are fewer taxis in New York City, the price of a taxi ride is higher.

perishables cannot be held back) to have more to sell at the higher future price. Therefore the present supply curve shifts leftward. For example, if oil producers expect the price of oil to be higher next year, some may hold oil off the market this year to be able to sell it next year. Similarly, if they expect the price of oil to be lower next year, they might pump more oil this year than previously planned.

Taxes and Subsidies. Some taxes increase per-unit costs. Suppose a shoe manufacturer must pay a $2 tax per pair of shoes produced. This would lead to a leftward shift in the supply curve, and the manufacturer would want to produce and sell fewer pairs of shoes at each price. If the tax is eliminated, the supply curve would shift rightward.

Subsidies have the opposite effect. Suppose the government subsidizes the production of corn. It promises to pay corn farmers $2 for every bushel of corn they produce. Because of the subsidy, the quantity supplied of corn is greater at each price, and the supply curve of corn shifts rightward. Removal of the subsidy shifts the supply curve of corn leftward. A rough rule of thumb is that we get more of what we subsidize and less of what we tax.

Government Restrictions. Sometimes government acts to reduce supply. Consider the U.S. import quota on Japanese television sets. An import quota, or quantitative restriction on foreign goods, reduces the supply of Japanese television sets. It shifts the supply curve leftward. The elimination of the import quota allows the supply of Japanese television sets in the United States to shift rightward.

Licensure has a similar effect. With licensure individuals must meet certain requirements before they can legally carry out a task. For example, owner-operators of day-care centers must meet certain requirements before they are allowed to sell their services. No doubt this reduces the number of day-care centers and shifts the supply curve of day-care centers leftward.

A Change in Supply versus a Change in Quantity Supplied

A *change in supply* refers to a shift in the supply curve as illustrated in Exhibit 3-10a. For example, saying that the supply for oranges has increased is the same as saying that the supply curve for oranges has shifted rightward. As we discussed earlier, the factors that can change supply (shift the supply curve) include prices of relevant resources, technology, number of sellers, expectations of future price, taxes and subsidies, and government restrictions.

A *change in quantity supplied* refers to a movement along a supply curve as in Exhibit 3-10b. What can cause a change in the quantity supplied of a good? The answer is a change in the price of the good, or own price.

The Market Supply Curve

An *individual supply curve* represents the price-quantity combinations for a single seller (or firm). The *market supply curve* represents the price-quantity combinations for all sellers of a particular good. In Exhibit 3-11 we have derived a market supply curve by "summing up" the individual supply curves. In (a) a **supply schedule,** the

Supply Schedule

The numerical tabulation of the quantity supplied of a good at different prices.

■ **EXHIBIT 3-10**
A Change in Supply versus a Change in Quantity Supplied

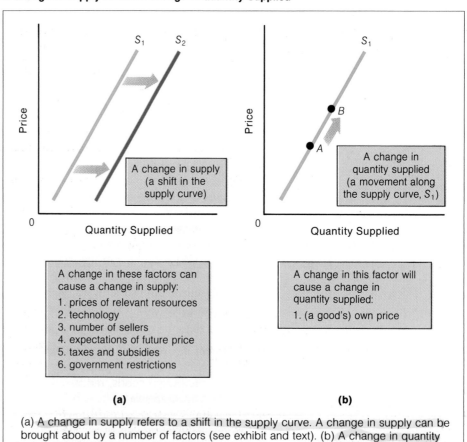

(a) A change in supply refers to a shift in the supply curve. A change in supply can be brought about by a number of factors (see exhibit and text). (b) A change in quantity supplied refers to a movement along a given supply curve. A change in quantity supplied is only brought about by a change in (a good's) own price.

(a) The market supply schedule is derived by adding up the quantity supplied by each party at each price. (b) The data points are plotted, giving us a market supply curve. Only two points on the market supply curve are noted.

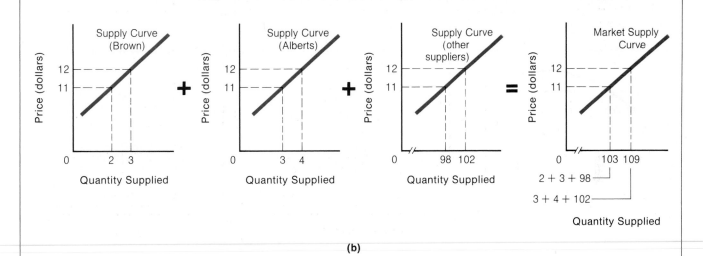

		Quantity Supplied		
PRICE	BROWN	ALBERTS	OTHER SUPPLIERS	ALL SUPPLIERS
$10	1	2	96	99
11	2	3	98	103
12	3	4	102	109
13	4	5	106	115
14	5	6	108	119
15	6	7	110	123

(a)

(b)

numerical tabulation of the quantity supplied of a good at different prices, is given for Brown, Alberts, and "all other suppliers." The market supply schedule is then obtained by adding up the quantity supplied by each party at each price, *ceteris paribus*. In (b) the data points are plotted, giving us a market supply curve.

THE MARKET: PUTTING SUPPLY AND DEMAND TOGETHER

The English economist Alfred Marshall (1842–1924) compared supply and demand to the two blades of a pair of scissors. It is impossible to say which blade does the actual cutting. In the same way it is impossible to say whether demand or supply is responsible for the market price we observe: Price is determined by both sides of the market.

Biography
Alfred Marshall
1842–1924

Brief Biography

Alfred Marshall was born in Bermondsey, a London suburb, on July 26, 1842. He died at his home in Cambridge, England, on July 13, 1924, at the age of 81. William Marshall, Alfred Marshall's father, was a strict disciplinarian who pushed his son to the point of mental and physical exhaustion. Alfred Marshall refused a classics scholarship at Oxford and instead studied mathematics at Cambridge. Marshall taught both at Oxford and at Cambridge. In July 1877 he married his former student Mary Paley, who was an economist and the great-granddaughter of the theologian and philosopher William Paley.

The Issue of Poverty

Marshall was greatly concerned with social issues, especially poverty, which he believed was at the root of many social problems. He hoped that the study of economics would enable him to better understand the causes of poverty and to find a solution to it and related problems.

Ceteris Paribus

Marshall derived a number of important economic tools that economists use today, including the condition of *ceteris paribus*. Marshall used *ceteris paribus* to handle the problem of continuous change in economics. With this tool, Marshall believed he could focus precisely on narrow issues and use the knowledge gained to analyze broader issues.

Supply and Demand

Marshall's *magnum opus*, his *Principles of Economics*, has had a major impact on the economics profession. Often referred to as the Bible of British economics, it introduced many economic concepts that are still used today. Marshall's discussion of supply and demand in the *Principles* includes his famous scissors analogy:

We might reasonably dispute whether it is the upper or the under blade of a pair of scissors that cuts a piece of paper, as whether value is governed by utility (consumer demand) or cost of production (supply).*

A Personal Note

Marshall's marriage to Mary Paley required him to give up his position at Cambridge under the celibacy rules then in force. For most of his life, Marshall was a hypochondriac.

*Alfred Marshall, *Principles of Economics*, 8th ed. (London: Macmillan, 1920), p. 348.

Supply and Demand at Work at an Auction

Think of yourself at an auction where bushels of corn are bought and sold. Suppose (just for a short while) that the supply curve of corn is vertical as in Exhibit 3-12. It cuts the horizontal axis at 30,000 bushels; that is, quantity supplied is 30,000 bushels. The demand curve for corn is downward sloping. Furthermore, suppose each potential buyer of corn is sitting in front of a computer that registers the number of bushels he or she wants to buy. For example, if Nancy Bernstein wants to buy 5,000 bushels of corn, she simply types the number "5,000" into her computer.

The auction begins. (Follow along in Exhibit 3-12 as we relay to you what is happening at the auction.) The auctioneer calls out the price:

■ $7.50. The potential buyers think for a second, and then each registers the number of bushels he or she wants to buy at that price. The total is 12,000 bushels, which is the quantity demanded of corn at $7.50. The auctioneer, realizing that 18,000

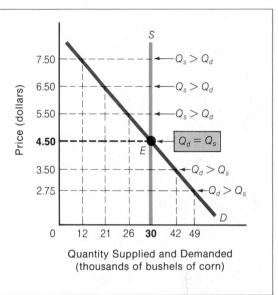

Q_d = quantity demanded; Q_s = quantity supplied. The auctioneer calls out different prices, and buyers record how much they are willing to buy. At prices $7.50, $6.50, and $5.50, quantity supplied is greater than quantity demanded. At prices $2.75 and $3.50, quantity demanded is greater than quantity supplied. At $4.50, quantity demanded equals quantity supplied.

Quantity Supplied and Demanded
(thousands of bushels of corn)

bushels of corn (30,000 − 12,000 = 18,000) will go unsold at this price, decides to lower the price per bushel to:

■ $6.50. The quantity demanded increases to 21,000 bushels, but still the quantity supplied of corn at this price is greater than the quantity demanded. The auctioneer calls out:

■ $5.50. The quantity demanded increases to 26,000 bushels, but the quantity supplied at $5.50 is greater than the quantity demanded. The auctioneer drops the price down to:

■ $2.75. At this price the quantity demanded jumps to 49,000 bushels and is greater than quantity supplied by 19,000 bushels. The auctioneer calls out a higher price:

■ $3.50. The quantity demanded drops to 42,000 bushels, but still buyers want to buy more corn at this price than there is corn to be sold. The auctioneer calls out:

■ $4.50. At this price the quantity demanded of corn is 30,000 bushels, and the quantity supplied of corn is 30,000 bushels. The auction stops. The 30,000 bushels of corn are bought and sold at $4.50 per bushel.

Learning the Language of Supply and Demand: A Few Important Terms

If quantity supplied is greater than quantity demanded, a **surplus** or **excess supply** exists. If quantity demanded is greater than quantity supplied, a **shortage** or **excess demand** exists. In Exhibit 3-12 a surplus exists at $7.50, $6.50, and $5.50. A shortage exists at $2.75 and $3.50. The price at which quantity demanded equals quantity supplied is the **equilibrium price** or **market-clearing price.** In our example $4.50 is the equilibrium price. The quantity that corresponds to the equilibrium price is the **equilibrium quantity.** In our example it is 30,000 bushels of corn. Any price at which quantity demanded is not equal to quantity supplied is a **disequilibrium price.** A market that exhibits either a surplus ($Q_s > Q_d$) or a shortage ($Q_d > Q_s$) is said to

Surplus (Excess Supply)

A condition in which quantity supplied is greater than quantity demanded. Surpluses only occur at prices above equilibrium price.

Shortage (Excess Demand)

A condition in which quantity demanded is greater than quantity supplied. Shortages only occur at prices below equilibrium price.

Equilibrium Price (Market-Clearing Price)

The price at which quantity demanded of the good equals quantity supplied.

Equilibrium Quantity

The quantity that corresponds to equilibrium price. The quantity at which the amount of the good buyers are willing to buy equals the amount sellers are willing to sell, and both equal the amount actually bought and sold.

Disequilibrium Price

A price other than equilibrium price. A price at which quantity demanded does not equal quantity supplied.

Disequilibrium

A state of either surplus or shortage in a market.

Equilibrium

Equilibrium means "at rest." Equilibrium is the price-quantity combination in a market from which there is no tendency for buyers or sellers to move away. Graphically, equilibrium is the intersection point of the supply and demand curves.

be in **disequilibrium.** A market in which quantity demanded equals quantity supplied ($Q_d = Q_s$) is said to be in equilibrium. **Equilibrium** is identified by the letter "E" in Exhibit 3-12.

Question:

Some people use the words shortage *and* scarcity *as synonyms. Do they refer to the same thing?*

Answer:

No. Scarcity is the condition where wants are greater than the resources available to satisfy those wants. Shortage is the condition where quantity demanded is greater than quantity supplied. A shortage occurs at *some* prices: specifically, at any disequilibrium price that is *below* equilibrium price (for example, $2.75 in Exhibit 3-12). Scarcity occurs at *all* prices. Even at equilibrium price ($4.50 in Exhibit 3-12), where quantity demanded equals quantity supplied, scarcity exists.

Moving to Equilibrium: What Happens to Price When There Is a Surplus or a Shortage?

What did the auctioneer do when the price was $7.50 and there was a surplus of corn? He lowered the price. What did the auctioneer do when the price was $6.50 and there was still a surplus of corn? He lowered it again. What did the auctioneer do when the price was $3.50 and there was a shortage of corn? He raised the price. The behavior of the auctioneer can be summarized: If a surplus exists, lower price; if a shortage exists, raise price. This is how the auctioneer moved the corn market into equilibrium.

Not all markets have auctioneers. (When was the last time you saw an auctioneer in the grocery store?) But many markets act *as if* an auctioneer were calling out higher and lower prices until equilibrium price is reached. In many real-world auctioneerless markets, prices fall when there is a surplus and rise when there is a shortage. Why?

Why Does Price Fall When There Is a Surplus?   With a surplus, suppliers will not be able to sell all they had hoped to sell at a particular price. As a result, their inventories grow beyond the level they hold in preparation for demand changes. Sellers will want to reduce their inventories. Some will lower prices to do so; some will cut back on production; others will do a little of both. As we show in Exhibit 3-13, there is a tendency for price and output to fall until equilibrium is achieved.

Why Does Price Rise When There Is A Shortage?   With a shortage, buyers will not be able to buy all they had hoped to buy. Some buyers will bid up the price to get sellers to sell to them instead of to other buyers. Some sellers, seeing buyers clamor for the goods, will realize that they can raise the price on the goods they have for sale. Higher prices will also call forth added output. Thus there is a tendency for price and output to rise until equilibrium is achieved (see Exhibit 3-13).

Moving to Equilibrium: Maximum and Minimum Prices

Our discussion of surpluses and shortages has illustrated how a market moves to equilibrium, but there is another way to show this. Exhibit 3-14 depicts the market for good *X*. Look at the first unit of good *X*. What is *the maximum price buyers would*

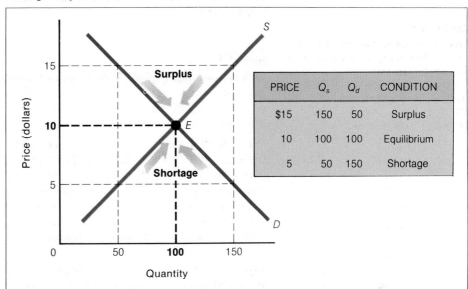

PRICE	Q_s	Q_d	CONDITION
$15	150	50	Surplus
10	100	100	Equilibrium
5	50	150	Shortage

If there is a surplus, sellers' inventories rise above the level they hold in preparation for demand changes. Sellers will want to reduce their inventories. As a result, price and output fall until equilibrium is achieved. If there is a shortage, some buyers will bid up price to get sellers to sell to them instead of to other buyers. Some sellers will realize they can raise the price on the goods they have for sale. Higher prices will call forth added output. Price and output rise until equilibrium is achieved. (Note: Recall that price, on the vertical axis, is price per unit of the good; and quantity, on the horizontal axis, is for a specific time period. In this text we do not specify this on the axes themselves, but consider it to be understood.)

■ EXHIBIT 3-14
Moving to Equilibrium in Terms of Maximum and Minimum Prices

As long as the maximum price buyers are willing to pay is greater than the minimum price suppliers need to receive, an exchange will occur. This condition is met for units 1–4. The market converges on equilibrium through a process of making mutually beneficial exchanges.

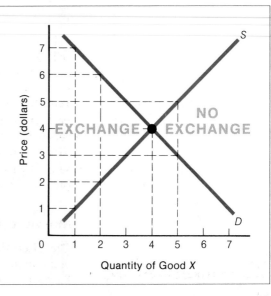

be *willing to pay* for it? The answer is $7. This can be seen by following the dotted line up from the first unit of the good to the demand curve.

What is the *minimum price sellers need to receive before they would be willing to sell* this unit of good X? It is $1. This can be seen by following the dotted line up from the first unit to the supply curve. Since the maximum price buyers are willing to pay is greater than the minimum price sellers need to receive, we can be sure that the first unit of good X will be exchanged.

What happens to the second unit? Here the maximum price buyers are willing to pay is $6, and the minimum price sellers need to receive is $2. We can be sure that the second unit of good X will be exchanged. In fact, we can be sure exchange will occur as long as the maximum price buyers are willing to pay is greater than the minimum price sellers need to receive. The exhibit shows that a total of four units of good X will be exchanged. The fifth unit will not be exchanged because the maximum price buyers are willing to pay ($3) is less than the minimum price suppliers need to receive ($5).

In the process just described, buyers and sellers exchange money for goods as long as both benefit from the exchange. The market converges on a quantity of 4 units of good X and a $4 price per unit. This is equilibrium. This way of explaining the movement to equilibrium illustrates two points that were hidden from view when we discussed it in terms of surpluses and shortages: (1) *At equilibrium all the mutually beneficial gains from the exchange have been obtained.* (2) *At equilibrium price, maximum price (for the buyer) and minimum price (for the seller) are the same.*

Changes in Equilibrium Price and Quantity

Equilibrium price and quantity are determined by supply and demand. Anytime either demand or supply changes or both change, equilibrium price and quantity change. Exhibit 3-15 illustrates 14 different cases where this occurs. We briefly note the effects on equilibrium price and quantity in each case.

■ (a) Demand rises (the demand curve shifts rightward), and supply is constant (the supply curve does not move). Equilibrium price rises, equilibrium quantity rises, too.

■ (b) Demand falls, supply is constant. Equilibrium price falls, equilibrium quantity falls.

■ (c) Supply rises, demand is constant. Equilibrium price falls, equilibrium quantity rises.

■ (d) Supply falls, demand is constant. Equilibrium price rises, equilibrium quantity falls.

■ (e) Demand rises and supply falls by an equal amount. Equilibrium price rises, equilibrium quantity is constant.

■ (f) Demand falls and supply rises by an equal amount. Equilibrium price falls, equilibrium quantity is constant.

■ (g) Demand rises by a greater amount than supply falls. Equilibrium price and quantity rise.

■ (h) Demand rises by a lesser amount than supply falls. Equilibrium price rises, equilibrium quantity falls.

■ (i) Demand falls by a greater amount than supply rises. Equilibrium price and quantity fall.

■ (j) Demand falls by a lesser amount than supply rises. Equilibrium price falls, equilibrium quantity rises.

■ (k) Demand rises by a greater amount than supply rises. Equilibrium price and quantity rise.

Equilibrium Price and Quantity Effects of Supply Curve and Demand Curve Shifts

The exhibit illustrates the effects on equilibrium price and quantity of a change in demand, a change in supply, or a change in both. Below each diagram the condition leading to the effects are noted, using the following symbols: (1) A bar over a letter means *constant* (thus, $\bar{S}$ means that supply is constant); (2) a downward-pointing arrow ($\downarrow$) indicates a fall; (3) an upward-pointing arrow ($\uparrow$) indicates a rise. A rise (fall) in demand is the same as a rightward (leftward) shift in the demand curve. A rise (fall) in supply is the same as a rightward (leftward) shift in the supply curve.

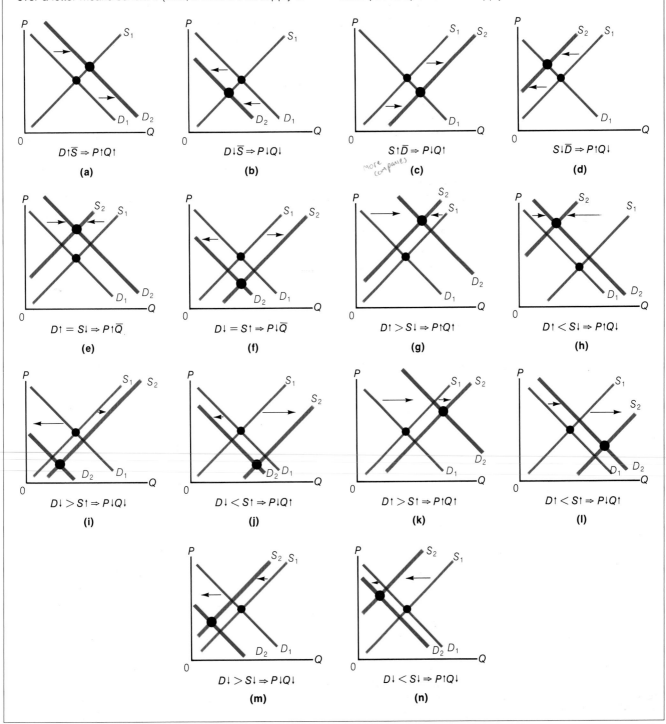

$D{\uparrow}\bar{S} \Rightarrow P{\uparrow}Q{\uparrow}$
(a)

$D{\downarrow}\bar{S} \Rightarrow P{\downarrow}Q{\downarrow}$
(b)

$S{\uparrow}\bar{D} \Rightarrow P{\downarrow}Q{\uparrow}$
(c)

$S{\downarrow}\bar{D} \Rightarrow P{\uparrow}Q{\downarrow}$
(d)

$D{\uparrow} = S{\downarrow} \Rightarrow P{\uparrow}\bar{Q}$
(e)

$D{\downarrow} = S{\uparrow} \Rightarrow P{\downarrow}\bar{Q}$
(f)

$D{\uparrow} > S{\downarrow} \Rightarrow P{\uparrow}Q{\uparrow}$
(g)

$D{\uparrow} < S{\downarrow} \Rightarrow P{\uparrow}Q{\downarrow}$
(h)

$D{\downarrow} > S{\uparrow} \Rightarrow P{\downarrow}Q{\downarrow}$
(i)

$D{\downarrow} < S{\uparrow} \Rightarrow P{\downarrow}Q{\uparrow}$
(j)

$D{\uparrow} > S{\uparrow} \Rightarrow P{\uparrow}Q{\uparrow}$
(k)

$D{\uparrow} < S{\uparrow} \Rightarrow P{\downarrow}Q{\uparrow}$
(l)

$D{\downarrow} > S{\downarrow} \Rightarrow P{\downarrow}Q{\downarrow}$
(m)

$D{\downarrow} < S{\downarrow} \Rightarrow P{\uparrow}Q{\downarrow}$
(n)

■ (l) Demand rises by a lesser amount than supply rises. Equilibrium price falls, equilibrium quantity rises.

■ (m) Demand falls by a greater amount than supply falls. Equilibrium price and quantity fall.

■ (n) Demand falls by a lesser amount than supply falls. Equilibrium price rises, equilibrium quantity falls.

■ CHAPTER SUMMARY

Demand

■ The law of demand states that as the price of a good rises, the quantity demanded of the good falls, and as the price of a good falls, the quantity demanded of the good rises, *ceteris paribus*. The law of demand holds that price and quantity demanded are inversely related.

■ Quantity demanded is the total amount of a good that buyers are willing to buy at a particular price.

■ A demand curve is the graphical representation of the law of demand.

■ Factors that can shift the demand curve include income, preferences, prices of related goods (substitutes and complements), number of buyers, and expectations of future price.

■ A change in quantity demanded is directly brought about by a change in a good's own price.

Absolute and Relative Prices

■ The absolute price of a good is its price in money terms. The relative price of a good is its price in terms of another good.

■ As the absolute price of a good rises, its relative price may rise *or* fall. What happens depends on the percentage increase in the absolute price of other goods. For example, if the absolute price of Y rises by a greater percentage than the absolute price of X, the relative price of X falls, even though its absolute price has risen.

Supply

■ The law of supply states that as the price of a good rises, the quantity supplied of the good rises, and as the price of a good falls, the quantity supplied of the good falls, *ceteris paribus*. The law of supply asserts that price and quantity supplied are directly related.

■ The law of supply does not hold when there is no time to produce more units of a good, or for goods that cannot be produced (over any period of time).

■ The upward-sloping supply curve is the graphical representation of the law of supply. More generally, a supply curve (no matter how it slopes) represents the relationship between price and quantity supplied.

■ Factors that can shift the supply curve include prices of relevant resources, technology, number of sellers, expectations of future price, taxes and subsidies, and government restrictions.

■ A change in quantity supplied is directly brought about by a change in a good's own price.

The Market

■ Both demand and supply establish equilibrium price and quantity.

■ A surplus exists in a market if, at some price, quantity supplied is greater than quantity demanded. A shortage exists if, at some price, quantity demanded is greater than quantity supplied.

■ If there is a surplus in a market, price and output tend to fall. If there is a shortage, price and output tend to rise.

■ At the equilibrium price, the quantity demanded of a good equals the quantity supplied.

■ QUESTIONS TO ANSWER AND DISCUSS

1. True or false? As the price of oranges rises, the demand for oranges falls, *ceteris paribus*. Explain your answer.

2. "The price of a bushel of wheat was $4.00 last month and is $5.00 today. The demand curve for wheat must have shifted rightward between last month and today." Discuss.

3. "Some goods are bought largely because they have 'snob appeal.' For example, the residents of Palm Beach gain prestige by buying expensive items. In fact, they won't buy some items unless they are expensive. The law of demand, which holds that people buy more at lower prices than higher prices, obviously doesn't hold for Palm Beachers. In short, the following rule applies in Palm Beach: high prices, buy; low prices, don't buy." Discuss.

4. "The price of T-shirts keeps rising and rising, and people keep buying more and more. T-shirts must have an upward-sloping demand curve." Identify the error.

5. "Demand is more important to the determination of price than supply." Discuss.

6. Predict what would happen to the equilibrium price of marijuana if it were legalized.

7. Compare the ratings for television shows with prices for goods. How are ratings like prices? How are ratings different from prices? (Hint: How does rising demand for a particular television show manifest itself?)

8. In this chapter we showed that because the relative price of high-quality apples is lower in New York than in Washington State, New Yorkers consume relatively more high-quality apples. Apply this principle in different areas. For example, ask yourself if you would consume relatively more expensive meals on vacation in Mexico than at home. (Hint: Might there be a transportation cost of going on vacation that is analogous to the transport cost of moving apples from Washington State to New York?)

9. Does the law of demand hold for friendship? Do you "buy" less (more) friendship the higher (lower) the "price" of friendship, *ceteris paribus*? Explain your answer. Does the law of demand hold for criminal activity? Do potential criminals "buy" less (more) crime the higher (lower) the "price" of crime, *ceteris paribus*? Explain your answer.

10. Many movie theaters charge a lower admission price for the first show on weekday afternoons than for a weeknight or weekend show. Explain why.

Chapter 4

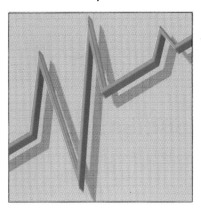

Supply, Demand, and Price: Applications

■ INTRODUCTION

Some courses, such as chemistry and biology, include lectures and a lab. There are no labs in economics, which, in a way, is too bad.

On the other hand, economics has certain advantages that chemistry lacks. The economics student may not have the same kind of lab the chemistry student has, but he or she has a whole lot more. All the world is his or her lab. As we explain in this chapter, economics is not only in this book or on the chalkboard or overhead projector in your classroom. It is on a freeway, in a Las Vegas showroom, and in the admissions office of your university or college. Open your eyes and ears to what is around you, wherever you may be, and ask: Does economics have something to say? You'll find out that it can't keep its mouth shut.

■ WHAT THIS CHAPTER IS ABOUT

We begin with a discussion of price as a rationing device and as a transmitter of information. Building on this, we turn next to price controls. Finally, we give some real-world examples of supply and demand and price at work.

Key Questions to Keep in Mind as You Read

1. What does it mean to say price is a rationing device?
2. What does it mean to say price is a transmitter of information?
3. What is a price ceiling? What is a price floor?
4. What are the effects of a price ceiling? What are the effects of a price floor?
5. Why are GPAs, ACTs, and SATs used for admission to universities and colleges?
6. Why is there bumper-to-bumper traffic on the freeways at some times and not at other times?

PRICE

Price performs two major tasks: It serves as a *rationing device* and as a *transmitter of information*. We discuss both here.

Price as a Rationing Device

Wants are virtually unlimited; resources are limited. In short, scarcity exists. Consequently, a rationing device is needed to determine who gets what of the available limited resources and goods. (Because resources are limited, goods are also since the production of goods requires resources.) Price serves as a rationing device. It rations scarce resources to those producers who pay the price for the resources. It rations scarce goods to those buyers who pay the price for the goods. It is as simple as this: Pay the price, and the resources or goods are yours. Don't pay the price, and they aren't.

Resources and goods need not be rationed by price. They could be rationed by *political power, ethnic background, physical appearance, religion, favoritism, brute force,* or on a *first-come-first-served basis,* to name only a few possibilities. All these are means that could be used to decide who gets what. Therefore all could be rationing devices.

Consider a world where brute force is the only rationing device. There the only way you could get what you want is by physically taking it from someone else. Of course, other people would be trying to take things away from you. Suppose you build a canoe to go fishing in, but your next-door neighbor, a burly fellow, hits you over the head and takes the canoe. He gets what he wants, not by paying a price, but through brute force. The strongest persons most willing to use their muscle to get what they want would rule. How would you fare in this world?

Consider a world where religion (backed up by the power of the state) is used as a rationing device. If you want a car, or food, or an education you must be a member of the "right" religion as determined by the persons that rule.[1]

Consider a world where ethnic background is used as a rationing device. Who gets what is decided by whether a person is the "right" ethnic background.[2]

Question:

Clearly, rationing devices such as brute force, religion, and ethnic background work to the disadvantage of the weak and people of the "wrong" religion and ethnic background. But price as a rationing device also works to the disadvantage of some people: specifically, the people who do not have the money to pay the prices—in other words, the poor. Isn't this correct?

Answer:

Undoubtedly, if price is the rationing device, poor people will not be able to buy some goods that rich people can buy. It is similar, in this sense, to using ethnic background as the rationing device and prohibiting the Chinese, for example, from

---

[1]In some countries religion is partly used to ration goods. For example, in Ayatollah Khomeini's Iran buying many goods is illegal unless you are a Moslem. Members of the Baha'i and Jewish faiths are discriminated against in this regard.

[2]There are numerous cases throughout history where persons of a particular ethnic background could not buy certain goods. In the United States the most notable example is that blacks were at one time prohibited from buying food in "white" restaurants.

buying some goods that the non-Chinese can buy. However, a poor person can sometimes earn the income to pay the price, but a Chinese person can never change his or her ethnic background. There are thousands of examples of poor people becoming rich people, but there is not one example of a Chinese person becoming English, Spanish, or French.

Finally, we need to understand that no matter what rationing device is used, it will be of greater benefit to some people than others. This is a consequence of living in a world of inherently unequal individuals.

Follow-up Question:

Why not use need *as the rationing device?*

Answer:

There are some problems here. First, who would determine need? Would Republicans argue that they should determine need and Democrats argue that they should? Second, what is it that people really need? We might agree that all people need a certain amount of food, water, clothing, and shelter. But what else? Do people need television sets, VCRs, trips to Aspen in the winter, personal computers, and so forth? Third, if need were the rationing device, would there be an incentive to work? With price as a rationing device, people have to produce goods and services to earn the income necessary to buy goods. If they could obtain these goods and services without working—by simply expressing a "need"—would anything be produced? Would anyone actually work under such a system?

Price as a Transmitter of Information

On the surface, price is a number with a dollar sign ($) in front of it. Below the surface, price is a transmitter of information, much as telephones, letters, and smoke signals are transmitters of information. To illustrate, consider the following set of events.

On Saturday, Noelle walks into a local grocery store and purchases a half-gallon of orange juice for $2.50. On Sunday, unknown to her, a cold spell hits Florida and wipes out one-quarter of the orange crop. The cold spell shifts the supply curve of oranges leftward and leads to a rise in the equilibrium price of oranges. Higher orange prices shift the supply curve of orange juice leftward and drive up its equilibrium price. Next Saturday Noelle returns to the grocery store and notices that the price of a half-gallon of orange juice is $3.50. She decides to buy a quart of orange juice for $1.75 instead of a half-gallon for $3.50. (Her demand curve for orange juice is downward sloping; she buys less at higher prices than at lower prices.)

But how exactly is price a transmitter of information? By moving up and down, it transmits information on the *relative scarcity of a good*. The higher price for orange juice is saying (once we translate its message into English): "There has been a cold spell in Florida resulting in less orange juice. The gap between people's wants for orange juice and the amount of orange juice available to satisfy those wants has widened."

Notice too that because Noelle directly responded to the higher price of orange juice by cutting back on her consumption, she indirectly responded to the information of the increased relative scarcity of orange juice, even without being informed about Florida weather conditions.

Theory in Practice

Prices and Prisoners of War

We are all aware of the thousands of markets around us. If we want to buy goods such as bread, lightbulbs, or cars, we can find sellers of these goods. We are the buyers, others are the sellers, together we comprise a market. But what about a market in a place like a prisoner-of-war (POW) camp. Do supply and demand work in a POW camp? What would be used for money? Would there be prices?

During World War II, an American, R. A. Radford, was captured and imprisoned in a POW camp. During his stay in the camp, he made some observations about economic happenings, which he later described in the journal *Economica*. He noted that the Red Cross would periodically distribute packages to the prisoners that contained goods such as cigarettes, toiletries, chocolate, cheese, jam, margarine, and tinned beef. Not all the prisoners had the same preferences for the goods. For example, some liked chocolate more than others; some smoked cigarettes, others did not. Because of their different preferences, the prisoners began to trade, say, a chocolate bar for some cheese, and a barter system emerged. After a short while, money appeared on the scene, but it was not U.S. dollars or any other government currency. Instead it was cigarettes. Cigarettes were money in that they were generally accepted for purposes of exchange, and prices (for the goods) were quoted in terms of cigarettes. As Radford noted, "The cigarette became the standard of value. In the permanent camp people started by wandering through the bungalows calling their offers—'cheese for seven' (cigarettes) . . . ."*

Other market phenomena began to appear. There were entrepreneurs who would buy up certain goods in a bungalow where they were less valued and sell them in another bungalow where they were highly valued. There were also middlemen who began to profit on any differences in prices. Competition among suppliers and among buyers developed. And when a new ration of cigarettes (money) would arrive at the camp, the demand for goods would rise, pushing up prices.

*R. A. Radford, "The Economic Organization of a P.O.W. Camp," *Economica* (November 1945): 189–201.

PRICE CONTROLS

Price is not always permitted to be a rationing device and transmitter of information. Sometimes it is controlled. There are two types of price controls: price ceilings and price floors. In our discussion of price controls, we will use the word "price" in the generic sense. It refers to the price of an apple, for example, the price of labor (wage), the price of credit (interest rate), and the price of a rental unit (rent).

Price Ceiling: Definition and Effects

Price Ceiling

A government-mandated maximum price above which legal trades cannot be made.

A **price ceiling** is a government-mandated maximum price above which legal trades cannot be made. For example, suppose the government mandates that the maximum price at which good X can be bought and sold is $8. It follows that $8 is a price ceiling. If $8 is below the equilibrium price of good X, as in Exhibit 4-1, any or all of the following effects may arise.[3]

[3]If a price ceiling is above the equilibrium price (say, $8 is the price ceiling and $4 is the equilibrium price), it has no effects. Usually, however, a price ceiling is below the equilibrium price.

The price ceiling effects we discuss here hold for a particular market structure and not necessarily for all market structures. The relevant market structure is usually referred to as a perfectly competitive market, a price-taker market, or a perfect market. No matter what the term, we are assuming enough buyers and sellers so that no single buyer or seller can influence price.

The price ceiling is $8 and the equilibrium price $12. At $12, quantity demanded = quantity supplied. At $8, quantity demanded > quantity supplied. (Recall that price, on the vertical axis, always represents price per unit; and quantity, on the horizontal axis, always holds for a specific time period.)

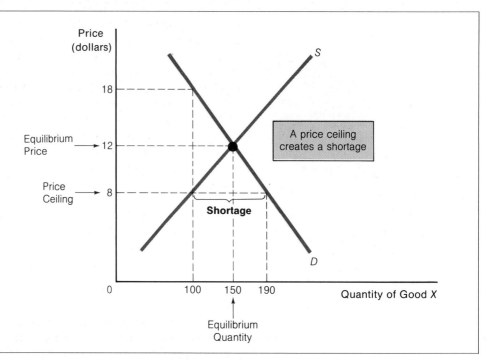

Shortages. At the $12 equilibrium price in Exhibit 4-1, the quantity demanded of good X (150) is equal to the quantity supplied (150). At the $8 price ceiling a shortage exists: The quantity demanded (190) is greater than the quantity supplied (100). In Chapter 3 we learned that when a shortage exists, there is a tendency for price and output to rise to equilibrium. But when a price ceiling exists, this tendency cannot be realized since it is unlawful to trade at the equilibrium price.

Fewer Exchanges. At equilibrium price, 150 units of good X are bought and sold. At the price ceiling in Exhibit 4-1, 100 units of good X are bought and sold. We conclude that price ceilings cause fewer exchanges to be made.

Nonprice Rationing Devices. If an equilibrium price of $12 *fully* rationed good X before the price ceiling was imposed, it follows that a (lower) price of $8 can only partly ration it. In short, price ceilings prevent price from rising to the level sufficient to ration goods fully. What then helps price do what it once did alone? The answer is some other (nonprice) rationing device, such as *first-come-first-served*.

In Exhibit 4-1, 100 units of good X will be sold at $8 although buyers are willing to buy 190 units at this price. What happens? Possibly, good X will be sold on a first-come-first-served basis for $8 per unit. In other words, to buy good X a person needs not only to pay $8 per unit but also to be one of the first persons in line.

Black Markets. A *black market* is an illegal market. There are principally two varieties: one in which illegal goods are bought and sold (cocaine and heroin in this country, for example, rock'n'roll records, Levis, and certain books in some other countries); and one in which goods are bought and sold at illegal prices (buying and selling goods above a price ceiling, for example). The latter type of black market

is relevant here. Buyers and sellers will regularly get around a price ceiling by making their exchanges "under the table." For example, some buyers of good X may offer some sellers of good X more than $8 per unit in order to buy the good. No doubt some sellers will accept the offers.

Question:

Why would some buyers offer more then $8 per unit when they can buy good X for $8?

Answer:

Not all buyers can buy the amount of good X they want at $8. As Exhibit 4-1 shows, there is a shortage: Buyers are willing to buy 190 units at $8, but sellers are only willing to sell 100 units. In short, 90 fewer units will be sold than buyers would like to buy. Some buyers will go unsatisfied. How then does any *one* buyer make it more likely that sellers will sell to him or her instead of to someone else? The answer is by offering to pay a higher price. Since it is illegal to pay a higher price, however, the transaction must be made "under the table." It is a black market transaction.

Tie-in Sale

A sale whereby one good can be purchased only if another good is also purchased.

Tie-in Sales. In Exhibit 4-1, what is the maximum price buyers would be willing to pay per unit for 100 units of good *X*? As we can see, it is $18. The maximum *legal* price, however, is $8. This difference between the two prices often prompts a **tie-in sale,** a sale whereby one good can be purchased *only if* another good is also purchased. For example, if Ralph's Gas Station only sells gasoline to customers if they buy a car wash, the two goods are linked together in a tie-in sale.

Suppose that the sellers of good *X* in Exhibit 4-1 also sell good *Y*. They might offer to sell buyers good *X* at $8 only if the buyers agree to buy good *Y* at, say, $10. We choose $10 as the price for good *Y* because that is the difference between the maximum per-unit price buyers are willing to pay for 100 units of good *X* (specifically, $18) and the maximum legal price ($8).

In New York City tie-in sales sometimes result from rent ceilings on apartments. Occasionally, in order to rent an apartment, an individual must agree to rent the furniture in the apartment.

Do Buyers Prefer Lower Prices to Higher Prices?

"Of course," someone might say, "buyers prefer lower prices to higher prices. What buyer in his right mind would want to pay a higher price for anything?" But wait a minute. Price ceilings are often lower than equilibrium prices. Does it follow that buyers prefer price ceilings to equilibrium prices? Not necessarily. As explained earlier, price ceilings have effects that equilibrium prices do not: shortages, use of first-come-first-served as a rationing device, tie-in sales, and so on. It could be that a buyer would prefer to pay a higher price (an equilibrium price) and avoid the effects of a price ceiling than pay a lower price and have to deal with them. All we can say for certain is that if *all other things are held constant,* buyers prefer lower prices to higher prices. As in many cases, the *ceteris paribus* condition makes all the difference.

Price Ceilings and False Information

Let's go back to the orange juice example we discussed previously. Suppose there is a price ceiling on orange juice at $2.50 per half-gallon, which happens to be the equilibrium price of orange juice before the cold spell in Florida. Furthermore, suppose the price ceiling is kept on even after the cold spell and subsequent fall in the supply of orange juice. Price is not permitted to rise to its new equilibrium level, $3.50, even though the supply curve of orange juice has shifted leftward. Can the information about the increased relative scarcity of orange juice (due to the cold spell) get through to orange juice buyers? No. Since price is prohibited from rising, it obviously cannot transmit this information. As far as buyers are concerned, nothing has changed, and they mistakenly think that they can go on drinking orange juice at the same rate as before. But this is a delusion. One way or the other, some people must curtail their consumption of orange juice, now that fewer oranges are available.

The lesson is simple. Price ceilings (below equilibrium price) distort the flow of accurate information to buyers. Buyers end up thinking that reality is something other than it is; they base their buying behavior on false information. Problems follow, and the unintended, unexpected, and undesirable effects of price ceilings are soon incurred.

Price Floor: Definition and Effects

Price Floor

A government-mandated minimum price below which legal trades cannot be made.

A **price floor** is a government-mandated minimum price below which legal trades cannot be made. For example, suppose the government mandates that the minimum price at which good X can be sold is $20. It follows that $20 is a price floor. (Exhibit 4-2). If the price floor is above the equilibrium price, the two following effects arise.[4]

Surpluses. At the $15 equilibrium price in Exhibit 4-2, the quantity demanded of good X (130) is equal to the quantity supplied (130). At the $20 price floor, a surplus exists; the quantity supplied (180) is greater than the quantity demanded (90). In

[4]If a price floor is below the equilibrium price (say, $20 is the price floor and $25 is the equilibrium price), it has no effects. Usually, however, a price floor is above the equilibrium price.

As with price ceilings, the price floor effects we discuss here hold for a perfectly competitive market. See footnote 3.

The price floor is $20 and the equilibrium price $15. At $15, quantity demanded = quantity supplied. At $20, quantity supplied > quantity demanded.

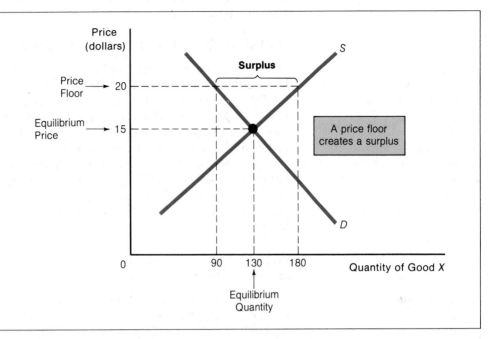

Chapter 3 we learned that a surplus is a temporary state of affairs. When a surplus exists, there is a tendency for price and output to fall to equilibrium. But when a price floor exists, this tendency cannot be realized since it is unlawful to trade at the equilibrium price.

Fewer Exchanges. At equilibrium price in Exhibit 4-2, 130 units of good X are bought and sold. At the price floor, 90 units are bought and sold. We conclude that price floors cause fewer exchanges to be made.

Two Cases of Price Floors

We turn now to two real-world examples of price floors. The first is *agricultural price supports;* the second is the *minimum wage law.*

Case 1: Agricultural Price Supports. A *price support* (in agriculture) is an example of a price floor. It is a government-guaranteed minimum price. Some of the agricultural products that either have or have had price supports include wheat, cotton, feed grains, dairy products, peanuts, and tobacco. Suppose the price support for wheat is set above the equilibrium price at $6 per bushel as in Exhibit 4-3. At this price, quantity supplied is greater than quantity demanded and there is a surplus of wheat. Also, the number of bushels of wheat bought by *private citizens* is less (10) at the price support (price floor) than at equilibrium price (18).[5] We would expect wheat buyers to dislike the price support program since they end up paying higher than equilibrium price for the wheat they buy.

What happens to the surplus? Farmers might want to get rid of the surplus of wheat and could do so by lowering price. But, of course, there is no need to lower price.

[5]We specify *private citizens* here because some of the wheat crop is purchased by government.

At a price support of $6 per bushel, consumers of wheat pay higher prices, a surplus results, fewer bushels of wheat are bought by private citizens, and government buys and stores the surplus (which taxpayers pay for).

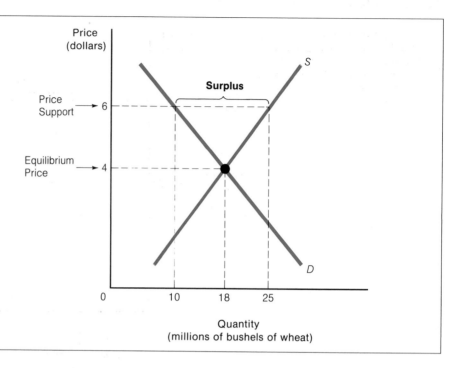

The price is supported by *government,* which buys the surplus at the price support.[6] Since the government's purchase of surplus wheat needs to be stored, sometimes huge storage costs result. For example, in the 1950s and early 1960s storage costs for wheat rose rapidly, reaching over $1 million per day at one period. For the taxpayers who ultimately had to pay the bill, this was not a happy state of affairs.

Thus, the effects of agricultural price supports are (1) a surplus, (2) fewer exchanges (less wheat bought by private citizens), (3) higher prices paid by consumers of wheat, and (4) government purchase and storage of the surplus wheat (taxpayers end up paying).[7]

Case 2: The Minimum Wage Law. The *minimum wage* is a price floor—a government-mandated minimum price for labor. It affects the market for unskilled labor. In Exhibit 4-4 the minimum wage is $3.35 an hour and the equilibrium wage is $2.50. At the equilibrium wage, N_1 workers are employed. At the higher minimum wage, N_3 workers want to work, but only N_2 actually do work. There is a surplus

[6]In practice the government does not just hand over so many dollars to the farmer for his or her surplus. The price support program works like this: Suppose a farmer harvests 10,000 bushels of wheat and the price support is $6 per bushel. If the harvest cannot be sold at $6 per bushel, the farmer can apply for a loan of $60,000 (10,000 bushels × $6 per bushel) from a government agency called the Commodity Credit Corporation (CCC). If the price of wheat rises above the price support, the farmer can later sell the wheat and repay the loan. If the farmer cannot sell any of the wheat, he or she can "repay" the loan by turning the wheat over to the CCC. If the farmer sells part of the wheat, say, 4,000 bushels, he or she can turn over 6,000 bushels to the CCC along with $24,000 (4,000 bushels × $6 per bushel) and keep the remainder ($36,000) of the loan. In this roundabout way, the farmer pays the price support for the farmer's surplus wheat.

[7]For more on agriculture in general and government policies that affect this industry in particular, see Chapter 15.

At a minimum wage of $3.35 an hour, there is a surplus of workers, and fewer workers are employed than would be at the equilibrium wage.

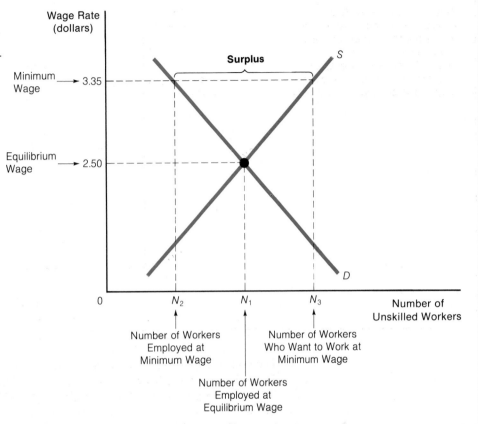

of workers equal to $N_3 - N_2$ in this unskilled labor market. In addition, fewer workers are working at the minimum wage (N_2) than at the equilibrium wage (N_1). Overall, the effects of the minimum wage are (1) a surplus of unskilled workers and (2) fewer workers employed.[8]

Question:

Isn't the minimum wage necessary to guarantee everybody a decent wage? If the minimum wage didn't exist, wouldn't employers hire workers for next to nothing?

Answer:

Employers may want to hire workers for "next to nothing," but the wages workers receive depend on the demand for and supply of labor. In other words, employers do not set wages at whatever level they like: In a competitive market setting, the forces of supply and demand determine equilibrium wages.

As to the minimum wage guaranteeing a decent wage, it is not clear that the minimum wage helps those people who have been priced out of the labor market by *the minimum wage*. For example, suppose Johnny Bates, a 17-year-old in Detroit,

[8]We remind the reader that the effects of the minimum wage are determined for a perfectly competitive (price-taker or perfect) market.

finds that his labor is worth $2.50 an hour to employers. If the government mandates that Johnny must be paid $3.35 an hour (85 cents more an hour than he's currently worth to employers), no employer will hire him. It is not clear how the minimum wage guarantees Johnny a decent wage. All it does for him is ensure that he earns a zero wage. Moreover, Johnny doesn't get an entry-level job where he can learn basic job skills that can help him get a better job in the future.

APPLICATIONS OF SUPPLY AND DEMAND

Do the tools of supply and demand help us to understand more about the real world? We think that they do, and we hope you agree. But if, by chance, you remain an unbeliever, then this section is for you. In it we present more applications of supply and demand.

Freeway Congestion

What does a traffic jam on a busy freeway in any large city have to do with supply and demand? Actually, it has quite a bit to do with supply and demand. Look at it this way: There is a demand for driving on the freeway, and a supply of freeway space. The supply of freeway space is fixed (freeways do not expand and contract over a day, week, or month). The demand, however, fluctuates. Sometimes it is higher than others. For example, we would expect the demand for driving on the freeway to be higher at 8 A.M. (rush hour) than at 11 P.M. But even though this may be the case, the money price for driving on the freeway is always the same—always zero.[9] A zero money price means that no tolls are paid to drive on the freeway.

Exhibit 4-5 shows two demand curves for driving on the freeway: $D_{8A.M.}$ and $D_{11P.M.}$. We have assumed the demand at 8 A.M. is greater than at 11 P.M. We have

[9]Although the money price may be zero, this does not imply that there is no cost to driving on the freeway. In Chapter 1 we learned that zero price does not imply zero opportunity cost.

■ **EXHIBIT 4-5**
Freeway Congestion and Supply and Demand

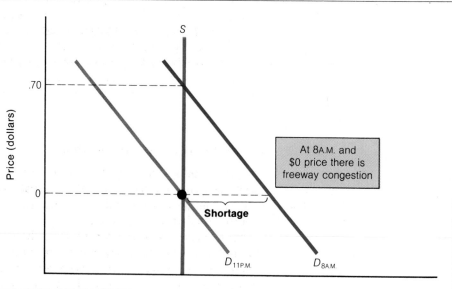

The demand for driving on the freeway is higher at 8 A.M. than at 11 P.M. At zero money price and $D_{11P.M.}$ the freeway market clears. At zero money price and $D_{8A.M.}$ there is a shortage of freeway space, which shows up as freeway congestion. At a price (toll) of 70 cents, the shortage is eliminated and freeway congestion disappears.

At 8A.M. and $0 price there is freeway congestion

Shortage

Price (dollars)

Freeway Space

also assumed that at $D_{11\text{P.M.}}$ and zero money price the freeway market clears: Quantity demanded of freeway space equals quantity supplied of freeway space. At the higher demand, $D_{8\text{A.M.}}$, however, this is not the case. At zero money price, a shortage of freeway space exists: The quantity demanded of freeway space is greater than the quantity supplied of freeway space. The shortage manifests itself in the form of freeway congestion, bumper-to-bumper traffic. One way to eliminate the shortage is through an increase in the money price of driving on the freeway at 8 A.M. For example, as Exhibit 4-5 shows, a toll of 70 cents would clear the freeway market at 8 A.M.

If charging different prices (tolls) at different times of the day on freeways sounds like an unusual idea, consider how Miami Beach hotels price their rooms. They charge different prices for their rooms at different times of the year. During the winter months when the demand for vacationing in Miami Beach is high, the hotels charge higher prices than when the demand is (relatively) low. If different prices were charged for freeway space at different times of the day, freeway space would be rationed the same way Miami Beach hotel rooms are rationed.

Question:

If this is correct, and freeway congestion can be eliminated by charging different tolls at different times of the day, why isn't this done?

Answer:

First, simply because a certain action will eliminate a problem, it does not necessarily follow that it is desirable to carry out that action. A system of tolls will reduce, if not eliminate, freeway congestion, but it may not be worth the cost to build and staff the toll booths. As technology for monitoring usage and billing improves, however, it's possible that we'll institute such a system. In some places in Hong Kong, this has already been done.

Second, freeways are "owned" by the taxpayers and managed by government, not privately owned and managed. The present owner-management team (taxpayers and government officials) is less likely to propose and implement a toll system than a privately owned and managed team that seeks to maximize profits.

Finally, some people argue that rationing freeway space by money price would hurt the poor by making it more expensive for them to get to work and to travel. Better a few traffic jams than this, they argue.

Tipping in a Las Vegas Showroom

To get a good seat in a Las Vegas showroom you have to tip (in advance) the person who seats you. Tourists in Las Vegas usually complain, "I don't know why I have to pay that guy $10 to walk me to my seat. It is ridiculous." But is it? Supply and demand explain what is going on.

In Las Vegas, all tickets for the same show sell for the same price (unlike tickets for a play in New York, say, where some tickets sell for higher prices than others). There are no seat assignments, however; buying a ticket guarantees you a seat, but it could be *any* seat from a good seat, center stage, to a bad seat, far in the back.

The showroom therefore has two markets: a market for good seats and a market for bad seats. In each market there is a demand for and a supply of seats. The bad

Economics in Our Times

What Does Price Have to Do with Being Late to Class?

Class starts at 10 o'clock in the morning. At 10:09, Pam Ferrario walks in late. She apologizes to the instructor, saying, "I've been on campus for 20 minutes, but I couldn't find a parking place." Her classmates nod, knowing full well what she is talking about. Here at the university, especially between the hours of 8 A.M. and 2 P.M., parking places are hard to come by.

This scene is replayed every day at many universities and colleges across the country. Students are late for class because on many days there isn't a parking space to be found.

What can be done about this? Students could start for class earlier. Suppose you have a class at 10 A.M., and you live in an apartment 5 miles from the campus. If you are lucky enough to find an open parking place as soon as you enter the campus parking lot, then you need only leave home at 9:35. However, you can't count on such good luck, so you'd better leave at 9:15, just to be on the safe side.

Who pays for the shortage of parking places under this scheme? The student does. He or she doesn't pay in money but in time.

Or, if you choose not to leave home earlier, then you might pay in being late to class, as we saw earlier.

Are there alternatives to the pay-in-time and pay-in-being-late-to-class schemes for rationing campus parking spots? Some economists have suggested a pay-in-price scheme. For example, the university could install meters in the parking lot and raise the fee high enough so that between the hours of 8 A.M. and 2 P.M., the quantity demanded of parking spaces equals the quantity supplied.

Such suggestions are sometimes criticized because students must pay the fee, no matter how high, in order to attend classes. Well, that's not exactly true. Parking off campus and using public transportation are sometimes alternatives. But this is not really the main point. The issue isn't paying or not paying, but choosing the form in which payment is made—dollar price, time, or being late for class.

Some economists have taken the pay-in-price scheme further and have argued that parking spots should be auctioned on a yearly basis. In other words, a student would rent a parking spot for a year. This way the student would always know that a parking spot would be open when he or she arrived at the campus. People who parked in someone else's spot would be ticketed by campus police.

Additionally, under this scheme, a student who rented a parking spot and chose not to use it between certain hours of the day could rent it out to someone else during this period. So we would expect to see notices like this on campus billboards:

Parking Spot for Rent
Near Arts Building and Student Union. Ideal for liberal arts students. Available on a 2–10 hour basis between 12 noon and 12 midnight. Rate: 50 cents per hour. Call 774-3022.

The argument is often heard that allocating campus parking spots according to price may be all right for rich and middle-income students, but that it hurts poor students. This is not a trivial argument, but it is often misleading. Poor students are not necessarily students without an income, they are simply students with relatively lower incomes than others. Poor students may choose to rearrange their purchases and buy more of one thing (a parking spot) and less of another (clothes, entertainment, and so on). We shouldn't jump to the conclusion that the poor would always prefer a nonmoney rationing scheme to a money rationing scheme.

Give price rationing for campus parking spots some thought. Consider what you believe to be its advantages and disadvantages. And the next time you're late for class and your instructor looks at you disapprovingly, simply say, "Is it my fault that we don't ration campus parking spots by price?"

seats market is shown in Exhibit 4-6a, the good seats market in Exhibit 4-6b. Notice that the demand is greater for good seats than bad seats (as we would expect).[10]

Normally, different market conditions (different demand and supply curves) would bring about different equilibrium prices. The showroom, however, sells all tickets

[10]We have drawn a vertical supply curve in both the good seats and bad seats markets. We are assuming here that the time period under consideration is so short that the quantity supplied of both good seats and bad seats cannot change even if price does. However, even with an upward-sloping supply curve in each market, the analysis is the same.

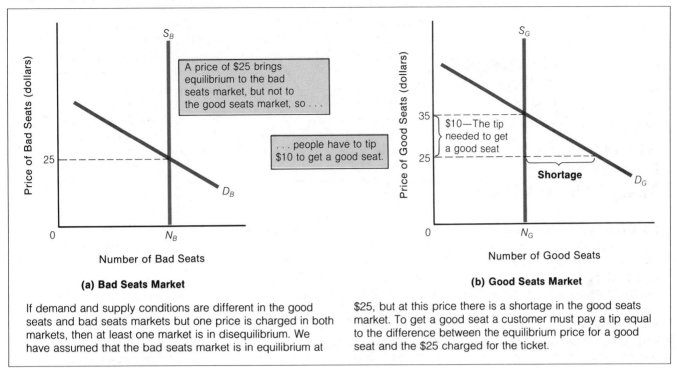

(a) Bad Seats Market

(b) Good Seats Market

If demand and supply conditions are different in the good seats and bad seats markets but one price is charged in both markets, then at least one market is in disequilibrium. We have assumed that the bad seats market is in equilibrium at

$25, but at this price there is a shortage in the good seats market. To get a good seat a customer must pay a tip equal to the difference between the equilibrium price for a good seat and the $25 charged for the ticket.

for the same price, $25. This is the equilibrium price in the bad seats market, but, as Exhibit 4-6b shows, it is a disequilibrium price (below equilibrium price) in the good seats market. The result is a shortage of good seats.

How are the "too few" good seats rationed? That is done by price in the form of a tie-in sale. To get a good seat, it is necessary to tip (in advance) the person who decides where you will sit. In short, first tip the person who does the seating, then get a good seat (assuming, or course, you tipped enough). The necessary tip to get a good seat is equal to the difference between the equilibrium price for a good seat and the $25 charged. In Exhibit 4-6 we have assumed the equilibrium price is $35; thus the tip is $10.

GPAs, ACTs, and SATs

In many colleges and universities students pay less than the equilibrium tuition (price) to attend. Usually, the student pays part of the price of his or her education (by way of tuition payments), and taxpayers and private donors pay part (by way of tax payments and charitable donations, respectively). To illustrate, suppose the student at University X pays the tuition, T_1, in Exhibit 4-7a. As we can see, this is below the equilibrium tuition, T_E. At T_1, the number of students who want to attend the university (N_1) is greater than the number of openings at the university (N_2): that is, quantity demanded is greater than quantity supplied. A shortage of university space exists. The university receives more applications for admission to the freshman class than there are places. Something has to be done. But what? The way the university rations its openings is by some combination of money price and other selected nonprice rationing devices. The student must pay the tuition, or have someone else pay it, *and* meet the standards of the nonprice rationing devices, which usually

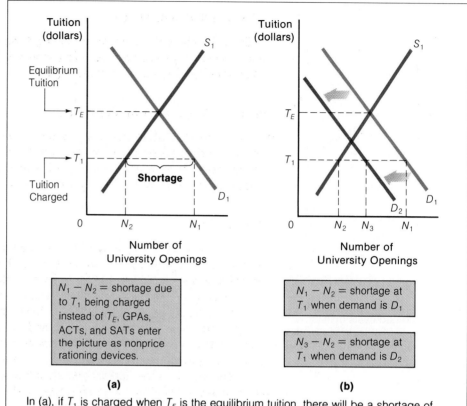

Tuition (dollars)

Equilibrium Tuition

T_E

T_1

Tuition Charged

Shortage

S_1

D_1

0 N_2 N_1

Number of University Openings

$N_1 - N_2$ = shortage due to T_1 being charged instead of T_E, GPAs, ACTs, and SATs enter the picture as nonprice rationing devices.

(a)

Tuition (dollars)

T_E

T_1

S_1

D_1

D_2

0 N_2 N_3 N_1

Number of University Openings

$N_1 - N_2$ = shortage at T_1 when demand is D_1

$N_3 - N_2$ = shortage at T_1 when demand is D_2

(b)

In (a), if T_1 is charged when T_E is the equilibrium tuition, there will be a shortage of university openings. The university will use GPAs, ACTs, and SATs as admission criteria (nonprice rationing devices). If the demand for the university falls, and T_1 is still charged (b), the shortage will become smaller, and, we predict, admission standards will be lowered.

include such things as GPAs (grade point average), ACTs (American College Test), and SATs (Scholastic Aptitude Test).

Question:

Suppose the demand for University X falls, but tuition T_1 is still charged. Would admission requirements be reduced?

Answer:

Yes. To illustrate, suppose the demand for university openings falls from D_1 to D_2 as in Exhibit 4-7b. The shortage of university openings falls from $N_1 - N_2$ to $N_3 - N_2$. As the shortage falls, the GPA, ACT, and SAT requirements do not need to be as stringent as before. We would predict that if the demand for University X falls, university admission standards would be reduced, *ceteris paribus*.

■ CHAPTER SUMMARY

Price as a Rationing Device

■ Scarcity implies the need for a rationing device. Possible rationing devices include price, political power, first-come-first-served, ethnic background, physical appearance, religion, favoritism, and brute force.

Price as a Transmitter of Information

■ In a market in which price is permitted to rise and fall according to supply and demand, price transmits information on the relative scarcity of a good. A higher (lower) price informs us that the gap between people's wants and the amount of resources or goods available to satisfy those wants has widened (narrowed).

Price Ceilings

■ A price ceiling is a government-mandated maximum price. If a price ceiling is below the equilibrium price, some or all of the following effects arise: shortages, fewer exchanges, nonprice rationing devices, black markets (of the variety in which it is illegal to sell at particular prices), and tie-in sales.

■ Consumers do not necessarily prefer (lower) price ceilings to (higher) equilibrium prices. They may prefer higher prices and none of the effects of price ceilings to lower prices and some of the effects of price ceilings. All we can say for sure is that consumers prefer lower to higher prices, *ceteris paribus*.

■ Freely flexible prices (prices that are allowed to respond to the forces of supply and demand) transmit accurate information (relevant to relative scarcities). Controlled prices transmit inaccurate or false information (relevant to relative scarcities).

Price Floors

■ A price floor is a government-mandated minimum price. If a price floor is above the equilibrium price, the following effects arise: surpluses and fewer exchanges.

■ Both agricultural price supports and the minimum wage are examples of price floors. The effects of agricultural price supports are (1) surpluses, (2) fewer exchanges, (3) higher prices for consumers, and (4) government purchase and storage (or other disposal) of the surplus (i.e., taxpayers pay). The effects of the minimum wage are (1) a surplus (of unskilled labor) and (2) fewer workers employed.

■ QUESTIONS TO ANSWER AND DISCUSS

1. "If price were outlawed as the rationing device (used in markets) there would be no need for another rationing device to take its place. We would have reached utopia." Discuss.

2. Many of the proponents of price ceilings argue that government-mandated maximum prices simply reduces producers' profits and do not affect the quantity supplied of a good on the market. What must the supply curve look like before a price ceiling does not affect quantity supplied?

3. The minimum wage hurts some unskilled workers because it prices them out of the labor market. For example, if the minimum wage is $3.35 per hour, and employers are only willing to pay a person $2.90 per hour, that person cannot legally be hired. Since the minimum wage largely applies to unskilled workers, would you expect all unskilled workers to argue against the minimum wage?

4. Some people argue that the minimum wage, by pricing many unskilled teenagers out of the labor market, causes these individuals to turn to selling drugs. After all, if a person can't get a job legally, he or she will get one illegally. The alternative is to starve. Other people disagree. They argue that the teenagers who sell drugs would do so even if there were no minimum wage. After all, there is usually a substantial monetary difference between working as a clerk in a hardware store for $2.50 an hour and selling drugs for, perhaps, hundreds of dollars a week. What do you think?

5. What kind of information does price transmit?

6. Suppose the price of IBM stock rises by $2 a share. Does the price rise transmit any information to you? What does it "say"?

7. Should grades in an economics class be "rationed" according to money price instead of how well a student does on the exams? If they were, and potential employers learned of this, what effect might this have on the value of your college degree?

8. The money price of driving on a freeway is always the same—zero. Is the (opportunity) cost always the same and zero, too? Explain your answer.

9. Think about ticket scalpers at a rock concert, a baseball game, and an opera. Might they exist because the tickets to these events were originally sold for less than the equilibrium price? Why or why not? In what way is a ticket scalper like and unlike your retail grocer, who buys food from a wholesaler and turns around and sells it to you?

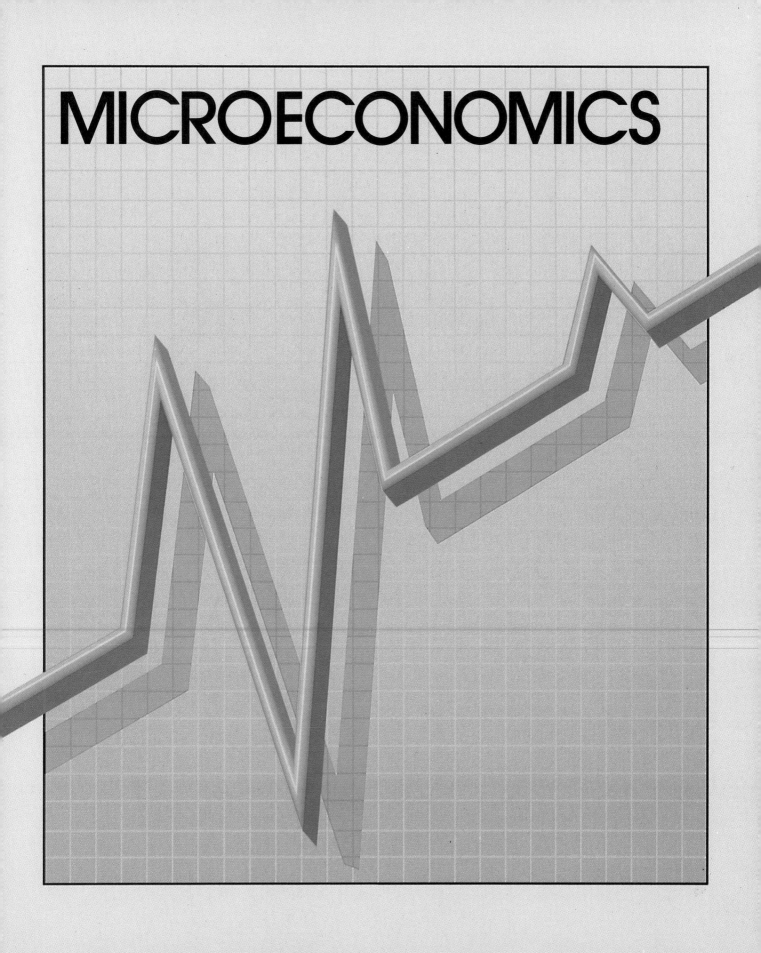

MICROECONOMICS

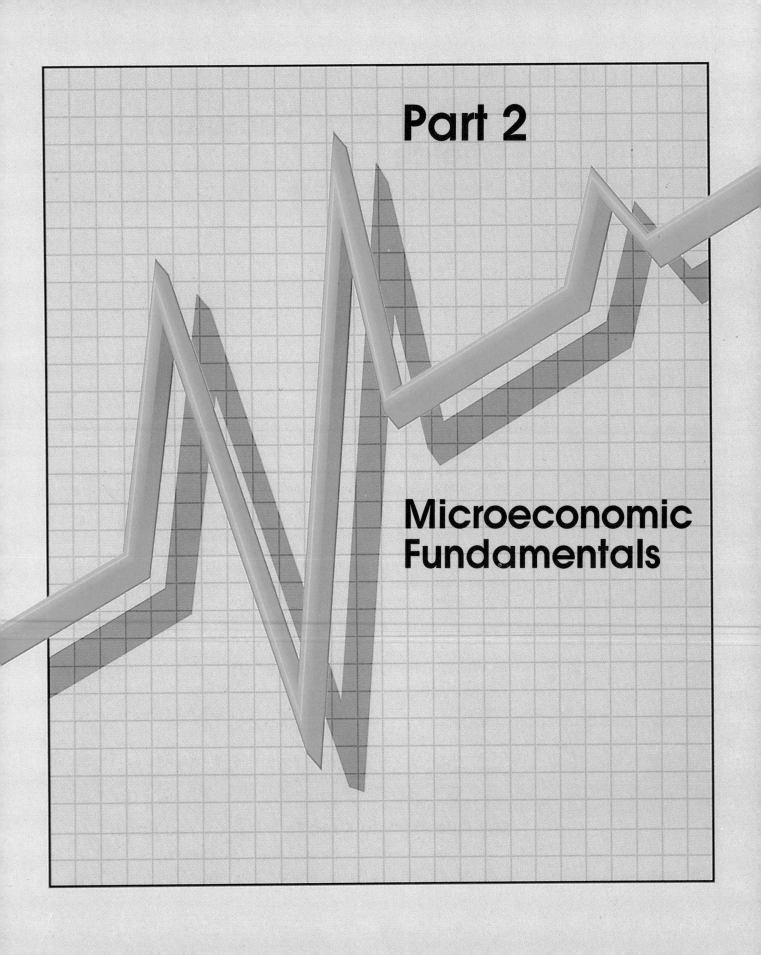

Part 2

Microeconomic Fundamentals

Chapter 5

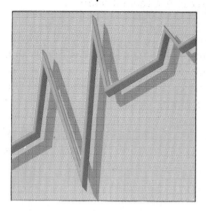

The Logic of Consumer Choice

■ INTRODUCTION

This chapter dispels a myth, presents a piece of shocking information, and untangles a paradox. We offer you the myth, the shocking information, and the paradox by posing three questions:

Question 1: Suppose you have two $1 bills. You give one to a millionaire and the other to a poor man. Who gets more satisfaction, or utility, from the extra dollar?

Question 2: Are rats like people when it comes to "buying" goods? Do they have downward-sloping demand curves? Are rats rational?

Question 3: Some goods have great value in use, others have little value in use. For example, water has great value in use because we need it to survive. Without water, there would be no life. Would you expect that the goods that have the greatest value in use will fetch the highest prices?

The answers to these questions form the substance of this chapter.

■ WHAT THIS CHAPTER IS ABOUT

It has been said that an educated person makes distinctions and that a very educated person makes *fine* distinctions. In this chapter we make fine distinctions. Specifically, we distinguish between *total* utility and *marginal* utility. This fine distinction is necessary to solving the age-old paradox of value and to paving the way for the development of marginal analysis in upcoming chapters. We also discuss the related issues of the law of diminishing marginal utility and consumer equilibrium.

Key Questions to Keep in Mind as You Read

1. What is the diamond-water paradox? What is its solution?

2. What is the difference between total utility and marginal utility?

3. What is the law of diminishing marginal utility?

4. What does it mean to equate marginal utilities per dollar? Do people do this?

5. Do rats have downward-sloping demand curves? Are rats rational?

UTILITY THEORY

Diamond-Water Paradox
The observation that those things that have the greatest value in use sometimes have little value in exchange and that those things that have little value in use sometimes have the greatest value in exchange.

Utility
A measure of the satisfaction, happiness, or benefit that results from the consumption of a good.

Util
An artificial construct used to "measure" utility.

Total Utility
Total satisfaction a person receives from consuming a particular quantity of a good.

Marginal Utility
The additional utility a person receives from consuming an additional unit of a particular good.

The economist Adam Smith wondered why something as valuable as water, which we need to survive, had a lower price than diamonds, which are not necessary for survival. He noted that often things that have the greatest *value in use,* or are the most useful, have little *value in exchange,* or have a relatively low price, and that things that have little or no value in use have the greatest value in exchange. Smith's observation came to be known as the **diamond-water paradox** (or the *paradox of value*). The paradox presented a challenge to economists, and they began to seek a solution to it. In this section, we begin to develop parts of the solution they found.

Utility, Total and Marginal

To say that a good gives you **utility** is to say that it has the power to satisfy wants, or that it gives you *satisfaction.* For example, suppose you buy your first unit of good X. You obtain a certain amount of utility. Economists refer to your receiving so many **utils**, where utils are an artificial construction with which to "measure" utility. (We realize you have never seen a "util"; no one has.)

You buy a second unit of good X. Once again, you get a certain amount of utility from this second unit. You receive *so many* utils. You purchase a third unit. As before, you derive a certain amount of utility from this third unit. If we were to sum the amounts of utility you obtained from each of the three units, we would have the **total utility** you received from purchasing good X. Total utility is the total satisfaction one receives from consuming a particular quantity of a good (in this example, three units of good X).

Total utility is different from **marginal utility.** If we consider only the *additional* utility gained from consuming an *additional* unit of good X, we would be referring to *marginal utility.* Marginal utility is the change in total utility divided by the change in the quantity consumed of a good (where the change in the quantity consumed of a good is usually equal to one unit): $MU = \Delta TU/\Delta Q$.

To illustrate, suppose you receive 50 utils of total utility from consuming one apple and 80 utils of total utility from consuming two apples. What is the marginal utility of the second apple? In other words, what is the additional utility of consuming an additional apple? It is 30 utils.

Law of Diminishing Marginal Utility

Do you think the marginal utility of the second unit is greater than, less than, or equal to the marginal utility of the first unit? Before answering, consider the difference in marginal utility between the third unit and the second unit, or between the fifth unit and the fourth unit (had we extended the number of units consumed). Basically we are asking whether the marginal utility of the unit that comes *next* is greater than, less than, or equal to the marginal utility of the unit that comes *before.*

Economists have generally answered "less than." This is because of the **law of diminishing marginal utility,** which states that for a given time period, *the marginal utility gained by consuming equal successive units of a good will decline as the amount consumed increases.* In terms of our artificial units "utils," this means that the number of utils gained by the consumption of the first unit of the good is greater

Law of Diminishing Marginal Utility
Holds that the marginal utility gained by consuming equal successive units of a good will decline as the amount consumed increases.

than the number of utils gained by the second (which is greater than the number gained by the third, which is greater than the number gained by the fourth, and so on). We illustrate the law of diminishing marginal utility in Exhibit 5-1.

In (a) we show both the total utility of consuming a certain number of units of a good and the marginal utility of consuming additional units. In (b) we have diagrammed total utility, and in (c) marginal utility. Notice in Exhibit 5-1b and c that total utility can increase as marginal utility decreases. This is important in helping us unravel the diamond-water paradox.

The law of diminishing marginal utility is based on the idea that if a good has a variety of uses but only one unit of the good is available, the consumer will use the first unit to satisfy his or her most urgent want. If two units are available, the consumer will use the second unit to satisfy a less urgent want.

To illustrate, suppose that good X can be used to satisfy wants A through E, with A being the most urgent want and E being the least urgent want, and B being more urgent than C, C being more urgent than D, and D being more urgent than E. We can chart the wants as follows:

		Wants		
A (most urgent)	B	C	D	E (least urgent)

Suppose the first unit of good X can satisfy any *one* (but only one) of the wants A through E. Which want will an individual choose to satisfy? The answer is "the most urgent want—A." The individual chooses to satisfy A instead of B, C, D, or E because people will ordinarily satisfy their most urgent want before all others. If you were dying of thirst in a desert (having gone without water for three days), and came across a quart of water, would you drink it or use it to wash your hands? You would drink it, of course. You would satisfy your most urgent want first. Washing your hands in the water would give you less utility than drinking the water.

Utility and the Hundredth Game of Chess

As we defined the law of diminishing marginal utility—the marginal utility gained by consuming equal successive units of a good will decline as the amount consumed increases—it follows that marginal utility begins to decline with the *second unit* of a good consumed. Occasionally, this doesn't appear to be the case. For example, someone will mention that his first chess game did not give him as much utility as his hundredth game because when he played his first chess game, he did not know how to play chess very well, but when he played his hundredth he did. The same can be said of other games such as golf and tennis. In short, sometimes you derive more utility from something as you get better at it. Does this invalidate the law of diminishing marginal utility? Some economists think not. They argue that a person's first game of chess may not be the same *good* as his hundredth game. Although to an onlooker the first and the hundredth games may appear to be much alike (they use the same board and so forth), from the viewpoint of the chess player, there may be a large difference between the first game of chess and the hundredth. In fact, the difference may be so large that we are dealing with two different goods.

This general problem has led some economists to refer to the less emphatic *principle* of diminishing marginal utility rather than to the *law* of diminishing marginal utility. Other economists have simply noted that there are *exceptions* to the law of diminishing marginal utility. Still others have said that it is important to define the law (or principle) of diminishing marginal utility as follows: The marginal utility associated with consuming equal successive units of a good will *eventually* decline as the amount consumed increases. The key word here is *eventually*. These econ-

Total Utility, Marginal Utility, and the Law of Diminishing Marginal Utility

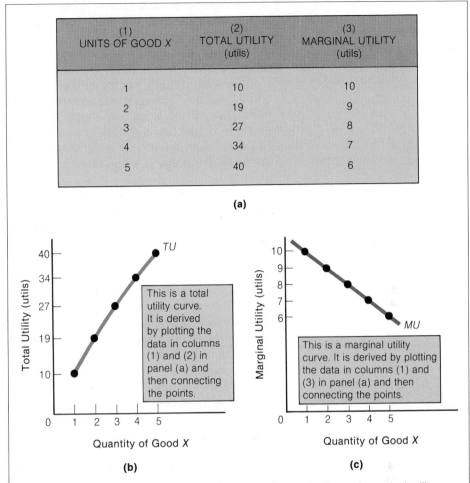

(1) UNITS OF GOOD X	(2) TOTAL UTILITY (utils)	(3) MARGINAL UTILITY (utils)
1	10	10
2	19	9
3	27	8
4	34	7
5	40	6

(a)

This is a total utility curve. It is derived by plotting the data in columns (1) and (2) in panel (a) and then connecting the points.

This is a marginal utility curve. It is derived by plotting the data in columns (1) and (3) in panel (a) and then connecting the points.

(b)

(c)

TU = total utility, and MU = marginal utility. (a) Both total utility and marginal utility are expressed in utils. Marginal utility is the change in total utility divided by the change in the quantity consumed of the good, $MU = \Delta TU/\Delta Q$. (b) Total utility. (c) Marginal utility. (b) and (c) together demonstrate that total utility can increase as marginal utility decreases.

omists argue that a person may enjoy, say, the first piece of pizza of the night immensely, and the second even more, but eventually there comes a point when one piece of pizza (say, the fourth) brings less utility than the previous piece (the third). In fact, this last version of the law of diminishing marginal utility is consistent with the law expressed by William Stanley Jevons, one of the founders of marginal utility theory. Jevons said that "the degree of utility varies with the quantity of commodity, and *ultimately* decreases as that quantity increases." See the biography of Jevons on p. 103 in this chapter.

The Millionaire and the Pauper: What the Law Says and Doesn't Say

Does a poor man get more or less utility from *one more dollar* than a millionaire? Most people would say that a poor man gets more utility from one more dollar than a millionaire because the poor man has so many fewer dollars than the millionaire.

"What's an extra dollar to a millionaire?" they ask. They then answer, "Nothing. A millionaire has so many dollars, one more doesn't mean a thing."

Some people think the law of diminishing marginal utility substantiates the claim that a millionaire gets less utility from one more dollar than a poor man. Unfortunately, though, this is a misreading of the law. In terms of our example, the law says that *for the millionaire* an additional dollar is worth less than the dollar that preceded it; and *for the poor man,* an additional dollar is worth less than the dollar that preceded it. Let's say the millionaire has $2 million, and the poor man has $1,000. We now give each of them one more dollar. The law of diminishing marginal utility says that the additional dollar is worth less to the millionaire than his two-millionth dollar; and the additional dollar is worth less to the poor man than his one-thousandth dollar. That is all the law says. We do not and cannot know whether the additional dollar is worth more or less to the millionaire than it is to the poor man. In summary, the law tells us something about the millionaire and about the poor man, but it does not tell us anything about the millionaire *in comparison with* the poor man.

To compare the utility the millionaire gets from the additional dollar with the utility the poor man gets from it is to fall into the trap of making an **interpersonal utility comparison**. The utility one person gets from something cannot be scientifically or objectively compared with the utility another person gets from the same thing, because *utility is subjective.* Who knows for certain how much satisfaction (utility) the millionaire gets from the additional dollar as compared with the poor man? The poor man may care little for money; he may shun it, consider it the root of all that is evil in the world, and prefer to consume the things in life that do not require money. On the other hand, the millionaire may be interested only in amassing more money. We should not be so careless as to "guess" at the utility one person obtains from consuming a certain item, compare it to our "guess" of the utility another person obtains from consuming the same item, and then call these "guesses" scientific facts.

Interpersonal Utility Comparison
Comparing the utility one person receives from a good, service, or activity with the utility another person receives from the same good, service, or activity.

The Solution to the Diamond-Water Paradox

Goods have both total utility and marginal utility. Take water, for example. Water is extremely useful; we cannot live without it. We would expect its total utility (its total usefulness) to be high. But we would also expect its marginal utility to be low. Why? We would expect this because water is in relatively plentiful supply, and as the law of diminishing marginal utility states, the utility of successive units of a good diminishes as consumption of the good increases. In short, water is immensely useful, but there is so much of it that individuals place relatively little value on another unit of it.

In contrast, diamonds are not as useful as water. We would expect the total utility of diamonds to be lower than the total utility of water. However, we would also expect the marginal utility of diamonds to be high. Why? Because there are relatively few diamonds in the world, the consumption of diamonds (in contrast to the consumption of water) takes place at relatively high marginal utility. Diamonds, which are rare, get used only for their few valuable uses. Water, being plentiful, gets used for its many valuable uses and for its not-so-valuable uses (such as spraying the car with the hose for two more minutes even though you are 99 percent sure that the soap is fully rinsed off.)

In conclusion, the total utility of water is high because water is extremely useful; the total utility of diamonds is low in comparison because diamonds are not as

Economics in Our Times

Should the Government Provide the Necessities of Life for Free?

Sometimes you will hear people say, "Food and water are necessities of life. No one can live without them. It is wrong to charge for these goods. The government should provide them free to everyone."

Or you might hear, "Medical care is a necessity to those who are sick. Without it, people will either experience an extremely low quality of life (you can't experience a high quality of life when you are feeling bad) or die. Making people pay for medical care is wrong. The government should provide it free to the people who need it."

Or someone might say, "A college education has become a necessity of life in this day and age. Without a college degree, you can't get a good job and earn a decent salary. You are stuck in a big hole with no way to get out. The government should provide a college education free to anyone who wants it."

Each of these statements labels

something as a necessity of life (food and water, medical care, college education) and then makes the policy proposal that government should provide the necessity for free.

Suppose government did give food and water, medical care, and college education to everyone for free—in other words, at zero price (although not at zero taxes). At zero price, people would want to consume these goods up to the point of *zero marginal utility* for each good. They would do so because if the marginal utility of the good (expressed in dollars) is greater than its price, one could derive more utility from purchasing the good than one would lose in parting with the dollar price of the good. In other words, if the price of a good is $5, an individual will continue purchasing it as long as the marginal utility she derives from its purchase is greater than $5. If the price is $0, she will continue to consume the good as long as the marginal utility she derives from it is greater than 0.

Since resources must be used to produce every unit of a good consumed, the government is using scarce resources to provide a good that has low marginal utility. Thus if some resources were withdrawn from producing these goods, total utility would fall very little. The resources could then be redirected to producing goods with a higher marginal utility, thus raising total utility.

The people who argue that certain goods should be provided free implicitly assume that the not-so-valuable uses of food and water, medical care, and college education are "valuable enough" to warrant a system of taxes to pay for the complete provision of these goods at zero price. It is questionable, however, if the least valuable uses of food and water, medical care, and college education are worth the sacrifices of other goods that would necessarily be forfeited if more of these goods were produced.

Think about these questions: Currently water is relatively cheap, and people use it to satisfy its more valuable uses and its not-so-valuable uses, too. But suppose water were cheaper than it is? Suppose it were zero price? Would it be used to satisfy its more valuable uses, not-so-valuable uses, and its *absolutely least valuable use*? If food had a zero price, would it follow that it too would be used to satisfy its more valuable uses, not-so-valuable uses, and its absolutely least valuable use (food fights perhaps)? Would the same be true of medical care? If medical care were free, would some people visit their doctor simply for a social outing? If college education were free, would some people go to college just to "hang out"?

useful as water. The marginal utility of water is low because water is so plentiful that people end up consuming it at low marginal utility; the marginal utility of diamonds is high because diamonds are so scarce that people end up consuming them at high marginal utility.

Do prices reflect total or marginal utility? We know that they reflect marginal utility; after all, diamonds are more expensive than water.

Question:

Aren't there times when water would be more expensive than diamonds?

Answer:

Yes, there are. If the supply of water is unusually limited for some reason, say, a drought, the price of water is likely to be higher than the price of diamonds. For example, in some arid parts of the world, water is in unusually short supply, and people have been known to trade their diamonds and precious metals as well as fight for some of it.

CONSUMER EQUILIBRIUM AND DEMAND

Our objective in this section is to identify the condition necessary for consumer equilibrium and then to discuss the relationship between it and the law of demand. The analysis that follows is based on the assumption that individuals seek to maximize utility.

Equating Marginal Utilities per Dollar

Suppose there are only two goods in the world, apples and oranges. At present a consumer is spending his entire income consuming 10 apples and 10 oranges a week. We assume that the marginal utility and price of each are as follows:[1]

$$MU_{oranges} = 30 \text{ utils}$$
$$MU_{apples} = 20 \text{ utils}$$
$$P_{oranges} = \$1$$
$$P_{apples} = \$1$$

The marginal (last) dollar spent on apples returns 20 utils per dollar and the marginal (last) dollar spent on oranges returns 30 utils per dollar. The ratio of MU_O/P_O (O = oranges) is greater than the ratio of MU_A/P_A (A = apples): $MU_O/P_O > MU_A/P_A$.

A consumer who found himself in this situation one week would redirect his purchases of apples and oranges the next week. He would think this: If I buy an orange, I receive more utility (30 utils) than if I buy an apple (20 utils). It's better to buy one more orange with a dollar and one less apple. I gain 30 utils from buying the orange, which is 10 utils more than if I buy the apple.

But what happens as the consumer buys one more orange and one less apple? The marginal utility of oranges falls (recall what the law of diminishing marginal utility says happens as a person consumes more of a good), and the marginal utility of apples rises (the consumer is consuming *fewer* apples). Because the consumer has bought one more orange and one less apple, he now has 11 oranges and 9 apples. At this combination of goods, the new situation looks like this:

$$MU_{oranges} = 25 \text{ utils}$$
$$MU_{apples} = 25 \text{ utils}$$
$$P_{oranges} = \$1$$
$$P_{apples} = \$1$$

[1]You may wonder where these marginal utility figures came from. These are points on hypothetical marginal utility curves, such as the one in Exhibit 5-1. What is important here is the fact that one number is greater than the other. We could easily have picked other numbers, such as 300 and 200, and so forth.

Here the ratio MU_O/P_O equals MU_A/P_A. The consumer is getting exactly the same amount of utility (25 utils) per dollar from the two goods. There is no way the consumer can redirect his purchases (buy more of one good and less of another good) and be made better off. Thus, the consumer is in equilibrium. In short, a consumer is in equilibrium when he or she derives the same marginal utility per dollar for all goods. The condition for **consumer equilibrium** is[2]

$$\frac{MU_A}{P_A} = \frac{MU_B}{P_B} = \frac{MU_C}{P_C} = \ldots = \frac{MU_Z}{P_Z}$$

where the letters A–Z represent all the goods a person buys.

Consumer Equilibrium
Occurs when the consumer has spent all income and the marginal utilities per dollar spent on each good purchased are equal: $MU_A/P_A = MU_B/P_B = MU_C/P_C = \ldots = MU_Z/P_Z$, where the letters A–Z represent all the goods a person buys.

Question:

If a person is in consumer equilibrium, does it follow that he has maximized his total utility?

Answer:

Yes, it does. By spending his dollars on goods that give him the greatest marginal utility and in the process bringing about the consumer equilibrium condition, he is adding as much to his total utility as he can possibly add.

Consumer Equilibrium and the Law of Demand

Suppose the consumer purchases 11 oranges and 9 apples and $MU_O/P_O = MU_A/P_A$. Then the price of oranges falls from $1 each to $.50. The situation is as follows:

$$MU_{oranges} = 25 \text{ utils}$$
$$MU_{apples} = 25 \text{ utils}$$
$$P_{oranges} = \$.50$$
$$P_{apples} = \$1.00$$

We now have $MU_O/P_O > MU_A/P_A$. The fall in the price of oranges has thrown the consumer out of equilibrium into disequilibrium. He will attempt to restore equilibrium by buying more of which good? He will buy oranges because he derives more utility per penny from buying oranges than apples. In short, a fall in the price of oranges throws the consumer out of equilibrium and causes him to buy more oranges to restore himself to equilibrium. Here we have the inverse relationship between (own) price and quantity demanded expressed in the law of demand.

Exhibit 5-2 presents another example that illustrates our point. There are two goods, A and B. Currently the price of both goods is $1 each. At this price the consumer buys 1 unit of good A and 6 units of good B. As we see from the exhibit, the marginal utility of the first unit of good A is 12 utils, and the marginal utility of the sixth unit of good B is also 12 utils. The consumer is in equilibrium where

$$\frac{MU_A}{P_A} = \frac{MU_B}{P_B}$$
$$\frac{12 \text{ utils}}{\$1.00} = \frac{12 \text{ utils}}{\$1.00}$$

[2]We are assuming here that the consumer exhausts his income and that saving is treated as a good.

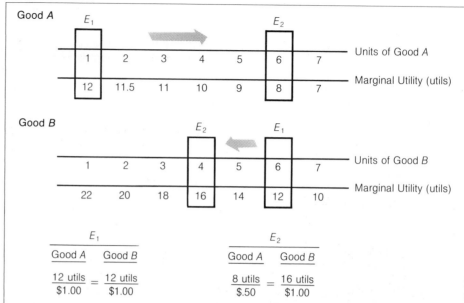

EXHIBIT 5-2
Consumer Equilibrium and a Fall in Price

$$\frac{E_1}{\begin{array}{cc} \text{Good } A & \text{Good } B \end{array}}$$

$$\frac{12 \text{ utils}}{\$1.00} = \frac{12 \text{ utils}}{\$1.00}$$

$$\frac{E_2}{\begin{array}{cc} \text{Good } A & \text{Good } B \end{array}}$$

$$\frac{8 \text{ utils}}{\$.50} = \frac{16 \text{ utils}}{\$1.00}$$

Initially the price of both good A and good B is $1. The consumer is in equilibrium buying 1 unit of good A and 6 units of good B. Then the price of good A falls to $.50. No longer is the consumer in equilibrium. To restore himself to equilibrium, he buys more of good A and less of good B. As he does this, the marginal utility of good A decreases and the marginal utility of good B increases. At the new set of prices, $.50 for A and $1.00 for B, the consumer is back in equilibrium when he purchases 6 units of good A and 4 units of good B.

Now suppose the price of good A falls to $.50. This changes the situation to the following:

$$\frac{MU_A}{P_A} > \frac{MU_B}{P_B}$$
$$\frac{12 \text{ utils}}{\$.50} > \frac{12 \text{ utils}}{\$1.00}$$

In this situation the consumer is gaining more utility per penny by purchasing good A than good B. He decides to buy more of good A and less of good B. In the exhibit, we see that he buys five more units of good A, to make a total of 6, and two less units of good B, to make a total of 4. As he buys more units of good A, the marginal utility of good A decreases (law of diminishing marginal utility). As we can see from the exhibit, the marginal utility of the sixth unit of good A is 8 utils. As the consumer cuts back on his purchases of good B, we notice that the marginal utility of good B increases. As the exhibit shows, the marginal utility of the fourth unit of good B is 16 utils. At the new set of prices, $.50 for good A and $1.00 for good B, the consumer is in equilibrium when he buys 6 units of good A and 4 units of good B. We have the following condition:

$$\frac{MU_A}{P_A} = \frac{MU_B}{P_B}$$
$$\frac{8 \text{ utils}}{\$.50} = \frac{16 \text{ utils}}{\$1.00}$$

The consumer receives equal utility per penny from purchasing goods A and B.

Biography
William Stanley
Jevons
(1835–1882)

Brief Biography

William Stanley Jevons only lived to age 47. He was born in Liverpool, England, where his childhood was shadowed by three dark events: the death of his mother when he was 10 years old, the mental illness of his brother, and the failure of the family business. At University College, London, he first studied chemistry, a natural science, but after spending some years as an assayer in Sydney, Australia, he developed an interest in economics, a social science. After his return to England in 1859, he resumed his studies at University College, taking his degree in political economy. Because Jevons exhibited a keen ability at collecting and classifying data, some economists refer to him as the founder of empirical economics. Jevons contributed to both theoretical and empirical economics, however. He

drowned in 1882 at a health resort in southern England.

The Big Three

Jevons's best-known book, *The Theory of Political Economy,* was published in 1871, the same year that the economist Carl Menger's *Grundsätze der Volkswirtschaftslehre* was published, and three years before economist Léon Walras's *Eléments déconomie politique pure.* These three—Jevons, Menger, and Walras—are said to be the fathers of marginal utility theory.

Total and "Final Degree" of Utility

Jevons distinguished between total utility and what he referred to as the "final degree of utility," which he defined as the "degree of utility of the last addition, or the next possible addition of a very small, or infinitely small, quantity to the existing stock." Here he was talking about marginal utility. He elaborated the law of diminishing marginal utility by saying that the "degree of utility varies with the quantity of commodity, and ultimately decreases as that quantity increases."

Interpersonal Utility Comparison

On the question of making interpersonal utility comparisons, Jevons said, "I see no means by which such comparisons can be made."

Jevons on Gambling

Jevons demonstrated that gambling in a fair game does not pay under the condition that people derive no pleasure from gambling; that is, if people gamble only to win and not for the

thrill. A fair game in gambling is one in which the value of the expected gain equals the wager made. For example, if you bet $1 to have a 10 percent chance to win $10, the game is fair: $1 (the wager) is equal to the probability of winning (10 percent) times the win ($10). Jevons pointed out that there is such a thing as the diminishing marginal utility of money: The last dollar brings less utility than the next-to-last dollar, and so on. This means that the money potentially lost from a wager has a higher per-unit utility than an equal amount of money potentially gained. Specifically, losing a dollar bet in a fair game causes you to lose more utility than winning a dollar causes you to gain utility.

A Personal Note

Jevons developed a "logical machine" that some people consider to be one of the ancestors of the modern computer.

Theory in Practice

Rats in Economics

How rational do you have to be to have a downward-sloping demand curve? Empirical research seems to say, "as rational as a white rat." Several researchers at Texas A&M University undertook to study the "buying" behavior of two white rats. The rats were put in laboratory cages with two levers: one they could push to obtain root beer, the other they could push to obtain nonalcoholic collins mix.

Each day each of the rats was given a "fixed income" of 300 pushes. (After 300 pushes the lever could not be pushed down until the next day.) The prices of root beer and collins mix were both 20 pushes per milliliter of beverage. Given this income and the price of root beer and collins mix, one rat settled in to consuming 11 milliliters of root beer and 4 milliliters of collins mix. The other rat settled in to consuming almost all root beer.

Then the prices of the two beverages were changed. The price of collins mix was halved while the price of root beer was doubled. Economic theory would predict that given these new prices the consumption of collins mix would increase and the consumption of root beer would decrease. This is exactly what happened. Both rats began to consume more collins mix and less root beer. In short, both rats had downward-sloping demand curves for collins mix and root beer.

Income and Substitution Effects

Consider what happens when the absolute price of one good falls and the absolute prices of all other goods remain constant. For example, suppose the absolute price of computers falls, and the absolute prices of all other goods remain constant. Two things occur: First, the relative price of computers falls.[3] Second, a consumer's **real income**, or purchasing power, rises.

A person's real income, or purchasing power, rises if with a given absolute (or dollar) income he or she can purchase more goods and services. To illustrate, suppose Barbara's income is $100 per week, and there are only two goods in the world, A and B, whose prices are $50 and $25, respectively. With her $100 income, Barbara purchases 1 unit of good A and 2 units of good B per week, for a total of 3 units of the two goods.

Suppose that the price of good A falls to $25, *ceteris paribus*. Now Barbara can purchase a greater combination of the two goods. She now purchases 2 units of good A and 2 units of good B, for a total of 4 units of the two goods. Given this, we say that Barbara's *real income* has risen as a result of the fall in the price of good A. With her $100 income, Barbara is able to purchase more goods.

To recap, a fall in the absolute price of a good leads to (1) a fall in the relative price of the good and (2) a rise in real income.

We learned in Chapter 3 that a fall in the relative price of a good *will*, and a rise in real income *can*, lead to greater purchases of the good.[4] That portion of the change in the quantity demanded of a good that is attributable to a change in its relative price is referred to as the **substitution effect**. That portion of the change in

Real Income

Income adjusted for price changes. A person has more (less) real income as the price of a good falls (rises), *ceteris paribus*.

Substitution Effect

That portion of the change in the quantity demanded of a good that is attributable to a change in its relative price.

[3]In Chapter 3 we explained the process by which a fall in absolute price brings about a decrease in relative price, *ceteris paribus*.

[4]Specifically, a rise in real income *will* lead to greater purchases of a good if the good is a normal good. It will not, if the good is an inferior good. Review the discussion of normal and inferior goods in Chapter 3, if necessary.

the quantity demanded of a good that is attributable to a change in real income, brought about by the change in absolute price, is referred to as the **income effect**.

To illustrate, suppose the price of normal good A falls from $10 to $8, *ceteris paribus*. As a result, the quantity demanded of good A rises from 100 units to 143 units. A portion of the 43-unit increase in the quantity demanded is due to the relative price of good A falling; and a portion of the 43-unit increase in quantity demanded is due to real income rising. Suppose quantity demanded rises from 100 to 129 units because the relative price of good A falls. This would be the extent of the substitution effect: People purchase 29 more units of good A because it has become relatively cheaper to purchase. The difference between 143 units and 129 units, or 14 units, constitutes the extent of the income effect: People purchase 14 more units of good A because their real incomes have risen.

■ CHAPTER SUMMARY

The Law of Diminishing Marginal Utility

■ The law of diminishing marginal utility holds that as the amount of a good consumed increases, the marginal utility of the good decreases.

■ The law of diminishing marginal utility should not be used to make interpersonal utility comparisons. For example, the law does not say that a millionaire receives less (or more) utility from an additional dollar than a poor man. Instead, it says that the last dollar has less value for both the millionaire and the poor man than the penultimate (next-to-last) dollar.

The Diamond-Water Paradox

■ The diamond-water paradox states that that which has great value in use sometimes has little value in exchange and that which has little value in use sometimes has great value in exchange. A knowledge of the difference between total utility and marginal utility is necessary to unravel the diamond-water paradox.

■ A good can have high total utility and low marginal utility. Take water, for example. Its total utility is high; but because water is so plentiful, its marginal utility is low. In short, water is immensely useful but it is so plentiful that individuals place relatively low value on another unit of it. In contrast, diamonds are not as useful as water, but because there are few diamonds in the world, the marginal utility of diamonds is high. To put it simply, a good can be extremely useful and have a low price if the good is in plentiful supply (high value in use, low value in exchange). On the other hand, a good can be of little use and have a high price if the good is in short supply (low value in use, high value in exchange).

Consumer Equilibrium

■ Individuals seek to equate marginal utilities per dollar. For example, if a person receives more utility per dollar spent on good A than B, she will reorder her purchases and buy more A and less B. There is a tendency to move away from this condition, $MU_A/P_A > MU_B/P_B$, to this condition, $MU_A/P_A = MU_B/P_B$. The latter condition represents consumer equilibrium (in a two-good world).

■ QUESTIONS TO ANSWER AND DISCUSS

1. If we take $1 away from a rich person and give it to a poor person, the rich person loses less utility than the poor person gains. Comment.

2. Is it possible to get so much of a good that it turns into a bad? If so, give an example.

3. If a person consumes fewer units of a good, will marginal utility of the good increase as total utility decreases?

4. If the marginal utility of good A is 4 utils and its price is $2, and the marginal utility of good B is 6 utils and its price is $1, is the individual consumer maximizing (total) utility if she spends a total of $3 buying one unit of each good? If not, how can more utility be obtained?

5. Individuals who buy second homes usually spend less for them than they do for their first homes. Why is this the case?

6. Think up five everyday examples where you or someone else makes an interpersonal utility comparison.

7. Is there a logical link between the law of demand and the assumption that individuals seek to maximize utility? (Hint: Think of how the condition for consumer equilibrium can be used to express the inverse relationship between price and quantity demanded.)

8. List five sets of two goods (each set is composed of two goods; for example, diamonds and water is one set) where the good with the greater value in use has lower value in exchange than the good with the lower value in use.

9. Do you think people with high IQs are in consumer equilibrium (equate marginal utilities per dollar) more often than people with low IQs? Why?

Appendix B Budget Constraint and Indifference Curve Analysis

In this chapter we used marginal utility theory to discuss consumer choice. Sometimes budget constraint and indifference curve analysis is used instead, especially in upper-division economics courses. We examine this important topic in this appendix.

THE BUDGET CONSTRAINT

Budget Constraint
All the combinations or bundles of two goods a person can purchase given a certain money income and prices for the two goods.

Societies have production possibilities frontiers (see Chapter 2), and individuals have **budget constraints**. The budget constraint is built on two prices and the individual's income. To illustrate, consider O'Brien who has a monthly income of $1,200. In a world of two goods, X and Y, O'Brien can spend his total income on X, he can spend his total income on Y, or he can spend part of his income on X and part on Y. Suppose the price of X is $100 and the price of Y is $80. Given this, if O'Brien spends his total income on X, he can purchase a maximum of 12 units; if he spends his total income on Y, he can purchase a maximum of 15 units. Locating these two points on a two-dimensional diagram and then drawing a line between them, as we have done in Exhibit 5B-1, gives us O'Brien's budget constraint. Any point on the budget constraint, as well as any point below it, represents a possible combination (bundle) of the two goods available to O'Brien.

The slope of the budget constraint has special significance. The absolute value of the slope represents the relative prices of the two goods, X and Y. This slope, or P_X/P_Y, is equal to 1.25, indicating that the relative price of 1 unit of X is 1.25 units of Y.

What Will Change the Budget Constraint?

As we stated, the budget constraint is built on two prices and the individual's income. This means that if any of the three variables changes (either of the prices or the individual's income), the budget constraint changes. Not all changes are alike, however. First, consider a fall in the price of good X from $100 to $60. With this change the maximum number of units of good X purchasable with an income of $1,200 rises from 12 to 20. The budget constraint revolves away from the origin in a counterclockwise direction, as shown in (Exhibit 5B-2a). Notice that the number of O'Brien's possible combinations of the two goods increases; there are more bundles of the two goods available after the price decrease than before.

An individual's budget constraint gives us a picture of the different combinations (bundles) of two goods available to the individual (this assumes a two-good world; for a many-good world, we could put one good on one axis and "all other goods" on the other). The budget constraint is derived by finding the maximum amount of each good an individual can consume (given his or her income and the prices of the two goods) and connecting these two points.

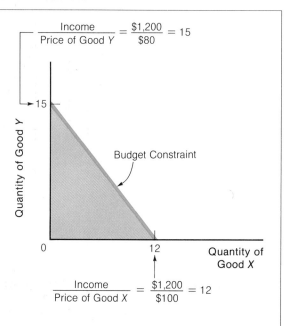

$$\frac{\text{Income}}{\text{Price of Good } Y} = \frac{\$1,200}{\$80} = 15$$

$$\frac{\text{Income}}{\text{Price of Good } X} = \frac{\$1,200}{\$100} = 12$$

Consider what happens to the budget constraint if the price of good X rises. If it goes from $100 to $150, the maximum number of units of good X falls from 12 to 8. The budget constraint revolves toward the origin in a clockwise direction. As a consequence, the number of bundles available to O'Brien decreases. We conclude that a change in the price of either good changes the slope of the budget constraint, with the result that relative prices and the number of bundles available to the individual also change.

We turn now to a change in income. If O'Brien's income rises to $1,600, the maximum number of units of X rises to 16 and the maximum number of units of Y rises to 20. The budget constraint shifts rightward (away from the origin) and is parallel to the old budget constraint. As a consequence, the number of bundles available to O'Brien increases (Exhibit 5B-2b). If O'Brien's income falls from $1,200 to $800, the extreme end points on the budget constraint become 8 and 10 for X and Y, respectively. The budget constraint shifts leftward (toward the origin) and is parallel to the old budget constraint. As a consequence, the number of bundles available to O'Brien falls (Exhibit 5B-2b).

INDIFFERENCE CURVES

An individual can, of course, choose any bundle of the two goods on or below the budget constraint. We assume that she spends her total income and therefore chooses a point on the budget constraint. This raises two important questions: (1) Which bundle of the many bundles of the two goods does the individual choose? (2) How does the individual's chosen combination of goods change given a change in prices or income? Both questions can be answered by combining the budget constraint with the graphical expression of the individual's preferences—that is, indifference curves.

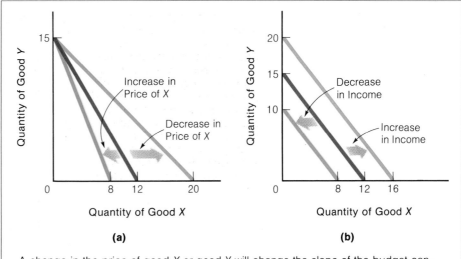

A change in the price of good X or good Y will change the slope of the budget constraint. A change in income will change the position of the budget constraint while the slope remains constant. Whenever a budget constraint changes, the number of combinations (bundles) of the two goods available to the individual changes, too.

Constructing an Indifference Curve

Is it possible to be indifferent between two bundles of goods? Yes, it is. Suppose bundle A consists of 2 pairs of shoes and 6 shirts and bundle B consists of 3 pairs of shoes and 4 shirts. A person who is indifferent between these two bundles is implicitly saying that it doesn't matter which bundle he ends up with; one is as good as the other. He is likely to say this, though, only if he receives equal total utility from the two bundles: If this were not the case, he would prefer one bundle to the other.

If we were to tabulate all the different bundles from which the individual receives equal utility, we would have an **indifference set**. If we then plotted the data in the indifference set, we would have an **indifference curve.** Consider the indifference set illustrated in Exhibit 5B-3a. There are four bundles of goods, A–D; each bundle gives the same total utility as every other bundle. These equal-utility bundles are plotted in Exhibit 5B-3b. Connecting these bundles in a two-dimensional space gives us an indifference curve.

Characteristics of Indifference Curves

Indifference curves for goods have certain characteristics that are consistent with reasonable assumptions about consumer behavior. We present a list of them here.

■ **Indifference curves are downward sloping** (from left to right). The assumption that consumers always prefer more of a good to less requires that indifference curves slope downward left to right. Consider the alternatives to downward sloping: vertical, horizontal, and upward sloping (left to right). A horizontal or vertical curve would combine bundles of goods some of which had more of one good and no less of

Indifference Set

Group of bundles of two goods that give an individual equal total utility.

Indifference Curve

Represents an indifference set. A curve that shows all the bundles of two goods that give an individual equal total utility.

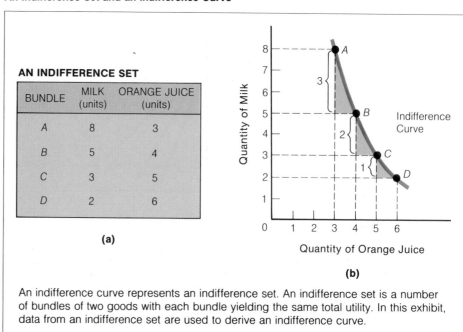

AN INDIFFERENCE SET

BUNDLE	MILK (units)	ORANGE JUICE (units)
A	8	3
B	5	4
C	3	5
D	2	6

(a)

(b)

An indifference curve represents an indifference set. An indifference set is a number of bundles of two goods with each bundle yielding the same total utility. In this exhibit, data from an indifference set are used to derive an indifference curve.

another good than other bundles Exhibit 5B-4a-b). (If bundle *B* contained more of one good and no less of another good than bundle *A*, would an individual be *indifferent* between the two bundles? No, he or she wouldn't. Individuals prefer more to less.) An upward-sloping curve would combine bundles of goods some of which had more of *both* goods than other bundles (Exhibit 5B-4c). A simpler way of putting it is to say that indifference curves are downward sloping because a person has to get more of one good in order to maintain his or her level of satisfaction (utility) when giving up some of another good.

■ **Indifference curves are convex to the origin.** This implies that the slope of the indifference curve becomes flatter as we move down and to the right along the indifference curve. For example, at 8 units of milk (point *A* in Exhibit 5B-3b), the individual is willing to give up 3 units of milk to get an additional unit of orange juice (and thus move to point *B*). At point *B*, where she has 5 units of milk, she is only willing to give up 2 units of milk to get an additional unit of orange juice (and thus move to point *C*). Finally, at point *C*, with 3 units of milk, she is now only willing to give up 1 unit of milk to get an additional unit of orange juice. We conclude that the more of one good that an individual has, the more units he or she will give up to get an additional unit of another good; the less of one good that an individual has, the fewer units he or she will give up to get an additional unit of another good. Is this reasonable? The answer is yes. Our observation is a reflection of diminishing marginal utility at work. As the quantity of a good consumed increases, the marginal utility of that good decreases; therefore we reason that the more of one good an individual has, the more units he or she can (and will) sacrifice to get an additional unit of another good and still maintain total utility. Stated differently, if the law of diminishing marginal utility did not exist, then it would not make sense to say that indifference curves of goods are convex to the origin.

An important peripheral point about marginal utilities is that *the absolute value of the slope of the indifference curve—which is called the* **marginal rate of substi-**

Marginal Rate of Substitution

The amount of one good an individual is willing to give up to obtain an additional unit of another good and maintain equal total utility.

Indifferences Curves for Goods Do Not Look Like This

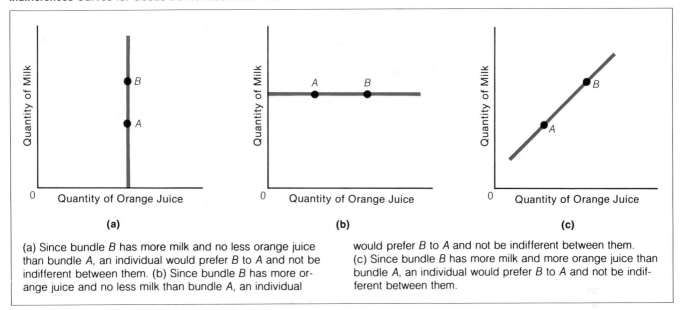

(a) Since bundle B has more milk and no less orange juice than bundle A, an individual would prefer B to A and not be indifferent between them. (b) Since bundle B has more orange juice and no less milk than bundle A, an individual would prefer B to A and not be indifferent between them.
(c) Since bundle B has more milk and more orange juice than bundle A, an individual would prefer B to A and not be indifferent between them.

tution—*represents the ratio of the marginal utility of the good on the horizontal axis to the marginal utility of the good on the vertical axis:*

$$\frac{MU_{\text{good on horizontal axis}}}{MU_{\text{good on vertical axis}}}$$

Let's look carefully at the words in italics. First, we said that the absolute value of the slope of the indifference curve is the marginal rate of substitution. The marginal rate of substitution (MRS) is the amount of one good an individual is willing to give up to obtain an additional unit of another good and maintain equal total utility. For example, in Exhibit 5B-3b we see that moving from point A to B, the individual is willing to give up 3 units of milk to get an additional unit of orange juice, with total utility remaining constant (between points A and B). The marginal rate of substitution is therefore 3 units of milk for 1 unit of orange juice in the area between points A and B. And as we said, the absolute value of the slope of the indifference curve, the marginal rate of substitution, is equal to the ratio of the MU of the good on the horizontal axis to the MU of the good on the vertical axis. How can this be? Well, if it is true that an individual giving up 3 units of milk and receiving 1 unit of orange juice maintains his total utility, it follows that (in the area under consideration) the marginal utility of orange juice is approximately three times the marginal utility of milk. In general terms

Absolute value of the slope of the indifference curve

$$= \text{marginal rate of substitution} = \frac{MU_{\text{good on horizontal axis}}}{MU_{\text{good on vertical axis}}}$$

■ **Indifference curves that are farther from the origin are preferable because they represent larger bundles of goods.** In Exhibit 5B-3b only one indifference curve was drawn. However, different bundles of the two goods exist and have indifference curves passing through them; these bundles have less of both goods or more of both goods than those illustrated in Exhibit 5B-3b. Illustrating a number of indifference

Indifference Curve Map

Represents a number of indifference curves for a given individual with reference to two goods.

curves on the same diagram gives us an **indifference curve map**. Strictly speaking, an indifference curve map represents a number of indifference curves for a given individual with reference to two goods. A "mapping" is illustrated in Exhibit 5B-5.

Notice that although only five indifference curves have been drawn, many more could have been added. For example, there are many indifference curves between I_1 and I_2.

Also notice that the farther away from the origin an indifference curve is, the higher total utility it represents. You can see this by comparing point A on I_1 and point B on I_2. At point B there is the same amount of orange juice as at point A, but more milk. Point B is therefore preferable to point A, and since B is on I_2 and A is on I_1, I_2 is preferable to I_1. The reason for this is simple: An individual receives more utility at any point on I_2 (because more goods are available) than at any point on I_1.

Transitivity

The principle whereby if A is preferred to B, and B is preferred to C, then A is preferred to C.

■ **Indifference curves do not cross.** The reason for this is that individuals' preferences are **transitive**. Look at the following example. If Kristin prefers Coca-Cola to Pepsi-Cola, and she also prefers Pepsi-Cola to root beer, then it follows that she prefers Coca-Cola to root beer. If she preferred root beer to Coca-Cola, she would be contradicting her earlier preferences. To say that an individual has transitive preferences means that he or she maintains a logical order of preferences during a given time period. Consider what indifference curves that crossed (intersected) would represent. In Exhibit 5B-6, indifference curves I_1 and I_2 intersect at point A. Notice that point A lies on *both* I_1 and I_2. Comparing A and B, we hold that the individual must be indifferent between them because they lie on the same indifference curve. The same holds for A and C. But if the individual is indifferent between A and B, and between A and C, it follows that she must be indifferent between B and C. But a quick glance at the exhibit tells us that C has more of both goods than B, and thus the individual will not be indifferent between B and C; she will prefer C to B. We cannot have transitive preferences and make sense of crossing indifference curves. We can, however, have transitive preferences and make sense of noncrossing indifference curves. We go with the latter.

■ **EXHIBIT 5B-5**
An Indifference Map

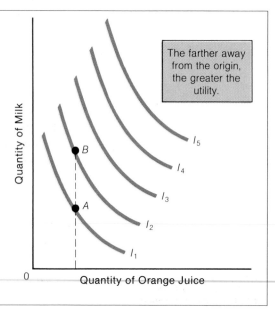

A few of the many possible indifference curves have been drawn. Any point in the two-dimensional space is on an indifference curve. Indifference curves farther away from the origin represent greater total utility than those closer to the origin.

The farther away from the origin, the greater the utility.

Crossing Indifference Curves Are Inconsistent with Transitive Preferences

Point *A* lies on both indifference curves I_1 and I_2. This means that the individual is indifferent between *A* and *B* and between *A* and *C*, which results in her (supposedly) being indifferent between *B* and *C*. But individuals prefer "more to less" (when it comes to goods) and would prefer *C* to *B*. We cannot have transitive preferences and make sense of crossing indifference curves.

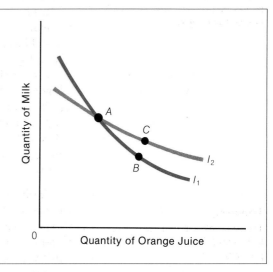

THE INDIFFERENCE MAP AND THE BUDGET CONSTRAINT COME TOGETHER

At this point we bring the indifference map and the budget constraint together to illustrate consumer equilibrium. We have the following facts: (1) The individual has a budget constraint. (2) The absolute value of the slope of the budget constraint is the relative prices of the two goods under consideration, say, P_X/P_Y. (3) The individual has an indifference map. (4) The absolute value of the slope of the indifference curve at any point is the marginal rate of substitution, which is equal to the marginal utility of one good divided by the marginal utility of another good; for example, MU_X/MU_Y. With this information, what is the necessary condition for consumer equilibrium? Obviously the individual will try to reach a point on the highest indifference curve she can reach. This point will be where the slope of the budget constraint is equal to the slope of an indifference curve (or where the budget constraint is tangent to an indifference curve). At this point consumer equilibrium is established and the following condition holds:

Slope of budget constraint = slope of indifference curve

or

$$\frac{P_X}{P_Y} = \frac{MU_X}{MU_Y}$$

This condition is met in Exhibit 5B-7 at point *E*. Note that it looks similar to the condition for consumer equilibrium that we found early in Chapter 5. By rearranging the terms in the condition, we get[1]

$$\frac{MU_X}{P_X} = \frac{MU_Y}{P_Y}$$

We now see that the condition for consumer equilibrium is the same whether we use a marginal utility approach or a budget constraint–indifference curve approach.

[1]Start with $P_X/P_Y = MU_X/MU_Y$ and cross multiply. This gives us $P_X MU_Y = P_Y MU_X$. Next divide both sides by P_X. This gives us $MU_Y = P_Y MU_X/P_X$. Finally, divide both sides by P_Y. This gives us $MU_Y/P_Y = MU_X/P_X$.

Consumer Equilibrium

Consumer equilibrium exists at
the point where the slope of the
budget constraint is equal to the
slope of an indifference curve, or
where the budget constraint is
tangent to an indifferent curve. In
this exhibit, this point is E. Here
$P_X/P_Y = MU_X/MU_Y$; or rearranging,
$MU_X/P_X = MU_Y/P_Y$.

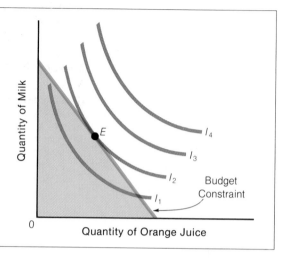

EXHIBIT 5B-8
From Indifference Curves to a Demand Curve

(a) At a price of $10 for good X,
consumer equilibrium is at point A
with the individual consuming 30
units of X. As the price falls to $5,
the budget constraint moves outward (away from the origin), and
the consumer moves to point B
and consumes 35 units of X. Plotting the price-quantity data for X
gives us a demand curve for X in
(b).

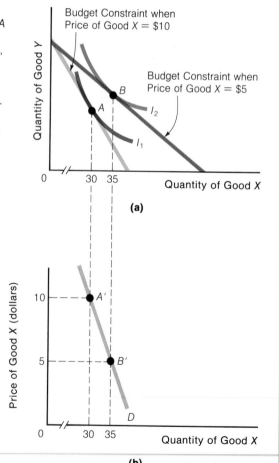

From Indifference Curves to a Demand Curve

We can now derive a demand curve within a budget constraint—indifference curve framework. In Exhibit 5B-8a there are two budget constraints, one reflecting a $10 price for good X and the other reflecting a $5 price for good X. Notice that as the price of X falls, the consumer moves from point A to B. At B, 35 units of X are consumed; at A, 30 units of X were consumed. We conclude that a lower price for X results in greater consumption of X. By plotting our relevant price and quantity data, we derive a demand curve for good X in (b).

Chapter 6

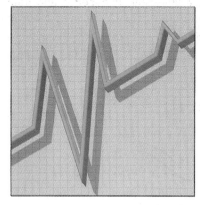

Elasticity

■ INTRODUCTION

John and Nicole Evans opened their own dry cleaning and laundry business on July 5, 1988. Before going into business, John had been a real estate agent and Nicole, a schoolteacher.

July 5 was an important date for them. They opened the shop bright and early at 7:00 A.M. Their first customer walked in at 7:15. He had four pairs of trousers, ten shirts, and a dark blue suit he wanted dry-cleaned. John and Nicole charged $2 each for the trousers, $1 per shirt, and $3 for the suit.

Months passed. John and Nicole were doing well in their business. Then one day Nicole said that she knew a way to do even better.

"John, if we'd lower our prices on trousers, I think we'd make more money."

"No way," said John. "You can't make more money by charging less. Pass me the iron."

Nicole, exasperated, said, "We might make less on each pair of trousers, but suppose we have a lot more trousers to clean. Wouldn't we make more money that way?"

John paused and thought a while. Let's see, less money for each pair of trousers we clean, but more trousers to clean.

Before he had completed the thought, Nicole spoke up, "For example, we charge $2 now and take in about 500 pairs of trousers per month. That's a $1,000. Suppose we lowered our price to $1.85 and took in 600 pairs of trousers per month. That would be $1,110 per month."

"But it could go the other way," said John. "Suppose we go to $1.85 and only take in 510 pairs of trousers. That's $943.50. What do you think of that?"

"That only means you could be right, or I could be right. That's a draw if you ask me."

John thought for a few seconds. "Okay," he said, "let's give it a try for a month or so to find out who is right."

Who do you think is right? Why? Could John and Nicole both be wrong?

■ WHAT THIS CHAPTER IS ABOUT

This chapter is divided into two parts. Part I defines price elasticity of demand, explains how it is calculated, and describes the relationship between it and total revenue (total expenditure). This information is important to understanding the firm and market structures, which is discussed in upcoming chapters. Part II discusses the determinants of price elasticity of demand, along with cross elasticity of demand, income elasticity of demand, and price elasticity of supply.

Key Questions to Keep in Mind as You Read

1. What is elasticity? What are the different types of elasticity?
2. How are elasticity concepts used in economics?
3. What is the relationship between total revenue (or total expenditure) and price elasticity of demand?
4. What are the determinants of price elasticity of demand?
5. What is cross elasticity of demand?
6. What is income elasticity of demand?
7. What is price elasticity of supply?
8. Who bears the burden of a tax?

ELASTICITY: PART I

As we learned in Chapter 3, the law of demand states that price and quantity demanded are inversely related, *ceteris paribus*. What we don't know is by *what percentage* quantity demanded changes as price changes. Suppose price rises by 10 percent. As a result, quantity demanded falls. But by *what percentage* does it fall? We can answer this question by applying the notion of *price elasticity of demand*. The general concept of *elasticity* provides a technique for estimating the response of one variable to changes in some other variable. It has numerous applications in economics.

Price Elasticity of Demand

Price Elasticity of Demand
A measure of the responsiveness of quantity demanded to changes in price.

Price elasticity of demand is a measure of the responsiveness of quantity demanded to changes in price. Who might be interested in price elasticity of demand? The answer is just about anyone who sells anything. The person who sells jogging shoes wants some idea of how much quantity demanded will fall if she raises shoe prices 5 percent. The car salesman wants to know how much quantity demanded will rise if he lowers car prices 10 percent. The university administration wants to know how much enrollment will drop if it raises tuition by 7 percent.

Economists measure price elasticity of demand quite simply: They divide the percentage change in the quantity demanded of a good by the percentage change in its price. For example, if the quantity demanded of good X falls by 20 percent as a result of a 10 percent rise in the price of good X, price elasticity of demand is 2 (20 percent/10 percent = 2). In short:

$$E_d = \frac{\text{percentage change in quantity demanded}}{\text{percentage change in price}} = \frac{\%\Delta Q_d}{\%\Delta P}$$

where E_d stands for "coefficient of price elasticity of demand," or simply "elasticity coefficient," and Δ stands for "change in."

Question:

Suppose the elasticity coefficient is 2. What does this mean?

Answer:

It means that if prices were raised from the prevailing rate, the percentage change in quantity demanded would be 2 times the percentage change in price. For example, if price were raised 1 percent, quantity demanded would fall 2 percent. Consider an example closer to home. Suppose the university raises tuition by 10 percent and the enrollment falls off by 20 percent. Here the elasticity coefficient is 2. This number is a shorthand way of saying that a 10 percent rise in tuition brought about a 20 percent (2 times the percentage change in price) fall in enrollment.

Follow-up Question:

If the elasticity coefficient is 2, which means quantity demanded falls by 2 times the percentage rise in price, shouldn't there be a minus sign (−) in front of the number 2?

Answer:

Strictly speaking, the answer is yes, since price and quantity demanded move in opposite directions. By convention, economists usually simplify things by using the *absolute value* of price elasticity of demand; thus they drop the minus sign.

Point Elasticity and Arc Elasticity

To calculate the elasticity coefficient, we must know how to calculate percentage changes—specifically the changes in both quantity demanded and price (since $E_d = \%\Delta Q_d/\%\Delta P$). The percentage change in anything equals the absolute change in that "something" divided by its base value. For example, if someone earns $1,000 per month and gets a raise to $1,100 per month, the percentage change in income is 10 percent, or $100, the absolute change in income, divided by $1,000, the original (base) income. We can rewrite $E_d = \%\Delta Q_d/\%\Delta P$ as

$$E_d = \frac{\Delta Q_d/Q_d}{\Delta P/P} \qquad (1)$$

There is a problem using this formula to calculate price elasticity of demand, especially the larger the changes in quantity demanded and price. To illustrate, suppose we calculate the elasticity coefficient between the two points, *A* and *B*, on a demand curve using formula 1.

$$\text{Point } A: P_1 = \$10 \qquad Q_{d1} = 100$$
$$\text{Point } B: P_2 = \$12 \qquad Q_{d2} = 50$$

If we start at point *A* and move to point *B* (price increases), the elasticity coefficient is 2.5 (absolute value). It is calculated this way:

$$E_d = \frac{\Delta Q_d/Q_d}{\Delta P/P} = \frac{50/100}{2/10} = 2.5$$

However, if we start at point *B* and move to point *A* (price decreases), the elasticity coefficient is 6.0. It is calculated this way:

$$E_d = \frac{\Delta Q_d/Q_d}{\Delta P/P} = \frac{50/50}{2/12} = 6.0$$

The basic problem here results from the standard practice of using the initial value as the base value when computing percentage changes. Such problems with percentage changes have led economists to compute price elasticity of demand using *midpoints* as the base values of changes in prices and quantities demanded. The midpoint formula for measuring arc elasticity is

$$E_d = \frac{\dfrac{\Delta Q_d}{(Q_{d1} + Q_{d2})/2}}{\dfrac{\Delta P}{(P_1 + P_2)/2}} \tag{2}$$

where, P_1 represents the first price, P_2 represents the second price, and Q_{d1} and Q_{d2} are the respective quantities demanded. To put it differently, we divide the change in quantity demanded by the *average* quantity demanded, all of which is then divided by the change in price divided by the *average* price. (Actually since we are finding the "average" of the two quantities demanded and the "average" of the two prices, it doesn't matter if P_1 in formula 2 is the first price or the second price, and the same for P_2. You may look on P_1 as one of the two prices and P_2 as the other price. The same, of course, applies to Q_{d1} and Q_{d2} in formula 2, too.)

If we use formula 2 to calculate the elasticity coefficient between points *A* and *B*, we get

$$E_d = \frac{\dfrac{\Delta Q_d}{(Q_{d1} + Q_{d2})/2}}{\dfrac{\Delta P}{(P_1 + P_2)/2}} = \frac{\dfrac{50}{(100 + 50)/2}}{\dfrac{2}{(10 + 12)/2}} = \frac{\dfrac{50}{75}}{\dfrac{2}{11}} = 3.7$$

Elastic, Inelastic, Unit Elastic, Perfectly Elastic, and Perfectly Inelastic Demand

If you look back at how we first defined price elasticity of demand, you will see

$$E_d = \frac{\text{percentage change in quantity demanded}}{\text{percentage change in price}} = \frac{\text{numerator}}{\text{denominator}}$$

Focusing on both the numerator and denominator, we realize that (1) the numerator can be greater than the denominator; (2) the numerator can be less than the denominator; or (3) the numerator can be equal to the denominator. These three cases, along with two peripherally related cases, are discussed in the following paragraphs. Exhibit 6-1 and 6-2 provide convenient summaries of the material.

Elastic Demand

The percentage change in quantity demanded is greater than the percentage change in price. Quantity demanded changes proportionately more than price changes.

Inelastic Demand

The percentage change in quantity demanded is less than the percentage change in price. Quantity demanded changes proportionately less than price changes.

Elastic Demand ($E_d > 1$). If the numerator (percentage change in quantity demanded) is greater than the denominator (percentage change in price), the elasticity coefficient is greater than one (1) and demand is **elastic.** This means, of course, that quantity demanded changes proportionately more than price changes. For example, a 10 percent increase in price brings about, say, a 20 percent reduction in quantity demanded ($E_d = 2$).

Inelastic Demand ($E_d < 1$). If the numerator (percentage change in quantity demanded) is less than the denominator (percentage change in price), the elasticity coefficient is less than one (1) and demand is **inelastic.** This means that quantity demanded changes proportionately less than price changes. For example, a 10

■ **EXHIBIT 6-1**
Price Elasticity of Demand

Demand may be elastic, inelastic, unit elastic, perfectly elastic, or perfectly inelastic.

ELASTICITY COEFFICENT	RESPONSIVENESS OF QUANTITY DEMANDED TO A CHANGE IN PRICE	TERMINOLOGY
$E_d > 1$	Quantity demanded changes proportionately more than price changes: $\%\Delta Q_d > \%\Delta P$.	Elastic
$E_d < 1$	Quantity demanded changes proportionately less than price changes: $\%\Delta Q_d < \%\Delta P$.	Inelastic
$E_d = 1$	Quantity demanded changes proportionately to price changes: $\%\Delta Q_d = \%\Delta P$.	Unit elastic
$E_d = \infty$	Quantity demanded is extremely responsive to even very small changes in price.	Perfectly elastic
$E_d = 0$	Quantity demanded does not change as price changes.	Perfectly inelastic

percent increase in price brings about, say, a 4 percent change in quantity demanded ($E_d = 0.4$).

Unit Elastic Demand ($E_d = 1$). If the numerator (percentage change in quantity demanded) equals the denominator (percentage change in price), the elasticity coefficient is one (1). This means quantity demanded changes proportionately to price changes. For example, a 10 percent increase in price brings about a 10 percent decrease in quantity demanded ($E_d = 1$). Demand exhibits unitary elasticity or is **unit elastic.**

Perfectly Elastic Demand ($E_d = \infty$). If quantity demanded is extremely responsive to changes in price, demand is **perfectly elastic.** For example, buyers are willing to buy all units of a seller's good at $5 per unit, but nothing at $5.10. A small percentage change in price brings about an extremely large percentage change in quantity demanded (from buying all to buying nothing). The percentage is so large, in fact, that economists say it is "infinitely large."

Perfectly Inelastic Demand ($E_d = 0$). If quantity demanded is completely unresponsive to changes in price, demand is **perfectly inelastic.** For example, buyers are willing to buy 100 units of good X at $10 each, and if price rises to $11, they are still willing to buy 100 units. A change in price brings about no change in quantity demanded.

Unit Elastic Demand

The percentage change in quantity demanded is equal to the percentage change in price. Quantity demanded changes proportionately to price changes.

Perfectly Elastic Demand

A small percentage change in price brings about an extremely large percentage change in quantity demanded (from buying all to buying nothing).

Perfectly Inelastic Demand

Quantity demanded does not change as price changes.

Question:

Suppose the price of "Cats Love It" cat food rises 10 percent, and Estelle doesn't buy any less of it per week for her cat, Fluffy. Does it follow that Estelle's demand for "Cats Love It" cat food is perfectly inelastic?

Answer:

Yes, it is, between the initial price and the 10 percent higher price. We qualify this because if price rises another 10 percent, Estelle may cut back on her weekly purchases of "Cats Love It" cat food and buy some other kind of cat food instead. In the next section, we show how price elasticity of demand changes as we move up some demand curves from lower to higher prices.

EXHIBIT 6-2
Price Elasticity of Demand

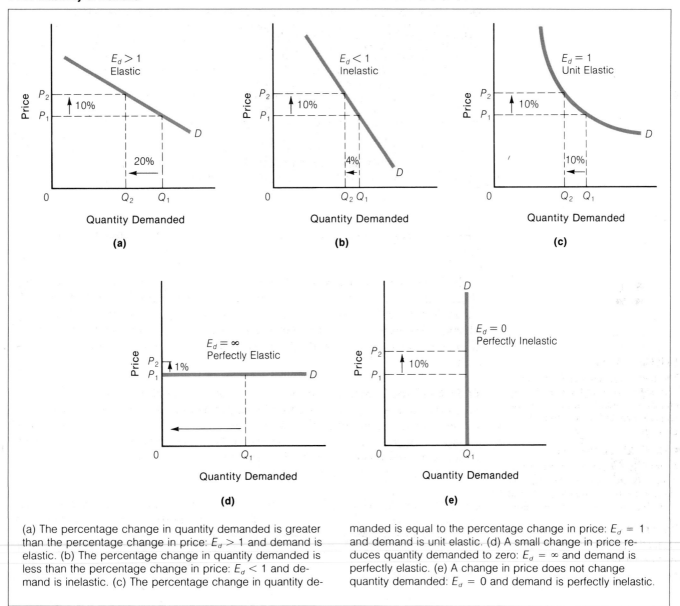

(a) The percentage change in quantity demanded is greater than the percentage change in price: $E_d > 1$ and demand is elastic. (b) The percentage change in quantity demanded is less than the percentage change in price: $E_d < 1$ and demand is inelastic. (c) The percentage change in quantity demanded is equal to the percentage change in price: $E_d = 1$ and demand is unit elastic. (d) A small change in price reduces quantity demanded to zero: $E_d = \infty$ and demand is perfectly elastic. (e) A change in price does not change quantity demanded: $E_d = 0$ and demand is perfectly inelastic.

Question:

Aren't all demand curves downward sloping because they express the inverse relationship between price and quantity demanded, ceteris paribus? In (d) and (e) in Exhibit 6-2, neither of the demand curves is downward sloping. What is going on?

Answer:

In the real world, there are no perfectly elastic or perfectly inelastic demand curves *at all prices.* Thus we ought to view the perfectly elastic and perfectly inelastic demand curves in Exhibit 6-2 as representations of the extreme limits between which all real-world demand curves fall.

We should add, however, that a few real-world demand curves *approximate* the perfectly elastic and inelastic demand curves in (d) and (e). In other words, they come very close. For example, the demand for a particular farmer's wheat approximates the perfectly elastic demand curve in (d). We discuss this in detail in Chapter 9.

Price Elasticity of Demand and Total Revenue (Total Expenditure)

Total Revenue
Price times quantity sold.

Total revenue equals the price of a good times the quantity of the good sold.[1] For example, if the hamburger stand down the street sells 100 hamburgers today at $1.50 each, its total revenue is $150.

Suppose the hamburger vendor were to raise the price of hamburgers to $2 each. What do you predict will happen to total revenue? Most people say it will increase; there is a widespread belief that higher prices bring higher total revenue. But total revenue may decrease, or it may remain constant. Suppose price rises to $2, but because of the higher price, the quantity of hamburgers sold falls to 50. Total revenue is now $100 (whereas it was $150). Whether total revenue rises, falls, or remains constant after a price change depends on whether the *percentage change in quantity demanded* is less than, greater than, or equal to the *percentage change in price*. We are back to price elasticity of demand.(Think back to John and Nicole's laundry business discussed in the introduction to the chapter.)

If demand is elastic, the percentage change in quantity demanded is greater than the percentage change in price. Given a price rise of, say, 5 percent, quantity demanded falls *by more than* 5 percent—say, 8 percent. What happens to total revenue? If quantity demanded falls, or sales fall off, by a greater percentage than price rises, total revenue decreases. In short, *if demand is elastic, a price rise decreases total revenue.*

But suppose demand is elastic and price falls? What happens to total revenue? In this case quantity demanded rises (price and quantity demanded are inversely related) by a greater percentage than price falls, causing total revenue to increase. In other words, sales increase by a greater percentage than price falls. In short, *if demand is elastic, a price fall increases total revenue.*

If demand is inelastic, the percentage change in quantity demanded is less than the percentage change in price. If price rises, quantity demanded falls, but by a smaller percentage than price rises. As a result, total revenue increases. *If demand is inelastic, a price rise increases total revenue.* If, however, price falls, quantity demanded rises by a smaller percentage than price falls. Total revenue decreases. *If demand is inelastic, a price fall decreases total revenue.*

If demand is unit elastic, the percentage change in quantity demanded equals the percentage change in price. If price rises, quantity demanded falls by the same percentage as price rises. Total revenue does not change. If price falls, quantity demanded rises by the same percentage as price falls. Once again, total revenue

---

[1]In the discussion here wherever the words "total revenue" appear the words "total expenditure" can be substituted. Total revenue, as we said, equals price times the quantity sold. Total expenditure equals price times the quantity purchased. If something is sold, it must be purchased, making total revenue equal to total expenditure. The term "total revenue" is used when looking at things from the point of view of sellers in a market. The term "total expenditure" is used when looking at things from the point of view of the buyers in a market. Buyers make expenditures, sellers receive revenues.

Theory in Practice

When Is a Half-Packed Auditorium Better Than a Packed One?

Suppose you are the manager of a famous rock group, which will soon go on a tour of 30 U.S. cities. In each of the 30 cities the group will play in an auditorium. The auditorium in St. Louis, Missouri, let's say, seats 20,000 people. Is it better to sell all 20,000 tickets for the rock group's performance or to sell less than 20,000 tickets, say, 10,000 tickets?

Most people will say that it is better to sell 20,000 tickets than 10,000 tickets. But is it necessarily better? To sell 20,000 tickets the price per ticket will have to be lower than the price per ticket to sell 10,000 tickets. For example, suppose that to sell all 20,000 tickets, the ticket price must be $10. In that case the total revenue will be $200,000. Suppose, however, that at $25 per ticket 10,000 tickets (and no more) can be sold. In that case the total revenue will be $250,000. In other words, a $10 ticket price fills the audito-

rium to capacity and generates $200,000 total revenue. A $25 ticket price only fills half the auditorium but generates $250,000 total revenue.

Question:

Doesn't the analysis implicitly assume that only one ticket price, either $25 or $10, can be charged? If more than one price can be charged, then the 10,000 good seats in the auditorium might be sold for $25 each, and the remaining 10,000 not-so-good seats might be sold for $10 each. The total revenue would be $350,000 ($25 × 10,000 + $10 × 10,000 = $350,000). In short, if only one price can be charged, a half-packed auditorium may, under certain conditions, generate more revenue than a packed auditorium. But if two prices can be charged, isn't a packed auditorium preferable to a half-packed auditorium?

Answer:

True, the assumption is that only one price can be charged; that is, all seats must be priced at either $10 or $25, not some seats at $10 and some seats at $25. Furthermore, charging a higher price for good seats and a lower price for not-so-good seats actually happens at rock concerts, plays, basketball games, and so forth. The example has demonstrated why.

does not change. *If demand is unit elastic, a rise or fall in price leaves total revenue unchanged.* For a quick review of the material in this section, see Exhibit 6-3.

ELASTICITY: PART II

In this section we discuss the elasticity ranges of a straight-line downward-sloping demand curve and the determinants of price elasticity of demand, along with cross price elasticity of demand, income elasticity of demand, and price elasticity of supply.

Price Elasticity of Demand Along a Demand Curve

The price elasticity of demand for a straight-line downward-sloping demand curve varies from highly elastic to highly inelastic. We illustrate this important point with the aid of Exhibit 6-4.

Notice that as we move down the demand curve from higher to lower prices, from $8 to $7 to $6 and so on, the price elasticity of demand (as measured by the elasticity coefficient in column 4) decreases, from 2.14 to 1.44 to 1.00 and so on. As we move up the demand curve from lower to higher prices, price elasticity of demand increases. There are three elasticity ranges on the demand curve: an inelastic range, and elastic range, and a unit elastic range.

If demand is elastic, a price rise leads to a decrease in total revenue and a price fall leads to an increase in total revenue. If demand is inelastic, a price rise leads to an increase in total revenue and a price fall leads to a decrease in total revenue. If demand is unit elastic, a rise or fall in price does not change total revenue.

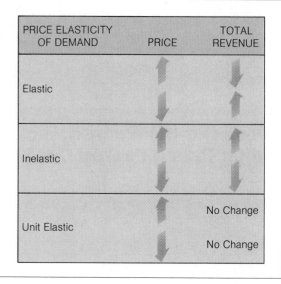

We can easily understand this result by recalling that price elasticity of demand is a ratio of the percentage change in quantity demanded to the percentage change in price. At the upper end of the demand curve, where quantities demanded are lower and prices are higher, a 1-unit change in quantity demanded is a relatively large percentage change in quantity demanded, and a $1 price change is a relatively small percentage change in price.

At the lower end of the demand curve, where quantities demanded are higher and prices are lower, the situation is reversed. A 1-unit change in quantity demanded is a relatively small percentage change in quantity demanded, and a $1 price change is a relatively large percentage change in price.

Determinants of Price Elasticity of Demand

There are three major determinants of price elasticity of demand: (1) the number of substitutes, (2) the percentage of one's budget spent on the good, and (3) time. Since all three factors interact, we discuss each holding all other things constant.

Number of Substitutes. Suppose good *A* has 2 substitutes and good *B* has 15 substitutes. We shall assume that each of the 2 substitutes for good *A* is as good (or close) a substitute for that good as each of the 15 substitutes is for good *B*.

Let the price of each good rise by 10 percent. The quantity demanded of each good decreases. Would we expect the "percentage change in quantity demanded of good *A*" to be greater or less than the "percentage change in quantity demanded of good *B*"? In short, will quantity demanded be more responsive to the 10 percent price rise in the good that has 2 substitutes (good *A*) or the good that has 15 substitutes (good *B*)? The answer is the good with 15 substitutes, good *B*. Why? This occurs because the more chance of substituting one good for another (there is more chance of substituting a good for *B* than for *A*), the less of a good will be purchased if its price rises. For example, when the price of good *A* rises 10 percent, people can turn to 2 substitutes; quantity demanded of good *A* falls, but not by as much as if there had been 15 substitutes, as there were for good *B*.

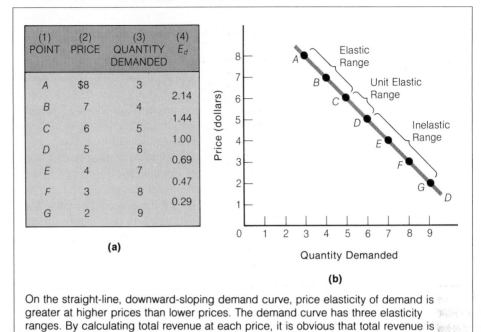

(1) POINT	(2) PRICE	(3) QUANTITY DEMANDED	(4) E_d
A	$8	3	
			2.14
B	7	4	
			1.44
C	6	5	
			1.00
D	5	6	
			0.69
E	4	7	
			0.47
F	3	8	
			0.29
G	2	9	

(a)

(b)

On the straight-line, downward-sloping demand curve, price elasticity of demand is greater at higher prices than lower prices. The demand curve has three elasticity ranges. By calculating total revenue at each price, it is obvious that total revenue is maximized where demand is unit elastic.

The relationship between the availability of substitutes and price elasticity is clear: *The more substitutes for a good, the higher the price elasticity of demand; the fewer substitutes for a good, the lower the price elasticity of demand.*

For example, the price elasticity of demand for Chevrolets is higher than the price elasticity of demand for all cars. This is so because there are more substitutes for Chevrolets than for cars. Everything that is a substitute for a car (bus, train, walking, bicycle, and so on) is also a substitute for a specific type of car, Chevrolet; but some things that are a substitute for a Chevrolet (Ford, Toyota, Chrysler, Mercedes-Benz, and so on) are not substitutes for a car. Instead, they are simply *types* of cars. Thus we can state the rule: The more broadly defined the good, the fewer the substitutes; the more narrowly defined the good, the greater the substitutes. There are more substitutes for this economics textbook than there are for all economics textbooks. There are more substitutes for Coca-Cola than there are for all soft drinks.

Percentage of One's Budget Spent on the Good. Claire Rossi has a monthly budget of $3,000. Of this monthly budget, she spends $30 per month on pens and $400 per month on dinners at restaurants. In percentage terms, she spends 1 percent of her monthly budget on pens and 13 percent of her monthly budget on dinners at restaurants. Suppose both the price of pens and the price of dinners at restaurants double. Would Claire be more responsive to the change in the price of pens or dinners at restaurants? The answer is the price of dinners at restaurants. The reason is that a doubling in price of a good on which a person spends 1 percent of her budget is not felt as strongly as a doubling in price of a good on which she spends 13 percent. Claire is more likely to shrug off the doubling in the price of pens than the doubling in the price of dinners at restaurants. Buyers are (and thus quantity demanded is) more responsive to price the larger the percentage of their budget that goes for the purchase of the good. In short, *the greater the percentage of one's budget that goes to purchase a good, the higher the price elasticity of demand; the smaller the percentage of one's budget that goes to purchase a good, the lower the price elasticity of demand.*

Time.   As time passes, buyers have greater opportunities to be responsive to a price change. For example, if the price of electricity went up today, and you knew about it, you probably would not change your consumption of electricity today as much as you will three months from today. As time passes, you have more chances to change your consumption by finding substitutes (natural gas), changing your lifestyle (buying more blankets and turning down the thermostat at night), and so on. We conclude that *the more time that passes (since the price change), the higher the price elasticity of demand for the good; the less time that passes, the lower the price elasticity of demand for the good.*[2] In other words, price elasticity of demand for a good is higher in the long run than in the short run.

Take the case of gasoline consumption patterns in the period 1973–75. Gasoline prices increased approximately 71 percent during this period. The consumption of gasoline didn't fall immediately and sharply. Motorists didn't immediately stop driving big gas-guzzling cars. As time passed, however, many car owners traded in their big cars for compact cars. Car buyers became more concerned with the miles-per-gallon (MPG) a car received. People began to form car pools. The short-run price elasticity of demand for gasoline was estimated at 0.2; the long-run price elasticity of demand for gasoline was estimated at 0.7, 3½ times larger.

Thinking through an Ad Campaign

The Coca-Cola Company's two slogans "Coke Is It" and "Coke, It's the Real Thing" are catchy and successful. But there is more to the story. If we examine the slogans carefully, we see that they are built on a firm understanding of the *relationship between the number of substitutes and price elasticity of demand* and *between price elasticity of demand and total revenue.* Consider the Coca-Cola Company's real message: Coke stands apart from the rest of the soft drinks. After all, Coke is *it*; Coke is the *real thing.* One naturally asks, How many soft drinks can be *it*? How many beverages can be the *real thing*? The answer the Coca-Cola Company hopes consumers will arrive at is "only one."

If the buying public accepts this message, if in fact buyers think that there are few (if any) substitutes for Coke (or at least decide there are fewer substitutes for it than they previously thought), the price elasticity of demand for Coke falls. Remember, the fewer the number of substitutes, the lower the price elasticity of demand.

And if it is possible to get the demand for Coca-Cola to become inelastic (at least for a short range of the demand curve above current price), the Coca-Cola Company can raise the price of Coke and raise total revenue. Remember, if demand is inelastic, an increase in price leads to higher total revenue.

The discussion of price elasticity of demand in this chapter and the discussions that go on in the offices of the "moguls of Madison Avenue" aren't so far removed.

---

[2]If we say, "The more time that passes (since the price change), the higher the price elasticity of demand," wouldn't it follow that price elasticity of demand gets steadily larger? For example, might it be that on Tuesday the price of good X rises, and 5 days later, $E_d = 0.70$, 10 days later is is 0.76, 20 days later it is 0.90, and so on until infinity? This is not exactly the case. Obviously there comes a time when quantity demanded is no longer adjusting to a change in price (just as there comes a time when there are no longer any ripples in the lake from the passing motorboat). Our conditional statement ("the more time that passes . . .") implies this condition.

OTHER ELASTICITY CONCEPTS

In this section we discuss three other elasticities: cross elasticity of demand, income elasticity of demand, and price elasticity of supply.

Cross Elasticity of Demand

Cross Elasticity of Demand
Measures the responsiveness in quantity demanded of one good to changes in the price of another good.

Cross elasticity of demand measures the responsiveness in the quantity demanded of one good to changes in the price of another good. It is defined as *the percentage change in the quantity demanded of one good divided by the percentage change in the price of another good.*

$$E_c = \frac{\text{percentage change in quantity demanded of one good}}{\text{percentage change in price of another good}}$$

where E_c stands for coefficient of cross elasticity of demand, or elasticity coefficient.[3]

This concept is often used to determine whether two goods are substitutes or complements and the degree to which one good is a substitute or complement to another. For example, consider two goods: Skippy peanut butter and Jif peanut butter. Suppose that there is a 10 percent increase in the price of Jif peanut butter and that the quantity demanded of Skippy peanut butter increases by 45 percent. The cross elasticity of demand for Skippy with respect to the price of Jif is written

$$E_c = \frac{\text{percentage change in quantity demanded of Skippy}}{\text{percentage change in price of Jif}}$$

This is a positive 4.5. When the elasticity coefficient is positive, we know that the percentage change in the quantity demanded of one good (numerator) moves in the same direction as the percentage change in the price of another good (denominator). This is representative of goods that are substitutes. In short, as the price of Jif rises, the demand curve for Skippy shifts rightward, causing the quantity demanded of Skippy to increase at each and every price.[4] We conclude that if $E_c > 0$, the two goods are substitutes.

If the elasticity coefficient is negative, $E_c < 0$, the two goods are complements. A negative number occurs when the percentage change in the quantity demanded of one good (numerator) and the percentage change in the price of another good (denominator) move in opposite directions. Consider an example. Suppose the price of cars increases by 5 percent and the quantity demanded of car tires decreases by 10 percent. To calculate the cross price elasticity of demand, we have -10 percent/5 percent $= -2$. Cars and car tires are complements.

Income Elasticity of Demand

Income Elasticity of Demand
Measures the responsiveness of quantity demanded to changes in income.

Income elasticity of demand measures the responsiveness of quantity demanded to changes in income. It is defined as *the percentage change in quantity demanded of a good divided by the percentage change in income.*

$$E_y = \frac{\text{percentage change in quantity demanded}}{\text{percentage change in income}}$$

where E_y = coefficient of income elasticity of demand, or elasticity coefficient.

[3]A question naturally arises: How can "E_d" and "E_c" both be the "elasticty coefficient"? It is a matter of convenience. When speaking about price elasticity of demand, the coefficient of price elasticity of demand is referred to as the "elasticity coefficient." When speaking about cross elasticity of demand, the coefficient of cross elasticity of demand is referred to as the "elasticity coefficient." This practice holds for other elasticities as well.

[4]In Chapter 3 we explained that if two goods are substitutes, a rise in the price of one good causes the demand for the other good to increase.

Normal Good

A good the demand for which rises (falls) as income rises (falls).

Inferior Good

A good the demand for which falls (rises) as income rises (falls).

Income Elastic

The percentage change in quantity demanded of a good is greater than the percentage change in income.

Income Inelastic

The percentage change in quantity demanded of a good is less than the percentage change in income.

Income Unit Elastic

The percentage change in quantity demanded of a good is equal to the percentage change in income.

Income elasticity of demand is positive, $E_y > 0$, for a normal good. A **normal good** is one whose demand, and thus quantity demanded, increases, given an increase in income; thus the variables in the numerator and denominator in the income elasticity of demand formula move in the same direction. Income elasticity of demand for an **inferior good** is negative, $E_y < 0$. In calculating the income elasticity of demand of a good, we use the same midpoint approach that we used for calculating price elasticity of demand.

$$E_y = \frac{\dfrac{\Delta Q_d}{(Q_{d1} + Q_{d2})/2}}{\dfrac{\Delta Y}{(Y_1 + Y_2)/2}}$$

where Y_1 represents the first income, Y_2 the second income, and Q_{d1} and Q_{d2} the respective quantities demanded.

Suppose income increases from \$500 to \$600 per month and that as a result quantity demanded of good X increases from 20 units to 30 units per month. We have

$$E_y = \frac{\dfrac{10}{(20 + 30)/2}}{\dfrac{100}{(500 + 600)/2}} = \frac{\dfrac{10}{25}}{\dfrac{100}{550}} = 2.2$$

Since E_y is a positive number, good X is a normal good. Also, since $E_y > 1$, demand for good X is said to be **income elastic.** This means the percentage change in quantity demanded of the good is greater than the percentage change in income. If $E_y < 1$, the demand for the good is said to be **income inelastic.** If $E_y = 1$, then it is **income unit elastic.**

Question:

Are there any real-world applications for income elasticity of demand?

Answer:

Yes, there are. Suppose Tara is considering buying stocks in the stock market. We'll assume her objective is to earn as much profit as possible. Furthermore suppose she believes that individuals' incomes will be increasing over the next few months and years. Would it be better for Tara to buy stocks in companies that produce inferior goods (income increases, demand for the good decreases) or in companies that produce normal goods (income increases, demand for the good increases)? Clearly the answer is "in companies that produce normal goods."

Having established this, would it be better for Tara to go with companies that produce normal goods that are highly income elastic, unit income elastic, or income inelastic? It would be better for her to go with companies that produce normal goods that are highly income elastic, where quantity demanded is highly responsive to increases in income.

We add a proviso: Simply because a good was highly income elastic last year, or for the past few years, it does not necessarily follow that it will be so this year or in the next few years. The future does not always mirror the past. This means that income elasticity of demand, if used as a predictive tool, should be used with caution.

Question:

Can a good be both normal and income inelastic?

Answer:

Yes, it can. A normal good means $E_Y > 0$. An income inelastic good means $E_Y < 1$. Suppose that for good X, $E_Y = 0.8$. This is a positive number (hence, X is a normal good) that is less than one (hence, X is income inelastic). Food, tobacco, and health-related drugs have been calculated to have elasticity coefficients greater than 0 but less than 1.

Price Elasticity of Supply

Price elasticity of supply measures the responsiveness of quantity supplied to changes in price. It is defined as the percentage change in quantity supplied of a good divided by the percentage change in the price of the good.

$$E_s = \frac{\text{percentage change in quantity supplied}}{\text{percentage change in price}}$$

where E_s stands for coefficient of price elasticity of supply, or elasticity coefficient. We use the midpoint approach to calculate price elasticity of supply.

Additionally, we may classify supply as *elastic, inelastic, unit elastic, perfectly elastic,* or *perfectly inelastic*. Elastic supply ($E_s > 1$) refers to a percentage change in quantity supplied that is greater than the percentage change in price. Inelastic supply ($E_s < 1$) refers to a percentage change in quantity supplied that is less than the percentage change in price. Unit elastic supply ($E_s = 1$) refers to a percentage change in quantity supplied that is equal to the percentage change in price. Perfectly elastic supply ($E_s = \infty$) represents the case where a small change in price changes quantity supplied by an infinitely large amount (and thus the supply curve, or a portion of the overall supply curve, is horizontal). Perfectly inelastic supply ($E_s = 0$) represents the case where a change in price brings no change in quantity supplied (and thus the supply curve, or a portion of the overall supply curve, is vertical). See Exhibit 6-5.

Price Elasticity of Supply and Time

The longer the period of adjustment to a change in price, the higher the price elasticity of supply. (We are speaking of goods whose quantity supplied *can* increase with time. This covers most goods. It does not, however, cover original Picasso paintings.) There is an obvious reason for this: Additional production takes time.

For example, suppose the demand increases for new housing in your city. To help us better illustrate the point, suppose this increase in demand comes all at once on Tuesday. This places upward pressure on the price of housing. Will the number of houses supplied be much different on Saturday than it was on Tuesday? No, it won't. It will take time for suppliers to figure out whether the increase in demand is permanent (if they consider it a temporary state of affairs, not much will be done). If contractors decide it is permanent, it takes time to move resources from the production of other things into the production of additional new housing. Simply put, the change in quantity supplied of housing is likely to be different in the long run than in the short run given a change in price. This translates into a higher price elasticity of supply in the long run than in the short run. See Exhibit 6-6 for a quick review of elasticity concepts.

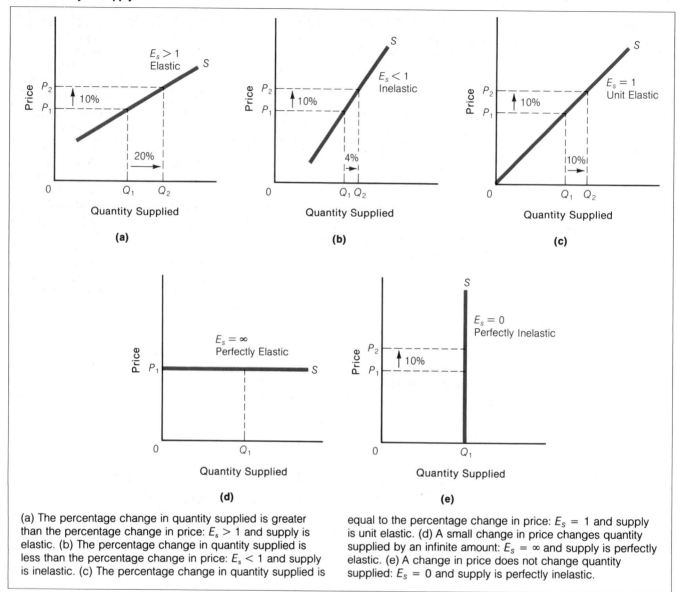

(a) The percentage change in quantity supplied is greater than the percentage change in price: $E_s > 1$ and supply is elastic. (b) The percentage change in quantity supplied is less than the percentage change in price: $E_s < 1$ and supply is inelastic. (c) The percentage change in quantity supplied is equal to the percentage change in price: $E_s = 1$ and supply is unit elastic. (d) A small change in price changes quantity supplied by an infinite amount: $E_s = \infty$ and supply is perfectly elastic. (e) A change in price does not change quantity supplied: $E_s = 0$ and supply is perfectly inelastic.

Don't Tax You, Don't Tax Me, Tax That Man Behind the Tree

Many people think that if government *places* a tax on firm X, firm X actually *pays* the tax. As we shall see, there is a difference between the placement and the payment of a tax, and furthermore placement does not guarantee payment.

Suppose the government places a tax on VCR tape producers: They are taxed $1 for every tape they sell. VCR tape producers are enjoined: Sell a tape, send $1 to government. This action changes equilibrium in the VCR tape market. To illustrate, in Exhibit 6-7, *before* the tax is imposed, the equilibrium price and quantity of tapes are $8 and Q_1, respectively. The tax per tape shifts the supply curve up and

Summary of the Four Elasticity Concepts

TYPE	DEFINITION	POSSIBILITIES	
Price elasticity of demand	percentage change in quantity demanded ÷ percentage change in price	$E_d > 1$ $E_d < 1$ $E_d = 1$ $E_d = \infty$ $E_d = 0$	Elastic Inelastic Unit elastic Perfectly elastic Perfectly inelastic
Cross elasticity of demand	percentage change in quantity demanded of one good ÷ percentage change in price of another good	$E_c < 0$ $E_c > 0$	Complements Substitutes
Income elasticity of demand	percentage change in quantity demanded ÷ percentage change in income	$E_y > 0$ $E_y < 0$ $E_y > 1$ $E_y < 1$ $E_y = 1$	Normal good Inferior good Income elastic Income inelastic Income unit elastic
Price elasticity of supply	percentage change in quantity supplied ÷ percentage change in price	$E_s > 1$ $E_s < 1$ $E_s = 1$ $E_s = \infty$ $E_s = 0$	Elastic Inelastic Unit elastic Perfectly elastic Perfectly inelastic

■ EXHIBIT 6-7
Who Pays the Tax?

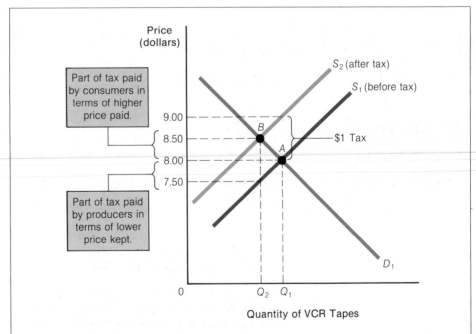

A tax placed on the producer of VCR tapes shifts the supply curve from S_1 to S_2 and raises the equilibrium price from $8.00 to $8.50. Part of the tax is paid by consumers through a higher price paid ($8.50 instead of $8.00), and part of the tax is paid by producers through a lower price kept ($7.50 instead of $8.00).

Theory in Practice

Elasticity Concepts Are Like Air, They Are Everywhere

The elasticity concepts are some of economists' favorite tools. Consider a few of the places they may pop up.

1. Before a Senate Health Subcommittee. During the debates on national health insurance in a Senate committee, one of the points usually discussed is how much of the medical bill the consumer should pay and how much the taxpayer should pay. Martin Feldstein, who later became chairman of the Council of Economic Advisors under President Reagan, argued before the Senate Health Subcommittee (during the Carter presidency) that consumers should pay at least 30 percent of their medical bills. Feldstein maintained that his studies on the price elasticity of demand for medical care showed that demand was highly elastic at low prices. This would translate into a large increase in the number of people going to doctors and hospitals if consumers paid much less than 30 percent of their medical bills; that is, the increase in quantity demanded of medical care would be proportionately larger than the decrease in price. Could doctors and hospitals handle all the extra work? Could the government (taxpayers) foot the bill?

2. In the oil fields. If the demand for the good a supplier sells is inelastic between the current price and a higher price, there will be a tendency to try to achieve the higher price. The reason is simple. If demand is inelastic, a higher

price brings greater total revenue. In the early and mid-1970s, OPEC (Organization of Petroleum Exporting Countries) saw the demand for oil as inelastic and sought to reduce the supply of oil in order to put upward pressure on price. OPEC hoped to decrease the supply of oil, push up its price, and generate greater total (oil) revenues. This in fact did happen in the short run. In the long run, the price elasticity of demand for oil increased, and OPEC's ability to increase oil revenues through supply reductions and price increases began to weaken.

3. In a public debate. Occasionally people propose that instead of giving poor people goods (such as food, housing, and medical care) free of charge, they should be given money. When this proposal is made, someone usually argues that it is better to give goods instead of cash because some of the poor people will spend the money on the "wrong" things; that is, on nonessentials. Instead of buying milk for the baby, they will spend the money on gambling or liquor. A study of 1,200 families in New Jersey who received cash grants between 1969 and 1972 showed, however, that most of their additional income was spent on better housing, washing machines, refrigerators, and other durable goods. In short, among the poor these items had a positive income elasticity of demand.

4. In the marketing department of a firm. Suppose a company sells cheese. A natural question might be, What goods are substitutes for cheese? The answer would shed some light on who the competitors of the company are. How might we go about finding out which goods are substitutes for cheese? The answer is that we could calculate the cross elasticity of demand between cheese and other goods. A positive cross elasticity of demand would indicate that the two goods were substitutes; and the higher the cross elasticity of demand, the greater the degree of substitution.

leftward from S_1 to S_2. The vertical distance between the two supply curves represents the $1 per tape tax. (Why does the vertical distance between the two curves represent the $1 per tape tax? This is because what matters to the producers is how much they get to keep for each tape sold, not how much the consumers pay. For example, if they get to keep $8 per tape for Q_1 tapes before the tax is imposed, then they must get to keep $8 per tape for Q_1 tapes after the tax is imposed. But if the tax is $1, the only way they can get to keep $8 per tape for Q_1 tapes is to charge $9 per tape. They receive $9 per tape from the consumer, turn over $1 to government, and keep $8 for themselves. In other words, each quantity on the new supply curve, S_2, corresponds to a $1 higher price than on the old supply curve, S_1. It does not follow, though, that the new equilibrium price will be $1 higher than the old equilibrium price.)

The new equilibrium comes at a price of $8.50 and quantity Q_2. Consumers pay $8.50 per tape (after the tax is imposed) as opposed to $8.00 (before the tax was imposed). The difference between the new price and the old price is the amount of the $1 tax that consumers pay per tape. In this example, consumers pay 50 cents, or one-half of the tax, of the $1 tax per tape.

The producers *receive* $8.50 per tape from consumers (after the tax is imposed) as opposed to $8.00 per tape (before the tax was imposed) but do not get to *keep* the $8.50 per tape. One dollar has to be turned over to the government, leaving the producers with $7.50. Before the tax was imposed, however, the producers received and kept $8.00 per tape.[5] As we noted, it is the price that the producers get to keep that is relevant to them. The difference between $8.00 and $7.50 is the amount of the tax per tape that the producers pay. In this example, the producers pay 50 cents of the $1 tax per tape. In short, the producers pay one-half of the tax. We conclude that the full tax was placed on the producers, but they paid only one-half of the tax, whereas none of the tax was placed on consumers but they paid one-half of the tax, too. What is the lesson? Government can place a tax on whomever it wants, but the determination of who ends up paying the tax depends on the laws of economics.

We can derive another lesson from this example. The percentage or share of the tax actually paid by consumers and producers depends on price elasticity of demand and supply. For example, you noticed that in this example both the consumers and the producers paid one-half of the tax. It did not have to be this way, however, as the following four cases illustrate.

Perfectly Inelastic Demand. To Exhibit 6-8a, demand is perfectly inelastic. A change in price brings no change in quantity demanded. In this case, consumers pay the full $1 tax per tape even though the tax is placed entirely on producers.

Perfectly Elastic Demand. In Exhibit 6-8b, demand is perfectly elastic. A small change in price brings an extremely large change in quantity demanded. In this case, producers pay the full tax.

Perfectly Elastic Supply. In Exhibit 6-8c, supply is perfectly elastic. A small change in price brings an extremely large change in quantity supplied. In this case, consumers pay the full tax.

Perfectly Inelastic Supply. In Exhibit 6-8d, supply is perfectly inelastic. A change in price brings no change in quantity supplied. If producers try to charge a higher price than $8.00 for their good (and thus try to get consumers to pay some of the tax), a surplus will result driving the price back down to $8.00. In this case, producers end up paying the full tax. Although we have not shown it in the exhibit, producers would receive $8.00, turn over $1 to the government, and keep $7 for each unit sold.

[5]Some economists would put it this way: The tax drives a *wedge* between what the producers receive from the consumers and what the producers are permitted to keep.

Different Elasticities and Who Pays the Tax

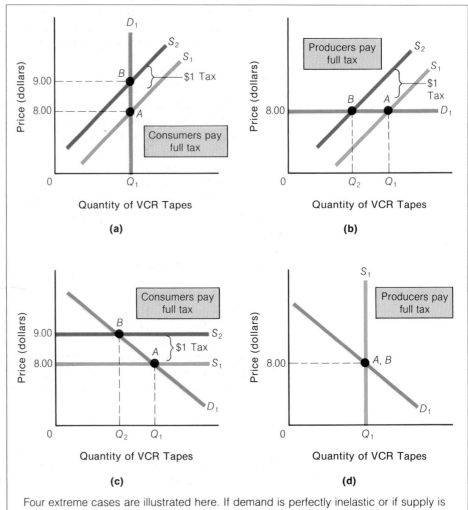

Four extreme cases are illustrated here. If demand is perfectly inelastic or if supply is perfectly elastic, consumers pay the full tax even though the tax may be placed entirely on producers. If demand is perfectly elastic or if supply is perfectly inelastic, the full tax is paid by producers.

■ CHAPTER SUMMARY

Part I
Price Elasticity of Demand

■ Price elasticity of demand is a measure of the responsiveness of quantity demanded to changes in price: E_d = percentage change in quantity demanded/percentage change in price.

■ If the percentage change in quantity demanded is greater than the percentage change in price, demand is elastic. If the percentage change in quantity demanded is less than the percentage change in price, demand is inelastic. If the percentage change in quantity demanded is equal to the percentage change in price, demand is unit elastic. If a small change in price brings on an infinitely large change in quantity demanded, demand is perfectly elastic. If a change in price brings on no change in quantity demanded, demand is perfectly inelastic.

■ The coefficient of price elasticity of demand (E_d) is negative, signifying the inverse relationship between price and quantity demanded. For convenience, however, the absolute value of the elasticity coefficient is used.

Total Revenue and Price Elasticity of Demand

■ Total revenue equals price times quantity sold. Total expenditure equals price times quantity purchased. Total revenue equals total expenditure.

■ If demand is elastic, price and total revenue are inversely related: As price rises (falls), total revenue falls (rises).

■ If demand is inelastic, price and total revenue are directly related: As price rises (falls), total revenue rises (falls).

■ If demand is unit elastic, total revenue is independent of price: As price rises (falls), total revenue remains constant.

Part II
Determinants of Price Elasticity of Demand

■ The more substitutes for a good, the higher the price elasticity of demand; the fewer substitutes for a good, the lower the price elasticity of demand.

■ The greater the percentage of one's budget that goes to purchase a good, the higher the price elasticity of demand; the smaller the percentage of one's budget that goes to purchase a good, the lower the price elasticity of demand.

■ The more time that passes (since a price change), the higher the price elasticity of demand; the less time that passes, the lower the price elasticity of demand.

Cross Elasticity of Demand

■ Cross elasticity of demand measures the responsiveness in the quantity demanded of one good to changes in the price of another good: E_c = percentage change in quantity demanded of one good/percentage change in the price of another good.

■ If $E_c > 0$, two goods are substitutes. If $E_c < 0$, two goods are complements.

Income Elasticity of Demand

■ Income elasticity of demand measures the responsiveness of quantity demanded to changes in income: E_y = percentage change in quantity demanded/percentage change in income.

■ If $E_y > 0$, the good is a normal good; if $E_y < 0$, the good is an inferior good.

■ If $E_y > 1$, demand is income elastic; if $E_y < 1$, demand is income inelastic; and if $E_y = 1$, demand is income unit elastic.

Price Elasticity of Supply

■ Price elasticity of supply measures the responsiveness of quantity supplied to changes in price: E_s = percentage change in quantity supplied/percentage change in price.

■ If the percentage change in quantity supplied is greater than the percentage change in price, supply is elastic. If the percentage change in quantity supplied is less than the percentage change in price, supply is inelastic. If the percentage change in quantity supplied is equal to the percentage change in price, supply is unit elastic.

■ Price elasticity of supply is higher in the long run than in the short run.

■ QUESTION TO ANSWER AND DISCUSS

1. Explain how a seller can determine whether the demand for his or her good is inelastic, elastic, or unit elastic between two prices.

2. Suppose the current price of gasoline at the pump is $1 per gallon and that one million gallons are sold per month. A politician proposes to add a 10 cents tax to the price of a gallon of gasoline. She says the tax will generate $100,000 tax revenues per month (one million gallons × 10 cents = $100,000). What assumption is she making?

3. A college in the South raises its annual tuition from $2,000 to $2,500, and its student enrollment falls from 4,877 to 4,705. Compute the price elasticity of demand. Is demand elastic or inelastic?

4. Suppose a straight-line, downward-sloping demand curve shifts rightward. Is the price elasticity of demand higher, lower, or the same between any two prices on the new (higher) demand curve than on the old (lower) demand curve?

5. Suppose Oklahoma City is hit by a tornado that destroys 25 percent of the housing in the area. Would you expect the total expenditure on housing after the tornado to be higher than, less than, or equal to what it was before the tornado?

6. Which of the following goods has the higher price elasticity of demand?
   a. Airline travel in the short run or airline travel in the long run
   b. Television sets or Sony television sets
   c. Cars or Toyotas
   d. Telephones or AT&T telephones
   e. Popcorn or Orville Redenbacker popcorn

7. How might you go about determining whether toothpaste and mouthwash manufacturers are in competition with each other?

8. Assume the demand for cocaine is perfectly inelastic. Further assume that the users of cocaine get the funds to pay for the cocaine by stealing. If the supply of cocaine decreases, what happens to the price of cocaine? What happens to the amount of crime committed by cocaine users?

9. In this chapter we showed that two advertising campaigns of the Coca-Cola Company were related to the concepts of price elasticity of demand, total revenue, and the number of substitutes. What other ad campaigns can you think of that are based on these concepts?

10. Suppose you learned that the price elasticity of demand for wheat is 0.7 between the current price for wheat and a price $2 higher per bushel. Do you think farmers collectively would try to reduce the supply of wheat and drive the price up $2 higher per bushel? Why? Assuming that they would try to reduce supply, what problems might they have in actually doing so?

11. It has been said that if government wishes to tax certain goods, it should tax goods that have inelastic rather than elastic demand. What is the rationale for this?

12. In 1947, the U.S. Justice Department brought a suit against the DuPont Company (which at the time sold 75 percent of all the cellophane in the United States) for monopolizing the production and sale of cellophane. In court the DuPont Company tried to show that cellophane was only one of several goods in the market in which it was sold. It argued that its market was not the cellophane market but the "flexible packaging materials" market, which included (besides cellophane) waxed paper, aluminum foil, and so forth. DuPont pointed out that it had only 20 percent of all sales in this more broadly defined market. Using this information, discuss how the concept of cross elasticity of demand would help establish whether DuPont should have been viewed as a firm in the cellophane market or as a firm in the "flexible packaging materials" market.

Chapter 7

The Firm

■ INTRODUCTION

"Everyone wants to be loved, and it always comes as a shock to discover that there are people who dislike you for what you really are rather than for what they mistakenly think you are. Indeed, most of us desperately resist such a conclusion. We keep insisting, to ourselves and others, that those people out there who are saying nasty things about us are merely ill-informed, or misguided, or have been seduced by mischievous propaganda on the part of a handful of irredeemably perverse spirits. And we remain confident, in our heart of hearts, that if they only understood us better, they would certainly dislike us less.

"In this respect businessmen are as human—and are as capable of self-deception—as anyone else. On any single day, all over the country, there are gatherings of corporate executives in which bewilderment and vexation are expressed at the climate of hostility toward business to be found in Washington, or in the media, or in academia—or even, incredibly, among their own children. . . .

"It is indeed amazing that, in a society in which business plays so crucial a role, so many people come to understand so little about it—and, at the same time, to know so much about it which isn't so. We have, for instance, managed to produce a generation of young people who, for all the education lavished on them, know less about the world of work—even the world of their fathers' work—than any previous generation in American history. They fantasize easily, disregard common observation, and appear to be radically deficient in that faculty we call common sense.

"Nor, it must be said, are their teachers in a much better condition. The average college professor in history, sociology, literature, political science, sometimes even economics, is just as inclined to prefer fantasy over reality. . . .

"So there is certainly room for all kinds of educational endeavors on the part of the business community, and I do not wish to be interpreted as in any way discouraging them. The fact that they seem so relatively ineffectual is not necessarily an argument against them. Education is at best a slow and tedious process, and that kind of education which tries to counteract a massive, original miseducation is even slower and more tedious. Too many businessmen confuse education with

advertising, and almost unconsciously impose the short time horizon of the latter on the former. The unit of time appropriate to the process of education is not a year but a generation."

—*Irving Kristol*[1]

■ WHAT THIS CHAPTER IS ABOUT

In this chapter we begin our discussion of the firm. It is unlikely that anyone reading these words has not come into contact with a firm. We deal with firms regularly and probably think we understand them; but that is not necessarily the case. In this chapter we want to know, first, why firms exist. Second, we want to know something about why firms are structured the way they are. For example, why aren't firms run more democratically? Why are most firms organized as a hierarchy? We think that answering these questions will give us important economic insights into the operations of the firm.

Key Questions to Keep in Mind as You Read

1. Why do firms exist?
2. Why are firms structured the way they are?
3. What are proprietorships, partnerships, and corporations?
4. What are the advantages and disadvantages of proprietorships, partnerships, and corporations?
5. What is unlimited liability?
6. What is the objective or goal of the firm?

WHY FIRMS EXIST

Business Firm

An entity that employs factors of production (resources) and produces goods and services to be sold to consumers, other firms, or the government.

A **business firm** is an entity that employs factors of production (resources) and produces goods and services to be sold to consumers, other firms, or the government. There are over 16 million firms in the United States today. We work for and buy goods from these firms; they are a part of our everyday lives. But why do firms exist?[2] Why aren't all producers *individuals*, contracting with each other to buy and sell goods? Why are some producers firms, which buy people's time ($100 for an eight-hour day, for example) and then tell them what to do?

The Market and the Firm: Invisible Hand vs. Visible Hand

The market we examined in Chapter 3 guides and coordinates individuals' actions. Moreover, the market does this in an impersonal manner. No one orders buyers to reduce quantity demanded when price increases; they just do it. No one orders sellers to increase quantity supplied when price increases; they just do it. No one orders more resources to be moved into the production of personal computers when

[1]Irving Kristol, *Two Cheers for Capitalism* (New York: Basic Books, 1978), pps. 23–24.

[2]The word "firm" usually refers to profit-seeking business enterprises, which is how we use it in this section of the chapter. Occasionally we speak of "business firms" or of "businesses" as a reminder that these terms can be used interchangeably with "firm." Of course there are other types of firms besides business firms. We discuss a few at the end of the chapter.

the demand and price for personal computers increase. The market *guides* individuals, from the production of one good into the production of another good, for example; and it *coordinates* individuals' actions, so that suppliers and demanders find mutual satisfaction at equilibrium, for example. As the economist Adam Smith observed, individuals in a market setting are "led by an invisible hand to promote an end which was no part of their intention."

Contrast the invisible hand of the market with the visible hand of a manager in a firm. Who tells the employee on the assembly line to make more computer chips? The manager does. Who tells the employee to design a new engine, to paint the lamps green, to put steak and lobster on the menu? The manager does. Obviously the visible hand of the manager of the firm also guides and coordinates individuals' actions. Thus both the *invisible hand* of the market and the *visible hand* of the manager of a firm guide and coordinate individuals' actions. There is, in other words, **market** and **managerial coordination**.

If the market is capable of guiding and coordinating individuals' actions, why did firms (and managers) ever arise in the first place? In other words, why do firms exist? Two economists have suggested a possible answer.

The Alchian and Demsetz Answer. Economists Armen Alchian and Harold Demsetz suggest that firms are formed when benefits can be obtained from individuals working as a team.[3] Sometimes the sum of what individuals can produce as a team is greater than the sum of what they can produce alone: sum of team production > sum of individual production. Consider 11 individuals, all making shoe boxes. Each working alone produces 10 shoe boxes per day, for a total daily output of 110. If they work as a team, however, the same 11 individuals can produce 140 shoe boxes; the added output (30 shoe boxes) is reason enough for them to work together as a team.

Shirking in a Team

Team production also brings disadvantages. One problem of team production is **shirking,** which refers to workers putting forth less than the agreed-to effort. The amount of shirking increases in teams because the costs of shirking to individual team members are lower than when they work alone.

Consider five individuals, Tom, Sue, Mark, Genia, and John, who form a team to produce lightbulbs because they realize that the sum of their team production will be more than the sum of their individual production. They agree to team-produce lightbulbs, sell the lightbulbs, and split the proceeds five equal ways. On an average day they produce 140 lightbulbs and sell each one for $2. Total revenue per day is $280, with each of the five team members receiving $56. Then Mark begins to shirk. Owing to his shirking, production falls to 135 lightbulbs per day, and total revenue falls to $270 per day; each person now receives $54. Notice that Mark did all the shirking and that total revenue fell by $10, but that Mark's reduction in pay was only $2, one-fifth of this amount.

In situations (such as team production), where one person receives all the benefits from shirking and pays only a part of the costs, we predict there will be more shirking than in the situation where the person who shirks bears the full cost of his or her shirking.

Market Coordination

The process in which individuals perform certain tasks, such as producing certain quantities of goods, based on changes in the market forces such as supply, demand, and price.

Managerial Coordination

The process in which managers direct employees to perform certain tasks.

Shirking

The behavior of a worker who is putting forth less than the agreed-to effort.

---

[3]Armen Alchian and Harold Demsetz, "Production, Information Costs and Economic Organization," *American Economic Review* 62 (December 1972): 777–95.

Question:

Suppose a firm is made up exclusively of extremely conscientious and hard-working people. Would shirking still be a problem?

Answer:

Even though individuals may have different inclinations to shirk (given the chance, some people will shirk more than others), this does not mean that their behavior is *independent* of a change in the cost of shirking. As long as shirking is considered a *good* (Isn't it a form of leisure?) from which individuals obtain utility, lowering the cost of shirking will cause individuals to "consume" more shirking, *ceteris paribus*.

The Monitor (Manager): Taking Care of Shirking

Monitor

Person in a business firm who coordinates team production and reduces shirking.

The **monitor** (or manager) plays an important role in the firm. He is the person who reduces the amount of shirking by firing shirkers and rewarding the productive members of the firm. In doing this, the monitor can preserve the benefits that often come with team production (increased output) and reduce, if not eliminate, the costs associated with team production (increased shirking). But this raises another question: *Who or what monitors the monitor?* In other words, how can the monitor be kept from shirking?

Residual Claimant(s)

Person(s) who share in the profits of a business firm.

One possibility is to give the monitor an incentive not to shirk by making him a **residual claimant** of the firm. A residual claimant receives the excess of revenues over costs (profits) as his income. If the monitor shirks, then profits are likely to be lower (or even zero or negative) and therefore the monitor will receive less income.

The Monitor-Employee Relationship: Exploitation or Mutual Benefit?

The monitor-employee relationship is often pictured as one where the monitor barks orders at the employees and threatens to fire them if they shirk. Some persons go farther and say that the monitor "exploits" the employee. We suggest a fundamentally different picture. Individuals join a firm because they expect to be made better off; later they realize that the benefits of team production are in jeopardy owing to shirking; the monitor solves this problem by firing shirkers and rewarding productive workers; the monitor has an incentive to monitor effectively because he is a residual claimant. In this scenario, employees voluntarily accept the monitor's commands because they realize that they are better off working as part of a team; and the employees also know that unless the entire team is monitored (themselves included), their portion of the benefits of working in the team will be less than they potentially can be.

The Objective of the Firm

Separation of Ownership from Control (or Management)

Refers to the significant division between owners and managers that often occurs in large business firms; owners and managers are not the same people.

What is the objective of the firm? Most economists say that the firm's goal or objective is to maximize profits. Not all economists agree, however. William Baumol, for example, claims that firms seek to maximize sales. A. A. Berle and Gardner Means maintain that **separation of ownership from control (or management)** in business firms (especially large firms) has allowed managers to pursue their own goals, such as increasing the size of the firm or increasing the number of employees working for them, at the expense of the profit-maximization goal of the stockholders (owners) of the firm. Richard Cyert, James March, and Herbert Simon argue that rather than trying to maximize profits, the firm seeks only to achieve some satisfactory target profit level (referred to by Simon as **satisficing behavior**) and then pursues other goals.

Satisficing Behavior
Behavior directed to meeting some satisfactory (not maximum) profit target.

Although these so-called sales and managerial theories of the firm explain some relevant aspects of the business firm, many economists argue that they do not offer a significant alternative to profit maximization as the goal of business firms. It may be true that business firms do not attempt only to maximize profits, and goals other than profit do sometimes motivate the behavior of firms. Nonetheless one must ask whether the theories built on the profit-maximization assumption satisfactorily describe, explain, and predict the firm's behavior. As you will see in later chapters, they apparently do this quite well.

Question:

Firm A decides to maximize profits over a three-year time span, while firm B decides to maximize profits over a shorter time period, say, one year. To the observer, who does not know the time span each firm has picked, firm B may appear to be attempting to maximize profits while firm A does not. In short, long-run profit maximization (three years in this example) may involve short-run behavior that appears contrary to profit maximization. And, of course, it may be contrary to profit maximization in the short run but not in the long run. Isn't this a problem with the profit-maximization hypothesis?

Answer:

That depends on how the word "problem" is used. Certainly this example does not call the profit-maximization hypothesis into question. In other words, nothing in this example suggests that firms do not attempt to maximize profits. Instead, the example correctly points out (1) that not all firms necessarily maximize profits over the same time period and (2) that failure to understand this can result in the idea that a firm does not maximize profits when in fact it does.

DIFFERENT TYPES OF BUSINESS FIRMS

Business firms differ in many ways. They differ as to what they produce, the number of people they employ, their revenues, their costs, where they are located, the type of advertising campaigns they run, their relationship with the government, the amount of taxes they pay, and hundreds of other details. Many of the differences among business firms are minor, but some are not. One major difference is the firm's legal categorization. Business firms commonly fall into one of three legal categories: proprietorships, partnerships, and corporations.

Proprietorship
A form of business that is owned by one individual who makes all the business decisions, receives the entire profits, and is legally responsible for the debts of the firm.

Proprietorships

A **proprietorship** is a form of business that is owned by one individual who makes all the business decisions, receives the entire profits, and is legally responsible for the debts of the firm.

Unlimited Liability
A legal term that signifies that the personal assets of the owner(s) of a firm may be used to pay off the debts of the firm.

Being legally responsible for the debts of the business means that the sole proprietor has **unlimited liability**; that is, a sole proprietor is responsible for settling all debts of the firm even if this means selling his or her personal property (the car, the house, and so on) to do so.

As Exhibit 7-1 shows, proprietorships are the most numerous form of business firm in the United States; in 1984, 70 percent of all firms were proprietorships. They accounted for only 5.9 percent of total business revenues, however. Using this latter criterion, the much less numerous corporations are the dominant form of business firm.

Advantages of Proprietorships.   There are certain advantages to proprietorships. The first advantage is that *proprietorships are easy to form and to dissolve.* To start a proprietorship one need only meet broadly defined health and zoning regulations and register the name of the business. To dissolve the proprietorship, one need only stop doing business. The second advantage is that *all decision-making power resides with the sole proprietor.* He or she need not consult anyone as to what product will be produced, how many units will be produced, or who will do what and when. The third advantage is that *the profit of the proprietorship is taxed only once.* The profit of the proprietorship is the income of the sole proprietor, and as such only personal income taxes apply to it.

Disadvantages of Proprietorships.   There are three major disadvantages of proprietorships. The first disadvantage is that *the sole proprietor faces unlimited liability.* As we noted, this means that the owner is responsible for all debts of the proprietorship and that his or her personal property can be used to settle these debts. In short, the liability of the firm can extend beyond the confines of the business to the proprietor's home, car, boat, and savings account. The second disadvantage is that *proprietorships have limited ability to raise funds for business expansion.* This partly explains why proprietorships are usually small business firms. Proprietorships do not find borrowing funds easy because lenders are not eager to lend funds to business firms whose success depends on only one person. The third disadvantage is that *proprietorships usually end with the death of the proprietor.* From the point of view of the business community and the firm's employees, this is a disadvantage. Employees usually like to work for firms that offer a degree of permanency and the possibility of upward career mobility.

Partnerships

Partnership

A form of business that is owned by two or more co-owners (partners) who share any profits the business earns; each of the partners is legally responsible for all debts incurred by the firm.

A **partnership** is a form of business that is owned by two or more co-owners, called partners, who share any profits the business earns and who are legally responsible

■ **EXHIBIT 7-1**
Forms of Business Organizations
Two criteria commonly used for classifying business firms include percentage of U.S. firms and percentage of total business revenues. Nearly three out of every four firms is a proprietorship, but they generate only 5.9 percent of total business revenues. Corporations, though relatively few in number, generate 89.8 percent of total business revenues. All data are for 1984.

TYPE OF FIRM	PERCENTAGE OF U.S. FIRMS	PERCENTAGE OF TOTAL BUSINESS REVENUES
Proprietorship	70.0%	5.9%
Partnership	10.2	4.3
Corporation	19.8	89.8

SOURCE: U.S. Bureau of the Census, *Statistical Abstract of the United States, 1988* (Washington, D.C.: U.S. Government Printing Office, 1988).

for any debts incurred by the firm. A partnership may be viewed as a proprietorship with more than one owner. Partners in a partnership may contribute different amounts of financial capital to the formation of the firm; they may agree to have different responsibilities within the firm; and they may agree to different "cuts" of the profit pie.

Advantages of Partnerships.   Since partnerships are much like proprietorships, they share many of the same advantages and disadvantages. First, *a partnership is easy to organize.* Second, *a partnership is usually an effective form of business organization in situations where team production involves skills that are difficult to monitor.* For example, physicians and attorneys often form partnerships. Names like the Smithies and Yankelovich law firm or the Matson, Bradbury, and Chan medical clinic are not uncommon. Monitoring the job performance of such professionals would be difficult. We could not know whether our fictional Dr. Matson was doing a good job or not when he talked gruffly to Mrs. Brown about her "moving aches and pains." Was he trying to short circuit her hypochondria, or was he simply being rude? Since Dr. Matson is a partner in the partnership, he is a residual claimant, and thus has an incentive to monitor his own work performance effectively.

Third, *in a partnership the benefits of specialization can be realized.* If, for example, one partner in an advertising agency is better at public relations and another is better at art work, then they can work at the tasks for which they are best suited.

Fourth, *the profit of the partnership is the income of the partners, and only personal income taxes apply to it.*

Disadvantages of Partnerships.   First, *the partners in a partnership have unlimited liability.* In a way this is even more of a disadvantage than it is in a proprietorship. In a proprietorship the proprietor incurs only his or her own debts and is solely responsible for them. In a partnership, one partner might incur the debts, but all partners are responsible for them. For example, if partner Matson incurs a debt by buying an expensive piece of medical equipment without the permission of partners Bradbury and Chan, that is too bad for partners Bradbury and Chan. They are still legally responsible for the debts incurred by Matson.

Second, *decision making in a partnership can be complicated or frustrating.* Suppose in our fictional law firm that Smithies wants to move the partnership in one direction, to specialize in corporate law, say, and Yankelovich wants to move it in another direction, to specialize in family law, say. Who makes the decision in this tug-of-war? Possibly no one will make the decision and things will stay as they are, which may not be a good thing for the growth of the partnership.

Third, *voluntary withdrawal by a partner from the firm, or the death of a member of a firm, can cause the partnership to dissolve or to be restructured.* This presents partnerships with a continuity problem, similar to the one proprietorships experience.

Question:

Isn't there such a thing as a limited partnership that avoids some of the problems of unlimited liability?

Answer:

Yes, in a **limited partnership** there are usually general partners and limited partners. General partners continue to have unlimited liability, but limited partners do not. The limited partner's liability is restricted to the amount he or she has invested in the firm. Usually limited partners do not participate in the management of the firm, nor do they enter into contractual agreements on behalf of the firm.

Limited Partnership
A form of business that is organized as a partnership, but which gives some of the partners the legal protection of limited liability.

Corporations

Corporation

A legal entity that can conduct business in its own name the way an individual does; ownership of the corporation resides with stockholders who have limited liability in the debts of the corporation.

A **corporation** is a legal entity that can conduct business in its own name in the same way an individual does; ownership of the corporation resides with stockholders who have limited liability in the debts of the corporation. As Exhibit 7-1 shows, in 1984 corporations made up only 19.8 percent of all U.S. firms but accounted for 89.8 percent of total business revenues. Corporations with which most of us are familiar include Exxon, Ford Motor Company, General Motors, AT&T, U.S. Steel (now USX), IBM, Procter & Gamble, and NBC, to name only a few.

Advantages of Corporations. First, *the owners of the corporation (the stockholders) are not personally liable for the debts of the corporation;* they have **limited liability**. Limited liability *assures the owners (stockholders) that if the corporation should incur debts that it cannot pay, creditors do not have recourse to the owners' personal property for payment.* This means that an owner of a corporation cannot lose more than his or her investment. For example, if a person buys 100 shares of stock in corporation XYZ at $50 a share for a total purchase price of $5,000, he cannot lose more than $5,000.

Limited Liability

A legal term that signifies that the owners (stockholders) of a corporation cannot be sued for the corporation's failure to pay its debts.

Second, *corporations continue to exist even if one or more owners of the corporation sell their shares or die.* This is because the corporation is a legal entity in and of itself.

Third, since the corporation's life is independent of the life of any one of the owners of the corporation, and because there is limited liability, *corporations are usually able to raise large sums of financial capital for investment purposes.* Limited liability is a plus from the point of view of the potential investor in a corporation. She knows that she can only lose her investment and nothing more. In addition, because corporations can sell bonds and issue stock, they have means of raising financial capital that do not exist for proprietorships or partnerships. We discuss bonds and stocks in more detail later in the chapter.

Disadvantages of Corporations The major disadvantage of corporations is the *double taxation of corporate income.* For example, suppose corporation XYZ makes a $3 million profit this year. This amount is subject to the corporate income tax. If the corporate tax is 25 percent, then $750,000 is paid in taxes and $2.25 million remains for **dividends** and other uses. Next, suppose half of this $2.25 million is distributed as dividends to stockholders. This is income for the stockholders and is taxed at personal income tax rates. In short, the $3 million profit was subject to both the corporate income tax and the personal income tax. Contrast this situation with the profit earned by a proprietorship. If a proprietorship had earned the $3 million in profit, it would only have been subject to one tax: the personal income tax.

Dividends

A share of profits distributed to stockholders.

A second disadvantage of corporations is that they are *often subject to problems associated with the separation of ownership from control,* where the owners of the corporation are different persons from the managers who control it on a day-to-day basis and owners and managers do not always agree on what the corporation's objectives should be.

The objective of the owners might be to increase profits and raise the value of the stock they hold. The manager might want to increase the size of the corporation or hire additional personnel or contribute to the local community—all of which may work against profitability.

Economics in Our Times

Greenmail: Or Was J. R. Ewing All That Bad?

If managers of a corporation fail to meet the stockholders' major objective of maximizing their wealth, the price of the corporate stock will probably not be an accurate reflection of the assets of the firm. The price of the stock is said to be "too low," given the corporation's assets, and the stock is referred to as being *underpriced*.

In situations such as this, entrepreneurially oriented persons usually enter the picture. They buy up large portions of the underpriced stock. The objective of the buyers is to obtain voting control of the corporation—in short, to "take it over." If they succeed, they can then replace the present management with new management who, they expect, will increase the profitability of the corporation.

During the *takeover threat*, the corporation's present management usually appeals to the stockholders and asks them not to sell their shares to the outside investors—even if they offer a higher price—but instead to stick with them. To defend themselves from a takeover and certain loss of their jobs, the present management uses corporate cash to buy back the corporation's stock from the outside investors at a profit to these investors. Millions of dollars have been made in this way. Texan T. Boone Pickens, chairman of the Mesa Petroleum Company, who has been compared to J. R. Ewing on television's "Dallas," is such an entrepreneurially oriented person. He has purchased the underpriced stock of poorly managed companies, issued takeover threats, and been bought out by the present management of these companies at prices well above those prevailing in the market. This practice is known as *greenmail*.

If Pickens appears to be working a get-rich-quick scheme without risk, look again. If Pickens or anyone else buys large blocks of a corporation's stock, thus bidding up its price, and later learns that the stock was not underpriced, millions will be lost instead of gained.

What are the consequences of greenmail for corporations? For one thing, the activities of greenmailers pressure managers into adopting and satisfying the objectives of stockholders of the corporation.

This possible difference in objectives between managers and owners is the subject of controversy in the economics profession. Many economists discount this problem. According to their argument, stockholders do not need to know what the managers of their corporation are doing on a daily basis; to find out how the managers are doing, stockholders can simply watch the value of their stock. If it goes down, they can reason that present management is not doing a good job and can organize to remove them; in short, they can monitor the managers by reading the stock pages of their local newspaper. Also, the stockholders can make the managers "one of them" by issuing stock to the managers. The idea here is to make the objectives of the managers the same as the objectives of the stockholders by making the managers stockholders. Finally, entrepreneurially oriented managers are usually waiting in the wings, willing and able to make the case to stockholders that the present management is doing a bad job and needs to be replaced (by them). Their presence restrains present management from satisfying its objectives at the expense of the objective(s) of stockholders.

Exhibit 7-2 summarizes the advantages and disadvantages of corporations and compares them with the advantages and disadvantages of proprietorships and partnerships.

Advantages and Disadvantages of Different Types of Business Firms

TYPE OF BUSINESS FIRM	EXAMPLES	ADVANTAGES	DISADVANTAGES
Proprietorship	1. Local barbershop 2. Many restaurants 3. Family farm 4. Carpet cleaning service	1. Easy to form and to dissolve. 2. All decision-making power resides with the sole proprietor. 3. Profit is taxed only once.	1. Proprietor faces unlimited liability. 2. Limited ability to raise funds for business expansion. 3. Usually ends with death of proprietor.
Partnership	1. Some medical offices 2. Some law offices 3. Some advertising agencies	1. Easy to organize. 2. Deals effectively with team production that involves skills difficult to monitor. 3. Benefits of specialization can be realized. 4. Profit is taxed only once.	1. Partners face unlimited liability (one partner can incur a debt and all partners are legally responsible for payment of the debt). 2. Decision making can be complex and frustrating. 3. Withdrawal or death of a partner can end partnership or cause its restructuring.
Corporation	1. IBM 2. AT&T 3. General Motors	1. Owners (stockholders) have limited liability. 2. Corporation continues if owners sell their shares of stock or die. 3. Usually able to raise large sums of financial capital.	1. Double taxation. 2. Problems may arise owing to separation of ownership from control (some suggest "separation of ownership from control" is more illusory than real).

THE BALANCE SHEET OF A FIRM

Balance Sheet

An accounting of the assets, liabilities, and net worth of a business firm.

Assets

Anything of value to which the firm has a legal claim.

Liabilities

A debt of the business firm.

Net Worth (Equity or Capital Stock)

Value of the business firm to its owners; it is determined by subtracting liabilities from assets.

All business firms—proprietorships, partnerships, and corporations alike—have a balance sheet. A **balance sheet** presents a picture of the financial status of a firm; it is an accounting of the assets and liabilities (and hence the net worth) of a firm. Exhibit 7-3 illustrates a balance sheet for a fictional corporation, American Computers, Inc.

On the left-hand side of the balance sheet **assets** are listed. An asset is anything of value to which the firm has a legal claim. On the right-hand side of the balance sheet, **liabilities** are listed. A liability is a debt of the firm. Also listed on the right-hand side of the balance sheet is **net worth**. Net worth, also known as **equity**, or **capital stock** (when dealing with a corporation), is the value of the business firm to its owners; it is determined by subtracting liabilities from assets. Thus according to American Computers' balance sheet, if the company sold off its assets and paid off its liabilities, it would have $90 million left over. This amount, or the net worth of the firm, represents the owners' claims on the assets of the firm. If liabilities should exceed assets, then the firm would have a negative net worth. Since a firm's net worth is equal to its assets minus its liabilities, it follows that liabilities plus net worth equal a firm's assets. In other words, the left-hand side of the balance sheet exactly "balances" the right-hand side.

$$\text{Net worth} = \text{assets} - \text{liabilities}$$

so it follows that

$$\text{Assets} = \text{liabilities} + \text{net worth}$$

A Balance Sheet for American Computers, Inc.

The left-hand side of the balance sheet lists the corporation's assets; the right-hand side of the balance sheet lists liabilities and net worth (equity or capital stock). The net worth of a business firm is equal to assets minus liabilities. This means liabilities plus net worth equal assets and the right-hand side of the balance sheet exactly "balances" the left-hand side.

ASSETS ($ MILLIONS)		LIABILITIES ($ MILLIONS)	
Cash	$ 5	Accounts payable	$ 10
Accounts receivables	15	Short-term debt	15
Inventory	25	Long-term debt	30
Equipment	40	Total liabilities	$ 55
Land and building	60	Net worth	90
Total assets	$145	Total liabilities and net worth	$145

FINANCING CORPORATE ACTIVITY

We mentioned earlier that corporations have options for raising financial capital that do not exist for proprietorships and partnerships. All firms can raise financial capital by borrowing from banks and other lending institutions. Corporations, however, have two other avenues: They can *sell bonds* (sometimes referred to as *issuing debt*), and they can *issue (or sell) additional shares of stock.*

Stocks and Bonds

Bond

An IOU statement that promises to pay a certain sum of money (the principal) at maturity and also to pay periodic fixed sums until that date.

Face Value (Par Value)

Dollar amount specified on the bond.

Coupon Rate

The percentage of the face value of the bond that is paid out regularly (usually quarterly or annually) to the holder of the bond.

(Shares of) Stock

A claim on the assets of a corporation that gives the purchaser a share of the ownership of the corporation.

A **bond** is a promise to pay for the use of someone else's money. More specifically, it is an IOU statement that promises to pay a certain sum of money (the principal) at maturity and also to pay periodic fixed sums until that date. All bonds specify the following: (1) the maturity date, which is some date in the future, say, 1999; (2) a dollar figure, which is called the **face value (par value)** of the bond, say, $1,000; (3) a **coupon rate** (of interest), which is stated in percentage terms. We shall pick 10 percent as our coupon rate.

When someone buys the bond we have just described from a corporation, the following process takes place: (1) The person who buys the bond pays some dollar amount for the bond (not necessarily the face value). Since this person will be receiving periodic payments, and will receive a fixed sum of money at the maturity date, we say that the person has lent money to the corporation, or that the corporation has borrowed money from the person who bought the bond. (2) The person who buys the bond receives annual payments from the corporation equal to the coupon rate times the face value of the bond. For our bond this amounts to $100 (10% × $1,000 = $100). These $100 payments will continue each year through 1999, the maturity date. (3) When the maturity date arrives, the person who bought the bond receives the face value of the bond—$1,000.

Instead of selling bonds, a corporation may issue **stock** to raise financial capital. A share of stock is a claim on the assets of the corporation that gives the purchaser a share of the ownership of the corporation. Whereas the buyer of a corporate bond is lending funds to the corporation, the buyer of a share of stock is acquiring an ownership right in the corporation.

Nonprofit Firms

There are firms other than business firms. It is important to know about them and to understand how and why they differ from business firms. In this short section we

The Monkey and the Economist

Here are two facts about stocks: (1) Stocks are bought and sold (traded) with the future in mind. Rollins might buy 100 shares of IBM because he thinks the price of IBM stock will rise. (2) People act quickly on information that relates to the future performance on a corporation whose stock is traded. If Carpenter, who owns stock in United Artists, hears that the company is headed for bad times, she won't wait long to act on this information. Taking the two facts together, we conclude that *stock prices quickly reflect individuals' most recently acquired information relating to the future performance of the corporations that issued the stock.*

With this conclusion in mind, consider two stocks: IBM stock and Ford Motor stock. Suppose both companies' stock is selling for the same price—$100 a share. One day individuals learn that IBM has made a major breakthrough in the market for computers and that it is headed for better times. On the same day individuals learn that one of Ford's models is about to be recalled, and the company is headed for rough times. What will happen to the prices of IBM and Ford stock? We would expect the price of IBM stock to be bid up and the price of Ford stock to fall. At the end of the

day, IBM stock will be selling for $100+ and Ford Motor stock will be selling for $100−

Many economists predict that the price of Ford Motor stock will fall sufficiently (and the price of IBM stock will rise sufficiently) so that Ford stock is no worse and no better a buy for the price than IBM stock. Furthermore, since individuals act quickly on information relating to future corporate performance, the new equilibrium between the stocks' prices is likely to be achieved rapidly.

What all this suggests is that there are no *uniquely* good or bad buys in the stock market. In equilibrium, IBM stock will be *as good or as bad a buy* as Ford stock, even though the expected future performances of the two corporations may not be the same. In theory, the prices of the two stocks will instantaneously adjust for the differences in the expected future performances of the two corporations.

Enter the monkey and the economist. Is one more capable than the other of choosing stocks within broad classes? In other words, is a monkey who "chooses" stocks by throwing darts at the stock market page of the newspaper any better or worse than an economist who sits at his desk pouring over stock market facts and figures? Unless the economist has *inside* information, or can *better evaluate given information*, he can do no better than the dart-throwing monkey at choosing stocks. As shocking as this sounds, it is simply a consequence of the extreme speed with which the stock market processes information relating to the future performance of companies whose stocks are traded.

As Paul Samuelson, a Nobel Prize winner in economics, has noted, "Even the best investors seem to find it hard to

---

discuss *nonprofit* firms, particularly private and public nonprofit firms. In Chapter 39, the worker-manager firm is discussed in the context of the Yugoslavian economy.

Nonprofit firms are firms in which there are no residual claimants; any revenues over costs must be plowed back into the operation of the firm so that "what comes in" equals "what goes out." Churches, charitable organizations, colleges, and mutual insurance companies are a few examples of nonprofit firms. All these organizations are without residual claimants. For example, in a college the college president does not pocket any of the funds over and above the costs of running the college. Any funds that come into the college—through tuition fees, state appropriations, or monetary gifts—must be used for the operation of the college.

It has been argued that since no residual claimants exist in a nonprofit firm, no one within the firm has an incentive (or, at least, as strong an incentive as in a profit-maximizing business firm with residual claimants) to monitor shirking. We predict then that there will be more shirking in a nonprofit firm than in a profit-seeking business firm. Also, since any funds in excess of costs cannot be taken out of the

Nonprofit Firms
Firms in which there are no residual claimants; any revenues over costs must be plowed back into the operation of the firm so that "what comes in" equals "what goes out."

do better than the comprehensive common-stock averages, or better on the average than random selection among stocks of comparable variability."* If you replace the words "random selection" with "monkey selection," you have the story we have told here.

A Postscript

In 1967, the editors of *Forbes* magazine taped the stock market page of a newspaper to the wall and threw darts at it 28 times. In each of the 28 "hit" companies, they invested a hypothetical $1,000.

By 1984, the original $28,000 had grown to $132,000 not counting dividends. This was a 370 percent gain, or ten times better than the performance of the Dow Jones Industrial Average (see the Appendix to this chapter for the definition of the Dow). Few highly trained professional stock analysts did as well.

Unfortunately for them, the editors of *Forbes* did not invest real money in the venture. Obviously they didn't trust the power of the dart.

Question:

Inside information, *just mentioned, has frequently been in the news in recent years. Some people have been sent to jail for using inside information. What is inside information? Is it hard to get?*

Answer:

Inside information is information that is not yet public; it is known only to a small group of people, called *insiders*. The following example explains how someone might get inside information.

Diana Jenkins works as an accountant for a major pharmaceutical company. She has a friend, David Thompson, who works as a researcher for the company. One day David tells Diana that he and others in the research department are working on a drug that represents a major advance in cancer treatment. Months pass, and then one day David tells Diana (in whispers) that the research team has perfected the drug and that it will soon be sold on the market. This is a piece of inside information. "No one knows about this except for a handful of people in the executive offices and the research team," says David to Diana, "so please be sure to keep it quiet."

Inside information is hard to get because companies often do not want to release it. For example, the company that David works for might not want the information to get out too soon because it is afraid that its competitors might speed up production of a cancer-curing drug they are working on. By releasing the inside information, David is probably breaking a contract with his employer to keep this information secret.

*Paul Samuelson, "Proof That Properly Discounted Present Values of Assets Vibrate Randomly," *The Bell Journal of Economics and Management Science* 4 (Autumn 1973): 369–74.

Inside Information
Information that is not yet public; it is known only to a small group of people called insiders.

firm, it is argued that top administrators in nonprofit firms will attempt to use these "surplus" funds to make their lives more comfortable *within* the firm. For example, the administrators might have large, luxurious offices and private dining rooms, pay out higher salaries than necessary in order to acquire a given quality of personnel, or take frequent pleasurable "business" trips.

Nonprofit firms are either private or public. A charitable organization such as the United Way is a private nonprofit firm. A police force that receives state-appropriated funds is a public nonprofit firm. One major difference between the two is who pays the costs of the firm.

In a private nonprofit firm, private citizens pay the costs. For example, the salaries of the persons who work for the local church are paid by private citizens mostly through voluntary contributions. In a public nonprofit firm, *taxpayers* pay the costs. The salaries of the police in your town are paid by taxpayers.

At times the difference is not so clear-cut. Sometimes a nonprofit firm will receive some funds from private citizens, who purchase the goods or services the nonprofit firm sells, and some funds from taxpayers. For example, state universities receive funds both from private citizens (students), as consumers of education, and also from taxpayers. Is the state university a private nonprofit firm or a public nonprofit firm? The answer is that it is a public nonprofit firm because it is operated by persons who must answer to members of the public sector: the state governor and the regents, who are elected or publicly appointed.

Public Nonprofit Firms and Taxes. A private nonprofit firm (such as a charitable organization) that doesn't satisfy the persons who contribute the funds—its customers, so to speak—is more likely to "go out of business" than is a public nonprofit firm that doesn't satisfy its customers. The reason is that the latter receives taxpayer funds whereas the former does not. If the customers of the private nonprofit firm do not wish to continue buying what the firm is selling or wish to stop contributing, they do just that. They show their change in preferences, or their dissatisfaction with the firm, by stopping the flow of dollars.

The customers-as-taxpayers of the public nonprofit firm are not in the same situation. They may not like the way the public nonprofit firm is treating them, or they may think the firm is doing an extremely poor job at delivering services, but unless they can convince their elected representatives to stop allocating tax funds for the public nonprofit firm, the flow of tax dollars is likely to continue.

■ CHAPTER SUMMARY

The Firm

■ Alchian and Demsetz argued that firms are formed when there are benefits from individuals working as a team; specifically, when the sum of what individuals can produce as a team is greater than the sum of what individuals can produce alone: sum of team production > sum of individual production.

■ There are both advantages and disadvantages to team production. The chief advantage (in many cases) is the positive difference between the output produced by the team and the sum of the output produced by individuals working alone. The chief disadvantage is the increased shirking in teams. The role of the monitor in the firm is to preserve the increased output and reduce or eliminate the increased shirking. The monitor has a monetary incentive not to shirk his monitoring duties because he is a residual claimant.

Different Types of Business Firms

■ A proprietorship is a form of business that is owned by one individual who makes all the business decisions, receives the entire profits, and is legally responsible for the debts of the firm. The sole proprietor has unlimited liability. The advantages of a proprietorship include the following: (1) It is easy to form and to dissolve. (2) All decision-making power resides with the sole proprietor. (3) The profits of the proprietorship are taxed only once. The disadvantages include the following: (1) The sole proprietor faces unlimited liability. (2) It has limited ability to raise funds for business expansion. (3) It usually ends with the death of the proprietor.

■ A partnership is a form of business that is owned by two or more co-owners (partners) who share any profits the business earns and who are legally responsible for any debts incurred by the firm. The advantages of a partnership include the following: (1) It is easy to organize. (2) It is an effective form of business organization in situations where team production involves skills that are difficult to monitor. (3) The benefits of specialization can be realized. (4) The profits of the partnership are taxed only once. The disadvantages include the following: (1) The partners have unlimited liability. (2) Decision making can be complicated and frustrating. (3) The voluntary withdrawal of a partner from the firm or the death of a partner can cause the partnership to be dissolved or restructured.

■ A corporation is a legal entity that can conduct business in its own name. Corporations account for the vast majority of total business revenues (approximately 90 percent). The advantages of a corporation include the following: (1) The owners (stockholders) of the corporation are not personally liable for the debts of the corporation; there is limited (not unlimited) liability. (2) The corporation continues to exist even when an owner sells his or her shares of stock or dies. (3) Corporations are usually able to raise large sums of financial capital for investment purposes. The disadvantages include the following: (1) There is double taxation of corporate income. (2) There are problems associated with separation of ownership from control (although some economists maintain that no serious problems exist here that cannot be solved).

The Balance Sheet of a Firm

■ A balance sheet is a picture of the financial status of a firm. Principally, a balance sheet lists a firm's assets, liabilities, and net worth. An asset is anything of value to which the firm has a legal claim. A liability is a debt of the firm. Net worth is the difference between assets and liabilities.

Financing Corporate Activity

■ Corporations can either issue bonds or additional shares of stock to raise funds. A bond is an IOU statement that promises to pay back a certain fixed sum of money at a specific point in time and to pay a fixed sum of money periodically. A share of stock is a claim on the assets of the corporation that gives the purchaser a share of the ownership of the corporation. A bondholder of corporation X, for example, does not have an ownership right in corporation X, but a stockholder of the corporation does.

Nonprofit Firms

■ Nonprofit firms are firms in which there are no residual claimants. There are both private and public nonprofit firms. One major difference between the two types is who pays the costs of the firms. In private nonprofit firms, private citizens as (voluntary) contributors or consumers do; in public nonprofit firms, taxpayers do. Since there are no residual claimants in nonprofit firms, we would expect the incentive to monitor shirking to be less, leading to more shirking than in business firms. In addition, since none of the "surplus" funds can be taken out of the firm, we would expect to see top administrators in nonprofit firms using the funds in personal ways: having big, luxurious offices and private dining rooms, paying out higher salaries than necessary to acquire a given quality of personnel, taking frequent pleasurable "business" trips, and so forth. Some economists believe the empirical evidence confirms this theory.

■ QUESTIONS TO ANSWER AND DISCUSS

1. Explain the difference between managerial coordination and market coordination.

2. Is the managerial coordination that goes on inside a business firm independent of market forces? Explain your answer.

3. Explain why even hard and conscientious workers will shirk more when the cost of shirking falls.

4. What does the phrase "separation of ownership from control" refer to?

5. Discuss the different types of liability (limited vs. unlimited) that proprietorships, partnerships, and corporations face.

6. In the chapter it was strongly hinted that business firms might operate differently than nonprofit firms. What might make this so?

7. Profit sharing is more often found in partnerships, where the number of owners is small, than in corporations where the number of owners tends to be relatively large. Might there be an economic reason for this? If so, what might it be?

8. Your economics class can be viewed as a team. You come together with other individuals to learn economics. There is a hierarchical scheme in the classroom. Your instructor is the monitor, and he or she instructs you as to what to read and when the tests will be given, and then grades your performance. Consider what would happen if, instead of this system, you were not graded. Would you shirk more or less? Explain your answer. In which setting would you expect to learn more economics? Why? Can you relate any of your answers to the performance of an employee in a firm? If so, explain how.

9. What differences, if any, do you think there might be between the behavior of the president of your college or university, as chief administrator of a nonprofit firm, and the behavior of the president of a business firm, as chief administrator of a business firm?

Appendix C

Stock Quotations, Bond Quotations, and the Dow

In this appendix we explain how to read the stock and bond market pages in the newspaper. Also, we explain what the Dow Jones Industrial Average is and what it means when the reporter on the nightly news says, "Today, the Dow was up 15 points."

Exhibit 7C-1 shows one row of the stock market page of a major daily newspaper. In each of the 11 columns there is a number or abbreviation, which has a specific meaning.

■ Column 1: **52-Week High.** The number is 39⅞. This means that the highest price paid for the stock within the last 52-week period was $39⅞ ($39.88).
■ Column 2: **52-Week Low.** The number is 29¾. This means that the lowest price for the stock within the last 52-week period was $29¾ ($29.75).
■ Column 3: **Stock.** This is where the name of the company that issued the stock or its abbreviation is noted. We have placed an X here.
■ Column 4: **Div. (Dividend).** The number is 1.20. This means that the last annual dividend was $1.20 per share of stock.
■ Column 5: **Yld % (Yield Percent).** The number is 3.4. This indicates the percentage of the closing share price that the dividend equals. It is obtained by dividing the dividend by the closing share price ($1.20/$35 = 3.4).
■ Column 6: **P-E Ratio (Price-Earnings Ratio).** The number is 31. This is the latest closing price per share divided by the latest available net earnings per share. For example, suppose a company's latest net earnings were $1 million, and that 100,000 shares of stock have been issued. This means that the earnings per share would be $10 ($1,000,000/100,000). If $120 is the latest closing price of the stock, then the P-E ratio is 12.

But what does a P-E ratio of 12 mean? Are P-E ratios that are higher than 12 better than those that are lower? Unfortunately, a P-E ratio, though easy to define, is not

■ **EXHIBIT 7C-1**
How to Read the Stock Market Page of a Newspaper
The exhibit illustrates one line from the stock market page of a newspaper.

(1)	(2)	(3)	(4)	(5)	(6)	(7)	(8)	(9)	(10)	(11)
52 Weeks				Yld	P-E	Sales				Net
High	Low	Stock	Div.	%	Ratio	100s	High	Low	Close	Chg.
39⅞	29¾	X	1.20	3.4	31	1435	35	34½	35	+ ⅜

so easy to explain. Roughly, however, what is in the numerator—the share price—reflects individuals' best guesstimate of the future; and what is in the denominator—the earnings per share in the last year—is a statement about the past. Thus two time periods are used in the derivation of the P-E ratio: the future and the past. Obviously the larger the P-E ratio (the greater the numerator is compared with the denominator), the more individuals think that the future will be different than the past; that is, they think that there will be a high growth in earnings. The closer the P-E ratio is to 1 (the closer the numerator is to the denominator), the more individuals think that future earnings will be similar to those in the past.

■ Column 7: **Sales 100s.** The number is 1435. This means 143,500 shares of this company's stock were traded on this day.

■ Column 8: **High.** The number is 35. This means the highest price at which the stock traded on this day was $35.

■ Column 9: **Low.** The number is 34½. This means the lowest price at which the stock traded on this day was $34½ ($34.50).

■ Column 10: **Close.** The number is 35. This is the price at which the stock closed at the end of the trading day ($35).

■ Column 11: **Net Chg. (Net Change).** The number is +⅜ of one dollar higher than the closing price on the previous trading day.

BOND QUOTATIONS

Here we follow the same procedure for bonds. Exhibit 7C-2 shows one row of the bond market page from a major daily newspaper.

■ Column 1: **Bonds.** This is where the name of the company that issued the bonds or its abbreviation is noted. We have placed an X in the spot. Next to the name 9s95 is written. This means the bond has a coupon rate of 9 percent and matures in 1995. Most corporate bonds have a $1,000 face value.

■ Column 2: **Cur Yld (Current Yield).** The number is 10. This means that if the bond is purchased today at the closing price (see column 6) it will provide a yield (effective interest rate) of 10 percent. This might be confusing since the coupon rate is 9 percent, but the coupon rate and the effective interest rate are not necessarily the same. The coupon rate = annual coupon payment/face value of the bond. The effective interest rate = annual coupon payment/price paid for the bond. In other words, the price one pays for a bond may not be equal to the face value of the bond. If it is not, then the coupon rate is different from the effective interest rate. If the price paid for the bond and the face value of the bond are the same, then the coupon rate equals the effective interest rate.

■ Column 3: **Vol (Volume).** The number is 105. This means the dollar volume for the day was $105,000.

■ Column 4: **High.** The number is 88⅜. Bond prices are quoted in points and fractions; each point is $10. Thus 88⅜ means that the highest price paid for this company's bonds on this day was $883.75 (83⅜ = 88.375 × $10 = $883.75).

■ **EXHIBIT 7C-2**
How to Read The Bond Market Page of A Newspaper
The exhibit illustrates one line from the bond market page of a newspaper.

(1)	(2)	(3)	(4)	(5)	(6)	(7)
	Cur					Net
Bonds	Yld	Vol	High	Low	Close	Chg.
X 9s 95	10	105	88⅜	88⅜	88⅜	+ ⅞

■ Column 5: **Low.** The number is 88⅜. The means that the lowest price paid for this company's bonds on this day was $883.75.

■ Column 6: **Close.** The number is 88⅜. This means that the closing price for this company's bonds on this day was $883.75.

■ Column 7: **Net Chg. (Net Change).** The number is +⅞. This means the closing price of the bond on this day was approximately $8.75 higher than on the previous trading day.

THE DOW JONES INDUSTRIAL AVERAGE (THE DOW)

Perhaps no piece of business news is heard by more people than the Dow Jones Industrial Average. Persons who know little about business, economics, or financial matters have heard of "the Dow." They know that it can go up, remain unchanged, or go down. On October 19, 1987, when the Dow fell 508 points, the news was broadcast around the world. Many people may not know exactly what it is, or how it operates, but they have a feeling that if it goes down, this is bad, and if it goes up, this is good. Our objective is to explain exactly what the Dow Jones Industrial Average is.

First, note that at present there is more than one Dow Jones Average. There is the Dow Jones Industrial Average, which is the most widely cited Dow Average, the Dow Jones Transportation Average, the Dow Jones Utility Average, and the Dow Jones Composite Average. We say more about the nonindustrial averages later.

The Dow Jones Industrial Average (DJIA) was first calculated in 1884 by Charles Dow, who used it as a measure of how the stock market was doing overall. He made this calculation by summing the prices of 11 major stocks and dividing by 11. In 1916 the list of stocks grew to 20; and in 1928 it grew to its present size, 30. The 30 companies included in the DJIA are listed in Exhibit 7C-3. (Some of the stocks included in the DJIA today were not always included; some stocks once included are no longer. For example, in 1982 Johns Manville was replaced by American Express.)

One might naturally think that the DJIA is calculated by summing the prices of the stocks that make up the list of industrials and dividing by the number of stocks. Since there are 30 stocks today, one would think the divisor would be 30. But the divisor is not 30. This is due to stock splits. To illustrate, consider two stocks: Y and Z. Suppose the price of stock Y is $50 and the price of stock Z is $100. To calculate

■ **EXHIBIT 7C-3**
The 30 Companies of the Dow Jones Industrial Index
The Dow Jones Industrial Index was originally a measurement of the stock price performance of 11 companies. Today, it measures the stock price performance of 30 companies.

Allied-Signal	Exxon	Philip Morris
Alcoa	General Electric	Primerica
American Express	General Motors	Procter & Gamble
AT&T	Goodyear Tire and Rubber	Sear Roebuck
Bethlehem Steel	IBM	Texaco
Boeing	International Paper	USX
Chevron	McDonald's	Union Carbide
Coca-Cola	Merck	United Technologies
DuPont	Minnesota Mining	Westinghouse Electric
Eastman Kodak	Navistar International	F. W. Woolworth

the average, we add $50 to $100 and divide by 2. We get $75. But suppose now that stock Y splits 2 for 1. This means that for every one share of stock Y a person held, he or she now has two shares. The new price of stock Y will be one-half what it was, or $25. Now if we calculate the average as before, we will add the price of stock Y ($25) to the price of stock Z ($100) and divide by 2. The average is $62.50. Notice that the average has changed although nothing of real substance has changed. To adjust for stock splits, the divisor used in calculating the average is changed from 2 to 1.66 since $125 divided by 1.66 gives us the true average of $75.

Besides the DJIA there are three other averages. The Dow Jones Transportation Average, made up of 20 transportation companies; the Dow Jones Utility Average, made up of 15 utility companies; and the Dow Jones Composite Average, made up of the 65 companies in all three indexes.

Chapter 8

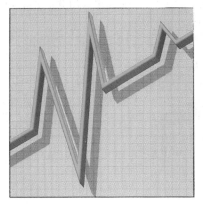

Production and Costs

■ INTRODUCTION

In the city of Philadelphia, Pennsylvania, there are thousands of stories to be told. This is one.

Alice Kerkland is a 32-year-old woman. Eleven years ago she was a college student, taking an economics course from Dr. Frank Williams. Back then, Alice was mildly interested in economics. She found supply-and-demand analysis both appealing and useful. She liked learning about the firm. She even liked learning about price elasticity of demand. The one economics topic Alice didn't like and wouldn't take the time to learn was production and costs.

Dr. Williams tried as hard as he could to interest Alice in the topic. But no matter what he did, Alice found it boring. She said it was too technical. Dr. Williams replied that the techniques had applications and that he would teach her some, but Alice was not interested.

Alice completed Dr. Williams's economics course. She did well on the final exam—except for the section on production and costs. As she walked out of the classroom after the exam, she mumbled, "Production and costs. Yech."

Years later, Alice got a good job with a new small firm in the city. For two or three years, the company did well. Everything looked great; the company was growing, sales were up, profits were increasing. Then things started getting shaky. They went from bad to worse. Part of Alice's job was to figure out what had happened and what should be done to turn things around.

She knew the problem had something to do with the company's costs, but she wasn't sure what. She decided to call her old economics professor and ask him for help. She couldn't reach him. He had died two years earlier.

She searched for her old economics textbook. She hoped that she could read up on production and costs and stumble across the answer. Although she hunted high and low, she couldn't find it. She remembered that she had resold it to the bookstore.

To make a long story short, Alice never did solve the company's problems. Things became even worse, and finally Alice, along with many others, was let go.

The last anyone heard, Alice hadn't found another job. She sits around her apartment all day (the house had to be sold) and watches soap operas. Her hus-

band left her, and the kids went with him. She wants to go to a psychiatrist for help, but she can't afford one. Her best friend's name is "Screwball," and worst of all, the name fits.

We've told you this story because you're now at the crossroads Alice was at when she was in college. She decided against learning about production and costs, and as you can see, she paid for it.

Please don't be another Alice Kerkland.

■ WHAT THIS CHAPTER IS ABOUT

Just as there are two sides to a market, a buying side (demand) and selling side (supply), there are two sides to a firm: a cost side and a revenue side. This chapter looks principally at the cost side.

Key Questions to Keep in Mind as You Read

1. What is the difference between accounting profit and economic profit? Which guides and directs economic activity?
2. What is the link between production and costs?
3. What is the short run? What is the long run?
4. Is it true that no matter how much fertilizer you use, you can't grow the world's supply of corn in a flowerpot?
5. What is marginal cost?
6. What is the long-run average total cost curve?
7. What are economies of scale, diseconomies of scale, and constant returns to scale?

ALL ABOUT COSTS

We discussed the concept of opportunity costs in Chapters 1 and 2. This chapter presents other types of costs—12 different cost concepts, to be specific. In this section we focus on three: explicit cost, implicit cost, and sunk cost.

Explicit Cost and Implicit Cost

Explicit Cost
A cost that is incurred when an actual (monetary) payment is made.

Implicit Cost
A cost that represents the value of resources used in production for which no actual (monetary) payment is made.

As we learned in Chapter 1, opportunity cost is a measure of what is given up when one action is taken instead of another. "What is given up" may either be explicit or implicit; hence, opportunity costs may be either **explicit costs** or **implicit costs.**

Consider a pizzeria in town. The owner of the pizzeria buys napkins, cheese, and soft drinks from her suppliers. The dollar payments she makes for these supplies are referred to as explicit costs (or accounting costs). An explicit cost is a cost that is incurred when an actual (monetary) payment is made. If Carol takes $25 out of her pocket and pays Shelly for selling her X, the $25 is an explicit cost for Carol.

An implicit cost is a cost that represents the value of resources used in production for which no actual (monetary) payment is made; it is a cost incurred as a result of a firm using resources that it owns or that the owners of the firm contribute to it.

Suppose that if the owner of the pizzeria had chosen not to own and work at the restaurant, she would have worked for an insurance company and earned $40,000 per year. In other words, by choosing to own and work at the pizzeria (and not to work for the insurance company), she *forfeits* a $40,000 salary. The $40,000 is an implicit cost.

With implicit costs, no money changes hands. But, of course, money need not change hands before a cost can be incurred. Cost connotes sacrifice; and sacrifices can be made, and alternatives can be forfeited, without money changing hands.

Question:

Are opportunity costs different in any way from explicit costs and implicit costs?

Answer:

No, they are not. There are two *subsets* of opportunity cost: the explicit-cost subset and the implicit-cost subset. Perhaps it would be clearer to say "explicit opportunity cost" and "implicit opportunity cost." But, as noted in Chapter 2, economists often leave out the word "opportunity" when speaking of costs.

Economic Profit and Accounting Profit

Economic Profit
The difference between total revenue and total (opportunity) cost, including both its explicit and implicit components.

Accounting Profit
The difference between total revenue and explicit costs.

Economic profit is the difference between total revenue and total opportunity cost, including both its explicit and implicit components.

$$\text{Economic profit} = \text{total revenue} - \text{total opportunity cost}$$

or

$$\text{Economic profit} = \text{total revenue} - (\text{explicit} + \text{implicit costs})$$

Accounting profit is the difference between total revenue and explicit costs.[1]

$$\text{Accounting profit} = \text{total revenue} - \text{explicit costs}$$

An example will help differentiate between economic profit and accounting profit. McDowell, an attorney working for the law firm of Zale and Zenzer, earns an annual salary of $60,000. One day he quits his job and opens up a copying shop across from the university. The first year of operation his explicit costs are $50,000. His total revenue is $130,000. What is his accounting profit? The answer is $80,000. We get this figure by subtracting $50,000 explicit costs from $130,000 total revenue. McDowell's economic profit is $20,000. We get this figure by subtracting both explicit costs ($50,000) and implicit costs ($60,000) from total revenue.

In calculating economic profit, we take into account the salary McDowell could be earning working for Zale and Zenzer (but is not earning because he chose to work for himself) and subtract it from total revenue. In calculating accounting profit, we do not take into account the salary McDowell could be earning working for Zale and Zenzer.

Question:

When most people use the word "profit," which profit do they mean? Which concept of profit is it better to use?

---

[1]Don't jump to the conclusion that accounting profit is what accountants calculate and economic profit is what economists calculate. What we have here are simply two different profit concepts. It is possible for anyone (an accountant, an economist, a computer analyst, a nurse, and so forth) to calculate either type of profit.

Answer:

When most noneconomists use the word "profit," they usually mean accounting profit. It is economic profit, however, that directs economic activity, as the following example illustrates.

Suppose one month after graduating from college, Marta gets a good-paying job working for a long distance telephone company. Three years later she thinks about leaving the company to start her own. Will what Marta has to give up to start her company, including her good-paying job, be important in her decision of whether to strike out on her own? We think she'll say yes. This then tells us that not only do explicit costs matter but that implicit costs matter, too.

We conclude that if we seek to understand and predict economic behavior, it is better to think in terms of economic profit than accounting profit.

Zero Economic Profit Is Not as Bad as It Sounds

Economic profit is usually lower (never higher) than accounting profit because economic profit is the difference between total revenue and total opportunity costs, including both explicit and implicit costs, whereas accounting profit is the difference between total revenue and only explicit costs. Thus it is possible for a firm to earn both a positive accounting profit *and* a zero economic profit. In economics, a firm that makes zero economic profit is said to be earning a **normal profit**: zero economic profit = normal profit.

Should an owner of a firm be worried if he has made zero economic profit for, say, the year just ending? No. A zero economic profit—as bad as it may sound—means the owner has generated total revenues sufficient to cover total opportunity costs; that is, both explicit *and* implicit costs. If, for example, the owner's implicit cost is a (forfeited) $100,000 salary working for someone else, then earning a zero economic profit means he has done as well as he could have in his next best (alternative) line of employment.

When we realize that zero economic profit (or normal profit) means "doing as well as could have been done," we understand that it isn't bad to make zero economic profit. Zero accounting profit is something altogether different; it implies that some part of total opportunity costs has not been covered by total revenue.

Sunk Cost

Sunk cost is a cost incurred in the past that cannot be changed by current decisions and therefore cannot be recovered. For example, suppose a firm must purchase a $10,000 government license before it can legally produce and sell lamp poles. Furthermore, suppose the government will not buy back the license, nor allow it to be resold. The $10,000 the firm spends to purchase the license is a sunk cost. It is a cost that, once it has been incurred (the $10,000 was spent), cannot be changed by a current decision (we cannot go back into the past and undo what was done), and cannot be recovered (the government will not buy back the license, nor allow it to be resold).

Question:

Suppose Alicia purchases a pair of shoes, wears them for a few days, and then realizes that they are uncomfortable. Furthermore, suppose she can't return the shoes

Normal Profit

Zero economic profit. A firm that earns normal profit is earning revenues equal to its total opportunity costs. This is the level of profit necessary to keep resources employed in that particular firm.

Sunk Cost

A cost incurred in the past that cannot be changed by current decisions and therefore cannot be recovered.

Theory in Practice

"Even Though I Hate Accounting, I Have To Get a Job as an Accountant"

Sunk cost is most often discussed in terms of the production of a good. We illustrate here how it might also be relevant to you or a friend in college.

Consider a senior in college who is about to graduate. She has spent a little over four years in college and has majored in accounting. In her last semester she finally admits to herself what she began to suspect in her junior year: She dislikes accounting work. She is, however, currently in-terviewing with accounting firms for a job as an accountant on graduation. A friend asks her why, if she dislikes accounting so intensely, she wants to be an accountant. She says that she has spent more than four years and a lot of money learning to be an accountant and that she must now become one to recapture some of the cost incurred.

But we ask, Is it possible to recapture some of the cost incurred? Aren't the costs she has incurred to learn accounting—the dollars spent on tuition and books, the time spent studying accounting—sunk? Yes, they are. There is no way to undo the past. Whether our senior becomes an accountant or not, the costs incurred in becoming an accountant cannot be recovered. Saying this does not imply that the senior should or should not work as an accountant, only that the decision to work as one is best made by ignoring the past. The relevant cost-related questions for the senior to ask herself when deciding whether to work as an accountant are, "What *will I give up* if I choose to work as an accountant?" Or, "What *will I give up* if I go back to school and learn something else?" It is not, "What *have I given up* to learn accounting?"

---

for a refund. Are the shoes considered a sunk cost? Would an economist recommend that Alicia continue wearing the shoes?

Answer:

The purchase of the shoes represents (1) a cost incurred in the past, that (2) cannot be changed by a current decision, and (3) cannot be recovered; therefore, it is a sunk cost. An economist would recommend that Alicia not base her current decision to wear or not wear the shoes on what has happened and cannot be changed.

Follow-up Question:

It seems a waste of money to buy the shoes and then not wear them. Isn't this correct?

Answer:

It is also a waste to compound mistakes.[2] We are simply saying (as all economists do) that sunk costs should not be considered in making present decisions, because if a person lets what she has done, *and can't undo,* influence her present decision, she runs the risk of compounding mistakes. For example, if Alicia decides to wear the uncomfortable shoes because she thinks it is a waste of money not to, then she may end up with an even bigger loss: certainly less comfort and possibly a trip to

[2]David Friedman, in his price theory text, puts it this way: "When, as a very small child, I quarreled with my sister and then locked myself in my room, my father would come to the door and say. 'Making a mistake and not admitting it is only hurting yourself twice.' When I got a little older he changed it to 'Sunk costs are sunk costs.' " (David Friedman is an economist and the son of an economist, Nobel Prize winner Milton Friedman.) *Price Theory: An Intermediate Text* (Cincinnati, Ohio: South-Western Publishing Co., 1986), 280.

the podiatrist later. The relevant question she must ask herself is, What *will* I give up by wearing the uncomfortable shoes? and not, What *did* I give up by buying the shoes? The message here is that only the future can be affected by a present decision, never the past. Bygones are bygones, sunk costs are sunk costs.

PRODUCTION AND COSTS IN THE SHORT RUN

Production Function

Expresses the relationship between different combinations of inputs and the maximum output that each combination produces.

Fixed Input

An input whose quantity cannot be changed as output changes in the short run.

Variable Input

An input whose quantity can be changed as output changes in the short run.

Fixed Costs

Costs that do not vary with output.

Variable Costs

Costs that vary with output.

162

Production involves costs and takes time to complete. In other words, there is a link between production, costs, and time. In this section, we discuss production and costs in the short run. In the next, we discuss production and costs in the long run.

The Production Function

We start with a **production function.** This expresses the relationship between different combinations of inputs and the maximum output that each combination produces. For example, we might say that if we combine 4 units of labor and 5 hours of a capital good (a particular machine, say), we will produce a maximum of 15 units of good X over some period of time. With a different combination of the two inputs, say, 2 units of labor and 5 machine hours, we will produce a maximum of 8 units of good X.

Two Time Periods, Two Types of Inputs, Three Types of Costs

The production of a good requires inputs; essentially there are two types: **fixed inputs** and **variable inputs.** A fixed input is an input whose quantity cannot be changed as output changes in the short run. A variable input is an input whose quantity can be changed as output changes in the short run. The following example illustrates a fixed input.

The McMahon and McGee Typewriter Company has rented a factory for which it has a six-month lease. In short, McMahon and McGee have contracted to pay the $2,300 monthly rent for six months—no matter what. This means whether McMahon and McGee produce 1 typewriter or 7,000 typewriters, the $2,300 rent on the factory must still be paid. The factory is an input in the production process of typewriters; specifically it is a fixed input.

Costs are associated with a fixed input. These are **fixed costs.** A fixed cost is a cost that does not change as output changes. The $2,300 rent for the factory is a fixed cost; it does not change with the number of typewriters McMahon and McGee produce. Whether they produce 0, 1, or 7,000, the rent is still the same. Such things as payments for fire insurance, payments for liability insurance, and the rental payments for a factory and machinery are usually considered fixed costs. They are independent of the level of output produced.

Examples of variable inputs for the McMahon and McGee Typewriter Company include typewriter ribbons, typewriter rollers, and plastic keys for the typewriter keyboards. These inputs can and (most likely) will change as the production of typewriters changes. As more typewriters are produced, more of these inputs will be purchased by McMahon and McGee; as fewer typewriters are produced, fewer of these inputs will be purchased. Labor might also be a variable input for McMahon and McGee. As they produce more typewriters, they might hire more employees; as they produce fewer typewriters, they might lay off some employees. Costs are associated with variable inputs. These costs are **variable costs.** A variable cost is a cost that changes as output changes.

Total Cost

The sum of fixed and variable costs.

Short Run

A period of time in which some inputs are fixed.

Long Run

A period of time in which all inputs can be varied (no inputs are fixed).

Average Fixed Cost

Fixed cost divided by quantity of output (output level): $AFC = FC/Q$.

Average Variable Cost

Variable cost divided by quantity of output: $AVC = VC/Q$.

Average Total Cost (Unit Cost)

Total cost divided by quantity of output: $ATC = TC/Q$.

Marginal Cost

The change in total cost that results from a change in output:
$MC = \Delta TC/\Delta Q = \Delta VC/\Delta Q$.

If we add fixed costs to variable costs, we have **total cost.** Total cost is the sum of fixed and variable costs.

We now turn to the two time periods in which production takes place: the **short run** and the **long run.** The short run is a period of time in which some inputs are fixed. This implies that any changes in output can only be brought about by a change in the quantity of variable inputs. The long run is a period of time in which all inputs can be varied (no inputs are fixed). See Exhibit 8-1 for a review of these points.

From Fixed, Variable, and Total Costs to Average and Marginal Costs

Fixed, variable, and total costs can all be turned into average magnitudes by dividing each by the firm's output. For instance, if fixed cost (FC) is $10,000, and quantity is 100 units, **average fixed cost** (AFC) is $1,000 (FC/Q = $10,000/100 = $100; "Q" stands for "quantity" or "quantity of output"). Maintaining quantity at 100 units, if variable cost (VC) is $40,000, **average variable cost** (AVC) is $400 (VC/Q = $40,000/100 = $400). And if total cost (TC) is $50,000, **average total cost** (ATC) or **unit cost** is $500 (TC/Q = $50,000/100 = $500).

Marginal cost (MC), an extremely important cost in economics, is *the change in total cost that results from a change in output.* Alternatively, we could say that marginal cost is the change in *variable cost* that results from a change in output. Since TC = FC + VC, and FC does not change as output changes, it follows that any change in VC will equal the change in TC. In our equation, for example, if VC rises by $10, then TC rises by $10, too.

Suppose the firm, having produced 100 units of good X at a total cost of $50,000, produces the 101st unit (an additional unit) and total cost rises to $55,000. This means marginal cost is $5,000. Simply put, it is the additional cost of producing an additional unit of output.

$$MC = \frac{\Delta TC}{\Delta Q} = \frac{\Delta VC}{\Delta Q}$$

See Exhibit 8-2 for a summary of the preceding points.

■ **EXHIBIT 8-1**

Time Periods, Inputs, and Costs

In the short run, there are both fixed and variable inputs and fixed and variable costs. In the long run, all inputs are variable and therefore the only costs are variable costs.

TIME PERIOD	INPUTS USED	COSTS ASSOCIATED WITH INPUTS	DEFINITION OF COSTS
Short run	Fixed	Fixed Costs	Costs that do not change as output changes. If there are 2 fixed inputs, A and B, then fixed costs equal $P_A Q_A + P_B Q_B$ where P_A = price of input A, P_B = price of input B, Q_A = quantity of input A, Q_B = quantity of input B.
	Variable	Variable Costs	Costs that change as output changes. If there are three variable inputs, X, Y, and Z, then variable costs equal $P_X Q_X + P_Y Q_Y + P_Z Q_Z$ where P_X = price of input X, Q_X = quantity of input X, and so on.
Long run	Variable	Variable Costs	Costs that change as output changes.

DEFINITION OF COST CONCEPT	SYMBOLS
Average fixed cost = Fixed cost ÷ Quantity of output	$AFC = FC/Q$
Average variable cost = Variable cost ÷ Quantity of output	$AVC = VC/Q$
Average total cost = Total cost ÷ Quantity of output	$ATC = TC/Q$
or	or
Average fixed cost + Average variable cost	$ATC = AFC + AVC$
Marginal cost = Change in Total cost ÷ Change in Quanitity of output	$MC = \Delta TC/\Delta Q$
or	or
Change in Variable cost ÷ Change in Quantity of output	$MC = \Delta VC/\Delta Q$

Question:

Once again, how can MC = ΔTC/ΔQ, and MC = ΔVC/ΔQ, when TC is not equal to VC?

Answer:

Total cost (*TC*) need not equal variable cost (*VC*), as long as the *change in total cost equals the change in variable cost.* For example, suppose *TC* = $100, and *VC* = $50. Now suppose *VC* rises to $80. This is a $30 change in variable cost. But it is also a $30 change in total cost since total cost equals variable cost plus fixed cost. In other words, when fixed cost is constant, a change in variable cost will be equal to the change in total cost. Consequently we can define marginal cost in either of these two ways.

From Definitions to Cost Curves

At this point, you know the definitions of fixed cost, variable cost, total cost, average fixed cost, average variable cost, average total cost, and marginal cost. See Exhibit 8-2 for a review. What does the cost curve for each of these cost concepts look like? We are about to lay the groundwork for this by (1) discussing the law of diminishing marginal returns to find out what the marginal cost curve looks like; and (2) discussing the average-marginal rule to find out what the average total cost and average variable cost curves look like in relation to the marginal cost curve.

The Law of Diminishing Marginal Returns

True or false: No matter how much fertilizer you use, you can't grow the world's supply of corn in a flowerpot. If you answered true, and it wasn't a guess, it should be easy for you to understand the (short-run) **law of diminishing marginal returns.**

In the nineteenth century, the English economist David Ricardo noted that agricultural land was essentially fixed in supply. He believed that as more and more variable inputs, such as labor and capital, were added to a fixed input, such as land, the variable inputs would yield smaller and smaller additions to output. Ricardo's theory came to be known as the law of diminishing marginal returns.

Law of Diminishing Marginal Returns
As ever larger amounts of a variable input are combined with fixed inputs, eventually the marginal physical product of the variable input will decline.

164

Specifically, the law states that *as ever larger amounts of a variable input are combined with fixed inputs, eventually the marginal physical product of the variable input will decline.*

To illustrate, consider the production of a good that requires two inputs. One input is labor, the other is capital. The capital input is fixed; the labor input is variable. (Note that we must be dealing in the *short run*, because the short run is the period of time in which some inputs are fixed.) We add more and more units of the variable input, labor, to the fixed input, capital. As we do this, output increases. This is illustrated in columns 1–3 in Exhibit 8-3.

We are interested next in *how much additional output is produced for each additional unit of variable input employed.* To put it differently, we are interested in the **marginal physical product** of the variable input, labor. The marginal physical product of a variable input is equal to the change in output that results from changing the variable input by one unit, holding all other inputs fixed.

For example, the marginal physical product of labor is equal to the change in output that results from changing labor by one unit ($MPP = \Delta Q/\Delta L$). This is calculated in column 4 of Exhibit 8-3. Notice that in column 4 the marginal physical product of labor first rises and then falls. The numbers go from 18 to 19 to 20, and then from 20 to 19 to 18 to 17 to 16. The point at which the marginal physical product of labor declines is the point at which diminishing marginal returns are said to have "set in."

Does the law of diminishing marginal returns make sense? Ask yourself what the world would look like *if the law of diminishing returns did not hold*. If the "law" *did not* hold, then it would be possible to continue to add additional units of a

Marginal Physical Product

The change in output that results from changing the variable input by one unit, holding all other inputs fixed.

■ **EXHIBIT 8-3**
The Law of Diminishing Marginal Returns

In the short run, as additional units of a variable input are added to a fixed input, the marginal physical product of the variable input increases at first, and marginal cost decreases. Eventually the marginal physical product of the variable input decreases, and marginal cost increases. The point at which marginal physical product decreases, or marginal cost rises, is the point at which diminishing marginal returns have set in.

(1) VARIABLE INPUT, LABOR (WORKERS)	(2) FIXED INPUT, CAPITAL (UNITS)	(3) QUANTITY OF OUTPUT (UNITS)	(4) MARGINAL PHYSICAL PRODUCT OF VARIABLE INPUT (UNITS) $\Delta(3) \div \Delta(1)$	(5) FIXED COST (DOLLARS)	(6) VARIABLE COST (DOLLARS)	(7) TOTAL COST (DOLLARS) (5) + (6)	(8) MARGINAL COST (DOLLARS) $\Delta(7) \div \Delta(3)$ or $\Delta(6) \div \Delta(3)$
0	1	0		$40	$ 0	$ 40	
			18				$1.11
1	1	18		40	20	60	
			19				$1.05
2	1	37		40	40	80	
			20				$1.00
3	1	57		40	60	100	
			19				$1.05
4	1	76		40	80	120	
			18				$1.11
5	1	94		40	100	140	
			17				$1.17
6	1	111		40	120	160	
			16				$1.25
7	1	127		40	140	180	

variable input to a fixed input, and the marginal physical product of the variable input would never decline. Thus we could increase output indefinitely as long as we continued to add units of a variable input to a fixed input.

A firm produces television sets with two inputs, labor (the variable input) and a machine (the fixed input). If the law of diminishing marginal returns does not hold, it would be possible to add more laborers continually to the machine and produce ever more television sets. The logical implication of this would be that the world's supply of television sets could be produced by one firm operating one machine in one location. In agriculture, it would be possible to grow the world's supply of corn in a flowerpot.

We do not see the world's supply of television sets being produced by one firm using one machine in one location. Nor do we see the world's corn supply being grown in a flowerpot. Why? The law of diminishing marginal returns says that as more units of the variable input are hired, *each one has fewer units of the fixed input to work with*; consequently, output eventually rises at a *decreasing rate*.

The Law of Diminishing Marginal Returns and Marginal Cost

Marginal cost is a reflection of the marginal physical product of the variable input. We can see this arithmetically in Exhibit 8-3. Column 5 lists the fixed cost associated with the fixed input. Column 6 lists the variable cost associated with the variable input. We obtained the dollar figures in this column by first noting that each worker costs $20 per day and then multiplying this cost times the number of workers. Adding fixed cost and variable cost, we get total cost in column 7. Finally, we calculate marginal cost in column 8.

Notice that marginal cost first falls and then rises. Furthermore, notice the important relationship between marginal cost and the marginal physical product of labor: *As the marginal physical product of labor increases, marginal cost decreases; and as the marginal physical product of labor decreases, marginal cost increases.* This relationship can be seen in Exhibit 8-4 by comparing (a) and (b).

We see that as the marginal physical product curve is rising, the marginal cost curve is falling; and as the marginal physical product curve is falling, the marginal cost curve is rising. This is common sense: As marginal physical product rises, or to put it differently, as the productivity of the variable input rises, we would expect costs to decline. And as the productivity of the variable input declines, we would expect costs to rise.

In general, what does the marginal cost curve look like? It depends on what the marginal physical product curve looks like (which, we remind ourselves, must have a declining portion to it because of the law of diminishing marginal returns). If the marginal physical product curve has first a rising portion and then a falling portion, it follows that the marginal cost curve will have first a falling portion and then a rising portion.

An easy way to see that MPP and MC move in opposite directions is to define marginal cost as equal to the additional cost of hiring an additional unit of the variable input divided by its marginal physical product. In our example in Exhibit 8-3 using the variable input, labor, this turns out to be **$MC = W/MPP$,** where MC = marginal cost, W = wage, and MPP = marginal physical product. The following table, which reproduces columns 4 and 8 from Exhibit 8-3, and notes the wage, shows what we mean.

EXHIBIT 8-4
Marginal Physical Product and Marginal Cost

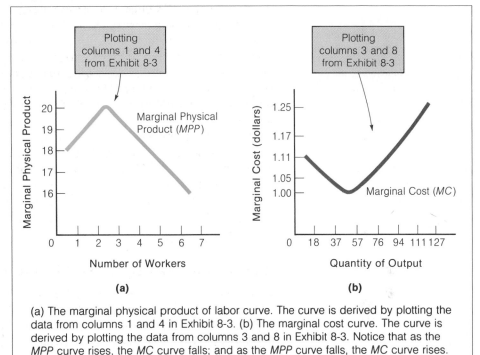

(a) The marginal physical product of labor curve. The curve is derived by plotting the data from columns 1 and 4 in Exhibit 8-3. (b) The marginal cost curve. The curve is derived by plotting the data from columns 3 and 8 in Exhibit 8-3. Notice that as the *MPP* curve rises, the *MC* curve falls; and as the *MPP* curve falls, the *MC* curve rises.

MPP	VARIABLE COST (W)	MC = W/MPP
18 units	$20	$20/18 = $1.11
19	20	20/19 = 1.05
20	20	20/20 = 1.00
19	20	20/19 = 1.05
18	20	20/18 = 1.11
17	20	20/17 = 1.17
16	20	20/16 = 1.25

As you can see by comparing the marginal cost figures in the last column in the table with the marginal cost figures in column 8 in Exhibit 8-3, whether we define MC as equal to $\Delta TC/\Delta Q$ $(= \frac{\Delta VC}{\Delta Q})$ or as equal to W/MPP, we get the same results. The latter way of defining marginal cost, however, *explicitly* shows that as *MPP* rises, *MC* falls, and as *MPP* falls, *MC* rises.

$$\downarrow MC = \frac{W}{MPP \uparrow}$$

$$\uparrow MC = \frac{W}{MPP \downarrow}$$

The Average-Marginal Rule

What do the average total and average variable cost curves look like in relation to the marginal cost curve? To explain, we need to discuss the **average-marginal rule,** which is best illustrated by an example.

Suppose there are 20 persons in a room and each person weighs 170 pounds. Your task is to calculate the average weight. This is accomplished by summing the individual weights and dividing by 20. Obviously this average weight will be 170 pounds. Now let an additional person enter the room. We shall refer to this *additional* person as the *marginal* person and the *additional* weight he brings to the room as the *marginal* weight.

Let the weight of the marginal person be 275 pounds. If we were to calculate a new average weight based on 21 persons instead of 20, it would be 175 pounds. The new average weight is greater than the old average weight. It was pulled up by the weight of the last person. In short, *when the marginal magnitude is above the average magnitude, the average magnitude rises*. This is one part of the average-marginal rule.

Suppose, however, that the weight of the marginal person had been less than the average weight of 170 pounds, for example, 65 pounds. Then the new average would have been 165 pounds. It was pulled down by the weight of the last person. Thus, *when the marginal magnitude is below the average magnitude, the average magnitude falls*. This is the other part of the average-marginal rule.

Now suppose we apply the average-marginal rule to find out what the average total and average variable cost curves look like in relation to the marginal cost curve. The following analysis holds for both the average total cost curve and the average variable cost curve, although we speak only in terms of the latter.

We reason that if marginal cost is below (less than) average variable cost, average variable cost is falling; and if marginal cost is above (greater than) average variable cost, average variable cost is rising. This reasoning implies that the relationship between the average variable cost curve and the marginal cost curve must look like that in Exhibit 8-5a. In Region 1 of (a) marginal cost is below average variable cost and, consistent with the average-marginal rule, average variable cost is falling. In Region 2 of (a) marginal cost is above average variable cost, and average variable cost is rising. In short, the relationship between the average variable cost curve and the marginal cost curve in Exhibit 8-5a is consistent with the average-marginal rule.

Additionally, since average variable cost is being pulled down when marginal cost is below it, and is being pulled up when marginal cost is above it, it follows that the marginal cost curve *must* intersect the average variable cost curve at the latter's lowest point. This lowest point is labeled "L" in Exhibit 8-5a.

In Exhibit 8-5c there are three average cost curves and a marginal cost curve. We now know that (1) the marginal cost curve has the shape it has because of the marginal physical product curve and the law of diminishing marginal returns; and (2) when the marginal cost curve is below the average variable and average total cost curves, the two curves are falling; when the marginal cost curve is above the average variable and average total cost curves, the two curves are rising.

But what about the average fixed cost curve? Is there any relationship between it and the marginal cost curve? The answer is no. We indirectly see why by recalling that average fixed cost is simply fixed cost (which is constant over output) divided by output ($AFC = FC/Q$). As output (Q) increases and fixed cost (FC) remains constant, it follows that average fixed cost (FC/Q) must decrease continuously. See Exhibit 8-5c.

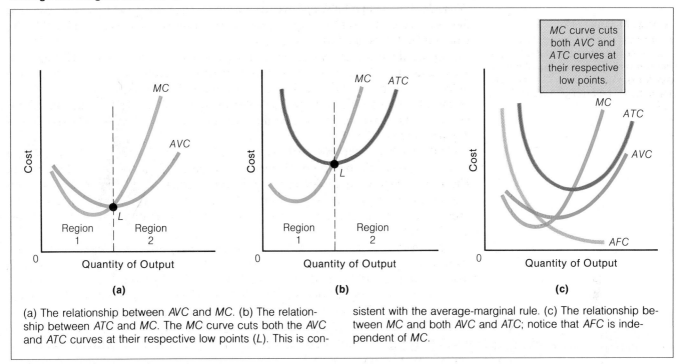

MC curve cuts both AVC and ATC curves at their respective low points.

(a) The relationship between *AVC* and *MC*. (b) The relationship between *ATC* and *MC*. The *MC* curve cuts both the *AVC* and *ATC* curves at their respective low points (*L*). This is consistent with the average-marginal rule. (c) The relationship between *MC* and both *AVC* and *ATC*; notice that *AFC* is independent of *MC*.

PRODUCTION AND COSTS IN THE LONG RUN

In this section we discuss production and long-run costs. As we noted previously, in the long run there are no fixed inputs and no fixed costs. Consequently the firm has greater flexibility in the long run than in the short run.

Long-Run Average Total Cost Curve

In the long run, variable costs *are* total costs. The reason is simple: In the short run, there are fixed costs and variable costs; therefore total cost is the sum of the two. But in the long run there are no fixed costs, so variable costs are total costs.

Here we focus on (1) what the long-run average total cost (*LRATC*) curve is and (2) what it looks like.

Consider the manager of a firm that produces bedroom furniture. When all inputs are variable, the manager must decide what situation he wants to be in in the (upcoming) short-run period. For example, when it comes to plant size, he must decide whether the plant will be small, medium-sized, or large. Once this decision is made, he is locked in to a specific plant size; he is locked in for the short run.

Suppose the manager must choose from among three different plant sizes. Associated with each size is a short-run average total cost (*SRATC*) curve. (Since here we discuss both short-run and long-run average total cost curves, we distinguish between the two with prefixes: *SR* for short run and *LR* for long run. In the previous section it was not necessary to add the prefix "*SR*" for short run, since short-run costs were the only costs we were discussing.) The three short-run average total cost curves, representing the different plant sizes, are illustrated in Exhibit 8-6a.

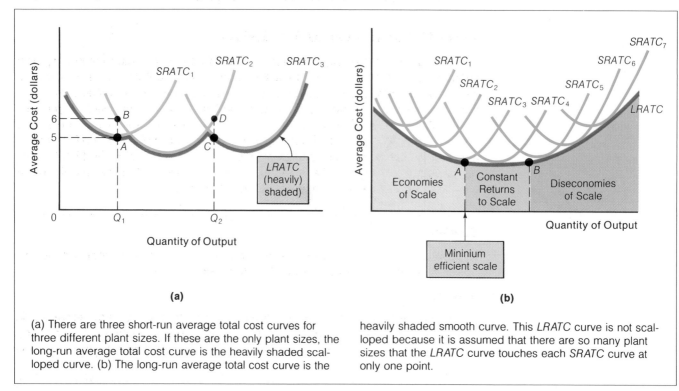

(a) There are three short-run average total cost curves for three different plant sizes. If these are the only plant sizes, the long-run average total cost curve is the heavily shaded scalloped curve. (b) The long-run average total cost curve is the heavily shaded smooth curve. This *LRATC* curve is not scalloped because it is assumed that there are so many plant sizes that the *LRATC* curve touches each *SRATC* curve at only one point.

Long-Run Average Total Cost Curve

A curve that shows the lowest (unit) cost at which the firm can produce any given level of output.

Suppose the manager of the firm wants to produce output level Q_1. Which plant size will he choose? Obviously the plant size represented by $SRATC_1$, since this gives him a lower unit cost of producing Q_1 than the plant size represented by $SRATC_2$. The latter plant size comes with a higher unit cost of producing Q_1 ($6 as opposed to $5).

Suppose, though, the manager chooses to produce Q_2. Which plant size will he choose now? He will choose the plant size represented by $SRATC_3$, because the unit cost of producing Q_2 is lower with the plant size represented by $SRATC_3$ than it is with the plant size represented by $SRATC_2$.

If we were to ask the same question for every (possible) output level, we would derive the **long-run average total cost curve.** The long-run average total cost curve shows the lowest unit cost at which the firm can produce any given level of output. In Exhibit 8-6a it is the heavily shaded portion of the three short-run average total cost curves.

In Exhibit 8-6b we also have a host of short-run average total cost curves and a long-run average total cost curve. In this case you will notice that the heavily shaded long-run average total cost curve is not scalloped, as it was in (a), but instead is smooth. The reason is that in (b) we assume there are many plant sizes in addition to the three represented in (a). In other words, although they have not been drawn, in (b) there exist short-run average total cost curves representing different plant sizes between $SRATC_1$ and $SRATC_2$ and between $SRATC_2$ and $SRATC_3$ and so on. In this case, the long-run average total cost curve would be smooth and would only touch each short-run average total cost curve at one point.[3]

The *LRATC* Curve Separates Two Regions

It is easy to think of the long-run average total cost curve as separating two regions: an attainable region and an unattainable region, as in Exhibit 8-7. For example, if the firm wants to produce Q_1, the lowest attainable cost level is ATC_1 (any cost level lower is unattainable); thus A_1 is on the *LRATC* curve. If the firm wants to produce Q_2, the lowest attainable cost level is ATC_2; thus A_2 is on the *LRATC* curve, too. We see, then, that any cost level (any unit cost) on or above the *LRATC* curve is attainable, whereas any cost level below the curve is unattainable. The *LRATC* curve separates the two regions; the curve itself thereby represents the lowest unit cost at which the firm can produce any given level of output.

Question:

If a firm currently producing Q_1 in Exhibit 8-7 desires to increase production to Q_2, would it be able to produce Q_2 at ATC_2 in the short run?

Answer:

No, it wouldn't. In the short run the firm can't vary all inputs, and therefore would have to accept unit costs higher than ATC_2; perhaps ATC_3 in Exhibit 8-7. In the long run, though, a plant optimal for the production of Q_2 can be built, and ATC_2 can be achieved.

---

[3]Sometimes the long-run average total cost curve is referred to as the *envelope* of all the short-run average total cost curves. In mathematics, a curve that just touches all of a number of curves is known as the *envelope* of the curves.

■ **EXHIBIT 8-7**
The *LRATC* Curve Separates the Attainable from the Unattainable

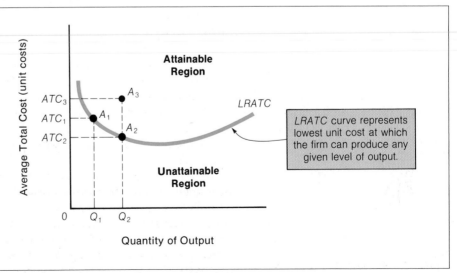

If the firm wants to produce Q_1, the lowest (unit) cost level is ATC_1; any lower cost level is unattainable. If the firm wants to produce Q_2, the lowest cost level is ATC_2; any lower cost level is unattainable. The *LRATC* curve separates the unattainable cost levels from the attainable.

LRATC curve represents lowest unit cost at which the firm can produce any given level of output.

Economies of Scale, Diseconomies of Scale, and Constant Returns to Scale

Economies of Scale

Exist when inputs are increased by some percentage and output increases by a greater percentage, causing unit costs to fall.

Constant Returns to Scale

Exist when inputs are increased by some percentage and output increases by an equal percentage, causing unit costs to remain constant.

Diseconomies of Scale

Exist when inputs are increased by some percentage and output increases by a smaller percentage, causing unit costs to rise.

Minimum Efficient Scale

The lowest output level at which average total costs are minimized.

Suppose two inputs, labor and capital, are used together to produce a particular good. If inputs are increased by some percentage (say, 100 percent), and output increases by a greater percentage (say, more than 100 percent), unit costs fall, and **economies of scale** are said to exist.

If inputs are increased by some percentage and output increases by an equal percentage, unit costs remain constant, and **constant returns to scale** are said to exist.

If inputs are increased by some percentage and output increases by a smaller percentage, unit costs rise, and **diseconomies of scale** are said to exist.

Here is an arithmetical example that illustrates economies of scale. Good X is made with two inputs, Y and Z, and it takes 20Y and 10Z to produce 5 units of X. The cost of each unit of input Y and Z is $1. Thus a total cost of $30 is required to produce 5 units of X; the unit cost (average total cost) of good X is $6 ($ATC = TC/Q$).

Now consider a doubling of inputs Y and Z to 40Y and 20Z, and a more than doubling in output, say, to 15 units. This means a total cost of $60 is required to produce 15 units of X, and the unit cost (average total cost) of good X is $4.

If, in the production of a good, economies of scale give way to constant returns to scale or diseconomies of scale, as in Exhibit 8-6b, the point at which this occurs is referred to as the **minimum efficient scale.** The minimum efficient scale is the lowest output level at which average total costs are minimized. Point A represents the minimum efficient scale in Exhibit 8-6b.

Question:

Is there any special significance to the minimum efficient scale of output?

Answer:

Yes, there is. If we look at the long-run average total cost curve in Exhibit 23-6b, we see that between points A and B there are constant returns to scale; the average total cost is the same over the various output levels between the two points. This means that larger firms (firms producing greater output levels) within this range do not have a cost advantage over smaller firms that operate at the minimum efficient scale.

Question:

Are economies of scale, diseconomies of scale, and constant returns to scale relevant to the short run, the long run, or both?

Answer:

They are only relevant to the long run. Implicit in the definition of the terms, and explicit in the arithmetical example of economies of scale, all inputs necessary to the production of a good are changeable. Since no input is fixed, economies of scale, diseconomies of scale, and constant returns to scale must be relevant only to the long run.

Additionally, the three conditions can be easily seen in the *LRATC* curve. If economies of scale are present, the *LRATC* curve is falling; if constant returns to scale are present, the curve is flat, and if diseconomies of scale are present, the curve is rising (see Exhibit 8-6b).

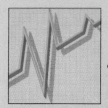

Theory in Practice

Minimum Efficient Scale and Number of Firms in an Industry

Some industries are composed of a smaller number of firms than other industries. Or, we can say there is a different degree of concentration in different industries.

The table lists the *minimum efficient scale (MES)* for six industries as a percentage of U.S. consumption or total sales for that industry. Notice that firms in some industries continue to experience economies of scale up to output levels that are a higher percentage of industry sales than firms in other industries. For example, cigarette firms reach the minimum efficient scale of plant, and thus exhaust economies of scale, at an output level of 6.6 percent of total industry sales. On the other hand, petroleum refining firms experience economies of scale only up to an output level of 1.9 percent of total industry sales. Consequently, we would expect to find fewer firms in the cigarette industry than in the petroleum refining industry. Specifically, by dividing the *MES* as a percentage of U.S. consumption into 100, we can estimate the number of efficient firms it takes to satisfy U.S. consumption for a particular product. For cigarettes, it takes 15 firms (100/6.6 = 15). For petroleum refining, it takes 52 firms.

INDUSTRY	MES AS A PERCENTAGE OF U.S. CONSUMPTION
Refrigerators	14.1%
Cigarettes	6.6
Beer brewing	3.4
Petroleum refining	1.9
Paints	1.4
Shoes	0.2

SOURCE: F. M. Scherer, Alan Beckenstein, Erich Kaufer, and R. D. Murphy, *The Economics of Multiplant Operation* (Cambridge, Mass.: Harvard University Press, 1975), p. 80.

We must not confuse *diminishing (marginal) returns* with *diseconomies of scale.* Diminishing returns are the result of using, say, a given plant size more intensively. Diseconomies of scale result from changes in the size of the plant.

Why Economies of Scale?

Up to a certain point, long-run unit costs of production fall as a firm grows. There are two main reasons for this: (1) In growing firms there are greater opportunities for employees to specialize. Individual workers can become highly proficient at more narrowly defined tasks, often producing more output at lower unit costs. (2) Growing firms (especially large, growing firms) can take advantage of highly productive mass production techniques and equipment that ordinarily require large setup costs and thus are only economical if they can be spread over a large number of units. For example, assembly line techniques are usually "cheap" when millions of units of a good are produced, and are "expensive" when only a few thousand units are produced.

Why Diseconomies of Scale?

Diseconomies of scale usually arise at the point at which a firm's size produces coordination, communication, and monitoring problems. In very large firms managers often find it difficult to coordinate work activities, communicate their directives to the right persons in satisfactory time, and monitor personnel effectively. The business operation simply gets "too big." There is, of course, a monetary incentive not to pass the point of operation where diseconomies of scale exist. Firms will usually find ways to avoid diseconomies of scale. They will reorganize, divide operations, hire new managers, and so on.

SHIFTS IN COST CURVES

In discussing the shape of short-run and long-run cost curves, we assumed that certain factors remained constant. We discuss a few of these factors here and illustrate how changes in them can shift cost curves.

Taxes

Consider a tax on each unit of a good produced. Suppose Company X has to pay $3 for each unit of X it produces. What effects will this have on the firm's cost curves? First, will the tax affect the firm's fixed costs? No, it won't. The reason is that the tax is paid only when output is produced, and fixed costs are present even if output is zero. (Note that if the tax had been a lump-sum tax, requiring the company to pay a "lump sum" no matter how many units of goods it produced, this would have affected fixed costs.) We conclude that the tax does not affect fixed costs and therefore cannot affect average fixed cost.

Will the tax affect variable cost? Yes, it will. As a consequence of the tax, the firm has to pay out more for each unit of the good it produces. Variable costs rise along with total cost. This means that average variable cost and average total cost rise, and the representative cost curves shift upward. Finally, since marginal cost is the change in total cost (or variable cost) divided by the change in output, marginal cost rises and the marginal cost curve shifts upward.

The shifts in the average total and marginal cost curves due to a tax on each unit of output are shown in Exhibit 8-8.

■ **EXHIBIT 8-8**
Shifts in Cost Curves Due to a Tax

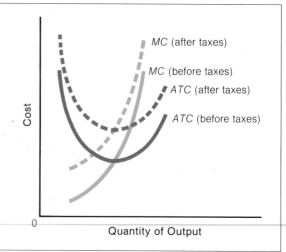

A tax on each unit of output produced increases variable cost, average variable cost, total cost, average total cost, and marginal cost (since variable cost and total cost have increased, and marginal cost is the change in either divided by the change in quantity of output). Only shifts in *ATC* and *MC* are shown here.

Input Prices

A rise or fall in input prices brings about a corresponding change in the firm's average total, variable, and marginal cost curves. For example, if the price of steel rises, the variable costs of building skyscrapers rise, and so must the average variable cost, the average total cost, and the marginal cost. The cost curves shift upward. If the price of steel falls, we get the opposite effects.

Technology

Technological changes often bring either (1) the capability of using fewer inputs to produce a good (for example, the introduction of the personal computer reduced the hours necessary to type and edit a manuscript) or (2) lower input prices (for example, technological improvements in the area of transistors have led to price reductions in the transistor components of calculators). In either case, technological changes of this variety lower variable costs, and consequently lower average variable cost, average total cost, and marginal cost.

■ CHAPTER SUMMARY

Explicit and Implicit Cost

■ An explicit cost is incurred when an actual (monetary) payment is made. An implicit cost represents the value of resources used in production for which no actual (monetary) payment is made.

Economic and Accounting Profit

■ Economic profit is the difference between total revenue and total opportunity cost, including both its explicit and implicit components. Accounting profit is the difference between total revenue and explicit costs. Economic profit is usually lower (never higher) than accounting profit. Economic profit (not accounting profit) motivates economic behavior.

Sunk Cost

■ Sunk cost is a cost incurred in the past; it is a cost that cannot be changed by current decisions. A person or firm that wants to minimize losses will hold sunk costs to be irrelevant to present decisions. For example, Janet buys good X for $10 on Monday with the idea of reselling it at a higher price in the near future. A week passes and the price of good X falls to $6. Some people argue that Janet should not sell good X because she will incur a loss. According to their argument, Janet should look over her shoulder, note the higher price she paid for the good, and let this fact influence her present decision. But bygones are bygones. Janet needs to ask herself: Do I expect the price of good X to go up or down? If the answer is down, then it is better to sell today at $6 than to sell tomorrow at an even lower price. If the answer is up, then Janet may want to sell later.

Production and Costs in the Short Run

■ The short run is a period of time in which some inputs are fixed. The long run is a period of time in which all inputs can be varied. The costs associated with fixed and variable inputs are referred to as fixed costs and variable costs, respectively.

■ Marginal cost is the change in total cost (or variable cost) that results from a change in output. It is an extremely important cost concept in economics.

The law of diminishing marginal returns states that as ever larger amounts of a variable input are combined with fixed inputs, eventually the marginal physical product of the variable input will decline. As this happens, marginal cost rises.

■ The average-marginal rule states that if the marginal magnitude is above (below) the average magnitude, the average magnitude rises (falls).

■ The marginal cost curve intersects the average variable cost curve at its lowest point. The marginal cost curve intersects the average total cost curve at its lowest point. There is no relationship between marginal cost and average fixed cost.

Production and Costs in the Long Run

■ In the long run, there are no fixed costs so variable costs equal total costs.

■ The long-run average total cost curve is the envelope of the short-run average total cost curves. It shows the lowest unit cost at which the firm can produce any given level of output.

■ If inputs are increased by some percentage and output increases by a greater percentage, unit costs fall, and economies of scale exist. If inputs are increased by some percentage and output increases by an equal percentage, unit costs remain constant, and constant returns to scale exist. If inputs are increased by some percentage and output increases by a smaller percentage, units costs rise, and diseconomies of scale exist.

■ The minimum efficient scale is the lowest output level at which average total costs are minimized.

■ QUESTIONS TO ANSWER AND DISCUSS

1. Illustrate the average-marginal rule in a noncost setting.

2. "People who earn big salaries are less likely to go into business for themselves than people who earn small salaries because their implicit costs are higher." Do you agree or disagree? Explain your answer.

3. A quick glance at Exhibit 8-5c shows that the average variable cost curve and the average total cost curve get closer to each other as output increases. What explains this?

4. When would total costs equal fixed costs?

5. Is studying for an economics exam subject to the law of diminishing marginal returns? If so, what is the fixed input? What is the variable input?

6. Some individuals decry the decline of the small family farm and its replacement with the huge corporate megafarm. Discuss the possibility that this is a consequence of economies of scale.

7. We know that there is a link between productivity and costs. For example, recall the link between the marginal physical product of the variable input and marginal cost. With this in mind, what link might there be between productivity and prices?

8. Some people's everyday behavior suggests that they do not hold sunk costs irrelevant to present decisions. Give some examples.

9. Explain why a firm might want to produce its good even after diminishing marginal returns have set in and marginal cost is on the rise. (Hint: Wouldn't a firm want to produce more if "what was coming in" was greater than "what was going out"—even if "what was going out" was on the rise?)

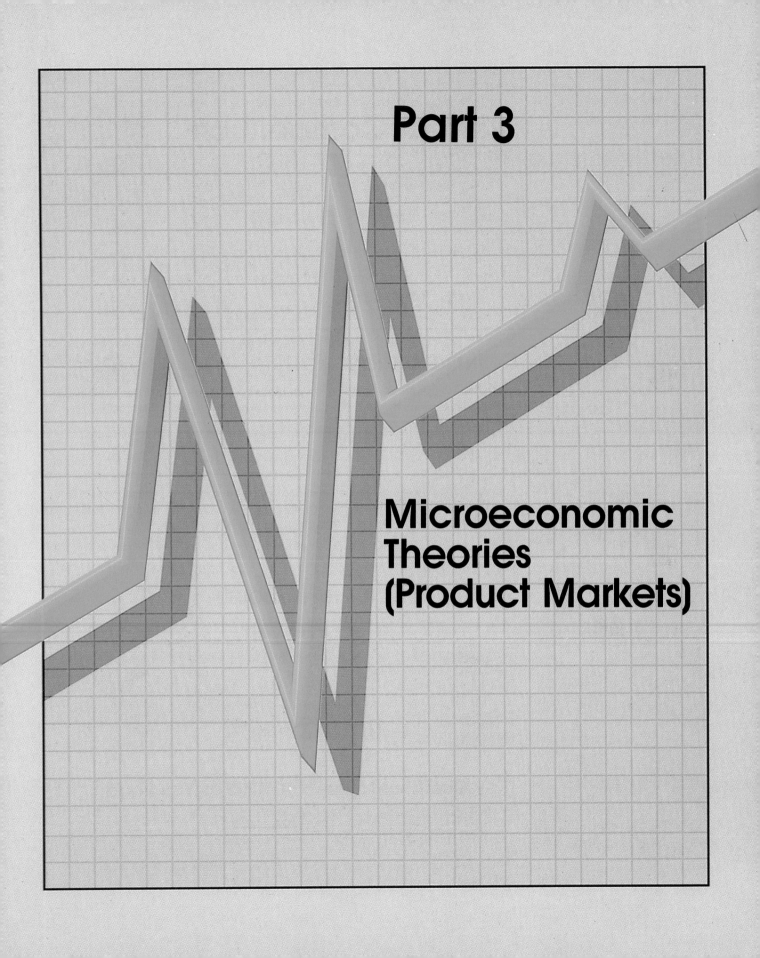

Part 3

Microeconomic Theories (Product Markets)

Chapter 9

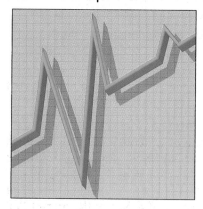

Perfect Competition

■ INTRODUCTION

All those things are realistic, but they are part of a theory that doesn't tell us any-thing that is seriously interesting, different, or more insightful than the abstract theory of perfect competition.[1]

—George Stigler
Winner of the 1982 Nobel Prize in Economics

In the competition between economic models, the theory of perfect competition holds a dominant market share: no set of ideas is so widely and successfully used by economists as is the logic of perfectly competitive markets.[2]

—John Roberts

■ WHAT THIS CHAPTER IS ABOUT

The farmer in Iowa and the Ford Motor Company find themselves in different *market structures*. The term *market structure* refers to the particular environment of a firm, the characteristics of which influence the firm's pricing and output decisions. In particular, it refers to the number of firms in an industry, the degree of similarity among the products of different firms, and the ease of entry into and exit from the market. In this and the following two chapters, we discuss four theories of market structures: perfect competition (Chapter 9), monopoly (Chapter 10), and monopo-listic competition and oligopoly (Chapter 11).

Key Questions to Keep in Mind as You Read

1. What are the assumptions of the theory of perfect competition?

2. What is a price taker?

---

[1]This statement is from our interview with Nobel Prize winner George Stigler in this chapter.
[2]John Roberts, "Perfectly and imperfectly competitive markets" in *The New Palgrave: A Dictionary of Economics*, vol. 3 (London: The Macmillan Press, 1987), p. 837.

3. Under what conditions does the firm continue to produce its output in the short run? Under what conditions does the firm shut down in the short run?

4. Why does the firm want to produce the quantity of output at which $MR = MC$?

5. What role do profits and losses play in perfect competition?

6. What conditions characterize long-run competitive equilibrium?

THE THEORY OF PERFECT COMPETITION

Market Structure
The particular environment a firm finds itself in, the characteristics of which influence the firm's pricing and output decisions.

Perfect competition
A theory of market structure based on four assumptions: there are many sellers and buyers, sellers sell a homogeneous good, buyers and sellers have all relevant information, and there is easy entry into and exit from the market.

The theory of **perfect competition,** or the theory of the perfectly competitive **market structure,** is built on four assumptions:

1. **There are many sellers and many buyers, none of which is large in relation to total sales or purchases.** This assumption speaks to both demand (number of buyers) and supply (number of sellers). Since there are many buyers and sellers, it is reasonably assumed that each buyer and each seller acts independently of other buyers and sellers, respectively, and is *so small a part of the market that he or she has no influence on price.*

2. **Each firm produces and sells a homogeneous product.** This means each firm sells a product that is indistinguishable from all other firms' products in a given industry (for example, the buyer of wheat cannot distinguish between Farmer Stone's and Farmer Gray's wheat). As a consequence, buyers are indifferent as to whom they buy the product from.

3. **Buyers and sellers have all relevant information about prices, product quality, sources of supply, and so forth.** Buyers and sellers know who is selling what, at what prices, at what quality, and what terms. In short, they know everything that relates to buying, producing, and selling the product.

4. **There is easy entry and exit.** New firms can enter the market easily and existing firms can exit the market easily. There are no barriers to entry or exit.

Examples of perfect competition include some agricultural markets and a small subset of the retail trade. The stock market, where there are hundreds of thousands of buyers and sellers of stock, is also sometimes cited as an example of perfect competition.

Question:

In the stock market not all buyers and sellers have all relevant information. Some buyers, for example, have inside information. *Doesn't it follow, then, that the stock market is* not *an example of a perfectly competitive market?*

Answer:

It is true that, strictly speaking, the stock market does not meet one of the assumptions of a perfectly competitive market, but the same general point can be made for other "perfectly competitive" markets. For example, surely not all buyers and sellers in the wheat market (a market that is widely said to be perfectly competitive) have *all* relevant information. No doubt some buyers and sellers are better informed than others. Still, the real-world wheat market may behave *as if* it satisfies all the assumptions of the theory of perfect competition. The assumptions of all economic theories or models deviate from reality. Nonetheless, this does not mean the theories are without value. Many economists contend that a theory is best judged by its predictive and explanatory power, not the realism of its assumptions.

Price Taker

A seller that does not have the ability to control the price of the product it sells; it "takes" the price determined in the market.

A perfectly competitive firm is a **price taker.** A price taker is a seller that does not have the ability to control the price of the product it sells; it *takes* the price determined in the market. For example, if Farmer Stone is a price taker, it follows that he can increase or decrease his output without significantly affecting the price of the product he sells.

Why is a perfectly competitive firm a price taker? Specifically, a firm is restrained from being anything but a price taker if it finds itself one among many firms where its supply is small relative to the total market supply (assumption 1 from the previous section), and it sells a homogeneous product (assumption 2) in an environment where buyers and sellers have all relevant information (assumption 3).

Question:

So given the assumptions of the theory of perfect competition, the perfectly competitive firm cannot be anything but a price taker. Is this correct?

Answer:

Yes, that is correct.

Follow-up Question:

If the assumptions of the theory guarantee that the perfectly competitive firm is a price taker, then aren't economists choosing the assumptions necessary to give them what they want?

Answer:

No, they aren't. Economists *do not* start out (1) wanting the perfectly competitive firm to be a price taker, and then (2) choose the assumptions that will make this so. Instead, economists start out (1) with certain assumptions, and then (2) logically conclude that the firm for which these assumptions hold, or behaves *as if* these assumptions hold, is a price taker; that is, it has no control over price. Afterward, economists test the theory by observing whether it accurately predicts and explains the real-world behavior of some firms.

The Demand Curve of the Perfectly Competitive Firm

In the perfectly competitive setting there are many sellers and many buyers. Together all buyers make up the market demand curve; together all sellers make up the market supply curve. An equilibrium price is established at the intersection of the market demand and market supply curves (Exhibit 9-1a). Once the equilibrium price has been established, we ask, What does the demand curve for the output of a single perfectly competitive firm look like? The answer is shown in Exhibit 9-1b; it is horizontal (flat, perfectly elastic) at the equilibrium price. The firm "takes" the equilibrium price as given—hence the firm is a price taker—and sells all quantities of output at this price.[3]

If the perfectly competitive firm were to charge a price higher than the market-established equilibrium price, it wouldn't sell any of its product. This is because the

---

[3]The horizontal demand curve does not mean that the firm can sell an *infinite* amount at the equilibrium price; rather, it means that price will be virtually unaffected by the variations in output that the firm may find it practicable to make.

Market Demand Curve and Firm Demand Curve in Perfect Competition

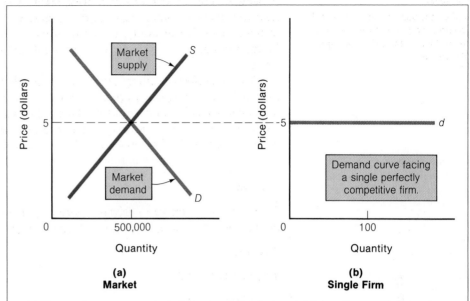

(a) The market, composed of all buyers and sellers, establishes the equilibrium price.
(b) A single perfectly competitive firm then faces the horizontal (flat, perfectly elastic) demand curve. We conclude that the firm is a price taker; it "takes" the equilibrium price established by the market and sells any and all quantities of output at this price. (The large "*D*" represents the market demand curve; the small "*d*" represents the single firm's demand curve.)

firm sells a homogeneous product, its supply is small relative to the total market supply, and all buyers are informed as to where they can obtain the product at the lower price.

And if the firm is attempting to maximize profits, it would not offer to sell its good at a lower price than the equilibrium price. Why should it? It can sell all it wants at the market-established equilibrium price. Therefore, this is the only relevant price for the perfectly competitive firm.

Question:

An earlier chapter said that demand curves are downward sloping. Now it appears that the demand curve for a perfectly competitive firm is not downward sloping, but horizontal. How can this be?

Answer:

The *market demand curve* in Exhibit 9-1a is downward sloping, thus positing an inverse relationship between price and quantity demanded, *ceteris paribus*. The demand curve faced by a *single* perfectly competitive firm does not contradict this relationship; it simply represents the pricing situation in which the single perfectly competitive firm finds itself. Specifically, it says that a single perfectly competitive firm's supply is such a small percentage of the total market supply that the firm cannot perceptibly influence price by changing its quantity of output. To put it differently, the firm's supply is so small compared with the total market supply that the inverse relationship between price and quantity demanded, although present, cannot be observed on the firm's level, although it is observable on the market level.

The Marginal Revenue Curve of the Perfectly Competitive Firm

Consider a simple numerical example. If the equilibrium price is $5, as in Exhibit 9-1, and the perfectly competitive firm sells 100 units of its good, its total revenue is $500 ($5 × 100 = $500). Now suppose the firm sells an additional unit, bringing the total number of units sold up to 101. Its total revenue is now $505 ($5 × 101 = $505).

But what is the firm's **marginal revenue**—the change in total revenue that results from selling one additional unit of output ($MR = \Delta TR/\Delta Q$)? This is $5. Notice that marginal revenue ($5) at any output level is always equal to the equilibrium price ($5). We conclude that for a perfectly competitive firm, price is equal to marginal revenue ($P = MR$). It follows that if price is equal to marginal revenue, the marginal revenue curve for the perfectly competitive firm is the same as its demand curve.

Specifically, a demand curve plots price against quantity, whereas a marginal revenue curve plots marginal revenue against quantity. If price equals marginal revenue, then the demand curve and marginal revenue are the same curve (Exhibit 9-2).

Marginal Revenue
The change in total revenue that results from selling one additional unit of output.

PERFECT COMPETITION IN THE SHORT RUN

We have seen that the perfectly competitive firm is a price taker, that (for it) price is equal to marginal revenue, and therefore the perfectly competitive firm's demand curve is the same as its marginal revenue curve. We turn now to a discussion of how much output the firm will produce in the short run.

■ **EXHIBIT 9-2**
The Demand Curve and Marginal Revenue Curve for a Perfectly Competitive Firm

(1) PRICE	(2) QUANTITY	(3) TOTAL REVENUE = (1) × (2)	(4) MARGINAL REVENUE = $\Delta TR/\Delta Q$ = $\Delta(3)/\Delta(2)$
$5	1	$5	$5
5	2	10	5
5	3	15	5
5	4	20	5

Plotting columns 1 and 2 gives us the demand curve; plotting columns 2 and 4 gives us the marginal revenue curve.

(a)   **(b)**

By computing marginal revenue we find that it is equal to price. By plotting columns 1 and 2, we obtain the firm's demand curve; by plotting columns 2 and 4 we obtain the firm's marginal revenue curve. The two curves are the same.

The Profit-Maximization Rule: $MR = MC$

Consider the situation in Exhibit 9-3. The perfectly competitive firm's demand curve and marginal revenue curve (one and the same) are drawn at the equilibrium price of $5. The firm's marginal cost curve is also shown. On the basis of these curves, what quantity of output will the firm produce?

The firm will continue to produce units of output as long as marginal revenue is greater than marginal cost; that is, as long as more is coming in than is going out on the marginal unit. It will not produce units of output for which marginal revenue is less than marginal cost. We conclude that the firm will stop producing when marginal revenue and marginal cost are equal. The **profit-maximization rule** for the firm says, *Produce the quantity of output at which MR = MC.*[4] In Exhibit 9-3 this comes at 125 units of output. For the perfectly competitive firm, the profit-maximization rule can be rewritten as $P = MC$ (since for the perfectly competitive firm $P = MR$). In perfect competition, $P = MR = MC$ when profit is maximized.

Profit-maximization Rule

Profit is maximized by producing the quantity of output at which $MR = MC$.

Question:

Why doesn't the firm in Exhibit 9-3 stop producing at 50 units of output? This is where the largest difference between marginal revenue and marginal cost occurs. Why does the firm continue to produce until marginal revenue equals marginal cost?

Answer:

Suppose the firm did stop producing with the 50th unit of output. Then it wouldn't have produced the 51st, which, as Exhibit 9-3 illustrates, comes with a greater marginal revenue than marginal cost. Nor would it have produced the 52d unit, for

[4]The profit-maximization rule is the same as the loss-minimization rule since it is impossible to maximize profits without minimizing losses. The profit-maximization rule also holds for all firms, whether they are perfectly competitive or not.

■ **EXHIBIT 9-3**
The Quantity of Output the Perfectly Competitive Firm Will Produce

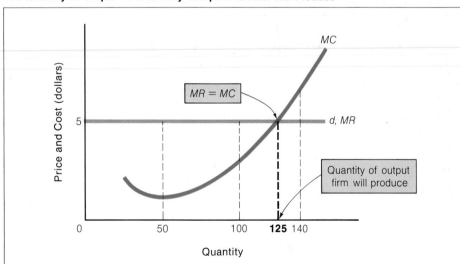

The firm's demand curve is horizontal at the equilibrium price. Its demand curve is its marginal revenue curve. The firm produces that quantity of output at which $MR = MC$.

which marginal revenue is also greater than marginal cost. In short, the firm would have not produced some units of output for which a marginal (additional) profit could have been made; thus it would not have been maximizing profit. What matters is whether *MR is greater* than *MC, not how much greater MR is than MC*.

To Produce or Not to Produce: Three Cases

The following cases illustrate three applications of the profit-maximization (loss-minimization) rule by a perfectly competitive firm.

Case 1: Price Is above Average Total Cost. Exhibit 9-4a illustrates the perfectly competitive firm's demand and marginal revenue curves. If the firm follows the profit-maximization rule, and produces the quantity of output at which marginal revenue equals marginal cost, it will produce 100 units of output. This will be the profit-maximizing quantity of output. Notice that at this quantity of output, price is above average total cost. Using the information in the exhibit, we can make the following calculations:

Case 1

Equilibrium price	= $15
Quantity of output produced	= 100 units
Total revenue ($P \times Q = \$15 \times 100$)	= $1,500
Total cost ($ATC \times Q = \$11 \times 100$)	= $1,100
Variable cost ($AVC \times Q = \$7 \times 100$)	= $700
Fixed cost ($TC - VC = \$1,100 - \$700$)	= $400
Profits ($TR - TC = \$1,500 - \$1,100$)	= $400

We conclude that if price is above average total cost for the perfectly competitive firm, the firm maximizes profits by producing the quantity of output at which $MR = MC$.

Case 2: Price Is below Average Variable Cost. Exhibit 9-4b illustrates the case in which price is below average variable cost. The equilibrium price at which the perfectly competitive firm sells its good is $4. At this price total revenue is less than both total cost and variable cost, as the following calculations indicate. To minimize its loss the firm should shut down.

Case 2

Equilibrium price	= $4
Quantity of output indicated by profit-maximization rule	= 50 units
Total revenue ($P \times Q = \$4 \times 50$)	= $200
Total cost ($ATC \times Q = \$13 \times 50$)	= $650
Variable cost ($AVC \times Q = \$5 \times 50$)	= $250
Fixed cost ($TC - VC = \$650 - \$250$)	= $400
Losses ($TR - TC = \$200 - \$650$)	= −$450

As one can see from the computation, if the firm produces in the short run, it will take a loss of $450. If it shuts down, its loss will be less. Specifically, it will lose its fixed costs, which amount to the difference between total cost and variable cost

Profit Maximization and Loss Minimization for the Perfectly Competitive Firm: Three Cases

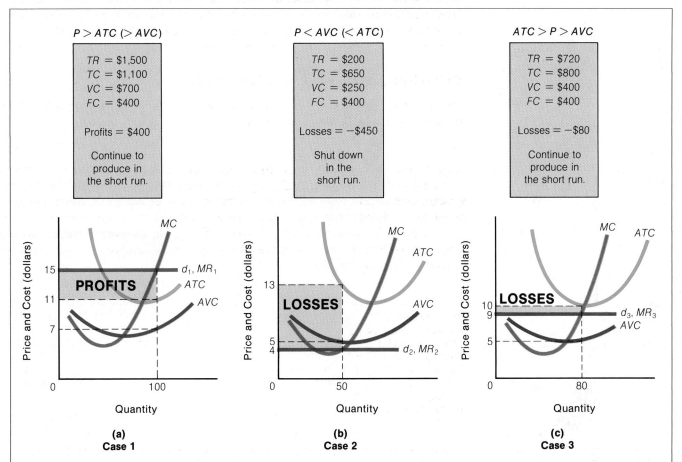

$P > ATC (> AVC)$

$TR = \$1,500$
$TC = \$1,100$
$VC = \$700$
$FC = \$400$
Profits = $\$400$
Continue to produce in the short run.

$P < AVC (< ATC)$

$TR = \$200$
$TC = \$650$
$VC = \$250$
$FC = \$400$
Losses = $-\$450$
Shut down in the short run.

$ATC > P > AVC$

$TR = \$720$
$TC = \$800$
$VC = \$400$
$FC = \$400$
Losses = $-\$80$
Continue to produce in the short run.

(a)
Case 1

(b)
Case 2

(c)
Case 3

In Case 1, (a), $TR > TC$ and the firm earns profits. It continues to produce in the short run. In Case 2, (b), $TR < TC$ and the firm takes a loss. It shuts down in the short run since it minimizes its losses by doing so; it is better to lose $400 in fixed costs than to take a loss of $450. In Case 3, (c), $TR < TC$ and the firm takes a loss. It continues to produce in the short run since it minimizes its losses by doing so; it is better to lose $80 by producing than to lose $400 in fixed costs.

(since $FC + VC = TC$, then $TC - VC = FC$). This is $400 ($650 − $250). Between the two options of producing in the short run or shutting down, the firm minimizes its losses by choosing to shut down; it will lose $400 by shutting down, whereas it will lose $450 by producing in the short run.

We conclude that if price is below average variable cost, the perfectly competitive firm minimizes losses by choosing to shut down; that is, by not producing.

Case 3: Price Is below Average Total Cost but above Average Variable Cost. Exhibit 9-4c illustrates the case in which price is below average total cost but above average variable costs. Here the equilibrium price at which the perfectly competitive firm sells its good is $9. If the firm follows the profit-maximization rule, it will produce 80 units of output. At this price and quantity of output, total revenue will be less than total cost (hence there will be a loss), but total revenue will be greater than variable cost.

Case 3

Equilibrium price	=	$9
Quantity of output produced	=	80 units
Total revenue ($P \times Q = \$9 \times 80$)	=	$720
Total cost ($ATC \times Q = \$10 \times 80$)	=	$800
Variable cost ($AVC \times Q = \$5 \times 80$)	=	$400
Fixed cost ($TC - VC = \$800 - \$400$)	=	$400
Losses ($TR - TC = \$720 - \$800$)	=	−$80

If the firm decides to produce in the short run it will take a loss of $80. Should it shut down instead? If it does, it will lose its fixed costs, which, in this case, will be $400 ($TC - VC = \$800 - \$400 = \$400$). It is better to continue to produce in the short run than to shut down: Losses are minimized by producing.

We conclude that if price is below average total cost but above average variable cost, the perfectly competitive firm minimizes its losses by continuing to produce in the short run instead of shutting down.

We also conclude that a firm produces in the short run as long as price is *above* average variable cost (Cases 1 and 3). Or, a firm shuts down in the short run if price is *less than* average variable cost (Case 2).

We can summarize the same information in terms of total revenue and variable costs. A firm produces in the short run as long as total revenue is greater than variable costs (Cases 1 and 3). A firm shuts down in the short run if total revenue is less than variable costs (Case 2).

Question:

Case 2 says that if P < AVC, the firm shuts down. Case 3 says that if P > AVC, the firm continues to operate in the short run. But suppose P = AVC. What does the firm do then?

Answer:

The firm is indifferent between shutting down and continuing to produce. Either way, it loses its fixed costs.

Question:

It seems to go against common sense to propose that a firm should continue to produce when it is taking a loss. Shouldn't a firm shut down whenever profits fall below zero?

Answer:

No, it shouldn't. If a firm takes a loss by producing where $MR = MC$, total cost is greater than total revenue. In the short run, the firm has fixed costs, which means that it is impossible for the firm to reduce its total costs to zero; therefore it cannot reduce its losses to zero. So, if the firm can't reduce its losses to zero in the short run, what is the next best thing? Obviously it should *minimize* its losses. And sometimes (not always) the firm loses less by continuing to produce *in the short run* than by shutting down (as in Case 3). Specifically, the firm minimizes its losses by producing if it can cover its variable costs.

The Perfectly Competitive Firm's Short-Run Supply Curve

Short-Run (Firm) Supply Curve

The portion of the firm's marginal cost curve that lies above the average variable cost curve.

Since the firm produces (supplies output) in the short run if price is above average variable cost, and it shuts down if price is below average variable cost (does not supply output), it follows that the **short-run supply curve** of the firm is that portion of its marginal cost curve that lies above the average variable cost curve. In other words, only a price above average variable cost will induce the firm to supply output. The short-run supply curve of the firm is illustrated in Exhibit 9-5.

From Firm to Industry Supply to Short-Run Competitive Equilibrium

Short-Run Industry (Market) Supply Curve

The horizontal summation of all existing firms' short-run supply curves.

Once we know that the firm's short-run supply curve is that part of its marginal cost curve that is above its average variable cost curve, it is a simple matter to derive the **short-run industry (or market) supply curve.**[5] We horizontally sum the short-run supply curves for all firms in the industry.

Consider, for simplicity, an industry made up of two firms, A and B. At a price of $4, firm A supplies 100 units of good X and firm B supplies 150 units. One point on the industry supply curve thus corresponds to $4 on the price axis and 250 units (100 units + 150 units) on the quantity axis.[6] By following this procedure for all prices, we would have the short-run industry (market) supply curve.

The industry (market) demand curve, as we saw in Chapter 3, is obtained using the same approach; this time, however, we sum the quantity demanded by each demander at every price. The interplay of industry (market) demand and short-run industry (market) supply finally establishes equilibrium price and quantity; thus this interplay characterizes the process and outcome of short-run competitive equilib-

---

[5]In discussion of market structures, the words "industry" and "market" are often used interchangeably when a single-product industry is under consideration, which is the case here.

[6]We add one qualification: Each firm's supply curve is drawn on the assumption that the prices of its variable inputs are constant.

■ **EXHIBIT 9-5**
The Perfectly Competitive Firm's Short-Run Supply Curve

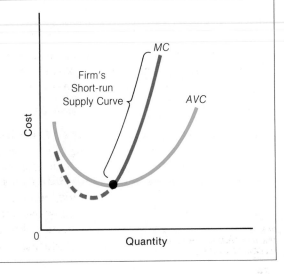

The short-run supply curve is that portion of the firm's marginal cost curve that lies above the average variable cost curve.

Theory in Practice

Job Security and Fixed Costs In the Short Run

Consider two firms X and Y, each with the same total costs but with different variable and fixed costs, as illustrated in Exhibit 9-6. For firm X, fixed costs are 33 percent of total costs, and for firm Y fixed costs are 17 percent of total costs. This difference will affect the shut-down decision for the two firms. Firm Y will shut down if total revenue falls to the level of variable cost ($500). But for firm X, total revenue has to fall to a lower level of variable cost ($400) before it will shut down. In short, when total revenue is between $500 and $400, firm X will still operate, but firm Y will shut down. Note that this result holds for firms that have the same total cost.

We can conclude that the greater the fixed cost–total cost ratio (*FC/TC*), the more likely the firm will operate in the short run; the smaller the fixed cost–total cost ratio, the less likely the firm will operate in the short run, *ceteris paribus*.

Now consider the input, labor. Suppose that labor's objective is to attain as much job security as possible. Given this objective, which firm would employees prefer to work for? The answer is firm X. The reason is that total revenue can fall farther for firm X than for firm Y without it shutting down.

Employees who value job security have not ignored the fact that the firms with higher fixed cost–total cost ratios are less likely to shut down in the short run. For example, in the past two decades in particular labor representatives have often argued for greater fringe benefits as an alternative to taking all gains in higher hourly wages. These fringe benefits often take the form of health, life, and accident insurance, contributions to pension funds, and the like. What is important to our discussion is that these fringe benefits are often negotiated so that the firm has to pay them for a period of time (six months to a year is common) after *it has shut down*. This means that part of the employees' payment-and-fringe-benefit package is a fixed cost to the firm. Since this compensation is a fixed cost (as opposed to wages which are a variable cost to the firm), it follows that fixed costs will be higher for a given level of total costs, and the firm's fixed cost–total cost ratio will also be higher. Consequently the firm is less likely to shut down in the short run, and job security increases.

A simple numerical example illustrates the point. For a given time period, a firm has total costs of $10,000, variable costs (which are exclusively labor costs) of $7,000, and fixed costs of $3,000 per week. Employees then propose to their employer that their total wages be reduced to $6,000, but that they now receive health insurance benefits worth $1,000 (they received $0 before) that will continue for a period of six months after the firm has shut down. The total costs of the firm will not change if this proposal is accepted, but fixed costs as a percentage of total costs will rise from 30 percent to 40 percent. If the firm does not accept the employees' proposal, it will shut down if total revenue falls to $7,000. If it does accept the employees' proposal, it will shut down if total revenue falls to $6,000. The firm's acceptance of the employees' proposal increases employee job security—at least in the short run.

■ **EXHIBIT 9-6**
Fixed (and Variable) Costs as a Percentage of Total Cost and the Shut-Down Decision

Both firms have the same total cost; however, firm X has a higher fixed cost–total cost ratio than firm Y. It follows that firm X is less likely to shut down in the short run. Firm X will shut down when total revenue falls to $400. Firm Y will shut down when total revenue falls to $500. It follows that firm Y would shut down before firm X would (since total revenue could fall to $500 and not fall to $400, but the reverse isn't true.)

FIRM X	FIRM Y
$TC = \$600$	$TC = \$600$
$VC = \$400$	$VC = \$500$
$FC = \$200$	$FC = \$100$
$\dfrac{VC}{TC} = \dfrac{\$400}{\$600} = .66$	$\dfrac{VC}{TC} = \dfrac{\$500}{\$600} = .83$
$\dfrac{FC}{TC} = \dfrac{\$200}{\$600} = .33$	$\dfrac{FC}{TC} = \dfrac{\$100}{\$600} = .17$

rium. The derivation of the short-run industry (market) supply curve, the industry (market) demand curve, and short-run competitive equilibrium is illustrated in Exhibit 9-7.

PERFECT COMPETITION IN THE LONG RUN

The number of firms in a perfectly competitive market may not be the same in the short run as in the long run. For example, if the typical firm is making economic profits in the short run, new firms will be attracted to the industry, and the number of firms will expand. If the typical firm is sustaining losses, some existing firms will exit the industry, and the number of firms will contract. We explain the process in greater detail in later sections. First, however, a detour is necessary to outline the conditions of long-run competitive equilibrium.

The Conditions of Long-Run Competitive Equilibrium

Long-Run Competitive Equilibrium
The condition where $P = MC = SRATC = LRATC$. There are zero economic profits, firms are producing the quantity of output at which price is equal to marginal cost, and no firm has an incentive to change its plant size.

The following conditions characterize **long-run competitive equilibrium:**

1. **Economic profit is zero: Price is equal to short-run average total cost ($P = SRATC$).** "SR" = short run and "LR" = long run. The logic of this condition can be understood by asking what would happen if price were above or below short-run average total cost.

   If it were above, positive economic profits would attract firms to the industry in order to obtain the profits. If price were below short-run average total cost, losses would result and some firms would want to exit the industry. We could not have long-run competitive equilibrium if firms have an incentive to enter or exit the industry in response to positive economic profits or losses, respectively. For long-run equilibrium to exist, there can be no incentive for firms to enter or

■ **EXHIBIT 9-7**
The Process of Short-Run Competitive Equilibrium

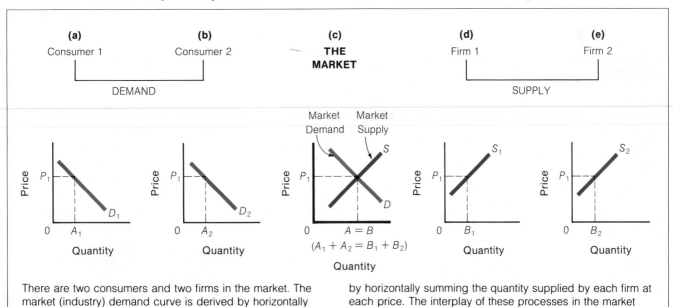

There are two consumers and two firms in the market. The market (industry) demand curve is derived by horizontally summing the quantity demanded by each consumer at each price; the short-run industry (market) supply curve is derived by horizontally summing the quantity supplied by each firm at each price. The interplay of these processes in the market setting establishes short-run competitive equilibrium.

exit the industry. This condition is brought about by zero economic profit (normal profit), which is a consequence of the equilibrium price being equal to short-run average total cost.

2. **Firms are producing the quantity of output at which price is equal to marginal cost ($P = MC$).** As previously noted, perfectly competitive firms naturally move toward the output level at which marginal revenue (or price, since $MR = P$ for a perfectly competitive firm) equals marginal cost.

3. **No firm has an incentive to change its plant size to produce its current output; that is, $SRATC = LRATC$ at the quantity of output at which $P = MC$.** To understand this condition, suppose $SRATC > LRATC$ at the quantity of output established in condition 2. The firm then has an incentive to change plant size in the long run because it wants to produce its product with the plant size that will give it the lowest average total cost (unit cost). It will have met this condition, and thus have no further incentive to change plant size, when it is producing the quantity of output at which price equals marginal cost and $SRATC$ equals $LRATC$.

The three conditions necessary for long-run competitive equilibrium can be stated: *Long-run competitive equilibrium exists when $P = MC = SRATC = LRATC$* (Exhibit 9-8).

■ **EXHIBIT 9-8**
Long-Run Competitive Equilibrium

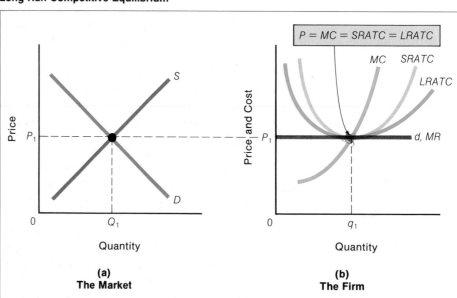

(a) Equilibrium in the market. (b) Equilibrium for the firm. In (b), $P = MC$ (the firm has no incentive to move away from the quantity of output at which this occurs, q_1); $P = SRATC$ (there is no incentive for firms to enter or exit the industry); and $SRATC = LRATC$ (there is no incentive for the firm to change its plant size). Note that the MC curve in the exhibit is the short-run marginal cost curve. Although not illustrated, the long-run marginal cost ($LRMC$) curve would also pass through the point where the demand, $LRATC$, and $SRATC$ curves are tangent. In short, long-run competitive equilibrium may be specified as $P = SRMC = LRMC = SRATC = LRATC$.

Question:

It appears that long-run competitive equilibrium exists when there is no incentive for firms to make any changes. Is this correct?

Answer:

Yes, it is. Specifically, long-run competitive equilibrium exists when all of the following occur:

1. **There is no incentive for firms to enter or exit the industry.** This means there are no economic profits or losses. There is, instead, zero economic profit (or normal profit), which can only come about if $P = SRATC$.

2. **There is no incentive for firms to produce more or less output.** This requires firms to produce the quantity of output at which P (MR) $= MC$, since any other output level does not maximize profits or minimize losses.

3. **There is no incentive for firms to change plant size.** Firms naturally want to produce at the lowest average total cost (unit cost) possible. If, for example, $SRATC > LRATC$ at the output level at which $MR = MC$, the firm has an incentive to change its plant size in the long run in order to produce the same output level at lower unit costs.

Industry Adjustment to an Increase in Demand

Suppose we start at long-run competitive equilibrium, where, as noted, $P = MC = SRATC = LRATC$. Then market demand rises for the goods produced by the firms in the industry. What happens? Equilibrium price rises; as a consequence, the demand curve faced by an individual firm (which is its marginal revenue curve) shifts upward; next, existing firms in the industry increase quantity of output since marginal revenue now intersects marginal cost at a higher quantity of output. In the long run, new firms begin to enter the industry since price is currently above average total cost and there are positive economic profits. As new firms enter the industry, the industry (market) supply curve shifts rightward. As a consequence, equilibrium price falls. It falls until long-run competitive equilibrium is reestablished; that is, until there is, once again, zero economic profit.

Review the process again, from the initial increase in the market demand to the reestablishment of long-run competitive equilibrium. Notice that price first increased in the short run (owing to the increase in demand), and then later decreased in the long run (owing to the increase in supply). Also, profits first increased (owing to the increase in demand and consequent increase in price) and then later decreased (owing to the increase in supply and consequent decrease in price); they went from zero to some positive amount and then back to zero.

We emphasize the up-and-down movements in both price and profits in response to an increase in demand. Too often people only see the primary upward movements in both price and profits and ignore or forget the secondary downward movements. The secondary effects in price and profits are as important as the primary effects.

The process of adjustment we have described brings up an important question. If price first rises owing to an increase in market demand, and later falls owing to an increase in market supply, will the new equilibrium price be greater than, less than, or equal to the original equilibrium price? For example, if equilibrium price is $10 before the increase in market demand, will the new equilibrium price (after market and firm adjustments have taken place) be greater than, less than, or equal to $10? The answer depends on whether increasing cost, decreasing cost, or constant cost, respectively, describes the industry in which the increase in demand has taken place. We discuss the three cases.

Constant-Cost Industry

An industry in which average total costs do not change as (industry) output increases or decreases, as firms enter or exit the industry, respectively.

Constant-Cost Industry. A **constant-cost industry** is an industry in which average total costs (unit costs) do not change as (industry) output increases or decreases, as firms enter or exit the industry. If market demand increases for a good produced by firms in a constant-cost industry, price will initially rise and finally fall to its *original level*. This is illustrated in Exhibit 9-9a.

We start from a position of long-run competitive equilibrium where there are zero economic profits. This is at point 1, which is one point on the long-run supply curve (*LRS*). We now experience an increase in demand. Price rises from P_1 to P_2; at P_2 there are positive profits, which cause the firms currently in the industry to expand output. We move up the supply curve, S_1, from point 1 to point 2. Next, new firms, drawn by the profits, enter the industry, causing the supply curve to shift rightward.

For a constant-cost industry, output is increased without a change in the price of inputs. Because of this, the firms' cost curves do not shift. But, of course, if costs do not rise to reduce the profits in the industry, then this means price must fall. (Profits can be reduced in two ways: through a rise in costs or a fall in price.) We know then that price must fall to its original level (P_1) before profits are zero. This implies that the supply curve shifts rightward by the same amount that the demand curve shifts rightward. In the exhibit this is a shift from S_1 to S_2. Connecting the two

■ **EXHIBIT 9-9**
Long-Run Industry Supply Curves

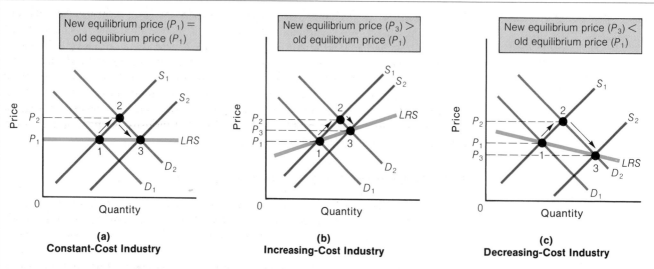

(a)
Constant-Cost Industry

(b)
Increasing-Cost Industry

(c)
Decreasing-Cost Industry

LRS = long-run industry supply. Each part illustrates the same scenario, but with different results depending on whether the industry has (a) constant costs, (b) increasing costs, or (c) decreasing costs. In each part we start at long-run competitive equilibrium (point 1). Demand increases, price rises from P_1 to P_2, and there are positive economic profits. Consequently existing firms expand output, and new firms are attracted to the industry.

In (a) input costs remain constant as output increases, so the firms' cost curves do not shift. Profits fall to zero through a

decline in price. This implies that in a constant-cost industry the supply curve shifts rightward by the same amount as the demand curve shifts rightward.

In (b) input costs increase as output increases. Profits are squeezed by a combination of rising costs and falling prices. The new equilibrium price (P_3) for an increasing-cost industry is higher than the old equilibrium price (P_1).

In (c) input costs decrease as output increases. The new equilibrium price (P_3) for a decreasing-cost industry is lower than the old equilibrium price (P_1).

Long-Run Industry Supply Curve

Graphic representation of the quantities of output that the industry is prepared to supply at different prices after the entry and exit of firms is completed.

Increasing-Cost Industry

An industry in which average total costs increase as (industry) output increases and decrease as (industry) output decreases, as firms enter and exit the industry, respectively.

long-run equilibrium points (1 and 3), where economic profits are zero, gives us the **long-run (industry) supply curve.** A constant-cost industry is characterized by a horizontal long-run supply curve.

Increasing-Cost Industry. An **increasing-cost industry** is an industry in which average total costs (unit costs) increase as (industry) output increases and decrease as (industry) output decreases, as firms enter and exit the industry, respectively. If market demand increases for a good produced by firms in an increasing-cost industry, price will initially rise and finally fall to a level *above its original level.*

Consider the situation in Exhibit 9-9b. We start, as before, in long-run competitive equilibrium. Demand increases and price rises from P_1 to P_2. This brings about positive economic profits, which cause firms in the industry to expand output and new firms to enter the industry. So far this is the same process we described for a constant-cost industry. The difference, however, is that in an increasing-cost industry as firms purchase more inputs to produce more output, some input prices rise and cost curves shift. In short, as industry output expands, profits are caught in a two-way squeeze: Price is coming down, and costs are rising. (If costs are rising as price is falling, then it is not necessary for price to fall to its original level before zero economic profits rule once again. Price will not have to fall as far to restore long-run competitive equilibrium in an increasing-cost industry as in a constant-cost industry). We would expect then that given an increase in demand in an increasing-cost industry, the new equilibrium price will be higher than the old equilibrium price. This means the supply curve shifts rightward by less than the demand curve shifts rightward. An increasing-cost industry is characterized by an upward-sloping long-run supply curve.

Decreasing-Cost Industry

An industry in which average total costs decrease as (industry) output increases and increase as (industry) output decreases, as firms enter and exit the industry, respectively.

Decreasing-Cost Industry. A **decreasing-cost industry** is an industry in which average total costs (unit costs) decrease as (industry) output increases and increase as (industry) output decreases, as firms enter and exit the industry, respectively. If market demand increases for a good produced by firms in a decreasing-cost industry, price will initially rise and finally fall to a level *below its original level.* In Exhibit 9-9c price initially moves from P_1 to P_2 and then to P_3. In such an industry, average total costs decrease as new firms enter the industry, so price must fall below its original level in order to eliminate profits. A decreasing-cost industry is characterized by a downward-sloping long-run supply curve.

Industry Adjustment to a Decrease in Demand

Demand can decrease as well as increase. The analysis we outlined for an increase in demand can be reversed to explain industry adjustment to a decrease in demand. Starting at long-run competitive equilibrium, market demand decreases; as a consequence, in the short run the equilibrium price falls, effectively shifting the firm's demand curve (marginal revenue curve) downward; following this, some firms in the industry will decrease production since marginal revenue intersects marginal cost at a lower level of output, and some firms will shut down.

In the long run, some firms will leave the industry because price is below average total cost and they are taking continuous losses. As firms leave the industry, the industry (market) supply curve shifts leftward. As a consequence, the equilibrium price rises. It will rise until long-run competitive equilibrium is reestablished; that is, until there are, once again, zero economic profits (instead of negative economic profits). Whether the new equilibrium price is greater than, less than, or equal to the original equilibrium (market) price depends on whether decreasing cost, in-

Theory in Practice

Calculators, VCRs, and Computers

In 1969, the first hand-held calculator was introduced in the United States; it sold for $395. In 1975, Sony sold the first videocassette recorder (VCR) for a price of $1,400. In 1977, Apple Computer Corporation sold the first personal computer—it had only 4K random access memory (RAM)—for just under $1,300.* In 1987, the prices of all three goods were much lower and the quality was generally considered much higher than in the years when the goods were first introduced. Hand-held calculators of higher quality than the one introduced in 1969 were selling for approximately $18. Videocassette recorders of higher quality than those in 1975

*It is important to note that $395 in 1969 was equivalent to approximately $1,200 in 1987; $1,400 in 1975 was equivalent to approximately $2,900 in 1987; and $1,300 in 1977 was equivalent to approximately $2,200 in 1987. This adjustment is necessary if we want to compare the 1987 prices of these three goods with the prices in the years noted.

were selling for approximately $400. Personal home computers of higher quality than those in 1977 were selling for approximately $600.

What brought about this sharp decrease in price and increase in quality? The entry of new firms into the calculator, VCR, and personal computer industries was responsible. Positive economic profits, realized by the first companies in the different industries, attracted new firms, the supply of the goods increased, and prices fell.** In 1970, one year after the first hand-held calculator was introduced, Texas Instruments, Inc., entered the industry. It was quickly followed by Canon, Sharpe, Hewlett-Packard, National Semi-Conductor, and Sears, to name only a few well-known companies. In the VCR industry, Sony was soon followed by RCA, General Electric, Zenith, and many others. In the personal computer industry, Apple was quickly followed by Tandy (Radio Shack), Xerox, IBM, Nippon Electric, Casio, Digital Equipment, and a host of others.

These examples illustrate how easy entry into the market can affect price and profits. They also suggest the potential benefits that exist for incumbent firms that can successfully limit entry into the industry. (Consider the profits Sony would have realized if it could have legally prohibited other firms from entering the videocassette recorder industry.)

**Changes in technology also occurred around the same time.

creasing cost, or constant cost, respectively, describes the industry in which demand decreased.

Question:

What motivates long-run adjustment?

Answer:

Profit seeking by firms is behind long-run adjustment. For example, suppose that in the short run the typical firm is making profits. In the long run new firms will enter the industry, causing the number of firms to expand, supply to increase, and prices to fall.

Differences in Costs, Differences in Profits: Now You See It, Now You Don't

Suppose there are two farmers, Hancock and Cordero, who produce wheat. Farmer Cordero grows his wheat on fertile land; Farmer Hancock grows his wheat on poor soil. Both farmers sell their wheat for the same price, but because of the difference in the quality of their land, Cordero has lower average total costs than Hancock. This is represented in Exhibit 9-10.

If we compare initial situations for the two farmers (see each farmer's ATC_1), we notice that Cordero is making profits and Hancock is not. Cordero is making profits because he pays lower average total costs than Hancock as a consequence of his farming higher quality land than Hancock. But is this situation likely to continue? Is Cordero likely to continue making profits? The answer is no. Individuals will bid up the price of the fertile land that Cordero farms vis-à-vis the poor quality land that Hancock farms. In other words, if Cordero is renting his farmland, the rent he pays will increase to reflect the superior quality of the land. The rent will increase by an amount equal to the profits per time period; that is, an amount equal to the shaded portion in (b). If Cordero owns the land, the superior quality of the land will have a higher implicit (opportunity) cost attached to it (Cordero can rent it out for more than Hancock can rent out his land, assuming Hancock owns his land), and this fact will be reflected in the average total cost curve.

In Exhibit 9-10b ATC_2 reflects either the higher rent Cordero must pay for the superior land or the full implicit opportunity cost he incurs by farming land he owns. In either case, once the average total cost curve reflects *all costs*, Cordero will be in the same situation as Hancock; he, too, will be making zero economic profits.

Where has the profit gone? It has gone for payment to the higher quality, more productive resource responsible for the lower average total costs in the first place. Consequently average total costs are no longer relatively lower for the person or firm that employs the higher quality, more productive resource or input.

■ **EXHIBIT 9-10**
Differences in Costs, Differences in Profits: Now You See It, Now It's Gone

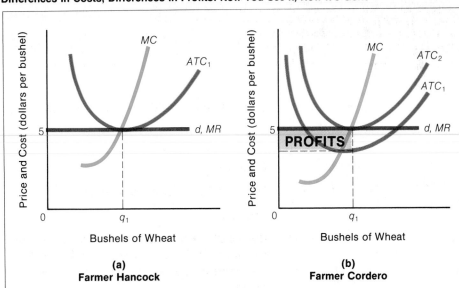

(a)
Farmer Hancock

(b)
Farmer Cordero

At ATC_1 for both farmers, Cordero makes profits and Hancock does not. The reason Cordero is making profits is because the land he farms is of higher quality (more productive) than Hancock's land. Eventually this fact is taken into account, either by Cordero paying higher rent for his land or by incurring higher implicit opportunity costs for it. This moves Cordero's ATC curve upward to the same level as Hancock's, and Cordero makes zero economic profits. The profits have gone as payment (implicit or explicit) for the higher quality, more productive land.

PERFECT COMPETITION AND RESOURCE ALLOCATIVE EFFICIENCY

Perfect competition is often put forth as a benchmark against which other market structures are judged. Some of the reasons for this involve the concept of *resource allocative efficiency*.

A firm that produces the quantity of output at which $P = MC$ is said to exhibit **resource allocative efficiency.** A perfectly competitive firm is such a firm. It produces the quantity of output at which $MR = MC$, and since for it $P = MR$, it follows that $P = MC$.

Resources are allocated efficiently when the (exchange) value of the resources to demanders equals the opportunity cost of the resources. Put differently, resource allocative efficiency is said to exist when the marginal benefit to demanders of the resources in the goods they purchase is equal to the marginal cost to suppliers of the resources they use in producing the goods. Resource allocative efficiency is established when firms produce the quantity of output at which price, or the market representation of the exchange value or marginal benefit of the resources to demanders, is equal to marginal cost. Continuing to produce a good until its price

Resource Allocative Efficiency
The situation that exists when firms produce the quantity of output for which price equals marginal cost.

equals its marginal cost ensures that all those units of the good are produced that are of greater value to demanders than the alternative goods that might have been produced.

An important point to notice is that for a perfectly competitive firm, profit maximization and resource allocative efficiency are not at odds. (Might they be for other market structures? See the next two chapters.) The firm seeks to maximize profit by producing the quantity of output at which $MR = MC$, and since for the firm $P = MR$, it automatically accomplishes resource allocative efficiency ($P = MC$) when it maximizes profit ($MR = MC$).

TOPICS FOR ANALYSIS WITHIN THE THEORY OF PERFECT COMPETITION

In this section we briefly analyze three topics within the theory of perfect competition: higher costs and higher prices, advertising, and setting prices.

Do Higher Costs Mean Higher Prices?

Suppose there are 600 firms in an industry. Each firm sells the identical product at the same price. Suppose that one of these firms experiences a rise in its marginal costs of production. Someone immediately comments, "Higher costs for the firm today, higher prices for the consumer tomorrow." Her assumption is that firms that experience a rise in costs simply "pass on" these higher costs to consumers in the form of higher prices.

Will this occur in a perfectly competitive market structure? Remember that each firm in the industry is a price taker; furthermore, only one firm has experienced a rise in marginal cost. Since this firm supplies only a tiny percentage of the total market supply, it is unlikely that there will be anything other than a negligible change in the market (industry) supply curve. And if the market supply curve does not change, neither will equilibrium price. In short, a rise in costs incurred by one of many firms does not mean consumers will pay higher prices. The situation would have been different, of course, if many of the firms in the industry had experienced a rise in costs. In this case the market supply curve would have been affected, along with price.

Will the Perfectly Competitive Firm Advertise?

Do individual farmers advertise? Have you ever seen an advertisement, say, for Farmer Johnson's wheat? We think not. First, since Farmer Johnson sells a homogeneous product, advertising her wheat is the same as advertising every wheat farmer's wheat. Second, since Farmer Johnson finds herself in a perfectly competitive market, she can sell all the wheat she wants at the going price. So, why should she advertise? From her viewpoint, advertising has costs and no benefits.

Will a perfectly competitive *industry* advertise? For example, if Farmer Johnson won't advertise her wheat, will the wheat industry advertise wheat? It may. The industry as a whole may join together to advertise wheat in the hope of shifting the market demand curve for wheat to the right. This is what happened in 1986 and 1987 in the California raisin industry. No individual California raisin producer sought to advertise his or her raisins, but the California raisin industry, as a whole, did advertise. You may remember the television commercial, where snazzy-looking raisins were dancing and singing, "I heard it through the grapevine. . . ."

Economics in Our Times

Interview: George Stigler

George Stigler won the Nobel Prize in Economics in 1982. His major contributions in economics have been in the areas of industrial structures, the functioning of markets, and the ef-

fects of public regulatory activities. Stigler is currently at the University of Chicago. We interviewed Professor Stigler on May 25, 1988.

Professor Stigler, What is it that sometimes makes theories built on unrealistic assumptions predict better than theories built on realistic assumptions?

The main explanation for the power of an abstract theory is that it has not specified a lot of factual content. If I specify factual content, if I get descriptive in my assumptions, there is a great danger that while I can tell a very good story, it doesn't tell me anything about the world. A striking example is the theory of monopolistic competition of the Chamberlinian variety which now is no longer used. It paid attention to things such as the fact that every seller differs from every other seller in location, or the charm of his personality, or the fact that his brand of toothpaste is advertised differently from another brand, and so forth. All those things are realistic, but they are part of a theory that doesn't tell us anything that is seri-

ously interesting, different, or more insightful than the abstract theory of perfect competition.

You once said that abstraction and generality are virtually synonyms. Is this your point here—that an abstract theory is a general theory, that it has the potential to tell us more about the world?

Yes, you can subject it to a wider range of challenging applications. For example, consider the standard assumption of competition: that the rate of return tends to equality in all the areas in which returns are allowed to flow. We can use that in a million applications.

Some economists have suggested that there is more agreement in microeconomics than in macroeconomics because economists ask harder questions in macroeconomics than in microeconomics. Do you agree or disagree?

I think many of the people in macroeconomics are extremely bright people and they certainly have a good command of the techniques of econom-

Supplier-set Price vs.
Market-determined Price: Collusion or Competition?

Suppose the only thing you know about a particular industry is that all firms within it sell their products at the same price. To explain this, some people argue that the firms are colluding. They believe the firms come together, pick a price, and stick to it.

This, of course, is one way all firms can arrive at the same price for their products. But it is not the only way. Another way has been described in this chapter. It could be that all firms are price takers; that is, the firms find themselves in a perfectly competitive market structure. There is no collusion here.

THE IMPORTANCE OF "AS IF" IN ECONOMIC THEORIES

The theory of perfect competition describes how firms act in a market structure where (1) there are many buyers and sellers, none of which is large in relation to total sales or purchases; (2) sellers sell a homogeneous product; (3) buyers and sellers have all relevant information; and (4) easy entry and exit exist. As noted earlier,

ics. Given this, I have to conclude that they are singularly less successful in predicting and understanding the phenomena they work with because they are working with a harder set of phenomena than the microeconomist deals with. Macroeconomics has not reached anything like the stability or universality of acceptance that microeconomics has achieved. If I compare the Ph.D.'s from different universities, they all use the same microeconomics, but they still vary a good deal in their macroeconomics. So probably I'm a lazy man: I'd rather work on subjects which we economists are awfully good at rather than those subjects, which however important, we're not as good at.

If you could snap your fingers and have the answer to any economic question, what question would you like to have answered?

There are some things anyone would like to solve. For example, if we could finally nail down the true theory of oligopoly, of the behavior of small groups or of coalitions, that would be an enormous contribution both to in-

dustrial organization in the private sector and to the theory of interest groups and their influence on political phenomena. It would be a stunning advance if we could show the logic of collusion and competition among groups.

Economics is interesting, don't you think, because there are so many challenging puzzles to solve?

If a field ever got to the dreadful state that there were no more interesting questions left, it would be terrible. I always say that just as in science we owe it to our successors to leave them a lot of unsolved problems—a duty, by the way, we completely fulfill—it is also true in social affairs.

You joined the faculty of the University of Chicago in 1958. You had been recommended by the Department of Economics for a position there 12 years earlier, but the university's acting president rejected the appointment because he was unimpressed by the results of his interview of you. Could you tell us a little more of this story?

On that occasion when I was interviewed, I was on a kick on how important empirical studies are to a scientist. Most likely the acting president of the university thought I was overdoing it. By the way, he, too, was a man of limited skill on that day. I thought at the time what an outrage it was. But a few weeks later they took that same job and offered it to Milton Friedman. I said to myself, What a wonderful contribution I have made to the university.

these assumptions are closely met in some real-world markets; for example, many agricultural markets, the stock market, and the commodity market.

It is important to realize, though, that these assumptions are *approximated* in some other markets. In such markets, the number of sellers may not be large enough so that every firm is an absolute price taker, but still the amount of control the firm has over price may be negligible. The amount of control may be so neglible, in fact, that the firm acts *as if* it were a perfectly competitive firm.

Similarly, buyers may not have all relevant information concerning price and quality, but they may still have a great deal of information, and the information they do not have may not matter. The products the firms in the industry sell may not be homogeneous, but the differences may be inconsequential. In short, a market that does not meet the assumptions of perfect competition may nonetheless approximate those assumptions to such a degree that it behaves *as if* it were a perfectly competitive market. If so, it follows that the theory of perfect competition can be used to predict the market's behavior.

■ CHAPTER SUMMARY

The Theory of Perfect Competition

■ The theory of perfect competition is built on four assumptions: (1) There are many sellers and many buyers, none of which is large in relation to total sales or purchases. (2) Each firm produces and sells a homogeneous product. (3) Buyers and sellers have all relevant information with respect to prices, product quality, sources of supply, and so on. (4) There is easy entry into and exit from the industry.

■ The theory of perfect competition predicts the following: (1) Economic profits will be squeezed out of the industry in the long run by the entry of new firms—that is, zero economic profit exists in the long run. (2) In equilibrium, firms produce the quantity of output at which price equals marginal cost. (3) In the short run firms will stay in business as long as price covers average variable costs. (4) In the long run firms will stay in business as long as price covers average total costs. (5) In the short run, an increase (decrease) in demand will lead to a rise (fall) in price; whether the price in the long run will be higher than, lower than, or equal to its original level depends on whether the firm finds itself in an increasing-, decreasing-, or constant-cost industry.

The Perfectly Competitive Firm

■ A perfectly competitive firm is a price taker. It sells its product only at the market equilibrium price.

■ The perfectly competitive firm faces a horizontal (flat, perfectly elastic) demand curve. Its demand curve and marginal revenue curve are one and the same.

■ The perfectly competitive firm (as well as all other firms) maximizes profits (or minimizes losses) by producing the quantity of output at which $MR = MC$.

■ For the perfectly competitive firm, price equals marginal revenue.

Production in the short run

■ If $P > ATC$, the firm earns economic profits and will continue to operate in the short run.

■ If $P < AVC < ATC$, the firm takes losses. It will shut down since the alternative (continuing to produce) increases the losses.

■ If $ATC > P > AVC$, the firm takes losses. Nevertheless, it will continue to operate in the short run since the alternative (shutting down) increases the losses.

■ If $P = AVC$, the firm is indifferent between continuing to produce and shutting down.

■ Since the firm only produces in the short run when price is greater than average variable cost, the portion of its marginal cost curve that lies above the average variable cost curve is the firm's short-run supply curve. (This statement is not always *exactly* correct since the firm may choose to produce when price equals average variable cost. Recall that the firm is indifferent between continuing to produce and shutting down when $P = AVC$.)

Conditions of Long-Run Competitive Equilibrium

■ Long-run competitive equilibrium exists when (1) there is no incentive for firms to enter or exit the industry; (2) there is no incentive for firms to produce more or less output; (3) there is no incentive for firms to change plant size. We formalize these conditions as follows: (1) Economic profits are zero (this is the same as saying there is no incentive for firms to enter or exit the industry). (2) Firms are producing the quantity of output at which price is equal to marginal cost (this is the same as saying there is no incentive for firms to produce more or less output; after all, when $P = MC$, it follows that $MR = MC$ for the perfectly competitive firm, and thus the firm is maximizing profits). (3) $SRATC = LRATC$ at the quantity of output at which $P = MC$ (this is the same as saying firms do not have an incentive to change plant size).

Industry Adjustment to a Change in Demand

■ In a constant-cost industry, an increase in demand will result in a new equilibrium price equal to the original equilibrium price (before demand increased); in an increasing-cost industry, an increase in demand will result in a new equilibrium price that is higher than the original equilibrium price; in a decreasing-cost industry, an increase in demand will result in a new equilibrium price that is lower than the original equilibrium price.

■ The long-run supply curve for a constant-cost industry is horizontal (flat, perfectly elastic); the long-run supply curve for an increasing-cost industry is upward sloping; the long-run supply curve for a decreasing-cost industry is downward sloping.

Perfect Competition and Resource Allocative Efficiency

■ A perfectly competitive firm is resource allocative efficient because it produces the quantity of output at which $P = MC$; that is, the exchange value of resources to demanders equals the opportunity cost of the resources. As is seen in Chapters 10 and 11, firms in other market structures do not exhibit resource allocative efficiency.

■ QUESTIONS TO ANSWER AND DISCUSS

1. True or false. The firm's entire marginal cost curve is its short-run supply curve.

2. Suppose each firm in a perfectly competitive market structure is in long-run equilibrium. Then demand for the firms' product increases. Initially price and economic profits rise. Soon afterward, the government decides to tax away most (but not all) of the economic profits, arguing that the firms in the industry did not earn them. Policymakers argue that the profits were simply the result of an increase in demand. What effect, if any, would the tax have on market adjustment?

3. Explain why one firm sometimes appears to be making higher profits than another, but in reality is not.

4. Profit maximization for a perfectly competitive firm does not conflict with resource allocative efficiency. Do you agree or disagree? Explain your answer.

5. Do higher costs mean higher prices in a perfectly competitive industry?

6. The perfectly competitive firm does not increase its quantity of output without limit even though it can sell all it wants at the going price. Why not?

7. Suppose you read in a business magazine that computer firms are reaping high profits. With the theory of perfect competition in mind, what would you expect to happen over time to the following: computer prices, the profits of computer firms, the number of computers on the market, the number of computer firms?

8. In your own words, explain resource allocative efficiency.

9. The term "price taker" can apply to buyers as well as sellers. A price-taking buyer is one who cannot influence price by changing the amount she buys. What goods do you buy for which you are a price taker? What goods do you buy for which you are not a price taker?

Chapter 10

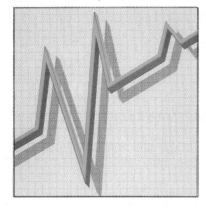

Monopoly

■ INTRODUCTION

Certain words are familiar to everyone, but when you ask what the words mean, few persons can come up with a good definition. Monopoly is such a word.

Once an economics instructor entered a classroom and asked the students for a definition of monopoly. Here are some of their definitions:

"Monopoly, that is a big company. Really big."

"John D. Rockefeller, the oil millionaire, he was a monopolist."

"A monopoly has no competition. It's the only guy in town."

"Monopolists make up the top ten companies of the Fortune 500. I think AT&T is a monopolist."

"I'm not sure, but I know that monopolists charge a high price."

"Monopoly is 180-degrees away from perfect competition."

Are any of these statements correct?

■ WHAT THIS CHAPTER IS ABOUT

This chapter presents the theory of monopoly. With respect to the first word, theory, remember that what we say in this chapter may not be perfectly descriptive of any real-world market. Our objective is not to describe with 100 percent accuracy, but rather to put forth a theory that, we hope, will explain and predict the behavior of some real-world markets. In short, we deal with the real world not by describing it (to do this we would need no theories, we could just describe what we see), but by trying to explain it and predict its movements.

With respect to the second word, monopoly, we ask you to lay aside any preconceived notions of what you think monopoly is, how it operates, and whether it is "good" or "bad." We begin with a definition of monopoly and proceed from there.

Key Questions to Keep in Mind as You Read

1. What are the assumptions of the theory of monopoly?
2. What is a price searcher?
3. Does a monopoly seller always receive monopoly profits?
4. Why is it difficult for firms to enter a monopoly market?
5. How do perfect competition and monopoly differ?
6. What is rent seeking? What does it mean to say that rent seeking is socially wasteful?
7. What is price discrimination? What are the conditions under which firms can price discriminate?

THE THEORY OF MONOPOLY

Monopoly
A theory of market structure based on three assumptions: there is one seller, it sells a product for which no close substitutes exist, and there are extremely high barriers to entry.

The theory of **monopoly** (or monopoly market structure) is built on three assumptions:

1. **There is one seller.** This means that the firm *is* the industry. Contrast this situation with perfect competition. In perfect competition, many firms make up the industry; in monopoly, only one firm makes up the industry.

2. **The single seller sells a product for which there are no close substitutes.** Because there are no close substitutes for its product, the single seller, the *monopolist* or *monopoly firm,* faces little if any competition.

3. **There are extremely high barriers to entry.** In the theory of perfect competition, we assumed it was easy for a firm to enter the industry. In the theory of monopoly, we assume it is very hard (if not impossible) for a firm to enter the industry; there are extremely high barriers that keep new firms out. We discuss the nature of these barriers shortly.

Examples of monopoly include many public utilities (local public utilities such as electricity, water, gas, and local telephone service) and the postal service (in the delivery of first-class mail).

Question:

One of the assumptions in the theory of monopoly is that the single seller sells a product for which there are no close substitutes. Isn't deciding what constitutes a close substitute for a product a subjective matter?

Answer:

Yes, it is. For example, someone might argue that writing a letter is a close substitute for making a telephone call, and someone else might argue that it is not. Whenever someone tries to draw a line between products that are close substitutes and products that are not close substitutes, there will be arguments as to where the line should be drawn.

Recall, however, that we are simply *assuming* that there are no close substitutes. This is part of our theory, which we hope will explain and predict the behavior of firms in some real-world markets. If, for example, the theory accurately predicts behavior in market X, even though some people argue that market X does not *perfectly* meet the assumption that there should be no close substitutes, some economists would say, "No matter, the market behaves *as if* the assumption were met."

We add that even if the critics are right and a range of substitutes exists, it is impossible to know beforehand how close a substitute must be before the theory (that assumes no close substitutes) is not useful. In other words, even if there is a "slightly close" substitute for a seller's product, "slightly close" may not be close enough to matter.

High Barriers to Entry

If a firm is a single seller of a product, why don't other firms enter the market and produce the same product? Legal barriers, economies of scale, or one firm's exclusive ownership of a scarce resource may make it difficult or impossible for new firms to enter the market.

Public Franchise

A right granted to a firm by government that permits the firm to provide a particular good or service and excludes all others from doing the same.

1. **Legal barriers.** These include public franchises, patents, and government licenses. A **public franchise** is a right granted to a firm by government that permits the firm to provide a particular good or service and excludes all others from doing the same (thus eliminating potential competition by law). For example, the U.S. Postal Service has been granted the exclusive franchise to deliver first-class mail. Many public utilities operate under state and local franchises, as do food and gas suppliers along many state turnpikes.

   In the United States, *patents* are granted to inventors of a product or process for a period of 17 years. During this time, the patent holder is shielded from competitors; no one else can legally produce and sell the patented product or process. The rationale behind patents is that they are necessary to encourage innovation in an economy. It's argued that few persons will waste their time and money trying to invent a new product if their competitors can immediately copy the product and sell it.

   Entry into some industries and occupations requires a government-granted *license*. For example, radio and television stations cannot operate without a license from the Federal Communications Commission (FCC). In most states, a person needs to be licensed to join the ranks of schoolteachers, physicians, dentists, architects, nurses, embalmers, barbers, veterinarians, and lawyers, among others.

2. **Economies of scale.** In some industries low average total costs are only obtained through large-scale production. This means that if new entrants are to be competitive in the industry, they must enter it on a large scale. But this is risky and costly and acts as a barrier to entry. If economies of scale are so pronounced in an industry that only one firm can survive in the industry, this firm is called a **natural monopoly.** Often-cited examples of natural monopoly include public utilities that provide gas, water, electricity, and local telephone service.

Natural Monopoly

The condition where economies of scale are so pronounced in an industry that only one firm can survive.

3. **Exclusive ownership of a scarce resource.** Existing firms may be protected from the entry of new firms by the exclusive or near-exclusive ownership of a resource needed to enter the industry. The classic example here is the Aluminum Company of America (Alcoa), which for a time controlled almost all sources of bauxite in the United States; Alcoa was the sole producer of aluminum in the country from the late nineteenth century until the 1940s.[1] Many people today view the DeBeers Company of South Africa as a monopoly because it controls a large percentage of diamond production and sales. Strictly speaking, though, DeBeers is more of a *marketing cartel* than a monopolist, although, as we see in the next chapter, a successful cartel acts much like a monopolist.

[1]We say more about Alcoa, and the important antitrust suit connected with it, in Chapter 17.

High Barriers to Entry and the Legal Prohibition of Competition: Government Monopoly and Market Monopoly

As we have seen, sometimes high barriers to entry exist because competition is legally prohibited; sometimes they exist independently. Where high barriers take the form of public franchises, patents, or government licenses, competition is legally prohibited. In contrast, where high barriers take the form of economies of scale or exclusive ownership of a resource, competition is not legally prohibited. In these cases nothing *legally* prohibits rival firms from entering the market and competing, even though they may choose not to do so. The high barrier to entry does not have a sign attached to it that reads "No competition allowed."

Some economists use the word *government monopoly* to refer to monopolies that are legally protected from competition. They use the word *market monopoly* to refer to monopolies that are not legally protected from competition.

Do not assume that because some monopolies are called "government monopolies" and others are called "market monopolies," that one type is better or worse than the other. The point we are making is simply that some sellers in the real world are legally protected from competition and some are not.

MONOPOLY PRICING AND OUTPUT DECISIONS

Price Searcher
A seller that has the ability to control to some degree the price of the product it sells.

A monopolist is a **price searcher;** that is, it is a seller that has the ability to control to some degree the price of the product it sells. In contrast to a price taker, a price searcher can raise its price and still sell its product—although not as many units as it could sell at the lower price. The pricing and output decisions of the price-searching monopolist are discussed in the next sections.

The Monopolist's Demand and Marginal Revenue

In the theory of monopoly, the monopoly firm is the industry, the industry is the monopoly firm—they are one and the same. It follows that the monopoly firm faces the market demand curve, which is downward sloping. A downward-sloping demand curve posits an inverse relationship between price and quantity demanded: More is sold at lower prices than at higher prices, *ceteris paribus*. Unlike the perfectly competitive firm, the monopolist can raise its price and still sell its product (though not as much).

Suppose the monopolist wants to sell an additional unit of its product. What must it do? Since it faces a downward-sloping demand curve, it must necessarily lower price. For example, if the monopoly seller is selling two units of X at $10 each, and it wishes to sell three units, it must lower price, say, to $9.75. It sells all three units at $9.75.[2] To sell an *additional* unit, it must lower price on all *previous units.*

The monopoly seller both gains and loses by lowering price, as Exhibit 10-1 shows. Specifically, it gains $9.75, the price of the additional unit sold because price was lowered. It loses 50 cents—25 cents on the first unit it used to sell at $10, plus 25 cents on the second unit it used to sell at $10. Gains are greater than losses here; the monopolist's net gain from selling the additional unit of output is $9.25 ($9.75 − .50 = $9.25). This is its marginal revenue: the change in total revenue that results from selling one additional unit of output. (Check this out. Total revenue is $20 when two units are sold at $10 each. Total revenue is $29.25 when three units are sold at $9.75 each. The change in total revenue that results from selling one additional unit of output is $9.25.)

[2]We are discussing here how a *single-price monopolist* behaves. This a monopolist that sells all units of its product for the same price. Later we discuss a *price-discriminating monopolist.*

The Dual Effects of a Price Reduction on Total Revenue

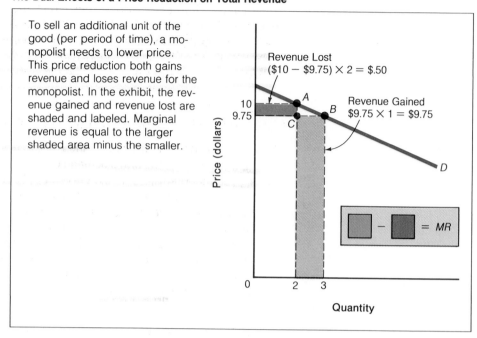

To sell an additional unit of the good (per period of time), a monopolist needs to lower price. This price reduction both gains revenue and loses revenue for the monopolist. In the exhibit, the revenue gained and revenue lost are shaded and labeled. Marginal revenue is equal to the larger shaded area minus the smaller.

Notice that the price of the good ($9.75) is greater than the marginal revenue ($9.25), $P > MR$. This is the case for a monopoly seller, or any price searcher. (Remember that for the firm in perfect competition, $P = MR$.)

Step by step, the effects of a price reduction can be summarized as follows:

1. To sell an additional unit of a good (per time period), the monopolist must lower price. In our example the monopolist must lower price from $10 to $9.75.

2. The monopolist gains and loses by doing this.

3. What is gained equals the price of the product times one (one additional unit). Let's call this the *revenue gained*. In our example this is $9.75 × 1 = $9.75. We see that price equals revenue gained (P = revenue gained).

4. What is lost equals the difference between the new lower price ($9.75) and the old higher price ($10) times the units of output sold *before* price was lowered. In our example this is 25 cents × 2 = 50 cents. Let's call this the *revenue lost*.

5. Marginal revenue can be defined as revenue gained minus revenue lost.

6. Since P = revenue gained
   and MR = revenue gained − revenue lost
   and revenue lost is > 0
   therefore $P > MR$.

Question:

Earlier it was said that to sell an additional unit, the monopolist must lower price on all previous units. This is confusing. How does the monopolist lower price on units it has already sold?

Answer:

We shouldn't think of "previous" and "additional" as referring to an actual sequence of events. The firm doesn't sell 100 units of a good and then decide to sell one more unit. The firm is in an either-or situation. *Either* the firm sells 100 units over some period of time, *or* it sells 101 units over the same period of time. If it wants to sell 101 units, the price per unit has to be lower than if it wants to sell 100 units.

The Monopolist's Demand and Marginal Revenue Curves

In perfect competition, the firm's demand curve is the same as its marginal revenue curve. In monopoly, the firm's demand curve is not the same as its marginal revenue curve. The monopolist's demand curve lies above its marginal revenue curve.

The demand curve plots price and quantity (*P* and *Q*); the marginal revenue curve plots marginal revenue and quantity (*MR* and *Q*). Because for a monopolist price is *greater than* marginal revenue, its demand curve necessarily lies *above* its marginal revenue curve. (Note that price and marginal revenue are the same for the first unit of output so the demand curve and the marginal revenue curve will share one point in common.) The correct relationship between a monopolist's demand and marginal revenue curves is illustrated in Exhibit 10-2.

A Digression: The Revenue-maximizing Price Is Usually Not the Profit-maximizing Price

We assume that all firms, whether price searchers or price takers, seek to maximize profits. Many of us easily fall into the trap of thinking that the price that maximizes revenues is necessarily the price that maximizes profits. Only under one condition is this the case: when the firm has no variable costs.

Profit is the difference between total revenue and total cost: profit = $TR - TC$. If the firm has no variable costs, then total cost equals fixed cost (remember that

■ **EXHIBIT 10-2**
Demand and Marginal Revenue Curves

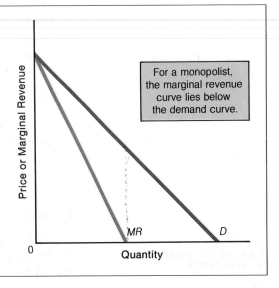

The demand curve plots price and quantity. The marginal revenue curve plots marginal revenue and quantity. Since for a monopolist $P > MR$, the marginal revenue curve must lie below the demand curve. (Note that when a demand curve is a straight line, the marginal revenue curve bisects the horizontal axis halfway between the origin and the point where the demand curve intersects the horizontal axis.)

For a monopolist, the marginal revenue curve lies below the demand curve.

fixed cost is constant as output changes). Thus profit can be rewritten as the difference between total revenue and fixed cost: profit = $TR - FC$, since $TC = FC$. It follows that maximizing total revenue is the same as maximizing profit, since every time total revenue increases, the difference between it and total cost (fixed cost)—that is, profit—increases, too.

We conclude that maximizing revenues is the same as maximizing profits only when the firm has no variable costs. It is unlikely, though, that the firm will be without variable costs. In the numerous cases in which variable costs exist, the price that maximizes revenues is not the same as the price that maximizes profits.

Monopoly Price and Output for a Profit-maximizing Monopolist

The monopolist that seeks to maximize profits produces the quantity of output at which $MR = MC$ (as did the profit-maximizing perfectly competitive firm) and *charges the highest price per unit at which this quantity of output can be sold.* In Exhibit 10-3, the highest price at which Q_1, the quantity at which $MR = MC$, can be sold is P_1. Notice that at Q_1 the *monopolist charges a price that is greater than marginal cost, $P > MC$.*

Whether profits are earned depends on whether P_1 is greater or less than average total cost at Q_1. In short, the profit-maximizing price may be the loss-minimizing price. Both monopoly profits and monopoly losses are illustrated in Exhibit 10-4.

■ **EXHIBIT 10-3**
The Monopolist's Profit-Maximizing Price and Quantity of Output

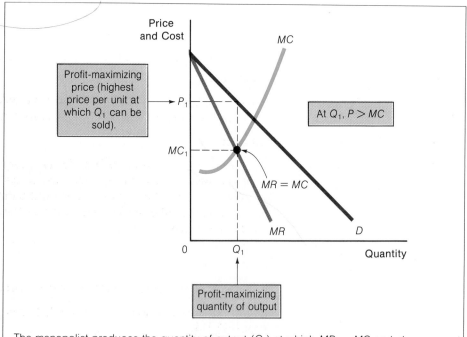

The monopolist produces the quantity of output (Q_1) at which $MR = MC$ and charges the highest price per unit at which this quantity of output can be sold at (P_1). Notice that at the profit-maximizing quantity of output, price is greater than marginal cost, $P > MC$.

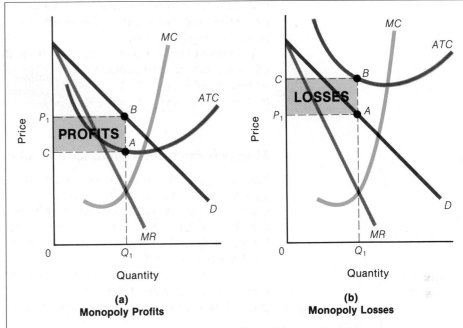

(a)
Monopoly Profits

(b)
Monopoly Losses

A monopoly seller is not guaranteed any profits. In (a), price is above average total cost at Q_1, the quantity of output at which $MR = MC$, and therefore TR (the area $0P_1BQ_1$) is greater than TC (the area $0CAQ_1$) and profits equal the area CP_1BA. In (b), price is below average total cost at Q_1, and TR (the area $0P_1AQ_1$) is less than TC ($0CBQ_1$) and losses equal P_1CBA.

Question:

Isn't it unrealistic to suggest that the monopolist can take a loss? After all, if the monopolist is the only seller in the industry how can it take a loss?

Answer:

Just because a firm is the only seller of a particular product does not guarantee it will earn profits. Remember, a monopolist cannot charge *any* price it wants for its goods; it charges the highest price that the demand curve allows it to charge. In some instances, the highest price may be lower than its average total costs (unit costs). If so, there is a loss.

Differences between Perfect Competition and Monopoly

There are some important differences between perfect competition and monopoly. Here are two.

1. **For the perfectly competitive firm, $P = MR$; for the monopolist, $P > MR$.** The perfectly competitive firm's demand curve is its marginal revenue curve; the monopolist's demand curve lies above its marginal revenue curve.

Theory in Practice

Stephen King: What's a Horror Writer Doing in an Economics Textbook Anyway?

The killer was slick.

He sat on a bench in the town park near the bandstand smoking a Marlboro and humming a song from the Beatles' white album—"you don't know how lucky you are, boy, back in the, back in the, back in the USSR. . . ."

—From The Dead Zone by Stephen King

Stephen King, the well-known horror writer, sells millions of books (including *Carrie, Christine, The Shining, It, Misery, Firestarter,* and *Pet Semetary*). As far as he's concerned, all those books are priced too high. King, like any author,

wants his books to be priced lower than the publisher wants them to be priced. This is because the author earns more income if they are priced lower.

Consider the facts. There are two main entities involved in producing a Stephen King novel: Stephen King, who writes the book, and the publishing company, which prints, markets, and distributes the book. Stephen King incurs no costs in publishing or selling the book; the publishing company does. This means that once King finishes writing the book and turns it over to the publishing company, he incurs no further costs. His marginal costs of publishing and selling the book are zero (in terms of our earlier discussion, he has no variable costs).

But this is not the situation for the publishing company. Its marginal costs are positive. The publishing company incurs an additional cost for each copy of the book that is published and sold. This difference in cost positions between the author and the publisher affects the price at which each wishes to sell the book.

Let's look at Exhibit 10-5, which shows a demand curve and marginal revenue curve for the book. Note that there are two marginal cost curves. The one for the publishing company is positive and (we have assumed) constant. The

▪ EXHIBIT 10-5
The Publisher and the Author Opt for Different Prices

The author faces zero costs of publishing and selling the book; the publishing company faces positive (and we assume) constant marginal costs. Both the author and the publishing company want to equate *MR* and *MC*. The difference, though, is that they do not have the same marginal cost. The author wants Q_A books produced and sold at a price of P_A; the publishing company wants Q_{PC} books produced and sold at a price of P_{PC}.

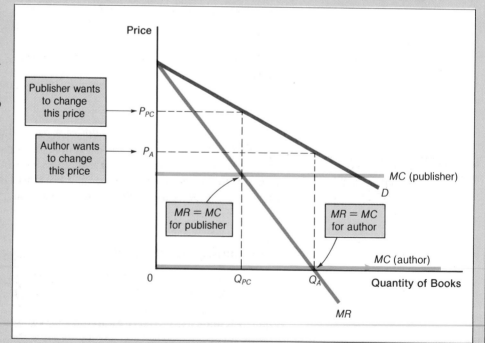

other marginal cost curve is for the author and is zero at all levels of output. In all, the exhibit shows one demand curve, one marginal revenue curve, and two marginal cost curves. (Since most authors receive a fixed percentage of total receipts from the sale of the book, the publisher's demand and marginal revenue curves are relevant to the author.) The author wants to sell the quantity of books at which marginal revenue equals his marginal cost. This is at Q_A. The highest price per book at which this quantity of books can be sold is P_A. This is the author's best price. Since the au-

thor is paid a fixed percentage of total sales revenues, he wants to maximize revenues. This occurs where $MR = 0$.

Assuming that the publishing company wants to maximize profits, it will want to sell the quantity of books at which marginal revenue equals its marginal cost. This is at Q_{PC}. The highest price per book at which this quantity of books can be sold is P_{PC}. Notice that P_{PC} is higher than P_A—the best price for the publisher is higher than the best price for the author.

2. **The perfectly competitive firm charges a price equal to marginal cost; the monopolist charges a price greater than marginal cost.** See Exhibit 10-3 for the monopoly case and Exhibit 9-3 in the last chapter for the perfect competition case.

$$\text{Perfect competition: } P = MR \quad \text{and} \quad P = MC$$
$$\text{Monopoly: } P > MR \quad \text{and} \quad P > MC$$

Question:

The last chapter pointed out that if a firm charges a price equal to marginal cost, P = MC, it exhibits resource allocative efficiency. Since the monopolist charges a price greater than marginal cost, P > MC, this must mean it does not exhibit resource allocative efficiency. Isn't this right?

Answer:

That is right. This point is addressed later in this chapter in the section, "The Case against Monopoly."

MONOPOLY PROFITS IN THE LONG RUN

In perfect competition, economic profits were reduced to zero in the long run by the entry of new firms. In monopoly, profits cannot be reduced to zero by the entry of new firms because extremely high barriers to entry prevent this. However, other forces may reduce profits. These include the capitalization of profits and monopoly rent-seeking activity.

The Capitalization of Profits

Suppose the owners of a profit-earning monopoly firm decide to sell it. What price will they ask for it? No doubt they will ask a price that reflects the value of the profits. As a result, the buyers of the monopoly firm will be faced with higher average total costs than were faced by the former owners of the firm. It is likely that the average total costs will be higher by an amount sufficient to return only zero economic profits to the new owners. This is illustrated in Exhibit 10-6.

The Capitalization of Profits

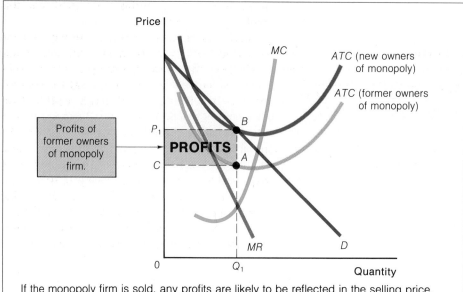

If the monopoly firm is sold, any profits are likely to be reflected in the selling price. The new owners' *ATC* curve is likely to be sufficiently higher than the former owners' *ATC* curve such that the new owners will receive zero economic profits.

The former owners of the monopoly firm had an *ATC* curve that was low enough to provide them with profits equal to the area CP_1BA. When they sold the monopoly firm, they asked for a price that reflected the value of the monopoly profits. The new owners have a higher *ATC* curve as a result; this *ATC* curve is likely to be high enough to provide only zero economic profits to the new owners. In short, through the capitalization of future profits into the firm's market value, the new owners of a monopoly firm will receive only zero economic profits.

Question:

If the new owners are paying a price that reflects the value of profits, and therefore end up receiving zero economic profits, why would they buy the monopoly firm?

Answer:

Perhaps they think they can operate the monopoly firm more efficiently and at lower cost than the previous owners; that is, they believe they can lower their *ATC* curve over time and make profits in the future. Or perhaps they believe the demand for the product the monopoly firm produces will rise. Of course, simply making their opportunity cost (which is what they do when they earn zero profits) may be enough to induce them to buy the monopoly firm.

Monopoly Rent Seeking

If profits are earned by a monopoly, these monopoly profits are sometimes referred to as **economic rent** or **monopoly rent.** Economic or monopoly rent is a payment in excess of opportunity cost.

Economic or Monopoly Rent

A payment in excess of opportunity cost.

How is it that monopoly profits are monopoly rents? The answer is simple. The opportunity costs of the monopolist are reflected in its *ATC* curve. If price is above average total costs, profits are earned, and this payment over and above costs is rent.

Market participants normally compete for monopoly profits or rent. Activity directed to the accomplishment of this goal is referred to as rent seeking.[3]

Consider the following example of rent seeking. Assume the government plans to award some firm a monopoly right to produce good *X*. Suppose firms desiring to produce *X* believe this right is worth $40 million. How will these firms compete for this right? Each firm will spend money (use resources) to convince government officials that it should be awarded the right. Each firm will hire lobbyists, donate money to political campaigns, wine and dine politicians, and so forth to improve its chances of being awarded the monopoly right. How much will each firm be expected to spend on rent seeking? If firm A is 40 percent sure it can win the right, we predict it will spend $16 million ($40 million × .40 = $16 million). Such an expenditure will dissipate some of the monopoly rents the firm is seeking. In a later section we explain why this rent-seeking activity is socially wasteful even though it is rational economic activity for the individual firm.

Rent Seeking

Actions of individuals and groups who spend resources to influence public policy in the hope of redistributing (transferring) income to themselves from others.

PRICE DISCRIMINATION

Sometimes monopoly sellers and other price searchers are able to practice price discrimination. Price discrimination brings with it a certain unsuspected consequence: the production of a quantity of output by the monopolist that is equal to the quantity of output that would be produced under perfectly competitive conditions.

What Is Price Discrimination?

Our discussion so far has assumed that the monopoly seller sells all units of its product for the same price (it is a single-price monopolist). Under certain conditions, though, it could practice **price discrimination.** This occurs when the seller charges different prices for the product it sells, and the price differences do not reflect cost differences.

There are three types of price discrimination: perfect price discrimination, second-degree price discrimination, and third-degree price discrimination.

Suppose a monopolist produces and sells 1,000 units of good *X*. If it sells each unit separately and charges the highest price each consumer would be willing to pay for the product rather than go without it, the monopolist is said to practice **perfect price discrimination.** This is sometimes called *discrimination among units*.

If it charges a uniform price per unit for one specific quantity, a lower price for an additional quantity, and so on, the monopolist practices **second-degree price discrimination.** This is sometimes called *discrimination among quantities*. For example, the monopolist might sell the first 10 units for $10 each, the next 20 units at $9 each, and so on.

If it charges a different price in different markets, or charges a different price to different segments of the buying population, the monopolist practices **third-degree price discrimination.** This is sometimes called *discrimination among buyers*. For example, if your local pharmacy charges senior citizens lower prices for medicine than it charges non-senior citizens, it practices third-degree price discrimination.

Price Discrimination

Occurs when the seller charges different prices for the product it sells, and the price differences do not reflect cost differences.

Perfect Price Discrimination

Occurs when the seller charges the highest price each consumer would be willing to pay for the product rather than go without it.

Second-Degree Price Discrimination

Occurs when the seller charges a uniform price per unit for one specific quantity, a lower price for an additional quantity, and so on.

Third-Degree Price Discrimination

Occurs when the seller charges different prices in different markets, or charges a different price to different segments of the buying population.

[3]The term ''rent seeking'' was introduced into economics in the context we are discussing here by economist Anne Krueger in her article ''The Political Economy of the Rent-Seeking Society,'' *American Economic Review* 64 (June 1974): 291–303.

Why Might the Monopolist Want to Price Discriminate?

Suppose these are the maximum prices at which the following units of a product can be sold: first unit, $10; second unit, $9; third unit, $8; fourth unit, $7. If the monopolist wants to sell four units, and it charges the same price for each unit (it is a single-price monopolist), its total revenue is $28 ($7 × 4).

Now suppose the monopolist *can* and *does* practice perfect price discrimination. It charges $10 for the first unit, $9 for the second unit, $8 for the third unit, and $7 for the fourth unit. Its total revenue is $34 ($10 + $9 + $8 + $7). A comparison of total revenue when the monopolist does and does not price discriminate tells us why the monopolist would want to price discriminate. A perfectly price-discriminating monopolist receives the maximum price for each unit of the good it sells; a single-price monopolist does not.

If the monopolist *perfectly price discriminates*, then for it price equals marginal revenue, $P = MR$. To illustrate, when the monopolist sells its second unit for $9 in our example (having sold the first unit for $10), its total revenue is $19—or its marginal revenue is $9, which is equal to price.

Conditions of Price Discrimination

It is obvious why the monopolist would want to price discriminate. But what conditions must exist before it can? To price discriminate, the following conditions must hold.

1. The seller must exercise some control over price; it must be a price searcher.

2. The seller must be able to distinguish among customers who would be willing to pay different prices.

3. It must be impossible or too costly for one buyer to resell the good to other buyers. The possibility of **arbitrage**, or "buying low and selling high", must not exist.

Arbitrage
Buying a good in a market where its price is low, and selling the good in another market where its price is higher.

If the seller is not a price searcher, it has no control over price and therefore cannot sell a good at different prices to different buyers. Also, unless the seller can distinguish among buyers who would pay different prices, it cannot price discriminate. After all, how would it know to whom to charge the higher (lower) prices? Finally, if a buyer can resell the good, there can be no price discrimination because buyers who buy the good at a lower price will simply turn around and sell the good to other buyers for a price lower than the seller's higher price. In time no one will pay the higher price.

Many movie theaters charge lower prices to matinee moviegoers than to evening moviegoers. It is possible to price discriminate this way because matinee moviegoers cannot resell their seats to evening moviegoers.

Moving to $P = MC$ through Price Discrimination

The perfectly competitive firm exhibits resource allocative efficiency; it produces the quantity of output at which $P = MC$.

What about the single-price monopolist? It produces the quantity of output at which $P > MC$. A quick glance back at Exhibit 10-3 confirms this. At Q_1, price is P_1, which is higher than marginal cost (MC_1). The single-price monopolist produces an inefficient level of output. But what about the monopolist that can and does practice perfect price discrimination? Does it, too, produce an inefficient level of output?

The answer is no. A perfectly price-discriminating monopolist does not lower price on all previous units in order to sell an additional unit of its product. For it, $P =$

MR (as was the case for the perfectly competitive firm). Naturally when the perfectly price-discriminating monopolist produces the quantity of output at which $MR = MC$, it automatically produces the quantity where $P = MC$. In short, the perfectly price-discriminating monopolist and the perfectly competitive firm both exhibit resource allocative efficiency.

Some important points are reviewed in Exhibit 10-7. In (a) we see that the perfectly competitive firm produces where $P = MC$. In (b) the single-price monopolist produces where $P > MC$. In (c) the perfectly price-discriminating monopolist produces where $P = MC$. Notice one important difference between the perfectly competitive firm and the perfectly price-discriminating monopolist. Although both produce where $P = MC$, the perfectly competitive firm charges the same price for each unit of the good it sells, and the perfectly price-discriminating monopolist charges a different price for each unit of the good it sells.

Question:

Suppose a firm charges one person $40 for its product and charges another person only $33. Isn't the first person paying a higher price so that the second person can pay a lower price?

Answer:

No, this is not the case. Suppose there are two persons, O'Neill and Stevens. The maximum price O'Neill will pay for good X is $40; the maximum price Stevens will pay for good X is $33. If a monopolist can and does perfectly price discriminate, it charges O'Neill $40 and Stevens $33.

■ **EXHIBIT 10-7**
Comparison of a Perfectly Competitive Firm, Single-price Monopolist, and Perfectly Price-discriminating Monopolist

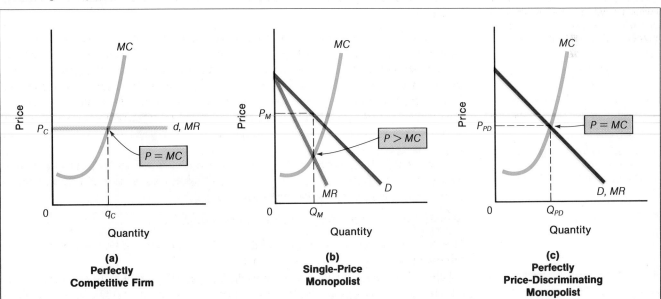

(a)
Perfectly Competitive Firm

(b)
Single-Price Monopolist

(c)
Perfectly Price-Discriminating Monopolist

For both the perfectly competitive firm and the perfectly price-discriminating monopolist, $P = MR$ and the demand curve is the marginal revenue curve. Both produce where $P = MC$. The single-price monopolist, however, produces where $P > MC$ since for it $P > MR$ and its demand curve lies above its marginal revenue curve. One difference between the perfectly competitive firm and the perfectly price-discriminating monopolist is that the former charges the same price for each unit of the good it sells, and the latter charges a different price for each unit of the good it sells.

Theory in Practice

It Looks Like a Deal, It Sounds Like a Deal, but Is It a Deal?

Sellers sometimes advertise one unit of their good for $X, but two units of the same good for less than $2X. For example, a department store might advertise one pair of men's trousers at $40, but two pairs for $70 (which is $10 less than $40 twice). At first sight this might appear to be quite a deal. Whether it is or not is a personal judgment. What it is for certain, however, is an act of price discrimination.

Look at the situation in terms of the department store's marginal cost curve and an individual's demand curve for trousers. In Exhibit 10-8 Brennen's demand curve tells us

he will buy only one pair of trousers if the price is $40 a pair, but that he will buy two pairs if the price is $30 a pair.

Suppose the department store wishes to sell Brennen two pairs of trousers. How might it go about this? It could price trousers at $30 a pair, and Brennen would buy two pairs. Under this pricing scheme the department store receives $60 total revenue. Or it could price the first pair at $40, and the second pair at $30—for a total of $70 for two. Will Brennen be willing to pay $40 for the first pair of trousers and $30 for the second pair? From his demand curve, we see that he will. Under this pricing scheme the department store receives $70 total revenue.

Here's another point to think about. Trousers can be resold. It is possible for Brennen to buy hundreds of pairs of trousers—at $70 for each two pairs—and then resell them for, say, $39 a pair; thus he is undercutting the department store by a dollar (assuming there are numerous buyers who have the same demand curve, or close to the same demand curve, that Brennen has for trousers). In short, there is room for arbitrage here. However, taking advantage of buying low and selling high may be too costly for Brennen.

■ EXHIBIT 10-8
It Looks Like a Deal, It Sounds Like a Deal, but Is It a Deal?

Given the demand curve in the exhibit, two different pricing schemes present themselves. First, $30 can be charged for each pair of trousers, at which price two pairs of trousers will be sold and total revenue will be $60. Second, $40 can be charged for the first pair of trousers, $30 for the second, and two pairs of trousers will be sold bringing in total revenue of $70.

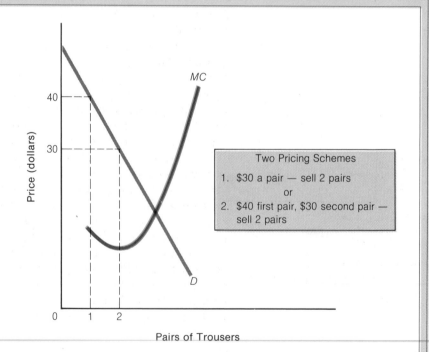

Two Pricing Schemes

1. $30 a pair — sell 2 pairs
   or
2. $40 first pair, $30 second pair — sell 2 pairs

Is O'Neill somehow paying the higher price so that Stevens can pay the lower price? It is easy to see that O'Neill is not by asking if the monopolist would have charged O'Neill a price under $40 if Stevens's maximum price had been $39 instead of $33. Probably it wouldn't—why should it when it could have received O'Neill's maximum price of $40?

Our point is that the perfectly price-discriminating monopolist tries to get the highest price from each customer, irrespective of what other customers pay. In short, the price O'Neill is charged is independent of the price Stevens is charged.

THE CASE AGAINST MONOPOLY

Monopoly is often said to be inefficient in comparison with perfect competition. Here we examine some of the shortcomings that are associated with monopoly.

The Welfare Cost Triangle

Exhibit 10-9 shows demand, marginal revenue, marginal cost, and average total cost curves. We have made the simplifying assumption that the product is produced under constant-cost conditions; as a consequence, marginal cost equals long-run average total cost.[4]

If the product is produced under perfect competition, output Q_C would be produced and sold at a price of P_C. At the competitive equilibrium output level, $P = MC$. If the product is produced under monopoly, output Q_M would be produced and sold at a price of P_M. At the monopoly equilibrium, $P > MC$.

Notice that greater output is produced under perfect competition than monopoly. The net value of the difference in these two output levels is said to be the **welfare cost of monopoly.** In Exhibit 10-9 we can see that the value to buyers of increasing output from Q_M to Q_C is equal to the maximum amount they would pay for this increase in output. This amount is designated by the area Q_MCAQ_C. The costs that would have to be incurred to produce this additional output are designated by the area Q_MBAQ_C. The difference between the two is the triangle BCA. This is the amount buyers value the additional output over and above the opportunity costs of producing the additional output. It is the welfare loss attached to not producing the competitive quantity of output. The triangle BCA is referred to as the **welfare cost triangle.** We conclude that monopoly produces a quantity of output that is "too small" in comparison to the quantity of output produced in perfect competition; thus this difference in output results in a welfare loss to society.

Welfare Cost of Monopoly

The net value (value to buyers over and above costs to suppliers) of the difference between the monopoly quantity of output (where $P > MC$) and the competitive quantity of output (where $P = MC$).

Welfare Cost Triangle

A diagrammatical representation of the welfare cost to society associated with monopoly.

[4]A simplifying assumption makes the analysis simpler without significantly affecting the results.

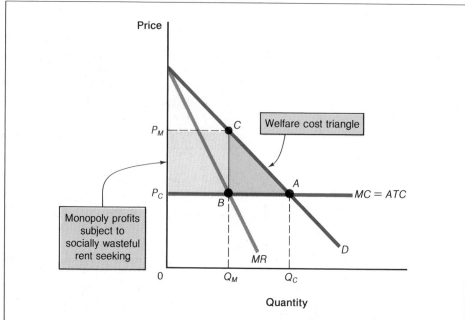

The monopolist produces Q_M and the perfectly competitive firm produces the higher output level Q_C. The welfare cost of monopoly is the triangle between these two levels of output, *BCA*. Rent-seeking activity is also directed to obtaining the monopoly profits, represented by the area P_CP_MCB. Rent seeking is socially wasteful activity in that resources are expended to affect a transfer and not to produce goods and services.

Arnold Harberger was the first economist who tried to determine the actual size of the welfare cost of monopoly in the manufacturing sector of the U.S. economy.[5] He estimated the welfare cost to be a small percentage of the economy's total output. Additional empirical work by other economists puts the figure at approximately 1 percent of total output.

Question:

If the monopolist can and does practice perfect price discrimination, it wouldn't produce "too small" an output level—would it?

Answer:

No, it wouldn't. The analysis of the welfare cost triangle assumes a single-price monopolist.

Rent Seeking is Socially Wasteful

The economist Gordon Tullock has argued that the welfare cost is not the only cost of monopoly to society.[6] Having identified the monopoly profits as P_CP_MCB in Exhibit

[5]Arnold Harberger, "Monopoly and Resource Allocation," *American Economic Review* 44 (May 1954): 77–87.
[6]Gordon Tullock, "The Welfare Cost of Tariffs, Monopolies, and Theft," *Western Economic Journal* 5 (June 1967): 244–32.

Economics in Our Times

Interview: Gordon Tullock

Gordon Tullock is considered one of the founders of public choice theory along with James Buchanan (see Chapter 19). Tullock is also the major developer of the theory of rent seeking. He is currently at the University of Arizona. We interviewed Professor Tullock on March 7, 1988.

Professor Tullock, a major point in your 1967 article on rent seeking was that the welfare cost of monopoly was greater than economists thought. The article has sparked an outpouring of research efforts in rent-seeking theory. Please tell us how you came to write this article.

The story is somewhat amusing. You may remember the first X-efficiency article by Harvey Leibenstein. In some ways, this article shocked me; in other ways, the argument put forth in it seemed plausible. My most seri-

ous criticism of it, though, was that I didn't think allocative efficiency meant *only* the absence of tariffs and monopoly. Nevertheless, the empirical data, which Leibenstein mentioned and I had read elsewhere, did indicate that neither tariffs nor monopoly led to very much inefficiency.

I wrote a response to this article and sent if off to the *American Economic Review*. I got a negative referee report from someone I thought had not understood it at all, along with an apologetic letter from John Gurley, the managing editor, who agreed that the referee hadn't understood the article, but nevertheless said he wasn't going to publish it. Soon afterward, I received a letter from Alice Vandermeulen who was working for the new *Western Economic Journal*. She asked me if I had anything to submit to the journal. I looked over my rent-seeking article, made some minor changes, and sent it to her. At this point, the article was entitled "The welfare effects of tariffs and monopolies." She decided to add the word "theft" to the title, so it became "The welfare effects of tariffs, monopolies, and theft."

I incorporated this paper into my standard lecture which I gave traveling around to various places. At the time I was convinced that my arguments were right and that the whole matter of rent seeking should be given more attention by economists. But I didn't realize the outpouring of further research that would occur.

In fact, the word "outpouring" is somewhat symbolic here. If a number of logs are drifting downstream and get jammed, old-fashioned lumberjacks would look for a single log, called the "key log," which when pulled out would cause things to

break loose. In my opinion, we have something of the same thing here. A very large amount of research which should have been done in the last 30 to 40 years had not been done because this particular "rent-seeking" key log still remained in place. When it was pulled out, an immense volume of research burst forth.

You have said that rent seeking is a socially wasteful activity. How might things be changed so that there is less rent seeking in the world and thus less waste?

This is a difficult question. It is easy to think of ways to remedy particular situations, but the general issue is very difficult. In fact, most governments throughout history have been dominated by rent-seeking activity. For some time in the nineteenth century, most of northwestern Europe was not—but this is an exceptional period. I think we ought to look for explanations of why that period was the way it was, instead of explanations of why we have returned to the normal, yet less desirable, state of affairs.

Anyway, all I can recommend is that economists talk about the social wastefulness of rent seeking and try to convince people that it is undesirable. Some economists have said that economic education does pay off. It seems to me that nineteenth-century northwestern Europe is an example of a place and a time where it did, and with some pressure it may do so again. In any case, David Ricardo and his friends were successful, and I see no reason why we can't be, too.

You have said that the term "rent seeking" is an unfortunate one. Would you explain why?

The problem with the term "rent seeking" is that rents are a perfectly fine thing to seek. For example, if a restaurant decides to improve its decor and increase its rents, we don't object to this.

Jagdish Bhagwati has been pushing the term "DUP," which stands for directly unproductive profit seeking and is pronounced "dupe." I am not sure this is the ideal term, but I think it is better than rent seeking.

Unfortunately one of the characteristics of language development is that once you get started with a term, you stick with it. I am happy to say that in this case I can't be blamed for starting this term.

Professor Tullock, you were trained as a lawyer at the University of Chicago, but have devoted most of your professional life to economics.

Obviously economics won you over. What was it about economics that first attracted you? What is it about economics that still excites you today?

I don't know what is was about economics that won me over. Probably it was somehow or other that I have the type of mind to which economics appeals. I took my only economics course from Henry Simons at the University of Chicago and he got me interested in the subject. (To engage in a little advertising here, I have arranged to have the syllabus of this course reprinted so that it is not lost altogether. I will sell it to anyone interested in it for $4.65.) Simons was an exceptionally good teacher for the brighter students in his class, al-

though I think the duller students detested him. He made his class very interesting, and from the time I finished this course until I became an economist, I read extensively in the economic journals. In fact, I read more extensively then than I do now. It was easier to read the journals back then than it is now.

What still interests me in economics is quite literally the fact that one can hope to improve the world by simply studying it. I must admit that I simply find economics of great interest even in those cases where it has no practical application. I am a very fortunate man to be paid a high salary to pursue my hobby.

10-9, and having noted that they may reasonably be viewed as a transfer from consumers to the monopolist, he asks two questions: First, will individuals compete for this transfer? Second, what are the consequences of people competing for transfers?

The answer to the first question is yes. There is no reason to believe that individuals will turn their backs on monopoly rents; they can be expected to compete for them. As a consequence, individuals will expend resources to bring about a simple transfer from others to themselves. Such rent-seeking behavior is socially wasteful, in the sense that resources that could be used to produce goods and services are used instead to transfer income from one group of persons to another.

For example, suppose group A is currently receiving monopoly rents of $20 million. Groups B, C, and D compete to take the monopoly position away from group A, and with it the monopoly rents. Groups B, C, and D hire lawyers, accountants, lobbyists, secretaries, and research staffs to accomplish their goal. Resources are expended. In the end, group B unseats group A and takes over the monopoly position and the monopoly rents (if any are left after the resource expenditure necessary to obtain the monopoly position). From society's perspective, it does not matter whether group A or group B receives the monopoly rents. What does matter is that the resources used in rent seeking were used in nonproductive instead of productive ways. *Resources were used to obtain a transfer, not to produce more goods.* Moreover, if the desire for the monopoly profits is intense, it is possible that resources valued at the total amount of the transfer—the monopoly rent of $20 million—will be wasted in seeking the transfer. This is area P_CP_MCB. When added to the welfare cost triangle, this increases the cost of monopoly to society.

Question:

Is the motivation for rent seeking the same or different from the motivation for profit seeking?

Answer:

It is the same since monopoly profit is monopoly rent. Notice, however, that there is a difference between profit seeking under perfect competition and monopoly profit (rent) seeking under monopoly. In the former, where there is easy entry into the industry, profit seeking leads to the entry of new firms into the industry, an increase in industry output, and a decrease in price. In monopoly, where high barriers to entry exist, monopoly profit (rent) seeking does not lead to additional output and lower price. Often it simply leads to a transfer of profits or rents and a socially wasteful expenditure of resources.

X-Inefficiency

Economist Harvey Leibenstein maintained that the monopolist is not under pressure to produce its product at the lowest possible cost.[7] It is possible for the monopolist to produce its product above the lowest possible unit cost and still survive. Certainly the monopolist benefits if it can and does lower its costs, but the point is that it doesn't have to in order to survive (with the proviso that average total costs cannot rise so high as to be higher than price). Leibenstein referred to monopolists operating at higher than lowest possible costs, and to the organizational slack that is directly tied to this, as **X-inefficiency.**

It is hard to obtain accurate estimates of X-inefficiency, but whatever its magnitude there are forces working to mitigate it. For example, if a market monopoly is being run inefficiently, persons realizing this may attempt to buy the monopoly, and if successful, lower costs to make higher profits.

X-Inefficiency
The increase in costs and organizational slack in a monopoly resulting from the lack of competitive pressure to push costs down to their lowest possible level.

■ CHAPTER SUMMARY

The Theory of Monopoly

■ The theory of monopoly is built on three assumptions: (1) There is one seller. (2) The single seller sells a product for which there are no close substitutes. (3) There are extremely high barriers to entry into the industry.

■ High barriers to entry may take the form of legal barriers (public franchise, patent, government license), economies of scale, and exclusive ownership of a scarce resource.

Monopoly Pricing and Output

■ The profit-maximizing monopolist produces the quantity of output at which *MR* = *MC* and charges the highest price per unit at which this quantity of output can be sold.

[7]Harvey Leibenstein, "Allocative Efficiency vs. X-Efficiency," *American Economic Review* 56 (June 1966): 392–415.

- For the single-price monopolist, $P > MR$; therefore its demand curve lies above its marginal revenue curve.
- The single-price monopolist sells its output at a price higher than its marginal cost, $P > MC$.

Monopoly Profits in the Long Run

- Monopoly profits are not competed away by the entry of new firms into the industry (as profits are in perfect competition). In monopoly, there are barriers to entering the industry. However, profits may be capitalized into the price of the monopoly firm if it is being sold or competed for indirectly through rent-seeking actions.

Rent Seeking

- Economic or monopoly rent is a payment in excess of opportunity cost. Monopoly profits are rents. Activity directed at competing for and obtaining rent is referred to as rent seeking. From society's perspective, rent seeking is a socially wasteful activity. People use resources to affect a transfer of the rent from others to themselves instead of producing goods and services.

Price discrimination

- Price discrimination occurs when a seller charges different prices for its product, and the price differences are not due to cost differences.
- Before a seller can price discriminate, certain conditions must hold: (1) The seller must be a price searcher. (2) The seller must be able to distinguish between customers who would be willing to pay different prices. (3) It must be impossible or too costly for a buyer to resell the good to others.
- A seller that practices perfect price discrimination (charges the maximum price for each unit of product sold) sells the quantity of output at which $P = MC$. It exhibits resource allocative efficiency.
- The single-price monopolist is said to produce too little output, since it produces less than would be produced under perfect competition. This is not the case for a perfectly price-discriminating monopolist.

■ QUESTIONS TO ANSWER AND DISCUSS

1. The perfectly competitive firm exhibits resource allocative efficiency ($P = MC$) and the single-price monopolist does not. What is the reason for this difference?

2. Since the monopolist is a single seller of a product with no close substitutes, is it able to obtain any price for its good that it wants?

3. When a single-price monopolist maximizes profits, price is greater than marginal cost. This means that consumers would be willing to pay more for additional units of output than they cost to produce. Given this, why doesn't the monopolist produce more?

4. Is there a welfare cost triangle if the firm produces the quantity of output at which price equals marginal cost?

5. It has been noted that rent seeking is individually rational, but socially wasteful. Explain.

6. Occasionally students accuse their instructors, rightly or wrongly, of practicing grade discrimination. What these students mean is that the instructor "charges" some students a higher price for a given grade than other students (in the sense of requiring some students to do more or better). Grade discrimination involves no money, price discrimination does. Discuss the similarities and differences between the two types of discrimination. Which do you prefer less or perhaps dislike more? Why?

7. Make a list of real-world price discrimination practices. Do they meet the conditions posited for price discrimination?

8. For many years in California, car washes would advertise "Ladies Day." This was one day out of the week when a woman could have her car washed for a price lower than a man could have his car washed. It was argued that this was a form of sexual discrimination. The argument was accepted, and a California court ruled that there could no longer be a "Ladies Day." Do you think that this was a case of sexual discrimination or price discrimination? Explain your answer.

9. Make a list of both market monopolies and government monopolies. Which list is longer? Why do you think this is so?

10. Fast-food stores often charge higher prices for their products in high-crime areas than in low-crime areas. In this an act of price discrimination? Why?

Chapter 11

Monopolistic Competition and Oligopoly

■ INTRODUCTION

In our interview with George Stigler in Chapter 9, he said that "if a field ever got to the dreadful state that there were no more interesting questions left, it would be terrible."

In economics, things are far from terrible. There are hundreds of interesting questions left. This chapter touches on many of them.

For instance, is competition wasteful? Adam Smith viewed the process of competition as beneficial to society at large. According to Smith, competition pushes entrepreneurs to search for new profits; in the process they provide goods and services that people want to buy. It also protects the consumer by keeping prices down, quality up, and sellers civilized. Smith was not in favor of restricting the number of sellers, which he believed would hurt the general public. Discussing the number of ale-houses, in a colorful passage, he says, "It is not the multitude of ale-houses, to give the most suspicious example, that occasions a general disposition to drunkenness among the common people; but that disposition arising from other causes necessarily gives employment to a multitude of ale-houses."[1]

In the 1930s economists in a formal way began to question some of the benefits of competition. Edward Chamberlin, whose name, along with Joan Robinson, is linked to the theory of monopolistic competition, put forth the "excess capacity theorem," which some called the "carcicature of wasteful competition." For Chamberlin and others, it was possible to have too many small firms. For cost purposes, it was sometimes better to have fewer, big firms than more, smaller firms.

Another question considered in this chapter is, How do small numbers of competitors compete? For example, do they band together to make themselves better off at the expense of their customers and thus compete very little if at all? Or do they compete with each other intensely, long, and often? Do they follow one policy under certain circumstances and another policy under another set of circumstances? What is the role of strategic behavior or game playing when there are only a few sellers? Is game playing rampant or minimal?

The following pages explore some of these issues.

[1]Adam Smith, *An Inquiry into the Nature and Causes of The Wealth of Nations*, vol. 1 (Chicago: University of Chicago Press, 1976), p. 383.

■ WHAT THIS CHAPTER IS ABOUT

In this chapter we discuss monopolistic competition and oligopoly. Monopolistic competition is a market structure that is said to combine elements of both perfect competition and monopoly. Oligopoly is a market structure that is dominated by a small number of firms, for which several theories have been developed. The discussions of monopolistic competition and oligopoly follow the format we used in Chapters 9 and 10. First, we outline the theories, focusing on their assumptions. Second, we discuss the predicted behavior of both monopolistic competitors and oligopolists.

Key Questions to Keep in Mind as You Read

1. What is monopolistic competition? How is it similar to and different from perfect competition and monopoly?

2. What does it mean to say that monopolistic competitors produce with excess capacity? What is the excess capacity theorem?

3. What is oligopoly? Why are there more theories of oligopoly than of other market structures?

4. What is a cartel? What are the problems of forming and maintaining a cartel?

5. What factor does the theory of contestable markets emphasize? How does the theory of contestable markets challenge orthodox market structure theory?

THE THEORY OF MONOPOLISTIC COMPETITION

Monopolistic Competition
A theory of market structure based on three assumptions: many sellers and buyers, firms producing and selling slightly differentiated products, and easy entry and exit.

The theory of **monopolistic competition** (or monopolistically competitive market structure) is built on three assumptions:

1. **There are many sellers and buyers.** This assumption held for perfect competition, too. For this reason, you might think the monopolistic competitor is a price taker, but this is not the case. It is a price searcher, basically because of the following assumption.

2. **Each firm (in the industry) produces and sells a slightly differentiated product.** Differences among the products may be due to brand names, packaging, location, credit terms connected with the sale of the product, friendliness of the sales people, and so forth. Product differentiation may be real or imagined. For example, aspirin may be aspirin, but if some people view a name brand aspirin (such as Bayer) as better than a generic brand, product differentiation exists.

3. **There is easy entry and exit.** Monopolistic competition resembles perfect competition in this respect. There are no barriers to entry and exit, legal or otherwise.

Examples of monopolistic competition include retail clothing, restaurants, textbook publishing, and service stations.

Question:

Is the breakfast cereal industry an example of monopolistic competition? After all, there are many different cereals on the market: for example, Crispix, Cracklin' Oat Bran, Apple Cinnamon Squares, Frosted Mini-Wheats, Cheerios, Cocoa Krispies, Rice Krispies, Raisin Bran, Corn Flakes, Frosted Flakes, Nutri-Grain, Product 19, Apple Raisin Crisp, to name only a few.

Answer:

With the exception of Cheerios, all the cereals mentioned are produced by *one* firm, Kellogg's. Cheerios is made by General Mills. Just because there are many different cereals, it does not necessarily follow that many firms make these cereals. In fact, there are relatively few firms in the cereal industry; thus the cereal industry is an example of oligopoly (few sellers). We discuss this market structure soon.

You Already Know More about Monopolistic Competition than You Think: Answer These Questions and See

You have already studied two theories of market structures, perfect competition and monopoly. Using your knowledge of these theories and the assumptions of the theory of monopolistic competition, what do you think the theory of monopolistic competition predicts?

First, do you think the monopolistic competitor (or monopolistic competitive firm) faces a horizontal or downward-sloping demand curve? The answer is downward sloping. The assumption of product differentiation tells us this. Because of product differentiation, each monopolistic competitor has some control over the price of the product it sells. Because its product is slightly different from other firms', it can raise price and still sell some of its product. In short, it is a *price searcher*.

Second, is the demand curve facing the monopolistic competitive firm flatter or steeper than the demand curve facing the monopoly seller? It is flatter. Why? As the discussion of elasticity in Chapter 6 explained, the more substitutes a product has, the greater the price elasticity of demand for the good. In monopolistic competition, there are substitutes; in monopoly, there are none. Therefore we predict that the demand curve facing a monopolistic competitor will be flatter than the demand curve facing a monopoly seller.

Third, will $P = MR$ (as in perfect competition), or will $P > MR$ (as in monopoly)? The answer is $P > MR$. The reason is that, as we said, the monopolistic competitor faces a *downward-sloping* demand curve. This means it has to lower price to sell an additional unit of the good. It follows that in monopolistic competition, the demand curve facing the firm lies above its marginal revenue curve.

Fourth, does the monopolistic competitor exhibit resource allocative efficiency? The answer is no. Since it maximizes profits by producing the quantity of output at which $MR = MC$ (all firms, no matter what the market structure, do this), and $P > MR$, it follows that $P > MC$ at the quantity of output at which the monopolistic competitive firm produces. Like the monopolist, the monopolistic competitor produces the quantity of output at which $MR = MC$ and charges the highest possible price per unit for the output. See Exhibit 11-1.

Fifth, will there be economic profits in the long run? Mostly likely, there won't be. The assumption of easy entry and exit precludes this. If firms in the industry are earning profits, new firms will enter the industry and compete them away. The long-run position in monopolistic competition is illustrated in Exhibit 11-2.

Question:

To the question of whether there will be profits in the long run, the answer was "Most likely, there won't be." Why was the answer qualified by "most likely"? Why not simply "no"?

The monopolistic competitor produces the quantity of output at
which $MR = MC$ and charges the
highest price per unit consistent
with this output. Notice that at q_1,
$P > MC$. This seller is receiving
short-run profits. It is not likely
that these profits will continue,
however, because there is easy
entry in the theory of monopolistic
competition.

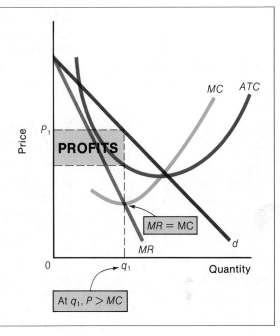

■ **EXHIBIT 11-2**
Monopolistic Competition in the Long Run: Zero Economic Profits

Because of easy entry and exit,
any short-run profits will most
likely be competed away in the
long run by new firms entering
the industry. Any short-run losses
will disappear in the long run owing to some firms exiting the industry. In long-run equilibrium,
price equals short-run average total cost and there will be zero
economic profits.

Because of easy entry
and exit, $P = ATC$ and
there are zero economic
profits in long-run
equilibrium. Notice
that A is not the lowest
point on ATC curve.

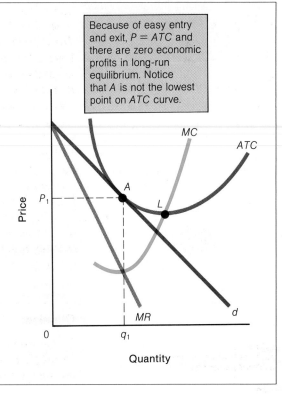

Biography
Joan Robinson
(1903–1983)

Brief Biography

Joan Violet Robinson was born in Surrey, England, on October 31, 1903, and died in Cambridge on August 5, 1983. Her great-grandfather, Frederick Denison Maurice, lost his position at King's College, London, for refusing to believe in eternal damnation. Like him she was tough in character and a nonconformist (for example,

she bought most of her clothing in India). She inspired strong feelings of both love and hate. Many economists in the 1970s expected that Joan Robinson would receive the Nobel Prize in Economics. The magazine *Business Week* even went so far as to publish a long article about her in anticipation of the event. She never did win the Nobel Prize.

The Two Cambridges

Joan Robinson published her theory of monopolistic competition at about the same time that Edward Chamberlin presented his. Joan Robinson launched her theory from Cambridge University, Cambridge, England. Chamberlin launched his from Harvard University, Cambridge, Massachusetts.

A Box of Tools

Robinson believed that she and Chamberlin had introduced a new technical apparatus—"a box of analytical tools"—that would deal with more general market conditions than

perfect competition (Robinson believed perfect competition to be a special case, not the general case).

Critic of the Market System

Robinson was a strong and vocal critic of the market system. First, she accepted the view that the market economy is inherently unstable. Second, she thought that the market economy is subject to the problems of income inequality, manipulation of demand, and extreme business concentration.

A Personal Note

Joan Robinson and Edward Chamberlin are given joint credit for developing the theory of monopolistic competition. Chamberlin resented this and worked obsessively most of his life to refine and differentiate his ideas and work from Robinson's. Robinson, on hearing of Chamberlin's anguish and obsession, is reported to have said, "I am sorry I ruined his life."

Answer:

The answer was qualified by "most likely" because monopolistic competition differs from perfect competition, where short-run profits attract new firms that produce the *identical* product produced by existing firms in the industry. In monopolistic competition new firms usually produce a *close substitute* for the product produced by existing firms. Is this enough of a difference to upset the zero economic profit condition in the long run? In some instances, it may be. An existing firm may differentiate its product sufficiently in the minds of the buying public that although new firms enter the industry and compete with it, it still continues to earn profits. Firms that try to differentiate their products from those of other sellers in ways other than in price are said to be engaged in *nonprice competition*. This may take the form of advertising or trying to establish a brand name that is well respected, among other things. For example, soft drink companies' advertising often tries to stress the uniqueness of their product. Dr. Pepper has been advertised as "the unusual one," 7-Up as "the uncola." IBM has a well-respected name in personal computers, Bayer in aspirin, Hilton in hotels. Such well-respected names sometime differentiate products enough in the minds of the buying public so that short-run profits are not easily, or completely, competed away by the entry of new firms into the industry.

Excess Capacity: What Is It, and Is It "Good" or "Bad"?

Excess Capacity Theory

States that a monopolistic competitor in equilibrium produces an output smaller than the one that would minimize its costs of production.

The theory of monopolistic competition makes one major prediction which is generally referred to as the **excess capacity theorem.** It states that in equilibrium a monopolistic competitor will produce an output smaller than the one that would minimize its costs of production.

To illustrate, look at point *A* in Exhibit 11-3b. At this point the monopolistic competitor is in long-run equilibrium since profits are zero ($P = ATC$). Now notice that point *A* is *not* the lowest point on the average total cost curve. The lowest point on the average total cost curve is point *L*. We conclude that in long-run equilibrium, when the monopolistic competitor earns zero economic profits, it is not producing the quantity of output at which average total costs (unit costs) are minimized for the given scale of plant.

In Exhibit 11-3 we also extend the analysis and graphics and contrast the perfectly competitive firm and the monopolistic competitor in long-run equilibrium. In (a) the

■ **EXHIBIT 11-3**

A Comparison of Perfect Competition and Monopolistic Competition: The Issue of Excess Capacity

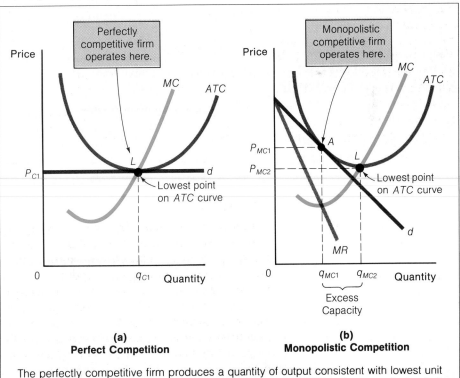

**(a)
Perfect Competition**

**(b)
Monopolistic Competition**

The perfectly competitive firm produces a quantity of output consistent with lowest unit costs. The monopolistic competitor does not. If it did, it would produce q_{MC2} instead of q_{MC1}. The monopolistic competitor is said to underutilize its plant size or to have excess capacity.

perfectly competitive firm is earning zero economic profits and price (P_{C1}) equals average total cost (ATC). Furthermore, the point at which price equals average total cost (point L) is the lowest point on the average total cost curve. In long-run equilibrium, the perfectly competitive firm produces the quantity of output at which unit costs are minimized.

Now look at (b). Here the monopolistic competitor is earning zero economic profits and price (P_{MC1}) equals average total cost. As previously noted, the monopolistic competitor does not produce the quantity of output at which unit costs are minimized. If it did, it would produce quantity of output q_{MC2}. Because of this, it has been argued that the monopolistic competitor produces "too little" output (q_{MC1} instead of q_{MC2}) and charges "too high" a price (P_{MC1} instead of P_{MC2}). With respect to the former, "too little" output translates into the monopolistic competitor *under-utilizing* its present plant size. It is said to have *excess capacity*. In (b) the excess capacity is equal to the difference between q_{MC2} and q_{MC1}.

It is sometimes argued that the monopolistic competitor operates at excess capacity because it faces a downward-sloping demand curve. To see this, once again turn to Exhibit 11-3b. Notice that the only way the firm would *not operate* at excess capacity is if its demand curve were tangent to point L—the lowest point on the ATC curve. But for this to occur the demand curve must be horizontal, which would require *homogeneous products*. There is no possible way for a downward-sloping demand curve to be tangent to point L. In short, the monopolistic competitor operates at excess capacity as a consequence of its downward-sloping demand curve, and its downward-sloping demand curve is a consequence of differentiated products. We leave you with a question many economists ask, but do not always answer the same way: If excess capacity is the price we pay for differentiated products (more choice), is it too high a price to pay?

OLIGOPOLY: EMPHASIS ON INTERDEPENDENCE

Oligopoly

A theory of market structure based on three assumptions: few sellers and many buyers, firms producing either homogeneous or differentiated products, and significant barriers to entry.

There is no one theory of **oligopoly** as there is for perfect competition, monopoly, and monopolistic competition. The different theories of oligopoly do make some common assumptions, however:

1. **There are few sellers and many buyers.** It is usually assumed that the few firms of an oligopoly are mutually interdependent; each one is aware that its actions will influence the other firms and that the actions of other firms affect it. The interdependence among firms is a key characteristic of oligopoly.

2. **Firms produce and sell either homogeneous or differentiated products.** Steel is a homogeneous product produced in an oligopolistic market; cars are a differentiated product produced in an oligopolistic market. The oligopolist is a price searcher. It, too, like all other types of firms, produces the quantity of output at which $MR = MC$.

3. **There are significant barriers to entry.** Economies of scale are perhaps the most significant barrier to entry in oligopoly theory, but patent rights, exclusive control over an essential resource, and legal barriers also act as barriers to entry here.

Oligopoly in the Real World

Concentration Ratio

The percentage of industry sales (or assets, output, labor force, or some other factor) accounted for by x-number of firms in the industry.

Which industries today are dominated by a small number of firms? Economists have developed the **concentration ratio** to help answer this question. This is the percentage of industry sales (or assets, output, labor force, or some other factor) accounted for by x-number of firms in the industry. The "x-number" in the definition is usually four or eight, but it can be any number (although it is usually small). It follows from

Theory in Practice

You Can Have the Comics, Just Give Me the Coupons Section

In Chapter 10 on monopoly we introduced the topic of price discrimination. Not only do monopolists sometimes price discriminate, but occasionally so do other price searchers, such as monopolistic competitors and oligopolists.

Some economists argue that *third-degree price discrimination,* or discrimination among buyers, is sometimes employed through the use of cents-off coupons. (Remember that third-degree price discrimination exists if a seller sells the same product at different prices to different segments of the population.)

As you know, one of the conditions of price discrimination is that the seller has to be able to distinguish among customers who would be willing to pay different prices.

Ask yourself this: Would people who value their time highly be more willing to pay a higher price for a product then people who do not? Some sellers think so. They argue that people who place a high value on their time want to economize on the *shopping time* connected with the pur-

chase of the product. If sellers want to price discriminate between these two types of customers—charging more to customers who value time more and charging less to customers who value time less—they must determine the category into which each of their customers falls.

How would you go about this if you were a seller? What many real-world sellers do is place cents-off coupons in newspapers and magazines. They hypothesize that people who value their time relatively low will spend it clipping and sorting coupons. The people who place a relatively high value on their time will not.

In effect, things work much like this in, say, a grocery store:

1. The posted price for all products is the same for all customers.
2. Both Linda and Josh put product *X* in their shopping carts.
3. When Linda gets up to the counter, the clerk asks, "Do you have any coupons today?" Linda says no. She is therefore charged the posted price for all products, including *X.*
4. When Josh gets up to the counter, the clerk asks, "Do you have any coupons today?" Josh says yes and pulls out a coupon for product *X.* Josh pays a lower price for product *X* than Linda pays.

In conclusion, one of the uses of the cents-off coupon is to make it possible for the seller to charge a higher price to one group of customers than to another group. (We say *one* of the uses, because cents-off coupons are also used to induce customers to try a product and so forth.)

the definition of a concentration ratio that a high ratio implies that few sellers make up the industry; a low concentration ratio implies that more than a few sellers make up the industry.

Suppose we calculate a four-firm concentration ratio for industry Z. Total industry sales for a given year are $5 million, and the four largest firms in the industry account for $4.5 million in sales. The four-firm concentration ratio would be .90 or 90 percent ($4.5 million is .90 of $5 million). Industries with high four- and eight-firm concentration ratios in recent years include cigarettes, cars, tires and inner tubes, cereal breakfast foods, telephone and telegraph, farm machinery, and soap and other detergents, to name a few.

Note, however, that although concentration ratios are often used to determine the extent (or degree) of oligopoly, they are not perfect guides to industry concentration. Most importantly, they do not take into account foreign competition and competition from substitute domestic goods. For example, the U.S. automobile industry is highly concentrated (.93 four-firm concentration ratio in 1982), but it still faces stiff competition from abroad. A more relevant concentration ratio for this particular industry might be computed on a worldwide basis.

PRICE AND OUTPUT UNDER OLIGOPOLY: THREE THEORIES

Oligopoly is often a more difficult market structure to analyze than perfect competition, monopoly, and monopolistic competition. This is largely due to the interdependence among firms in oligopoly. When interdependence among firms exists, the significant concept becomes the reaction of one firm to the actions of one or more of the other firms. Because many possible assumptions can be made about a firm's reactions, a number of different oligopoly theories exist. Here we discuss three: the kinked demand curve theory, the price leadership theory, and the cartel theory.

The Kinked Demand Curve Theory

Kinked Demand Curve Theory
A theory of oligopoly that assumes that if a single firm in the industry cuts price, other firms will do likewise, but if it raises price, other firms will not follow suit. The theory predicts price stickiness or rigidity.

The behavioral assumption in the **kinked demand curve theory** is that if a single firm lowers price, other firms will do likewise, but if a single firm raises price, other firms will not follow suit. Suppose there are five firms in an industry, A, B, C, D, and E. If firm A raises its price, the other firms maintain their prices. If firm A cuts its price, the other firms match the price cut.

The kinked demand curve theory, developed in the 1930s by Paul Sweezy, is portrayed in Exhibit 11-4. The current price being charged by the firm is $19. If the firm raises its price to $20, other firms will not match it, and therefore the firm's sales will drop off (from 20 to 10). In short, the demand curve for the firm above $19 is highly elastic. However, if the firm should lower its price to, say, $18, other firms will match the price cut, and therefore the firm's sales will not increase by much (only from 20 to 21). Demand is much less elastic below $19 than above it. We conclude that there is a *kink* in the firm's demand curve at the current price. We have designated the kink by the letter "K" in Exhibit 11-4. The kink signifies that other firms respond radically differently to a single firm's price hikes than to its price cuts.

Actually, there are two demand curves and two marginal revenue curves as we have shown in the window in Exhibit 11-4. Only the thicker portions of the curves in the window are relevant, however, and thus appear in the main diagram. To illustrate, starting at a price of $19, the firm believes price cuts will be matched but price hikes will not. This says that when considering a price cut, the firm believes it faces the more inelastic of the two demand curves, d_2 instead of d_1, and the corresponding marginal revenue curve, MR_2 instead of MR_1. But when considering a price hike, the firm believes it faces the more elastic of the two demand curves, d_1 instead of d_2, and the corresponding marginal revenue curve, MR_1 instead of MR_2. It follows that *the* demand curve and *the* marginal revenue curve the firm faces are part of d_2 and part of MR_2, and part of d_1 and part of MR_1, respectively, depending on whether it is considering a price cut or hike.

Question:

Why do firms match price cuts but not price hikes?

Answer:

It has been argued that firms match price cuts because failure to do so will result in their losing a large share of the market. They do not match price hikes because they hope to gain in market share.

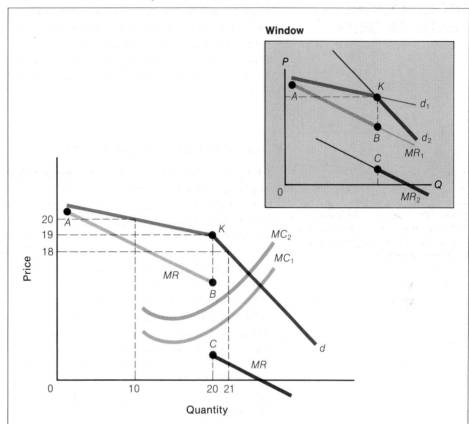

The key behavioral assumption of the theory is that rival firms will not match a price hike but will match a price cut. The theory predicts that changes in marginal costs in area *B* to *C* will not bring changes in price or output. In the window in the exhibit, we see two demand curves and two marginal revenue curves. The firm believes it faces d_2, the more inelastic demand curve, if it cuts price; the firm believes it faces d_1, the more elastic demand curve, when it raises price. The relevant portions of each demand curve are indicated by heavy lines. We show only the relevant parts of the demand curves in the main diagram in the exhibit.

Price Rigidity and Oligopoly

Notice the marginal revenue curve for the oligopolist in the main diagram of Exhibit 11-4. Directly below the kink, it drops off sharply. In fact, we may see the marginal revenue curve as three segments: a line from point *A* to point *B*, which corresponds to the upper part of the demand curve; a gap between points *B* and *C*, which comes directly below the kink in the demand curve; and a line from point *C* onward, which corresponds to the lower part of the demand curve from point *K* onward.

The gap between points *B* and *C* represents the sharp change in marginal revenue that comes about once price is lowered below the kink on the demand curve. The gap helps explain why prices might be less flexible (more rigid) in oligopoly than other market structures. We recall that the oligopolistic firm produces the output at which marginal revenue equals marginal cost. For the firm in Exhibit 11-4, though, marginal cost can change between points B and C, and the firm will continue to produce the same quantity of output and charge the same price. For example, an increase in marginal cost from MC_1 to MC_2 will not lead to a change in production levels or price.

To put it differently, prices are "sticky" if oligopolistic firms face kinked demand curves. Costs can change within certain limits, and such firms will not change their prices because they expect that none of their competitors will follow their price hikes, but that all will match their price cuts.

Criticisms of the Kinked Demand Curve Theory. As previously noted, the kinked demand curve (and resulting MR curve) posits that prices in oligopoly will be less flexible (or more rigid) than in other market structures. The theory has been criticized on both theoretical and empirical grounds. On a theoretical level, looking at Exhibit 11-4, the theory fails to explain how the original price of $19 came about. In other words, why does the *kink* come at $19? It is a theory that is better at explaining things once the kink (the current price) has been identified than in explaining the placement of the kink.

On empirical grounds the theory has been challenged as a *general theory of oligopoly*. For example, economist George Stigler found no evidence that the oligopolists he examined were more reluctant to match price increases than price cuts, which calls into question the behavioral assumption behind the kinked demand curve.[2]

Question:

Are there any real-world examples of firms behaving the way the kinked demand curve theory predicts?

Answer:

In the years following airline deregulation, the airline industry seemed to follow the pricing patterns specified in the theory. For example, United, Eastern, TWA, and Pan American began to lower fares in 1981 and 1982; they were followed by other major airlines. At one time in 1981 United raised fares and the other airlines did not. In 1984, Braniff lowered fares and was followed by American and Delta.

The Price Leadership Theory

Price Leadership Theory

In this theory of oligopoly the dominant firm in the industry determines price, and all other firms take their price as given.

The key behavioral assumption in the **price leadership theory** is that one firm in the industry—called the dominant firm—determines price and all other firms take this price as given. For example, suppose there are ten firms in an industry, A–J, and that firm A is the dominant firm; assume also that it is much larger than its rival firms (although the dominant firm need not be the largest firm in the industry, it could be the low-cost firm). The dominant firm sets the price that maximizes its profits, and all other firms take this price as given. All other firms, then, are seen as price takers; thus they will equate price with their respective marginal costs.

This explanation suggests that the dominant firm does not concern itself with the other firms in the industry but rather simply forces other firms to adapt. This is not

[2]George Stigler, "The Kinky Oligopoly Demand Curve and Rigid Prices," *Journal of Political Economy* 55 (October 1947): 432–49.

quite correct. The dominant firms sets the price based on information it has on the other firms in the industry. We see this in Exhibit 11-5.

In (a) the market demand curve and the horizontal sum of the marginal cost curves of the fringe firms (all firms other than the dominant firm) are shown. Since these fringe firms are price takers, the marginal cost curve in (a) is the supply curve. The dominant firm observes that at a price of P_1 the fringe firms alone can supply the entire market. They will supply Q_1. In short, P_1 and Q_1 is the situation in the industry or market *that excludes the dominant firm*.

Now add the dominant firm. It derives its demand curve, D_{DN}, by noting how much is left over for it to supply at each given price. For example, at a price of P_1 we noted that the fringe firms would supply the entire market and nothing would be left for the dominant firm to supply. So a price of P_1 and an output of zero is one point on the dominant firm's demand curve, which we see in (b). (Note that sometimes the dominant firm's demand curve is referred to as the "residual demand curve" for obvious reasons.) The dominant firm continues to locate other points on its demand curve by noting the difference between the market demand curve (D) and MC_F at each price.

Once the dominant firm calculates its residual demand curve, it produces the quantity of output at which its marginal revenue equals its marginal cost. This level is q_{DN} in Exhibit 11-5b. It charges the highest price for this quantity of output, which is P_{DN}. This price is the price that the dominant firm sets and the fringe firms take.

■ **EXHIBIT 11-5**
Price Leadership Theory

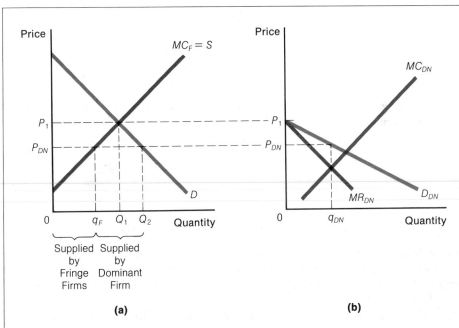

Here we have a dominant firm and a number of fringe firms. (a) The horizontal sum of the marginal cost curves of the fringe firms gives us the supply curve. At P_1, the fringe firms supply the entire market. (b) The dominant firm derives its demand curve by computing the difference between market demand (D) and MC_F at each price below P_1. It then produces q_{DN} and charges P_{DN}. P_{DN} becomes the price that the fringe firms take. They equate price and marginal cost and produce q_F in (a). The remainder of the output—the difference between Q_2 and q_F—is produced by the dominant firm.

Since they act as price takers here, they equate P_{DN} with marginal cost and produce q_F, as shown in (a). The remainder of the total output produced by the industry—the difference between Q_2 and q_F—is produced by the dominant firm. This means that the distance from the origin to q_{DN} in (b) is equal to the difference between Q_2 and q_F in panel (a).

At one time or another, the following firms have been price leaders in their industries: R. J. Reynolds (cigarettes), General Motors (autos), Kellogg's (breakfast cereals), Goodyear Tire and Rubber (tires).

The Cartel Theory

Cartel Theory

In this theory of oligopoly oligopolistic firms act in a manner consistent with having only one firm in the industry.

Cartel

An organization of firms that reduces output and increases price in an effort to increase joint profits.

The key behavioral assumption of the **cartel theory** is that oligopolists in an industry act in a manner consistent with there being only one firm in the industry. In short, they form a **cartel** in order to capture the benefits that would exist for a monopolist. A *cartel* is an organization of firms that reduces output and increases price in an effort to increase joint profits. Before turning to the specifics of cartel theory, we need to illustrate the benefits that may arise from forming and maintaining a cartel.

In Exhibit 11-6 we show an *industry* in long-run competitive equilibrium. The price is P_1 and the quantity of output is Q_1. The industry is producing the output at which price equals marginal cost and there are zero economic profits. Now suppose the firms that make up the industry form a cartel and reduce output to Q_C. The new price becomes P_C (cartel price), and there are profits equal to CP_CAB, which can be shared among the members of the cartel. With no cartel, there were no profits; with a cartel, profits are made. Thus an incentive exists to form a cartel and behave cooperatively rather than competitively. But even though the incentive exists to form a cartel, this does not mean that one can be formed, or if formed, that it will be successfully maintained. Several problems await firms that wish to form and maintain a cartel, in addition to the fact that legislation prohibits certain types of cartels in the United States.

■ **EXHIBIT 11-6**
The Benefits of a Cartel (to Cartel Members)

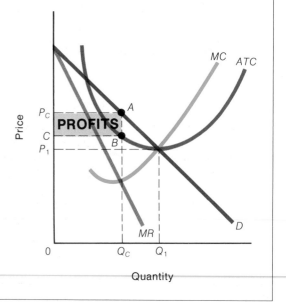

We assume the industry is in long-run competitive equilibrium, producing Q_1 and charging P_1. There are no profits. A reduction in output to Q_C through the formation of a cartel raises price to P_C and brings profits of CP_CAB. (Note: You are accustomed to seeing long-run competitive equilibrium for a firm, not the industry. See Chapter 9 where we worked with a horizontal demand curve that faced the firm. Here we work with a downward-sloping demand curve that faces the industry. Don't be misled by this difference. No matter what type of demand curve we use, long-run competitive equilibrium comes where $P = MC = SRATC = LRATC$.)

Code Names, Cheating, and Cartels

Economics is sometimes full of intrigue. Consider what has come to be known as "the incredible electrical conspiracy."* Between 1956 and 1959 the executives of General Electric Company, Westinghouse Electric Corporation, Allis-Chalmers, Southern States Equipment, and a few other companies entered into a cartel agreement. They conspired among themselves to fix prices as follows: Buyers of electrical equipment often asked for sealed (secret) bids from sellers. The sellers of the electrical equipment decided to enter into an agreement whereby they would rotate among themselves the "right" to make the lowest bid. One company would

*"The Incredible Electrical Conspiracy," *Fortune* (April 1961): 132; (May 1961): 161.

make the lowest bid one time, another company would make the lowest bid the next time, and so on. This is called *bid rigging*. With bid rigging, the low bid is likely to be higher than it would have been otherwise.

The business executives who entered into this agreement tried to maintain the secrecy of their actions. Their meetings were clandestine, often at nonbusiness places such as the golf course. When they registered at hotels, they did not use their company's name. Letters were sent without a return address; code names were used.

There was one problem: The conspirators began to cheat on the agreement. Companies that had agreed not to submit a low bid submitted the lowest bid. During the trial, some of the defendants argued that cheating was so rampant that profitability was greater without the cartel than with it. In any case, the trial ended with the companies being fined $2 million, 6 executives going to jail, and 23 others receiving suspended sentences.

Another cartel in which cheating has been prominent is OPEC (Organization of Petroleum Exporting Countries), perhaps the most famous cartel in history (with the possible exception

of the "cartel" on "Dallas"). It was formed in 1960 and consisted then of Iran, Iraq, Kuwait, Saudi Arabia, and Venezuela. By 1973 OPEC had 13 members. For the first ten years, OPEC had little success. During this time oil prices actually fell in real terms. In the 1970s, however, OPEC began to assert itself, and oil prices increased dramatically. A number of events led to OPEC's success, including some that were external to OPEC itself. For example, it has been argued that misguided U.S. domestic oil policy at that time kept U.S. oil production low and thus gave OPEC a stronger hand.

OPEC's success began to falter in 1982, however. Owing to a reduced demand for oil and a more market-oriented U.S. domestic policy in oil, oil markets began to be characterized by surpluses. Cheating by OPEC members began. Almost every news magazine and newspaper reported that many of the OPEC countries were offering the buyers of oil "under-the-table" discounts. In short, the price set at Geneva was one thing (OPEC oil ministers often held their meetings in Geneva, Switzerland), but actual selling prices were something else. In 1986, the oil market collapsed and prices fell to about 35 percent of their earlier levels.

The Problem of Forming the Cartel. Even if it were legal, getting the sellers of an industry together to form a cartel can be costly especially when the number of sellers is large. Each potential cartel member might resist incurring the costs of forming the cartel because it stands to benefit more if someone else does it. In other words, each potential member has an incentive to become a free rider: to stand by and take a free ride on the actions of others. This being the case, we cannot simply assume that because there are benefits to organizing and forming a cartel, one will automatically be formed. There are costs as well as benefits in organizing and forming a cartel.

The Problem of Formulating Cartel Policy. Suppose the first problem is solved, and potential cartel members form a cartel. Now comes the problem of formulating

So You Want to Be a Cartel? Call 1-800-777-Gov't (Government)

We often here that the government is in the business of breaking up cartels. As Economics in Our Times, "Code Names, Cheating, and Cartels," pointed out, the government has prosecuted executives in firms that were engaged in implementing a cartel agreement. However, the role government has played and continues to play in cartels is mixed. On occasion government has actually helped to create and maintain a cartel instead of breaking it up. There are even cases where the cartel in question wouldn't exist without the government's assistance.

For example, in the area of agriculture, the acreage allotment program (in which the government restricts the number of acres a farmer can plant of a given crop) is aimed at reducing the supply of a crop; this is an objective of farmers who expect a reduction in supply to bring about higher prices, higher revenues, and higher profits. Could the farmers collectively reduce the supply of their crop without government assistance? Would a cartel agreement specifying a lower level of output work? It's not likely. The problems of forming and maintaining a noncheating cartel would probably be too great to overcome. However, a government program that restricts production gets around these problems. In the end, a government program that restricts production and a cartel that restricts production have the same outcome.

Along the same lines, consider the Civil Aeronautics Board (CAB) in the days of airline regulation. The CAB was created to protect the airlines from "cutthroat competition." It had the power to set air fares, allocate air routes, and prevent the entry of new carriers into the airline industry. In the days before deregulation the federal government's General Accounting Office estimated that airline fares would have been, on average, as much as 52 percent lower if the CAB had not been regulating them. A striking conclusion presents itself: The CAB was doing for the airlines—preventing price competition among airlines, allocating routes, and preventing competition—what an airline cartel would have done.

As to the Interstate Commerce Commission (ICC), Judge Richard Posner has observed that "the railroads supported the enactment of the first Interstate Commerce Act, which was designed to prevent railroads from price discrimination, because discrimination was undermining the railroad's cartels."[*]

Government is not always the glue that holds a cartel together, but there are numerous examples where it is.

[*]Richard A. Posner, "Theories of Regulation," *Bell Journal of Economics and Management Science* 5 (Autumn 1984): 337.

policy. For example, firm A might propose that each cartel member reduce output by 10 percent, while firm B advocates that all bigger cartel members reduce output by 15 percent and all smaller members reduce output by 6 percent. There may be as many policy proposals as there are cartel members. Reaching agreement may be difficult. Such disagreements are harder to resolve the greater the differences between cartel members in costs, size, and so forth.

The Problem of Entry into the Industry. Even if the cartel members manage to agree on a policy that generates high profits, those high profits will provide an incentive for firms outside the industry to join the industry. If current cartel members cannot keep new suppliers from doing this, the cartel is likely to break up. For example, high prices and profits achieved by the OPEC (Organization of Petroleum Exporting Countries) cartel led to additions in the world's oil supply. In 1973, OPEC produced 56 percent of the world's oil supply; in 1985, OPEC's share was down to 30 percent.

The Problem of Cheating. As paradoxical as it at first appears, once the cartel agreement is made, there is an incentive for cartel members to cheat on the agreement. With this in mind, consider Exhibit 11-7. Here we show a representative firm of the cartel. We compare three situations for this firm: first, the situation before the cartel is formed; second, the situation for the firm after the cartel is formed when all members adhere to the cartel price; third, the situation for the firm if it cheats on the cartel agreement, but the other cartel members do not.

Before the cartel is formed, the firm is in long-run competitive equilibrium; it produces q_1 and charges price P_1. It makes zero economic profits. Next, it reduces its output to q_C as directed by the cartel (the cartel has set a quota for each member), and it charges the cartel price of P_C. It makes profits equal to CP_CAB. Now note what happens if the firm cheats on the cartel agreement and produces q_{CC} instead of the stipulated q_C. As long as other firms do not cheat, this firm views its demand curve as horizontal at the cartel price (P_C). The reason is simple: It is one of a number of firms so it cannot affect price by changing output. Therefore it can produce and sell additional units of output without lowering price. We conclude that if the firm decides to cheat on the cartel agreement, and other firms do not, then the cheater-

■ **EXHIBIT 11-7**
The Benefits of Cheating on the Cartel Agreement

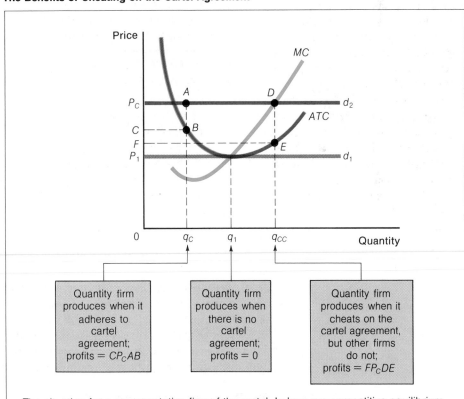

The situation for a representative firm of the cartel. In long-run competitive equilibrium it produces q_1 and charges P_1, making zero economic profits. As a consequence of the cartel agreement, it reduces output to q_C and charges P_C. Its profits are CP_CAB. If it cheats on the cartel agreement and others do not, the firm will increase output to q_{CC} and reap profits of FP_CDE. Note, however, that if this firm can cheat on the cartel agreement, so can others. Given the monetary benefits that exist from cheating, it is unlikely that the cartel will be around long.

firm can increase its profits from the smaller amount CP_CAB to the larger amount FP_CDE. Of course, if all firms cheat, we are back where we started—with no cartel agreement and at price P_1.

This illustrates a major theme of cartels: Firms have an incentive to form a cartel, but once it is formed, they have an incentive to cheat. As a result some economists have concluded that even if cartels can be formed successfully, it is unlikely that they will be effective for long.

THE THEORY OF CONTESTABLE MARKETS: CHALLENGING ORTHODOXY

Contestable Market
A market in which entry is easy and exit is costless.

Our discussion of market structures, from perfect competition to oligopoly, has emphasized the number of sellers in each market structure. In perfect competition there were many sellers; in monopoly there was only one; in monopolistic competition there were many; in oligopoly there were few. The message was that the number of sellers in a market influences the behavior of the sellers within the market. For example, the monopoly seller is more likely to restrict output and charge higher prices than the perfect competitor.

Recently economists have shifted emphasis from the number of sellers in a market toward the issue of entry into and exit from an industry. This new focus is a result of the work of economists like William Baumol and others who have put forth the idea of contestable markets.[3]

A **contestable market** is one in which the following conditions are met: (1) There is easy entry into the market and costless exit from the market. (2) New firms entering the market can produce the product at the same cost as current firms. (3) Firms exiting the market can easily dispose of their fixed assets by selling them elsewhere (less depreciation; thus fixed costs are not sunk but recoverable).

To illustrate, suppose there are currently eight firms in an industry, all of which are making profits. Firms outside the industry notice this and decide to enter the industry (nothing prevents entry). They acquire the necessary equipment and produce the product in question at the same cost as current producers. Time passes, and the firms that entered the industry decide to exit it. They can either switch their machinery into another line of production or sell their equipment for what they paid for it, less depreciation.

Notice the important element of "hit-and-run" entry and exit in a contestable market. New entrants can enter—hit—produce the product and compete away the profits of current firms; then they exit costlessly—run.

The theory of contestable markets has been criticized because of its assumptions—in particular the assumption that there is extremely free entry into, and costless exit from, the industry. It is important to note, however, that although this theory, like most theories, is a caricature of the real world, this does not in and of itself destroy its usefulness.

Currently, the theory of contestable markets is being tested. It is still relatively young (as market structure theories go), and it is difficult to tell what its overall worth will turn out to be. It has, at minimum, rattled orthodox market structure theory. Here are a few of its conclusions:

1. Even if an industry is composed of a small number of firms, or simply one firm, this is not evidence that the firms perform in a noncompetitive way. They might be extremely competitive if the market they are in is contestable.

[3]William J. Baumol, "Contestable Markets: An Uprising in the Theory of Industry Structure," *American Economic Review* 72 (March 1982): 1–15. For a critique of the contestable markets theory, see William G. Shepherd, "'Contestability' vs. Competition," *American Economic Review* 74 (September 1984): 572–87.

2. Profits can be zero in an industry even if the number of sellers in the industry is small.

3. If a market is contestable, inefficient producers cannot survive. Cost inefficiencies invite lower-cost producers into the market, driving price down to minimum ATC and forcing inefficient firms to change their ways or exit the industry.

4. If as conclusion 3 suggests, a contestable market encourages firms to produce at their lowest possible average total cost and charge $P = ATC$, it follows that they will also sell at a price equal to marginal cost. (Recall that the marginal cost curve intersects the average total cost curve at its minimum point.)

The theory of contestable markets has also led to a shift in policy perspectives. To some (but certainly not all) economists, the theory suggests that efforts directed at lowering entry and exit costs might do more to encourage firms to act as perfect competitors (such as selling at $P = MC$) than direct interference in the behavioral patterns of firms.

THE FOUR MARKET STRUCTURES REVIEWED

With the discussion of oligopoly, our examination of the four different market structures—perfect competition, monopoly, monopolistic competition, and oligopoly—comes to an end. Exhibit 11-8 reviews some of the characteristics and consequences of the different market structures.

The first four columns of the exhibit simply summarize the characteristics of the different market structures. In the last column we have noted the long-run market tendency between price and average total cost in the different market structures. This indicates whether long-run profits are possible. Note that for three of the four market structures (monopoly, monopolistic competition, and oligopoly) superscript letters beside the possible profits refer you to notes that describe alternative market tendencies given different conditions. For example, the market tendency in oligopoly is for $P > ATC$ and for profits to exist in the long run. The reason for this is that there are significant barriers to entry in oligopoly and short-run profits cannot be competed away through the entry of new firms into the industry. As we have just learned, however, the market tendency of price and average total cost may be different if the particular oligopolistic market is contestable.

■ **EXHIBIT 11-8**
Characteristics and Consequences of Market Structures

MARKET STRUCTURE	NUMBER OF SELL-ERS	TYPE OF PRODUCT	BARRIERS TO ENTRY	LONG-RUN MARKET TENDENCY OF PRICE AND ATC
Perfect competition	Many	Homogeneous	No	$P = ATC$ (zero economic profits)
Monopoly	One	Unique	Yes	$P > ATC$ (positive economic profits)[a,c]
Monopolistic competition	Many	Slightly differentiated	No	$P = ATC$ (zero economic profits)[b]
Oligopoly	Few	Homogeneous or differentiated	Yes	$P > ATC$ (positive economic profits)[c]

[a]It is possible for positive profits to turn to zero profits through the capitalization of profits or rent-seeking activities.
[b]It is possible for the firm to make positive profits in the long run if it can differentiate its product sufficiently in the minds of the buying public.
[c]It is possible for positive profits to turn to zero profits if the market is contestable.

Economics in Our Times

Interview: William Baumol

William Baumol is one of the key persons associated with the development of the contestable markets theory. Besides contestable markets, Baumol is well known for his work on the *sales maximization theory,* which says that firms maximize sales subject to a minimum-profit constraint, instead of attempting to maximize profits. Baumol is currently at New York University and Princeton University. We conducted the following interview with Professor Baumol on March 18, 1988.

Professor Baumol, what insights into the market process does the contestable markets theory provide?

One of its key insights is the suggestion that freedom of entry can act as a supplement to, or as a substitute for, actual competition.

One of the things contestable markets theory teaches us is that the number of firms in an industry may
not affect a firm's behavior as much as whether the industry is contestable. Would you go so far as to say that contestability is the major criterion by which we ought to measure markets?

Really you are asking here whether freedom of entry, or contestability, is more important than actual competition. And to this I would say no. The way I have presented it (including cases where I have testified) is to say that there are two sets of sufficient conditions for effective competitiveness of a market, and the presence of either or both is a sufficient guarantee for the purpose. To me the merger guidelines of the Department of Justice are precisely right when they say that the department will not interfere with a merger in a market if either there are enough competitors present in the market, or if entry is sufficiently easy, or both.

To your knowledge, what industries either are, or behave as if they are, contestable?

The answer is it's a matter of degree. For example, we had originally thought that airlines would be highly contestable, and there is still some evidence that they are characterized by a considerable degree of contestability, but we now believe that airlines are not nearly as contestable as we had thought earlier.

Two examples of industries that we do believe are highly contestable are barges and trucks. Let me explain why. Both trucks and barges deal primarily with industrial rather than consumer products. That means that much of their business is carried out by contract. And contract makes the difference here. For example, if the market is exploited by a monopolist, then a prospective entrant can say to the customers of the monopolist,

"Look, if I come in without a contract, the monopolist will undercut me and drive me out, and you'll be back in your old position. But if you sign a contract with me for five years, cutting their profits down by 90 percent, we will both benefit." This sort of thing makes that market contestable. In contrast, airlines deal with thousands and thousands of passengers so that contracts are unworkable and do not occur and therefore the incumbents can, if they choose, punish an entrant by cutting prices that drive him out.

Can you provide us with some specific examples of how contestable markets theory has been used by courts and government agencies?

Its most effective use by government agencies has been of two sorts. One is, in effect, acting in accord with, or in the spirit of, the merger guidelines. That is, saying in effect that before we will say a particular industry involves monopoly or market power, we must consider the combination of ease of entry and the number of incumbents, rather than the number of incumbents alone. And there have been a number of cases of that sort.

The second is that regulatory agencies have used it in formulating rules for regulation. That is to say, what they have rightly been persuaded to do is to act as substitutes for contestability in markets that were not contestable. The agencies therefore have required the regulated firms to tailor their behavior to that which would prevail if the market had been contestable. Now what this means is that they have removed those regulations that are unnecessary to achieve those results, and strengthened the regulations that were needed for the purpose.

My final comment is that the concept of market contestability has also been misused by lawyers who were tempted to claim that the entire world is contestable, a position that neither I nor my coauthors hold.

Is it somewhat surprising to you that the courts and government agencies have so readily adopted contestable markets theory?

I was surprised, and I was flattered. As I said before, my impression is that when the courts and the regulatory agencies have used it, it has been used sensibly. But when it was used for partisan purposes, it was in a number of cases abused. And it was embarrassing for me and my coauthors because we ended up

being characterized as believing what we do not believe—that is, that everything is all for the best, without government interference. It is my belief that you have to examine things case by case, you have to get the evidence to find out whether a particular market is or is not contestable. The only point we're making that is different from what was known before, but is crucial as I now hope to convince you, is that the perfectly competitive model, which had been used as a guide by regulators and the courts before, simply does not apply to most of the cases that are at issue because most of those cases are cases with economies of scale (which

makes for large firms). If the firms weren't large in the first place, nobody would worry about them, and it is not only by accident that the perfectly competitive model, with its multiplicity of tiny firms, must assume the existence of constant returns to scale. What our analysis says is that similar rules, which are equally demanding, and which are equally suitable for protecting consumers, can be applied for the first time to cases with large firms and with economies of scale. But I want to emphasize that we don't want to be any less tough when there is monopoly than does anyone else.

■ CHAPTER SUMMARY

Monopolistic Competition

■ The theory of monopolistic competition makes the following assumptions: (1) There are many sellers and buyers. (2) Each firm in the industry produces and sells a slightly differentiated product. (3) There is easy entry and exit.
■ The monopolistic competitor is a price searcher.
■ For the monopolistic competitor, $P > MR$, and its marginal revenue curve lies below its demand curve.
■ The monopolistic competitor produces the quantity of output at which $MR = MC$. It charges the highest price per unit for this output.
■ Unlike the perfectly competitive firm, the monopolistic competitor does not exhibit resource allocative efficiency.
■ The monopolistically competitive firm does not earn profits in the long run (because of easy entry into the industry) unless it can successfully differentiate its product (for example, by brand name) in the minds of the buying public.

Excess Capacity Theorem

■ The excess capacity theorem states that a monopolistic competitor will, in equilibrium, produce an output smaller than the one at which average total costs (unit costs) are minimized.

Oligopoly in General

■ There are many different oligopoly theories. All are built on the assumptions that (1) there are few sellers and many buyers, (2) firms produce and sell either homogeneous or differentiated products, and (3) there are significant barriers to entry.

■ One of the key characteristics of oligopolistic firms is their mutual interdependence.

Specific Oligopoly Theories

■ The kinked demand curve theory assumes that if a single firm lowers price, other firms will do likewise, but if a single firm raises price, other firms will not follow suit.

■ The price leadership theory assumes that the dominant firm in the industry determines price and all other firms take this price as given.

■ The cartel theory assumes that firms in an oligopolistic industry act in a manner consistent with there being only one firm in the industry.

■ The kinked demand curve theory predicts that an oligopolistic firm will experience price stickiness or rigidity. This is because there is a ''gap'' in its marginal revenue curve, along which the firm's marginal cost can rise or fall; hence, the firm can still produce the same quantity of output and charge the same price. The evidence in some empirical tests rejects the theory. For example, Stigler found no evidence that the oligopolists he examined were more reluctant to match price increases than price decreases.

■ Four problems are associated with cartels: (1) the problem of forming the cartel, (2) the problem of formulating policy, (3) the problem of entry into the industry, and (4) the problem of cheating.

The Theory of Contestable Markets

■ A contestable market is one in which the following conditions are met: (1) There is easy entry into the market and costless exit from it. (2) New firms entering the market can produce the product at the same costs as current firms. (3) Firms exiting the market can easily dispose of their fixed assets by selling them elsewhere (less depreciation). The theory of contestable markets lays more emphasis on the issue of entry into and exit from an industry and less emphasis (than orthodox market structure theories) on the number of sellers in an industry.

■ QUESTIONS TO ANSWER AND DISCUSS

1. Is there anything all firms in all four market structures have in common?

2. Why does the marginal revenue curve have the unusual look that it does in the kinked demand curve model?

3. Would you expect cartel formation to be more likely in industries comprised of a few firms or many firms? Explain your answer.

4. Does the theory of contestable markets shed any light on oligopoly pricing theories?

5. There are 60 types or varieties of product X on the market. Is product X made in a monopolistically competitive market?

6. Why does interdependence of firms play a major role in oligopoly, but not in perfect competition or monopolistic competition?

7. Airline companies sometimes fly airplanes that are one-quarter full between cities. Some people point to this as evidence of economic waste. What do you think? Would it be better to have fewer airline companies and more full planes?

8. Concentration ratios have often been used to note the "tightness" of an oligopoly market. A high concentration ratio indicates a tight oligopoly market, and a low concentration ratio indicates a "loose" oligopoly. Would you expect firms in tight markets to reap higher profits, on average, than firms in loose markets? Would it matter if the markets were contestable?

9. Coupons are usually more common on small-ticket items than big-ticket items. Explain why.

10. Market theories are said to have the happy consequence of getting individuals to think in more focused and analytical ways. Has this happened to you? Give examples to illustrate.

Appendix D Game Theory and Oligopoly

Game Theory
A mathematical technique used to analyze the behavior of decision makers who try to reach an optimal position for themselves through game playing or the use of strategic behavior, and who are fully aware of the interactive nature of the process at hand and anticipate the moves of other decision makers.

Game theory is a mathematical technique used to analyze the behavior of decision makers who try to reach an *optimal position* through game playing or the use of *strategic behavior,* and who are fully aware of the *interactive nature of the process* at hand and *anticipate the moves* of other decision makers. To illustrate, game theory is often used to study situations fundamentally like that of two persons playing chess. Chess has all the necessary ingredients. First, it has decision makers who are trying to reach an optimal position (I want to place my opponent in checkmate). Second, each player plans a strategy to meet his or her objective (I will move my pawn here and my castle there, so that my opponent will be forced to move his knight). Third, chess players are aware of the interactive nature of a chess game (what she does influences what I do), and they anticipate each others' moves (I think he will move here, so if I move there now, I will be in a better position). We begin by discussing a well-known game in game theory called *prisoner's dilemma.*

PRISONER'S DILEMMA

The prisoner's dilemma game illustrates a case where individually rational behavior leads to a jointly inefficient outcome. It has been described this way: "You do what is best for you, I'll do what is best for me, and somehow we end up in a situation that is not best for either of us."

The Mechanics of Prisoner's Dilemma

Here are the mechanics of the prisoner's dilemma game.

The Facts.   Two men, Bob and Nathan, are arrested and charged with jointly committing a crime. They are put in separate cells so that they cannot communicate with each other. The district attorney goes to each man separately and says the following:

■ If you confess to the crime and agree to turn state's evidence, and your accomplice does not confess, I will let you off with a $500 fine.
■ If your accomplice confesses to the crime and agrees to turn state's evidence, and you do not confess, I will fine you $5,000.
■ If both you and your accomplice remain silent and refuse to confess to the crime, I will charge you with a lesser crime (which I can prove you committed), and both you and your accomplice will end up paying a fine of $2,000.
■ If both you and your accomplice confess, I will fine each of you $3,000.

The Options and Consequences. Each man has two choices: confess or not confess. We show these choices on the grid in Exhibit 11D-1. According to the possibilities laid out by the district attorney, if both men do not confess, each pays a fine of $2,000. This is shown in Box 1 in the exhibit.

If Nathan confesses and Bob does not, then Nathan gets off with the light fine of $500, and Bob pays the stiff penalty of $5,000. This is shown in Box 2.

If Nathan does not confess and Bob confesses, then Nathan ends up with the stiff penalty of $5,000, and Bob pays the light fine of $500. This is shown in Box 3.

Finally, if both men confess, each pays $3,000. This is shown in Box. 4.

What Nathan Thinks. Nathan considers his choices and possible outcomes as outlined in Exhibit 11D-1. He reasons to himself, I have two options, confess or not confess, and Bob has the same two options. Let me ask myself two questions:

■ First, *if Bob chooses not to confess, what is the best thing for me to do?* The answer is confess, since if I do not confess, I will end up in Box 1 paying $2,000, but if I confess I will end up in Box 2 paying only $500. No doubt about it, if Bob chooses not to confess, I ought to confess.
■ Second, *if Bob chooses to confess, what is the best thing for me to do?* The answer is confess, since if I do not confess, I will end up in Box 3 paying $5,000, but if I confess I will pay $3,000. No doubt about it, if Bob chooses to confess, I ought to confess.

Nathan's Conclusion. Nathan concludes that no matter what Bob chooses to do, not confess or confess, he is always better off if he confesses. Nathan decides to confess to the crime.

■ **EXHIBIT 11D-1**
Prisoner's Dilemma

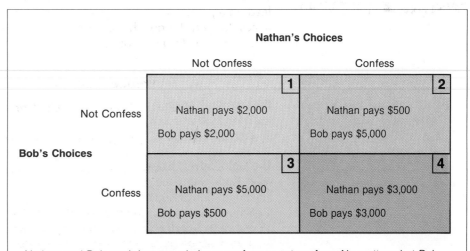

Nathan and Bob each has two choices: confess or not confess. No matter what Bob does, it is always better for Nathan to confess. No matter what Nathan does, it is always better for Bob to confess. Both Nathan and Bob confess and end up in Box 4 where each pays a $3,000 fine. Both men would have been better off had they not confessed. That way they would have ended up in Box 1 paying a $2,000 fine.

The Situation Is the Same for Bob.   Bob goes through the same mental process that Nathan does. Asking himself the same two questions Nathan asked himself, Bob gets the same answers and makes the same conclusion. Bob decides to confess to the crime.

The Outcome.   The DA goes to each man and asks what he has decided. Nathan says, "I confess." Bob says, "I confess." The outcome is shown in Box 4 with each man paying a fine of $3,000.

Look Where They Could Be.   Is there an outcome, represented by one of the four boxes, that is better for *both* Nathan *and* Bob than the outcome where each pays $3,000? Yes, there is; it is Box 1. In Box 1 both Nathan and Bob pay $2,000. To get to Box 1, all the two men had to do was keep silent and not confess.

Changing the Game.   What would happen if the DA gave Nathan and Bob another chance? Suppose she tells them that she will not accept their confessions. Instead, she wants them to *talk it over together* for ten minutes, after which time she will come back, place each man in a separate room, and ask for his decision. The second time she will accept each man's decision, no matter what.

   Will this change the outcome? Most people will say yes, arguing that Nathan and Bob will now see that their better choice is to remain silent, so that each ends up with a $2,000 fine instead of a $3,000 fine. Let's assume that this happens, that Nathan and Bob enter into a gentleman's agreement to remain silent.

Nathan's Thoughts on the Way to His Room.   The DA returns and takes Nathan to a separate room. On the way there, Nathan thinks to himself, I'm not sure I can trust Bob. Suppose he goes back on our agreement and confesses. If I hold to the agreement and he doesn't, he'll end up with a $500 fine and I'll end up paying $5,000. Of course, if I break the agreement and confess and he holds to the agreement, then I'll reduce my fine down to $500. Maybe the best thing for me to do is break the agreement and confess, hoping that he doesn't and I'll only pay $500. If I'm not so lucky, at least I'll protect myself from paying $5,000.

   Once in the room the DA asks Nathan what his decision is. He says, "I confess."

The Situation Is the Same for Bob.   Bob sees the situation the same way Nathan does and chooses to confess again.

The Outcome Again.   Both men end up confessing a second time. Each pays $3,000, realizing that if they had been silent and kept to their agreement, their fine would only be $2,000 each.

The Gold, Silver, Brass, and Paper Rings.   Look at Nathan and Bob's situation this way. Each wants the gold ring (the low $500 fine) instead of the paper ring (the maximum fine of $5,000). It is impossible to get the gold ring without a confession. If each reaches for the gold ring and confesses, each will end up with a brass ring (the $3,000 fine). If neither reaches for the gold ring, if neither confesses, each ends up with a silver ring (the $2,000 fine).

   The lesson: Sometimes reaching for the gold ring will get you a brass ring. Not reaching for the gold ring could get you a better ring than if you had reached for it—you could get a silver ring instead of a brass ring. The dilemma: If you don't reach for the gold ring, you could end up with the paper ring and that's like having no ring at all. In summary, going for the gold gets you brass. Not going for the gold could get you silver, but then it could get you paper.

What Do Prisoners, Rings, and Dilemmas Have to Do with Oligopolists?

Oligopolists are sometimes a lot like our prisoners, Nathan and Bob. Sometimes they too are in a prisoner's dilemma. To illustrate, suppose we approximate the situation using two firms, A and B, that sell the same product and are in stiff competition with each other. Currently the competition between them is so stiff that each earns only $10,000 profits. Soon the two firms decide to enter into a *cartel agreement* in which each agrees to raise prices and, once raised, not to undercut the other. If they hold to the agreement, each firm will earn profits of $50,000. But if one firm holds to the cartel agreement, and the other does not, the one that does not hold to the agreement will earn profits of $100,000, and the one that does will earn $5,000 profits. Of course, if neither holds to the agreement, then both will be back where they started—earning $10,000 profits. We have outlined the choices for the two firms and the possible outcomes in Exhibit 11D-2.

Each firm is likely to behave the way our two prisoners behaved. Each firm will see the chance to earn $100,000 by breaking the agreement (instead of $50,000 by holding to it); it will also realize that if it does not break the agreement and the other firm does, it will be in a worse situation than when it was in stiff competition with the other firm. Most economists hypothesize that the two firms will end up in Box 4 in Exhibit 11D-2, earning the profits they did before they entered into the agreement. In short, they will *cheat* on the cartel agreement and end up in competition—the very situation they wanted to escape.

■ **EXHIBIT 11D-2**
Cartels and Prisoner's Dilemma

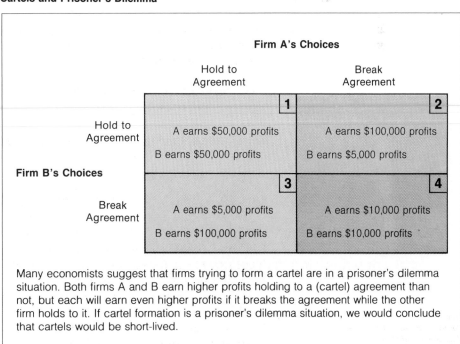

Many economists suggest that firms trying to form a cartel are in a prisoner's dilemma situation. Both firms A and B earn higher profits holding to a (cartel) agreement than not, but each will earn even higher profits if it breaks the agreement while the other firm holds to it. If cartel formation is a prisoner's dilemma situation, we would conclude that cartels would be short-lived.

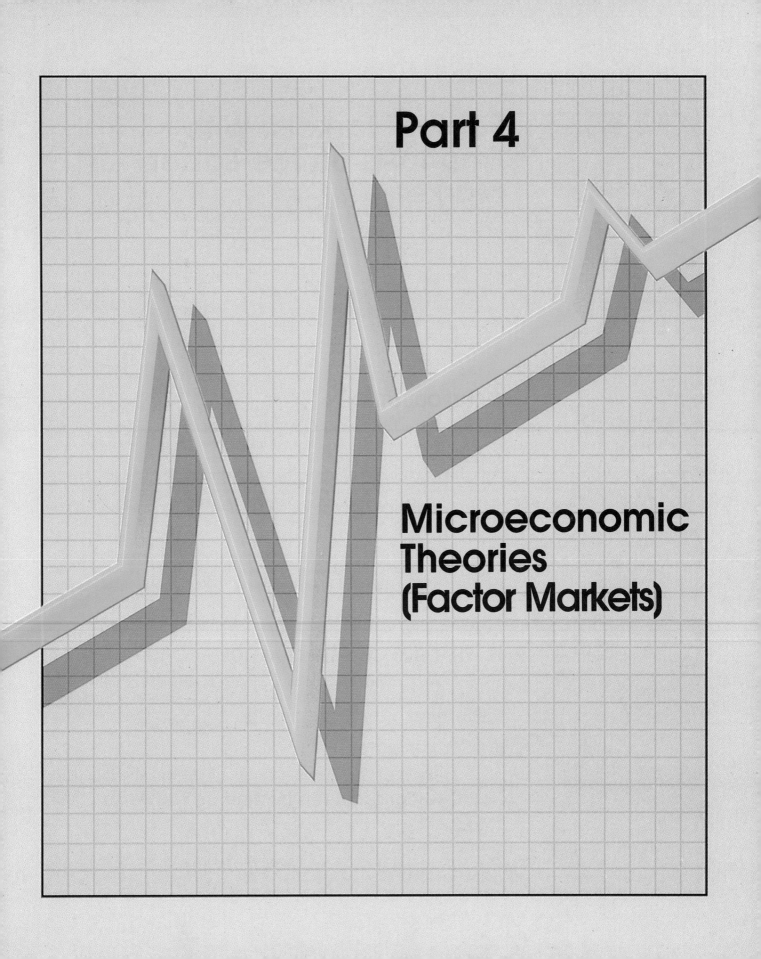

Part 4

Microeconomic Theories (Factor Markets)

Chapter 12

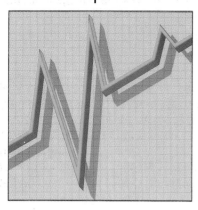

Factor Markets: With Emphasis on the Labor Market

■ INTRODUCTION

Between seven and nine o'clock every weekday morning, millions of people are driving, walking, running, bicycling, or flying (no one is skipping) to their jobs. For about eight hours a day, all these people—insurance salespersons, bank presidents, attorneys, plumbers, computer operators, dentists, carpenters, bus drivers— are members of the labor market.

This chapter is about factor markets in general and the labor market in particular. The latter should be especially interesting to you.

Perhaps you are getting ready to enter a particular labor market. Maybe you're a sociology or English major or a finance or education major who will be graduating in a few months. On graduation, you may be thrown full force into the labor market. This chapter should help you better understand what you'll encounter.

■ WHAT THIS CHAPTER IS ABOUT

In our chapters on perfect competition, monopoly, monopolistic competition, and oligopoly, the firm was a *seller* of products. In this chapter the firm is a *buyer* of factors (resources or inputs). We approach this subject by examining some general principles that are relevant to factor markets. Then we will turn to a specific factor market, the labor market.

Key Questions to Keep in Mind as You Read

1. What does it mean if a firm is a price taker in a factor market? What does it mean if a firm is a price searcher in a factor market?

2. Why do firms employ that factor quantity at which marginal revenue product equals marginal factor cost, *MRP = MFC*?

3. How should a firm combine its factors of production so that it minimizes costs?

4. Why do wage rates differ?

5. Why do employers sometimes want to know the GPAs of the college graduates they interview for jobs?

FACTOR MARKETS IN GENERAL

Product Price Taker

A firm that faces a horizontal demand curve for the product it sells. It can sell as many units of its good as it wants without affecting price. The perfectly competitive firm discussed in Chapter 9 is a product price taker.

Product Price Searcher

A firm that faces a downward-sloping demand curve for the product it sells. It sells fewer units at higher prices than lower prices. The monopoly, monopolistic competitive, and oligopoly firms discussed in Chapters 10 and 11 are product price searchers.

Factor Price Taker

A firm that can buy all of a factor it wants at the equilibrium price. It faces a horizontal (flat, perfectly elastic) supply curve of factors.

Factor Price Searcher

A firm that drives up factor price if it buys an additional factor unit. It faces an upward-sloping supply curve of factors.

A firm may be a buyer in one market and a seller in another. For example, IBM sells computers; thus it is a seller in the computer market. But IBM also buys paper, plastic, paint, and labor; thus it is a buyer in numerous factor markets.

As was explained in previous chapters, a seller may be a price taker or a price searcher. In short, the firm faces either a horizontal or a downward-sloping demand curve. In this chapter we refer to a seller that is a price taker in a product market as simply a **product price taker.** A seller that is a price searcher in a product market is called a **product price searcher.**

The "price taker–price searcher" terminology, which was used to describe the firm in its role as a seller of products, is also relevant to the firm in its role as a buyer of factors. For example, a firm is a price taker in a factor market—or **factor price taker**—if it can buy all of a factor it wants at the equilibrium price. Given this, it faces a horizontal (flat, perfectly elastic) supply curve of factors.

For example, suppose the department store at the local mall is a price taker in hiring salesclerks. This means the store can hire salesclerks one right after another, all for the same wage rate, and not drive up the wage rate.

A firm that is a price searcher in a factor market—a **factor price searcher**—faces an upward-sloping supply curve of factors. If it buys an additional factor unit, it drives up factor price. For example, if the department store is a price searcher in hiring salesclerks, then as it hires additional clerks, it must pay a higher wage rate not only to the extra person hired but to all those hired previously, too.

A firm may fall into four possible categories, which are illustrated in Exhibit 12-1:

1. A product price taker and a factor price taker (box I).

2. A product price searcher and a factor price taker (box II).

3. A product price taker and a factor price searcher (box III).

4. A product price searcher and a factor price searcher (box IV).

The exhibit shows the relevant demand and supply curves for each case.

We turn now to a discussion of two of the four categories: (1) the firm as product price taker and factor price taker (*PT-PT*) and (2) the firm as product price searcher and factor price taker (*PS-PT*).

The Firm as Product Price Taker and Factor Price Taker, *PT-PT*

Why do firms purchase factors? The answer is obvious—to produce products to sell. This goes for all firms, no matter what their classification. General Motors buys steel in order to build cars to sell to car buyers. Farmers buy tractors and fertilizer in order to produce grain to sell.

In short, the demand for factors is a **derived demand.** It is derived from, and directly related to, the demand for the product that the factors go to produce. If the demand for the product rises, the demand for the factors used to produce the product rises; if the demand for the product falls, the demand for the factors used to produce the product falls. For example, if the demand for a university education falls, so

Derived Demand

Demand that is the result of some other demand. For example, factor demand is the result of the demand for the products that the factors go to produce.

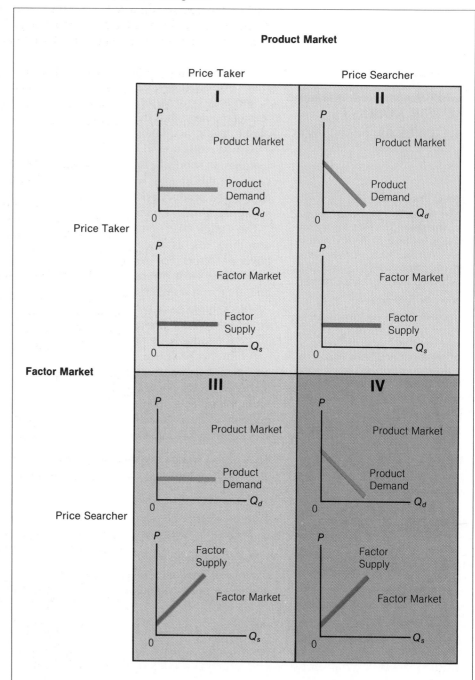

P = price. In the product and factor markets, P stands for "product price" and "factor price," respectively. A firm may be either a price taker or a price searcher in product markets; and it may be either a price taker or a price searcher in factor markets. Thus a firm may fall into one of four possible categories. The demand and supply curves for a firm in each category are depicted in the four boxes.

does the demand for university professors. If the demand for computers rises, so does the demand for skilled computer workers.

When the demand for a seller's product rises, the seller needs to have some idea of how much more of a factor it should buy. The concepts of marginal revenue product and marginal factor cost are relevant here.

Marginal Revenue Product

The additional revenue generated by employing an additional factor unit.

Marginal Revenue Product. Marginal revenue product (**MRP**) is the additional revenue generated by employing an additional factor unit. For example, if a firm employs one more unit of a factor, and its total revenue rises by $20, its MRP equals $20. Marginal revenue product can be calculated in two ways.

First,

$$MRP = \frac{\Delta TR}{\Delta \text{ factor}}$$

See Exhibit 12-2, where the data illustrate a product price taker since, according to column 4, $P = MR$. Total revenue is calculated in column 5 by multiplying price times quantity of output. Finally, MRP for factor X is calculated in column 6.

The other, more common way to calculate marginal revenue product is

$$MRP = MR \times MPP$$

The marginal physical product (*MPP*) of factor X is calculated in column 3 of Exhibit 12-2, using the method explained in Chapter 8 (recall the discussion of the law of diminishing marginal returns). MRP is then calculated by multiplying the numbers in column 3 by the dollar figures in column 4.

Marginal Factor Cost

The additional cost incurred by employing an additional factor unit.

Marginal Factor Cost. Marginal factor cost (**MFC**) is the additional cost incurred by employing an additional factor unit:

$$MFC = \frac{\Delta TC}{\Delta \text{ factor}}$$

For a factor price taker, marginal factor cost is constant and equal to factor price, $MFC = P$. For example, suppose a firm wants to purchase 1 unit of factor Y at a

■ **EXHIBIT 12-2**
Marginal Revenue Product Schedule

Using the data provided in the exhibit, MRP is calculated in two ways: $MRP = \Delta TR/\Delta$ factor, and $MRP = MR \times MPP$. Marginal revenue product is the additional revenue generated by employing one more factor unit. Note that we have assumed that the firm is a product price taker and that all factors other than X are fixed.

(1) UNITS OF FACTOR X	(2) QUANTITY OF OUTPUT	(3) MARGINAL PHYSICAL PRODUCT OF X (MPP_X) $MPP_X = \frac{\Delta(2)}{\Delta(1)}$	(4) PRODUCT PRICE, MARGINAL REVENUE ($P = MR$)	(5) TOTAL REVENUE $TR = P \times Q$ $= (4) \times (2)$	(6) MARGINAL REVENUE PRODUCT OF X (MRP_X) $MRP = \frac{\Delta TR}{\Delta X} = \frac{\Delta(5)}{\Delta(1)}$ $= MR \times MPP_X = (4) \times (3)$
0	10*	0	$5	$ 50	$ 0
1	19	9	5	95	45
2	27	8	5	135	40
3	34	7	5	170	35
4	40	6	5	200	30
5	45	5	5	225	25

*Seeing that the quantity of output is 10 at 0 units of factor X indicates that other factors (not shown in the exhibit) must also be used to produce the good.

price of $10. The total cost is $10. If it purchases a second unit, it pays $10, total cost rises to $20, and MFC equals $10. *The MFC curve, or the factor supply curve, is horizontal (flat, perfectly elastic) for the factor price taker.*[1]

The $MRP = MFC$ Rule: Maximizing Profits. The firm continues to purchase units of a given factor as long as $MRP > MFC$. It stops where $MRP = MFC$. By doing this, the firm maximizes profits; it buys factors as long as their purchase adds more to revenues than to costs. In Exhibit 27-3, MRP equals MFC at a factor quantity of Q_1.

Question:

In Exhibit 12-3, why is the MFC curve horizontal at P_1?

Answer:

The MFC curve is horizontal at P_1 because we have assumed that the firm is a factor price taker; it can buy all of a factor it wants at the equilibrium price without driving up the price of the factor.

The MRP Curve Is the Firm's Factor Demand Curve. The factor demand curve tells us how many factor units the firm will buy at different prices (for example, 500 units at $2 per unit, 600 units at $1.50 per unit, and so forth). As Exhibit 12-4

[1]Although the MFC, or factor supply, curve for the single factor price taker is horizontal, the *market* supply curve is upward sloping. This is similar to the situation for the perfectly competitive firm described in Chapter 9. There we noted that the firm's demand curve was horizontal, but that the market (or industry) demand curve was downward sloping. In factor markets, we are simply talking about the supply side of the market instead of the demand side. The firm's supply curve is flat because it can hire additional factor units without driving up the price of the factor; it buys a relatively small portion of the factor. For the industry, however, higher factor prices must be offered to entice factors (such as workers) from other industries. The difference in the two supply curves—the firm's and the industry's—is basically a reflection of the different sizes of the firm and the industry.

■ **EXHIBIT 12-3**
Equating MRP and MFC

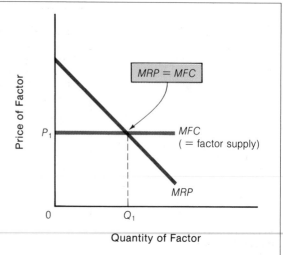

The firm continues to purchase a factor as long as its MRP exceeds its MFC. In the exhibit, the firm purchases Q_1.

illustrates, the firm's *MRP* curve is its factor demand curve because the *MRP* curve shows exactly how much of a factor the firm buys at different prices (which is what any demand curve shows).

To illustrate, suppose the price of the factor in Exhibit 12-4 is P_1. Since the firm is a factor price taker and thus can buy as many factor units at this price as it wants, P_1 equals MFC_1. At P_1, the firm chooses Q_1 factor units. If price rises to P_2, the firm chooses Q_2. At a lower factor price, the firm buys more factor units; at a higher factor price, the firm buys fewer factor units. The *MRP* curve maps out the quantity of factors the firm is willing to buy at different factor prices.

Question:

Why is the MRP curve downward sloping?

Answer:

The *MRP* curve is downward sloping because (after some point) the more of a factor that is used, the lower its *MRP* will be (because of the law of diminishing marginal returns). In short, since $MRP = MR \times MPP$, and *MPP* declines at some point, so must *MRP*.[2]

Value Marginal Product

The price of the good multiplied by the marginal physical product of the factor: $VMP = P \times MPP$. For a product price taker, $P = MR$, and thus $MRP = VMP$. For a product price searcher, $P > MR$, and $VMP > MRP$.

Value Marginal Product. Value marginal product (**VMP**) is equal to the price of the product times the marginal physical product of the factor:

$$VMP = P \times MPP$$

For example, if price is $10 and marginal physical product is 9 units, then *VMP* is $90. The *VMP* is a measure of the value that each factor unit adds to the firm's product. Think of it as the marginal physical product measured in dollars.

[2]If the firm is a product price searcher, there is an additional reason: namely, that higher levels of sales mean a lower *MR*, along with a declining *MPP*.

■ **EXHIBIT 12-4**
The *MRP* Curve Is the Firm's Factor Demand Curve

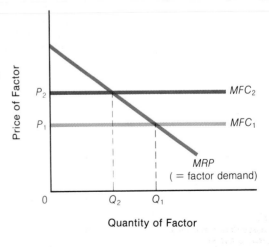

The *MRP* curve shows the various quantities of the factor the firm is willing to buy at different prices, which is what a demand curve shows. For example, at P_1 the firm buys Q_1; at P_2 it buys Q_2.

Question:

Is VMP = MRP *for a price taker in a product market?*

Answer:

Yes, it is. Since for a product price taker $P = MR$, and we know that $VMP = P \times MPP$ and $MRP = MR \times MPP$, it follows that $VMP = MRP$. Looking back at Exhibit 12-2 shows this. In the last column one way of calculating MRP is by multiplying MR times MPP, or multiplying the dollar amounts in column 4 times the unit amounts in column 3. If we were to calculate VMP, we would multiply P times MPP, which again would be column 4 times column 3.

A Summary.   The following conditions hold for a firm that is a price taker in both the product and factor markets:

1. The firm buys and employs the factor quantity at which $MRP = MFC$.
2. MFC = factor price. This is because the firm is a factor price taker.
3. The MRP curve is the firm's factor demand curve.
4. $VMP = MRP$. This is because the firm is a product price taker. It follows that this firm's VMP curve will be identical to its MRP curve. See Exhibit 12-5a.
5. At the profit-maximizing factor quantity, $VMP = MRP = MFC$ = factor price.

The Firm as Product Price Searcher and Factor Price Taker, *PS-PT*

For the product price searcher, $P > MR$; therefore VMP ($P \times MPP$) does not equal MRP ($MR \times MPP$). Instead, $VMP > MRP$. Therefore the following conditions hold:

1. The firm buys and employs the factor quantity at which $MRP = MFC$.
2. MFC = factor price. This is because the firm is a factor price taker.
3. The MRP curve is the firm's factor demand curve.
4. $VMP > MRP$. This is because the firm is a product price searcher. It follows from this that if we were to derive the firm's VMP and MRP curves, the MRP curve would lie *below* the VMP curve. See Exhibit 12-5b.
5. At the profit-maximizing factor quantity, $VMP > MRP = MFC$ = factor price.

The Least-Cost Rule: Applicable When There Is More Than One Factor

Suppose a firm requires two factors, labor and capital, to produce its product. How does it combine these two factors to minimize costs? Does it combine 20 units of labor with 5 units of capital, or perhaps 15 units of labor with 8 units of capital?

Simply put, the firm purchases the two factors until the ratio of MPP to price for one factor equals the ratio of MPP to price for the other factor. In other words,

$$\frac{MPP_L}{P_L} = \frac{MPP_K}{P_K}$$
(L = Labor and K = Capital)

This is the **least-cost rule.** To understand the logic behind it, suppose that (1) the price of labor is $5, (2) the price of capital is $10, (3) an extra unit of labor results

Least-Cost Rule

Specifies the combination of factors that minimizes costs. This requires that the following condition be met: $MPP_1/P_1 = MPP_2/P_2 = \ldots = MPP_n/P_n$, where the numbers stand for the different factors.

258

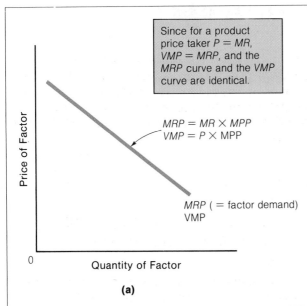

Since for a product price taker $P = MR$, $VMP = MRP$, and the MRP curve and the VMP curve are identical.

$MRP = MR \times MPP$
$VMP = P \times MPP$

MRP (= factor demand)
VMP

Price of Factor

Quantity of Factor

(a)

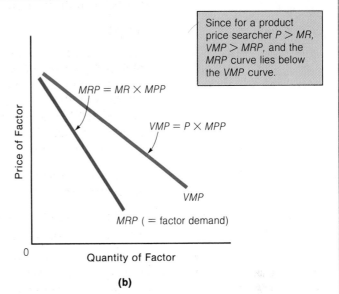

Since for a product price searcher $P > MR$, $VMP > MRP$, and the MRP curve lies below the VMP curve.

$MRP = MR \times MPP$

$VMP = P \times MPP$

VMP

MRP (= factor demand)

Price of Factor

Quantity of Factor

(b)

$MRP = MR \times MPP$ and $VMP = P \times MPP$. (a) The MRP (factor demand) curve and VMP curve. These are one and the same for a product price taker because for a product price taker, $P = MR$. (b) The MRP (factor demand) curve and

VMP curve for a product price searcher. The MRP curve lies below the VMP curve because for a product price searcher, $P > MR$.

in an increase in output of 25 units, and (4) an extra unit of capital results in an increase in output of 25 units. Finally, the firm currently spends an extra $5 on labor and an extra $10 on capital.

Notice that MPP_L/P_L is greater than MPP_K/P_K: 25/$5 > 25/$10. Thus in our example, a dollar spent on labor is more effective at raising output than a dollar spent on capital. In fact, it is *twice* as effective.

The firm is not minimizing costs. As is, it spends an additional $15 ($5 on labor and $10 on capital) and produces 50 additional units of output. Instead it could spend $10 on labor only, spending $0 on capital, and produce the 50 additional units of output, saving $5. To minimize costs, the firm will rearrange its purchases of factors until the least-cost rule is met.

Question:

If $MPP_L/P_L > MPP_K/P_K$, how does the firm equalize the two ratios?

Answer:

It buys more labor and less capital. As this happens, the MPP of labor falls, and the MPP of capital rises, bringing the two ratios closer in line. The firm continues to buy more of the factor whose MPP to price ratio is larger. It stops when the two ratios are equal. This type of equilibrating process was described in Chapter 5 when we discussed marginal utility and consumer choice.

Labor is a factor that is of special interest because at one time or another most people find themselves in the labor market. In this section, we first discuss the demand for labor, next the supply of labor, and finally the two together. We focus our discussion on the firm that is a price taker in both the product and factor markets.[3] (See box I in Exhibit 12-1.)

Shifts in the Firm's *MRP*, or Factor Demand, Curve

As we said earlier, the firm's *MRP* curve is its factor demand curve, and marginal revenue product equals marginal revenue times marginal physical product:

$$MRP = MR \times MPP \qquad (1)$$

Since for a product price taker, $P = MR$, we can rewrite (1) as

$$MRP = P \times MPP \qquad (2)$$

Now consider the demand for a specific factor input, labor. As the price of the product that labor produces changes, the factor demand curve for labor shifts. See Exhibit 12-6, where we start with a product price of $10 and curve MRP_1. At the wage rate of W_1, the firm hires Q_1 workers.

Suppose product price rises to $12. As we can see from equation (2), *MRP* rises. At each wage rate the firm wants to hire more workers. For example, at W_1, it wants

[3]It is important to keep in mind that the labor market we are discussing here is a labor market in which neither buyers nor sellers have any control over wage rates. Because of this, supply and demand, as discussed in Chapter 3, are our analytical tools. In the next chapter we modify this analysis.

■ **EXHIBIT 12-6**
Shifts in the Firm's *MRP*, or Factor Demand, Curve

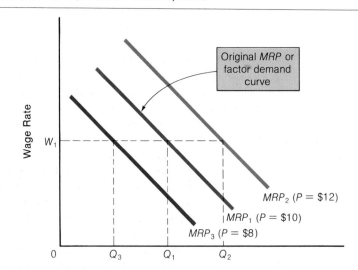

It is always the case that $MRP = MR \times MPP$. For a product price taker, since $P = MR$, it follows that $MRP = P \times MPP$. If P changes, *MRP* will change. For example, if product price rises, *MRP* rises, and the firm's *MRP* curve (factor demand curve) shifts rightward. If product price falls, *MRP* falls, and the firm's *MRP* curve (factor demand curve) shifts leftward. If *MPP* rises (reflected in a shift in the *MPP* curve), *MRP* rises, and the firm's *MRP* curve shifts rightward. If *MPP* falls, *MRP* falls, and the firm's *MRP* curve shifts leftward.

to hire Q_2 workers instead of Q_1. In short, a rise in product price shifts the firm's *MRP*, or factor demand, curve rightward.

If product price falls from \$10 to \$8, *MRP* falls. At each wage rate the firm wants to hire fewer workers. For example, at W_1 it wants to hire Q_3 instead of Q_1 workers. In short, a fall in product price shifts the firm's *MRP*, or factor demand, curve leftward.

It is also the case that changes in the *MPP* of the factor (reflected in a shift in the *MPP* curve) also change the firm's *MRP* curve. As we can see from equation (2), an increase in, say, the *MPP* of labor will increase *MRP* and shift the *MRP*, or factor demand, curve rightward. A decrease in *MPP* will decrease *MRP* and shift the *MRP*, or factor demand, curve leftward.

Question:

Considering the factor labor, if there is either a change in the price of the product labor produces, or a change in the MPP of labor (reflected in a shift in the MPP curve), the (factor) demand curve for labor shifts. Is this correct?

Answer:

Yes, that is correct.

Market Demand for Labor

Using the preceding section as background, we can now discuss the market demand curve for labor. Normally, we would expect this to be the horizontal summation of the firms' demand curves (*MRP* curves) for labor. However, this is not the case, as Exhibit 12-7 illustrates.

Here we have two firms, A and B, that we assume make up the buying side of the factor market. We also assume that the product price for both firms is P_1: Exhibit 12-7a and b show the *MRP* curve for the two firms based on this product price.

Starting at a wage rate of W_1, firm A purchases 100 units of labor. This is the amount of labor at which its marginal revenue product equals marginal factor cost (or the wage). At this same wage rate, firm B purchases 150 units of labor. If we horizontally sum the *MRP* curves of firms A and B, we get the *MRP* curve in (c), where the two firms together purchase 250 units of labor at W_1.

Now increase the wage rate to W_2. In (c) firms A and B move up the given MRP_{A+B} curve and purchase 180 units of labor. This may seem to be the end of the process, but, of course, it is not. A higher wage rate increases each firm's costs and thus shifts its supply curve leftward. This leads to an increase in product price to P_2.

Recall that the firm's marginal revenue product is equal to marginal revenue (and price, if the firm is a product price taker) times marginal physical product, *MRP* = MR or (P) × *MPP*. If price rises, so does *MRP*; thus each firm faces a *new MRP* curve at the wage rate W_2. Exhibit 12-7a and b illustrate these new *MRP* curves for firms A and B, and (c) shows the horizontal summation of the new *MRP* curves. The firms together now purchase 210 units of labor at W_2.

Once all adjustments have been made, connecting the units of labor purchased by both firms at W_1 and W_2 gives us the *market demand curve* in (c).

The Elasticity of Demand for Labor

The **elasticity of demand for labor** is the percentage change in the quantity demanded of labor divided by the percentage change in the price of labor (the wage rate).

Elasticity of Demand for Labor
Percentage change in the quantity demanded of labor divided by the percentage change in the wage rate.

$$E_L = \frac{\text{percentage change in quantity demanded of labor}}{\text{percentage change in wage rate}}$$

where E_L = coefficient of elasticity of demand for labor or simply elasticity coefficient. For example, if the wage rate were to change by 20 percent and the quantity demanded of a particular type of labor changed by 40 percent, the elasticity of demand for this type of labor would be 2 (40 percent/20 percent); the demand between the old wage rate and the new wage rate would be elastic. There are three main determinants of elasticity of demand for labor.

Elasticity of Demand for the Product that Labor Produces. If the demand for the product that labor produces is highly elastic, a small percentage increase in price will decrease quantity demanded of the product by a relatively large percentage. In turn, this will greatly reduce the demand for the labor that produces the product.

The relationship between the elasticity of demand for the product and the elasticity of demand for labor is as follows: *The higher the elasticity of demand for the product, the higher the elasticity of demand for the labor that produces the product; the lower the elasticity of demand for the product, the lower the elasticity of demand for the labor that produces the product.*

Ratio of Labor Costs to Total Costs. Labor costs are a part of total costs. Consider two situations: one where labor costs are 90 percent of total costs and one where labor costs are only 5 percent of total costs. Now suppose there is a $2 per hour increase in wages. Total costs are affected more where labor costs are 90 percent of total costs (the $2 per hour wage increase is being applied to 90 percent of all

■ **EXHIBIT 12-7**
The Derivation of the Market Demand Curve for Labor

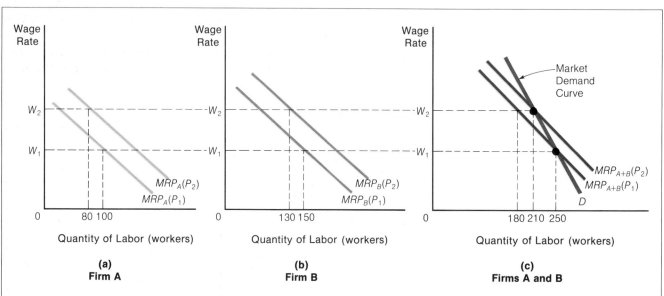

Two firms, A and B, make up the buying side of the market for labor. At a wage rate of W_1, firm A purchases 100 units of labor, and firm B purchases 150 units. Together they purchase 250 units, as illustrated in (c). The wage rate rises to W_2, and the amount of labor purchased by both firms initially falls to 180 units. Higher wage rates translate into higher

costs, a fall in product supply, and a rise in product price from P_1 to P_2. Finally, an increased price raises *MRP*. We obtain new *MRP* curves for each firm. The horizontal summation of the new *MRP* curves shows they purchase 210 units of labor. Connecting the units of labor purchased by both firms at W_1 and W_2 gives us the market demand curve.

costs) than where labor costs are only 5 percent. Price rises by more in the case where labor costs are a larger percentage of total costs. And, of course, the more price rises, the more quantity demanded of the product falls. It follows that labor, being a derived demand, is affected more. In short, the decline in the quantity demanded of labor is greater for a $2-per-hour wage increase when labor costs are 90 percent of total costs than when labor costs are 5 percent of total costs. The relationship between the labor cost–total cost ratio and the elasticity of demand for labor is as follows: *The higher the labor cost–total cost ratio, the higher the elasticity of demand for labor (the greater the cutback in labor for any given wage increase); the lower the labor cost–total cost ratio, the lower the elasticity of demand for labor (the less the cutback in labor for any given wage increase).*

Number of Substitute Factors. The more substitutes there are for labor, the more sensitive buyers of labor will be to a change in the price of labor. This is a principle we established in Chapter 6 when we discussed price elasticity of demand. The more chances of substituting other factors for labor, the more likely firms that purchase labor will cut back on their use of labor if the price of labor rises. *The more substitutes for labor, the higher the elasticity of demand for labor; the fewer substitutes for labor, the lower the elasticity of demand for labor.*

The Market Supply of Labor

As the wage rate rises, the quantity supplied of labor rises, *ceteris paribus*. The upward-sloping labor supply curve in Exhibit 12-8 illustrates this. At a wage rate of W_1, individuals are willing to supply 100 labor hours; at the higher wage rate of W_2, individuals are willing to supply 200 labor hours (this is because some individuals who were not willing to work at a wage rate of W_1 are willing to work at a wage rate of W_2, and also because some individuals who were working at W_1 will be willing to supply more hours at W_2); at the even higher wage rate of W_3, individuals are willing to supply 280 labor hours.

For any given individual, the wage he receives must cover his opportunity costs—the wage he could receive in his next best line of employment. If an employer does

■ **EXHIBIT 12-8**
The Market Supply of Labor

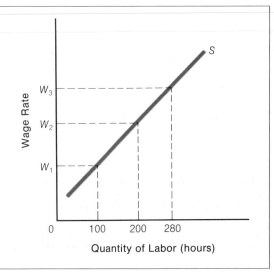

A direct relationship exists between the wage rate and the quantity of labor supplied. As the wage rate rises, more individuals will have their opportunity costs met and will be willing to supply their labor on the market. In short, as the wage rate rises, more individuals are willing to work.

Theory in Practice

Would You "Pay" $225,000 for a Job That Pays $89,500?

In 1988, the annual salary of a U.S. senator was $89,500. Many senators either spent much of their own money to become elected—sometimes the amounts were far in excess of $89,500—or forfeited high-paying jobs in order to become U.S. senators. Take the case of a hypothetical, but not untypical, senator.

Joe Ryan works for a law firm in Florida where his annual salary is $314,500 a year. One day he decides to run for the U.S. senate. He campaigns hard and wins the race. He leaves Florida and his $314,500 job to go to Washington and collect his $89,500 salary.

Why would an individual "pay" more than $89,500 a year to obtain a job that pays only $89,500 a year? Probably other considerations besides money are involved. The job is likely to offer nonpecuniary benefits such as respect, power, and privilege as well as being able to speak with the president and make key decisions.

How much are these nonpecuniary benefits worth? For Senator Ryan, who forfeited $314,500 a year to obtain $89,500 a year, the nonpecuniary benefits are worth at least the difference between the two sums, or $225,000 a year.

not pay this amount to an employee, the employee will not work for the employer. For example, if Miller can work for Cusack for $1,000 a month, and Richards offers Miller $500 a month, then Richards is not meeting Miller's opportunity costs and therefore will not be successful in employing him.

Question:

A person who could be working for a major corporation earning $150,000 a year instead works at a small private college where she earns $44,000 a year. Obviously her employer isn't paying her "next best alternative wage."

Answer:

In speaking about the supply of labor we assume that "all other things are held constant." This takes into account the nonmoney or nonpecuniary benefits individuals receive in their work. The person who chooses to work at the $44,000 job instead of the $150,000 job is probably receiving some nonmoney benefits at the private college that compensate her for the reduced income she is earning.

For example, she might be working at a more leisurely pace than she would in the big corporation, or maybe what she is doing is more enjoyable, or the hours are shorter. If we add nonmoney benefits to the overall pay package a person receives in his or her work, we conclude that an employer must provide an employee a wage-plus-nonmoney-benefits package at least equal to the employee's next best wage-plus-nonmoney-benefits package before the employee will work for that employer.

Changes in the Supply of Labor

As previously noted, changes in the wage rate change the quantity supplied of labor. But what changes the entire labor supply curve? Two factors of major importance are wage rates in other labor markets and the nonmoney or nonpecuniary aspects of a job.

Wage Rates in Other Labor Markets. Deborah currently works as a technician in a television manufacturing plant. She has job skills suitable for a number of jobs. One day she learns that the computer manufacturing plant on the other side of town is offering 33 percent more pay per hour. Since she is also trained to work as a computer operator, Deborah decides to leave her current job and apply for work at the computer manufacturing plant. In short, the wage rate offered in other labor markets can bring about a change in the supply of labor in a particular labor market.

Nonmoney or Nonpecuniary Aspects of a Job. Other things held constant, people prefer to avoid dirty, heavy, dangerous work in cold climates. An increase in the overall "unpleasantness" of a job (for example, an increased probability of contracting lung cancer working in an asbestos factory) will cause a decrease in the supply of labor to that firm or industry. An increase in the overall "pleasantness" of a job (employees are now entitled to a longer lunch break and use of the company gym) will cause an increase in the supply of labor to that firm or industry.

Putting Supply and Demand Together

Exhibit 12-9 illustrates a particular labor market. The equilibrium wage rate and quantity of labor hours are established by the forces of supply and demand. At a wage rate of W_2, there is a surplus of labor. Some people, who want to work at this wage rate, will not be able to find jobs. A subset of this group will begin to offer their services for a lower wage rate. The wage rate will move down until it reaches

■ **EXHIBIT 12-9**
Equilibrium in a Particular Labor Market

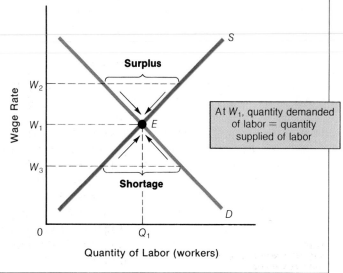

The forces of supply and demand bring about the equilibrium wage rate and quantity of labor. At the equilibrium wage rate, the quantity demanded of labor equals the quantity supplied. At any other wage rate there is either a surplus or a shortage of labor.

At W_1, quantity demanded of labor = quantity supplied of labor

W_1. At the wage rate W_3, there is a shortage of labor. Some demanders of labor will begin to bid up the wage rate until it reaches W_1. At the equilibrium wage rate, W_1, the quantity supplied of labor equals the quantity demanded of labor.

Why Wage Rates Differ

Why do wage rates differ? To answer this, we must ask what conditions would be necessary for everyone to receive the same pay.

Assume the following conditions hold: (1) The demand for every type of labor is the same. (Throughout our analysis, any wage differentials caused by demand are short-run differentials.) (2) There are no special nonpecuniary aspects to any job. (3) All labor is ultimately homogeneous and can costlessly be trained for different types of employment. (4) All labor is mobile at zero cost.

Given these conditions, there would be no difference in wages rates in the long run. Consider Exhibit 12-10, where two labor markets, A and B, are shown. Initially the supply conditions are different, with a greater supply of workers in labor market B (represented by S_B) than in labor market A (represented by S_A). Because of the different supply conditions, more workers are working in labor market B (Q_B) than in labor market A (Q_A), and the equilibrium wage rate in labor market B ($10) is lower than the equilibrium wage rate in labor market A ($30).

The differences in the wage rates between the two labor markets will not last. We have previously assumed that labor can move costlessly from one labor market to another (so why not move from the lower-paying job to the higher-paying job?), that there are no special nonpecuniary aspects to any job (there is no nonpecuniary

■ **EXHIBIT 12-10**
Wage Rate Equilization Across Labor Markets

Quantity of Labor (workers)

(a)
Labor Market A

Quantity of Labor (workers)

(b)
Labor Market B

Given the four necessary conditions, there will be no wage rate differences across labor markets. We start off with a wage rate of $30 in labor market A and a $10 wage rate in labor market B. Soon some individuals in B relocate to A, increasing the supply in one market, driving down the wage rate, and decreasing the supply in the other, thus driving up the wage rate. Equilibrium comes when the same wage rate is paid in both labor markets.

reason for not moving), that labor is ultimately homogeneous (workers who work in labor market B can work in labor market A), and that if workers need training to make a move from one labor market to another, they are not only capable of being trained, but can acquire the training costlessly. As a result, some workers in labor market B will relocate to labor market A, decreasing the supply of workers to S_B' in labor market B and increasing the supply of workers to S_A' in labor market A. The relocation of workers ends when the equilibrium wage rate in both markets is the same—$20.

We conclude that wage rates will not differ if our four conditions hold. But in reality, they do not hold. Therefore we can direct our attention to why wage rates differ. Obviously they differ because demand conditions are not the same in all labor markets (important to explain short-run wage differentials *only*), neither are supply conditions; there are nonpecuniary aspects to different jobs, labor is not homogeneous, labor cannot be retrained without cost, and labor is not costlessly mobile.

Why Demand and Supply Curves Differ in Different Labor Markets

Saying that wage rates differ because demand and supply conditions in different labor markets differ raises another question: Why do demand and supply conditions differ in different labor markets?

First, consider demand. We know that the firm's *MRP* curve is its factor demand curve, so we need to look at what affects the components of *MRP*, namely, *MR* and *MPP*. Product supply and demand conditions determine price and therefore indirectly affect marginal revenue (since $MR = \Delta TR/\Delta Q$ and $TR = P \times Q$) and factor demand. In short, since the supply and demand conditions in *product markets* are different, it follows that the demand for labor in different *labor markets* will be different, too.

The second factor, the marginal physical product of labor, is affected by individual workers' *own abilities and skills* (both innate and learned), the *degree of effort* they put forth on the job, and the *other factors of production* they work with. With respect to the latter, American workers are more productive than workers in many other countries because they work with many more capital goods and technical know-how. If all individuals had the same innate and learned skills and abilities, applied the same degree of effort on the job, and worked with the same amount and quality of other factors of production, wages would differ less than they currently do.

What about supply? Why are the supply conditions in different labor markets different? First, as we noted earlier, jobs come with *different nonpecuniary aspects*. Working as a coal miner in West Virginia is not as attractive a job as working as a gardener at a lush resort in Hawaii. We would expect this fact to be reflected in the supply of coal miners and gardeners.

Second, supply is also a reflection of *the number of persons who can actually do a job*. Williamson may want to be a nuclear physicist, but may not have the ability in science and mathematics to be one. Johnson may want to be a basketball player, but may not have the ability to be one.

Third, even if individuals have the ability to work at a certain job, they may perceive *the training costs as too high* (relative to the perceived benefits) to train for it. Miller may have the ability to be a brain surgeon, but views the years of schooling required to become one too high a price to pay.

Fourth, sometimes supply in different labor markets reflects a difference in the *cost of moving* across markets. Wage rates might be higher in Alaska than in Alabama for comparable labor because the workers in Alabama find the cost of relocating to Alaska too high relative to the benefits of receiving a higher wage.

Question:

Do the same factors that affect the demand for and supply of labor also affect the wage rate labor is paid?

Answer:

Yes, they do. Since the wage rate is determined by supply and demand forces, the factors that affect these forces indirectly affect wage rates. See Exhibit 12-11 for a summary.

Marginal Productivity Theory

Here are some things we know:

1. If a firm is a factor price taker, marginal factor cost is constant and equal to factor price, $MFC = P$. For example, suppose we have a factor price taker that hires labor. For the firm, $MFC = W$, where "W" is the wage rate.

■ **EXHIBIT 12-11**
The Wage Rate
A step-by-step framework for understanding the factors that affect the wage rate.

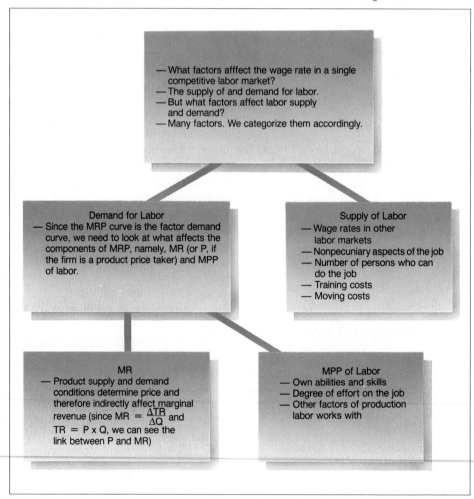

Economics in Our Times

If the Tax Is Divided Equally, Why Do I Pay It All?

When Congress established the Social Security system, it instituted Social Security taxes and split the tax between the employer and employees. By doing this it intended to split the cost of the system. In 1988, the tax was $15.02 per $100 on annual maximum taxable earnings of $45,000. Half of the $15.02 per $100, or $7.51, was *placed* on the employer, and the other half was *placed* on the employee.*

Economists know that sometimes taxes *placed* on one group of persons are actually *paid* for by another group. To a large extent, this is the case with the Social Security tax. Although half of the tax is placed on the employer, and half is placed on the employee, the employee ends up *paying* almost all of the tax.

We approximate this conclusion in Exhibit 12-12. We say "approximate" because most economists believe that the supply curve for labor *in the aggregate* is extremely inelastic. For simplicity, we have drawn the supply curve as perfectly inelastic, or vertical. In short, our supply curve approximates the actual supply curve. In a situation where no Social Security tax is placed on the employer, D_1 is

*The contribution rate is scheduled to rise to 7.51 percent in 1989 and to 7.65 percent in 1990.

the relevant demand curve for labor. The equilibrium wage rate is $9, meaning that employers are willing to pay a maximum of $9 per hour (per worker) for Q_1 workers. (Remember that a demand curve gives us the *maximum amount* per unit a buyer is willing to pay for alternative quantities. In the case of the labor market, this is the *maximum* wage rate per worker for alternative quantities of labor.)

Now consider placing the entire Social Security tax on the employer instead of half on the employer and half on the employee. Suppose employers

calculate the Social Security tax on an hourly basis and find that they have to "pay" $1 per hour for every employee they hire. If $9 was the equilibrium wage rate *before the tax*, then employers are not willing to pay any more for the same number of workers *after the tax.* Employers are only willing to pay labor $9 per hour *minus* the hourly computed tax. In short, from the employer's perspective, the demand curve for labor falls by $1 for each alternative quantity of labor. Employers are now willing to pay only a maximum of $8 per hour per worker

■ **EXHIBIT 12-12**
Who Pays the Social Security Tax?

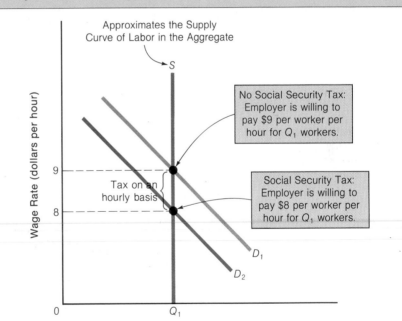

With no Social Security tax, the equilibrium wage rate is $9 per hour; employers are willing to pay a maximum of $9 per hour (per worker) for Q_1 workers. With the Social Security tax fully placed on employers, and computed on an hourly basis, employers are willing to pay $9 per hour *minus* the hourly computed tax for Q_1 workers. Since we have assumed the hourly tax is $1 per employee, and that the supply curve for labor is perfectly inelastic in the aggregate, the new equilibrium wage rate is $8. Under the conditions stated, the employee ends up paying the full Social Security tax in the form of lower wages.

2. Firms hire the factor quantity at which $MRP = MFC$.

3. Taking points 1 and 2 together, we know that a factor price taker pays labor a wage equal to its marginal revenue product, $W = MRP$. That is, since $MFC = W$ (point 1), and $MRP = MFC$ (point 2), it follows that $W = MRP$.

4. If a firm is a product price taker, $MRP = VMP$.

5. If a firm is both a product price taker *and* a factor price taker, it pays labor a wage equal to its value marginal product, $W = VMP$. That is, since $W = MRP$ (point 3), and $MRP = VMP$ (point 4), it follows that $W = VMP$.

Marginal Productivity Theory

States that firms in competitive or perfect product and factor markets pay factors their marginal revenue products.

This is the **marginal productivity theory,** which states that if a firm sells its product and purchases its factors in competitive or perfect markets (that is, it is a product price taker and a factor price taker; box I in Exhibit 12-1), it pays its factors their MRP or VMP (since the two are equal for a product price taker).

In other words, the theory holds that under the competitive conditions specified, if a factor unit is withdrawn from the productive process, and the amount of all other factors remain the same, the *decrease in the value of the product produced* equals the factor payment received by the factor unit. To illustrate, suppose Wilson works for price taker firm X producing good X. One day he quits his job (but nothing else relevant to the firm changes). As a result, the total revenue of the firm falls by $100. If Wilson was paid $100, then he received his MRP. He was paid a wage equal to his contribution to the productive process.[4]

___

Question:

Aren't some workers paid less than their MRPs (less than their contributions to the productive process)? If so, isn't this evidence sufficient to reject the marginal productivity theory?

___

[4]Recall that there are two ways to calculate MRP: $MRP = \Delta TR/\Delta$ factor, and $MRP = MR \times MPP$. In this example we used the first method. When Wilson quits his job, the change in the denominator is 1 factor unit. If, as a result, TR falls by $100, then the change in the numerator is $100.

Answer:

The theory specifies that the firm sells its product and purchases its factors in competitive, or perfect, markets. Not all firms fit into this category; thus, certainly some workers are not paid their MRPs. (We discuss marginal productivity theory and market imperfections in the next chapter.)

Follow-Up Question:

Are workers who work for firms that "sell their products and purchase their factors in competitive markets" paid their MRPs?

Answer:

The proponents of marginal productivity theory argue that employees in this setting are paid wages that over time closely approximate their MRPs. In other words, not all employees are paid their *exact* MRPs, but most employees in this setting are paid *close to* their MRPs. The critics of the theory point out that it is very difficult for firms to measure the value of their employees' marginal products accurately. The proponents argue that the firms have a monetary incentive to make a reasonable "guesstimate." They add that firms interview and screen potential employees, as well as regularly evaluate current employees, to acquire information on workers' MRPs.

LABOR MARKETS AND INFORMATION

We now look at job hiring, employment practices, and employment discrimination. All three topics are directly related to the issue of information.

Employee Screening: Or What Is Your GPA?

Employers typically do not know exactly how productive a potential employee will be on the job. What the employer wants, but lacks, is complete information about the potential employee's future job performance.

This raises two questions. First, why would an employer want complete information about a potential employee's future job performance? Second, what does the employer do because he or she lacks complete information?

The answer to the first question is obvious. Employers have a strong monetary incentive to hire good, stable, quick-learning, responsible, hard-working, punctual employees. One study found that corporate spending on training employees reached $40 billion annually. Obviously corporations would like to see the highest return possible for their training expenditures. This requires that they hire employees who will make the training pay off. This is where **screening** comes in.

Screening

The process used by employers to increase the probability of choosing "good" employees based on certain criteria.

Screening is the process used by employers to increase the probability of choosing "good" employees based on certain criteria. For example, an employer might ask a young college graduate searching for a job what his GPA was in college. This is a screening mechanism. The employer might know from past experience that people with high GPAs turn out to be better employees, on average, than persons with low GPAs.

Promoting from Within

Sometimes employers promote from within the company because they have more information on company employees than on potential employees.

Theory in Practice

Baseball Players, Soldiers, and Women in the Work Force

We know three things about the labor market: (1) Labor tends to be paid its marginal revenue product in competitive markets. (2) Individuals' wages must at least equal their opportunity costs (their next best alternative wage, all other things held constant). (3) The supply curve of labor is upward sloping, indicating that as wage rates rise, so does the quantity of labor supplied to the market. Do these principles hold in the real world? We cite three of the many cases where they do.

First, consider baseball players. Gerald Scully undertook to calculate the marginal revenue product of professional baseball players.* He found that star hitters had a marginal revenue product between $250,000 and $383,700 and that star pitchers had a marginal revenue product between $321,700 and $479,000. No baseball player, however, earned more than $125,000 when these marginal revenue products were computed. In short, baseball stars were being paid less than their *MRP*s.

What happened over the long run? Through the free agency system, players' salaries—and especially the salaries of star players—were upgraded. In the 1970s and 1980s, baseball stars experienced huge increases in salary, which moved their pay closer to their *MRP*s.

*Gerald W. Scully, "Pay and Performance in Major League Baseball," *American Economic Review* 64 (December 1974): 915–30.

Next, let's look at soldiers. Since 1973, the United States has operated an all-volunteer military service rather than using the military draft. With the draft, the government did not have to worry about paying soldiers a wage equal to their opportunity costs, since draft evasion carried a prison penalty. With the volunteer military service, however, the government must pay a wage that covers a soldier's opportunity costs. If it doesn't, the person will not volunteer. In the years immediately after the all-volunteer service was established, the military complained about the low quality and quantity of the volunteers. Pay increases in later years—between 1980 and 1982 pay increased approximately 29 percent—are said to have largely solved both problems.

Military recruiters now also recognize that economic recessions help recruitment and economic recoveries hurt it. During recessions, wage rates sometimes fall, making a given military wage look better. In economic recoveries, wage rates often rise, making a given military wage look worse.

Finally, take women in the labor force. In 1950, three out of every ten women worked outside the home; today the rate has approximately doubled. What has led to the relative increase in working women? Some commentators point to social phenomena such as the higher divorce rate (there are relatively more single women now), the more casual, less regimented lifestyles of Americans today than in the 1950s, and the greater social acceptance of women in the labor force. Although these changes may have been influential, economists generally point to the higher real wage rates in the economy as the primary cause. (Real wage rates are inflation-adjusted wage rates.) For example, in the early 1980s, an hour's work bought slightly more than one and a half times the amount of goods and services that an hour's work bought in the early 1950s. When the opportunity cost of staying out of the work force rises—which is what happens when real wage rates rise—fewer people choose not to work—women and men alike.

For example, suppose the executive vice-president in charge of sales is retiring from Trideck, Inc. The president of the company could, of course, hire an outsider to replace the vice-president, but often she will select an insider about whom she has some knowledge. What may look like discrimination to outsiders—"That company discriminates against persons not working for it"—may simply be a reflection of the difference in costs to the employer of acquiring relevant information on employees inside and outside the company.

Is It Discrimination or Is It an Information Problem?

Suppose the world is made up of people with characteristic X and people with characteristic Y. We call them X people and Y people, respectively. Over time we observe that most employers are X people and that they tend to hire and promote proportionally more X than Y people. Are the Y people being discriminated against?

It could be. Nothing that we have said so far would rule this out. But then it may be that X people rarely hire or promote Y people because over time X employers have learned that Y people on average do not perform as well as X people.

For purposes of illustration, we simply state that X people are not discriminating against Y people, but instead that Y people are not being hired and promoted as often as X people because, for whatever reason, Y people on average are not as productive as X people.

Suppose that in this environment an extremely productive Y person comes along and applies for a job with an X employer. The problem is, the X employer does not know—she lacks complete information—about the full abilities of the Y person; furthermore, it is costly to acquire complete information. She bases her decision to reject the Y person's job application based on what she knows about Y people, which is that on average they are not as productive as X people. She doesn't do this because she has something against Y people, but because it is simply *too costly* for her to acquire complete information on every potential employee—X or Y.

We do not mean to imply that everything that looks like discrimination is really a problem of the high cost of information. Nonetheless, sometimes what looks like discrimination ("he doesn't like me, I'm a Y person") is a consequence of living in a world where acquiring complete information is "too costly."

The Theme Played in a Different Arena

Despite the differences between the product market and the factor market, certain similarities also exist.

For example, in the product market the firm produces that quantity of output at which marginal revenue equals marginal cost, $MR = MC$. In the factor market, the firm buys the factor quantity at which marginal revenue product equals marginal factor cost, $MRP = MFC$. The economic principle of *equating additional benefits with additional costs* holds in both markets.

Next, compare the firm's least-cost rule with the way buyers allocate their consumption dollars. A buyer of goods in the product market chooses combinations of goods such that the marginal utility of good A divided by the price of a good A is equal to the marginal utility of good B divided by the price of good B; that is, $MU_A/P_A = MU_B/P_B$. A firm buying factors in the factor market does the same thing, except here the condition (for the two factors X and Y) reads $MPP_X/P_X = MPP_Y/P_Y$. Consumers do not buy goods any differently from the way that firms buy factors.

A good understanding of economics involves knowing that economic principles present themselves over and over again in different settings. Once you realize this, much of the mystery of economics disappears. You are then ready to move on to new and different topics, some of which may not even be discussed in economics texts, and analyze them based on economic principles you have learned earlier. To a large degree, this is the reason for studying economics in the first place.

CHAPTER SUMMARY

Price Takers, Price Searchers

■ The "price taker–price searcher" terminology can be used to describe firms as buyers in factor markets, just as it is used to describe firms as sellers in product markets.

■ A factor price taker can buy all of a factor it wants at the equilibrium price. It faces a horizontal (flat, perfectly elastic) supply curve of factors.

■ A factor price searcher drives up factor price if it buys an additional factor unit. It faces an upward-sloping supply curve of factors.

■ In this chapter we discussed two types of firms: (1) the product price taker and factor price taker and (2) the product price searcher and factor price taker.

Derived Demand

■ The demand for a factor is derived—hence it is called a derived demand. Specifically, it is derived from, and directly related to, the demand for the product that the factor goes to produce. For example, the demand for auto workers is derived from the demand for autos.

MRP, MFC, VMP

■ Marginal revenue product (MRP) is the additional revenue generated by employing an additional factor unit. Marginal factor cost (MFC) is the additional cost incurred by employing an additional factor unit. The profit-maximizing firm buys that factor quantity at which $MRP = MFC$.

■ The MRP curve is the firm's factor demand curve; it shows how much of a factor the firm buys at different prices.

■ Whereas $MRP = MR \times MPP$, $VMP = P \times MPP$. For a product price taker, $P = MR$, so $MRP = VMP$. For a product price searcher, $P > MR$, so $VMP > MRP$. The VMP is a measure of the value that each factor unit adds to the firm's product.

■ For the firm that is a price taker in both product and factor markets, $VMP = MRP = MFC = factor\ price$ at the profit-maximizing factor quantity.

■ For the firm that is a price searcher in the product market and a price taker in the factor market, $VMP > MRP = MFC = factor\ price$ at the profit-maximizing factor quantity.

The Least-Cost Rule

■ The firm minimizes costs by buying factors in the combination at which the MPP-price ratio for each is the same. For example, if there are two factors, labor and capital, the least-cost rule reads

$$\frac{MPP_\text{L}}{P_\text{L}} = \frac{MPP_\text{K}}{P_\text{K}}$$

Labor and Wages

■ A change in the price of the product labor produces, or a change in the marginal physical product of labor (reflected in a shift in the MPP curve), will shift the demand curve for labor.

Theory in Practice

Are Interest, Land Rent, and Profit All That Bad?

Throughout history, interest, land rent, and profits have often been attacked. For example, at various times some philosophers and religious leaders have maintained that interest is improper and unjust and that it is wrong for a person to make a loan to another person and charge interest. The early communists also considered interest to be unjust.

As for land rents, Henry George (1839–1897), who wrote the influential book *Progress and Poverty*, felt that all land rents were pure economic rents and should be heavily taxed. Landowners benefited simply because they had the good fortune to own land. In George's view, landowners did nothing productive. For example, he maintained that the early owners of land in the American West reaped higher land rents, not because they made their land more productive, but because individuals from the East began to move West. George argued for a heavy tax on land rents and said that there would be no supply response in land owing to the tax because land was in fixed supply.

Profits have also frequently come under attack. High profits are somehow thought to be evidence of corruption or manipulation. Those who earn profits are often considered no better than thieves.

A few things are overlooked by those who speak of interest, land rent, and profits being improper and unfair. One is the idea that interest, land rents, and profits are returns to genuine factors of production. Most people find it easy to understand that labor is a factor of production and that wages are the return to this factor. But understanding that land, capital, and entrepreneurship are also genuine factors of production with returns that flow to them seems to be more difficult.

Another point that is overlooked is that interest exists largely because individuals naturally have a positive rate of time preference. Those who dislike interest are in fact criticizing individuals because of the way they naturally happen to be. If they could somehow make individuals not weight present consumption over future consumption, interest would diminish.

A similar point can be made about profit. Some say profit is the consequence of living in a world of uncertainty. If those who do not like profit could make this world of ours less uncertain, or bring certainty to it, then profit would disappear.

Question:

Do interest, rent, and profits together (interest + rent + profits) make up a larger or smaller percentage of national income than wages alone do?

Answer:

The percentage is quite a bit smaller. In most years, wages' share of national income is about 75 percent, leaving 25 percent for interest, rent, and profit together.

Remember, however, that monopoly profits may be competed for, may become capitalized, and may disappear altogether if the monopoly market is contestable. For a review, see Chapter 10.

Profit and Loss as Signals

Too often we simply see profit and loss in terms of the benefit or hurt they bring to particular persons. We need to go beyond this and see both profit and loss as *signals*.[3]

For example, when one firm makes a profit, other firms view this as a signal that the profit-making firm is producing and selling a good that buyers value more than the factors that go to make the good. The profit causes resources to move into the

[3]In our chapters on market structures, we discussed profit and loss as signals. We repeat the essence of that discussion here.

production of the particular good to which the profit is linked. In short, resources follow profit.

On the other hand, if a firm is taking a loss, this is a signal to the firm that it is producing and selling a good that buyers value less than the factors that go to make the good. The loss causes resources to move out of the production of the particular good to which the loss is linked. Resources turn away from losses.

■ CHAPTER SUMMARY

Interest

■ The word *interest* refers to (1) the price paid by borrowers for loanable funds and (2) the return on capital in the production process. There is a tendency for these two to become equal.

■ The equilibrium interest rate (in terms of the price for a loanable fund) is determined by the demand for, and supply of, loanable funds. The supply of loanable funds comes from savers, people who consume less than their current incomes. The demand for loanable funds comes from the demand for consumption and investment loans.

■ Consumers demand loanable funds because they have a positive rate of time preference; they prefer earlier availability of goods to later availability. Investors (or firms) demand loanable funds so that they can invest in productive roundabout methods of production.

■ The nominal interest rate is the interest rate determined by the forces of supply and demand in the loanable funds market. It is the interest rate in current dollars, unadjusted for expected inflation. The real interest rate is the nominal interest rate adjusted for expected inflation. Specifically, real interest rate = nominal interest rate − expected inflation rate (which means nominal interest rate = real interest rate + expected inflation rate).

Rent

■ Economic rent is a payment in excess of opportunity costs. A subset of this is pure economic rent, which is a payment in excess of opportunity costs when opportunity costs are zero. Historically, the term ''pure economic rent'' was used to describe the payment to the factor, land, since land (in total) was assumed to be fixed in supply (perfectly inelastic supply curve). Today, the terms economic rent and pure economic rent are also often used when speaking about economic factors other than land.

■ David Ricardo argued that grain prices weren't high because land rents were high, but that rents were high because grain prices were high. Land rents are price determined, not price determining.

■ How much economic rent a factor receives depends on the perspective from which the factor is viewed. For example, a university librarian earning $50,000 a year receives $2,000 economic rent if his next best alternative income at another university is $48,000. Or the economic rent may be $10,000 if his next best alternative in a nonuniversity position pays $40,000.

Profit

■ Several different theories of profit address the question of the "source" of profit. (From where does profit come?). One theory holds that profit would not exist in a world of certainty; hence, uncertainty is the source of profit. Another theory holds that profit is the return for alertness to arbitrage opportunities. A third theory holds that profit is the return to the entrepreneur as innovator.

■ Taking the three profit theories together, we can say that profit is the return to entrepreneurship, where entrepreneurship entails bearing uncertainty, being alert to arbitrage opportunities, and exhibiting innovativeness.

■ QUESTIONS TO ANSWER AND DISCUSS

1. What type of people are most willing to pay high interest rates?

2. Some persons have argued that in a moneyless (or barter) economy, interest would not exist. Is this true?

3. In what ways are a baseball star who can do nothing but play baseball and a parcel of land similar?

4. What is the overall economic function of profits?

5. "The more economic rent a person receives in his job, the less likely he is to leave the job, and the more contented he will be on the job." Do you agree or disagree? Explain your answer.

6. It has been said that a society with a high savings rate is a society with a high standard of living. What is the link (if any) between saving and a relatively high standard of living?

7. Make an attempt to calculate the present value of your future income.

8. What do you think each of the following events would do to individuals' rate of time preference, and thus to interest rates?
  a. A technological advance that raises longevity.
  b. An increased threat of war.
  c. Growing older.

9. "As the interest rate falls, firms are more inclined to buy capital goods." Do you agree or disagree? Explain your answer.

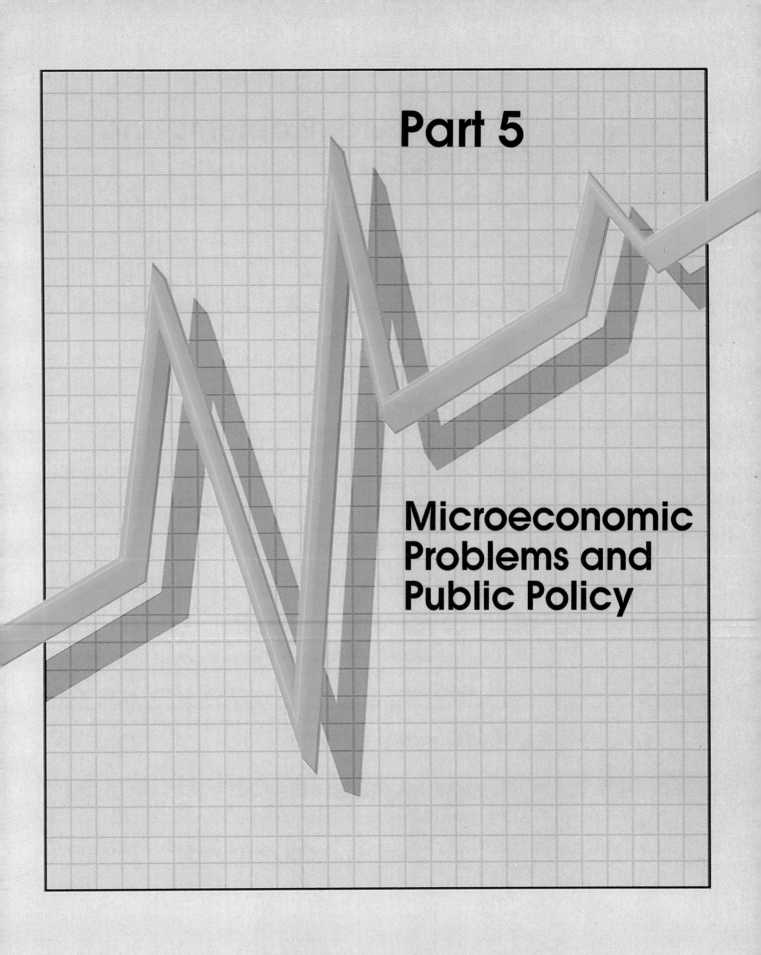

Part 5

Microeconomic Problems and Public Policy

Chapter 15

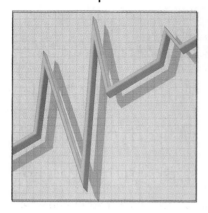

Agriculture: Problems and Policies

■ INTRODUCTION

What pictures come to mind when someone mentions agriculture, or farming? Here are three of the many pictures we could draw.

The first is a rather romantic, Norman Rockwell–like picture of gently rolling lands with crops planted in the west fields, cattle grazing in the foreground, and a clean white farmhouse with years of family written all over it. The sky is blue, the sun is warm, and a big lovable dog is following a little boy toward the house where his mother waits on the front porch with a pitcher of lemonade.

The second picture is not so serene, peaceful, or pretty. It shows a farmer opening a letter he has just received from the bank. The letter states that he has missed the last four mortgage payments and informs him that if he doesn't pay up by the end of the month, the bank will foreclose on his farm. Feeling sick, the farmer sits down. He stares into space for hours, wondering what he will do.

The third picture shows a lobbyist in Washington. He is asking the senator from New Hampshire to support the upcoming farm legislation in the Congress. The senator argues that the budget is out of control, the farmers are already getting $26 billion or more per year, and enough is enough. The lobbyist leaves the senator's office disappointed. Later that day, the senator from Kansas pays a visit to the senator from New Hampshire and personally asks him to support the upcoming farm legislation. In return, the senator from Kansas promises to look favorably upon the New Hampshire senator's tax bill.

■ WHAT THIS CHAPTER IS ABOUT

This chapter discusses the problems in agriculture, the policies enacted to deal with them, and the effects of those policies. Three groups of people are involved in the story we tell here: farmers, consumers, and taxpayers. And, of course, there is government, which, as you will see, through its policies, affects all three.

Key Questions to Keep in Mind as You Read

1. What effect does high productivity have on farmers?
2. What effect does income inelasticity have on farmers?
3. What effect does price inelasticity have on farmers?
4. Why do farmers as a group sometimes prefer bad weather to good weather? (Wouldn't you think it would be the opposite?)
5. How do price supports, supply-restricting policies, and target prices work?

AGRICULTURE: THE ISSUES

From the perspective of some farmers, there are three issues (some would say problems) of major concern: high productivity in the agricultural sector, income inelasticity for specific foods (income elasticity less than 1), and price inelasticity for specific foods (price elasticity of demand less than 1). Related to these three issues is the issue of price instability in the agricultural sector.

Agriculture and High Productivity

At the beginning of this century, one farmer produced enough food to feed 8 people. Today, one farmer produces enough food to feed 35 people. Obviously farmers have become more productive over the years. In fact, the productivity of the agricultural sector has increased faster than productivity in the economy as a whole. The 1987 *Economic Report of the President* reads: "Over much of the 20th century, agriculture has been one of the most innovative and productive sectors in the U.S. economy. . . . Farmers in the United States represent less than 3 percent of the civilian labor force, but they produce enough food to feed the entire domestic population, while maintaining the capacity to export large quantities to the rest of the world."[1]

Increased productivity in the agricultural sector has pushed the supply curve of farm products rightward. From the perspective of the consumer, this is good. Increased supply means more food at lower prices. But from the perspective of farmers, lower prices do not necessarily mean higher revenues. For example, if the demand curve for a particular food is inelastic, a lower price brings lower, not higher, revenues. See Exhibit 15-1.

Here we have illustrated a rightward shift in the supply curve for some particular food item, due to an increase in productivity. As a result, equilibrium price falls and equilibrium quantity rises. Since the demand curve between the two equilibrium points, E_1 and E_2, is inelastic, total revenue is less at E_2 than at E_1. In summary, increased productivity results in lower prices for consumers and lower revenues for farmers.

Question:

Why don't farmers simply agree among themselves to be less productive, since greater productivity seems to work to their disadvantage?

---

[1]Council of Economic Advisers, *Economic Report of the President, 1987* (Washington, D.C.: U.S. Government Printing Office, 1987), pp. 147–8.

High Productivity Doesn't Always Benefit Farmers as a Group

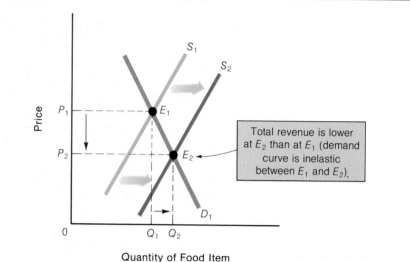

Owing to increased agricultural productivity, the supply curve shifts rightward from S_1 to S_2. As a result, equilibrium price falls and equilibrium quantity rises. The demand curve between E_1 and E_2 is inelastic, so total revenue is lower at E_2 than at E_1. In summary, increased productivity results in lower prices for consumers and lower revenues for farmers.

Answer:

That is easy to say but hard to do. Ideally, each farmer wants to be as productive as possible, while wanting his fellow farmers to be as unproductive as possible. We can see why by considering the following hypothetical example.

Suppose on Tuesday all farmers agree to restrict output in one of two ways: indirectly, by being less productive, or directly, by taking certain acreage out of production.[2] On Wednesday, Farmer Jenkins thinks to himself, If everyone abides by the agreement to restrict output, the supply curve will shift leftward and a higher price will result. It certainly would be nice if once that higher price arrives on the scene, I have a lot to sell. So it seems that the best thing for me to do is forget the agreement and, in fact, increase output (or at least do nothing to decrease it), and in the interim hope that all other farmers do not think and behave the way I do.

The problem here is that Jenkins is not the only farmer who can or will think this way. Other farmers will behave similarly. In the end, any farmers' agreement to restrict output is not likely to hold, because each farmer will reason that he will be better off if he increases output while others do not.[3]

---

[2]The transaction costs of getting all farmers together are probably so high that all farmers wouldn't meet to make an agreement like the one described here. We omit this real-world complexity to make our main point: Even if all farmers could get together to agree to be less productive, the agreement probably wouldn't last.

[3]Those of you who read the Appendix to Chapter 11 will recognize that farmers are in a prisoner's dilemma situation.

Agriculture and Income Inelasticity

In Chapter 6 we defined income elasticity of demand as

$$E_y = \frac{\text{percentage change in quantity demanded}}{\text{percentage change in income}}$$

If $E_y < 1$, the percentage change in quantity demanded is less than the percentage change in income—and the demand for the good in question is *income inelastic*. In the United States, studies show that as real income has been increasing, the per-capita demand for food has been increasing by much less. Many studies put U.S. income elasticity for food at less than 0.2, which means that as income increases 10 percent, food purchases increase by less than 2 percent.

If we put the income inelasticity of demand for food together with high agricultural productivity, we see that while demand for food has been increasing (due largely to population growth), the supply of food has been increasing even more (see Exhibit 15-2). Of course, supply increases that outstrip demand increases lead to falling prices.

In fact, if we look at the **parity price ratio,** which is a ratio of an index of prices that farmers receive to an index of prices that farmers pay, it is evident that in much of this century prices of agricultural products have fallen *relative* to other prices (see Exhibit 15-3). The ratio uses the years 1910–14, which were a period of unusual peace time prosperity for farmers, as a base period. If the ratio falls below the base-period ratio of 100, this means that prices of agricultural products have fallen relative

Parity Price Ratio

A ratio of an index of prices that farmers receive to an index of prices that farmers pay.

■ **Exhibit 15-2**
High Productivity and Income Inelasticity Together

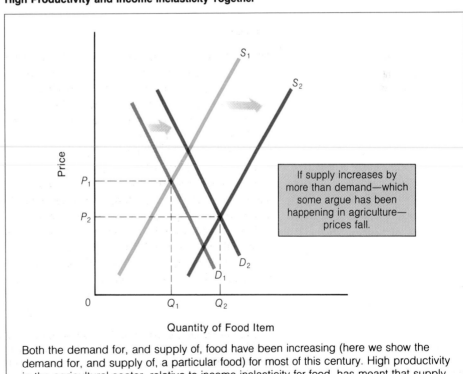

Both the demand for, and supply of, food have been increasing (here we show the demand for, and supply of, a particular food) for most of this century. High productivity in the agricultural sector, relative to income inelasticity for food, has meant that supply has increased by more than demand. As a result prices have fallen.

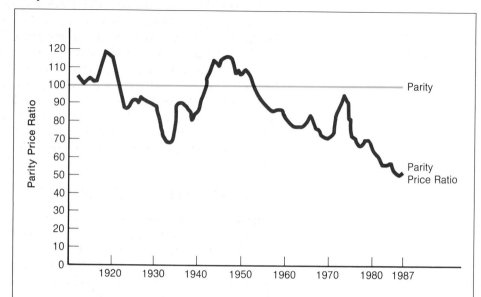

Parity Price Ratio in the 1980s	
Year	Parity Price Ratio
1980	65
1981	61
1982	56
1983	56
1984	57
1985	52
1986	51

For much of this century prices of agricultural products have fallen relative to the prices of other goods. When the parity price ratio falls below the base-period ratio of 100, prices of agricultural products have fallen relative to other prices. When the ratio rises above the base-period ratio of 100, prices of agricultural products have risen relative to other prices.

SOURCES: Department of Agriculture; U.S. Bureau of the Census, *Statistical Abstract of the United States, 1988* (Washington, D.C.: U.S. Government Printing Office, 1988).

to other prices; if the ratio rises above the base-period ratio of 100, this means that prices of agricultural products have risen relative to other prices. As we can see from Exhibit 15-3, for most of the period measured, prices of agricultural products have fallen relative to the prices of other goods.

Question:

What do farmers want when they ask for parity? Do they want the same prices for their products today that existed in the period 1910–14?

Answer:

They want the same *relative* prices today that existed in the period 1910–14. For example, suppose that in 1910–14, a bushel of wheat sold for $1 and a shirt could be purchased for $1. This meant that the price of wheat in terms of a shirt (or the *relative price* of a bushel of wheat) was one shirt: 1 bushel of wheat = 1 shirt. Now suppose that in 1989 one bushel of wheat sells for $6 and a shirt can be purchased for $12. The relative price of a bushel of wheat has fallen to ½ shirt. Parity would be 50 percent. When farmers argue for full, or 100 percent, parity, they are arguing for a price for their wheat that maintains the same relative relationship between wheat and shirts (in our example) as existed in the period 1910–14. In our example, a $12 price for a bushel of wheat in 1989 would maintain full parity.

Agriculture and Price Inelasticity

If market demand is inelastic, and supply is subject to severe shifts from season to season, it follows that (1) price changes are likely to be large, and (2) total revenue is likely to be highly volatile. This is the case in agriculture.

First, the demand for many agricultural products is inelastic. For example, the following estimates of price elasticity of demand have been made: cattle, 0.68; chickens, 0.74; corn, 0.54; eggs, 0.23; milk used for cheese, 0.54; potatoes, 0.11; and soybeans, 0.61.

Second, the supply of many food products changes from one year to the next, because not only is the supply of food products a function of technological and productivity changes but it is also dependent on the weather—and as we know, the weather is subject to sharp changes. For example, in some years in the Midwest the weather is excellent, and the corn and wheat crops are plentiful. And in some years the weather is bad, and the corn and wheat crop are in "short" supply.

To illustrate, Exhibit 15-4 shows two supply curves: S_B, which represents the supply of a food item when there is bad weather, and S_G, which represents the

■ **Exhibit 15-4**
Large Price Changes and Volatile Total Revenue

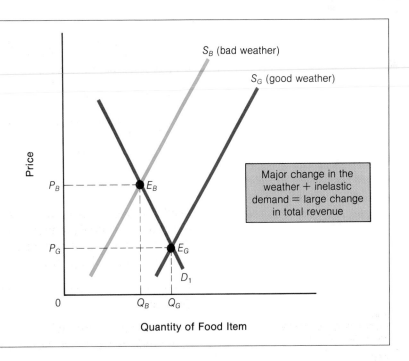

If demand is inelastic and supply is subject to severe changes from season to season, price changes will be large and total revenue (farmers' gross income) will be volatile. Suppose the supply curve shifts from S_B to S_G. As a result, price falls from P_B to P_G, and total revenue falls from $P_B \times Q_B$ to $P_G \times Q_G$.

Major change in the weather + inelastic demand = large change in total revenue

supply when there is good weather. The demand curve, D_1, is inelastic in the region relevant to our discussion. Whether we start at S_B (bad weather) and move to S_G (good weather), or start at S_G and move to S_B, there is a large change in price due to the relatively high inelasticity of demand for the food item. We would expect then that large changes in supply, brought about by changes in weather conditions, would in turn bring about relatively large fluctuations in the price of agricultural products.

If there are large changes in price when demand is inelastic, it follows that there will be large changes in total revenue or farmers' gross income. Suppose demand is perfectly inelastic and quantity demanded is thus completely insensitive to changes in price. If price is $10 and quantity demanded is 100, total revenue is $1,000. If price drops by 50 percent to $5, total revenue falls by 50 percent to $500, too, since quantity demanded does not change at all. Thus, large changes in price bring about large changes in total revenue (farmers' gross income) when demand is inelastic. See Exhibit 15-5, which shows the large variations in farmers' gross income and net income that occurred between 1977 and 1987.

The instability in price and total revenue (gross income) increases the uncertainties of farming. Typically farmers argue that they have no idea what prices they will get for their products or what they will earn from one season to the next. Farmers see this as a major agricultural problem.

Why Bad Weather Is Sometimes Good

An individual farmer prefers good weather to bad weather, but farmers as a group prefer bad weather to good weather. What's the explanation for this seeming inconsistency?

One of the things an individual farmer is interested in is his or her total revenue, or price times quantity ($P \times Q$). The P is determined by the market, and Q is largely determined by the individual farmer and the weather. The individual farmer prefers good weather to bad weather because the better the weather (up to some limit), the greater his Q, or output, and therefore the greater total revenue is. Farmers as a group prefer bad weather to good weather (up to some limit) because bad weather shifts the supply curve for their product leftward and raises P, and if demand is inelastic, total revenue rises.

Ideally, an individual farmer would want good weather for himself and bad weather for all other farmers. In other words, an individual farmer might "vote" for good weather for himself so that his Q will be high, but "vote" for bad weather for all other farmers so that total supply will be less and P will be high.

The Changing Farm Picture

Because of the problems directly and indirectly related to high productivity, income inelasticity, and price inelasticity, the farm picture today is different from what it was in years past. For example, there are fewer farms in this country today than there were earlier in this century. As Exhibit 15-6 shows, the number of farms in 1987 was barely 37 percent of the number in 1900. The number of people living on farms also steadily decreased. The farm population, which is defined as the civilian population living on farms in rural areas (regardless of occupation), has gone from approximately 25 million in the late 1940s to a little over 5 million in the 1980s (see Exhibit 15-7a). Farm employment, which is defined as persons working on

Farmers' Gross Income and Net Income, 1977–87

It is not unusual for farmers' gross income and net income to be up one year and down the next.

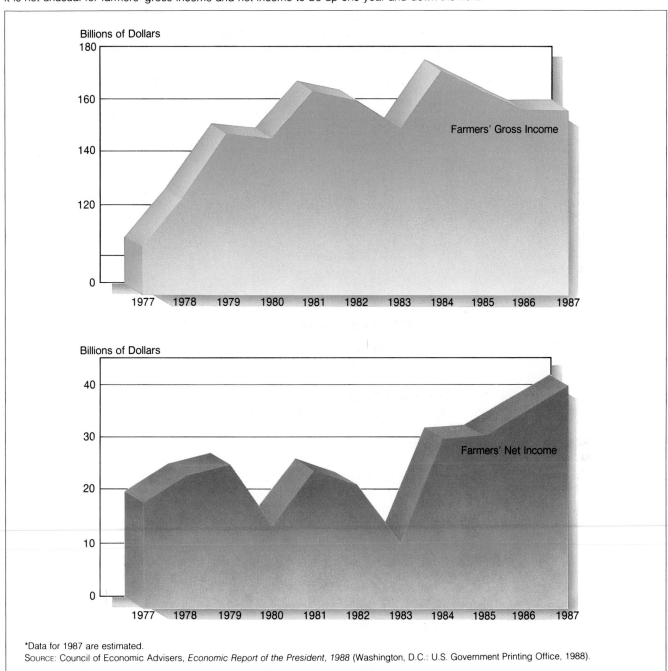

Billions of Dollars

Farmers' Gross Income

Billions of Dollars

Farmers' Net Income

*Data for 1987 are estimated.
SOURCE: Council of Economic Advisers, *Economic Report of the President, 1988* (Washington, D.C.: U.S. Government Printing Office, 1988).

farms, has also declined, from approximately 10 million in the late 1940s to approximately 3.2 million in the 1980s (see Exhibit 15-7b). Thus there is little doubt that in the latter half of this century not only have the number of farms been shrinking but the farm population and number of farm workers have been shrinking, too.

The Number of Farms in the United States, Selected Years
The number of farms in the United States has declined during this century.

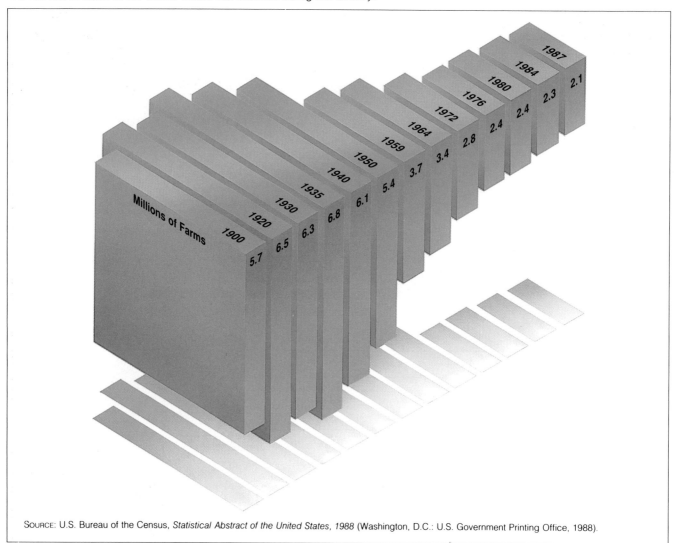

Source: U.S. Bureau of the Census, *Statistical Abstract of the United States, 1988* (Washington, D.C.: U.S. Government Printing Office, 1988).

Question:

Do small family farms account for a much smaller percentage of (total) gross farm income today than in past years?

Answer:

Yes, they do. The traditional family farm has annual sales between $40,000 and $100,000. Such farms make up roughly 11–12 percent of all farms and account for roughly 6.5 percent of gross farm income. Large farms, which have annual sales of over $500,000, make up roughly 1 percent of all farms and account for roughly 27 percent of gross farm income.

Farm Population and Farm Employment, Selected Years

Both the farm population and farm employment have declined over the latter half of this century.

*Farm population figures after 1979 are based on the Census Bureau's new definition of a farm family.
SOURCE: Council of Economic Advisers, *Economic Report of the President, 1988* (Washington, D.C.: U.S. Government Printing Office, 1988).

Farm Population in Millions

1949	1954	1959	1964	1969	1974	1979	1985	1986
25.8	19.0	16.5	12.9	10.3	9.2	6.2	5.3	5.2

Farm Employment in Millions

1948	1954	1959	1964	1969	1974	1979	1985	1986
10.3	8.6	7.3	6.1	4.5	4.3	3.7	2.9	2.7

AGRICULTURE: POLICIES

Farmers could solve many of their problems if they could control the supply of their products. As we explained in the previous section, many of their problems arise because (1) supply has grown faster than demand (the high productivity problem combined with the income inelasticity problem), which brings about falling relative prices for agricultural products, and (2) supply can and does severely change from season to season, which, together with the price inelasticity problem, brings about sharply fluctuating farm prices and total revenues, or farm incomes.

But farmers have not been able to control supply by themselves. And so they have turned to government for help. In this section we discuss a few of the major government-implemented policies designed to help farmers. We also discuss the effects of these agricultural policies on consumers and taxpayers.

Price Supports

Price Support

A government-mandated minimum price for agricultural products; an example of a price floor.

An agricultural **price support** is an example of a price floor. It is a government-guaranteed minimum price. Some of the agricultural products that either have or have had price supports include wheat, cotton, feed grains, dairy products, peanuts, and tobacco. Suppose the price support for wheat is set at $6 per bushel, which is above the equilibrium price (see Exhibit 15-8). At this price quantity supplied is greater than quantity demanded, and there is a surplus of wheat. In addition, the amount of wheat bought *by private citizens* is less (Q_2) at the price support (price floor) than at the equilibrium price (Q_1). (We specify *private citizens* here because some of the wheat crop is purchased by government.) We would expect wheat buyers to dislike the price support program since they end up paying higher than equilibrium price for the wheat they buy.

What happens to the surplus? Farmers want to get rid of the surplus and could do so by lowering price. But, of course, there is no need to lower price. The price is supported *by government*, which buys the surplus at the support price.[4] The government's surplus wheat purchase needs to be stored, resulting in sometimes huge storage costs. For example, in the 1950s and early 1960s storage costs for wheat escalated, reaching over $1 million per day at one period. For the taxpayers who ultimately had to pay the bill, this was not a happy state of affairs.

Thus the effects of agricultural price supports are (1) a surplus, (2) fewer exchanges (less wheat bought by private citizens), (3) higher prices paid by consumers of wheat, and (4) government purchase and storage of the surplus wheat (for which taxpayers pay).

Restricting Supply

Prices of agricultural products can be increased directly by price supports or indirectly by restricting supply. Suppose the government and farmers want to raise the price of wheat from $4 to $6 per bushel. As we have just seen, one way is to set a price support for wheat at $6. Another way is to restrict the supply of wheat by enough so that price will automatically rise to $6 per bushel. The objective is to shift the supply curve leftward from S_1 to S_2, as shown in Exhibit 15-9. Historically, govern-

---

[4]In practice the government does not just hand over dollars to the farmer for his or her surplus. The price support program works like this: Suppose a farmer harvests 10,000 bushels of wheat and the price support is $6 per bushel. If the harvest cannot be sold at $6 per bushel, the farmer can apply for a loan of $60,000 (10,000 bushels × $6 per bushel) from a government agency called the Commodity Credit Corporation (CCC). If the price for wheat rises above the price support the farmer can later sell the wheat and repay the loan. If the farmer cannot sell any of the wheat, he or she can "repay" the loan by turning the wheat over to the CCC. If the farmer sells part of the wheat, say, 4,000 bushels, he or she can turn over 6,000 bushels to the CCC along with $24,000 (4,000 bushels × $6 per bushel) and keep the remainder ($36,000) of the loan. In this roundabout way, the government pays the price support for the farmer's surplus wheat.

Effects of an Agricultural Price Support

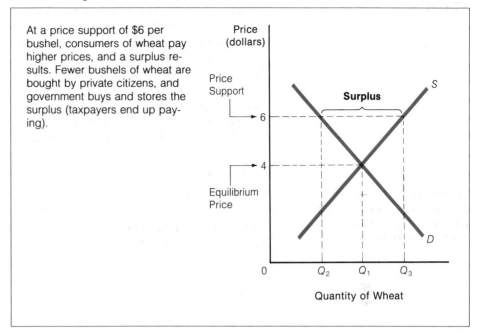

At a price support of $6 per bushel, consumers of wheat pay higher prices, and a surplus results. Fewer bushels of wheat are bought by private citizens, and government buys and stores the surplus (taxpayers end up paying).

■ Exhibit 15-9
The Objective of Supply-Restricting Agricultural Policies

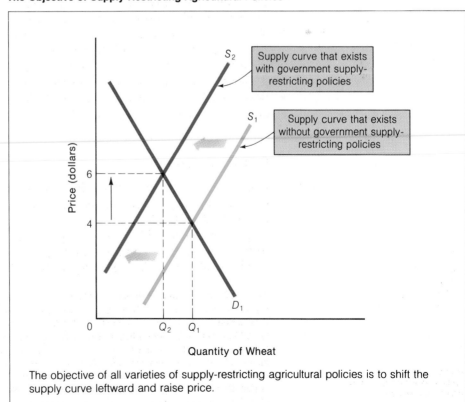

Supply curve that exists with government supply-restricting policies

Supply curve that exists without government supply-restricting policies

The objective of all varieties of supply-restricting agricultural policies is to shift the supply curve leftward and raise price.

ment has used three methods to accomplish this objective: (1) assigning acreage allotments, (2) assigning market quotas, and (3) paying farmers not to produce as much of their crops. These three ways are called the acreage allotment program, the marketing quota system, and the soil bank program, respectively.

Acreage Allotment Program. The acreage allotment program restricts output by limiting the number of farm acres that can be used to produce a particular crop. The allowable (total) acreage is distributed among farmers in a predetermined manner. In some cases, acreage allotment is based on a farmer's history of production.

To illustrate how the program works, suppose Farmer Thompson has a 10,000-acre farm on which he plants wheat. When the acreage allotment program is put into effect, he is limited to plant only 7,500 acres. The idea here is that if all wheat farmers reduce the number of acres they plant in wheat, the quantity of wheat brought to market will fall. As this happens, price rises, *ceteris paribus*.

One consequence of this program is that farmers begin to take their least-productive land out of production and to farm their remaining (allowable) acreage more intensively. Because of this effect, government is not always able to restrict the output of a crop to the degree it seeks.

Economists often remark that the acreage allotment program makes it more costly to produce crops. If farmers have an incentive to farm their alloted land more intensively, they tend to substitute more expensive resources such as fertilizer for less expensive resources such as land. (If farmers are combining resources such as fertilizer, land, and labor in the cheapest way possible before the program, any disturbance, such as restricting the use of land, causes a shift from a less costly to a more costly means of production.)

Marketing Quota System. Under a marketing quota system, government does not restrict land usage, but instead sets a limit on the quantity of a product that a farmer is allowed to bring to market. In 1981, a large crop of oranges was harvested in California. As part of the marketing quota system, "excess" oranges were destroyed by dumping them in cow pastures.

Soil Bank Program. In 1956 the Eisenhower administration initiated the soil bank program. Under this program farmers were paid to take part of their land out of cultivation. (The difference between the acreage allotment program and the soil bank program is that under the former, farmers do not receive a direct payment.) Under the soil bank program, as under the acreage allotment program, farmers tend to take their least-productive land out of production and to farm their remaining acreage more intensively. The most recent version of the soil bank program is the Payment in-Kind (PIK) program, which is discussed in this chapter's Economics In Our Times.

Target Prices

Target Price

A guaranteed price; if the market price is below the target price, the farmer receives a deficiency payment equal to the difference between the market price and the target price.

Another way in which government tries to aid farmers is by setting a guaranteed price called a **target price**. This is different from a price support in that consumers do not necessarily pay the target price. Also, with a target price there is no surplus for the government to purchase and store. We show how it works with the aid of Exhibit 15-10.

Suppose government sets a target price for wheat at $6 per bushel. At this price, farmers choose to produce Q_1 bushels of wheat. However, consumers will not buy Q_1 bushels of wheat at $6 per bushel. The maximum price consumers will pay per

Economics in Our Times

Grain Instead of Cash

In 1983 the Reagan administration established a supply-restricting program called *Payment-in-Kind*, or PIK. Under PIK, farmers agreed to set aside certain acres of farmland, not in exchange for cash, but for grain that the government had purchased and stored as a result of previous price support programs. The farmers could store the grain or sell it. The PIK program was supposed to (1) reduce supply, (2) stabilize prices and raise farm income, and (3) reduce or eliminate government stockpiles and reduce storage costs. Under PIK it was possible for a farmer to take an entire farm out of production. The Department of Agriculture announced that farmers had taken 231 million acres out of production as a result of the program. As things turned out, more farmers signed up for the program than had been expected (some say because the grain payments to farmers were too generous), and as a result the government depleted its entire stockpile of grain. In fact, the government did not have sufficient stockpiles to meet its commitments and had to buy grain on the market to do so. The PIK program was phased out after its first year.

Critics of PIK say that the problem lies with trying to fine-tune the farm economy. They point out that at the time the PIK program was in full force, a drought reduced the corn crop below normal levels; as a result, the combination of PIK and the bad weather reduced supply by more than government officials had wanted. Also, the supply of crops not affected by the drought did not fall by as much as expected. This was because farmers set aside their least-productive farmland and farmed their productive acreage more intensively. In short, supply fell by more than expected for some crops and by less than expected for other crops.

■ **Exhibit 15-10**
The Target Price System

With target prices, the government guarantees farmers a (target) price per unit of food produced. For example, if government sets the target price of wheat at $6 per bushel, farmers produce Q_1 bushels. When this quantity is placed on the market, consumers will end up paying $2 per bushel. The difference between the $6 target price and the $2 price consumers pay is the deficiency payment per bushel that government pays farmers.

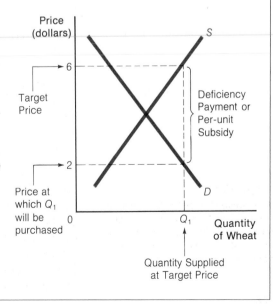

Theory in Practice

Oatmeal with a Little Sugar and Milk

We're told that hot oatmeal with a little sugar and milk makes a good, tasty breakfast. Here is a story about each of the three main ingredients in such a breakfast.

The Oatmeal

In the spring of 1988, the Quaker Oats Company ran some 60-second radio commercials in which it promised midwestern farmers "high bids for top-quality grain." One ad said, "We want to help you supply us." Another ad invited farm youths to enter an oats-growing contest. It said, "Quaker Oats is looking for you."

The Quaker Oats company was advertising for oats because U.S. oats production was off. Oats production had declined because, as one South Dakota farmer said, "Why should I raise oats when I can get more money for barley?" (*Wall Street Journal,* June 10, 1988).

Producing less oats when the demand for oats is down is understandable, but producing less oats when the demand for oats is up would seem to be irrational. In the mid-1980s oats production was down at the same time that the demand for oatmeal and oats-based cereal was rising. In 1985 approximately 500 million bushels of oats were produced; by 1987, production had declined to 374 million bushels. Many economists point to the fact that subsidies for barley were 96 cents higher than for oats as the reason for the decline. Farmers, they argue, were acting rationally given the incentive structure that government agricultural policy had established. Because of the subsidy differences between barley and oats, General Mills in 1988 was adding to its surplus of barley at the same time that it was importing oats from Argentina.

The Sugar

Government price supports give rise to incentives to import those goods [that are supported], potentially displacing the farmers the government seeks to help. Thus, governments have two choices: introduce barriers to trade, or purchase domestic and imported supplies until the world market price is bid up to the internal level. Because the latter policy would require extraordinary government outlays, most governments impose trade restrictions that involve no budgetary expenditures but impose losses on consumers. With few exceptions, trade restrictions instituted through border measures are in place solely to validate domestic farm programs. Hence, a country's agricultural trade policy is derived largely from its domestic support programs.

—Economic Report of the President, 1987, p. 165.

At the urging of U.S. sugar producers, Congress restricts the supply of sugar to U.S. consumers through the use of sugar quotas. As a result, in recent years the price of sugar in the United States has been double the world price for sugar.

This may not be the end of the story, however. Because foreigners cannot sell as much sugar in the United States as they would like, their incomes are affected adversely. One study, cited in the *Economic Report of the President,* estimated that industrialized countries' sugar policies reduced the real income of people living in the developing countries by $2.1 billion. Some economists have argued that in some Caribbean and Central American countries, one-time sugar producers have turned to planting and selling marijuana and other illegal drugs to make up the lost income.

The Milk

The Congress passed the 1985 Food Security Act in an attempt to remove government gradually from agriculture. However, economists estimate that the annual cost to consumers of corn, sugar, milk, cotton, wheat, rice, peanuts, and tobacco as a result of the 1985 act are $6–10 billion. The annual cost to the taxpayers is $20 billion, and the annual producer gain is $20–23 billion. This makes the annual net loss (all losses minus all gains) somewhere between $3 and $10 billion. Consumer losses for milk alone have been estimated at between $1.6 and $3.1 billion per year, and taxpayer losses at $1 billion per year. In 1985, then Secretary of Agriculture Richard Lyng said that the federal government planned to pay some dairy farmers to slaughter their cattle and go out of business. The objective behind the plan was to reduce milk production. As a result, milk consumers ended up paying higher prices for milk.

Source: Wall Street Journal, June 10, 1988; Council of Economic Advisers, *Economic Report of the President, 1987* and *1988* (Washington, D.C.: U.S. Government Printing Office, 1987 and 1988).

bushel for Q_1 is \$2. Under the target price system, this is exactly what consumers pay. In fact, \$2 is the market (clearing) price for this quantity of output. Since the government has guaranteed a target price of \$6 per bushel to farmers, it makes a *deficiency payment* of \$4 per bushel to farmers (deficiency payment per bushel = target price per bushel − market price per bushel). The total deficiency payment that government makes to farmers equals \$4 times Q_1 [(\$6 − \$2) × Q_1]. With the target price system, consumers end up getting a lot of cheap wheat for which the government (taxpayers) pay. A problem with the target price program is that deficiency payments go to rich and poor farmers alike. For example, in fiscal 1986, farmers received a total of \$26 billion in deficiency payments. It has been estimated that 15 percent of these payments went to farmers who had a net worth in excess of \$1 million.

■ CHAPTER SUMMARY

Agriculture and High Productivity

■ Productivity in the agricultural sector has increased faster than productivity in the economy as a whole. This has not always been a blessing for farmers, because when productivity increases, the supply curve for their products shifts rightward and price falls. Decreases in price often lead to decreased revenues since the demand for many farm products is inelastic.

Agriculture and Income Inelasticity

■ The demand for many farm products is income inelastic, which means that quantity demanded changes by a smaller percentage than income changes. When combined with the high productivity problem, this means that the supply of farm products is likely to increase by more than the demand for them. Once again, this puts downward pressure on price.

Agriculture and Price Inelasticity

■ In addition to high productivity and income inelasticity, which tend to put downward pressure on farm prices, the demand for many agricultural goods is inelastic, which means falling price leads to falling total revenue (or gross farm income). Also, because demand is inelastic, shifts in supply—which are commonplace in agriculture owing to changes in weather conditions—bring about (sometimes) large changes in price and total revenue. Such unexpected (sometimes) large changes in price and total revenue increase the uncertainties of farming.

Parity Price Ratio

■ The parity price ratio is a ratio of an index of prices that farmers receive to an index of prices that farmers pay. The ratio uses the years 1910–14, which was a period of unusual peacetime prosperity for farmers, as a base period. For much of this century the parity price ratio has been below 100, which means that prices of agricultural products have fallen relative to other prices.

Agricultural Policies

■ Three major agricultural policies are price supports, which attempt to set the prices of agricultural products directly; supply-restricting policies, which attempt to decrease supply and bring about a higher price for agricultural products indirectly; and target prices, which neither try to set prices directly nor decrease supply, but instead pay farmers a deficiency payment if the market price for their goods does not equal the target price.

■ A price support is a government-guaranteed minimum price; it is an example of a price floor. If the price support is set above the equilibrium price (which is customary), then a surplus results. Historically, government has purchased the surplus and stored it.

■ The acreage allotment program, the market quota system, the soil bank program, and the Payment-in-Kind (PIK) program are all examples of supply-restricting agricultural policies. In the acreage allotment program, farmers are only permitted to produce crops on a percentage of their total acreage. In the market quota system, government sets the amount of a product that a farmer is allowed to bring to market. In the soil bank program, farmers are paid to take part of their land out of production. In the PIK program, farmers are paid in crops (instead of cash) to take a part of their land out of production.

■ In the target price program, government sets a target price for an agricultural product and then pays farmers the difference between the target price and the market price.

■ QUESTIONS TO ANSWER AND DISCUSS

1. What is the connection between inelastic demand and price instability?

2. Why don't all supply-restricting agricultural policies work as intended?

3. Some people argue that unless small family farms are assisted through price supports, target prices, or supply-restricting policies, they will soon disappear, and large (corporate) farms will control food production in this country. Some go even further and say that without government assistance to small farmers, agriculture will cease to be a perfectly competitive market and will become an oligopolistic market. Today 5 percent of all farms have annual sales over $200,000 and are considered large farms. If the agriculture industry comes to be dominated by these large farms, is it likely that agriculture will become an oligopolistic market?

4. How might government reduce the amount of farm payments in the federal budget, and still assist farmers?

5. According to the *1988 Economic Report of the President* (page 361), the price index that represents prices received by farmers was 127 in 1987, and the price index that represents prices paid by farmers was 162. Did farmers have full parity in 1987?

6. There are approximately 2 million farms in the United States and in 1986 farmers received a total of $26 billion in deficiency payments. This is $13,000 per farm. Critics of farm programs often argue that other businesses in the United States do not receive (on average) a $13,000 subsidy, so why should farmers? What do you think? Are there special problems associated with farming that would warrant a $13,000 per-farm subsidy? Discuss in detail.

7. Critics of present-day agricultural policies argue that government does for farmers what they can't do for themselves: restrict supply and push prices up. Do you agree or disagree? Why?

8. Some people contend that the majority of Americans realize that they subsidize farmers through various government programs, but they don't mind doing this because they know they are preserving a way of life. For example, a person living in New York City doesn't mind paying higher taxes so that farmers can receive deficiency payments because the New Yorker receives utility from knowing that he or she is preserving the family farm and a wholesome way of life. This argument assumes that America wouldn't be the same without family farms and that it is worth paying taxes to preserve them. What do you think of this argument? How would you go about determining how much truth there is in it?

9. Do you think the number of farmers in the United States will increase, decrease, or stay roughly the same in the next 20-year period? Why?

Chapter 16

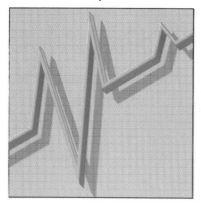

The Distribution of Income and Poverty

■ INTRODUCTION

Every year, Forbes magazine lists the 400 richest Americans. As soon as the magazine appears, newspapers in cities across the country publish front-page stories, giving the names of many of the people who made the list. There is no doubt about it, we are interested in and excited by rich people. Such television shows as "Dallas," "Dynasty," and "Lifestyles of the Rich and Famous" confirm this.

Americans are also interested in (although not excited by) the poor. Almost every year, the major television networks broadcast shows about the poor and the homeless in America. Almost always, the shows do well in the ratings.

But unlike the rich, few people care about the names of the poor. There are only pictures: the homeless sleeping on the streets, the young woman with the old face surrounded by young children, and the old man sitting alone in a rocking chair in a tiny apartment.

In this chapter, we go behind the headlines and the news stories to discuss these two income groups: the rich and the poor.

■ WHAT THIS CHAPTER IS ABOUT

Why are some persons rich and others poor? What does it mean to be poor? How is income inequality measured?

In this chapter, we seek answers to these and many other questions. We discuss the facts surrounding the distribution of income, the ways economists measure the degree of income inequality, the reasons income inequality exists, and the problem of, and proposed solutions to, poverty.

Key Questions to Keep in Mind as You Read

1. Who are the rich and how rich are they?

2. What are transfer payments? What are in-kind transfer payments? How do transfer payments affect the distribution of income?

3. What are the Lorenz curve and the Gini coefficient?
4. Why does income inequality exist?
5. What is the poverty line?
6. What causes poverty?
7. What are some ways poverty might be reduced or eliminated?

SOME FACTS ABOUT INCOME DISTRIBUTION

People often discuss public policy issues without a firm grasp of the reality behind the issues. We also sometimes speak of a *fact,* when we should speak of *facts.* A (single) fact is usually not as informative as facts are, in much the same way that a single snapshot (in time) does not tell as much of a story as a moving picture (which is a succession of snapshots through time). This section presents a few *facts* about the distribution of income.

Who Are the Rich and How Rich Are They?

By many interpretations the *lowest fifth* (lowest 20 percent) of family income groups is considered poor, the top fifth is considered rich, and the three-fifths in between are considered middle income. Given this breakdown, what income do you think a family of four had to receive in 1986 to be considered rich—that is, to be in the top fifth of all income earners? The answer is $50,371. Many people regard that figure as low. They usually think the ranks of the rich are filled exclusively with millionaires and multimillionaires. Of course, millionaires and multimillionaires are rich, but then so is the family that earned $50,371 in 1986.

If we define as rich only those families that make up the *top 5 percent* of income earners, we find that a family in 1986 was rich if it had an income of $82,273 or more. In 1986 the lowest 20 percent (the poor) earned 4.6 percent of the total money income, and the highest 20 percent (the rich) earned 43.7 percent, or almost ten times as much as the poor. The highest 5 percent received 17 percent of the total money income, meaning that in 1986 they received approximately four times as much as the bottom 20 percent received (see Exhibit 16-1).

The Income Distribution over a Period of Time

Has income distribution in the United States become less equal, more equal, or stayed about the same over time?[1] Exhibit 16-2 shows the income shares of family income groups in 1929 and 1986. In 1929 the highest (top) fifth income group accounted for 54.4 percent of all income; in 1986, the percentage had fallen to 43.7. In 1929, the top 5 percent received 30 percent of all income; in 1986, the percentage had fallen to 17 percent. (not shown in exhibit). At the other end of the income spectrum, in 1929 the lowest fifth received 3.9 percent of all income; in 1986, the percentage had risen to 4.6. The middle groups—the three -fifths of income recipients between the lowest fifth and the highest fifth—accounted for 41.7 percent of all income in 1929 and 51.6 percent in 1986. Thus the facts show that the income distribution in this country became more equal between 1929 and 1986.

[1]Grammatically speaking, "less nearly equal" and "more nearly equal" are preferable to "less equal" and "more equal." However, we will adopt the more familiar usage. Note also that whenever we say "more equal" or "less equal," we could just as easily have said "less unequal" and "more unequal," respectively. To avoid confusion, though, we will speak of more or less equality for the most part (and not more or less inequality).

Distribution of Family Income and Income Shares, 1986

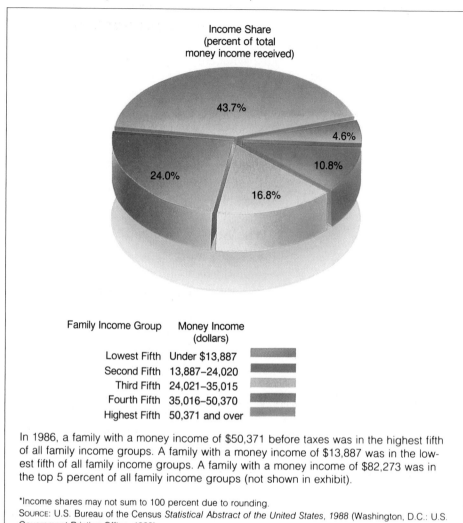

Income Share
(percent of total
money income received)

43.7%

4.6%

10.8%

24.0%

16.8%

Family Income Group	Money Income (dollars)	
Lowest Fifth	Under $13,887	
Second Fifth	13,887–24,020	
Third Fifth	24,021–35,015	
Fourth Fifth	35,016–50,370	
Highest Fifth	50,371 and over	

In 1986, a family with a money income of $50,371 before taxes was in the highest fifth of all family income groups. A family with a money income of $13,887 was in the lowest fifth of all family income groups. A family with a money income of $82,273 was in the top 5 percent of all family income groups (not shown in exhibit).

*Income shares may not sum to 100 percent due to rounding.
SOURCE: U.S. Bureau of the Census *Statistical Abstract of the United States, 1988* (Washington, D.C.: U.S. Government Printing Office, 1988).

But if a shorter time period is considered, we must conclude the opposite. For example, between 1979 and 1986, the income share received by the lowest fifth fell, while the income share received by the highest fifth increased (see Exhibit 16-3). We conclude that during this period the income distribution became less equal.

The Income Distribution Adjusted for Taxes and In-Kind Transfer Payments

Ex Ante Distribution (of Income)

The before-tax-and-transfer-payment distribution of income.

Ex Post Distribution (of Income)

The after-tax-and-transfer-payment distribution of income.

Government can change the distribution of income. One of the ways it does this is through the use of taxes and transfer payments. Economists speak of **ex ante** and **ex post distributions** of income. The ex ante distribution of income is the before-tax-and-transfer-payment distribution of income. The ex post distribution of income is the after-tax-and-transfer-payment distribution of income. Transfer payments include

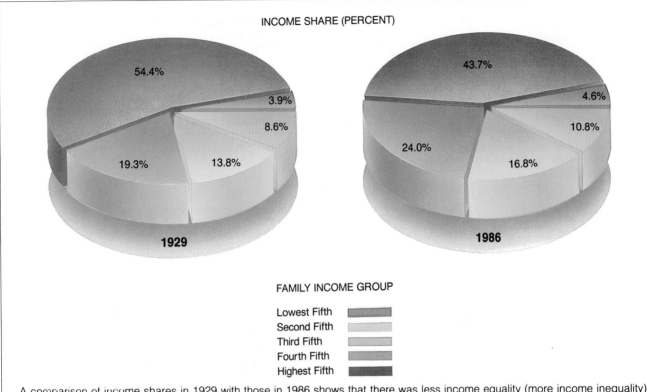

INCOME SHARE (PERCENT)

1929: 54.4% · 3.9% · 8.6% · 19.3% · 13.8%

1986: 43.7% · 4.6% · 10.8% · 24.0% · 16.8%

FAMILY INCOME GROUP

Lowest Fifth
Second Fifth
Third Fifth
Fourth Fifth
Highest Fifth

A comparison of income shares in 1929 with those in 1986 shows that there was less income equality (more income inequality) in 1929 than in 1986. Note that income shares have not been adjusted for direct taxes.

SOURCES: U.S. Bureau of the Census, *Historical Statistics of the United States*, (Washington, D.C.: U.S. Government Printing Office, 1960). U.S. Bureau of the Census, *Statistical Abstract of the United States, 1988* (Washington, D.C.: U.S. Government Printing Office, 1988).

Transfer Payments

Payments to persons that are not made in return for goods and services currently supplied.

In-Kind Transfer Payments

Transfer payments, such as food stamps, medical assistance, and subsidized housing, that are made in a specific good or service.

welfare payments (such as, Aid to Families with Dependent Children [AFDC]), food stamps, housing, education, and health care. **Transfer payments** are payments to persons that are not made in return for goods and services currently supplied.

The income distributions in Exhibits 16-2 and 16-3 do not take into account taxes, nor do they take into account **in-kind transfer payments,** that is, transfer payments, such as food stamps, medical assistance, and subsidized housing, that are paid in a specific good or service rather than cash. However, the exhibits do take into account cash (monetary) transfer payments, such as direct monetary welfare assistance.

Economists Edgar Browning and William Johnson undertook to identify the ex post distribution of income in 1976 by adjusting for taxes (specifically, income and payroll taxes) and all transfers, both cash and in-kind transfer payments. Exhibit 16-4, which is based on their findings, shows that the adjusted income shares present a more equal income distribution than the unadjusted income shares do. For example, the unadjusted income share of the lowest fifth income group in 1976 was 2.6 percent, but its adjusted income share was 6.2 percent. On the other end, the unadjusted income share for the highest fifth income group in 1976 was 50.1 percent, but its adjusted income share was 42.0 percent.

Income Distribution, 1979–86

Over the period 1979–86 income distribution became less equal. Note that income shares have not been adjusted for direct taxes.

FAMILY INCOME GROUP	INCOME SHARE (PERCENT)*							
	1979	1980	1981	1982	1983	1984	1985	1986
Lowest fifth	5.2%	5.1%	5.0%	4.7%	4.7%	4.7%	4.6%	4.6%
Second fifth	11.6	11.6	11.3	11.2	11.1	11.0	10.9	10.8
Third fifth	17.5	17.4	17.4	17.1	17.1	17.0	16.9	16.8
Fourth fifth	24.1	24.3	24.4	24.3	24.3	24.4	24.2	24.0
Highest fifth	41.7	41.6	41.9	42.7	42.8	42.9	43.5	43.7

SOURCE: U.S. Bureau of the Census, *Statistical Abstract of the United States*, 1988 (Washington, D.C.: U.S. Government Printing Office, 1988).
*Income shares may not sum to 100 percent due to rounding.

The Effect of Age on the Income Distribution

We need to distinguish between people who are poor for long periods of time (sometimes their entire lives) and people who are poor temporarily. For example, consider Sherri Holmer who attends college and works part-time as a waitress at a nearby restaurant. Currently, her income is so low that she falls into the lowest fifth of income earners. But it isn't likely that this will always be the case. After college her income will probably rise. If she is like most people, her income will rise during her twenties, thirties, and forties. In her late forties or early fifties, her income will take a slight downturn and then level off.

It is possible, in fact highly likely, that a person in her *late* twenties, thirties, or forties will have a higher income than another person in her *early* twenties or sixties, even though their total lifetime incomes will be identical. That is, if we view each person *over time*, income equality is greater than if we view each person at a particular point in time (say, when one is 58 years old and the other is 68).

To illustrate, consider the case of John and Stephanie in different years. Starting in 1988 in Exhibit 16-5, John is 18 years old and earning $10,000 per year and Stephanie is 28 years old and earning $30,000. Thus the income distribution between John and Stephanie is unequal in 1988.

■ Exhibit 16-4
Income Distribution Adjusted for Taxes and Transfers

Adjusted income shares (adjusted for taxes and transfers, both cash and in-kind) portray greater income equality than unadjusted income shares.

FAMILY INCOME GROUP	INCOME SHARE (UNADJUSTED)	INCOME SHARE (ADJUSTED FOR IN-KIND AND CASH TRANSFERS AND INCOME AND PAYROLL TAXES)*
Lowest fifth	2.6%	6.2%
Second fifth	8.4	12.0
Third fifth	15.5	16.9
Fourth fifth	23.4	23.0
Highest fifth	50.1	42.0

SOURCES: Edgar K. Browning and William R. Johnson, *The Distribution of the Tax Burden* (Washington, D.C., American Enterprise Institute, 1979); Edgar K. Browning and Jacqueline M. Browing, *Public Finance and the Price System*, 3d ed. (New York: Macmillan, 1987), 243.
*Income shares do not sum to 100 percent due to rounding.

■ **Exhibit 16-5**
Income Distribution at One Point in Time and over Time

In each year the income distribution between John and Stephanie is unequal with either Stephanie earning more than John (1988, 1998, 2008, and 2018) or John earning more than Stephanie (2028). However, the total income earned by each person in the five years specified is $236,000, giving us a perfectly equal income distribution over time.

YEAR	JOHN'S AGE	JOHN'S INCOME	STEPHANIE'S AGE	STEPHANIE'S INCOME
1988	18 years	$ 10,000	28 years	$ 30,000
1998	28	35,000	38	45,000
2008	38	52,000	48	60,000
2018	48	64,000	58	75,000
2028	58	75,000	68	26,000
Total		$236,000		$236,000

Ten years later, the income distribution is still unequal with Stephanie earning $45,000 and John earning $35,000. In fact, income distribution is unequal in every year shown in the exhibit. However, if we look at the total income earned by each person in the five years specified, we see that each person earned $236,000, giving us a perfectly equal income distribution over time.

A Simple Equation

Before we discuss the possible sources or causes of income inequality, we should mention the factors that determine a person's income. Here we have combined four of them—labor income, asset income, transfer payments, and taxes—in a simple equation:

Individual income = labor income + asset income + transfer payments − taxes

Labor income is equal to the wage rate an individual receives times the number of hours he or she works. Asset income consists of such things as the return to saving, the return to capital investment, and the return to land. Transfer payments and taxes we have already discussed. This equation gives us a quick way of focusing on the direct and indirect factors that affect an individual's income and the degree of income inequality. Before we examine this topic in more detail, we take a short detour to explain the conventional ways that income inequality is measured.

Question:

The equation includes transfer payments, which may come in the form of cash or in-kind payments. According to the equation, if a person receives an in-kind transfer—such as free food—his income increases. But this doesn't make sense. How can a free good increase a person's income? After all, food isn't money.

Answer:

We are interested in how much a person can consume. An individual who earns $10,000 per year and doesn't have to pay apartment rent is better off (in having more goods and services) than a person who earns $10,000 per year and does have to pay apartment rent. The first person is better off than his absolute level of money income would lead us to believe. By including in-kind transfers, among other things, in individual income, we are trying to take into account this quality of being "better off." Although most government income figures do not take into account in-kind transfers, most economists would argue that simple money income is not as accurate a measure of one's command over goods and services as is a measurement of income that adjusts for in-kind transfers.

MEASURING INCOME INEQUALITY

There are two commonly used measurements of income inequality. One is the Lorenz curve; the other is the Gini coefficient.

The Lorenz Curve

Lorenz Curve

A graph of the income distribution. It expresses the relationship between cumulative percent of families and cumulative percent of income.

The **Lorenz curve** represents the distribution of income; it expresses the relationship between *cumulative percent of families* and *cumulative percent of income*. Exhibit 16-6 shows a hypothetical Lorenz curve.

The data in (a) are used to plot the Lorenz curve in (b). According to (a), the lowest fifth income group has an income share of 10 percent, the second fifth has an income share of 15 percent, and so on. The Lorenz curve in (b) is derived by plotting five points. Point *A* represents the *cumulative* income share of the lowest fifth income group (10 percent of income goes to the lowest fifth income group). Point *B* represents the *cumulative* income share of the lowest fifth income group *plus* the second fifth (25 percent of income goes to two-fifths, or 40 percent, of the income recipients). Point *C* represents the *cumulative* income share of the lowest fifth income group *plus* the second fifth *plus* the third fifth (45 percent of income goes to three-fifths,

■ **Exhibit 16-6**
A Hypothetical Lorenz Curve

Family Income Group	Income Share (percent)	Cumulative Income Share (percent)
Lowest fifth	10%	10%
Second fifth	15	25
Third fifth	20	45
Fourth fifth	25	70
Highest fifth	30	100

(a)

(b)

The Lorenz curve in (b) was derived using the data in (a). The Lorenz curve shows the cumulative percent of income earned by the cumulative percent of families. If all family income groups received the same percentage of total income, the Lorenz curve would be the line of perfect income equality. The bowed Lorenz curve shows an unequal distribution of income. The more bowed the Lorenz curve is, the more unequal the distribution of income.

or 60 percent, of the income recipients). The same procedure is used for points *D* and *E*. Connecting these points gives us the Lorenz curve that represents the data in (a); thus the Lorenz curve is another way of depicting the income distribution in (a). (It is a picture of the data.) Exhibit 16-7 illustrates the Lorenz curve for the United States based on the (money) income shares in Exhibit 16-1.

What would the Lorenz curve look like if there were *perfect income equality* among the different income groups? In this case every income group would receive exactly the same percentage of total income, and the Lorenz curve would be the line of perfect income equality illustrated in Exhibit 16-6b. This is a 45° line, along which at any point cumulative percent of income (on the vertical axis) equals cumulative percent of families (on the horizontal axis). We can see this by examining the characteristics of any point on the line of perfect income equality. For example, at point *F*, 60 percent of the families receive 60 percent of the total income.

The Gini Coefficient

Gini Coefficient

A measurement of the degree of inequality in the income distribution.

The **Gini coefficient,** which is a measurement of the degree of inequality in the income distribution, is used in conjunction with the Lorenz curve. It is equal to the area between the line of perfect income equality (or 45° line) and the actual Lorenz curve divided by the entire triangular area under the line of perfect income equality.

$$\text{Gini coefficient} = \frac{\text{area between line of perfect income equality and actual Lorenz curve}}{\text{entire triangular area under the line of perfect income equality}}$$

Exhibit 16-8 illustrates both the line of perfect income equality and an actual Lorenz curve. The Gini coefficient is computed by dividing the shaded area (the area be-

■ **Exhibit 16-7**
Lorenz Curve For The United States, 1986

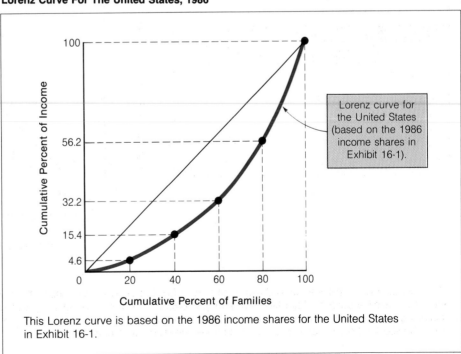

This Lorenz curve is based on the 1986 income shares for the United States in Exhibit 16-1.

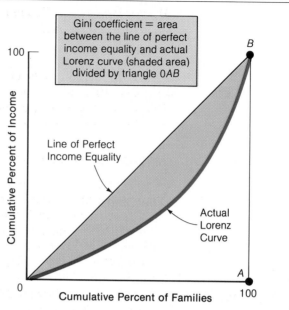

Gini coefficient = area between the line of perfect income equality and actual Lorenz curve (shaded area) divided by triangle 0*AB*

Cumulative Percent of Income

100

Line of Perfect Income Equality

Actual Lorenz Curve

0

Cumulative Percent of Families

100

The Gini coefficient is a measurement of the degree of income inequality. It is equal to the area between the line of perfect income equality and the actual Lorenz curve divided by the entire triangular area under the line of perfect income equality. In the diagram this is equal to the shaded portion divided by the triangular area 0*AB*. A Gini coefficient of 0 means perfect income equality; a Gini coefficient of 1 means complete income inequality. The larger the Gini coefficient, the greater the income inequality; the smaller the Gini coefficient, the less the income inequality.

tween the line of perfect income equality and the actual Lorenz curve) by the area 0*AB* (the entire triangular area under the line of perfect income equality).

The Gini coefficient is a number between 0 and 1. On the one extreme, the Gini coefficient equals 0 if the numerator in the equation is 0. A numerator of 0 means there is no area between the line of perfect income equality and the actual Lorenz curve, implying that they are one and the same. It follows that a Gini coefficient of 0 means perfect income equality.

At the other extreme, the Gini coefficient equals 1 if the numerator in the equation is equal to the denominator. If this is the case, the actual Lorenz curve is as far away from the line of perfect income equality as is possible. It follows that a Gini coefficient of 1 means complete income inequality. (What would the actual Lorenz curve look like if there were complete income inequality? If would represent a situation where one person had all of total income and no one else had any income. In Exhibit 16-8, a Lorenz curve representing complete income inequality would lie along the horizontal axis from 0 to *A* and then move from *A* to *B*.)

If a Gini coefficient of 0 represents perfect income equality and a Gini coefficient of 1 represents complete income inequality, then it follows that the larger the Gini coefficient, the greater the degree of income inequality; the smaller the Gini coefficient, the less the degree of income inequality.

Question:

What is the Gini coefficient of the United States? How does it compare with other countries' coefficients?

Answer:

The Gini coefficient of the United States has been computed at .369. Sweden (.271), Norway (.301), and Canada (.348) have lower Gini coefficients. Spain (.397) and France (.417) have higher Gini coefficients.[2]

A Limitation of the Gini Coefficient

Although we can learn the degree of inequality in the income distribution from the Gini coefficient, we should be careful not to misread what it is saying. For example, suppose the Gini coefficient is .33 in country 1 and .25 in country 2. We know that the income distribution is more equal in country 2 than in country 1. But would we know in which country the lowest income group receives the larger percentage of income? The natural inclination is to answer in the country with the more equal income distribution—country 2. However, this may not be true.

To see this, consider Exhibit 16-9, where two Lorenz curves are drawn. Overall Lorenz curve 2 is closer to the line of perfect income equality than Lorenz curve 1; thus the Gini coefficient for Lorenz curve 2 is smaller than the Gini coefficient for Lorenz curve 1. But notice that the lowest 20 percent income group has a lower percentage of total income with Lorenz curve 2 than with curve 1.

Our point is that the Gini coefficient lacks the ability to tell us what is happening in different income groups. We should not jump to the conclusion that because in country 2 the Gini coefficient is lower than in country 1, the lowest income group has a greater percentage of total income in country 2 than in country 1.

[2]These figures are from Lars Osberg, *Economic Inequality in Canada* (Toronto: Butterworths, 1981).

■ **Exhibit 16-9**
Limitation of the Gini Coefficient

By itself the Gini coefficient cannot tell us anything about the income share of a particular income group. Although there is a tendency to believe that the bottom income group receives a larger percentage of total income the lower the Gini coefficient, this need not be the case. In the diagram, the Gini coefficient for Lorenz curve 2 is lower than the Gini coefficient for Lorenz curve 1. But, as we can see, the bottom 20 percent income group obtains a smaller percentage of total income in the lower Gini coefficient case.

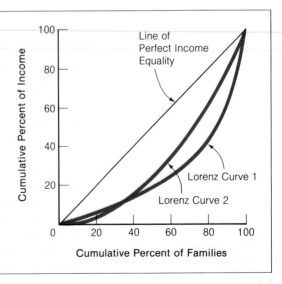

WHY INCOME INEQUALITY EXISTS

Why does income inequality exist? How might income inequality be lessened? Both questions can be answered by focusing on the simple equation we briefly discussed in an earlier section: *Individual income = labor income + asset income + transfer payments − taxes.* Obviously and most generally, income inequality exists because people do not receive the same labor income, asset income, and transfer payments or pay the same taxes. If the objective is to reduce income inequality, one means of doing so is to increase transfer payments going to, and decrease taxes paid by, those persons with low labor and asset incomes; and decrease transfer payments going to, and increase taxes paid by, those with high labor and asset incomes. Leaving the discussion of how transfer payments and taxes can make the distribution of income more equal until later (in our section on poverty), we concentrate now on why income inequality exists.

Factors Contributing to Income Inequality

In this section we discuss six factors that contribute to income inequality. The list includes innate abilities and attributes, work and leisure, education and other training, risk taking, luck, and wage discrimination.

Innate Abilities and Attributes. Individuals are not all born with the same innate abilities and attributes. Not everyone is born with the same degree of intelligence, common sense, good looks, and creativity. Some individuals have more marketable innate abilities and attributes than others. For example, the man or woman born with exceptionally good looks is more likely to earn a high salary as an actor or model than the man or woman with average looks. The person who is born with the ability to write and a sharp sense of creativity will probably become a well-paid novelist.

Work and Leisure. There is a trade-off between work and leisure: more work means less leisure, less work means more leisure. Some individuals will choose to work more hours (or take on a second job) and thus have less leisure. This choice will be reflected in their labor income. They will earn a larger income than those persons who choose not to work more, *ceteris paribus.*

Education and Other Training. Economists usually refer to schooling and other types of training as an "investment in human capital." Remember from the discussion of physical capital goods in Chapter 14 that in order to buy a capital good, or invest in one, a person had to forgo present consumption. A person did so in the hope that the capital good would increase his or her future consumption.

Schooling can be looked on as capital. First, one must forgo present consumption to obtain it. Second, by providing individuals with certain skills and knowledge, schooling can increase their future consumption over what it would be without the schooling. Schooling, then, is **human capital.** In general, human capital refers to education, the development of skills, and anything else that is particular to the individual and increases his or her productivity.

Contrast a person who has obtained an education with a person who has not. The educated person is likely to have certain skills, abilities, and knowledge that the uneducated person lacks. Consequently he or she is likely to be worth more to an employer. Most college students know this. It is part of the reason they are college students.

Human Capital

Education, development of skills, and anything else that is particular to the individual and increases his or her productivity.

Risk Taking. Individuals do not all have the same attitude toward risk. Some individuals are more willing to take on risk than others. Some of the individuals who are willing to take on risk will do well and rise to the top of the income distribution, and some will fall to the bottom. Those individuals who exhibit a preference for playing it safe aren't as likely to reach the top of the income distribution or hit the bottom.

Luck. When individuals can't explain why something has happened to them, they often say it was the result of good or bad luck. At times the good or back luck explanation makes sense; at other times, it is more a rationalization than an explanation.

There are times when good and bad luck influence incomes. For example, the college student who studies biology only to find out in her senior year that the bottom has fallen out of the biology market has experienced bad luck. The farmer who hits oil while digging a well has experienced good luck. An automobile worker who is unemployed owing to a recession he had no part in causing is experiencing bad luck. A person who trains for a profession in which there is an unexpected increase in demand experiences good luck.

Although luck can and does influence incomes, it is not likely to have (on average) a large or long-run effect on incomes. The person who experiences good luck today, and whose income reflects this fact, isn't likely to experience luck-boosting income increases time after time. In the long run, such factors as innate ability and attributes, education, and personal decisions (how much work, how much leisure?) are more likely to have a larger, more sustained effect on income than good and bad luck.

Wage Discrimination

The situation that exists when individuals of equal ability and productivity (as measured by their contribution to output) are paid different wage rates.

Wage Discrimination. **Wage discrimination** exists when individuals of equal ability and productivity, as measured by their marginal revenue products, are paid different wage rates. It is a fact that the median income of blacks in the postwar period as a whole has been approximately 60 percent that of whites, and that since the late 1950s, women working full-time have earned approximately 60 percent of the male median income. Are these differences between white and black incomes, and between male and female incomes, due wholly to discrimination? Most empirical studies show that approximately half the differences are due to differences in educational, productivity, and job training differences (although one may ask if discrimination has anything to do with the educational, productivity, and job training differences). The remainder is due to other factors, one of which is hypothesized to be discrimination.

Most persons agree that discrimination exists, although they differ on the degree to which they think it affects incomes. Additionally, we should note that discrimination is not always directed at employees by employers. For example, consumers may practice discrimination—some white consumers, for example, may wish to deal only with white physicians and lawyers; some nonwhites may wish to deal only with nonwhite physicians and lawyers. Wage discrimination and a proposed means of dealing with it are discussed further in the Theory in Practice about comparable worth.

Income Differences: Some are Voluntary, Some are Not

Even in a world with absolutely no discrimination, differences in income would still exist. Other factors account for this. Some individuals would have more marketable skills than others, some individuals would decide to work harder and longer hours

Theory in Practice

Comparable Worth: What Is a Truck Driver Really Worth?

Accepting the view that discrimination does negatively affect the incomes of certain groups, in 1963 the Congress passed the Equal Pay Act, which mandated equal pay for equal work. The next year Title VII of the Civil Rights Act of 1964 prohibited employers from discriminating against women. These rules were relatively straightforward, but during the 1970s, a new concept, *comparable worth,* began to be discussed. The idea behind comparable worth is that equal pay should be paid for comparable work. The difficulty comes when we try to define "comparable." Equal work is one thing, comparable work quite another. For example, most people believe that a woman who drives a truck loaded with oranges from Florida to Illinois does the same work as a man who drives a truck loaded with oranges from Florida to Illinois. But what is comparable work? Is working as a secretary in a major corporation comparable to working as an electrician? Is working as a registered nurse in a hospital comparable to working as a truck driver?

In one comparable worth case, a state employees' union brought a suit against the State of Washington, charging that the state had discriminated because it had paid lower wages to women in female-dominated jobs than it had paid men in "comparable" male-denominated jobs. Although the union ultimately lost the case, the state agreed to institute a comparable worth policy over a ten-year period.

To implement the program, the state had to determine which state jobs were comparable. Independent consultants were hired to conduct a study, and it was agreed that jobs would be evaluated on a point system according to four criteria: knowledge and skills, mental demands, accountability, and working conditions. The higher the number of points a job received, the higher the pay would be for the person occupying the job. Jobs receiving equal points were considered comparable; thus workers in comparable jobs were to receive equal pay.

In the Washington study, a registered nurse received more points than a computer-systems analyst. A clerical supervisor received more points than a beginning secretary. Truck drivers received fewer points than retail clerks. The study found that clerk-typists were comparable to warehouse workers.

Skeptics wonder how the consultants evaluating different jobs could make sensible evaluations based on a factor such as "mental demands." How, they ask, does one evaluate the mental demands of a warehouse worker as compared with a secretary? More importantly, though, critics charge that if expert-determined wage rates replace supply-and-demand-determined wage rates, undesirable consequences will emerge—even for those persons who initially think they will benefit from the implementation of the comparable worth doctrine.

For example, suppose the expert-determined wage for a secretary is $12 per hour while the supply-and-demand-determined wage is $7 per hour. Furthermore, suppose the expert-determined wage for an engineer is $13 per hour while the supply-and-demand-determined wage is $16 per hour. What will happen if the supply-and-demand-determined wages are overturned by the legislatures or the courts and replaced by expert-determined wages? At minimum, we would expect a surplus of secretaries and a shortage of engineers.

Consider specifically what would happen in the market for secretaries. First, employers of secretaries would hire fewer secretaries at $12 per hour than at $7 per hour (the demand curve for secretaries is downward sloping, no law can change that). Second, we would expect that more individuals will want to become secretaries at a wage rate of $12 per hour than at $7 per hour. Moreover, these persons are likely to be more qualified (higher skilled) than the persons working as secretaries at $7 per hour. Can you explain why? The persons who would not work as secretaries at $7 per hour largely did not because their opportunity costs were higher than $7 per hour. With a longer line of potential secretaries, and fewer secretarial positions, employers are likely to ration the available jobs to the most highly qualified persons. For the most part, the most highly qualified persons will be the persons who would not work as secretaries at $7 per hour, but will work as secretaries at $12 per hour. In the end, persons working as secretaries before comparable worth might not be working as secretaries after comparable worth.

than others, some individuals would take on more risk than others, some individuals would undertake more schooling and training than others. Thus, some degree of income inequality is due to the fact that individuals are innately different and that they make different choices. Of course, saying this also implies that some degree of income inequality is due to factors unrelated to innate ability or choices; it might be due to discrimination or luck.

An interesting debate continues to be waged on the topic of discrimination-based income inequality. The opposing sides weight different factors differently. Some persons argue that wage discrimination would be lessened if markets were allowed to be more competitive, more open, more free. They believe that in an open and competitive market, with few barriers to entry and no government protection of privileged groups, discrimination would have a high price. Firms that didn't want to hire the best and the brightest—no matter what color, religion, or sex a person was—would suffer. They would ultimately pay for their act of discrimination. Proponents of this argument usually propose that government deregulate, reduce legal barriers to entry, and in general not hamper the workings of the free market mechanism.

Other persons contend that even if the government were to follow this script, much wage discrimination would still exist. They think government should play an active legislative role in reducing both wage discrimination and other types of discrimination that they believe ultimately result in wage discrimination. The latter include discrimination in education and discrimination in on-the-job training. Proponents of an active role for government usually believe that such policy programs as quotas (minimum numbers of certain employees), equal pay for equal work, and comparable worth (equal pay for comparable work) are beneficial in reducing both the amount of wage discrimination in the economy and the degree of income inequality.

NORMATIVE STANDARDS OF INCOME DISTRIBUTION

For hundreds of years, economists, political philosophers, and political scientists, among others, have debated what constitutes a proper, just, or fair distribution of income and have proposed different normative standards. Here we discuss three of the more well-known normative standards of income distribution. These include the marginal productivity normative standard, the absolute (complete) income equality normative standard, and the Rawlsian normative standard.

The Marginal Productivity Normative Standard

The marginal productivity theory of factor prices (discussed in Chapter 12) states that in a competitive setting people tend to be paid their marginal revenue products.[3] The marginal productivity normative standard of income distribution holds that people *should be* paid their marginal revenue products.

We illustrate this idea in Exhibit 16-10a. The first "income pie" in (a) represents the actual income shares of eight individuals, A–H, who work in a competitive setting and are paid their respective MRPs. As we can see, the income distribution is unequal, since the eight persons do not contribute equally to the productive process. Some individuals are more productive than others.

The second income pie, which is the same as the first, is the income distribution

[3]You may recall that in a competitive setting value marginal product (VMP) equals marginal revenue product (MRP). Thus we can say that the marginal productivity theory holds that in a competitive setting people tend to be paid their VMPs or MRPs.

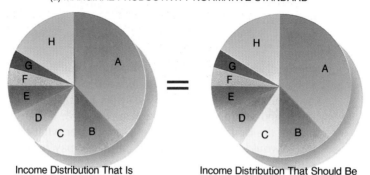

(a) MARGINAL PRODUCTIVITY NORMATIVE STANDARD

Income Distribution That Is   Income Distribution That Should Be

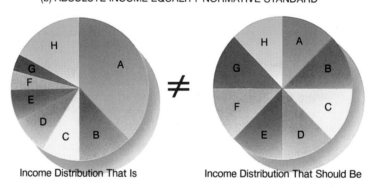

(b) ABSOLUTE INCOME EQUALITY NORMATIVE STANDARD

Income Distribution That Is   Income Distribution That Should Be

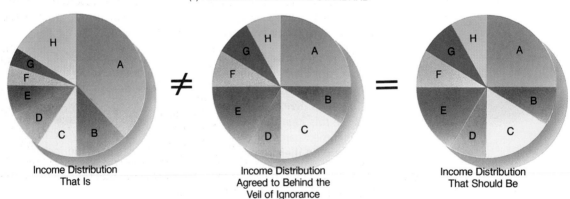

(c) RAWLSIAN NORMATIVE STANDARD

Income Distribution
That Is

Income Distribution
Agreed to Behind the
Veil of Ignorance

Income Distribution
That Should Be

(a) The marginal productivity, (b) absolute, and (c) Rawlsian normative standards of income distribution. Note that the income pies do not change as income distribution changes. In reality the size of the income pies might depend on the income distribution. We are not concerned with this point here, but only with illustrating what different income distributions, based on different normative standards, look like at one point in time.

that the proponents of the marginal productivity normative standard believe should exist. In short, individuals should be paid their marginal revenue products.

Proponents of this position argue that it is just for individuals to receive their contribution (high, low, or somewhere in-between) to the productive process, no more and no less. They also argue that paying people according to their productivity gives them an incentive to become more productive. For example, individuals have an incentive to learn more and to become better trained if they know that they will be paid more as a consequence. According to this argument, without such incentives work effort would decrease, laziness would increase, and in time the entire society would feel the harmful effects. Critics of this position respond that some persons are innately more productive than others and that rewarding them for innate qualities is unfair.

Question:

This discussion assumed a competitive setting where people were paid their MRPs. Suppose a person is in a monopsony setting (discussed in Chapter 13) and is not being paid his or her MRP. Would the proponents of the marginal productivity normative standard argue that he or she should be?

Answer:

Yes, they would. Here we are focusing on *normative standards*; thus we are discussing people who think the marginal productivity standard *should be* applied no matter what the current situation *is*. In short, it is possible to be a proponent of the marginal productivity normative standard whether or not you believe people are currently being paid their marginal revenue products.

The Absolute Income Equality Normative Standard

Exhibit 16-10b illustrates the viewpoint of those persons who advocate the absolute income equality normative standard. The first income pie represents the income distribution that exists—there is income inequality. The second income pie represents the income distribution that the persons who argue for absolute income equality believe should exist. Notice that each individual receives an equal percentage of the income pie. No one has any more or any less than anyone else.

Some hold that an equal distribution of income will lead to the maximization of total utility (in society). The argument goes this way: (1) Individuals are alike when it comes to how much satisfaction they receive from an added increase in income. (2) Receiving additional income is subject to the law of diminishing marginal utility; that is, each additional dollar is worth less to the recipient than the dollar that preceded it. (3) From points 1 and 2 it follows that redistributing income from the rich to the poor will raise total utility The rich will not lose as much utility from the redistribution as the poor will gain. Overall, total utility (of society) will rise through the redistribution of income from the rich to the poor. Total utility will be maximized when all persons receive the same income.

Opponents of this position hold that it is impossible to know if all individuals receive equal utility from an added dollar of income, and that a rich person may receive far more utility from an added dollar of income than a poor person receives. If so, then redistributing income until it is equalized would not maximize total utility.

The Rawlsian Normative Standard

In *A Theory of Justice,* philosopher John Rawls states that individuals will argue for a different income distribution if they know what their position is in the current income distribution than if they don't know their position in the current income distribution.[4] We give an example to illustrate.

Consider Patricia Jevons. She is thought to be a rich person; since her income is $300,000 per year, she is in the top 5 percent of income earners. Furthermore, the income distribution in which she occupies this position is largely unequal. There are few rich people and many poor people. Given that Patricia *knows* her position in the income distribution and considers it a comfortable position to occupy, she is less likely to argue for a more equal income distribution (and the high taxes that will be needed to bring it about) than if she were placed behind John Rawls's fictional **veil of ignorance**.

The veil of ignorance is the imaginary veil or curtain behind which a person does not know his position in the income distribution; that is, a person does not know whether he will be rich or poor once the veil is removed. Rawls argues that behind the veil a person would be more likely to ''vote'' for a more equal income distribution than she would ''vote'' for without the veil.

The full power of Rawls's veil of ignorance idea, and its impact on the income distribution, can be seen in the following scenario. On Monday everyone knows his position in the income distribution. Some people are arguing for more income equality, but a sizable group do not want this. They are satisfied with the status-quo income distribution.

On Tuesday everyone is somehow magically transmitted behind Rawls's veil of ignorance. Behind it, no one knows his position on the other side of the veil. No one knows whether he is rich or poor, innately talented or not, lucky or unlucky. As a group, the persons behind the veil must decide on the income distribution they wish to see once the veil is removed. Rawls argues that they will opt for a more equal distribution than currently exists—the tendency will be toward (but need not hit) income equality. Rawls believes that individuals are largely risk avoiders and will not want to take the chance that once the veil is removed, they will end up poor. They will opt for an income distribution such that if they do end up (relatively) poor, their standard of living is not too low.

The Rawlsian normative standard is illustrated in Exhibit 16-10c, which shows three income pies. The first represents the income distribution that currently exists. The second represents the income distribution that individuals behind the veil of ignorance would accept. Notice that it is a more equal income distribution than the first. The third and last income pie, which is the same as the second, represents the income distribution that Rawls holds should exist—since it was agreed to in an environment where individuals were, in a sense, equal: no one knew how he or she would fare once the veil was removed.

Critics of the Rawlsian position state that individuals behind the veil of ignorance might not reach a consensus on the income distribution that should exist, and that they might not be risk avoiders to the degree Rawls assumes they will be.

Furthermore, the individuals behind the veil of ignorance will consider the trade-off between less income inequality and more output. As we hinted earlier, in a world where there is likely to be an unequal income distribution because of unequal individual productivities (sharply different marginal revenue products), reducing income inequality requires higher taxes and a lower reward for productive effort. In the end, this will lead to less productive effort being expended and less output for

Veil of ignorance
The imaginary veil or curtain behind which a person does not know his or her position in the income distribution.

[4]John Rawls, *A Theory of Justice* (Cambridge: Harvard University Press, 1971).

consumption. In short, the *size* of the income pie might change given different income distributions. Rawls's critics argue that this information is likely to be considered to a greater degree than Rawls assumes it will be.

Question:

To expand on the last point: The way the income pies have been drawn, the size of the pie does not change no matter what the income distribution is. Isn't this unlikely? For example, isn't it possible that the income pie over time will be larger with an unequal income distribution than with an absolutely equal income distribution? After all, it isn't likely that individuals will work as hard if they know that government is determined to make all incomes the same.

Answer:

That is correct. The income pies are drawn to illustrate what different income distributions, based on different normative standards, look like at one point in time, not over time. Over time the size of the pies might indeed change.

POVERTY

This section presents some facts about poverty and examines its causes and some proposed solutions.

What Is Poverty, and Who Are the Poor?

There are principally two views of poverty. One view holds that poverty should be defined in absolute terms; the other holds that poverty should be defined in relative terms.

A definition of poverty in absolute terms might be the following: Poverty exists if a family of a four receives an income below $10,000 per year. A definition of poverty in relative terms might be the following: Poverty exists if a family of four receives an income that places it in the lowest 10 percent of family income recipients.

Viewing poverty in relative terms means that poverty will always exist—unless, of course, there is absolute income equality. Given any unequal income distribution, some persons will always occupy the bottom rung of the income ladder; thus there will always be poverty. This holds no matter how high the absolute standard of living of the members of the society. For example, in a community of ten persons, where nine earn $1 million per year, and one earns $400,000 per year, the person earning $400,000 per year is in the bottom 10 percent of the income distribution and therefore is considered to be living in poverty if poverty is defined in relative terms.

The U.S. government defines poverty in absolute terms. The absolute poverty measurement was developed in 1964 by the Social Security Administration, based on the findings of the Department of Agriculture. Called the **poverty income threshold** or **poverty line,** it refers to the income below which people are considered to be living in poverty. Individuals or families with incomes below the poverty income threshold, or poverty line, are considered poor.

In 1986, the poverty income threshold was $11,203 for a family of four. It was $5,701 for an individual between 15 and 64 years of age and $5,255 for an individual 65 years of age or older. The poverty threshold is updated yearly to reflect changes in the consumer price index. Exhibit 16-11 shows both the absolute number of

Poverty Income Threshold (Poverty Line)

Income level below which people are considered to be living in poverty.

Persons Below the Poverty Line, 1970–86

YEAR	NUMBER OF PERSONS BELOW THE POVERTY LINE (MILLIONS)	PERCENTAGE OF THE POPULATION IN POVERTY
1970	25.4 million	12.6%
1971	25.6	12.5
1972	24.5	11.9
1973	23.0	11.0
1974	23.4	11.2
1975	25.9	12.3
1976	25.0	11.8
1977	24.7	11.6
1978	24.5	11.4
1979	26.1	11.7
1980	29.3	13.0
1981	31.8	14.0
1982	34.4	15.0
1983	35.3	15.2
1984	33.7	14.4
1985	33.1	14.0
1986	32.4	13.6

SOURCE: Council of Economic Advisers, *Economic Report of the President, 1988* (Washington, D.C.: U.S. Government Printing Office, 1988).

persons living below the poverty line and the percentage of the total population living in poverty for the period 1970–86.

Limitations of the Official Poverty Income Statistics

We need to be aware of certain limitations and shortcomings of the official poverty income statistics. First, the poverty figures are based solely on money incomes. Many money-poor persons receive in-kind benefits. For example, a family of four with a money income of $10,000 in 1988 was defined as poor, although it might have received in-kind benefits worth, say, $4,000. If the poverty figures are adjusted for in-kind benefits the percentage of persons living in poverty drops, usually quite substantially. In 1986, on the basis of money income only, 13.6 percent of the population was said to be living in poverty, but when in-kind benefits were taken into account, the percentage dropped to 11.6. It has been estimated that the U.S. government currently spends $1.50 in in-kind benefits for every $1 cash benefit.

In addition, poverty figures are not adjusted for unreported or illegal income, leading to an overestimate of poverty. Furthermore, poverty figures are not adjusted for regional differences in the cost of living, leading to both over- and under-estimates of poverty.

Finally, government counters are unable to find some poor persons—such as some illegal aliens and some of the homeless—which leads to an underestimate of poverty.

Who Are the Poor?

The poor are made up of persons of all religions, colors, sexes, ages, and ethnic backgrounds. However, some groups are represented much more prominently in the poverty figures than others. For example, a greater percentage of blacks and Hispanics are poor than whites. To illustrate, in 1986, 31.1 percent of blacks, 27.3

Persons below the Poverty Line, by Race for 1986

	NUMBER OF PERSONS BELOW THE POVERTY LEVEL (MILLIONS)			PERCENTAGE BELOW THE POVERTY LEVEL		
Year	**White**	**Black**	**Hispanic**	**White**	**Black**	**Hispanic**
1980	19.7	8.6	3.5	10.2%	32.5%	25.7%
1981	21.6	9.2	3.7	11.1	34.2	26.5
1982	23.5	9.7	4.3	12.0	35.6	29.9
1983	24.0	9.9	4.6	12.1	35.7	28.0
1984	23.0	9.5	4.8	11.5	33.8	28.4
1985	22.9	8.9	5.2	11.4	31.3	29.0
1986	22.2	9.0	5.1	11.0	31.1	27.3

SOURCE: U.S. Bureau of the Census, *Statistical Abstract of the United States, 1988* (Washington, D.C.: U.S. Government Printing Office, 1988).

percent of Hispanics, and 11 percent of whites were poor. A greater percentage of families headed by females are poor than families headed by males, and families with seven or more persons are much more likely to be poor than families with fewer than seven persons. Additionally, a greater percentage of young persons are poor than others, and the uneducated and poorly educated are more likely to be poor than the educated. Overall, a disproportionate percentage of the poor are black or Hispanic and live in large families headed by a female who is young and has little education. See Exhibits 16-12 through 16-15.

If we look at things in terms of absolute numbers, instead of percentages, then most poor persons are white. This largely stems from the fact that there are more whites in the total population than other groups.

The Causes of Poverty: How Many, What Weight, Which One?

Why are some people poor? To a large degree, the causes and sources of poverty are the same as the causes and sources of inequality in the income distribution, which we discussed earlier.

It would be easier if there were one simple reason why some people are poor. Some persons speak as if there is. They argue that people are poor because they do not want to work. Others argue that people are poor because they are discriminated against in the workplace. Although most economists today believe poverty has more than one cause, they differ as to the weights they assign to the causes. And sometimes

■ Exhibit 16-13
Persons below the Poverty Line, by Age for 1986

AGE	NUMBER OF PERSONS BELOW THE POVERTY LEVEL (MILLIONS)	PERCENTAGE BELOW THE POVERTY LEVEL
Under 16 years old	11.6	21.0%
16–21 years old	3.6	16.6
22–44 years old	9.5	10.8
45–64 years old	4.0	9.1
65 years old and over	3.4	12.4

SOURCE: U.S. Bureau of the Census, *Statistical Abstract of the United States, 1988* (Washington, D.C.: U.S. Government Printing Office, 1988).

■ Exhibit 16-14
Families below the Poverty Line, by Family Size for 1986

SIZE OF FAMILY	NUMBER OF FAMILIES BELOW THE POVERTY LEVEL (MILLIONS)	PERCENTAGE BELOW THE POVERTY LEVEL
2 persons	2.3	8.9%
3 persons	1.6	11.0
4 persons	1.3	10.1
5 persons	0.8	13.7
6 persons	0.4	20.0
7 persons or more	0.3	31.9

Source: U.S. Bureau of the Census, *Statistical Abstract of the United States, 1988* (Washington, D.C.: U.S. Government Printing Office, 1988).

they (along with others) differ as to the cause of poverty in a particular case. We explain this latter point through a short fictional story.

Christine Berkley is 25 years old; she has only a seventh-grade education; she has three small children and no husband. She spends her days watching television, taking care of her children, and generally staying around her apartment. Christine and her children live in poverty. Their total income comes from government cash and in-kind assistance.

Viewing this situation, one person comments that Christine is poor because of her own choosing. She chose not to get an education, to get pregnant outside of marriage, and to stay at home instead of work. This person argues that the life Christine is living now—in poverty—is the consequence of decisions that she made years ago.

Another person argues differently. He says that Christine was unlucky to be born in a family where her father was an alcoholic and her parents didn't stress the importance of getting an education. He says that when Christine was young and attending school, she couldn't really do her homework because her father was yelling at her mother, and the television was always turned up loud. Additionally, Christine has been discriminated against in the workplace. Besides, with her lack of education, any job she could get would probably pay so little that she would not be able to afford day care for her children. He concludes that Christine is living in poverty because of bad luck and discrimination.

In broad terms, one person sees voluntary choice as the cause of Christine's poverty, the other sees factors outside her control as the cause. This is not the place to wage a full discussion about which person is closer to the truth or to try to answer

■ Exhibit 16-15
Families below the Poverty Line, by Education for 1986

EDUCATION OF HOUSEHOLDER	NUMBER OF FAMILIES BELOW THE POVERTY LEVEL (MILLIONS)	PERCENTAGE BELOW THE POVERTY LEVEL
Elementary: Less than 8 years	1.0	25.5%
8 years	0.5	15.5
High School: 1 to 3 years	1.3	18.5
4 years	2.1	9.5
College: 1 year or more	0.9	4.0

Source: U.S. Bureau of the Census, *Statistical Abstract of the United States, 1988* (Washington, D.C.: U.S. Government Printing Office, 1988).

the century-old question, Is one's life the result of fate or choice? Our purpose is simply to show that even though individuals may agree that poverty has more than one cause, it does not follow that they can agree about the specific cause in a specific case.

Proposed and Existing Ways of Reducing or Eliminating Poverty

In this section, we discuss three ways of reducing or eliminating poverty: the current welfare system, the negative income tax, and the market-oriented program.

The Current Welfare System. The current welfare system largely aids the poor in two ways: by providing cash benefits and by providing in-kind benefits. The major cash payment program is Aid to Families with Dependent Children (AFDC). In 1985 this program paid out $15.1 billion with an average monthly payment per family of $342.

The major in-kind forms of assistance to the poor include food stamps, public housing, and Medicaid. In 1986, the food stamp program paid out slightly more than $13.4 billion (which includes administrative expenses) to approximately 20 million recipients. In 1986, for a family of four the maximum monthly food stamp allotment was $264. This is $8.80 per day for a family of four, or $2.20 per person.

Some critics of the current welfare system usually comment that too little money is being spent to get people out of poverty. Other critics either comment that too much money is being spent, or that much that is being spent isn't reaching the right people (for example, in the past there have been reports of college students from rich families sometimes receiving food stamps).

Additionally, they charge that the current welfare system has the unintended consequence of distorting the incentive individuals have to lessen their need. Consider the case of the fictional Barbara Sullivan. Barbara receives $496 per month in AFDC payments and $204 per month in food stamps. Barbara is currently not working, but she is seriously considering trying to find work soon. There is a problem, though: If she works and earns an income, her AFDC payments and food stamps will be cut. On the one hand, she earns income if she works; but on the other hand, she loses money (AFDC) and in-kind benefits (food stamps) if she works. The real question is how much she benefits by working relative to how much she loses. In many instances, the net benefit from working is small. In such instances, some individuals choose not to work; thus we can reasonably say that welfare assistance acts as a disincentive to work.

In October 1988 the Congress passed by a wide margin of acceptance, legislation that requires welfare recipients who have children over the age of three to participate in work, training, or education programs approved of or established by the states. The measure also requires that states extend welfare benefits to two-parent families in which both parents are unemployed as long as one parent works a minimum of 16 hours a week in a community-service job. This provision becomes effective on October 1, 1993.

The Negative Income Tax. The negative income tax was designed to lessen the disincentive effects of the current welfare system. In popular jargon, the negative income tax is the program that would solve the problem of poverty with a check. We explain how it would work with the aid of Exhibit 16-16.

The income and negative income tax figures in Exhibit 16-16 are hypothetical. The process of finding a family's negative income tax payment is quite easy. For example, if a family earns zero income (column 1), it would receive a negative

Economics in Our Times

Interview: John Kenneth Galbraith

To the public at large, one of the best known economists is John Kenneth Galbraith. Two of his many books, *The Affluent Society* and *The New Industrial State* have had a major impact on the way many people think about economics and the economy. Galbraith is a vocal critic of the free market system. He *argues against* giant corporations, which he believes manipulate the American economy, and he *argues for* more responsible government that will adequately address, among other things, the legitimate concerns of the poor. Galbraith is currently at Harvard University. We interviewed Professor Galbraith on March 18, 1988.

Professor Galbraith, people are often moved to action by their vision of the way (they believe) the world

could be. Could you give us some specifics as to your vision of the way the world could be?

If I were asked what I would most like to see changed, it would come down to two things. First, that we escape from the hideous military competition that we now have with the Soviet Union. I think increasingly this is being seen as a competition between the military establishments of the two superpowers unrelated to any purpose designed to enhance the security of the two countries. The second thing I would like to see in any vision of the future is relief for what we have now come to call "the underclass." These are the people who do not have access to anything approaching the American way of life—who are ill, homeless, psychologically disturbed, or, in the much more common case, devoid of the minimum of income necessary for decent life.

You have had much to say about the poor and about income inequality. What do you consider an intolerable level of poverty and income inequality? What public actions would you propose on this front?

Certainly I don't want to see anybody falling below the prescribed poverty level, but beyond that I would like to see greater equality of income distribution. And as to the instruments, there is none that is new. The government has to repair the substantial defaults of capitalism by an adequate minimum wage, a strong housing program (there is no industrialized country where capitalism builds good houses for the poor), and a strong health program for those who do not have access to medical care.

Do you think that the government spending pie is big enough and

needs only to be split up differently? Or do you prefer not only a different division of the pie but also a bigger pie?

I certainly hope for some redistribution of government income from defense to the social programs, but I have no doubt that an effective program on behalf of the poor probably does require an increased role for the federal government.

Do you think most Americans have the same priorities you do but that these priorities are not being transmitted properly through the political process, or do they have different priorities than you?

I don't think it is necessarily the role of an economist to be with the majority. The role of the economist is to state what he or she believes is right and should be done. I confess to the feeling that those of us who are asking for a more equitable society, and a more responsible and effective role for government, may well be in the minority.

Your critics have argued that you place too much faith or trust in government to do the right thing. What do you say to those who argue that you are naïve when it comes to what government can and will do?

We always have critics who are looking for reputable applause.

In your opinion what topics do mainstream academic economists spend too little time analyzing, researching, and writing about?

I would say three are important. First, the obvious pressing problems of the social concerns of the poor. Second, the economic role of the military-industrial complex, which is extremely important and should attract much

Guaranteed Income Level

Income level below which people are not allowed to fall.

Implicit Marginal Tax Rate

The rate at which the negative income tax payment, or any cash grant or subsidy, is reduced as earned income rises.

income tax payment, or cash grant, of $5,000 (column 2). This would make its total income (column 3) $5,000. It follows that no family would be permitted to fall below an income of $5,000; this income would then be the **guaranteed income level.** Exactly what dollar figure would constitute the guaranteed income level would be decided through the political process.

Suppose now that the family that previously earned $0 earns $1,000. How will it be affected? Its negative income tax payment will fall—from $5,000 to $4,500—but not by the amount its earned income increased. For a $1,000 increase in earned income, its negative income tax payment decreases by $500. This means the family's **implicit marginal tax rate** is 50 percent. The implicit marginal tax rate is the rate at which the negative income tax payment, or any cash grant or subsidy, is reduced as earned income increases.

For the family in our example, the implicit marginal tax rate is 50 percent for every $1,000 increase in earned income up to $10,000. The essence of the negative income tax is that a family can make itself substantially better off—as measured by its total income (column 3)—by working and earning income. This contrasts with many present welfare assistance programs that, at certain levels of assistance and in certain circumstances, impose a 100 percent implicit marginal tax rate on the welfare recipient. The message of such a (high-tax) welfare system is clear: Earn an additional dollar of income, lose a dollar of welfare assistance. With such a high

■ **Exhibit 16-16**
Hypothetical Negative Income Tax

The negative income tax here has an implicit marginal tax rate of 50 percent and guaranteed income of $5,000. A family that earns $0 receives a negative income tax payment of $5,000. If this same family earns $1,000, the negative income tax payment falls to $4,500.

(1) EARNED INCOME	(2) NEGATIVE INCOME TAX PAYMENT (CASH GRANT)	(3) TOTAL INCOME = EARNED INCOME + NEGATIVE INCOME TAX PAYMENT
$ 0	$5,000	$ 5,000
1,000	4,500	5,500
2,000	4,000	6,000
3,000	3,500	6,500
4,000	3,000	7,000
5,000	2,500	7,500
6,000	2,000	8,000
7,000	1,500	8,500
8,000	1,000	9,000
9,000	500	9,500
10,000	0	10,000

Theory in Practice

Rich Man, Poor Man: Possible Justifications of Government Welfare Assistance

What is the justification for government involvement in welfare assistance, in redistributing income and goods from the rich to the poor? Some individuals would answer that there is no justification for government providing welfare assistance. They say that this function is outside the proper role of government, that playing Robin Hood is not the proper task of government. Persons who make this argument say they are not against helping the poor (for instance, they are usually in favor of private charitable organizations), but that they are against government using its powers to take from some to give to others.

Persons who believe differently usually present the *public good–free rider* justification and/or the *social-insurance* justification for government welfare assistance.

Proponents of the public good–free rider position make the following arguments: (1) Most individuals in society would feel better if there were little or no poverty; it is distressing to view the sights of poverty—slums, hungry and poorly clothed people, the homeless. Therefore there is a demand for reducing or eliminating poverty. (2) The reduction or elimination of poverty is a *public good*, a good, which if consumed by one person can be consumed by other persons to the same degree, and the consumption of which cannot be denied to anyone.* That is, once poverty is reduced or eliminated, everyone will benefit from no longer viewing the ugly and upsetting sights of poverty, and no one can be excluded from such benefits. (3) If no one can be excluded from experiencing the benefits of poverty reduction, then individuals will not have any incentive to pay for what they can get for free, thus they will become *free riders*. The economist Milton Friedman sums up the force of the argument this way:

I am distressed by the sight of poverty: I am benefited by its alleviation; but I am benefited equally whether I or someone else pays for its alleviation; the benefits of other people's charity therefore partly accrue to me. To put it differently we might all of us be willing to contribute to the relief of poverty, *provided* everyone else did. We might not be willing to contribute the same amount without such assurance.**

The acceptance of the public good–free rider argument leads individuals to conclude that government is justified in taxing all persons to pay for welfare assistance for some.

The social-insurance justification is a different type of justification for government welfare assistance. It holds that individuals currently not receiving welfare think they might one day need welfare assistance and thus are willing to take out a form of insurance for themselves by supporting welfare programs (with their tax dollars and votes) today.

*We discuss public goods in Chapter 18.
**Milton Friedman, *Capitalism and Freedom* (Chicago: University of Chicago Press, 1952), p. 191.

implicit marginal tax rate, the disincentive to work and earn income is strong, as is the incentive to remain on welfare.

Question:

Wouldn't the negative income tax provide people with a sharp disincentive to work if the guaranteed income level were set too high? After all, if the guaranteed income level were set at $17,000 many people currently earning that income might decide to quit their jobs and collect negative income tax payments. Isn't this likely to be the case?

Answer:

Certainly if the guaranteed income level is set too high, individuals currently not receiving welfare assistance would have an incentive to put themselves into a position where they would receive it. In this case, the negative income tax program might lead to more instead of fewer individuals receiving welfare assistance. The dollar amount of the guaranteed income is critical to the program having the desired effect.

The Market-Oriented Program. In both the current welfare system and the negative income tax scheme, government is actively involved in trying to reduce or eliminate poverty. Both use the approach of assisting poor persons directly by giving them cash or goods and services. The market-oriented program for reducing poverty does not take the direct assistance approach but rather advocates breaking down the existing legal barriers to employment, thereby indirectly assisting poor persons.

For example, advocates of this approach hold that the minimum wage actually hurts poor, unskilled persons by pricing them out of the labor market. They argue that a poor person with low skills is trapped into a life of idleness if he or she cannot get a job, and that the person isn't likely to get a job if the minimum wage law mandates that an employer must pay the person more than he or she is worth.

Consider another example. As we noted in Chapter 3, in many major cities of the country a person must obtain an expensive medallion (license) before opening a taxi business. Advocates of the market-oriented approach to reducing poverty argue that such licensing procedures keep some people in poverty. The removal of such licensing procedures would promote a more open and entry-free market. They say that the poor will benefit immensely if job opportunities that are currently closed are opened up to them. This group often predicts that if government were to become more involved in opening up the market, instead of working alongside those who wish to close it, poverty would quickly decrease, and the need for welfare-type programs would diminish.

■ CHAPTER SUMMARY

The Distribution of Income

■ The distribution of income is determined first in factor markets. The government can change the distribution of income through taxes and transfer payments. The evidence available shows that the ex post distribution of income is more equal than the ex ante distribution of income.

■ Individual income = labor income + asset income + transfer payments − taxes. Government affects the latter factors, transfer payments and taxes.

■ The Lorenz curve represents the income distribution. The Gini coefficient is a measurement of the degree of inequality in the distribution of income. A Gini coefficient of 0 means perfect income equality; a Gini coefficient of 1 means complete income inequality.

■ Income inequality exists because individuals differ in their innate abilities and attributes, their choices of work and leisure, their education and other training, their attitudes about risk taking, the luck they experience, and the amount of wage discrimination directed against them. Some income inequality is the result of voluntary choices, some is not.

■ There are three major normative standards of income distribution: the marginal productivity normative standard, which holds that income distribution should be based on workers being paid their marginal revenue products: the absolute income equality normative standard, which holds that there should be absolute or complete income equality; and the Rawlsian normative standard, which holds that the income distribution decided on behind the veil of ignorance (where individuals are equal) should exist in the real world.

Poverty

■ The income poverty threshold or poverty line is the income level below which a family or person is considered poor and living in poverty.

■ It is important to be aware of the limitations of poverty income statistics. The statistics are usually not adjusted for (1) in-kind benefits, (2) unreported and illegal income, and (3) regional differences in the cost of living; and (4) the statistics do not count the poor who exist but are out of sight, such as illegal aliens and some of the homeless.

■ Different ways of dealing with the problem of poverty have been proposed; some have been implemented. The current welfare system aids people through cash and in-kind payments. The negative income tax establishes a guaranteed level of income below which no one is allowed to fall; as a family earns income, its negative income tax payment is reduced by less than its earned income rises (up until a certain income level). An important consideration in this program is the level at which the guaranteed income is set. The market-oriented approach to reducing or eliminating poverty stresses breaking down the barriers to poor persons earning income.

■ QUESTIONS TO ANSWER AND DISCUSS

1. "The Gini coefficient for country A is .35, and the Gini coefficient for country B is .22. From this it follows that the bottom 10 percent of income recipients in country B have a greater percentage of the total income than the bottom 10 percent of the income recipients in country A." Do you agree or disagree? Why?

2. Would you expect greater income inequality in country A, where there is great disparity in age, or in country B, where there is little disparity in age? Explain your answer.

3. What is a major criticism of the absolute income equality normative standard?

4. Would the work-disincentive effect of the negative income tax be less with a 10 percent implicit marginal tax rate than with a 50 percent implicit marginal tax rate, *ceteris paribus*?

5. A good welfare system is said to be one that takes care of the deserving without encouraging people to become undeserving. In short, it helps the people who deserve to be helped, but doesn't distort incentives to the degree that the undeserving put themselves into situations where they can cash in on people's generosity. Discuss the current welfare system, the negative income tax, and the market-oriented program with this thought in mind.

6. In what ways does the Rawlsian technique of hypothesizing individuals behind a veil of ignorance help or not help us decide whether we should have a 55 mph speed limit or a higher one, a larger or smaller welfare system, and higher or lower taxes placed on the rich?

7. Welfare recipients would rather receive their benefits in cash than in-kind, but much of the welfare system provides benefits in-kind. Is there any reason for not giving recipients their welfare benefits the way they want to receive them? Would it be better to move to a welfare system that only provides benefits in cash?

8. Critics of the market-oriented program of reducing poverty often remark that it does too little and that it does not really address the root causes of poverty, such as discrimination. Do you agree or disagree? Why?

Chapter 17

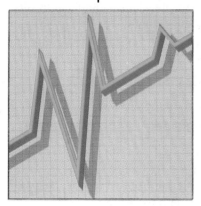

Antitrust, Business Regulation, and Deregulation

■ INTRODUCTION

An economics professor reminisced:

    When I was an economics student at college, I would often be persuaded by the last argument I heard. Once two economists came to campus and discussed the government's role in the economy. One economist was in favor of a larger role for government to play in the economy, the other was in favor of a smaller role. When the first economist spoke, I believed he was right and the second economist was wrong. When the second economist spoke, I believed he was right and the first economist was wrong. . . .

    Probably everyone, at some time or another, has been in this situation: persuaded by the last argument heard. This is often the case for beginning economics students, especially when they study certain topics, including the topics in this chapter. On questions of antitrust policy, regulation, and deregulation, economists can be found on both sides of the fence, and a few are sitting squarely on top of it. This is not good or bad, it simply is. And because it is, the student hears many different views, all of which seem to have merit.

    We're telling you this to prepare you for what's to come. As you read and study this chapter, it's likely that at times you will feel yourself being pulled in different directions. That's not bad, for part of learning economics is learning to grapple with the real world and the many different ways of viewing things that you'll encounter there. The real world is sometimes messy, and debates in economics simply mirror this fact.

■ WHAT THIS CHAPTER IS ABOUT

The television reporter sits across from the economist and asks him to explain what the recent economic news means. The economist responds. He talks about an economic theory (cleverly disguised) and cites a few facts and figures. The reporter, knowing that time is short and the attention span of the viewers is even shorter, cuts to the important question: So, what do we do? The reporter wants to know what *policy* we (the American public, the government, the regulators, whoever) should implement. News reporters and laypersons are far more interested in economic policy than economic theories and economic facts and figures. This is natural.

This chapter is largely about economic policy, specifically, economic policy that relates to business—antitrust law and business regulation and deregulation.

Key Questions to Keep in Mind as You Read

1. What are some different ways of dealing with monopoly power?
2. What are antitrust laws? What is their stated purpose?
3. What is a natural monopoly?
4. What are the different ways of regulating a natural monopoly?
5. Why are the effects of regulation sometimes different from what was intended?
6. What is the public interest theory of regulation?
7. What is the capture hypothesis?

ANTITRUST

Antitrust Law
Legislation passed for the stated purpose of controlling monopoly power and preserving and promoting competition.

In Chapter 10, we learned that a monopoly produces a smaller output than is produced by a perfectly competitive firm with the same revenue and cost considerations, charges a higher price, and causes a welfare loss to society. Some economists argue that based on these facts government should place certain restrictions on monopolies. They also say that government should restrict the activities of cartels, since the objective of a cartel is to behave as if it were a monopoly.

The opponents of this view hold that monopolies do not have as much market power as some people think—witness the competition some monopolies face from broadly defined substitutes and imports. They also maintain that cartels usually contain the seeds of their own destruction—therefore it is only a matter of time (usually short) before they naturally crumble.

In this chapter we are not concerned with the debate about *whether* to restrict monopoly power. Instead, we examine the ways government has dealt with, and continues to deal with, monopoly power. Two of the ways government has dealt with monopoly power are through the antitrust laws and through regulation. We examine **antitrust law** in this section, regulation in the next.

Antitrust law is legislation passed for the stated purpose of controlling monopoly power and preserving and promoting competition. First, let's look at how a few of the major antitrust acts have been used and at the effects they have had.

Antitrust Acts

The seven major acts that constitute U.S. antitrust policy are the Sherman Act (1890), the Clayton Act (1914), the Federal Trade Commission Act (1914), the Robinson-Patman Act (1936), the Wheeler-Lea Act (1938), the Celler-Kefauver Antimerger Act (1950), and the Hart-Scott-Rodino Antitrust Procedural Improvements Act (1980).

The Sherman Act (1890). The Sherman Act was passed during a period when mergers of companies were common. At that time, the organization that companies formed by combining together was called a **trust;** this in turn gave us the word "antitrust."

Trust
A combination of firms that come together to act as a monopolist.

360

The Sherman Act contains two major provisions:

1. "Every contract, combination in the form of trust or otherwise, or conspiracy, in restraint of trade or commerce among the several states, or with foreign nations, is hereby declared to be illegal."

2. "Every person who shall monopolize, or attempt to monopolize, or combine or conspire with any other person or persons to monopolize any part of the trade or commerce . . . shall be guilty of a misdemeanor."

Some people have argued that the provisions of the Sherman Act are vague. For example, the act never explains which specific acts constitute "restraint of trade," although it declares such acts illegal.

The Clayton Act (1914). The Clayton Act made the following business practices illegal when their effects "may be to substantially lessen competition or tend to create a monopoly":

1. Price discrimination—charging different customers different prices for the same product where the price differences are not related to cost differences.

2. Exclusive dealing—selling to a retailer on the condition that the seller not carry any rival products.

3. Tying contracts—arrangements whereby the sale of one product is dependent on the purchase of some other product(s).

4. The acquisition of competing companies' stock if the acquisition reduces competition (some say a major loophole of the act is that it did not ban the acquisition of competing companies' physical assets, and therefore did not prevent anticompetitive mergers as it was designed to do).

Finally the act made interlocking directorates illegal, irrespective of their effects (that is, interlocking directorates are illegal at all times, not just when their effects "may be to substantially lessen competition . . ."). An *interlocking directorate* is an arrangement whereby the directors of one company sit on the board of directors of another company in the same industry.

The Federal Trade Commission Act (1914). The Federal Trade Commission Act contained the broadest and most general language of any antitrust act. It declared illegal "unfair methods of competition in commerce." In essence, this amounts to declaring illegal those acts that are judged to be "too aggressive" in competition. The problem is how to decide what is fair and what is unfair, what is aggressive but not too aggressive. This act also set up the Federal Trade Commission to deal with "unfair methods of competition."

The Robinson-Patman Act (1936). The Robinson-Patman Act was passed in an attempt to decrease the failure rate of small businesses by protecting them from the competition of large and growing chain stores. The large chain stores were receiving price discounts from their suppliers and, in turn, were passing the discounts on to their customers. As a result, small businesses had a difficult time competing, and many of them failed. The Robinson-Patman Act prohibited suppliers from offering special discounts to large chain stores unless they also offered the discounts to everyone else. Many economists believe that, rather than preserving and strengthening competition, the Robinson-Patman Act limited it. The act seemed to be more concerned about a certain group of competitors than about the process of competition and the buying public as a whole.

The Wheeler-Lea Act (1938).   The Wheeler-Lea Act empowered the Federal Trade Commission (FTC) to deal with false and deceptive acts or practices. Major moves in this area have been against advertising that the FTC has deemed false and deceptive.

The Celler-Kefauver Antimerger Act (1950).   The Celler-Kefauver Act was designed to close the "loophole" that remained in the Clayton Act with respect to mergers (see point 4 of the Clayton Act). It banned anticompetitive mergers that occurred as a result of one company acquiring the physical assets of another company.

The Hart-Scott-Rodino Antitrust Procedural Improvements Act (1980).   This act required that pending mergers be reported in advance to the Federal Trade Commission and the Justice Department.

Unsettled Points in Antitrust Policy

It is not always clear where lines should be drawn in implementing antitrust policy. Which firms should be allowed to enter into a merger, which firms should be prohibited? What constitutes restraint of trade? Which firms should be termed "monopolists" and broken into smaller firms, and which firms should be left alone?

As we might guess, not everyone answers these questions the same way. In short, some points of antitrust policy are still unsettled. A few of the more important unsettled points are noted here.

Definition of the Market.   Should a market be defined broadly or narrowly? The way it is defined will help determine whether a particular firm is considered a monopoly or not. For example, in an important antitrust suit in 1945, a court ruled that Alcoa (Aluminum Company of America) was a monopoly because it had 90 percent of the virgin aluminum ingot market. If the market Alcoa operated within had been broadened to include stainless steel, copper, tin, nickel, and zinc (some of the goods it had to compete with), it is unlikely that Alcoa would have been ruled a monopoly.

Later court rulings have tended to define markets broadly rather than narrowly. For instance, in the DuPont case in 1956, the market relevant to DuPont was ruled to be the flexible wrapping materials market rather than the narrower cellophane market.

In a well-publicized antitrust suit, the Justice Department filed antitrust charges against IBM, saying that it had monopolized the "general-purpose computer and peripheral-equipment" industry. After 13 years and 66 million pages of documents, the government decided to drop the suit. It did so largely on the basis of a broad interpretation of IBM's market. Although IBM did dominate the mainframe computer industry, there was little evidence that it dominated the minicomputer, wordprocessor, or computer-services markets.

Concentration Ratios.   Concentration ratios have often been used to gauge the amount of competition in an industry. As we pointed out in Chapter 11, there are problems with using concentration ratios. First, concentration ratios do not address the issue of foreign competition. For example, the four-firm concentration ratio might be very high, but still the four firms that make up the concentration ratio may face stiff competition from abroad. Furthermore, it is possible for a four-firm concentration ratio to remain stable over time even though there is competition among the four major firms in the industry.

Herfindahl Index

Measures the degree of concentration in an industry. It is equal to the sum of the squares of the market shares of each firm in the industry.

In 1982 the Justice Department replaced the four- and eight-firm concentration ratios with the Herfindahl index, although it too is subject to some of the same criticisms as the concentration ratios. The **Herfindahl index** measures the degree of concentration in an industry. It is equal to the sum of the squares of the market shares of each firm in the industry:

$$\text{Herfindahl index} = (S_1)^2 + (S_2)^2 + \ldots + (S_n)^2$$

where S_1 through S_n are the market shares of firms 1 through n. For example, if there are 10 firms in an industry, and each firm has a 10 percent market share, the Herfindahl index is 1,000 ($1{,}000 = 10^2 + 10^2 + 10^2 + 10^2 + 10^2 + 10^2 + 10^2 + 10^2 + 10^2 + 10^2$).

Exhibit 17-1 compares the Herfindahl index and the four-firm concentration ratio. Looking at the top four firms A–D, we notice that together they have a 48 percent market share, which generally is thought to describe a concentrated industry. A merger between any of the top four firms and any other firm (say, between firm B and firm G) would give the new merger firm a greater market share than any existing firm and usually would incur frowns from the Justice Department. The Herfindahl index for the industry is 932, however, and the Justice Department considers any number less than 1,000 to be representative of an unconcentrated industry. Furthermore, a merger between two firms that does not raise the Herfindahl index by more than 200 points (assuming the index is below 1,000 before the merger) will not bring on an antitrust action. For example, a merger between firm B (with a 12 percent market share) and firm G (with a 7 percent market share) will raise the Herfindahl index by 168 and is therefore likely to be permitted. (We obtain the

■ **EXHIBIT 17-1**

A Comparison of the Four-Firm Concentration Ratio and the Herfindahl Index

Using the old method (in this case, the four-firm concentration ratio), the top four firms in the industry have a 48 percent market share. A proposed merger between any of the top four firms and any other firm would likely be frowned on by the Justice Department. However, the Herfindahl index of 932 is representative of an unconcentrated industry, and any merger that didn't increase the index by more than 200 would most likely be allowed.

FIRMS	OLD METHOD (MARKET SHARE)	HERFINDAHL INDEX (MARKET SHARE SQUARED)
A	15%	225
B	12	144
C	11	121
D	10	100
E	8	64
F	7	49
G	7	49
H	6	36
I	6	36
J	6	36
K	6	36
L	6	36
Total	100%	932
	Four-firm concentration ratio = .48 or 48 percent	Herfindahl Index = 932

Economics in Our Times

Antitrust Decisions: Some Hits, Some Misses

The stated purpose of the antitrust laws may be worthwhile. Most people agree that promoting and strengthening competition is a noble cause. Often, however, a difference arises between the stated purpose or objective of a policy and its effects. Some economists have argued that the antitrust laws have not, in all instances, accomplished their stated objective. (We have already hinted at this in our short discussion of the Robinson-Patman Act.) Here are a few representative cases that illustrate some of the ways the courts and government policy-makers have approached antitrust issues.

Case 1: In 1966 the U.S. Supreme Court ruled on the legality of a merger between Von's Grocery Co. and

Shopping Bag Food Stores, both of Los Angeles. Together the two grocery chains had a little over 7 percent of the grocery market in the Los Angeles area. However, the Supreme Court ruled that a merger between the two companies violated the Clayton Act. It based its ruling largely on the fact that between 1950 and the early 1960s, the number of small grocery stores in Los Angeles had declined sharply. The court took this as an indication of increased concentration in the industry.

Economists are quick to point out that the number of firms in an industry might be falling owing to technological changes, and when this happens, the average size of an existing firm rises. Justice Potter Stewart, in a dissenting opinion to the 1966 decision, argued that the Court had erroneously assumed that the "degree of competition is invariably proportional to the number of competitors."

Case 2: In 1967, the Salt Lake City–based Utah Pie Co. charged that three of its competitors in Los Angeles, Continental Baking Company, Carnation Company, and Pet Milk Company, were practicing price discrimination. Utah Pie charged that these companies were selling pies in

Salt Lake City for lower prices than they were selling pies for near their plants of operation. The Supreme Court ruled in favor of Utah Pie.

Some economists note, though, that Utah Pie charged lower prices for its pies than did its competitors, and that it continued to increase its sales volume and make a profit during the time its competitors were supposedly exhibiting anticompetitive behavior. They suggest that Utah Pie was using the antitrust laws to hinder its competitors.

Case 3: In 1978, Continental Airlines set out to acquire National Airlines. The Justice Department opposed the merger of the two companies because it said the merged company would dominate the New Orleans air-traffic market. The Civil Aeronautics Board (CAB) did not oppose the merger because it said the market under consideration was contestable. As we noted in Chapter 11, firms in a contestable market that operate inefficiently, or consistently earn positive economic profits, will be joined by competing firms. It was implicitly argued that statistical measures, such as concentration ratios, mean less than whether the market is contestable.

number 168 by first finding the market share of the merged firm—which is 12 percent + 7 percent, or 19 percent—then squaring this, giving us 361, and finally finding the *difference* between 361 and the sum of the market share squared of both firms before the merger (which is 144 + 49, or 193; that is, 361 − 193 = 168).

The advantage of the Herfindahl index over the four- and eight-firm concentration ratios is that it provides information about the dispersion of firm size in an industry. For example, the Herfindahl index will be different between setting A, where 3 firms together have a 50 percent market share and there are only 4 other firms in the industry, and setting B, where 3 firms together have a 50 percent market share and there are 150 other firms in the industry.

The Herfindahl index and the four- and eight-firm concentration ratios have been criticized for implicitly arguing *from firm size to market power*. Both assume that firms that have large market shares have market power that they are likely to be abusing. But, of course, size could be a function of efficiency, serving the buying public well.

REGULATION

In 1988, approximately 60,000 persons were employed in 27 regulatory agencies of the United States. Many more persons were employed in smaller regulatory agencies in the federal government, and tens of tousands more were employed by state and local regulatory agencies. This section examines the stated objectives of these regulatory agencies and the effects of regulation.

The Case of Natural Monopoly

Natural Monopoly
The condition where economies of scale are so pronounced in an industry that only one firm can survive; an industry in which it is not economical to have more than one firm providing a good.

The discussion of monopoly in Chapter 10 briefly mentioned a **natural monopoly.** There we noted that if economies of scale are so pronounced or large in an industry that only one firm can survive, that firm is called a *natural monopoly*. Firms that supply local electricity, gas, water, and telephone service are usually considered natural monopolies.

Consider the natural monopoly setting represented in Exhibit 17-2. Suppose there is one firm in the market and that it produces Q_1 units of output at an average total cost of ATC_1. At Q_1, we have an inefficient allocation of resources. Why? As we learned in Chapter 9, resource-allocative efficiency exists when the marginal benefit to demanders of the resources used in the goods they buy equals the marginal cost to suppliers of the resources they use in the production of the goods they sell. In Exhibit 17-2, resource-allocative efficiency exists at Q_2, corresponding to the point where the demand curve intersects the MC curve.

There are two ways to reach the higher, efficient quantity of output, Q_2: (1) The firm currently producing Q_1 could increase its output to Q_2. (2) Another firm could enter the market and produce Q_3—the difference between Q_2 and Q_1.

■ **EXHIBIT 17-2**
The Natural Monopoly Situation

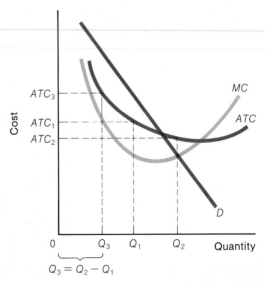

Here the only existing firm produces Q_1 at an average total cost of ATC_1. The resource-allocative efficient output level is Q_2. There are two ways to obtain this output level: (1) The only existing firm can increase its production to Q_2, or (2) a new firm can enter the market and produce Q_3, which is the difference between Q_2 and Q_1. The first way minimizes total cost, the second way does not. This then is a natural monopoly situation: One firm can supply the entire output demanded at a lower cost than two or more firms could.

$$Q_3 = Q_2 - Q_1$$

Different costs are associated with each way. For example, if a new firm enters the market and produces Q_3, it incurs an average total cost of ATC_3. Thus, both firms *together* produce Q_2, but one firm incurs average total costs of ATC_3, and the other firm incurs average total costs of ATC_1.

If, instead, the firm currently in the market increases its production to Q_2, it incurs average total costs of ATC_2. As long as the objective is to increase output to the resource-allocative efficient level, it is cheaper (lower total costs) to do this by getting the firm currently in the market to increase its output to Q_2 than to have two firms together produce Q_2.

Natural monopoly exists where one firm can supply the entire output demanded at lower cost than two or more firms can. (From this, some economists argue that a natural monopoly is best defined as an industry in which it is not economical to have more than one firm produce a good.)

Will the natural monopolist charge the monopoly price? Some economists say yes. See Exhibit 17-3, where the natural monopoly firm produces Q_1, at which marginal revenue equals marginal cost, and charges price P_1, which is the highest price per unit consistent with the output it produces.

Because it charges the "monopoly price," some persons argue that the natural monopoly firm should be regulated. What form should the regulation take? We address this question next.

Question:

In many towns, because the local gas company is considered to be a natural monopoly, local government officials argue that no other firm can successfully compete with it (it can produce gas at a lower ATC than all other firms, therefore outcompeting them). Furthermore the government officials prohibit other firms from even trying to compete with the gas company.

But why does government need to prohibit other firms from competing with the local gas company? If the gas company really is a natural monopolist, it can out-

■ **EXHIBIT 17-3**
The Profit-Maximizing Natural Monopoly

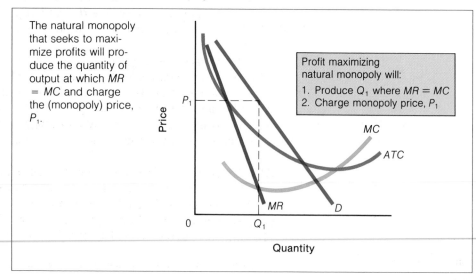

The natural monopoly that seeks to maximize profits will produce the quantity of output at which $MR = MC$ and charge the (monopoly) price, P_1.

Profit maximizing natural monopoly will:

1. Produce Q_1 where $MR = MC$
2. Charge monopoly price, P_1

compete all newcomers. Why does it need government protection from the competitors it can outcompete anyway?

Answer:

Some economists say that government isn't so much protecting the natural monopolist (the gas company) from competition as it is protecting the public from *inefficient entry* into the natural monopoly setting. According to this argument, if new firms are permitted to enter a natural monopoly setting to compete against the natural monopolist, they will be outcompeted, leave the industry, and the resources they used to enter the industry will have been wasted. The situation is analogous to preventing a 135-pound weakling from getting into the boxing ring with a 250-pound professional boxer. If you know the 135-pound weakling is going to lose anyway, it may be better (some say) to prevent him from wasting his time, and "society's" scarce resources, trying to do something he can't possibly do.

Other economists do not accept this argument. They point out that we don't protect the public from "inefficient entry" in other market structures, and therefore we should not do so here. Additionally, they sometimes note that it is difficult to know for certain whether a particular firm's entry into an industry will turn out to waste resources or not.

Ways of Regulating the Natural Monopoly

The natural monopoly may be regulated through price, profit, or output regulation.

Price Regulation. *Marginal-cost regulation* is one form of price regulation. The objective is to set a price for the natural monopoly firm that equals marginal cost at the quantity of output at which demand intersects marginal cost. In Exhibit 17-4, this price is P_1. Notice that at this price the natural monopoly takes a loss. At Q_1, average total cost is greater than price, and thus total cost is greater than total revenue.[1] Obviously the natural monopoly would rather go out of business than be subject to this type of regulation; that is, unless it receives a subsidy for its operation.

Profit Regulation. Government may want the natural monopoly to earn only zero economic profits. If so, it will be required to produce Q_2 and charge a price of P_2 (where $P_2 = ATC$; for this reason this form of regulation is often called *average-cost pricing*).

On the surface this may seem like a good way to proceed, but in practice things often turn out differently. The problem is that if the natural monopoly is always held to zero economic profits—and is not allowed to fall below, or rise above, this level—then it has an incentive to let costs rise. Higher costs—in the form of higher salaries or more luxurious offices—simply mean higher prices to cover the higher costs. In this case, it is unlikely that average cost pricing is an efficient way to proceed.

Output Regulation. The government could mandate a quantity of output it wants the natural monopoly to produce. Suppose this is Q_3 in Exhibit 17-4. Here there are positive economic profits, since price is above average total cost at Q_3. It is possible that the natural monopoly would want higher profits. At a fixed quantity of output, this can be obtained by lowering costs. In this setting the natural monopolist

[1]Remember that $TC = ATC \times Q$ and $TR = P \times Q$. Since here $ATC > P$, it follows that $TC > TR$.

Ways of Regulating a Natural Monopoly

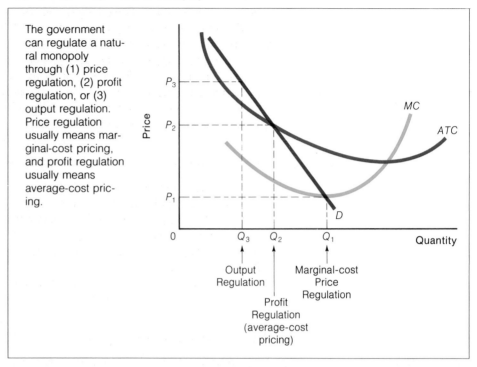

The government can regulate a natural monopoly through (1) price regulation, (2) profit regulation, or (3) output regulation. Price regulation usually means marginal-cost pricing, and profit regulation usually means average-cost pricing.

might lower costs by reducing the quality of the good or service it sells, knowing that it faces no direct competition and that it is protected (by government) from competitors.

Problems with Regulating a Natural Monopoly

Regulation does not always turn out the way it was intended. The major problems with regulating a natural monopoly have to do with *incentives* and *information*.

As we have noted, government regulation of a natural monopoly—whether it takes the form of price, profit, or output regulation—can distort the incentives of those who operate the natural monopoly. To repeat, if profit is regulated to the extent that zero economic profits are guaranteed, then there will be little incentive to hold costs down. Furthermore, the owners of the natural monopoly also have an incentive to try to influence the government officials or other persons who are regulating the natural monopoly (more on this later).

In addition, each of the three types of regulation we have discussed requires information. For example, if the government wishes to set price equal to marginal cost or average cost for the natural monopoly, it must know the cost conditions of the firm. Three problems arise here: (1) The cost information is not easy to come by, even for the natural monopoly itself. (2) The cost information can be "rigged" (to a degree) by the natural monopoly, and therefore the regulators will not get a true picture of the firm. (3) The regulators have little incentive to obtain accurate information, since they are likely to keep their jobs and prestige even if they work with less-than-accurate information (This raises another question: Who will ensure that the regulators do a good job?).

Last, there is the issue of **regulatory lag,** which is indirectly related to information. Regulatory lag refers to the period between the time when a natural monopoly's

Regulatory Lag

The period between the time when a natural monopoly's costs change and the time when the regulatory agency adjusts prices for the natural monopoly.

368

costs change and the time when the regulatory agency adjusts prices for the natural monopoly. For example, suppose the gas rates your local gas company charges customers are regulated. Next the gas company's costs rise, and it seeks a rate hike through the local regulatory body. This is not likely to happen quickly. The gas company will probably have to submit an application for a rate hike, document its case, have a date set for a hearing, argue its case at the hearing, and then wait for the regulatory agency to decide on the merits of the application. The time between the beginning of the process and the end may be many months; during that time the regulated firm is operating in ways and under conditions that both the firm and the regulatory body might not have desired.

Regulating Industries That Are Not Natural Monopolies

Some firms are regulated even though they are not natural monopolies. For instance, government has regulated both the airline and trucking industries.[2] In the trucking industry the Interstate Commerce Commission (ICC) fixed routes, set minimum freight rates, and erected barriers to entry. In the airline industry, the Civil Aeronautics Board (CAB) did much the same. Some economists view the regulation of competitive industries as unnecessary; when it exists, they see it as evidence that the firms that are being regulated are controlling the regulation to reduce their competition. We discuss this in greater detail next.

The Capture Hypothesis

Capture Hypothesis

Holds that no matter what the motive for the initial regulation and the establishment of the regulatory agency, eventually the agency will be "captured" (controlled) by the special interests of the industry that is being regulated.

The **capture hypothesis** holds that no matter what the motive for the initial regulation and the establishment of the regulatory agency, eventually the agency will be "captured" (controlled) by the special interests of the industry that is being regulated.[3] The following are a few of the interrelated points that have been put forth to support this hypothesis:

1. In many cases, persons who have been in the industry will be asked to regulate the industry since they know the most about it. Such regulators are likely to feel a bond with those persons remaining in the industry, see their side of the story more often than not, and thus, in a way, cater to them.

2. At regulatory hearings, members of the industry will be there in greater force than taxpayers and consumers. For the industry, the regulatory hearing can affect it substantially and directly; for taxpayers and consumers, the effect (spread over millions of people) is usually small and indirect. Thus regulators are much more likely to hear and respond to the side of the story presented by the groups being regulated.

3. Members of the regulated industry will make a point of getting to know the members of the regulatory agency. They will talk frequently on business matters, perhaps they will socialize together. The bond between the two groups will grow stronger over time. This will have an impact on regulatory measures.

Public Interest Theory of Regulation

Holds that regulators are seeking to do and will do through regulation what is in the best interest of the public or society at large.

The capture hypothesis is markedly different from what has come to be called the **public interest theory of regulation.** This theory holds that regulators are seeking to do and will do through regulation what is in the best interest of the public or society at large. Here then are two interesting, different, and at first sight, believable hy-

[2]We speak in the past tense here because in recent years there has been a move to deregulate airlines and trucking. We discuss this in more detail shortly.

[3]See George Stigler, *The Citizen and the State: Essays on Regulation* (Chicago: University of Chicago Press, 1975).

potheses or theories of regulation. Economists have directed much effort to testing the two theories. There is no clear consensus yet, but in the area of business regulation, the adherents of the capture hypothesis have been increasing.

DEREGULATION

In recent years there has been a move to deregulate some industries. Three notable examples include airlines, trucking, and railroads.

The Deregulation of Airlines

The Civil Aeronautics Act, which was passed in 1938, gave the Civil Aeronautics Authority (CAA) the authority to regulate air fares, the number of carriers on interstate routes, and the pattern of routes. The CAA's successor, the Civil Aeronautics Board (CAB), regulated fares in such a way that major air carriers could meet their average costs. An effect of this was that fares were raised so that high-cost, inefficient air carriers could survive. Additionally, the CAB did not allow price competition between air carriers. As a result, air carriers usually competed in a nonprice dimension: by offering more scheduled flights, better meals, more popular in-flight movies, and so forth.

In 1978 things began to change. Under CAB chairman Alfred Kahn, an economist, the airline industry was deregulated. Under deregulation airlines can compete on fares, initiate service along a new route, or discontinue a route. Empirical research after deregulation showed that airline fares fell with many airline carriers offering "Super Saver" fares. In 1978, fares fell 20 percent, and between 1979 and 1984, fares fell approximately 14 percent. In 1976, 15 percent of travelers received discount fares, whereas in 1987 this number had grown to 90 percent.[4] Additionally, new airlines joined the industry after deregulation.

Question:

Hasn't airline deregulation also affected such things as airline safety, airport congestion, and quality of service? For example, if airline deregulation makes it cheaper but less safe to fly, most people might "vote" for regulation and higher prices and more safety.

Answer:

Economists are not agreed about the nonprice effects of airline deregulation. Some argue that deregulation, having brought on more airlines, has indirectly produced greater airport congestion and reduced safety in the skies. They also argue that greater price competition has resulted in existing airlines shortchanging safety maintenance.

Other economists disagree, saying there is no evidence that air travel is less safe today than during the days of regulation. In fact, the *Economic Report of the President, 1988* says that "the accident and fatal accident rates for all scheduled passenger and cargo operations have declined dramatically during the last 30 years, reaching an all-time low in the period since [airline] deregulation."[5]

As to the airport congestion problem, the proponents of airline deregulation see this as only partially due to more airlines. A more important reason for airport congestion, they say, is that government-owned airports do not ration arrival and

---

[4]Council of Economic Advisers, *Economic Report of the President, 1988* (Washington, D.C.: U.S. Government Printing Office, 1988), p. 203.

[5]Council of Economic Advisers, *Economic Report of the President, 1988* (Washington, D.C.: U.S. Government Printing Office, 1988), p. 208.

departure times by price (that is, the airports do not use price to allocate takeoffs and landings at the most desirable times; thus there is little incentive for airlines to transfer peak traffic to off-peak periods). In short, these economists believe that the problem of airport congestion lies not so much with airline deregulation as it does with the airport authorities. Airline deregulation combined with a sensible price-rationing system for airports, they say, would not produce as much airport congestion as airline deregulation combined with a nonprice rationing system for airports.

The Deregulation of Railroads

Since its establishment in 1887, the Interstate Commerce Commission (ICC) had set rates and established routes for the railroads and also limited entry to and exit from the industry. In the late 1970s things began to change. Today railroads have greater flexibility in setting rates and in dropping unprofitable routes. In 1979, when the ICC exempted fresh fruits and vegetables from rate regulations (on railroads), the railroads responded by lowering their rates and picking up additional business. The same thing occurred when the ICC exempted coal and piggyback traffic (trucks on railroad flatcars) from rate regulation. The ICC still sets limits on the prices railroads may charge where there is evidence of "market dominance."

The Deregulation of Trucking

In the trucking industry, the ICC established freight rates, set routes, and erected barriers to entry. The benefit to existing trucking companies from the ICC-created barriers to entry was most clearly evident in the price of a trucking license. In 1976, before deregulation of the trucking industry, the average price for a license was over $500,000. In 1981, after deregulation, the average price had fallen to approximately $13,000. Deregulation removed many of the restrictions to firms entering the trucking industry and, as expected, resulted in a huge increase in firms entering the industry. Within five years of deregulation, the number of trucking companies went from 18,000 to 30,000. This increase put downward pressure on prices; inflation-adjusted truck rates fell 25 percent between 1977 (the year before entry restrictions were relaxed) and 1982.

Other Deregulation

Deregulation has made inroads into other areas as well. Since 1972, the FCC has been deregulating the television-broadcasting industry by doing such things as removing barriers to satellite broadcasting, licensing low-power television stations, and removing restrictions on cable television. In the area of telephone service, entry into the long-distance end of the business has been eased by the government mandating "equal access" to local telephone service facilities for all long-distance telephone companies. The Depository Institutions Deregulation and Monetary Control Act of 1980 eased some regulations on banks and savings and loans. For example, it eliminated interest-rate ceilings on bank savings deposits.

A Question for George Stigler

Nobel Prize winner George Stigler, whose interview appeared in Chapter 9, is closely associated with the capture hypothesis we discussed earlier. Stigler has argued that special interest groups tend to "capture" the regulatory system and use it to promote their own narrowly defined self-interest. In practice this usually means that

Economics in Our Times

Why, If You Fly, Do You Always Have To Go Through Dallas or Chicago?

The shortest distance between two points is a straight line. Some say that the airline industry doesn't care much about straight lines (or obviously about short distances). It cares about *hubs* and *spokes*.

To illustrate, suppose you want to go from Phoenix to New York City. The shortest route to take is the direct route: Phoenix *directly to* New York. Very likely, however, you won't be able to get a direct flight. Often (but not always) you will be routed through Dallas.* In other words, you will get on the plane in Phoenix, get off the plane in Dallas, get on another plane in Dallas, fly to New York, and finally get off the plane in New York. This is the hub-and-spoke delivery system illustrated in Exhibit 17-5 (it looks like a bicycle wheel). The hub represents the center of an airline network; the spokes, representing origin and destination cities, are always linked up through the hub.

The hub-and-spoke system has been used more often since airline deregulation. In several instances airline departures from major hubs (such as Dallas and Chicago) have doubled. Most economists believe the increased use of the hub-and-spoke system, which makes average travel

*If not Dallas, there is always Chicago.

time longer, is the result of increased price competition brought on by deregulation. Airlines after deregulation were under greater pressure to compete on price; thus it became more important to cut costs. One way to cut costs is to use bigger planes since bigger planes cost less to operate per seat mile. Also, the bigger planes have to be filled. To accomplish both objectives—flying bigger planes that are more fully occupied—it became necessary to gather passengers at one spot—the hub—and from there fly more of them to their destination at once. For example, instead of flying people in Phoenix and people in Albuquerque directly but separately to New York, both groups of people are

flown first to Dallas, and then the combined group is flown to New York.

On the positive side, some people argue that it is better to pay lower airline ticket prices and reach one's destination a little later than to pay higher prices and get there sooner. Also, it is generally argued that increased use of the hub-and-spoke system has given passengers more options to travel on different airlines (once in Dallas, numerous airlines can fly you to New York) at more convenient times (numerous flights leave Dallas every hour).

Source: Council of Economic Advisers, *Economic Report of the President, 1988* (Washington, D.C.: U.S. Government Printing Office, 1988), pp. 203–5.

▪ EXHIBIT 17-5
The Hub-and-Spoke System

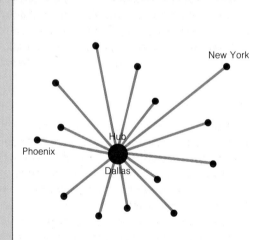

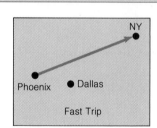

Fast Trip

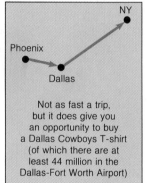

Not as fast a trip, but it does give you an opportunity to buy a Dallas Cowboys T-shirt (of which there are at least 44 million in the Dallas-Fort Worth Airport)

Since airline deregulation, the hub-and-spoke delivery system has been used increasingly. There are both benefits and costs to this system. A cost is longer average travel time. A benefit is a lower ticket price.

the regulated firms get the regulations they want. But this raises an interesting question about deregulation, which we asked Professor Stigler:

Does it follow that where deregulation exists, the broadly based public interest has somehow come to outweigh the special interests?

I wish that were true, and people talk about the deregulation movement and some are occasionally so kind as to say that we economists at the University of Chicago were important in it. I don't really believe that is what happened. I believe that situations arise where the old regulatory schemes no longer work. For example, consider the cartel that fixed commission rates on the New York Stock Exchange. This held for 180 years or so. But it finally gave way because important new developments like the growth of large traders who were no longer using the New York Stock Exchange, and were working in a third market, brought enormous pressure for change. Then the SEC went along and agreed to the deregulation of fixed commission rates. I assume that the same theory that explains why interest groups get regulation explains why sometimes they want to get rid of it.

■ CHAPTER SUMMARY

Dealing with Monopoly Power

■ A monopoly produces less than a perfectly competitive firm produces (assuming the same revenue and cost conditions), charges a higher price, and generally causes a welfare loss to society. This is the monopoly power problem, and solving it is usually put forth as a reason for antitrust laws and/or government regulatory actions. Some economists note, though, that government antitrust and regulatory actions do not always have the intended effect. Additionally, sometimes they are implemented where there is no monopoly power problem to solve.

Antitrust Laws

■ Two major criticisms have been directed at the antitrust acts. First, some argue that the language in the antitrust acts is vague; for example, even though the words "restraint of trade" are used in the Sherman Act, the act does not clearly explain what actions constitute a restraint of trade. Second, it has been argued that some antitrust acts appear to hinder, rather than promote, competition; for example, the Robinson-Patman Act.

■ There are a few unsettled points in antitrust policy. One centers around the proper definition of a market. Should a market be defined narrowly or broadly? Answering this question one way or the other will have an impact on which firms are considered monopolies. In addition, the use of concentration ratios for identifying monopolies or deciding whether to allow two firms to enter into a merger has been called into question. Recently, concentration ratios have been largely replaced (for purposes of implementing antitrust policy) with the Herfindahl index. This index is subject to some of the same criticisms as the concentration ratios.

Regulation

■ Even if we assume that the intent of regulation is to serve the public interest, it does not follow that this will be accomplished. To work as desired, regulation must be based on complete information (the regulatory body must know the cost conditions of the regulated firm, for example), and it must not distort incentives (to keep costs down, for example). Many economists are quick to point out that neither condition is likely to be fully met. In itself, this does not mean that regulation should not be implemented. It only brings out the point that regulation may not have the effects one expected.

■ Government uses three basic types of regulation to regulate natural monopolies: price, profit, or output regulation. Price regulation usually means marginal-cost price regulation: setting $P = MC$. Profit regulation usually means zero economic profits. Output regulation specifies a particular quantity of output that the natural monopoly must produce.

■ QUESTIONS TO ANSWER AND DISCUSS

1. Explain why defining a market narrowly or broadly can make a difference in how antitrust policy is implemented.

2. What is the implification of saying that regulation is likely to affect incentives?

3. What is the major difference between the capture hypothesis (or capture theory of regulation) and the public interest theory of regulation?

4. A study of both unregulated and regulated electric utilities by George Stigler and Claire Friedland found no difference in the rates charged by regulated and unregulated electric utilities. The conclusion one might easily draw from this study is that regulation is ineffective when it comes to utility rates. What ideas or hypotheses presented in this chapter might have predicted this?

5. The courts have ruled that it is a *reasonable restraint of trade* (and therefore permissible) for the owner of a business to sell his business and sign a contract with the new owner saying he will not compete with her within a vicinity of, say, 100 miles, for a period of, say, 5 years. If this is a reasonable restraint of trade, can you give an example of what you would consider an unreasonable restraint of trade? Explain how you decide what is a reasonable restraint of trade and what isn't.

6. In your opinion what is the best way to deal with the monopoly power problem? Do you advocate antitrust laws or regulation, or something else we didn't discuss? Give reasons for your answer.

7. It is usually asserted that public utilities such as electric companies and gas companies are natural monopolies. But an assertion is not proof. How would you go about trying to "prove" (disprove) that electric companies and the like are (are not) natural monopolies? (Hint: You might consider comparing the average total cost of a public utility that serves many customers with the average total cost of a public utility that serves relatively few customers.)

8. Discuss the advantages and disadvantages of the deregulation of business.

Chapter 18

Market Failure: Externalities and Public Goods

■ INTRODUCTION

Economics is not just about profits, costs, market structures, antitrust laws, prices, and supply and demand. It is about

- *cattle grazing in an open field*
- *cigarette smoking in a restaurant*
- *acid rain*
- *national defense*
- *lighthouses*
- *charity*
- *pollution*
- *traffic congestion*
- *people who play their stereos too loud*
- *outer space*

What do economists know about acid rain? you may ask. What do they know about cigarette smoking in a restaurant or lighthouses or charity? Well, let's see.

■ WHAT THIS CHAPTER IS ABOUT

Market Failure

A situation in which the market does not provide the ideal or optimal amount of a particular good.

Market failure is a situation in which the market does not provide the ideal or optimal amount of a particular good. We saw an example of this in our discussion of monopoly; monopoly produced too little output. In this chapter, we discuss two other cases where some economists believe the market fails. The first deals with externalities, the second with public goods.

Key Questions to Keep in Mind as You Read

1. What are negative externalities and positive externalities?
2. How might we deal with externalities?
3. What is the significance of the Coase theorem?
4. What is a public good?
5. What is the difference between a public good and a government-provided good?
6. What is the free-rider problem?
7. How do we guard against satellite congestion in outer space?

EXTERNALITIES

Externality
A side effect of an action that affects the well-being of third parties.

Sometimes, when goods are produced and consumed, side effects (spillover or third-party effects) occur that are felt by people who are not directly involved in the market exchanges. In general, these side effects are called **externalities** because the costs or benefits are *external* to the person(s) who caused them. In this section, we discuss two types of externalities, negative and positive.

Negative Externalities

Negative Externality
Exists when a person's or group's actions cause a cost (adverse side effect) to be felt by others.

Suppose Ramon lives in a house near an airport. Occasionally, airplanes fly over his home, creating noise and causing him some discomfort. The airplane pilot, who works for the airline company, undertakes an action (flying) in which a cost external to him is felt by some other person. In short, the flying generates an externality, and because it imposes a cost on a third party (sometimes called an "external cost"), it is referred to as a **negative externality.** A negative externality exists when a person's or group's actions cause a cost (adverse side effect) to be felt by others. A consequence of a negative externality is that *social costs* do not equal *private costs,* and the *socially optimal level of production* is not naturally obtained. We illustrate this in Exhibit 18-1.

In Exhibit 18-1 we see a downward-sloping demand curve for the good. The supply curve, S_1, represents the *private costs* of the producers of the good. We make this point explicitly by speaking of a *marginal private cost (MPC)* curve instead of simply a marginal cost curve. Equilibrium in this market setting is at E_1; Q_1 is the output—specifically, the *market output.*

Now assume that negative externalities arise as a result of the production of the good. If the external costs, linked with the negative externalities, are to be taken into account, we "add" them (as best we could) to the marginal private costs and end up with a *marginal social cost (MSC)* curve, represented in Exhibit 18-1 by S_2. If *all* costs are taken into account (both external costs and private costs), equilibrium comes at E_2 at the quantity Q_2. This is sometimes referred to as the **socially optimal output.**

Socially Optimal Output
The output level at which all benefits (external as well as private) and all costs (external as well as private) have been taken into account and adjusted for.

Notice that the market output (Q_1) is greater than the socially optimal output (Q_2) when negative externalities exist. The market is said to "fail" (hence, market failure) because it *overproduces* the good that is connected with the negative externality. The triangle noted in Exhibit 18-1 is the visible manifestation of the market failure: It is the net social cost of producing the market output (Q_1) instead of the socially optimal output (Q_2), or of moving from the socially optimal output to the market output.

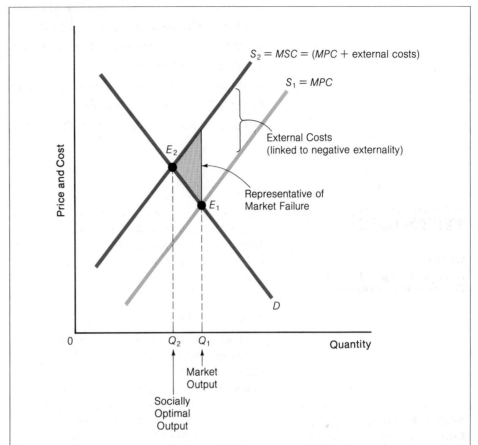

Because of a negative externality, marginal social costs (*MSC*) are greater than marginal private costs (*MPC*), and the market output is greater than the socially optimal output. The market is said to fail in that it overproduces the good.

Question:

How exactly does the triangle in Exhibit 18-1 represent the net social cost of moving from the socially optimal output to the market output?

Answer:

We explain this concept with the aid of Exhibit 18-2 where Q_2 is the socially optimal output. If "society" moves from Q_2 to Q_1, who specifically benefits and how do we represent these benefits? Buyers benefit (they are a part of society) since they will be able to buy more output at prices they are willing to pay; thus the area under the *demand curve* between Q_2 and Q_1 represents the benefits of moving from Q_2 to Q_1 (see the shaded area in Window 1 in Exhibit 18-2).

Next we ask, If "society" moves from Q_2 to Q_1, how can we illustrate the costs that are incurred? Sellers and third parties incur costs (sellers incur private costs,

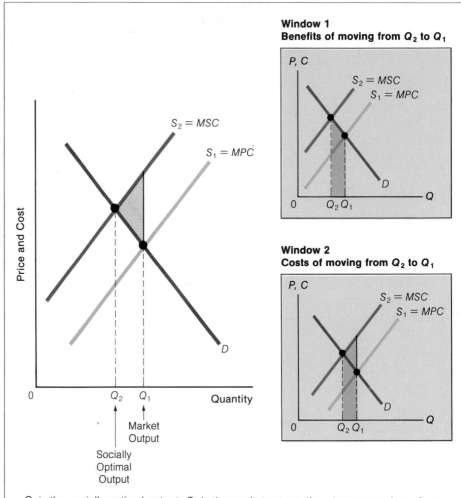

Window 1
Benefits of moving from Q_2 to Q_1

Window 2
Costs of moving from Q_2 to Q_1

Q_2 is the socially optimal output, Q_1 is the market output. If society moves from Q_2 to Q_1, buyers benefit by an amount represented by the shaded area in Window 1, but sellers and third parties together incur greater costs, represented by the shaded area in Window 2. The triangle (the difference between the two shaded areas) represents the net social costs to society of moving from Q_2 to Q_1, or producing Q_1 instead of Q_2.

and third parties incur external costs), so the area under S_2 (not S_1, because S_1 only takes into account part of society—sellers—and ignores third parties) between Q_2 and Q_1 represents the full costs of moving from Q_2 to Q_1 (see the shaded area in Window 2).

Since the shaded area in Window 2 is larger than the shaded area in Window 1, the costs to sellers *and* third parties of moving from Q_2 to Q_1 outweigh the benefits to buyers of moving from Q_2 to Q_1. Specifically, the difference between the shaded areas is the triangle; thus costs outweigh benefits by the triangle. In short, the triangle in this example represents the "net social cost" of moving from Q_2 to Q_1 or producing Q_1 instead of Q_2.

Positive Externalities

Suppose Erica Evans is a beekeeper who lives near an apple orchard. Erica's bees occasionally fly over to the orchard and pollinate the blossoms, in the process making the orchard more productive. Thus Erica undertakes an action—keeping bees—in which a benefit external to the action is felt by some person—namely, the orchard owner. Erica's beekeeping generates an externality, and because it results in a benefit to a third party (sometimes called an "external benefit"), it is referred to as a **positive externality.** A positive externality exists when a person's or group's actions cause a benefit (beneficial side effect) to be felt by others. A consequence of a positive externality is that social benefits do not equal private benefits, and the socially optimal level of production is not naturally obtained. We illustrate this in Exhibit 18-3.

The demand curve, D_1, represents the *private benefits* of the demanders of the good. We make this point explicitly by speaking of a *marginal private benefit (MPB)* curve. Equilibrium in this market setting is at E_1; Q_1 is the market output.

Now assume that positive externalities are generated as a result of the production of the good. If the external benefits, linked with the positive externalities, are to be

Positive Externality

Exists when a person's or group's actions cause a benefit (beneficial side effect) to be felt by others.

■ **EXHIBIT 18-3**
The Positive Externality Case

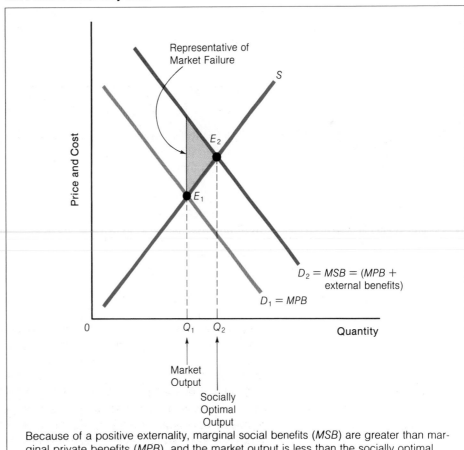

Because of a positive externality, marginal social benefits (*MSB*) are greater than marginal private benefits (*MPB*), and the market output is less than the socially optimal output. The market is said to fail in that it underproduces the good.

taken into account, we would "add" them (as best we could) to the marginal private benefits and end up with a *marginal social benefit (MSB)* curve, represented in Exhibit 18-3 by D_2. If all benefits are taken into account (private and external benefits), output is Q_2. This is the socially optimal output.

Notice that the market output is less than the socially optimal output. The market is said to fail because it *underproduces* the good that is connected with the positive externality. The triangle in Exhibit 18-3 shows the market failure: It is the net social benefit of moving from the market output to the socially optimal output.

Question:

If Q_2 is the socially optimal output, does this mean that it is better to be at Q_2 than at Q_1?

Answer:

That is not necessarily the case. Economists usually answer this question by adding conditions. If the cost of moving from the market output to the socially optimal output—that is, if the cost of adjusting for the negative or positive externality—is less than the benefits, the answer is yes; if not, the answer is no.

All we have shown so far is that where negative and positive externalities exist, benefits can be gained (in the case of positive externalities) or costs can be lessened (in the case of negative externalities) by moving from the market output to the socially optimal output. Remember, though, that there are costs associated with this adjustment. (A person doesn't simply snap his fingers and move to where he wants to be.) We say more about this in a later section of the chapter.

INTERNALIZING EXTERNALITIES

Internalizing Externalities

An externality is *internalized* if the person(s) or group that generated the externality incorporate into their own private or *internal* cost-benefit calculations the external benefits (in the case of a positive externality) or the external costs (in the case of a negative externality) that third parties bear.

An externality is **internalized** if the person(s) or group that generated the externality incorporate into their own private or *internal* cost-benefit calculations the external benefits (in the case of a positive externality) or the external costs (in the case of a negative externality) that third parties bear. Simply put, internalizing externalities is the same as adjusting for externalities. An externality has been internalized or adjusted for *completely* if, as a result, the socially optimal output emerges. A few of the numerous ways to adjust for, or internalize, externalities are presented in this section.

Persuasion

Many negative externalities in particular arise partly because persons or groups do not consider other individuals when they decide to undertake an action. Consider the person who plays his stereo loudly at three o'clock in the morning. Perhaps if he had considered the external cost his action imposes on his neighbors, he would either have not played the stereo at all or would have played it low. The option of trying to persuade those who impose external costs on us to adjust their behavior to take these costs into account is one way to adjust for—or internalize—externalities. In today's world, such slogans as "Don't Drink and Drive" and "Don't Litter" are attempts to persuade individuals to take into account the fact that their actions affect others. The religious commandment "Do unto others as you would have them do unto you" makes the same point.

Assigning Property Rights

Consider the idea that air pollution and ocean pollution—both of which are examples of negative externalities—are the result of the air and oceans being unowned. No one owns the air, no one owns the oceans, and because no one does, many individuals *feel free* (no pun intended) to emit wastes into them. If private property, or ownership, rights in air and oceans could be established, the negative externalities would likely become much less. If someone owns the resource, then actions that damage the resources come with a price; namely, the resource owner can sue for damages.

For example, in the early West when grazing lands were unowned (common property) and open, many cattle ranchers allowed their herds to overgraze. The reasons for this were simple. No one owned the land, no one could stop the overgrazing to preserve the value of the land, and if one rancher decided not to allow his herd to graze, this simply meant that there was more grazing land for other ranchers. As a consequence of the overgrazing, a future generation had to face overgrazed, barren, wasted land. From the point of view of future generations, the cattle ranchers who allowed their herds to overgraze were generating negative externalities.

What would have happened if the western lands had been privately owned? In this case, there would not have been any overgrazing, because the monetary interests of the owner of the land would not have permitted it. The landowner would have charged the rancher a fee for grazing his cattle, and thus more grazing would have entailed additional fees. There would have been less grazing of cattle at a positive fee than at a zero fee (the case when the lands were open and unowned). The externalities would have been internalized.

Question:

In the example of grazing lands, assigning private property rights, or establishing ownership rights, to unowned land lessened the externality problem. Establishing ownership rights in land is possible, but can this be done with the air and oceans?

To return to the case of the person who plays his stereo loudly at three o'clock in the morning, surely the negative externality would be less (or nonexistent) if someone owned the air. If Amy Cohan owned the air over her property and lived next door to the stereo-player, she could charge him for sending those music sounds through her air. This would put a price on his behavior, and thus the externalities would be internalized. But is it possible to assign property rights in air?

Answer:

It is very difficult and costly to establish ownership rights in air. Consequently, assigning property rights is not likely to be the method chosen to deal with externalities that arise as a consequence of unowned air. There are other ways of dealing with the problem, however, as we explain in the next sections.

Voluntary Agreements

Externalities can sometimes be internalized through individual voluntary agreements. Consider two persons, Pete and Sean, living on a deserted island. Pete and Sean have agreed between themselves that Pete owns the northern part of the island and that Sean owns the southern part. Pete occasionally cooks early in the morning, and the breeze carries the cooking smells over to Sean's part of the island where he is sleeping. Often the cooking smells awaken Sean, who has a keen sense of smell. Pete and Sean have a problem. Pete wants to be free to cook in the morning, and Sean would like to continue to sleep. They have a negative externality problem.

Suppose that Sean values his sleep in the morning by a maximum of 6 oranges—he would give up 6 oranges to be able to sleep without Pete cooking. On the other hand, Pete values cooking in the morning by 3 oranges—he would give up a maximum of 3 oranges to be able to cook in the morning. Since Sean values his sleep by more than Pete values cooking in the morning, they have an opportunity to strike a "deal." Sean can offer Pete some number of oranges greater than 3, but less than 6, to refrain from cooking in the morning. The deal will make both Pete and Sean better off. In this example, the negative externality problem is successfully addressed through the individuals voluntarily entering into an agreement. The condition for this outcome is that the **transaction costs,** costs associated with making and reaching the agreement, must be low relative to the expected benefits of the agreement.

These last two ways of internalizing externalities—property rights assignments and voluntary agreements—can be combined as in the following example.[1]

A rancher's cattle occasionally stray onto the adjacent farm and damage some of the farmer's crops. If the court assigns liability to the cattle rancher and orders him to prevent his cattle from straying, then a property rights assignment solves the externality problem. As a result, the rancher might put up a strong fence to prevent his cattle from damaging his neighbor's crops.

But there may be another solution. It is possible that the court's property rights assignment will be undone by the farmer and the cattle rancher if they find it in their mutual interest to do so. Suppose the rancher is willing to pay $100 a month to the farmer for permission to allow his cattle to stray onto the farmer's land, but that the farmer is willing to give permission for only $70 a month. Assuming trivial or zero transaction costs, the farmer and the rancher will undo the court's property rights assignment. For a payment of $70 or more a month, the farmer will allow the rancher's cattle to stray onto his land.

Before we go on, ask yourself what the resource allocative outcome would have been if the court, instead of assigning liability to the cattle rancher, had given him the property right to allow his cattle to stray. With this (opposite) property rights assignment, the cattle would have been allowed to stray (which was exactly the outcome of the previous property rights assignment once the cattle rancher and farmer voluntarily agreed to undo it). We conclude that *in the case of trivial or zero transaction costs, the property rights assignment does not matter to the resource allocative outcome.* In a nutshell, this is the **Coase theorem.** The theorem can be expressed in other ways, two of which we mention here: (1) In the case of trivial or zero transaction costs, a property rights assignment will be undone if it benefits the relevant parties to undo it. (2) In the case of trivial or zero transaction costs, the resource allocative outcome will be the same no matter who is assigned the property right.

The Coase theorem is significant for two reasons: (1) It shows that under certain conditions the market can internalize externalities. (2) It provides a benchmark for analyzing externality problems—that is, it shows what would happen if transactions costs were trivial or zero.

Transaction Costs

The costs associated with the time and effort needed to search out, negotiate, and consummate an exchange.

Coase Theorem

Says that in the case of trivial or zero transaction costs, the property rights assignment does not matter to the resource allocative outcome.

[1]See Ronald Coase, "The Problem of Social Cost," *Journal of Law and Economics* 3 (October 1960): 1–44.

Theory in Practice

Pigou vs. Coase

The first editor of the *Journal of Law and Economics* was Aaron Director. In 1959, Director published an article by Ronald Coase entitled "The Federal Communications Commission." In the article Coase took issue with economist A.C. Pigou, a trailblazer in the area of externalities and market failure, who had argued that government should use taxes and subsidies to adjust for negative and positive externalities, respectively. Coase argued that in the case of negative externalities, it is not clear that the state should tax the person imposing the negative externality. First, Coase stressed the *reciprocal* nature of externalities; specifically, he pointed out that it takes two to make a negative externality (it is not always clear who is harming whom). Second, Coase proposed a "market solution" to externality problems that was not implicit in Pigou's work.

Aaron Director and others believed that Coase was wrong and that Pigou was right. Coase, who was teaching at the University of Virginia at the time, was invited to discuss his thesis with Director and a handful of well-known economists. The group included Martin Bailey, Milton Friedman, Arnold Harberger, Reuben Kessel, Gregg Lewis, John McGee, Lloyd Mints, George Stigler, and, of course, Director.

The group met at Aaron Director's house one night. Before Coase began to outline his thesis, the group took a vote and found that everyone (with the exception of Coase) sided with Pigou. Then the sparks began to fly. Friedman, it is reported, "opened fire" on Coase. Coase withstood the intellectual attacks of his colleagues. At the end of the debate, another vote was taken. Everyone sided with Coase against Pigou. It is reported that as the members of the group left Director's home that night, they said to themselves and aloud to one another that they had witnessed history in the making. The Coase theorem had taken hold in economics.

Source: Steven N. S. Cheung, "Ronald H. Coase," in *The New Palgrave: A Dictionary of Economics,* vol. 1, (London: Macmillan Press, 1987), pps. 455–57.

Taxes and Subsidies

Taxes and subsidies are sometimes used as corrective devices for a market failure. Specifically, a tax adjusts for a negative externality, a subsidy for a positive externality. First, consider the negative externality case in Exhibit 18-1.

The objective of the corrective tax is to move the supply curve from S_1 to S_2 (recall from our discussion in earlier chapters that a tax can shift a supply curve) and therefore move from the market-determined output, Q_1, to the socially optimal output, Q_2.

In the case of a positive externality, illustrated in Exhibit 18-3, the objective is to subsidize the demand side of the market so that the demand curve moves from D_1 to D_2 and output moves from Q_1 to the socially optimal output, Q_2.

We need to keep in mind that there are costs and consequences to taxes and subsidies. For example, suppose government misjudges the external costs illustrated in Exhibit 18-4 and imposes a tax on the supplier of the good that moves the supply curve, not from S_1 to S_2, but instead from S_1 to S_3. As a result, the output level will be farther away from the socially optimal output than it was before the "corrective" tax was supplied.

It is possible for government to miscalculate external costs and impose a tax that moves the supply curve from S_1 to S_3 instead of from S_1 to S_2. As a result, the output level will be farther away from the socially optimal output than before the "corrective" tax was applied. Q_3 is farther away from Q_2 than Q_1 is from Q_2.

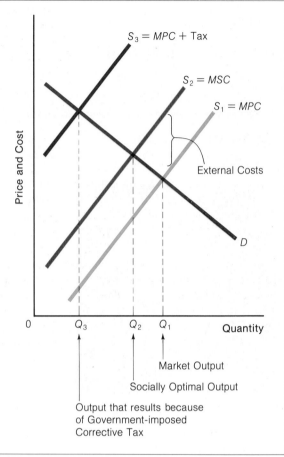

Beyond Internalizing: Setting Regulations

One way to deal with externalities, in particular with negative externalities, is for government to apply regulations directly to the activity that generates the externalities. For example, factories producing goods also produce smoke that rises up through the smokestacks. The smoke is often seen as a negative externality. Government may decide that the factory must install pollution-reducing equipment, or that it can only put so much smoke into the air per day, or that it must move to an area that is less populated.

The critics of this approach often note that regulations, once instituted, are difficult to remove even if conditions warrant removal. Also, regulations are often applied across the board when circumstances dictate otherwise. For example, factories in relatively pollution-free cities might be required to install the same pollution control equipment as factories in smoggy, pollution-ridden cities.

Finally, there is the cost of regulation. If government is going to regulate, there must be regulators (whose salaries must be paid), offices (to house the regulators), paper (to type out the regulations), typewriters and typists (to do the typing), and

Economics in Our Times

Interview: Harold Demsetz

Harold Demsetz is well-known and respected for his work in the area of property rights theory. His article, *Toward a Theory of Property Rights,* is considered a classic in the field. Demsetz is currently at the University of California, Los Angeles. We interviewed Professor Demsetz on September 26, 1988.

Professor Demsetz, you have argued that property rights change to internalize externalities. Would you give us a few examples to illustrate this principle at work.

In my paper, *Toward a Theory of Property Rights,* I focused on the privatizing of lands by Indians in the eastern United States on the Canada-U.S. border. Anthropologists had discovered a correlation through time and across geography between the fur trade whose source was in Europe and the privatization of land among these Indians. I explain this correlation, and its absence among Indians in the Southwest, by considering the externality associated with treating animals as a free good. All hunters had access to fur-bearing animals that inhabited the forests of this region, and no hunter had a rational incentive to refrain from hunting in order to preserve or increase the stock of animals in these forests. This is because an animal left unhunted was an animal that other hunters had free access to hunt. Hence, refraining from hunting would neither enrich a hunter nor guarantee an increase in the stock of animals. There existed no incentive for hunters in the present to take account of the cost that might be borne by future generations as a result of depleting the stock of animals.

Before the coming of the fur trade, the treating of these animals as if access to them were costless probably did not do much damage to the stock of animals. The scale of hunting could not have been great when its only purpose was to meet the purely personal needs of these Indians. The coming of the fur trade changed this by increasing the value of these furs and the scale of hunting. The stock of animals must have been put into jeopardy. What the Indians did to solve this problem was privatize land. This land had been treated as communal property, freely accessible to all. By privatizing the land, the Indians in effect privatized access to the animals because it is in the nature of forest animals to stay within fairly narrow territorial areas. Now, an Indian who refrained from hunting preserved the stock of animals on his land, so that the value of doing so accrued to him. An incentive to husband these animals was created by this act of privatization. The coming of the fur trade, by changing the benefits from husbanding the animals, made it profitable for the Indians to resolve the externality problem through this act of privatization.

In the southwestern United States, things were different. Here the animals were grazing animals not forest animals. Someone with a right to land doesn't automatically get a right to the animals, too, because they graze over wide tracts of land and thus are very likely to go off to someone else's land. In this case it is very costly to husband animals because the Indians would need to fence in a very large tract of land. In cost-benefit terms, the situation did not argue for the privatizing of lands in the Southwest. In fact, the Indians did not privatize land in the Southwest and buffalo herds were not able to withstand the scale of hunting that came about once Indians came into possession of rifles and horses.

Another example relates to the exploration of minerals under the earth. When it came to exploring for minerals, the general rule of law that governed the activity was called "rule of capture." What that meant was that anyone who wanted to could go down into his land and take the minerals out. With mineral resources, this doesn't cause any serious externality. A person takes iron ore or gold from his mine and no one else is affected. But when oil was discovered, what we had was a resource that flowed under pressure. And in this case sinking a well and pumping crude oil reduced the pressure in the oil field and made it more costly to retrieve all the oil in the field.

With the rule of capture, there is a great incentive for people to take crude oil out as fast as they can because if they don't someone else will (since the pool of oil is large enough to extend across tracts of private lands owned by different persons). The response to this was the unitization of the oil field, which means that no longer can an owner of an oil well take as much oil out of the ground as he wants. Instead, he can take only the amount that is determined jointly by all owners of the land holding the oil pool.

A third example concerns air space. With the coming of air transport, something that once was a free good—air space—became a scarce good, especially air space near the ground. As a result we got a change in property rights such that owners of land or homes near airports are entitled to quiet at certain times of the day.

You can go through a whole litany of cases in which you can see the relevance of externalities in the development of property rights. But I would put the proposition more generally than just in terms of externalities. We can look at property rights arrangements in cost-benefit terms. In some cases, demands and supplies change, and therefore the costs and benefits of privatizing change so that new rights replace old rights.

Within the property rights literature, two articles are widely cited. There is your article, "Toward a Theory of Property Rights," and Ronald Coase's "The Problem of Social Cost." What are the key insights provided in these two articles?

The articles appear to deal with the same subject but they really don't. The Coase article is not strictly about property rights. Coase takes the property rights system as completely defined and existing, then he gets into a debate with the Pigovians about externalities, showing that when transaction costs are zero, externali-

ties don't exist. If transaction costs are positive, the usual prescription for dealing with them in the Pigovian framework is not necessarily the correct prescription.

In my paper I am not really dealing with the externality problem in the same way, or even arguing with the Pigovians. What I'm trying to do is to explain why certain kinds of bundles of rights arise, and externalities (being a cost) are one clue as to why they arise. But as I stated earlier, a more general view is to look at costs and benefits of devising new property rights without special reference to the external costs associated with externalities.

In recent years, the media has reported on, and many people have viewed on television, the cruel clubbing to death of baby seals off Prince Edward Island in the Gulf of St. Lawrence. You have explained how this event is related to a particular property rights assignment. Will you repeat the main points of your argument for us?

There has been a legitimate public outcry about the hunt. The outcry has been about the inhuman behavior of the hunters, which is very paradoxical since the hunters are human. One shouldn't look to inhuman behavior to explain human behavior. One has to look elsewhere, and not very far.

The legal arrangement is such that annually some branch of the Canadian government decides how many seals are allowed to be taken, say, 50,000. Then the government allows a certain period of time—say one or two weeks—for anybody to come in and take the seals until the total of 50,000 is taken. That means the hunters treat the seals as a free good up to 50,000. At 50,000, seals become

an infinitely scarce good if the hunters abide by the law. That kind of legal arrangement is guaranteed to get very human people to hunt very quickly in order to get a large share of the seals before other people do and before the hunt ends. There is a great premium placed on fast hunting, and in hiring people who are agile, and on hiring people whose stomach doesn't turn when they hunt in this fashion.

You could of course avoid this behavior by prohibiting the hunt. But if you wanted to allow the hunt, you can get behavior that people would call more humane very easily. All you would have to do is sell people the right to take a number of seals. The hunters would then pay for the license to take a certain number of seals, with the total licenses being sold equal to the total number of seals the Canadian government wants to allow to be taken. And then the hunter could very patiently and with greater humanity, take the seals that he is entitled to by virtue of now having a property right in those seals. The only way he could get the property right in the seals in the previous arrangement was by killing them and by killing them quickly he got more. Under the arrangement I am proposing, the property right is created by the purchase, and the hunter is entitled to the seal, and he can take his time and handle the problem in a way that is more congenial to those people that have been complaining about the nature of the hunt.

Theory in Practice

Is No Pollution Worse Than Some Pollution?

Question: When might some pollution be preferred to no pollution? Answer: When all other things are not held constant. In short, most of the time.

Certainly if all other things are held constant, less pollution is preferred to more pollution, and therefore no pollution is preferred to some pollution. But the world would be different with no pollution—and not only in terms of having cleaner air, rivers, and oceans. Pollution is a byproduct of the production of many goods and services. For example, it is unlikely that steel could be produced without some pollu-

tion as a byproduct. Given the current state of pollution technology, less steel pollution means less steel and fewer products made from steel.

Pollution is also a byproduct of many of the goods we use daily, including our cars. We could certainly end car pollution tomorrow, but this would mean that we would have to give up driving cars. Are there any benefits to driving cars? If there are, then perhaps we wouldn't choose zero car pollution (since it probably would mean no cars and no driving). In short, zero pollution is not preferable to some positive amount of pollution once we take into consideration that we'll have fewer goods and services if we have less pollution.

The same conclusion can be reached through Coasian-type analysis. Suppose there are two groups: polluters and nonpolluters. For certain units of pollution, the value to polluters of polluting might be greater than the value of a less polluted environment to nonpolluters. In the presence of trivial or zero transaction costs, a deal will be struck. The outcome will be characterized by some positive amount of pollution.

more. As we previously noted, there may be benefits to dealing with externalities successfully, but the costs of dealing with them need to be taken into account as well.

Question:

Is there any one best way of dealing with externalities? It is not clear whether it is better to use persuasion to deal with externalities, or to use, say, taxes and subsidies.

Answer:

Almost all economists would agree that some methods of dealing with externalities are better in some situations than in others. For example, if the smoke from your neighbor's barbecue comes into your yard and bothers you, it is unlikely that any economist would think the negative externality situation at hand would warrant direct governmental involvement in the form of regulation or taxes. In this rather trivial case, persuasion may be the best way to proceed. In the case of a factory emitting smoke into the air, however, persuasion might not be effective. Nor might voluntary agreements, since the transaction costs of entering into an agreement would very likely be high (getting together all or most persons affected by the factory's smoke, is difficult, for example). In this case, the inclination to propose taxes or regulations would be strong.

Economics in Our Times

Interview: Murray Weidenbaum

Murray Weidenbaum was chairman of the Council of Economic Advisers under President Reagan from February 27, 1981, until August 25, 1982. The council offers economic analysis and advice to the president. Professor Weidenbaum is well known and respected for his work in the area of government regulation. He is currently at Washington University in St. Louis, Missouri, where he is the director of the Center for the Study of American Business. We conducted this interview with Professor Weidenbaum on March 11, 1988.

Professor Weidenbaum, for years you have studied government regulation in this country. Would you give us a few of (what you consider to be) the "right" reasons for regulation and a few of the "wrong" reasons?

One of the right reasons for regulation is to deal with situations where large externalities are present. The best example I can think of is air and water pollution, where cleaning up a dirty river, or reducing the pollutants in the air, may generate far more benefits than costs to the society. More specifically, the situation is one where sometimes the polluter faces greater private costs than benefits from doing so, and so he does not clean up the pollution. But society as a whole receives greater benefits than costs from having the pollution cleaned up. This is the standard case for government intervention. There are debates, of course, as to what is the best way for the government to intervene, but that is a different matter.

Let me give another example. Consider the case where the consumer does not have adequate information about a product and thus does not know of the hidden hazards of the product. The important thing here is to provide the consumer with additional information. In technical areas, the simplest thing may be for the Consumer Product Safety Commission to set standards that companies must meet. In other cases, it may be more effective to give the consumer more information as to the nature of the hazard. The same thing applies to the workplace.

As to the wrong reasons for regulation, examples include regulations that interfere with competition. Interstate trucking is an excellent example. Import restrictions are another. They reduce the choice to the consumer and raise price.

Most people suspect that regulation comes with a price tag, but they are uncertain how high or low that price is. Could you shed some light on this subject?

Let me first say that I view the costs of complying with regulation as a "hidden tax." And the very fact that it is hidden presents the basic problem for policy. Too often policymakers in promoting regulation crow about the visible benefits and do not have to worry about the costs because they are hidden in the form of higher prices paid for by the consumer.

So people see the benefits of regulation, but they don't realize the costs they are paying?

Precisely. Which of course brings up the need for cost-benefit analysis of proposed regulations. But of course we must be aware that there is a natural tendency on the part of regulators, and the proponents of regulation, to overestimate the benefits and underestimate the costs, and conversely those persons (potentially) subject to the regulation tend to overestimate the costs and underestimate the benefits. A certain sense of detachment needs to be present in evaluating any specific set of numbers.

It has been hypothesized that if the Gramm-Rudman-Hollings Act and other limits on deficits succeed in restricting government spending, legislators will try to satisfy the pressure from powerful special interest groups through regulations on the private sector. As a hypothetical example, instead of providing subsidized day care, Congress will simply enact a law requiring companies to provide day care on the premises. Is this kind of thing likely if government expenditures are cut to balance the budget?

The short answer is yes. In fact, you don't have to be hypothetical; the Congress is seriously considering legislation that will impose various types of social requirements on busi-

PUBLIC GOODS

Many economists argue that the market fails to produce public goods. A **public good** is a good that, once produced and provided to one person, gives benefits to more than that one person. The two characteristics of a public good are nonrivalry in consumption and nonexcludability.

Nonrivalry in Consumption

A good is **nonrivalrous in consumption** if its consumption by one person does not reduce its consumption by others. Consider national defense. Once produced, national defense protects all persons—not just some—in the protected georgraphical area (which may be as large as the entire United States). It is impossible to protect one person in Newark, New Jersey, from incoming missiles and not protect another person in New York City as well. And just as important, protecting the person in Newark does not reduce the degree of protection for the person in New York. National defense is nonrivalrous in consumption.

A good is **rivalrous in consumption** if its consumption by one person reduces its consumption by others. Let's look at an apple. If one person takes a bite out of an apple, there is that much less of the apple for someone else to consume. Many goods are rivalrous in consumption, such as cars, shoes, dresses, shirts, medical services, typewriters, pizzas, and hammocks. All such goods are known as private goods.

Nonexcludability

A good is **nonexcludable** if it is impossible, or prohibitively costly, to exclude someone from obtaining the benefits of the good once it has been produced. Consider national defense again. Once produced, it is impossible (or "prohibitively costly" if your penchant is to see nothing as impossible) to exclude someone from "consuming" its services. The same holds for flood control or large-scale pest control. Once the dam has been built, once the pest spray has been sprayed, it is impossible to exclude persons from benefiting from it.

Public Good

A good characterized by nonrivalry in consumption and nonexcludability.

Nonrivalrous in Consumption

A good is nonrivalrous in consumption if its consumption by one person does not reduce its consumption by others.

Rivalrous in Consumption

A good is rivalrous in consumption if its consumption by one person reduces its consumption by others.

Nonexcludability

A good is nonexcludable if it is impossible, or prohibitively costly, to exclude someone from receiving the benefits of the good once it has been produced.

A good is **excludable** if it is possible, or not prohibitively costly, to exclude someone from obtaining the benefits of the good once it has been produced. For example, a movie in a movie theater is excludable, in that persons who do not pay to see the movie can be excluded from seeing it. Other goods that fit into this category include typewriters, radios, rock concerts, swimming pools, tennis courts, and hotel rooms.

Nonrivalry Does Not Necessarily Imply Nonexcludability

There is a tendency to believe that any good that is nonrivalrous in consumption is also nonexcludable. This is erroneous. It is possible to have a good that is both nonrivalrous in consumption and excludable. Once again, consider a movie in a movie theater. The movie can be seen equally (or very nearly equally) by everyone in the theater. If Gloria views the movie, this does not prevent Franco from viewing it, too.

It is possible, though, to exclude someone from viewing the movie. If a person does not pay the admittance fee to see the movie, he will not be permitted into the movie theater—he will be excluded. A movie, then, is an example of a good that is both nonrivalrous in consumption and excludable.

Does this mean a movie in a movie theater is a public good? No, it doesn't, because the movie doesn't possess both characteristics of a public good: nonrivalry in consumption and nonexcludability. It only possesses nonrivalry in consumption.

What about national defense? Is it a public good? Yes, it is, since it is both nonrivalrous in consumption and nonexcludable.

The Free Rider

When a good is nonexcludable, it is possible for individuals to obtain the benefits of the good without paying for it. Persons who do so are referred to as **free riders.** It is because of the so-called free rider problem that most economists hold that the market will fail to produce public goods, or fail to produce them at a desired level.

Consider someone contemplating the production of public good X. The good is nonrivalrous in consumption and nonexcludable; therefore once it has been produced and provided to one person, there is no incentive for others to pay for it (even if they demand it) since they can receive its benefits without paying. No one is likely to supply a good for which no one has to pay in order to consume. The market, it is argued, will not produce public goods. The door then is opened to government involvement in the production of public goods. It is often stated that if the market will not produce public goods, although they are demanded, then the government must.

The free rider argument is the basis for accepting government (the public or taxpayers) provision of public goods. We need remind ourselves, though, that there is a difference between a *public good* and a *government-provided good.* A public good has already been defined: It is a good that is nonrivalrous in consumption and nonexcludable. A government-provided good is any good provided by government (or by the public or taxpayers). In some instances, a government-provided good is a public good, such as when government furnishes national defense. But it need not be. Government furnishes mail delivery and education, two goods that are also provided privately, and are excludable and thus not subject to free riding.

Question:

It seems that the market only fails to produce a demanded good when the good is nonexcludable, because the free rider problem only arises if the good is nonexcludable. The rivalry vs. nonrivalry issue is not relevant to the issue of market failure; that is, a good can be rivalrous in consumption or nonrivalrous in consumption and still be produced by the market. Isn't this correct?

Answer:

That is correct. As we noted earlier, a movie may be nonrivalrous in consumption, but be excludable, too. And we know that the market has no problem producing movies and movie theaters. The free rider problem only occurs with goods that are nonexcludable.

Also relevant to the question is the case of "the lighthouse in economics."[2] For a long time, a lighthouse was thought to have the two characteristics of a public good: (1) It is nonrivalrous in consumption—any ship can use the light from the lighthouse, and one ship's use of the light does not detract from another's. (2) It is also nonexcludable—it is difficult to exclude any nonpaying ships from using the light. Thus the lighthouse seemed to be a perfect good for government provision.

There is only one problem. The economist Ronald Coase found that in the eighteenth and early nineteenth centuries many lighthouses were privately owned, which meant that the market had not failed to provide lighthouses. Economists were left to conclude either that the market could provide public goods, or that the lighthouse wasn't a public good as had been thought. Closer examination showed the lighthouse was nonrivalrous in consumption, but that the costs of excluding others from using it were fairly low. Lighthouse owners knew that usually only one ship was near the lighthouse at a time and that they could turn off the lights if a ship did not exhibit the flag of a paying vessel.

SOME INTERESTING EXTERNALITY AND PUBLIC GOODS ISSUES

Externality and public goods theory has a number of interesting "real-world" applications. Here we present a few interesting issues that relate to externalities and public goods.

Acid Rain

Acid rain is a "rain" or "mist" that carries a mixture of sulfur-dioxide gases and nitrous-oxide emissions. When it falls to the earth, it is thought to destroy forests and pollute lakes and rivers, killing fish. Scientists are not agreed on the causes of acid rain. Some blame the emissions from industrial plants. Others say it is principally due to car exhausts.

Additionally, scientists and nonscientists disagree as to where acid rain first arises. The Canadians say it originates largely in the United States. Individuals who live in the East say it originates in the Midwest. Midwesterners say it originates in the East. Obviously we have a problem here—specifically, a negative externality problem. But how do we solve it? Should we use persuasion? What about assigning property rights in the air? If we did this, we would still have a problem because even if a

[2]See Ronald Coase, "The Lighthouse in Economics," *Journal of Law and Economics* 19 (October 1976).

group of people owned the air, how would they know exactly who was polluting it? Will voluntary agreements work? One problem with voluntary agreements is that no one knows for sure who is creating the acid rain and to what degree? We could tax the activities that we think are generating the negative externality, but this does not place us on very solid ground. What about direct regulation? We still do not know who to regulate and to what degree. Besides there are costs to regulation. Thus the problem of acid rain—a negative externality problem—is a sticky one that is not likely to be dealt with in a way that is satisfactory to everyone.

Question:

What is the significance of this acid rain example?

Answer:

First, it shows that acid rain is a negative externality problem, which may help some people to view it in a new way. Second, it illustrates that some negative externalities are more difficult to deal with than others. Acid rain is particularly difficult to deal with because, among other things, not everyone is agreed as to its cause or its birthplace.

Traffic Congestion

In most cases, roads are provided by government. The often-cited justification for this is that roads are public goods; they are nonrivalrous in consumption (for the most part, one person's driving on the road does not prevent another person from driving on the road) and nonexcludable (it might be prohibitively costly to exclude someone from driving on the road; there would have to be gates everywhere).

The payment scheme worked out for the production of roads is quite simple. Taxes are raised and spent to construct roads; then once the roads are constructed, no one has to make a direct monetary payment to drive on most roads (turnpikes are the notable exception). We conclude that once a person has paid his or her taxes, there is a zero (money) price to driving on roads. And economists are quick to point out that the quantity demanded of a good is greater at a zero price than at some positive price.

The zero price of driving on roads often leads to traffic congestion (see Chapter 4). In many big cities around the world, traffic is bumper to bumper on major roadways during the "rush hour" period early in the morning and in the evening. Can anything be done about rush hour traffic or must individuals simply grin and bear it?

Some economists have argued that roads are not, and never have been, public goods. First, although they are nonrivalrous in consumption at some times, such as when there are few cars on the roads, at other times, such as rush hour, they are rivalrous in consumption. Second, they are not nonexcludable (which means they are excludable). The existence of tolls and the like proves this. Does this mean government should sell the roads to private investors and permit private roads and private pricing schemes?

In Hong Kong the government has started to experiment with a market approach to rationing road space. Cars are fitted with an electronic number plate, which is read by electronic devices buried under the roads at frequently congested intersections. The license number is relayed to a central computer that adds a fee to the car owner's monthly bill. A car owner can lower his monthly bill by deciding not to drive on certain roads. It is also possible for the price of driving on certain roads to increase at certain times of the day. For example, when the demand for the road space is high, the price will be higher than when the demand for the road space is low. By selling road space on a market basis, critics of government-provided roads charge, the continuing problems of "shortages" and "surpluses" of road space will be solved.

Smoking Sections in Restaurants

Recall the days before there were smoking and nonsmoking sections in most restaurants. Shelly Blevins, a nonsmoker, is seated at a table next to Diane Mueller, a chain smoker. Shelly is quietly eating her meal when cigarette smoke wafts its way over to her nose. She gives Diane a dirty look, but the latter doesn't notice because she is busy lighting up another cigarette. We have a negative externality situation that raises the question: Who has the right to do what? Does Shelly have the right to sit quietly in the restaurant and eat her meal in a smokeless environment? Does Diane have the right to sit quietly in the restaurant and enjoy herself by smoking a few cigarettes?

Can this externality problem be resolved through persuasion or voluntary agreement? Shelly could lean over to Diane and ask her to refrain from smoking. That might work. Or Shelly and Diane might try to enter into a voluntary agreement. If eating in a smokeless environment is worth more to Shelly than smoking cigarettes is to Diane, then Shelly could pay Diane not to smoke. Most likely, though, time is short in a restaurant and most people will not work out voluntary agreements relevant to smoking and not smoking, nor will most persons try to persuade others to change their habits. Thus the negative externality problem in the restaurant is not likely to be solved through persuasion or voluntary agreements.

Restaurant owners have largely solved the problem by separating the two groups of customers. Most restaurants now have smoking and nonsmoking sections. The negative externality problem has been solved, one would assume, in the least costly manner.

Is Charitable Giving Subject to Free Riding?

Some persons contend that charitable giving is a public good and subject to free riding. Consider a particular case. Bill McDonald is the type of person who receives utility when individuals less fortunate than he are being helped. When a homeless person is given a home, he feels good inside. When he learns that a rich entrepreneur in Dallas has decided to pay the college tuition of 20 poor, college-age students, it makes his day. Notice that charitable giving appears to be a public good. It is nonrivalrous in consumption and nonexcludable. If the rich entrepreneur in Dallas pays the tuition of 20 poor, college-age students, Bill McDonald receives utility from such a gesture as easily as the rich entrepreneur; and it is impossible to exclude him from receiving the utility once the rich entrepreneur's charitable giving has been reported.

We explained earlier that a public good is subject to free riding. Is Bill McDonald a free rider? Will he take a free ride on the charitable giving of others? Using the following line of reasoning, many persons argue that he will: (1) The average person's charitable contribution is a tiny percentage of total charitable contributions ($75 out of many millions). (2) Consequently, the average person realizes that even if he or she does not make a charitable contribution, charitable giving by others will not be

Economics in Our Times

Economics 22,300 Miles High, or You Can See for Miles and Miles

Economics has moved beyond the classroom, the city, the state, and the nation. It has moved into outer space. The reason is simple; space has become scarce (and as you will recall from Chapter 1, the bedrock upon which economics rests is scarcity). Space is scarce today because of the increased use of satellites. These satellites are used to transmit live news reports or telephone calls from the other side of the world, to monitor weather conditions (for example, hurricanes), and to monitor the military operations of other countries. The best place to put these satellites for transmission purposes is 22,300 miles above the earth in an area called the geostationary orbital arc. The arcs of the orbital paths that are of greatest interest to the United States lie between 60 degrees and 135 degrees west longitude because a satellite placed in this area can serve the entire continental United States. Unfortunately for the United States, this orbital arc is also of great interest to Canada, Mexico, and Latin America.

Owing to space congestion, these countries and companies in these countries cannot put as many satellites as they want into this area of space. To minimize the chance of collisions, as well as signal interfer-

ence, satellites must be positioned a certain distance from each other. For example, technical considerations require that each satellite be placed approximately 2–3 degrees away from any other satellite using the same transmission frequency. This means that there are only so many space slots for satellites to occupy. INTELSAT, the international telecommunications satellite organization, has projected that slots in some orbital arcs will be filled by the early 1990s.

Space congestion exists in outer space because no one owns space. In 1967, the United Nations Committee on the Peaceful Uses of Outer Space drafted the Outer Space Treaty, which said that all nations have equal rights to the resources of space. In other words, space is communal property—all nations "own" it. But as we know, communal property rarely provides the incentives necessary for efficient use. Many economists predict that the present system of rationing space slots according to first-come-first-served (zero price) is bound to produce negative externalities in the future.

For example, suppose a particular space area already is congested. If one more satellite is launched into the area, it will increase the risks of signal interference and collision for all the other satellites in the area and will be viewed as a negative externality by the owners of the other satellites.

This situation is similar to the cattle rancher–farmer example we discussed earlier. What are each party's rights in the congested area? If space is "owned" by everyone, doesn't the nation that wants to put a satellite into space have the right to do so? But on the other hand, don't the nations and companies that already have satellites in space have the right to use "their"

space property in a way that minimizes the risks to their satellites?

One of the ways to solve the externality problem is to *assign property rights* in space slots. Let's say Space Slot 1 is assigned (we will skirt the issue for now of who or what assigns the property right to whom) to company X. Since company X's computations show that Space Slot 1 can safely accommodate three satellites of a certain size and transmission frequency, it figures that it can maximize profits by limiting its satellite occupants to three. Therefore it leases space in its space slot for $Y per time period. Any intruder satellites in its space will be dealt with harshly—after all, they will be on private property without permission.

If space is private property, space slots are likely to be put to their highest-valued use (in much the same way that an acre of land in the center of the city will be purchased by the person(s) who will put the land to its highest-valued use.) The situation in space is analogous to the situation in a city with high rent districts, say, New York City. Just as prime lots in New York fetch high prices, prime slots in space would fetch high prices. The persons who buy the high-priced lots in New York make it worth their while by building tall skyscrapers and renting office space to thousands of tenants. The persons who buy high-priced slots in space would make it worth their while by building large satellites that carry many transponders, the devices that bounce back communication signals. Then the company that owns the satellite can rent out the transponders to clients. Since space is scarce, it may be better to have a few large satellites in space with many transponders than many small satellites with a few transponders. Clearly, allocating property rights in space will force people to economize on this scarce resource.

To Whom Do the Space Slots Go?

Property rights in space can be allocated in numerous ways, none of which seems to generate unanimous approval. Some economists have proposed that space slots be auctioned off, but this has been criticized on the ground that poor countries will be at a disadvantage in the bidding. Some have proposed that each nation should receive a quota of slots. Then nations that currently lack the technology to put a satellite in space could rent out their slots or sell them. Others have proposed that a lottery be held with the "winners" chosen at random. As these proposals suggest, deciding the distribution of space slots raises the issue of equity. In many ways, equity is the stumbling block to assigning property rights in space since it is doubtful that the nations of the world will agree on what is equitable here.

We don't know when property rights will be assigned in space, nor do we know how these property rights will be assigned. We do predict, however, that sooner or later space will be subject to property rights assignments. The impending externality problems are the reason why.

much different (total charitable contributions will be less by only $75—a mere drop in the bucket). (3) A person has an incentive to become a free rider once the person realizes that his or her contribution will not affect total charitable contributions by more than the tiniest amount and that he or she can benefit from the charitable giving of others. What is the moral of the story? When a person feels that his contribution is insignificant to the total contribution, or that the benefits he receives from a good will not be appreciably different in the absence of his paying for it, then he has a strong incentive to become a free rider.

Free Riders and the Size of the Group: Can Committees Get Too Big?

As we have just seen, a person has a strong incentive to become a free rider if his contribution is insignificant to the total contribution, or the benefits he receives from a good will not be appreciably different in the absence of his paying for it. Now we ask, Is there anything, that if changed, would affect both the way a person views his contribution vis-à-vis the total contribution and the benefits received from a good in the absence of paying for it? The answer is *the size of the group*. All other things held constant, the larger the group size, the smaller or less significant the individual's contribution relative to the total contribution, and the less likely the benefits received from a good will be appreciably different in the absence of paying for it.

For example, if the group size is one million, then one person's contribution is a smaller percentage of the total contribution than if the group size is ten. We conclude that as the group size decreases, the incentive to become a free rider becomes less; as the group size increases, the incentive to become a free rider becomes greater. We would expect to find fewer free riders in small groups than in large groups.

Relate this to the size of a committee. A large committee of 20–30 persons is likely to contain more free riders than a committee of 4–6 persons. In a large committee, each individual's contribution is a smaller percentage of the total contribution of the group, and therefore doing little or nothing does not appreciably affect the results as much as it would in a small committee. One person taking a free ride in a large committee is not as likely to be noticed or felt as one person taking a free ride in a small committee. We would expect more free riding in large committees than in small committees. It follows from this, that small committees are likely to accomplish more than large committees.

■ CHAPTER SUMMARY

Externalities

■ An externality is a side effect of an action that affects the well-being of third parties. There are two types of externalities: negative and positive. A negative externality exists when an individual's or group's actions cause a cost (adverse side effect) to be felt by others. A positive externality exists when an individual's or group's actions cause a benefit (beneficial side effect) to be felt by others.

■ When either negative or positive externalities exist, the market output is different from the socially optimal output. In the case of a negative externality, the market is said to overproduce the good connected with the negative externality (the socially optimal output is less than the market output). In the case of a positive externality, the market is said to underproduce the good connected with the positive externality (the socially optimal output is greater than the market output). See Exhibits 18-1 and 18-3.

■ Negative and positive externalities can be internalized or adjusted for in a number of different ways, including persuasion, the assignment of property rights, voluntary agreements, and taxes and subsidies. Additionally, regulations may be used to adjust for externalities directly.

The Coase Theorem

■ The Coase theorem holds that in the case of trivial or zero transaction costs, the property rights assignment does not matter to the resource allocative outcome. To put it differently, a property rights assignment will be undone if it benefits the relevant parties to undo it. The Coase theorem is significant for two reasons: (1) It shows that under certain conditions the market can internalize externalities. (2) It provides a benchmark for analyzing externality problems—that is, it shows what would happen if transactions costs were trivial or zero.

Public Goods

■ A public good is a good characterized by nonrivalry in consumption and nonexcludability. The market is said to fail in the provision of public goods. The market's failure is a consequence of the nature of a public good; a supplier of the good would not be able to extract payment for the good since its benefits can be received without making payment. In short, the market fails because of the free rider problem associated with public goods.

■ There is a difference between a public good and a government-provided good. A public good is a good that is nonrivalrous in consumption and nonexcludable. A government-provided good is any good provided by government. Sometimes a public good and a government-provided good are the same; for example, national defense. Sometimes they are not.

■ QUESTIONS TO ANSWER AND DISCUSS

1. Give an example that illustrates the difference between private costs and social costs.

2. Consider two types of divorce laws. Law A allows either the husband or the wife to obtain a divorce without the other person's consent. Law B permits a divorce only if both parties agree to the divorce. Will there be more divorces under law A or law B, or will there be the same number of divorces under both laws?

3. People have a demand for sweaters, and the market provides sweaters. There is evidence that people also have a demand for national defense, yet the market does not provide national defense. What is the reason the market does not provide national defense? Is it because government is providing national defense and therefore there is no need for the market to do so, or because the market won't provide national defense?

4. Education is often said to generate positive externalities. How might it do this?

5. Give an example of each of the following:
   a. A good rivalrous in consumption and excludable
   b. A good nonrivalrous in consumption and excludable
   c. A good rivalrous in consumption and nonexcludable
   d. A good nonrivalrous in consumption and nonexcludable

6. Some individuals argue that with increased population growth, negative externalities will become more common, and there will be more instances of market failure and more need for government to solve externality problems. Other individuals argue that as time passes, technological advances will be made and used to solve negative externality problems. They conclude that over time there will be fewer instances of market failure and less need for government to deal with externality problems. What do you believe will happen? Give reasons to support your position.

7. Name at least five government-provided goods that are not public goods.

8. Some individuals hold that "life is one big externality." Just about everything that someone does affects someone else either positively or negatively. To permit government to deal with externality problems is to permit government to tamper with everything in life. There is no clear dividing line between externalities government should and should not become involved in. Do you support this position? Why or why not?

9. Economists sometimes shock noneconomists by stating that they do not favor the complete elimination of pollution. Explain the rationale for this position.

Chapter 19

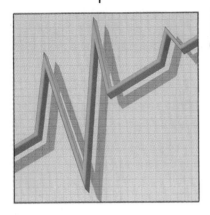

Public Choice: Economic Theory Applied to Politics

■ INTRODUCTION

The time has come for all of us, rich and poor, black and white, urban and rural, to work together for the betterment of our children's lives. We must begin today to make sure that they have a bright future.

—A politician running for office

I don't know. There doesn't seem to be much difference between the two candidates. I guess I'll flip a coin.

—A voter

I think he'll vote our way.

—A member of a special-interest group

I'm sick and tired of the public thinking we don't work hard. I work extremely hard. No one really understands how hard.

—A bureaucrat

■ WHAT THIS CHAPTER IS ABOUT

The last chapter was about *market failure*. To a large degree, this chapter is about *government failure*. Government failure is said to exist when government enacts policies that produce inefficient and/or inequitable results as a consequence of the rational behavior of the participants in the political process—politicians, voters, special-interest groups, and bureaucrats.

   In this chapter we examine the workings of government; specifically, we take a look at politicians, voters, special-interest groups, and government bureaucracy. Our subject is *public choice*: the branch of economics that deals with the application of economic principles and tools to public-sector decision making.

Key Questions to Keep in Mind as You Read

1. What is public choice?

2. Why do political candidates in a two-person race move toward the middle of the political spectrum?

3. Why do politicians speak in general terms instead of getting specific on the issues?

4. Why are so many voters largely uninformed on the issues? What is rational ignorance?

5. Why is there so much special-interest legislation?

PUBLIC CHOICE

Public Choice
The branch of economics that deals with the application of economic principles and tools to public-sector decision making.

Before turning to specific topics within the domain of **public choice,** we examine some of the analytical methods used by public choice theorists.

Individuals and Institutional Arrangements

Public choice theorists reject the notion that people are schizophrenic, exhibiting greed and selfishness in their transactions in the private (market) sector and altruism and public spirit in their actions in the public sector. The same people who are employers, employees, and consumers in the market sector are the politicians, bureaucrats, special-interest group members, and voters in the public sector. According to public choice theorists, differences between the behavior of people in the market sector and people in the public sector are due not to different motives (or the way people are), but to the different institutional arrangements in the two sectors.

To illustrate, consider a simple example. Erin Bloom currently works for a private, profit-seeking firm that makes radio components. Erin is cost conscious, does her work on time, and generally works hard. She knows that she must exhibit this particular work behavior if she wants to be promoted.

Time passes. Erin leaves her job at the radio components company and takes a job with the Department of Health and Human Services (HHS) in Washington, D.C. Is Erin a different person (with different motives) working for HHS than she was working for the radio components company? Public choice theorists would say no.

But simply because Erin is the same person in and out of government, it does not necessarily follow that she will exhibit the same work behavior. The reason is that the costs and benefits of certain actions may be substantially different at HHS than at the radio components company.

For example, perhaps the cost of being late for work is less in Erin's new job at HHS than at her old job. In her job at the radio components company, she had to work overtime if she came in late; in her new job, her boss doesn't say anything when she comes in late. We predict that Erin is more likely to be late in her new job than she was in her old one. She is simply responding to costs and benefits as they exist in her new work environment.

Question:

Some people talk as if government is made up exclusively of good and giving people, who have nothing but the public good in mind. Other people talk as if government is made up exclusively of bad and grabbing people, who have nothing but their own welfare at stake. Are public choice theorists saying that both are caricatures of the real people who work in government?

Answer:

Yes, they are. As one of the first public choice theorists, James Buchanan, has said: "If men should cease and desist from their talk about and their search for evil men [and his sentiments include "purely good men," too] and commence to look instead at the institutions manned by ordinary people, wide avenues for genuine social reform might appear."[1]

THE POLITICAL MARKET

Positive economists want to understand the world they live in. This means not only understanding such things as the production and pricing of goods, unemployment, inflation, and the firm but also understanding political outcomes and political behavior. This section is an introduction to the political market.

Moving Toward the Middle

I never lied to you, I always been cool
I want to be elected.
I got to get the votes, I talk about schools
I want to be elected.
Elected
Elected
I want to be elected . . .
　　　　　　　　　—From the song *Elected* by Alice Cooper

During political elections, voters often complain that the candidates for office are "too much alike." Some find this frustrating; they say they would prefer to have more choice.

As Exhibit 19-1 illustrates, two candidates running for the same office often sound alike because of the competition for votes: (a), (b), and (c) show a distribution of voters. The political spectrum goes from the "Far Left" to the "Far Right," and it should be noticed that (relatively) few voters hold positions in either of the two extreme wings—that is, in the Far Left wing or the Far Right wing.

Additionally, we assume that voters will vote for the candidate who comes closest to matching their own ideological or political views. For example, the person whose views are in the Far Left of the political spectrum will vote for the candidate closest to the Far Left.

Our election process begins with two candidates, a Democrat and a Republican, occupying the positions D_1 and R_1 in (a), respectively. If the election were held today, the Republican would receive more votes than his Democratic opponent. The Republican would receive all the votes of the voters who position themselves to the right of R_1, the Democrat would receive all the votes of the voters who position themselves to the left of D_1, and the voters between R_1 and D_1 would be split down the middle between the two candidates. Given this, the Republican would receive more votes than the Democrat.

If, however, the election were not held today, the Democrat would likely notice (through polls and the like) that his opponent was doing better than he, and to offset this he would move toward the center, or middle, of the political spectrum to pick up some votes; (b) illustrates this move by the Democrat. Relative to his position in

[1]James Buchanan, *The Limits of Liberty, between Anarchy and Leviathan* (Chicago: University of Chicago Press, 1975), p. 149. An interview with Buchanan appears near the end of this chapter.

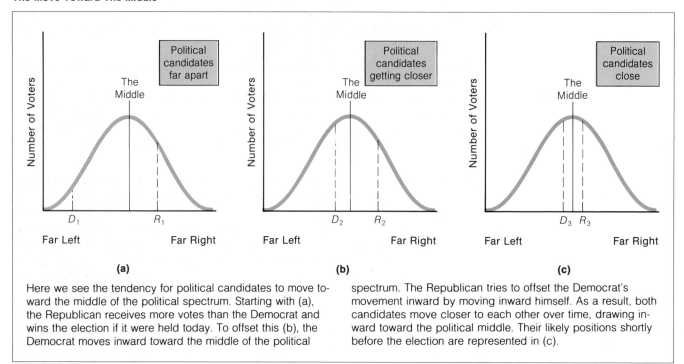

Here we see the tendency for political candidates to move toward the middle of the political spectrum. Starting with (a), the Republican receives more votes than the Democrat and wins the election if it were held today. To offset this (b), the Democrat moves inward toward the middle of the political spectrum. The Republican tries to offset the Democrat's movement inward by moving inward himself. As a result, both candidates move closer to each other over time, drawing inward toward the political middle. Their likely positions shortly before the election are represented in (c).

(a), the Democrat is closer to the middle of the political spectrum, and as a result he picks up votes. Voters to the left of D_2 vote for the Democrat, voters to the right of R_2 vote for the Republican, and the voters between the two positions split their votes equally between the two candidates. If the election were held now, the Democrat would win the election.

In (c) each candidate, in an attempt to get more votes than his or her opponent, moves toward the middle of the political spectrum. At election time, the likely position of the two candidates is *side-by-side at the political center or middle*. Notice that in (c) both candidates have become "middle-of-the-roaders" in their attempt to pick up votes. This tendency to move to a position at the center of the distribution is what causes many voters to complain that there is not much difference between the candidates for political office.

What Does the Theory Predict?

The theory we have just presented has explanatory power; it explains why politicians running for the same office often sound alike. But what does the theory predict? Here are a few of its predictions:

1. **Candidates will label their opponents as either "too far right" or "too far left."**
   The candidates know that the one closer to the middle of the political spectrum (in a two-person race) will win more votes and thus the election. As we noted earlier, to accomplish this feat, they will move toward the political middle. At the same time, they will say that their opponent is a member of the political fringe (that is, a person far from the center).

For example, a Democrat will argue that his Republican opponent is "too conservative." A Republican will argue that his Democratic opponent is "too liberal." You may have noticed this phenomenon in the 1988 presidential election between George Bush and Michael Dukakis when, for example, Bush frequently referred to Dukakis as being "out of the mainstream."

2. **Candidates will call themselves "middle-of-the-roaders," not right- or left-wingers.** In their move toward the political middle, candidates will try to portray themselves as moderates. In their speeches, they will make the point that they represent the majority of voters, that they are practical, not ideological, persons. They will not be likely to refer to themselves as "ultra-liberal" or "ultra-conservative," or as right- or left-wingers, because to do so would send the wrong message to the voters.[2]

3. **Candidates will take polls, and if they are not doing well in the polls and their opponent is, they will modify their positions to become slightly more like their opponent.** Polls tell candidates who the likely winner of the election will be. A candidate who finds out that she would lose the election (she is down in the polls) in not likely to sit back and do nothing. The candidate will change her positions. Often this means becoming more like the winner of the poll; that is, becoming more like her opponent in the political race. We illustrated this process in Exhibit 19-1.

4. **Candidates will speak in general instead of specific terms.** Voters agree more on *ends* than on the *means* to accomplishing those ends. For example, voters of the left, right, and middle believe that a strong economy is better than a weak economy. They do not all agree, however, on the best way to obtain a strong economy. The person on the right might advocate less government intervention as a way to strengthen the economy, while the person on the left might advocate more government intervention. Most political candidates soon learn that addressing the issues specifically involves discussing "means," and that doing so

[2]The headline in the *Wall Street Journal* on October 11, 1988 captures the essence of what we are talking about. It reads: "Bush's Speeches Are Moving Closer to the Middle In Bid to Broaden Base of Support Among Voters."

"He stands there all day, saying nothing, promising everything. He calls it politics."

Theory in Practice

Simple Majority Voting and Inefficiency: The Case of the Statue in the Public Square

The simple majority decision rule is often used to decide public questions. Most people think this is the fair and democratic way to do things. However, there are instances where a simple majority vote leads to a project being undertaken whose costs are greater than its benefits.

Consider a ten-person community. The names of the individuals in the community are listed in column 1 of Exhibit 19-2. The community is considering whether to purchase a statue (a replica of the Statue of Liberty) to put in the center of the public square. The cost of the statue is $1,000, and the community has previously agreed that if the statue is purchased, the ten individuals will share the cost equally—that is, each will pay $100 in taxes (see column 3).

Column 2 notes the dollar value of the benefits each individual will receive from the statue. For example, Applebaum places a dollar value of $150 on the statue, Browning

places a dollar value of $140 on the statue, and so on. Column 4 notes the net benefit (+) or net cost (−) of the statue to each individual. There is a net benefit for an individual if the dollar value he or she places on the statue is greater than the tax (cost) he or she must incur. There is a net cost if the reverse holds true. Finally, column 5 indicates how each of the ten individuals would vote. If an individual believes there is a net benefit to the statue, he or she will vote "for" it. If an individual believes there is a net cost to the statue, he or she will vote "against" it. Six individuals vote for the statue, and four individuals vote against it. The majority rules, and the statue is purchased and placed in the center of the public square.

Notice, though, that the total dollar value of benefits to the community ($812) is less than the total tax cost to the community ($1,000). In short, using the simple majority decision rule has resulted in a situation where a statue has been purchased although the benefits of the statue to the community are *less* than the costs of the statue to the community.

This outcome should not be shocking once it is understood that the simple majority decision rule does not take into account the intensity of individuals' preferences. No matter how strongly a person feels about the issue, he or she simply registers one vote. For example, even though Emerson places a net benefit of $1 on the statue, and Isley places a net cost of $90 on the statue, for purposes of voting, each individual has only one vote. There is no way for Isley to register that he does not want the statue more than Emerson wants it.

■ **EXHIBIT 19-2**
Simple Majority Voting and Inefficiency
The simple majority decision rule sometimes generates inefficient results. Here the statue is purchased even though the total dollar value of the benefits of the statue is less than the total dollar costs.

(1) INDIVIDUALS	(2) DOLLAR VALUE OF BENEFITS TO INDIVIDUAL	(3) TAX LEVIED ON INDIVIDUAL	(4) NET BENEFIT (+) OR NET COST (−)	(5) VOTE FOR OR AGAINST
Applebaum	$150	$ 100	+ $50	For
Browning	140	100	+ 40	For
Carson	130	100	+ 30	For
Davidson	110	100	+ 10	For
Emerson	101	100	+ 1	For
Finley	101	100	+ 1	For
Gunter	50	100	− 50	Against
Harris	10	100	− 90	Against
Isley	10	100	− 90	Against
Janowitz	10	100	− 90	Against
Total	$812	$1,000		

increases the probability that they will have an extreme-wing label attached to them.

For example, the candidate who advocates less government intervention in the economy is more likely to be labeled a "right-winger" than a candidate who simply calls for a stronger national economy without discussing the specific means he would use to bring this about. In the candidate's desire to be perceived as a middle-of-the-roader, he is much more likely to talk about ends, on which voters agree, than about means, on which voters disagree.

VOTERS AND RATIONAL IGNORANCE

The preceding section explained something about the behavior of politicians, especially near or at election time. We turn now to a discussion of voters.

The Costs and Benefits of Voting

Political commentators often remark that the voter turnout for a particular election was low. They might say, "Only 54 percent of the registered voters actually voted." Are voter turnouts low because Americans are apathetic or because they do not care who wins an election? Are they uninterested in politics, government, and related issues? Public choice economists often explain low voter turnouts in terms of the costs and benefits of voting.

Consider Mark Quincy who is thinking about voting in a presidential election. Mark may receive many benefits from voting. He may feel more involved in public affairs, he may feel that he has met his civic responsibility, he may feel more patriotic, he may feel he has a greater right to criticize government if he takes an active part in it. In short, he may benefit from seeing himself as a doer instead of a talker. Ultimately, however, he will weigh these positive benefits against the costs of voting, which include driving to the polls, standing in line, and so on. If, in the end, Mark perceives the benefits of voting as greater than the costs, he will vote.

But suppose Mark believes that he only benefits from voting if his vote will have an impact on the election outcome. In other words, if his vote will make the difference between candidate X winning and candidate Y winning, then Mark sees voting as worthwhile; if not, he sees voting as a waste of time. In that case, it is not likely that Mark will vote. For example, in a presidential election, where millions of votes will be cast, the probability that one voter's vote will affect the election outcome is very small. The truth of the matter is (probably) that with or without Mark's vote, the election outcome will be the same.

The point that public choice economists make is that *if* many individual voters will only vote if they perceive their vote as making a difference, *then* it is not likely they will vote because it is not likely that their vote will make a difference. Once again, in most elections, a single vote is a tiny percentage of the total votes cast. We conclude that the low turnouts that appear to be a result of voter apathy may instead be a result of cost-benefit calculations.

Rational Ignorance

"Democracy would be better served if only the voters took more of an interest in, and became better informed about, politics and government. They don't know much about the issues." How often have you heard this?

The problem is not that voters are too stupid to learn about the issues. Many persons who know little about politics and government are quite capable of learning about both, *but they choose not to learn.*

But why would many voter-citizens choose to be uninformed about politics and government? The answer is perhaps predictable: because the benefits of becoming informed are often outweighed by the costs of becoming informed. In short, many persons believe that becoming informed is simply not worth the effort; hence, on an individual basis, it makes sense to be uninformed about politics and government, to be in a state of **rational ignorance.**

Rational Ignorance
The state of not acquiring information because the costs of acquiring the information are greater than the benefits.

Look at the case of Shonia Tyler. Shonia has many things she could be doing with her time: She could be earning a living, reading a good novel, watching a television program, going out with friends. Shonia could also be becoming better informed about the candidates and the issues in the upcoming U.S. Senate race.

There are costs associated with becoming informed, however. If Shonia stays home and reads up on the issues, she can't go out with her friends. If she stays up late to watch a news program, she might be tired at work the next day. These costs have to be weighed against the benefits of becoming better informed about the candidates and the issues. For Shonia, as for many people, the benefits aren't likely to be greater than the costs. Many persons see little personal benefit to becoming more knowledgeable about political candidates and issues. Very likely this is linked to the small impact any single individual can have in a large-numbers setting (see the preceding section, "The Costs and Benefits of Voting").

Question:

Earlier it was said that politicians move toward the middle of the political spectrum to increase the probability that they will win the election. Now it turns out that the voter in the middle of the political spectrum, or any other voter for that matter, isn't likely to be knowledgeable about the issues. Doesn't this imply that politicians are trying to match the political preferences of a group of largely uninformed voters?

Answer:

Yes, it does. Many persons believe this is one of the deficiencies of representative democracy.

SPECIAL-INTEREST GROUPS

Special-Interest Groups

Subsets of the general population that hold (usually) intense preferences for or against a particular government service, activity, or policy. Often special-interest groups gain from public policies that may not be in accord with the interests of the general public.

Special-interest groups are subsets of the general population that hold (usually) intense preferences for or against a particular government service, activity, or policy. Often special-interest groups gain from public policies that may not be in accord with the interests of the general public. In recent decades they have played a major role in government.

Special-Interest Groups: Informational Content and Lobbying Efforts

For the most part, the general voter will be uninformed on the issues. The same does not hold for members of a special-interest group. For example, it is likely that teachers will know a lot about government education policies; farmers will know a lot about government farm policies; union members will know a lot about government union policies. On "their" issue, the members of a particular special-interest group will know much more about the issue at hand than the general voter will know. The reason for this is simple: The more directly and intensely issues affect them, the greater the incentive of individuals to become informed on the issues.

When we bring together the uninformed general voters and the informed members of a special-interest group, what we often observe is that the special-interest group

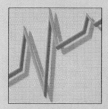

Theory in Practice

A Simple Quiz You Are Likely to Fail (but That's Not Bad)

Rational ignorance is usually easier to see in others than in ourselves. We understand that most people are not well informed on politics and government, but we often fail to put ourselves into the same category, even when we deserve to be there. We can take a giant leap forward in understanding rational ignorance and special-interest legislation if we see ourselves more clearly. With this in mind, try to answer the following ten questions about politics or government.

1. What is the name of your most recently elected U.S. senator, and what party does he or she belong to?
2. How has your congressional representative voted in any of the last 20 votes in Congress?
3. What is the approximate dollar-amount of federal government spending? What is the approximate dollar-amount of federal government tax revenues?
4. Which political party controls the House of Representatives?

5. What is the name of your representative in the state legislature?
6. Name just one special-interest group and note how much it received in federal monies (within a broad range) in the last federal budget.
7. Explain what was at issue in the most recent local political controversy that did not have to do with someone's personality or personal life.
8. Approximately how many persons sit in your state's legislature?
9. What political positions (if any) did the governor of your state hold before becoming governor?
10. In what month and year will the next congressional election in your area be held?

If you know the answers to only a few of the questions, then consider yourself rationally ignorant about politics and government. This is what we would expect.

Now ask yourself if you don't know the answers to the questions because they are too hard (and almost impossible) to answer or because you have not been interested in answering such questions.

Finally, ask yourself if you will now take the time to find the answers to the questions you couldn't answer. For example, if you do not know the answer to question 6, are you going to take the time to find the answer? We think not. If we're right, then you should now understand—on a personal level—what rational ignorance is all about.

is able to sway politicians in its direction—even if it means that the general public will be made worse off by such actions (which of course is not always the case).

Suppose special-interest group A, composed of 5,000 individuals, favors a policy that will result in the redistribution of $50 million from the general taxpayers to the group. The dollar benefit for each member of the special-interest group is $10,000. Given this substantial dollar amount, it is likely that the members of the special-interest group (1) will know about the proposed legislation, and (2) will find it worthwhile to lobby the politicians who will decide the issue.

But will the politicians also hear from the general voter (general taxpayer)? First, the general voter-taxpayer will be less informed on the legislation than the member of the special-interest group, and even if he or she were informed, it would be necessary for each person to calculate the benefits and the costs of lobbying against the proposed legislation. If the legislation passes, the average taxpayer will pay out approximately 50 cents. The benefits of lobbying against the legislation are probably not greater than 50 cents. Therefore we would reasonably conclude that *even if* the general taxpayer were informed on the legislation at hand, he or she would not be likely to argue against it. It just wouldn't be worth the time and effort. We conclude that much of the legislation passed in our legislatures is likely to be special-interest legislation.

Question:

Is special-interest legislation necessarily bad legislation? Can't legislation proposed and lobbied for by a special-interest group benefit not only the special interest (directly) but also the public interest (perhaps indirectly)?

Answer:

Special-interest legislation is not necessarily "bad" legislation, and certainly it is possible that such legislation can benefit the public interest. It is not always one way or the other. What we are saying is simply this: The costs and benefits of being informed on particular issues and the costs and benefits of lobbying for and against issues are different for the member of the special-interest group and the member of the general public, and this can make a difference as to the type of legislation that will be proposed, passed, and implemented.

Congressional Districts as Special-Interest Groups

Most people do not ordinarily think of congressional districts as special-interest groups. (Special-interest groups are commonly thought to include the ranks of public school teachers, steel manufacturers, automobile manufacturers, farmers, environmentalists, bankers, truck drivers, doctors, and so on). With some issues, however, a particular congressional district may be a special-interest group.

Suppose an air force base is located in one of the congressional districts of Texas. Along comes a Pentagon study that says that the air force base is not needed; it advises the Congress of the United States to close it down. The Pentagon study demonstrates that the cost to the taxpayers of keeping the base open is greater than the benefits to the country of maintaining the base.

But closing the air force base would hurt the pocketbooks of the people in the congressional district that houses the base. Their congressional representative knows as much; she also knows that if she can't keep the base open, she isn't as likely to be reelected to office.

Therefore she speaks to other members of Congress about the proposed closing. In a way, she is a lobbyist for her congressional district. Will the majority of the members of Congress be willing to go along with the representative of the congressional district of Texas? If they do, they know that their constituents will be paying more in taxes than the Pentagon has said is necessary to assure the national security of the country. But if they don't, when they need a vote on one of their own special-interest (sometimes the word "pork-barrel" is used) projects, the representative from Texas may not be forthcoming. In short, members of Congress sometimes trade votes: my vote on your air force base for your vote on subsidies to dairy farmers in my district.[3] This type of vote trading is commonly referred to as **logrolling.** It is the exchange of votes to gain support for legislation.

Logrolling
The exchange of votes to gain support for legislation.

---

[3]Congressman Leon Panetta of California, speaking of the ways of Congress, said: "There is an unwritten rule around here. If I go to a member for help, at some point down the road they'll remember." *Wall Street Journal,* May 13, 1988, p. 18R.

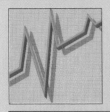

Public-Interest Talk, Special-Interest Legislation

Special-interest legislation usually isn't called special-interest legislation by the special-interest group lobbying for it. Instead, it is said to be "in the best interest of the general public." A number of examples, both past and present, come to mind.

In the early nineteenth century, the British Parliament passed the factory acts, which put restrictions on women and children working. Those who lobbied for the restrictions said they did so for humanitarian reasons; for example, they said they did not want young children and women working hard in the cotton mills. There is evidence, however, that male workers in the factories were the main "lobbyists" for the factory acts and that a reduced supply of women and children directly benefited them by raising wages. Some economists argue that the male factory workers chose to push for the factory acts by appealing to individuals' higher sensibilities and to their humanitarian instinct, instead of letting it be known that they would benefit at the expense of others.

Today, those interests calling for, say, economic protectionism from foreign competitors or greater federal subsidies rarely explain that they favor this measure because it will make them better off while someone else foots the bill. Instead, they usually voice the public-interest argument. Economic protectionism isn't necessary to protect industry X, it is necessary to protect American jobs and the strength of the domestic American economy. The subtle special-interest message often is "Help yourself by helping us."

Sometimes this message holds true, and sometimes it does not. But it is likely to be as forcefully voiced in the latter case as in the former.

GOVERNMENT BUREAUCRACY

Government Bureaucrat
An unelected person who works in a government bureau and is assigned a special task that relates to a law or program passed by the legislature.

A discussion of politics and government is not complete without mention of the government bureau and bureaucrat. A **government bureaucrat** is an unelected person who works in a government bureau and is assigned a special task that relates to a law or program passed by the legislature.

A Few Facts about Government Bureaus

Consider a few facts about government bureaus:

1. A government bureau receives its funding from the legislature. Often its funding in future years depends on how much it spends carrying out its specified duties in the current year.

2. A government bureau does not maximize profits.

3. There are no transferable ownership rights in a government bureau. There are no stockholders in a government bureau.

4. Many government bureaus provide services for which there is no competition. For example, if a person wants a driver's license, there is usually only one place to go, the Department of Motor Vehicles.

5. If the legislation that established the government bureau in the first place is repealed, there is little need for the government bureau.

These five facts about government bureaus cause many economists to argue as follows:

1. Government bureaus are not likely to end the current year with surplus funds. If they do, then funding for the following year is likely to be less than it was for the current year. The motto is "spend the money, or lose it."

2. Since a government bureau does not attempt to maximize profits the way a private firm would, it does not watch its costs as carefully. Combining points 1 and 2, we conclude that government bureau costs are likely to remain constant or rise, but are not likely to fall.

3. No one has a monetary incentive to watch over the government bureau because no one "owns" the government bureau, and no one can sell an "ownership right" in the bureau. Stockholders in private firms have a monetary incentive to ensure that the managers of the firms do an efficient job. Since there is no analog to stockholders in a government bureau, there is no one to ensure that the bureau managers operate the bureau efficiently.

4. Government bureaus and bureaucrats are not as likely to try to please the "customer" as private firms because (in most cases) they have no competition and are not threatened by any in the future. If the lines are long in the Department of Motor Vehicles, then this is just too bad. Customers have no place else to go to get what they need.

5. Government bureaucrats are likely to lobby for the continued existence and expansion of the programs they administer. To behave differently would go against their own best interests. To argue for the repeal of a program, for example, is to argue for the abolition of their jobs.

Question:

This description makes it sound as if government bureaucrats are petty, selfish people. Aren't many government bureaucrats nice, considerate people who work hard at their jobs?

Answer:

The point is *not* that government bureaucrats are bad people set on taking advantage of the general public, but that ordinary people will behave in certain predictable ways in a government bureau that is funded by the legislature, does not maximize profits, has no analog to private-sector stockholders, has little (if any) competition, and whose existence depends on the continuance of certain legislation.

A View of Government

The view of government presented in this chapter is perhaps much different from the view presented by your elementary school social studies teacher. He may have described government as made up of people who were kind, charitable, altruistic, generous, and, above all else, dedicated to serving the public good. No doubt some will say that the view of government in this chapter is cynical and exaggerated. It may very well be. But remember it is based on a *theory*, and most theories are not descriptively accurate. The real question, though, is whether the theory of public-sector decision making presented in this chapter meets the test that any theory must meet: that of explaining and predicting real-world events. Many economists and political scientists have concluded that it does.

Economics in Our Times

Interview: James Buchanan

James Buchanan won the Nobel Prize in Economics in 1986 for his work in public choice theory. Most economists today view Buchanan and his long-time colleague, Gordon Tullock, as the founders of public choice. Buchanan is currently Director of the Center for Study of Public Choice and University Professor at George Mason University in Fairfax, Virginia. We interviewed Professor Buchanan on March 9, 1988.

Professor Buchanan, many people regard *The Calculus of Consent,* which you wrote with Gordon Tullock, as the book that started public choice. Could you tell us something of the excitement you and Tullock felt when you developed the ideas in this book?

There was no sense of any startling new discovery when writing *The Cal-*

culus of Consent. Rather, Tullock and I considered ourselves to be extending—applying—very straightforward economic theory to the political process, and particularly to the choice among sets of constitutional rules.

Twenty-five years ago, when a college student took an economic course, he or she learned nothing about public choice theory because it was still in its infancy. Today, almost every economics principles text devotes a chapter to public choice. How is the college student better off because of this?

The college student who is exposed to any basic public choice theory takes away a more skeptical view of what government and politics can do and will do in response to social and economic problems that arise. The student learns to take on a more realistic and less romantic view of politics and politicians.

You are in favor of the balanced budget amendment, as are a majority of American citizens polled. However, so far the Congress has not passed it. What explains the Congress's failure to pass the amendment in the face of rather widespread popular approval? Is it likely the balanced budget amendment will be passed before the twenty-first century?

Congress will not surrender its power to spend without taxing unless it is forced to do so by constitutional limits. The Founders quite rightly allowed for one means of securing constitutional change without going through Congress. If 34 states pass resolutions (32 states have already done so), the Congress will act either to call a convention or to send an amendment back to the states for ratification. I would estimate that the

chances for favorable enactment of the balanced budget amendment during the next decade are quite good.

Part of the public choice message is that politicians edge their way to the middle of the political spectrum, voters exhibit rational ignorance, and special-interest groups lobby hard to receive benefits paid for by others. Given this, is there any hope for the future? If so, in whom or what does it lie?

Looking forward, it is easy to be pessimistic, since the rent seeking [actions of individuals and groups who spend resources to influence public policy in the hope of transferring income from others to themselves] seems more pervasive than ever. But blatant rent seeking is subject to more and more criticism, and if we look backward for two decades and measure the change in the dialogue about politics, then we can be a bit optimistic.

■ CHAPTER SUMMARY

Politicians and the Middle

■ In a two-person race, candidates for the same office will gravitate toward the middle of the political spectrum to pick up votes. If a candidate does not do this, and his opponent does, the opponent will win the election. Candidates do a number of things around election time that would cause us to believe that they understand where they are headed—that is, toward the middle. For example, candidates attempt to label their opponents as either "too far right" or "too far left." Candidates usually pick labels for themselves that represent the middle of the political spectrum, they speak in general terms, and they take polls and adjust their positions accordingly.

Voting and Rational Ignorance

■ There are both costs and benefits to voting. Many potential voters will not vote because the costs of voting—in terms of time spent going to the polls and so on—outweigh the benefits of voting measured as the probabilty of their single vote affecting the election outcome.

■ There is a difference between being unable to learn certain information and choosing not to learn certain information. Most voters choose not to be informed on political and government matters because the costs of becoming informed outweigh the benefits of becoming informed. They choose to be rationally ignorant.

Special-Interest Groups

■ Special-interest groups are usually well informed on "their" issue. Individuals have a greater incentive to become informed on issues the more directly and intensely the issue affects them.

■ Legislation that concentrates the benefits on a few and disperses the costs over many is likely to pass since the beneficiaries will have an incentive to lobby for it, whereas those who pay the bill will not lobby against it because each of them pays such a small part of the bill.

Bureaucrats

■ Public choice economists do not believe that government bureaucrats are bad people set on taking advantage of the general public. They believe that they are ordinary people (just like our friends and neighbors) who behave in predictable ways in a government bureau that is funded by the legislature, does not maximize profits, has no analog to private-sector stockholders, has little (if any) competition, and whose existence depends on the continuance of certain legislation.

■ QUESTIONS TO ANSWER AND DISCUSS

1. Critics often charge that not all politicians move toward the middle of the political spectrum to obtain votes. They often cite Barry Goldwater in the 1964 presidential election and George McGovern in the 1972 presidential election as examples. Are these exceptions to the theory developed in this chapter?

2. Would voters have a greater incentive to vote in an election in which there were only a few registered voters or many registered voters?

3. Most individuals learn more about the car they are thinking of buying than about the candidates running for the presidency of the United States. Explain why.

4. What type of legislation would we expect to see if the general voter is rationally ignorant, special-interest groups heavily lobby elected officials, and elected officials engage in logrolling?

5. If the model of politics and government presented in this chapter is true, what are some of the things we would expect to see?

6. It has often been remarked that Democratic candidates are more liberal in the Democratic primaries and that Republican candidates are more conservative in the Republican primaries than either is in the general election, respectively. Explain why.

7. What are some ways of reducing the cost of voting to voters?

8. What are some ways of making government bureaucrats and bureaus more cost conscious?

9. Some individuals see national defense spending as benefiting the special interests—in particular, the defense industry. Others see it as directly benefiting not only the defense industry but the general public as well. The issue here is that while some individuals see "special interest" only, others see special interest and public interest. This difference in view often leads to political arguments. Does this same difference in view exist for issues other than national defense? Name a few.

10. Evaluate each of the following proposals for reform in terms of the model presented in this chapter:

a. Linking all spending programs to a visible tax hike.

b. A balanced budget amendment that stipulates that the Congress cannot spend more than total tax revenues.

c. A budgetary referenda process whereby the voters actually vote on the distribution of federal dollars to the different categories of spending (X percentage to agriculture, Y percentage to national defense, and so on) instead of the elected representatives deciding.

THE WORLD ECONOMY

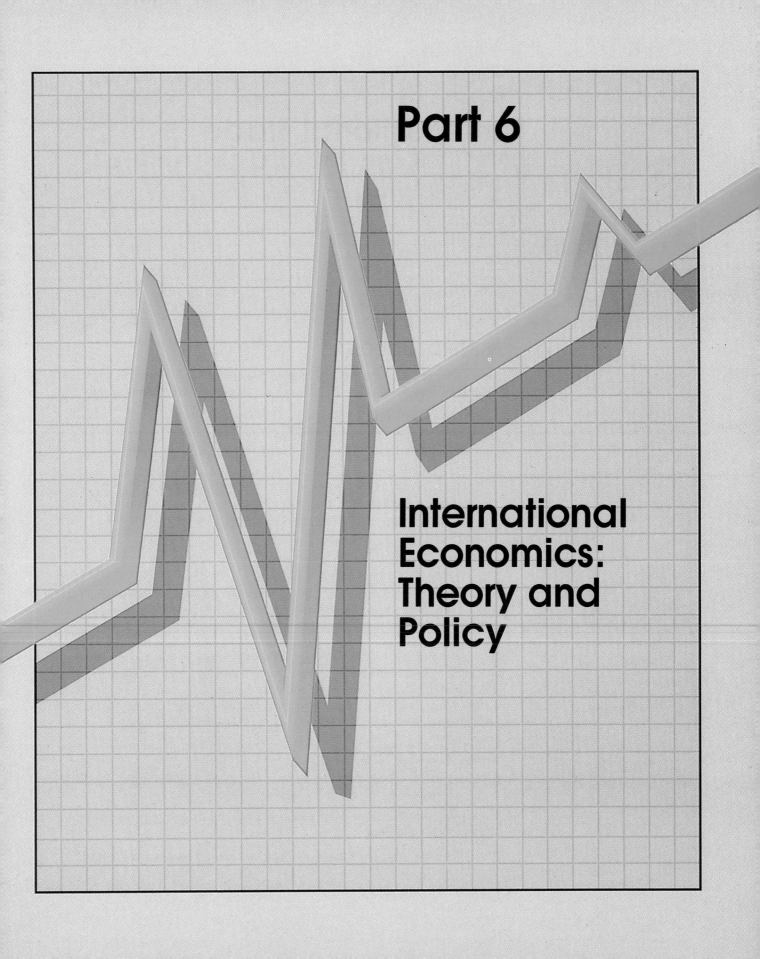

Part 6

International Economics: Theory and Policy

Chapter 20

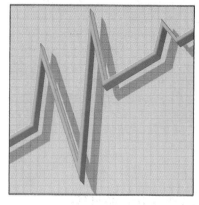

International Trade

■ INTRODUCTION

Stories on international trade and finance heat up and cool down. In 1987 and 1988, they were heating up. Headlines such as these were commonplace:

> *DOLLAR TUMBLES ON WIDENING OF TRADE GAP*
> *—Wall Street Journal, July 16, 1987*
>
> *DOLLAR, TRADE GAP RETURN SPOTLIGHT TO PROTECTIONISM*
> *—Wall Street Journal, January 4, 1988*
>
> *RECORD EXPORTS CUT TRADE GAP FOR 1st QUARTER*
> *—Wall Street Journal, May 26, 1988*
>
> *JAPAN IS PRESSING U.S. TO PREVENT BATTLE ON RICE*
> *—Wall Street Journal, October 7, 1988*
>
> *1987 NEED NOT BECOME 1929*
> *—Fortune, November 23, 1987*

During this time, people who had rarely spoken the words "international trade" began to engage in heated discussions. To the casual observer, it seemed to happen overnight.

What lies ahead? We predict that international trade and finance will continue to be a hot topic. The world is becoming a smaller place, national economies are becoming more interdependent; today, more than ever, what happens in Tokyo affects what happens in New York and what happens on Main Street, U.S.A.

How does international trade differ from domestic trade? The economist John Chipman has noted three differences:[1]

1. *Barriers (both natural and artificial) are more prevalent in international trade than in domestic trade.*

2. *International trade uses different currencies where domestic trade uses only one currency.*

3. *International trade takes place between autonomous governments where domestic trade does not.*

You will see the interplay of these three factors in this chapter and the next.

[1]See John Chipman's article on international trade in *The New Palgrave, A Dictionary of Economics* (London: The Macmillan Press, 1987).

■ WHAT THIS CHAPTER IS ABOUT

Economics is about trade, and trade does not stop at the borders of a city, state, or nation. People do not trade exclusively with people who live in their city, state, or nation. They trade with people in other countries, too. For example, a person in Denver, Colorado, may step into a department store and purchase a Sony television set made in Japan. This chapter examines both international trade and the prohibitions that are sometimes placed on it.

The organization of this chapter is slightly different from other chapters. In particular, we often discuss the material by answering specific questions. Perhaps a better title for this chapter would have been "Some Answers to Questions about International Trade That You Weren't Really Sure How to Ask."

Key Questions to Keep in Mind as You Read

1. What does it mean to say a country has an absolute advantage in the production of a good?

2. What does it mean to say a country has a comparative advantage in the production of a good?

3. Which matters more to international trade: a country's absolute advantage or its comparative advantage?

4. What is consumers' surplus?

5. What is producers' surplus?

6. What is a tariff? What are the effects of a tariff?

7. What is a quota? What are the effects of a quota?

INTERNATIONAL TRADE THEORY

In this section we discuss some of the facts and figures of international trade, especially as they relate to the United States. We also introduce the important *law of comparative advantage.*

Is International Trade Equally Important in All Countries?

One way of determining how "important" international trade is to different countries is to look at exports as a percentage of GNP (exports/GNP).[2] For example, in the United States in 1986, exports were 5.1 percent of GNP, and in Belgium, exports were 60.7 percent of GNP. Exhibit 20-1 shows that exports accounted for a lower percentage of GNP in the United States in 1986 than in other industrialized countries.

On an absolute basis, though, the United States is a major international trader. In 1986, it exported $217.3 billion worth of goods, more than all but one nation listed.

Question:

Which countries are the major trading partners of the United States?

[2]We could also look at imports as a percentage of GNP (imports/GNP) to measure how "important" international trade is in different countries. Both are shown in Exhibit 20-1.

■ **EXHIBIT 20-1**
Relative and Absolute Size of Exports, Selected Countries, 1986

In comparison with the other countries listed here, the export/GNP ratio in the United States is relatively small. In absolute terms, however, the United States exports more than all but one nation listed.

COUNTRY	TOTAL EXPORTS (BILLIONS OF 1986 DOLLARS)	EXPORTS AS A PERCENTAGE OF GNP	TOTAL IMPORTS (BILLIONS OF 1986 DOLLARS	IMPORTS AS A PERCENTAGE OF GNP
Belgium	$ 68.6	60.7%	$ 68.5	60.6%
Netherlands	80.6	48.0	75.4	44.8
Sweden	37.2	29.1	32.5	22.8
Denmark	21.2	27.4	22.8	29.4
West Germany	242.4	26.9	189.7	21.0
Switzerland	37.2	26.1	40.9	28.7
Canada	86.7	24.7	81.3	23.2
Italy	97.5	19.4	100.0	19.8
United Kingdom	107.0	19.3	126.2	22.7
France	119.3	16.8	128.8	18.1
Spain	27.1	11.9	34.9	15.3
Japan	210.8	10.6	127.7	6.4
United States	217.3	5.1	370.0	8.8

SOURCE: U.S. Bureau of the Census, *Statistical Abstract of the United States, 1988* (Washington, D.C.: U.S. Government Printing Office, 1988).

Answer:

The major, single-country trading partners of the United States are Canada and Japan. In 1987, Canada bought 24.2 percent of U.S. exports and supplied 17.7 percent of the U.S. imports. In the same year, Japan bought 10.7 percent of U.S. exports and supplied 20.5 percent of U.S. imports. As a block, western Europe bought 28.8 percent of U.S. exports and supplied 23 percent of U.S. imports. Other major trading partners of the United States include Mexico, the United Kingdom, West Germany, the Netherlands, France, South Korea, Belgium, Taiwan, Italy, Hong Kong, and Brazil.

What Does the United States Export and Import?

In 1987, major U.S. exports included automobiles, computers, aircraft, corn, wheat, soybeans, scientific instruments, coal, and plastic materials. Its major imports included petroleum, automobiles, clothing, iron and steel, office machines, footwear, fish, coffee, and diamonds. Exhibit 20-2 shows the percentage breakdowns for broad categories of U.S. exports and imports for 1986 and 1987.

Why Do People in Different Countries Trade with Each Other?

The reasons why we have international trade are the same as why we have any trade, at any level. Individuals trade to make themselves better off. Pat and Zach, both of whom live in St. Paul, Minnesota, trade because they both value something the other has more than they value some of their own possessions. On an international scale, Elaine in the United States trades with Cho in China because Cho has something that Elaine wants.

Obviously different countries have different terrain, climate, resources, skills, and so on. It follows that some countries will be able to produce some goods that other countries cannot produce or can produce only at extremely high costs.

For example, Hong Kong has no oil, Saudia Arabia has a large supply. Bananas

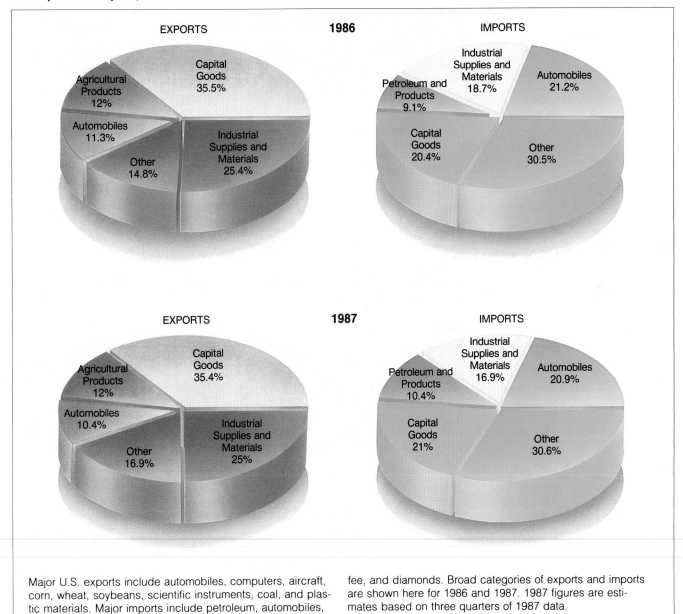

Major U.S. exports include automobiles, computers, aircraft, corn, wheat, soybeans, scientific instruments, coal, and plastic materials. Major imports include petroleum, automobiles, clothing, iron and steel, office machines, footwear, fish, coffee, and diamonds. Broad categories of exports and imports are shown here for 1986 and 1987. 1987 figures are estimates based on three quarters of 1987 data.

SOURCE: Council of Economic Advisers, *Economic Report of the President, 1988* (Washington, D.C.: U.S. Government Printing Office, 1988).

do not grow easily in the United States, but they flourish in Honduras. Americans could grow bananas, if they used hothouses, but it is cheaper for Americans to buy bananas from Hondurans than to produce bananas themselves.

How Do Countries Know What to Trade?

To explain how countries know what to trade, we need to discuss the concepts of *absolute advantage* and *comparative advantage*. Here is a simple model.

Absolute Advantage. Assume a two country–two good world. The countries are the United States and Japan, and the goods are food and clothing. Both countries can produce the two goods in the four different combinations listed in Exhibit 20-3. For example, with a given amount of resources, the United States can produce 90 units of food and 0 units of clothing, or 60 units of food and 10 units of clothing, and so on. With the same amount of resources used in the United States, Japan can produce 60 units of food and 0 units of clothing, and so on. Plotting the different combinations of the two goods each country can produce gives us the production possibilities frontiers in Exhibit 20-3.[3]

[3]Notice that these are straight-line production possibilities frontiers, not curved ones. A straight-line production possibilities frontier indicates that resources can be transferred from the production of one good into another at *constant* opportunity cost. For a review, see Chapter 2.

■ **EXHIBIT 20-3**
Production Possibilities in Two Countries

UNITED STATES			JAPAN		
Points on Production Possibilities Frontier	Food	Clothing	Points on Production Possibilities Frontier	Food	Clothing
A	90	0	A′	60	0
B	60	10	B′	40	20
C	30	20	C′	20	40
D	0	30	D′	0	60

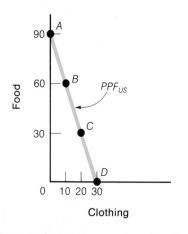
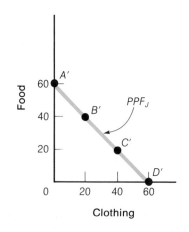

The United States has an absolute advantage in the production of food, Japan has an absolute advantage in the production of clothing. Initially, the United States produces at point B on its production possibilities frontier, and Japan produces at point C′ on its production possibilities frontier. If the United States specializes in food production, and Japan in clothing production, and the United States trades 20 units of food to Japan for 10 units of clothing, both countries will be made better off.

Notice that using the same amount of resources the United States can produce more of one good (food) than Japan can, but Japan can produce more of another good (clothing) than the United States can. For example, using the same quantity of resources, the United States can produce 90 units of food whereas Japan can produce only 60 units, but Japan can produce 60 units of clothing whereas the United States can produce only 30 units. Economists would say that the United States has an **absolute advantage** in the production of food and Japan has an absolute advantage in the production of clothing.

A country has an absolute advantage in the production of a good if, using the same amount of resources as another country, it can produce more of a particular good. To put it differently, a country has an absolute advantage in the production of a good if, with fewer resources, it can produce the same amount of a good as another country.

Suppose now that the United States is producing and consuming the two goods in the combination represented by point *B* on its production possibilities frontier, and Japan is producing and consuming the two goods in the combination represented by point *C'* on its production possibilities frontier. The United States is producing and consuming 60 units of food and 10 units of clothing, and Japan is producing and consuming 20 units of food and 40 units of clothing. We refer to this as the *no specialization–no trade (NS-NT)* case. See column 1 in Exhibit 20-4.

Now suppose the two countries decide to specialize and trade. We call this the *specialization-trade (S-T)* case. The United States specializes in the production of

Absolute Advantage

The situation where a country can produce more of a good than another country can produce with the same quantity of resources.

■ **EXHIBIT 20-4**
Comparing the No Specialization–No Trade Case With the Specialization-Trade Case

	NO SPECIALIZATION— NO TRADE CASE (*NS-NT*)	SPECIALIZATION—TRADE CASE (*S-T*)			
Country	(1) Production and Consumption in the *NS-NT* Case	(2) Production in the *S-T* Case	(3) Exports (−) Imports (+) Terms of Trade are 2F = 1C	(4) Consumption in the *S-T* Case (2) + (3)	(5) Gains from Specialization and Trade (4) − (1)
UNITED STATES					
Food	60 ⎱ Point *B* in	90 ⎱ Point *A* in	−20	70	10
Clothing	10 ⎰ Exhibit 35-3	0 ⎰ Exhibit 35-3	+10	10	0
JAPAN					
Food	20 ⎱ Point *C'* in	0 ⎱ Point *D'* in	+20	20	0
Clothing	40 ⎰ Exhibit 35-3	60 ⎰ Exhibit 35-3	−10	50	10

Column 1: Both the United States and Japan operate independently of each other. The United States produces and consumes 60 units of food and 10 units of clothing. Japan produces and consumes 20 units of food and 40 units of clothing.
Column 2: The United States specializes in the production of food; Japan specializes in the production of clothing.
Column 3: The United States and Japan agree to the terms of trade 2 units of food for 1 unit of clothing. They actually trade 20 units of food for 10 units of clothing.
Column 4: Overall, the United States consumes 70 units of food and 10 units of clothing. Japan consumes 20 units of food and 50 units of clothing.
Column 5: Consumption levels are higher for both the United States and Japan in the *S-T* case than in the *NS-NT* case.

food, producing 90 units, and Japan specializes in the production of clothing, producing 60 units. In short, the United States moves to point A on its production possibilities frontier, and Japan moves to point D' on its production possibilities frontier. See column 2 in Exhibit 20-4.

After they have specialized in production, the two countries must settle on the terms of trade: that is, how much food will trade for how much clothing. The United States faces the following situation: For every 30 units of food it does not produce, it can produce 10 units of clothing (see Exhibit 20-3). Thus, 3 units of food come at an opportunity cost of 1 unit of clothing ($3F = 1C$), or 1 unit of food comes at a cost of $\frac{1}{3}$ unit of clothing ($1F = \frac{1}{3}C$). Meanwhile Japan faces the following situation: For every 20 units of food it does not produce, it can produce 20 units of clothing. Thus 1 unit of food comes at an opportunity cost of 1 unit of clothing ($1F = 1C$). Recapping, for the United States $3F = 1C$, and for Japan $1F = 1C$.

With these cost ratios, it would seem likely that both countries could agree on terms of trade that specify $2F$ for $1C$. The United States would prefer to give up 2 units of food instead of 3 units for 1 unit of clothing, whereas Japan would prefer to give up 1 unit of clothing and get 2 units of food instead of only 1. Suppose the two countries agree to the terms of trade of $2F = 1C$ and trade, in absolute amounts, 20 units of food for 10 units of clothing. See column 3 in Exhibit 20-4.

Now the United States produces 90 units of food and trades (exports) 20 units to Japan, for which it receives in exchange (imports) 10 units of clothing. Thus the United States consumes 10 units of clothing (received in trade from Japan) plus 70 units of food it has left over (recall that it produced 90 units and only traded away 20 units). See the situation for the United States in column 4 in Exhibit 20-4.

Now Japan produces 60 units of clothing and trades (exports) 10 units to the United States and receives in exchange (imports) 20 units of food. Thus Japan consumes 20 units of food (received in trade from the United States) plus 50 units of clothing it has left over (it only traded away 10 of the 60 units of clothing it produced). See the situation for Japan in column 4 in Exhibit 20-4.

Comparing the consumption levels of both countries in the no specialization–no trade case with the specialization-trade case, we find that both countries consume more in the specialization-trade case. The United States consumes 10 more units of food and no less clothing; Japan consumes 10 more units of clothing and no less food. Both countries have made themselves better off through specialization and trade.

Question:

In the example, both countries had an absolute advantage in the production of one good. Isn't this why they both benefited from specialization and trade? Would both have benefited if one country, say, the United States, had had an absolute advantage in the production of both goods?

Answer:

Yes, they would. Even if the United States had had an absolute advantage in the production of both goods, it could still have gained through specialization and trade. The classical economist David Ricardo pointed this out in the early nineteenth century. The discussion of *comparative advantage* in the next section explains this point further.

Comparative Advantage. Notice in Exhibit 20-5 that the United States is better than Japan at producing both food and clothing; it has an absolute advantage in the production of both goods. Suppose the two countries are not specializing or trading. The United States is producing and consuming the combination of the two goods represented by point *B* on its production possibilities frontier, and Japan is producing and consuming the combination of the two goods represented by point *B'* on its production possibilities frontier. See column 1 in Exhibit 20-6.

Now suppose the two countries decide to specialize and trade. Since the United States is better than Japan in the production of both goods, which good does the United States specialize in? Similarly, which good does Japan specialize in since it is not as efficient as the United States in the production of either good? The general answer to both questions is the same: *Countries specialize in the production of the good in which they have a* **comparative advantage.** A country has a comparative advantage in the production of a good when it can produce the good at lower opportunity cost than another country.

Comparative Advantage

The situation where a country can produce a good at lower opportunity cost than another country.

■ **EXHIBIT 20-5**
Production Possibilities in Two Countries

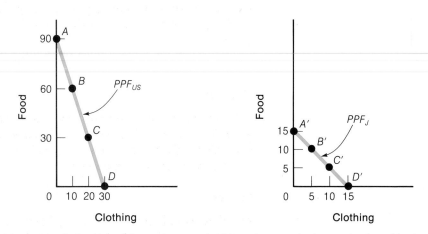

UNITED STATES			JAPAN		
Points on Production Possibilities Frontier	Food	Clothing	Points on Production Possibilities Frontier	Food	Clothing
A	90	0	A'	15	0
B	60	10	B'	10	5
C	30	20	C'	5	10
D	0	30	D'	0	15

Even though the United States has an absolute advantage in the production of both goods, both countries can be made better off by specializing in and trading the good in which each has a comparative advantage. Gains from specialization and trade depend on comparative advantage, not absolute advantage.

Even If One Country Has an Absolute Advantage in Both Goods, Both Countries Can Gain from Specialization and Trade

	NO SPECIALIZATION—NO TRADE CASE (NS-NT)		SPECIALIZATION—TRADE CASE (S-T)			
Country	(1) Production and Consumption in the NS-NT Case	(2) Production in the S-T Case	(3) Exports (−) Imports (+) Terms of Trade are $2F = 1C$	(4) Consumption in the S-T Case (2) + (3)	(5) Gains from Specialization and Trade (4) − (1)
UNITED STATES					
Food	60 ⎫ Point B in	90 ⎫ Point A in	−20	70	10
Clothing	10 ⎭ Exhibit 35-5	0 ⎭ Exhibit 35-5	+10	10	0
JAPAN					
Food	10 ⎫ Point B′ in	0 ⎫ Point D′ in	+20	20	10
Clothing	5 ⎭ Exhibit 35-5	15 ⎭ Exhibit 35-5	−10	5	0

Column 1: Both the United States and Japan operate independently of each other. The United States produces and consumes 60 units of food and 10 units of clothing. Japan produces and consumes 10 units of food and 5 units of clothing.

Column 2: The United States specializes in the production of food; Japan specializes in the production of clothing.

Column 3: The United States and Japan agree to the terms of trade 2 units of food for 1 unit of clothing. They actually trade 20 units of food for 10 units of clothing.

Column 4: Overall, the United States consumes 70 units of food and 10 units of clothing. Japan consumes 20 units of food and 5 units clothing.

Column 5: Consumption levels are higher for both the United States and Japan in the S-T case than in the NS-NT case.

For example, in the United States the opportunity cost of producing 1 unit of clothing is 3 units of food (since for every 10 units of clothing it produces, it forfeits 30 units of food) whereas the opportunity cost of producing 1 unit of food is ⅓ unit of clothing. In Japan, the opportunity cost of producing 1 unit of clothing is 1 unit of food (since for every 5 units of clothing it produces, it forfeits 5 units of food). To recap, in the United States the situation is $1C = 3F$ and $1F = \frac{1}{3}C$; in Japan the situation is $1C = 1F$ or, turning it around, $1F = 1C$.

We see that the United States can produce food at a lower opportunity cost ($\frac{1}{3}C$ as opposed to $1C$ in Japan) whereas Japan can produce clothing at a lower opportunity cost ($1F$ as opposed to $3F$ in the United States). Thus the United States has a comparative advantage in food, and Japan has a comparative advantage in clothing.

Suppose the two countries specialize in the production of the good in which they have a comparative advantage (see column 2 in Exhibit 20-6), agree to the terms of trade $2F = 1C$, and trade in absolute amounts 20 units of food for 10 units of clothing. See column 3 in Exhibit 20-6.

Now the United States produces 90 units of food and trades 20 units to Japan, receiving 10 units of clothing in exchange. It consumes 70 units of food and 10 units of clothing. See the listing for the United States in column 4 in Exhibit 20-6.

Now Japan produces 15 units of clothing and trades 10 to the United States, receiving 20 units of food in exchange. It consumes 5 units of clothing and 20 units of food. See the listing for Japan in column 4 in Exhibit 20-6.

Comparing the consumption levels in both countries in the two cases, the United States and Japan each consume 10 more units of food and no less clothing in the specialization-trade case than in the no specialization—no trade case. See column 5 in Exhibit 20-6.

We conclude that even when a country has an *absolute advantage* in the pro-duction of both goods (or when a country has an absolute disadvantage in the production of both goods), it stands to gain by specializing in the production of and trading the good in which it has a *comparative advantage*.

Question:

Specialization and trade appear to allow a country's inhabitants to consume at a level beyond its production possibilities frontier. Is this correct?

Answer:

Yes, that is correct. To see this, turn back to Exhibit 20-5 and look at the *PPF* for the United States. In the *NS-NT* case, the United States consumes 60 units of food and 10 units of clothing—that is, the United States consumes at point *B* on its *PPF*.

In the *S-T* case, however, it consumes 70 units of food and 10 units of clothing. A point that represents this combination of the two goods is outside the country's *PPF*.

How Do Countries Know When They Have a Comparative Advantage?

Government officials of a country do not sit down with piles of cost data before them and determine what their country should specialize in producing and then trade. Countries do not plot production possibilities frontiers on graph paper or calculate opportunity costs. Instead it is individuals' desire to make a dollar, a franc, or a pound that determines the pattern of international trade; it is the desire to earn a profit that determines what a country specializes in and trades.

Take the case of Geoffrey, an enterprising Englishman who visits the United States. Geoffrey observes that beef is relatively cheap in the United States (compared with the price he paid in England) and tea is relatively expensive. Noticing the price differences for beef and tea between his country and the United States, he decides to buy some tea in England, bring it to the United States, and sell it for the relatively higher U.S. price. With his profits on the tea transaction, he buys beef in the United States, ships it to England, and sells it for the relatively higher English price. It is obvious that what Geoffrey is doing is buying low and selling high; he is buying in the country where the good is cheap and selling it in the country where the good is expensive.

What are the consequences of Geoffrey's activities? First, he is making a profit. The larger the price differences in the two goods between the two countries, and the more he reshuffles goods between countries, the more profit Geoffrey makes.

Second, Geoffrey's activities are moving each country toward its comparative advantage. The United States ends up exporting beef to England, and England ends up exporting tea to the United States. Just as the pure theory predicts, individuals in the two countries specialize in and trade the good in which they have a comparative advantage. The outcome is brought about spontaneously through the actions of individuals trying to make themselves better off; they are simply trying to gain through trade.

TRADE RESTRICTIONS

International trade theory shows that countries gain from free international trade; that is, from specializing in the production of the goods in which they have a comparative advantage and trading these goods for other goods. In the real world, however, there are numerous types of trade restrictions, which raises the question: If countries gain from international trade, why are there trade restrictions? We answer this and related questions in this section.

Why Are There Trade Restrictions in the Real World?

In the previous section we learned that specialization and international trade benefit individuals in different countries. This occurs *on net*. Every person may not gain. For example, suppose Pam Dickson lives and works in the United States making clock radios. She produces and sells 12,000 clock radios per year for a price of $40 each. As the situation stands, there is no international trade. Individuals in other countries who make clock radios do not sell their clock radios in the United States. Then one day things change. The U.S. market is opened up to clock radios from Japan. It appears that the Japanese manufacturers have a comparative advantage in the production of clock radios. They sell their clock radios in the United States for

$25 each. Pam realizes that she cannot compete with this price. Her sales fall off to such a degree that she goes out of business. For Pam, personally, the introduction of international trade, *in this one instance,* has harmed her.

This raises the issue of the distributional effects of trade. Using the tools of supply and demand, we concentrate on two groups: U.S. consumers and U.S. producers. But first let's detour to discuss consumers' and producers' surplus.

Consumers' and Producers' Surplus

Consumers' Surplus

The difference between the price buyers pay for a good and the maximum or highest price they would have paid for the good. It is a dollar measure of the benefit gained by being able to purchase a unit of a good for less than one is willing to pay for it.

Producers' Surplus

The difference between the price sellers receive for a good and the minimum or lowest price for which they would have sold the good. It is a dollar measure of the benefit gained by being able to sell a unit of output for more than one is willing to sell it.

Consumers' surplus is the difference between the price buyers pay for a good and the maximum or highest price they would have paid for the good. It is a dollar measure of the benefit gained by being able to purchase a unit of a good for less than one is willing to pay for it. For example, if Yakov would have paid $10 to see the movie at the Cinemax, but only paid $4, his consumer surplus is $6.

Producers' surplus is the difference between the price sellers receive for a good and the minimum or lowest price for which they would have sold the good. It is a dollar measure of the benefit gained by being able to sell a unit of output for more than one is willing to sell it. For example, if Joan sold her book for $14, but would have sold it for as low (but no lower) than $4, her producer surplus is $10. Consumers' surplus is the consumers' net gain from trade, and producers' surplus is the producers' net gain from trade.

Both consumers' and producers' surplus are represented in Exhibit 20-7. In (a), consumers' surplus is the shaded triangle. This triangle is the area under the demand

■ **EXHIBIT 20-7**
Consumers' and Producers' Surplus

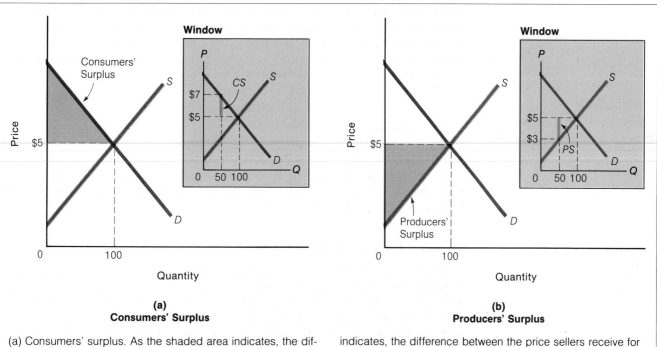

(a)
Consumers' Surplus

(b)
Producers' Surplus

(a) Consumers' surplus. As the shaded area indicates, the difference between the maximum or highest amount consumers would be willing to pay and the price they actually pay is consumers' surplus. (b) Producers' surplus. As the shaded area indicates, the difference between the price sellers receive for the good and the minimum or lowest price they would be willing to sell the good for is producers' surplus.

curve and above the equilibrium price out to the equilibrium quantity. To understand why this area is consumer's surplus, think of the definition of consumers' surplus (highest price − price paid). For example, notice in the window in (a) that consumers would have been willing to pay $7 for the 50th unit but instead paid $5. Thus the consumers' surplus on the 50th unit of the good is $2. If we add the consumers' surplus on each unit of the good between and including the first and the 100th (100 units being the equilibrium quantity), we obtain the shaded (consumers' surplus) triangle.

In (b), producers' surplus is represented by the shaded triangle. This triangle is the area above the supply curve and under the equilibrium price out to the equilibrium quantity. To understand why this area represents producers' surplus, think of the definition of producers' surplus (price paid − lowest price). For example, notice in the window in (b) that suppliers would have sold the 50th unit for as low as $3 but actually sold it for $5. Thus the producers' surplus on the 50th unit of the good is $2. If we add the producers' surplus on each unit of the good between and including the first and the 100th, we obtain the shaded (producers' surplus) triangle.

Exports Permitted and Prohibited: The Effects on U.S. Consumers and Producers

We now consider two cases: one where the U.S. government permits U.S. producers to export goods and one where it does not. With these two cases in mind, look at Exhibit 20-8, where (a) illustrates the world market for wheat. The equilibrium world market price is P_W. At this price U.S. consumers buy Q_1 amount of wheat in (b), and U.S. producers produce Q_2 amount of wheat. The difference between the two quantities $(Q_2 − Q_1)$ is the amount of wheat U.S. producers export to the rest of the world.

Now suppose exports are prohibited; U.S. producers are no longer allowed to export wheat to the rest of the world. Price is now determined by domestic demand and supply. In the short term, this results in a surplus of wheat in the United States and drives price down. As a result, the price that is relevant to American wheat buyers is P_N in (b). In equilibrium, U.S. consumers buy Q_3 amount of wheat, U.S. producers produce and sell Q_3 amount of wheat, and no U.S. wheat is exported. Now compare the situation for U.S. consumers and producers when exports are permitted and when they are prohibited.

Exports Permitted and Prohibited: The Effects on U.S. Consumers.   If exports are *permitted* consumers' surplus is represented by the area $P_W AB$. This is the area under the demand curve and above the world equilibrium price P_W (which is the relevant equilibrium price if exports are permitted).

If exports are *prohibited,* U.S. consumers receive consumers' surplus equal to the area $P_N AD$. This is the area under the demand curve and above the equilibrium price P_N (which is the relevant equilibrium price if exports are prohibited).

Consumers' surplus is greater when exports are prohibited than when they are permitted: $P_N AD > P_W AB$. U.S. consumers are helped by a policy that prohibits exports; they are hurt by a policy that permits exports.

Exports Permitted and Prohibited: The Effects on U.S. Producers.   If exports are permitted, producers' surplus is $P_W CE$. This is the area above the supply curve and under the world equilibrium price P_W (which is the relevant equilibrium price if exports are permitted).

Exports Permitted and Prohibited: The Effects on U.S. Consumers and Producers

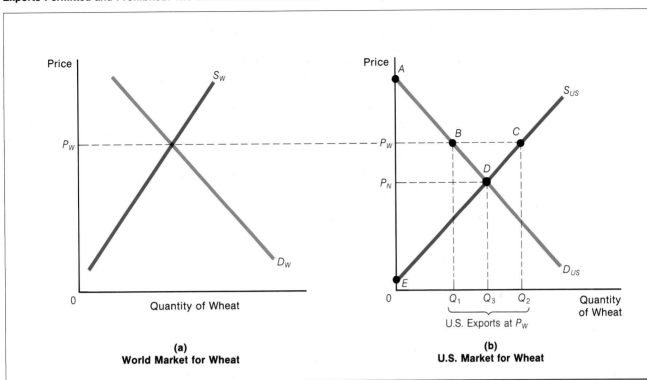

(a)
World Market for Wheat

(b)
U.S. Market for Wheat

U.S. CONSUMERS			U.S. PRODUCERS		
	Consumers' Surplus	Net Gain from Prohibiting Exports		Producers' Surplus	Net Gain from Permitting Exports
EXPORTS PERMITTED	P_WAB	$P_WBD\ P_N$	EXPORTS PERMITTED	P_WCE	$P_WCD\ P_N$
	Since $P_NAD > P_WAB$, U.S. consumers are better off if exports are prohibited.			Since $P_WCE > P_NDE$, U.S. producers are better off if exports are permitted.	
EXPORTS PROHIBITED	P_NAD		EXPORTS PROHIBITED	P_NDE	

$P_WCD\ P_N$ is greater than $P_WBD\ P_N$ by the area BCD. This area represents the net gain of a policy of permitting exports over a policy of prohibiting exports. In short, there are net gains to free trade.

(c)

If exports are permitted, consumers' surplus is P_WAB and producers' surplus is P_WCE. If exports are prohibited, consumers' surplus is P_NAD and producers' surplus is P_NDE. The net gain to consumers of a policy that prohibits exports over a policy that permits exports is P_WBDP_N. The net gain to producers of a policy that permits exports over a policy that prohibits exports is P_WCDP_N. Since $P_WCDP_N > P_WBDP_N$, there is a net gain to free trade represented by the area BCD.

If exports are prohibited, U.S. producers receive producers' surplus equal to P_NDE. This is the area above the supply curve and under the equilibrium price P_N (which is the relevant equilibrium price if exports are prohibited). Producers' surplus is greater if exports are permitted than if they are prohibited: $P_WCE > P_NDE$. U.S. producers are helped by a policy that permits exports; they are hurt by a policy that prohibits exports.

How much better off, on net, are U.S. consumers if exports are prohibited than if they are permitted? The answer is represented by the area P_WBDP_N in (b). Since consumers' surplus is larger when exports are prohibited (P_NAD) than when exports are permitted (P_WAB), the net gain to consumers of having exports prohibited is the difference between the two consumers' surplus areas, which is P_WBDP_N.

How much better off, on net, are U.S. producers if exports are permitted than if they are prohibited? Since producers' surplus is larger when exports are permitted (P_WCE) than when they are prohibited (P_NDE), the net gain to producers of having exports permitted is the difference between the two producers' surplus areas, which is P_WCDP_N. Looking at this area in (b), you will notice that it *includes* the net benefit to consumers of having exports permitted—that is, area P_WBDP_N. This means that the net gain to producers of having exports permitted is greater than the net gain to consumers of having exports prohibited. The former is greater than the latter by the area BCD. *The area BCD represents the net gain of a policy of permitting exports over a policy of prohibiting exports.* In other words, there are net gains to free trade. Exhibit 20-8c provides a summary of this analysis.

Imports Permitted and Prohibited: The Effects on U.S. Consumers and Producers

The analysis of permitting and prohibiting imports follows the same steps as in the previous section. We begin, as we did before, at the world equilibrium price of P_W (see Exhibit 20-9a). At this price for cars, U.S. consumers wish to buy Q_2 cars in (b); Q_1 of these cars will be bought from the U.S. producers of cars, and the difference between Q_2 and Q_1 ($Q_2 - Q_1$) will be bought from the foreign producers of cars. In short, U.S. consumers import $Q_2 - Q_1$ cars. In this case, where imports are permitted, consumers' surplus is represented by the area P_WAC, and U.S. producers receive producers' surplus equal to the area P_WDE.

Now suppose government passes legislation prohibiting foreign car imports. As a result, price rises to P_N. At this equilibrium price, U.S. consumers buy Q_3 cars and American producers sell Q_3 cars. U.S. consumers receive consumers' surplus equal to the area P_NAB, and U.S. producers receive producers' surplus equal to the area P_NBE.

Comparing the two situations, we notice that U.S. consumers receive higher consumers' surplus when imports are permitted ($P_WAC > P_NAB$), and U.S. producers receive higher producers' surplus when imports are prohibited ($P_NBE > P_WDE$).

The net gain to U.S. consumers of a policy that permits imports over one that prohibits them is represented by the area P_NBCP_W. The net gain to U.S. producers of a policy that prohibits imports over one that permits them is represented by the area P_NBDP_W. Since the net gain to consumers of a policy that permits imports is greater than the net gain to producers of a policy that prohibits imports ($P_NBCP_W > P_NBDP_W$), we conclude that there is a net gain, represented by the area BCD, to the former policy over the later. Once again, the area BCD may be viewed as the net gain from free trade. See Exhibit 20-9c for a summary of the analysis.

Imports Permitted and Prohibited: The Effects on U.S. Consumers and Producers

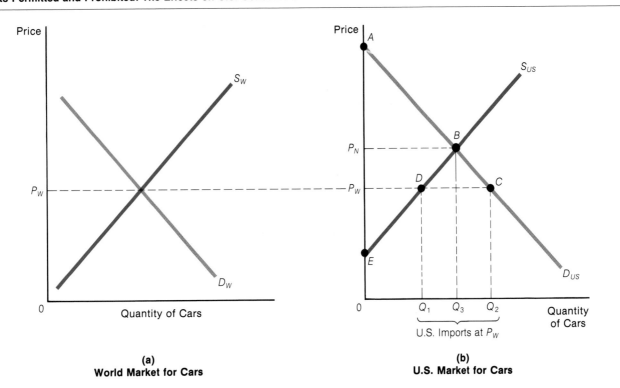

(a)
World Market for Cars

(b)
U.S. Market for Cars

U.S. CONSUMERS				U.S. PRODUCERS		
	Consumers' Surplus	Net Gain from Permitting Imports			Producers' Surplus	Net Gain from Prohibiting Imports
IMPORTS PERMITTED	P_WAC		$P_NBC\ P_W$	IMPORTS PERMITTED	P_WDE	$P_NBD\ P_W$
		Since $P_WAC > P_NAB$, U.S. consumers are better off when imports are permitted.				Since $P_NBE > P_WDE$, U.S. producers are better off when imports are prohibited.
IMPORTS PROHIBITED	P_NAB			IMPORTS PROHIBITED	P_NBE	

$P_NBC\ P_W$ is greater than $P_NBD\ P_W$ by the area BCD. This area represents the net gain of a
policy of permitting imports over a policy of prohibiting imports. In short, there are net gains to free trade.

(c)

If imports are permitted, consumers' surplus is P_WAC and producers' surplus is P_WDE. If imports are prohibited, consumers' surplus is P_NAB and producers' surplus is P_NBE. The net gain to consumers of a policy that permits imports over a policy that prohibits imports is P_NBCP_W. The net gain to producers of a policy that prohibits imports over a policy that permits imports is P_NBDP_W. Since $P_NBCP_W > P_NBDP_W$, there is a net gain to free trade represented by the area BCD.

If Free Trade Results in Net Gain, Why Do Nations Sometimes Restrict Trade?

Based on the preceding analysis, the case for free trade (no prohibitions on exports or imports) appears to be a strong one. The case for free trade has not gone unchallenged, however. Some persons maintain that at certain times free trade should be restricted or suspended. In almost all cases, they argue that it is in the best interest of the public or country as a whole to do so. In short, they advance a public-interest argument. Other persons contend that the public-interest argument is only superficial; down deep they say, it is a special-interest argument clothed in pretty words. As you might guess, the debate between the two groups is often heated.

Arguments for Trade Restrictions

There are numerous arguments for trade restrictions. We present a few of them here.

The National-Defense Argument. It is often argued that certain industries—such as aircraft, petroleum, chemicals, and weapons—are necessary to the national defense. For example, suppose the United States has a comparative advantage in the production of wheat and the Soviet Union has a comparative advantage in the production of weapons. Should the United States specialize in the production of wheat, and then trade wheat to the Soviet Union in exchange for weapons? Many Americans would answer no. It is too dangerous, they maintain, to leave weapons productions to another country—whether that country is the Soviet Union, or England, or Canada.

The national-defense argument may have some validity. But even valid arguments may be abused. Industries that are not really necessary to the national defense may maintain otherwise. In the past, the national-defense argument has been used by some firms in the following industries: pens, pottery, peanuts, papers, candles, thumbtacks, tuna fishing, and pencils.

The Infant-Industry Argument. Alexander Hamilton, the first U.S. secretary of the treasury, argued that "infant" or new industries often need to be protected from older, established foreign competitors until they are mature enough to compete on an equal basis. Today, some persons voice the same argument. The infant-industry argument is clearly an argument for temporary protection. Critics charge, however, that once an industry is protected from foreign competition, removing the protection is almost impossible; the once infant industry will continue to argue that it isn't old enough to go it alone. Critics of the infant-industry argument say that simple everyday politics will make it unlikely that a benefit once bestowed will be removed.

Finally, the infant-industry argument, like the national-defense argument, may be abused. It may well be that all new industries, whether they could currently compete successfully with foreign producers or not, would argue for protection on infant-industry grounds.

Dumping
The sale of goods abroad at a price below their cost and below the price charged in the domestic markets.

The Anti-Dumping Argument. **Dumping** is the sale of goods abroad at a price below their cost and below the price charged in the domestic market. If a French firm sells wine in the United States for a price below the cost of producing the wine and below the price charged in France, it is said to be *dumping* wine in the United States. Critics of dumping maintain that it is an unfair trade practice that puts domestic producers of substitute goods at a disadvantage. Additionally, they charge that dumpers seek only to penetrate a market, drive out domestic competitors, and then raise

Economics in Our Times

Interview: Lester Thurow

Lester Thurow is one of the few economists who is well known to the public. In recent years he has appeared on numerous news programs to discuss such topics as international trade, industrial policy, productivity, and the trade deficit. He is one of the more articulate, well-respected, and sometimes controversial economists on the public scene today. He is currently at the Massachusetts Institute of Technology. We conducted this interview with Professor Thurow on March 30, 1988.

Professor Thurow, in your essay on declining industries in *The New Palgrave: A Dictionary of Economics,* you say, "Almost all countries protect their declining industries to some extent." They do this despite the fact that most economists utilize simple economic models that show that protectionism comes with net costs to society. Why is there so much protectionism in the world?

I think the simple reason is that if you look at the pluses and the minuses from free international trade, the pluses may be bigger than the minuses but the pluses are spread over a very large number of people who all get a small addition to their incomes, and the minuses are spread over a relatively small number of people who take a huge cut in their incomes. For example, if we give $1 to all Americans, and take away $1,000 from each of 100 Americans, then the 100 Americans who are losing are going to put up a tremendous economic fight, and the millions of Americans who are winning are not, because what they are winning is a small amount of money ($1). And this would be the case even if the total winnings are greater than the total losses.

Most Americans appear to believe that Japan is much more protectionist than the United States. Do you think this is true?

If you mean protectionist in terms of formal government rules and regulations that keep out American products, I think the conventional answer is that Japan is slightly more protectionist than the United States. If you count private cultural things that stop outsiders from selling goods and services, then there are many of these things that are in the Japanese system, and are built into the culture, that make it very hard for foreigners to sell, and there are less of these kinds of things built into the American culture.

You have argued that a nation should not prevent declining industries from shrinking, but that it should manage the transition of human resources from old declining industries to new rising industries. Additionally, you have argued that government should pick and back the industries that have great potential for future success and assist them with research funds, subsidies (in some cases), and government contracts. Your critics charge that you have too much faith that government will manage resources in the way you think they ought to be managed. First, how do you respond to your critics? Second, do some countries manage this area of economic life as you think it should be managed in the United States?

Let me start with the last question and move backward. If you look at the Japanese Ministry of International Trade and Industry (MITI), it certainly seems to run a very effective industrial policy. So the answer is that there are some governments that do it.

I guess I would respond to the critics, however, by saying you can't have it both ways. They say, well, the American government can't do this, but then they scream and shout at the Japanese to try to stop them from doing what they say can't be done. You've got to be consistent. If you say it can't work, then you keep your mouth closed about what is happening in Japan. And if you start complaining about what is happening in Japan, then the correct answer is not to get the Japanese to change their behavior, but for Americans to figure out how, in their context, they can do likewise.

You have had more opportunities than most economists to deal with the press, since in recent years you have been interviewed on a number of news programs. Do most of the journalists and news reporters who have interviewed you have an excellent, good, average, or poor understanding of economics?

prices. However, some economists point to the infeasibility of this strategy. Once the dumpers have driven out their competition and raised prices, their competition is likely to return. The dumpers, in turn, would have obtained only a string of losses (owing to their selling below cost) for their efforts. Second, opponents of the anti-dumping argument point out that domestic consumers benefit from dumping. They end up paying lower prices.

The Foreign Export-Subsidies Argument. Some governments subsidize the firms that export goods. If a country offers a below-market (interest rate) loan to a company, it is often argued that the government subsidizes the production of the good the firm produces. If, in turn, that firm exports the good to a foreign country, domestic producers of substitute goods call "foul." They complain that the foreign firm has been given an unfair advantage that they should be protected against.[4] Critics of this position say that one should not turn his or her back on a gift (in the form of lower prices). If foreign governments want to subsidize their exports, and thus give a gift to foreign consumers at the expense of their own taxpayers, then the recipients should not complain. Of course, the recipients are usually not the ones who are complaining. Usually the ones complaining are the domestic producers who can't sell their goods at as high a price because of the gift domestic consumers are receiving from foreign governments.

The Low-Foreign-Wages Argument. It is sometimes argued that American producers can't compete with foreign producers because American producers pay high wages to their workers, and foreign producers pay low wages to their workers. The American producers insist that free trade must be restricted or they will be ruined. What the argument overlooks is the reason American wages are high and foreign wages are low in the first place. In a word, the reason is productivity. High productivity and high wages are usually linked, as are low productivity and low wages. If an American worker, who receives $20 per hour, can produce (on average) 100 units of X per hour, working with numerous capital goods, the cost per unit may be lower than in the case of a foreign worker, who receives $2 per hour, but produces (on average) 5 units of X per hour, working by hand. In short, a country's high-wage disadvantage may be offset by its productivity advantage; a country's low-wage advantage may be offset by its productivity disadvantage. Simply put, high wages do not necessarily mean high costs once productivity (and the costs of nonlabor resources) are factored in.

[4]Words are important in this debate. For example, domestic producers who claim that foreign governments have subsidized foreign firms say that they are not asking for economic *protectionism,* but only for *retaliation,* or *reciprocity,* or simply *tit-for-tat.* The words they use have less negative connotation than the words their opponents use.

The Saving-Domestic-Jobs Argument. Sometimes the argument against completely free trade is made in terms of saving domestic jobs. Actually, we have already discussed this argument in its different guises. For example, the low-foreign-wages argument is one form of it. That argument continues along this line: If domestic producers cannot compete with foreign producers because foreign producers pay low wages and domestic producers pay high wages, domestic producers will go out of business and domestic jobs will be lost. The foreign-export-subsidies argument is another. Its proponents generally state that if foreign-government subsidies give a competitive edge to foreign producers, not only will domestic producers fail but as a result of their failure, domestic jobs will also be lost. The low-foreign-wages and foreign-export-subsidies arguments are also applied to the saving-domestic-jobs argument (so we will not repeat them here). Additionally, critics of the saving-domestic-jobs argument (in all its guises) often argue that if a domestic producer is being outcompeted by foreign producers, and domestic jobs in a particular industry are being lost as a result, the world market is signaling that those labor resources could be put to better use in an industry in which the country holds a comparative advantage.

How Is Trade Restricted?

There are numerous ways to restrict free trade. Tariffs and quotas are two of the more commonly used methods.

Tariff
A tax on imports.

Tariffs. A **tariff** is a tax on imports. The primary effect of a tariff is to raise the price of the imported good to the domestic consumer. Exhibit 20-10 illustrates the effects of a tariff.

■ **EXHIBIT 20-10**
The Effects of a Tariff

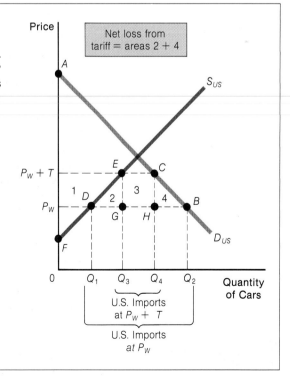

A tariff raises the price of cars from P_w to $P_w + T$, decreases consumers' surplus by areas $1 + 2 + 3 + 4$, increases producers' surplus by area 1, and generates tariff revenues collected by government equal to area 3. Since consumers lose more than producers and government gain, a net loss results from a tariff.

The world price for cars is P_W. At this price, U.S. consumers are buying Q_2 cars: Q_1 from U.S. producers and the difference between Q_2 and Q_1 ($Q_2 - Q_1$) from foreign producers. In other words, U.S. imports at P_W are $Q_2 - Q_1$. In this situation, consumers' surplus is $P_W AB$ and producers' surplus is $P_W DF$.

Now suppose a tariff is imposed. The new price for imported cars in the U.S. car market rises to $P_W + T$ (the world price plus the tariff). At this price, U.S. consumers buy Q_4 number of cars: Q_3 from U.S. producers of cars and $Q_4 - Q_3$ from foreign producers. U.S. imports are $Q_4 - Q_3$, which is a smaller number of imports than at the pretariff price. An effect of tariffs, then, is to reduce imports. At the price $P_W + T$, consumers' surplus is $(P_W + T)AC$, and producers' surplus is $(P_W + T)EF$.

Because of the tariff, consumers' surplus is reduced by an amount equal to the areas $1 + 2 + 3 + 4$, and producers' surplus is increased by an amount equal to area 1. The government collects tariff revenues equal to area 3. This area is obtained by multiplying the number of imports ($Q_4 - Q_3$) times the tariff itself, which is the difference between $P_W + T$ and P_W ($P_W + T - P_W = T$).

In conclusion, the effects of the tariff are a decrease in consumers' surplus, an increase in producers' surplus, and tariff revenues for government. Since the loss to

■ **EXHIBIT 20-11**
Tariff Rates In the United States Since 1860

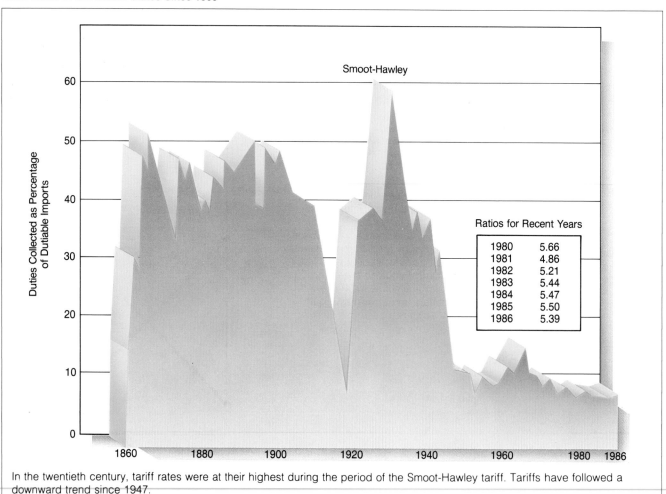

Ratios for Recent Years	
1980	5.66
1981	4.86
1982	5.21
1983	5.44
1984	5.47
1985	5.50
1986	5.39

In the twentieth century, tariff rates were at their highest during the period of the Smoot-Hawley tariff. Tariffs have followed a downward trend since 1947.

SOURCE: U.S. Bureau of the Census, *Historical Statistics of the United States* (Washington, D.C.: U.S. Government Printing Office, 1960); U.S. Bureau of the Census *Statistical Abstract of the United States,* (Washington, D.C.: U.S. Government Printing Office, 1988).

consumers (areas 1 + 2 + 3 + 4) is greater than the gain to producers (area 1) plus the gain to government (area 3), it follows that a net loss results from a tariff. This is the other side of the coin that reads "There is a net gain to free trade."

Exhibit 20-11 illustrates tariff rates in the United States since 1860. In this century, tariff rates were at their highest during the *Smoot-Hawley* tariff, enacted by the Congress in 1930. Numerous economists believe the Smoot-Hawley tariff deepened the depression in the 1930s.

Quota

A legal limit on the amount of a good that may be imported.

Quotas. A **quota** is a legal limit on the amount of a good that may be imported. For example, the government may decide to allow no more than 100,000 foreign cars to be imported, or 10 million barrels of OPEC oil, or 30,000 Japanese television sets. A quota, like a tariff, raises the price of imported goods to domestic consumers. We illustrate this in Exhibit 20-12, which looks much like Exhibit 20-10.

Once again consider the situation in the U.S. car market. At a price of P_W, U.S. consumers buy Q_1 cars from U.S. car producers and import $Q_2 - Q_1$ *from foreign car producers. Consumers' surplus is P_WAB (as it was in the tariff example) and producers' surplus is P_WDF. Suppose now that the U.S. government sets a quota equal to $Q_4 - Q_3$. Since this is the number of foreign cars U.S. consumers imported when the tariff was imposed in our previous example (see Exhibit 20-10), the new price of cars rises to P_Q in Exhibit 20-12 (which is equal to $P_W + T$ in Exhibit 20-10). At P_Q, consumers' surplus is P_QAC and producers' surplus is P_QEF. The decrease in consumers' surplus due to the quota is equal to the areas 1 + 2 + 3 + 4; the increase in producers' surplus is equal to area 1.

But what about area 3? Is this area transferred to government, as was the case when a tariff was imposed? No, it isn't. This area represents the additional revenue earned by the importers (and sellers) of $Q_4 - Q_3$. Without the quota, those importers

■ **EXHIBIT 20-12**
The Effects Of a Quota

A quota that sets the legal limit of imports at $Q_4 - Q_3$ causes the price of cars to increase from P_W to P_Q. As a result, consumers' surplus decreases by the areas 1 + 2 + 3 + 4, producers' surplus increases by area 1, and importers receive higher total revenues on imports $Q_4 - Q_3$, or area 3. Since consumers lose more than producers and importers gain, a net loss results from a quota.

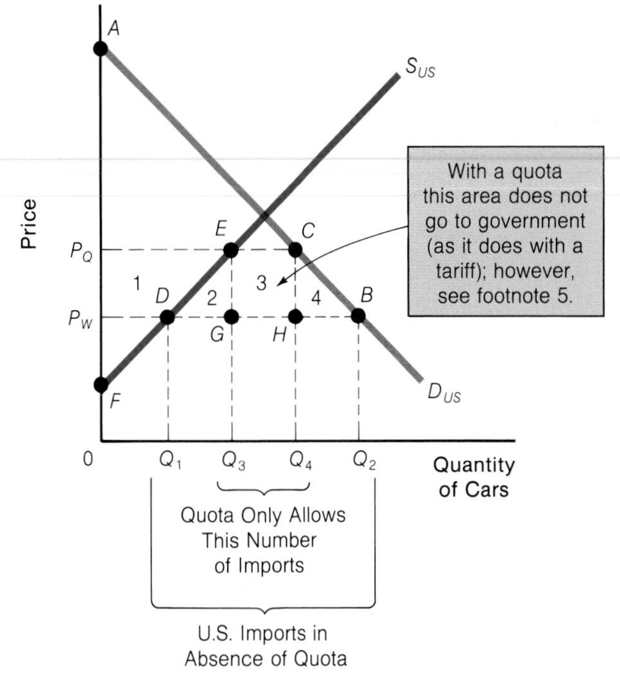

With a quota this area does not go to government (as it does with a tariff); however, see footnote 5.

Quota Only Allows This Number of Imports

U.S. Imports in Absence of Quota

Theory in Practice

Us Against Them, or Us Against Us?

The U.S. auto companies did not have a good year in 1980. The Big Three U.S. auto companies, General Motors, Ford, and Chrysler, sold over 1 million fewer cars in 1980 than in 1979. The Big Three blamed Japanese car imports for their problems and lobbied for protectionism. They said they needed a little time to catch their breath, retool for smaller cars, change their production processes, and cut costs. In a way, they were voicing the infant-industry argument. Given the age of the industries, some have preferred to call it the *senile-industry argument.*

In 1981, some members of Congress argued strongly for severe protectionist measures to be slapped on Japanese car imports. To prevent this, the Reagan administration proposed, and the Japanese agreed to, a **"voluntary" export restraint** (VER). A "voluntary" export restraint is an agreement between two countries in which the exporting country voluntarily agrees to limit its exports to the importing country. (The effects of a "voluntary" export restraint can be analyzed the same way we analyzed a quota.) We put the word *voluntary* in quotation marks because in this case the export restraint was not really voluntary in the way the word is usually understood. The Japanese accepted the VER because, some say, they feared much worse measures if they didn't.

What happened as a result of the VER? In a *Wall Street Journal* article, Robert Crandall of the Brookings Institution, reported that the effects of VER were:

1. In 1983, Japanese car imports were selling for about $1,500 more than they would have without the restraints.
2. In 1984, Japanese car imports were selling for about $2,500 more than they would have without the restraints.
3. In the period 1984–85, U.S. consumers paid about $10 billion more for Japanese cars than they would have in the absence of the restraints.
4. The restraints on imports allowed U.S. car companies to raise their prices by about $1,000 per car.
5. American consumers paid about $16.6 billion more for U.S.-produced cars in 1984–85 because of the restraints.*

*Robert W. Crandall, "Detroit Rode Quotas to Prosperity," *Wall Street Journal*, January 29, 1986, p. 30.

"Voluntary" Export Restraint

An agreement between two countries in which the exporting country "voluntarily" agrees to limit its exports to the importing country.

and sellers of $Q_4 - Q_3$ sold their imported cars for P_W. Their total revenue was therefore $P_W \times (Q_4 - Q_3)$, or the area Q_3GHQ_4. Because of the quota, the price rises to P_Q and their total revenue is $P_Q \times (Q_4 - Q_3)$, or the area Q_3ECQ_4. The difference between total revenues on $Q_4 - Q_3$ imports without a quota and with a quota is the area 3.

In conclusion, the effects of a quota are a decrease in consumers' surplus (areas 1 + 2 + 3 + 4), an increase in producers' surplus (area 1), and an increase in total revenue for the importers who sell the quota (area 3). Since consumers lose more than domestic producers and importers gain, a net loss results from a quota.[5]

---

[5]It is perhaps incorrect to imply that government receives *nothing* from a quota. Although it receives nothing directly, it may gain indirectly. Economists generally argue that since government officials are likely to be the persons who will decide which importers will get to satisfy the quota, they will naturally be lobbied by importers; thus government officials will likely receive *something*, if only dinner at an expensive restaurant, while the lobbyist makes his or her pitch. In short, in the course of the lobbying, resources will be spent by lobbyists as they curry favor with those government officials or politicians who have the power to make the decision as to who gets to sell the limited number of imported goods. In economics, lobbyists' activities, geared toward obtaining a special privilege, are referred to as *rent seeking.*

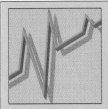

Theory in Practice

Brother, Do You Have $85,000 to Spare to Save a $24,000 Job?

Suppose the U.S. government imposes a tariff on imported good X. As a result, the domestic producers of good X sell their goods for higher prices, receive higher producers' surplus, and are generally better off. Some of the domestic workers who produce good X are better off, too. Perhaps without the tariff on imports of good X some of them would have lost their jobs.

Such scenarios raise two important questions: How many domestic jobs in the firms that produce good X are saved because of the tariff? How much do consumers have to pay in higher prices to save these jobs? Economists are inter-ested in answering such questions. Here are a few answers for different industries at different times.

In 1977, tariffs and quotas were imposed on imports of foreign footwear. An estimated 21,000 domestic jobs were protected in the domestic footwear industry as a result. The average worker in the industry earned $8,340 (in 1980 dollars). Domestic consumers paid $77,714 for *each* $8,340 domestic footwear job protected.

In 1977, tariffs and quotas were imposed on imports of carbon steel. An estimated 20,000 domestic jobs in the in-dustry were protected as a result. The average worker in the industry earned $24,329 (again in 1980 dollars). In this case domestic consumers paid $85,272 for *each* $24,329 job protected.

In 1981, "voluntary" export restraints were placed on Jap-anese car imports (see the Theory in Practice, "Us against Them, or Us against Us?"). The U.S. International Trade Commission estimated that 44,000 domestic jobs were pro-tected—at a cost of $193,000 per job.

Sources: Keith E. Maskus, "Rising Protectionism and International Trade Pol-icy," Federal Reserve Bank of Kansas City, *Economic Review* (July/August 1984): 3–17; *Washington Post*, February 21, 1985, p. A18.

Question:

It appears that the following statements are true:

1. *Tariffs and quotas generate a net loss (consumers lose more than producers, importers, and governments gain).*

2. *Tariffs and quotas exist in the real world.*

3. *Neither tariffs nor quotas would or could exist without government sanction.*

Given these facts, would it be reasonable to conclude that governments, at least on the issue of international trade, do not try to promote the general welfare?

Answer:

Many persons have come to this conclusion. However, other persons argue that things aren't quite as black and white as the diagrams may make them appear. They say that the reasons for limiting trade (see the earlier section) have to be considered alongside the diagrams that clearly show a net loss from limiting free trade.

Balancing Aggregate Benefits from Free Trade against Individual Losses

International trade is a place where economics and politics often do battle. The simple tools of supply and demand and consumers' and producers' surplus tell us that there are net gains from free trade; limiting exports or imports serves only to make living standards, on the whole, lower than they would be if free trade were permitted.

But, on the other hand, there are the harsh realities of life. Domestic producers may advocate quotas and tariffs to make themselves better off, but give little thought to the negative effects felt by foreign producers or domestic consumers. And domestic consumers may advocate policies that prohibit exports to make themselves better off, but give little thought to the negative effects felt by foreign consumers or domestic producers.

Perhaps the battle over international trade comes down to this: Policies are largely advocated, argued, and lobbied for based more on their *distributional effects* than on their aggregate or overall effects. On an aggregate level, free trade produces a net gain for society whereas restricted trade produces a net loss. But just because free trade *in the aggregate* produces a net gain does not mean that every single person benefits more from free trade than restricted trade. This chapter has presented numerous examples where a subset of the population gains more, in a particular instance, from restricted trade than from free trade. In short, perhaps real-world policies are often determined more by the answer to the question, How does it affect *me?* than by How does it affect *us?*

■ CHAPTER SUMMARY

Specialization and Trade

■ A country has an absolute advantage in the production of a good if, using the same amount of resources as another country, it can produce more of a particular good. A country has a comparative advantage in the production of a good it produces at lower opportunity cost than another country.

■ Individuals in countries that specialize and trade have a higher standard of living than would be the case if they did not specialize and did not trade.

■ Government officials do not sit down with cost data and determine what their country should specialize in and trade. Instead, the desire to earn a dollar, franc, or pound guides individuals' actions and produces the unintended consequence that countries specialize in and trade the good(s) in which they have a comparative advantage. However, trade restrictions can change this outcome.

International Trade: Distributional Effects

■ Consumers' surplus is greater if exports are prohibited than if they are permitted.

■ Producers' surplus is greater if exports are permitted than if they are prohibited.

■ Consumers' surplus is greater if imports are permitted than if they are prohibited.

■ Producers' surplus is greater if imports are prohibited than if they are permitted.

■ Producers lose more than consumers gain from a policy that prohibits exports. Thus prohibiting exports results in a net loss.

■ Consumers lose more than producers gain from a policy that prohibits imports. Thus prohibiting imports results in a net loss.

■ Producers gain more than consumers lose from a policy that permits exports. Thus permitting exports results in a net gain.

■ Consumers gain more than producers lose from a policy that permits imports. Thus permitting imports results in a net gain.

Arguments for Trade Restrictions

■ The national-defense argument states that certain goods—such as aircraft, petroleum, chemicals, and weapons—are necessary to the national defense and should be produced domestically whether the country has a comparative advantage in the production of them or not.

■ The infant-industry argument states that "infant" or new industries should be protected from free (foreign) trade so that they may have time to develop and compete on an even basis with older, more established foreign industries.

■ The anti-dumping argument states that domestic producers should not have to compete (on an unequal basis) with foreign producers that sell products below cost and below the prices they charge in their domestic markets.

■ The foreign-export-subsidies argument states that domestic producers should not have to compete (on an unequal basis) with foreign producers that have been subsidized by their governments.

■ The low-foreign-wages argument states that domestic producers cannot compete with foreign producers that pay low wages to their employees when domestic producers pay high wages to their employees. In order that high-paying domestic firms may survive, limits on free trade are proposed.

■ The saving-domestic-jobs argument states that either through low foreign wages or government subsidies (or dumping, and so forth), foreign producers will be able to outcompete domestic producers, and therefore domestic jobs will be lost. In order that domestic firms may survive, and domestic jobs not be lost, limits on free trade are proposed.

■ The arguments for trade restrictions are not accepted as valid by all persons. Critics often maintain that the arguments can be and are abused and, in most cases, are motivated by self-interest.

Tariffs and Quotas

■ A tariff is a tax on imports. A quota is a legal limit on the amount of a good that may be imported.

■ Both tariffs and quotas raise the price of imports.

■ Tariffs lead to a decrease in consumers' surplus, an increase in producers' surplus, and tariff revenues for the government. Consumers lose more through tariffs than producers and government (together) gain.

■ Quotas lead to a decrease in consumers' surplus, an increase in producers' surplus, and additional revenues for the importers that sell the quota. Consumers lose more through quotas than producers and importers (taken together) gain.

■ QUESTIONS TO ANSWER AND DISCUSS

1. A production possibilities frontier is usually drawn for a country. One could, however, be drawn for the world. Picture the world's production possibilities frontier in your mind. Is the world positioned at a point on the curve or below the frontier? Give a reason for your answer.

2. Using the data in the table answer the questions that follow.

POINTS ON PRODUCTION POSSIBILITIES FRONTIER	CANADA		ITALY	
	GOOD X	GOOD Y	GOOD X	GOOD Y
A	150	0	90	0
B	100	25	60	60
C	50	50	30	120
D	0	75	0	180

a. In which good does Canada have a comparative advantage?
b. In which good does Italy have a comparative advantage?
c. What might be a set of favorable terms of trade for the two countries?
d. Prove that both countries would be better off in the specialization-trade case than in the no specialization–no trade case.

3. "Whatever can be done by a tariff can be done by a quota." Discuss.

4. Consider two groups of domestic producers: domestic producers that compete with imports and domestic producers that export goods. Suppose the domestic producers that compete with imports convince the legislature to impose a high tariff on imports, so high in fact that almost all imports are eliminated. Does this policy in any way adversely affect domestic producers that export goods?

5. Suppose the U.S. government wants to curtail imports, would it be likely to favor a tariff or a quota to accomplish its objective? Why?

6. Suppose the land mass known to you as the United States of America had been composed over the past 200 years of 50 separate countries instead of 50 separate states. Would you expect the standard of living of the people who inhabit this land mass to be higher, lower, or equal to what it is today? Why?

7. Even though Jeremy is a better gardener and novelist than Bill is, he (Jeremy) still hires Bill as his gardener. Why?

8. Suppose that tomorrow a constitutional convention were called and you were chosen as one of the delegates from your state. You and the other delegates must decide whether it will be constitutional or unconstitutional for the federal government to impose tariffs and quotas or restrict international trade in any way. What would be your position?

9. Some economists have argued that since domestic consumers gain more from free trade than domestic producers gain from (import) tariffs and quotas, consumers should buy out domestic producers and rid themselves of costly tariffs and quotas. For example, if consumers save $400 million from free trade (through paying lower prices) and producers gain $100 million from tariffs and quotas, consumers can pay producers something more than $100 million but less than $400 million and get producers to favor free trade, too. Assuming this scheme were feasible, what do you think of it?

Chapter 21

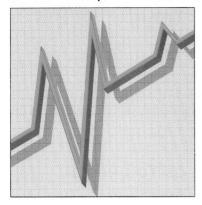

International Finance

■ INTRODUCTION

The meeting described here did not happen. But surely something very close to it did—many times.

It was nine o'clock in the morning at the White House. The president, the chairman of the Board of Governors of the Federal Reserve, and the secretary of the treasury met in the Oval Office. The president sat down in a big comfortable chair. The Treasury secretary sat on the sofa, and the Fed chairman sat across from him on a hard-backed chair. Together, they formed a triangle.

The president began. "What are we going to do about the trade figures and the dollar?" he asked. He looked at the two men as if he wanted a nice, simple answer.

The Treasury secretary spoke up, "We're in somewhat of a dilemma, Mr. President. The Fed eased up on the money supply after the recent scare in the stock market, and that seems to have calmed things here at home. But on the other hand, the action lowered interest rates and pushed the dollar down on the foreign exchange markets. We didn't really want that right now."

"There's been some support for the dollar from the French and the West Germans," the Fed chairman said. "But the markets are getting jittery; they don't seem to think this will continue."

"Will it?" the president asked.

"I'm not really sure," said the Fed chairman.

"Will the dollar stabilize soon?" the president asked.

"I think so," said the Treasury secretary. The Fed chairman nodded in agreement, but only half-heartedly.

The president wasn't sure exactly what that meant.

"Should we just wait it out, or take some action now?" the president asked.

"Well . . .," said the Fed chairman.

The meeting ended at 9:34 A.M.

◼ WHAT THIS CHAPTER IS ABOUT

Chapter 20 presented the *real* side of international transactions. Money did not figure prominently in the picture. Principally, we concentrated on the goods being produced in one country and traded in others.

Chapter 21 presents the *monetary* side of international transactions. Here money does figure prominently in the picture. All types of monies are involved: U.S. dollars, Japanese yen, English pounds, French francs, Indian rupees, and more.

In discussions of the monetary side of international transactions, two topics naturally appear: the balance of payments and exchange rates. We discuss both in this chapter.

Key Questions to Keep in Mind as You Read

1. What is the merchandise trade balance? What is the balance of payments?
2. What is a flexible exchange rate system? What is a fixed exchange rate system?
3. How is an international purchase different from a domestic purchase?
4. What does it mean to say a currency is overvalued or undervalued?
5. What causes a currency to depreciate in value or to appreciate in value?
6. What is the difference between devaluation and depreciation? What is the difference between revaluation and appreciation?
7. How would an international gold standard work?
8. What is the J-curve?

THE BALANCE OF PAYMENTS

Balance of Payments

A periodic statement (usually annual) of the money value of all transactions between residents of one country and residents of all other countries.

Debit

In the balance of payments, any transaction that either supplies the nation's currency or creates a demand for foreign currency in the foreign exchange market.

Credit

In the balance of payments, any transaction that either supplies a foreign currency or creates a demand for the nation's currency in the foreign exchange market.

Countries keep track of their domestic level of production by calculating their gross national product; similarly, they keep track of the flow of their international trade (receipts and expenditures) by calculating their **balance of payments.** The balance of payments is a periodic statement (usually annual) of the money value of all transactions between residents of one country and residents of all other countries. The balance of payments provides information relating to a nation's imports and exports, domestic residents' earnings on assets located abroad, foreign earnings on domestic assets, gifts to and from foreign countries (including foreign aid), and official transactions by governments and central banks.

Balance of payments accounts record both debits and credits. A debit is indicated by a minus (−) sign, and a credit is indicated by a plus (+) sign. *Any transaction that supplies the nation's currency in the foreign exchange market is recorded as a* **debit.**

For example, if Americans buy Japanese television sets, they must first buy Japanese yen by selling (supplying) U.S. dollars. This import transaction is listed as a debit in the U.S. balance of payments.

Similarly, *any transaction that supplies a foreign currency in the foreign exchange market is recorded as a* **credit.** If the Japanese buy American computers, they must first buy U.S. dollars by selling (supplying) Japanese yen. This export transaction is listed as a credit in the U.S. balance of payments.

The international transactions that occur, and are summarized in the balance of payments, can be grouped into three categories. Simply put, the balance of payments is composed of three accounts: the current account, the capital account, and the official reserve account—and a statistical discrepancy. We have illustrated a U.S. balance of payments account for year Z in Exhibit 21-1. The data in the exhibit are hypothetical (to make our calculations simpler), but not unrealistic.

EXHIBIT 21-1
U.S. Balance of Payments, Year Z

CURRENT ACCOUNT

1. EXPORTS OF GOODS AND SERVICES   +340
    a. Merchandise exports (including military sales)   +220
    b. Services   +30
    c. Income from U.S. assets abroad   +90

2. IMPORTS OF GOODS AND SERVICES   −390
    a. Merchandise imports (including military purchases)   −300
    b. Services   −40
    c. Income from foreign assets in U.S.   −50

Merchandise Trade Balance
Difference between value of merchandise exports (item 1a)
and value of merchandise imports (item 2a): +220 − 300 = −80

3. NET UNILATERAL TRANSFERS ABROAD   −11

Current Account Balance
Items 1, 2, 3: +340 − 390 −11 = ————————————————→   −61

CAPITAL ACCOUNT

4. OUTFLOW OF U.S. CAPITAL   −16
5. INFLOW OF FOREIGN CAPITAL   +60

Capital Account Balance
Items 4 and 5: −16 + 60 = ————————————————→   +44

OFFICIAL RESERVE ACCOUNT

6. INCREASE (−) IN U.S. OFFICIAL RESERVE ASSETS   −4
7. INCREASE (+) IN FOREIGN OFFICIAL ASSETS IN U.S.   +3

Official Reserve Balance
Items 6 and 7: −4 + 3 = ————————————————→   −1

STATISTICAL DISCREPANCY   +18

TOTAL $0 $0
                                                        (Always zero)

Balance of Payments =

Summary statistic of all ◇ items (items 1-7 and the statistical discrepancy)

+$340 − 390 −11 −16 + 60 − 4 + 3 + 18 = $0

or

Summary statistic of all ▮ items (current account balance, capital account balance,
official reserve balance, and the statistical discrepancy)

−$61 + 44 − 1 + 18 = $0

Note: the pluses (+) and minuses (−) in the exhibit serve two purposes. First, they
distinguish between credits and debits. A plus is always placed before a credit, and
a minus is always placed before a debit. Second, in terms of our calculations, we
view the pluses and minuses as operational signs. In other words, if a number has a
plus in front of it, we simply add it to our total. If a number has a minus in front of it,
we simply subtract it from our total.

The data in this exhibit are hypothetical but not unrealistic. All numbers are in billions
of dollars. The plus and minus signs in the exhibit should be viewed as operational
signs.

Question:

When Americans buy Japanese goods, they supply dollars and demand yen. When the Japanese buy American goods, they supply yen and demand dollars. Thus the first transaction is recorded as a debit (since it supplies the nation's currency) and the second as a credit (since it supplies a foreign currency) in the U.S. balance of payments. Is this correct?

Answer:

Yes, that is correct.

The Current Account

Current Account

Includes all payments related to the purchase and sale of goods and services. Components of the account include exports, imports, and net unilateral transfers abroad.

The **current account** includes all payments related to the purchase and sale of goods and services. There are three major components of the current account: exports of goods and services, imports of goods and services, and net unilateral transfers abroad.

Exports of Goods and Services. Americans export goods (say, cars), they export services (say, insurance, banking, transportation and tourism), and they receive investment income on assets they own abroad. All three activities increase the demand for U.S. dollars at the same time as they increase the supply of foreign currencies; thus they are recorded as credits (+). For example, if a foreigner buys a U.S. computer, payment must ultimately be made in U.S. dollars. Thus she is required to supply her nation's currency when she demands U.S. dollars. (Note that we use "foreigner" in this chapter to mean someone in a foreign country.)

Foreign Exchange Market

The market in which currencies of different countries are exchanged.

Merchandise Trade Balance

The difference between the value of merchandise exports and the value of merchandise imports.

Merchandise Trade Deficit

The situation where the value of merchandise exports is less than the value of merchandise imports.

Merchandise Trade Surplus

The situation where the value of merchandise exports is greater than the value of merchandise imports.

Imports of Goods and Services. Americans import goods and services, and foreigners receive income on assets they own in the United States. These activities increase the demand for foreign currencies at the same time as they increase the supply of U.S. dollars to the **foreign exchange market;** thus they are recorded as debits (−). For example, if an American buys a Japanese car, payment must ultimately be made in Japanese yen. Thus he is required to supply U.S. dollars when he demands Japanese yen. Exhibit 21-1 shows that exports of goods and services totaled +$340 billion in year Z, and imports of goods and services totaled −$390 billion.[1]

If we look at the difference between the value of merchandise exports (1a in Exhibit 21-1) and the value of merchandise imports (2a in the exhibit), ignoring for now export and import services as well as income from U.S. assets abroad and income from foreign assets in the United States, we have the **merchandise trade balance** (or balance of trade). Specifically, the merchandise trade balance is the difference between the value of merchandise exports and the value of merchandise imports. In year Z this was −$80 billion. If the value of a country's merchandise exports is less than the value of its merchandise imports, it is said to have a **merchandise trade deficit.** If the value of a country's merchandise exports is greater than the value of its merchandise imports, it is said to have a **merchandise trade surplus.** Exhibit 21-2 shows the U.S. merchandise trade balance from 1960 through 1987.

[1]We realize that in everyday language, people do not say, "Exports were a *positive* $X billion, and imports were a *negative* $Y." We do not mean to imply that they do by placing a plus sign (+) in front of exports and a minus sign (−) in front of imports. We are using the signs to reinforce the essential point that exports are credits and imports are debits. This specificity will be useful later when we calculate certain account balances.

EXHIBIT 21-2
U.S. Merchandise Trade Balance, 1960–87

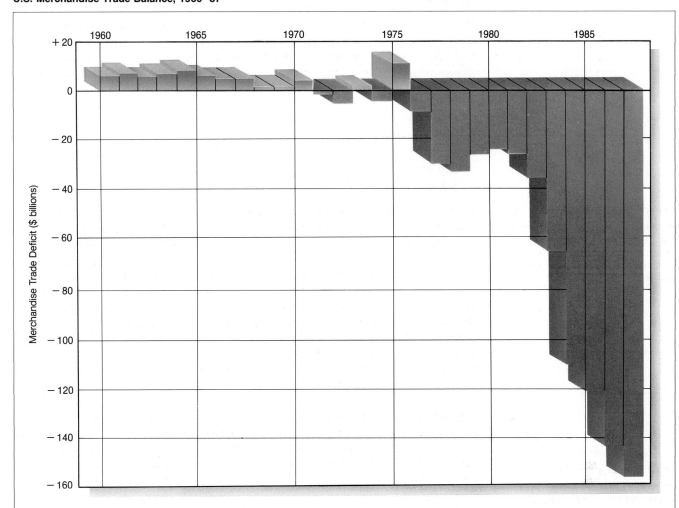

In the 1960s there were numerous years with a merchandise trade surplus. In the 1970s and 1980s there were numerous years with a merchandise trade deficit. The minus sign (−) in front of deficit figures signifies that merchandise exports were less than merchandise imports. The merchandise trade deficit for the first quarter of 1988 (not shown in the exhibit) was $39.5 billion.

SOURCE: Council of Economic Advisers, *Economic Report of the President, 1988* (Washington, D.C.: U.S. Government Printing Office, 1988). U.S. Commerce Department.

Question:

In Exhibit 21-1, merchandise exports are +$220 billion (item 1a) and merchandise imports are −$300 billion (item 2a). Can't the merchandise trade balance be calculated simply by subtracting the merchandise imports from merchandise exports?

Answer:

Yes, it can be calculated by subtracting merchandise imports from merchandise exports. But we must be careful not to make the mistake of *subtracting a minus $300 billion* from a *positive $220 billion*. In other words, we don't do this: Merchandise trade balance = $220 billion − (−$300 billion). This equals $520 billion.

Instead, we simply subtract the *value of the merchandise imports*, which is $300 billion, pure and simple, from the value of the merchandise exports, which is $220 billion. In other words, Balance of trade = $220 billion − $300 billion. This equals − $80 billion.

In terms of calculations, the positive and minus signs in Exhibit 21-1 are operational signs. When a minus sign (−) appears in front of a number, we simply subtract that number from the total. When a positive sign (+) appears in front of a number, we simply add that number to the total.

Net Unilateral Transfers Abroad. *Unilateral transfers* are one-way money payments. They can go from Americans or the U.S. government to foreigners or to foreign governments. If an American sends money to a relative in a foreign country, or the U.S. government gives money to a foreign country as a gift or grant, or an American decides to retire in a foreign country and receives a Social Security check there, all these transactions are referred to as *unilateral transfers.*

Unilateral transfers can also go from foreigners or foreign governments to Americans or to the U.S. government. If a foreign citizen sends money to a relative living in the United States, this is a unilateral transfer.

If an American makes a unilateral transfer abroad, this gives rise to a demand for foreign currency and a supply of U.S. dollars; thus it is entered as a debit item in the U.S. balance of payments accounts. If a foreigner makes a unilateral transfer to an American, this gives rise to a supply of foreign currency (and demand for U.S. dollars) and thus is entered as a credit item in the U.S. balance of payments accounts. For year Z we have assumed that unilateral transfers made by Americans to foreign citizens were greater than unilateral transfers made by foreign citizens to Americans; thus we get a negative *net* dollar amount, − $11 billion in this case. This is referred to as *net unilateral transfers abroad.*

Items 1, 2, and 3 in Exhibit 21-1—or simply, exports of goods and services, imports of goods and services, and net unilateral transfers abroad—are known as the current account. Specifically, the **current account balance** is the summary statistic for these three items. In year Z it is − $61 billion. The news media sometimes call the current account balance the *balance of payments*. To an economist, this is incorrect. As we shall soon see, the balance of payments includes several more items.

Capital Account

The **capital account** includes all payments related to the purchase and sale of assets and to borrowing and lending activities. Its major components are outflow of U.S. capital and inflow of foreign capital.

Outflow of U.S. Capital. American purchases of foreign assets and U.S. loans to foreigners are outflows of U.S. capital. As such, they give rise to a demand for foreign currency and a supply of U.S. dollars on the foreign exchange market. Hence they are considered a debit. For example, if an American wants to buy land in Brazil, U.S. dollars must be supplied to purchase (demand) Brazilian cruzados.

Inflow of Foreign Capital. Foreign purchases of U.S. assets and foreign loans to Americans are inflows of foreign capital. As such, they give rise to a demand for U.S. dollars and to a supply of foreign currency on the foreign exchange market. Hence, they are considered a credit. For example, if a West German buys a U.S. Treasury bill, German marks must be supplied to purchase (demand) U.S. dollars.

Current Account Balance
The summary statistic for exports of goods and services, imports of goods and services, and net unilateral transfers.

Capital Account
Includes all payments related to the purchase and sale of assets and to borrowing and lending activities. Components include outflow of U.S. capital and inflow of foreign capital.

Capital Account Balance

The summary statistic for the outflow of U.S. capital and the inflow of foreign capital. It is equal to the difference between the outflow of U.S. capital and the inflow of foreign capital.

Items 4 and 5 in Exhibit 21-1—or simply, outflow of U.S. capital and inflow of foreign capital—comprise the capital account. Specifically, the **capital account balance** is the summary statistic for these two items. It is equal to the difference between the outflow of U.S. capital and the inflow of foreign capital. In year Z it is $44 billion.

Official Reserve Account

A government possesses official reserve balances in the form of foreign currencies, gold, its reserve position in the International Monetary Fund (discussed later), and *special drawing rights* (also discussed later). Countries with a deficit in the current and capital accounts can draw on their reserves. For example, if the United States has a combined deficit in its current and capital accounts of $5 billion, it could draw down its official reserves to meet this combined deficit. Viewing item 6, we see that the United States increased its reserve assets by $4 billion in year Z. This is a debit item since if the United States acquires official reserves (say, through the purchase of a foreign currency), it has increased the demand for the foreign currency and supplied dollars. Thus an increase in official reserves is like an outflow of capital in the capital account and appears as a payment with a negative sign. It follows that an increase in foreign official assets in the United States is a credit item.

Statistical Discrepancy

If someone buys a U.S. dollar with, say, Swiss francs, someone must sell a U.S. dollar. Thus *dollars purchased = dollars sold*. In all the transactions discussed earlier—exporting goods, importing goods, sending money to relatives in foreign countries, buying land in foreign countries—dollars were bought and sold. The total number of dollars sold must always equal the total number of dollars purchased. However, balance of payments accountants do not have complete information; they can only record credits and debits that they observe. This means there may be more debits or credits than those observed in a given year. Suppose in year Z *all* debits are observed and recorded, but *not all* credits are observed and recorded—perhaps because of smuggling activities, secret bank accounts, people living in more than one country, and so on. To adjust for this, balance of payments accountants make use of the *statistical discrepancy*, which is that part of the balance of payments that adjusts for missing information. In Exhibit 21-1, the statistical discrepancy is +$18 billion. This means that $18 billion worth of credits (+) went unobserved in year Z. There were probably some hidden exports and unrecorded capital inflows that year.

What the Balance of Payments Equals

The balance of payments is the summary statistic for the following: exports of goods and services (item 1), imports of goods and services (item 2), net unilateral transfers abroad (item 3), the outflow of U.S. capital (item 4), the inflow of foreign capital (item 5), the increase in U.S. official reserve assets (item 6), the increase in foreign official assets in the United States (item 7), and the statistical discrepancy. Calculating the balance of payments, we have (in billions of dollars) $+340 - 390 - 11 - 16 + 60 - 4 + 3 + 18 = 0$.

Alternatively, the balance of payments is the summary statistic for the following: the current account balance, capital account balance, official reserve balance, and statistical discrepancy. Calculating the balance of payments we have (in billions of dollars) $-61 + 44 - 1 + 18 = 0$. The balance of payments for the United States in year Z equals *zero*. Fact is, the balance of payments *always* equals zero.

Question:

If the balance of payments is always zero, why do news reporters sometimes speak of a deficit in the U.S. balance of payments? Second, why does the balance of payments always equal zero?

Answer:

As we mentioned earlier, news reporters don't always use the term "balance of payments" as strictly as economists use the term. Some news reporters refer to the current account balance as the balance of payments. Other reporters refer to the current account balance *plus* the capital account balance as the balance of payments.

The reason the balance of payments always equals zero is that the three accounts that comprise the balance of payments, when taken together, plus the statistical discrepancy, include all of the *sources* and all of the *uses* of dollars in international transactions. And since every dollar used must have a source, adding the sources (+) to the uses (−) necessarily gives us zero.

FLEXIBLE EXCHANGE RATES

Exchange rate

The price of one currency in terms of another currency; e.g., 1 dollar = 2 marks.

Flexible Exchange Rate System

The system whereby exchange rates are determined by the forces of supply and demand for a currency.

If a U.S. buyer wants to purchase a good from a U.S. seller, the buyer simply turns over to the seller the required number of U.S. dollars. If, however, a U.S. buyer wants to purchase a good from a seller in France, it is a slightly different matter. First, the U.S. buyer must exchange her U.S. dollars for French francs, and then with the French francs she buys the good from the French seller. The market in which currencies of different countries are exchanged, as we mentioned earlier, is the foreign exchange market.

In the foreign exchange market, currencies are bought and sold for a price, or an **exchange rate.** For instance, it might take $1.50 to buy a British pound, 17 cents to buy a French franc, 58 cents to buy a West German mark, or seven-tenths of 1 cent to buy a Japanese yen. In this section we discuss how exchange rates are determined in the foreign exchange market when the forces of supply and demand are allowed to rule. Economists refer to this as a **flexible exchange rate system.** In the next section we discuss how exchange rates are determined under a fixed exchange rate system.

The Demand and Supply of Currencies

To simplify our analysis, we assume that there are only two countries in the world, the United States and Great Britain. This then means that there are only two currencies in the world, the dollar ($) and the pound (£). In this two-country two-currency world, what constitutes the demand for dollars or the supply of dollars on the foreign exchange market? What constitutes the demand for pounds or the supply of pounds?

Odd as it may appear at first sight, the demand for dollars and the supply of pounds are linked, as are the demand for pounds and the supply of dollars. To illustrate, suppose an American wants to buy a British Rolls Royce. Before he can purchase the Rolls Royce, the American must buy British pounds—hence, British pounds are demanded. But the American buys British pounds with dollars; that is, he supplies dollars to the foreign exchange market in order to demand British pounds. We conclude that the American demand for British goods leads to a demand for British pounds and to a supply of U.S. dollars on the foreign exchange market.

The story is similar if a British buyer wants to buy an American Cadillac. Before she can purchase the Cadillac, the British buyer must buy dollars—hence U.S. dollars are demanded. The British buyer buys the dollars with pounds. We conclude that the British demand for American goods leads to a demand for U.S. dollars and to a supply of British pounds on the foreign exchange market. This process is illustrated in Exhibit 21-3.

Exhibit 21-3a shows the market for British pounds. (Exhibit 21-3b shows the market for U.S. dollars, which mirrors what is happening in the market for British pounds.) On the horizontal axis we have placed the "quantity of pounds," and on the vertical axis, the exchange rate—specifically, the dollar price per pound. Notice that the demand curve for British pounds is downward sloping, indicating that as the dollar price per pound increases, Americans buy fewer pounds, and as the dollar price per pound decreases, Americans buy more pounds. For example, if it takes $1.90 to buy one pound, Americans will buy fewer pounds than they would if it takes $1.50 to buy one pound. Simply put, the higher the dollar price per pound, the more expensive British goods are for Americans and the fewer British goods Americans will buy; thus fewer pounds will be demanded.

The supply of pounds is upward sloping. It is easy to understand why if we recall that the supply of British pounds is linked to the British demand for American goods and U.S. dollars. Consider a $1.90 price for a pound compared with a price of $1.50 a pound. At $1.50 = £1, a British buyer gives up one pound for which he receives $1.50 in return. But at $1.90 = £1, a British buyer gives up one pound and receives $1.90 in return. At which exchange rate are American goods *cheaper* for the British? The answer is at the exchange rate of $1.90 = £1.

To see this explicitly, consider an American computer with a price tag of $1,000. At an exchange rate of $1.90 = £1, the British will have to pay approximately £526

■ EXHIBIT 21-3
Translating U.S. Demand for Pounds Into U.S. Supply of Dollars, and British Demand for Dollars into British Supply of Pounds

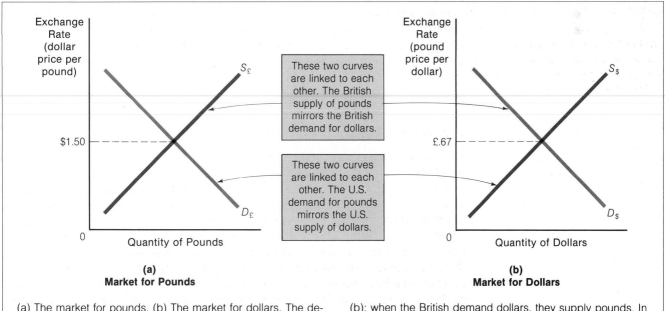

(a) The market for pounds. (b) The market for dollars. The demand for pounds in (a) is linked to the supply of dollars in (b): when Americans demand pounds, they supply dollars. The supply of pounds in (a) is linked to the demand for dollars in (b): when the British demand dollars, they supply pounds. In (a), the exchange rate is $1.50 = £1, which is equal to £.67 = $1 in (b). Exchange rates are the reciprocals of each other.

to buy the American computer ($1,000/$1.90 = £526). But at an exchange rate of $1.50 = £1, the British will have to pay approximately £667 pounds ($1,000/$1.50 = £667). To the British, the American computer is cheaper at the exchange rate of $1.90 per pound than at $1.50 per pound. It follows, then, that the higher the dollar price per pound, the more dollars will be demanded by the British (because American goods will be cheaper), and therefore the more pounds will be supplied to the foreign exchange market. The upward-sloping supply curve for pounds illustrates this.[2]

The Equilibrium Exchange Rate

In a completely flexible exchange rate system, where the forces of supply and demand are allowed to rule, the equilibrium exchange rate (dollar price per pound) will be $1.50 = £1 in Exhibit 21-4. At this dollar price per pound, the quantity demanded of pounds equals the quantity supplied of pounds. There are no shortages or surpluses of pounds. At any other exchange rate, however, either an excess demand for pounds or an excess supply of pounds exists.

Let's look at the exchange rate of $1.90 = £1. At this exchange rate, a surplus of pounds exists. As a result, downward pressure will be placed on the dollar price of a pound (just as downward pressure would be placed on the dollar price of an apple if there were a surplus of apples). If, however, the exchange rate were $1.10 = £1, there would be a shortage of pounds, and upward pressure would be placed on the dollar price of a pound.

It is also important to note that exchange rates are reciprocals of each other. To take a simple example, if 1 pound = 2 dollars, then 1 dollar = ½ pound.

Question:

Are the demand and supply curves in Exhibit 21-4 related in any way to the U.S. balance of payments in Exhibit 21-1?

[2]Actually, the supply curve here is upward sloping because we have assumed that the British demand for American goods is price elastic. This assumption will hold for most of this chapter. We bring price elasticity of demand into the discussion explicitly when we discuss the J-curve toward the end of the chapter.

■ **EXHIBIT 21-4**
The Foreign Exchange Market

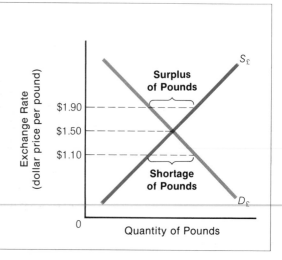

The demand for pounds is downward sloping: The higher the dollar price of pounds, the fewer pounds will be demanded; the lower the dollar price of pounds, the more pounds will be demanded. At $1.90 = £1, there is a surplus of pounds, placing downward pressure on the exchange rate. At $1.10 = £1, there is a shortage of pounds, placing upward pressure on the exchange rate. At the equilibrium exchange rate, $1.50 = £1, the quantity demanded of pounds equals the quantity supplied of pounds.

Answer:

Yes, they are. For example, U.S. exports represent a demand for U.S. dollars by foreigners (and therefore constitute the supply of foreign currencies) while U.S. imports represent the U.S. demand for foreign currencies (and therefore constitute the supply of U.S. dollars). In fact, any dollar amount with a plus sign (+) in front of it in Exhibit 21-1 represents a demand for U.S. dollars and a supply of foreign currencies, and any dollar amount with a minus sign (−) in front of it represents a demand for foreign currencies and a supply of dollars.

Changes in the Equilibrium Exchange Rate

In Chapter 3 we learned that a change in the demand for a good, or the supply of a good, or both would change the equilibrium price of the good. The same holds true for the price of currencies. A change in the demand for pounds, or a change in the supply of pounds, or a change in both will change the equilibrium dollar price per pound. If the dollar price per pound rises—say, from $1.50 = £1 to $1.80 = £1—the pound is said to have **appreciated** and the dollar to have **depreciated.**

A currency has appreciated in value if it takes more of a foreign currency to buy it. A currency has depreciated in value if it takes more of it to buy a foreign currency. For example, a movement in the exchange rate from $1.50 = £1 to $1.80 = £1 means that more dollars are necessary to buy one pound, so the pound has appreciated (the other side of the coin is that fewer pounds are necessary to buy one dollar). And since more dollars are necessary to buy one pound, the dollar has depreciated.

If the equilibrium exchange rate can change owing to a change in the demand for and supply of a currency, then it is important to understand what factors can change the demand for and supply of a currency. Three are presented here.

A Difference in Income Growth Rates. An increase in a nation's income will usually cause the nation's residents to buy more of both domestic and foreign goods. The increased demand for imports will result in an increased demand for foreign exchange.

Suppose U.S. residents experience an increase in income, but British residents do not. As a result, the demand curve for pounds shifts rightward, as illustrated in Exhibit 21-5. This causes the equilibrium exchange rate to rise from $1.50 = £1 to $1.80 = £1. We see that if one nation's income grows, and another's lags behind, the currency of the higher-growth-rate country *depreciates,* and the currency of the lower-growth-rate country *appreciates.* To many persons this is paradoxical; nevertheless, it is true.

Differences in Relative Price Levels. Suppose the U.S. price level rises 25 percent at a time when Great Britain experiences stable prices. An increase in the U.S. price level will make British goods relatively less expensive for Americans and American goods relatively more expensive for the British. As a result, the American demand for British goods will increase, and the British demand for American goods will decrease.

How will this affect the demand for and supply of British pounds in Exhibit 21-6? The demand for British pounds will increase (British goods are relatively cheaper than they were before the U.S. price level rose), and the supply of British pounds will decrease (since American goods are relatively more expensive, the British buy fewer American goods; thus they demand fewer U.S. dollars and supply fewer British pounds).

Appreciation

An increase in the value of one currency relative to other currencies.

Depreciation

A decrease in the value of one currency relative to other currencies.

The Growth Rate of Income and the Exchange Rate

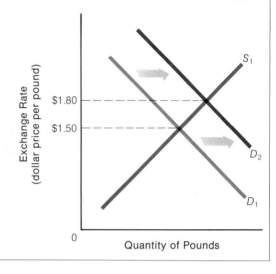

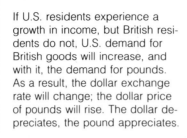

If U.S. residents experience a growth in income, but British residents do not, U.S. demand for British goods will increase, and with it, the demand for pounds. As a result, the dollar exchange rate will change; the dollar price of pounds will rise. The dollar depreciates, the pound appreciates.

Purchasing Power Parity Theory

States that exchange rates between any two currencies will adjust to reflect changes in the relative price levels of the two countries.

As Exhibit 21-6 shows, the result of an increase in the demand for British pounds and a decrease in the supply of British pounds is an appreciation in the pound and a depreciation in the dollar. It now takes more dollars and cents to buy one pound than it did before the U.S. price level increased 25 percent.

An important question is, How much will the U.S. dollar depreciate as a result of the rise in the U.S. price level vis-à-vis the British price level? (Recall that there is no change in the British price level). The **purchasing power parity (PPP) theory** predicts that the U.S. dollar will depreciate by 25 percent.[3] This requires the dollar price of a pound to rise to $1.88 (since $1.88 − $1.50 = 38 cents and 38 cents is approximately 25 percent of $1.50). A 25 percent depreciation in the dollar restores the original relative prices of American goods to British customers.

For example, consider a U.S. car with a price tag of $10,000. If the exchange rate is $1.50 = £1, a British buyer of the car will pay approximately £6,667. If the car price increases by 25 percent to $12,500, and the dollar depreciates 25 percent (to $1.88 = £1) the British buyer of the car will still only have to pay approximately £6,667 pounds.

In short, the purchasing power parity theory predicts that changes in the relative price levels of two countries will affect the exchange rate in such a way that one unit of a nation's currency will continue to buy the same amount of foreign goods as it did before the change in the relative price levels. In our example, because the higher U.S. inflation rate causes a change in the equilibrium exchange rate and leads to a depreciated dollar, one pound continues to have the same purchasing power it previously did.

On some occasions the PPP theory of exchange rates has predicted accurately, whereas on others it has not. For the period 1973–86 it accurately predicted the exchange rate between the U.S. dollar and the Canadian dollar. It did not accurately predict the exchange rate between the U.S. dollar and the Japanese yen for the period 1973–79. In the period 1972–86 the theory accurately predicted the *trend* of the exchange rate between the U.S. dollar and British pound, but still the *actual*

[3]The PPP theory is sometimes referred to as the "inflation theory of exchange rates."

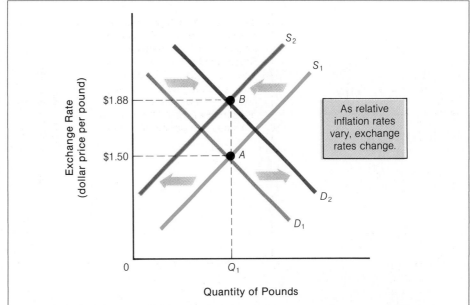

If the price level in the United States increases by 25 percent while the price level in Great Britain remains constant, the U.S. demand for British goods (and therefore pounds) will increase, and the supply of pounds will decrease. As a result, the exchange rate will change; the dollar price of pounds will rise. The dollar depreciates, and the pound appreciates. PPP theory predicts that the dollar will depreciate in the foreign exchange market until the original price (in pounds) of American goods and British customers is restored. In this example, this requires the dollar to depreciate 25 percent.

exchange rate between the two currencies diverged widely at times from the predicted exchange rate.

Many economists suggest that the theory does not always predict accurately because the demand for and supply of a currency are affected by more than the difference in inflation rates between countries. We have already noted that different income growth rates affect the demand for a currency and therefore the exchange rate. Shortly, we shall discuss other factors that affect the exchange rate. In the *long run,* however, and in particular when there is a *large difference* in inflation rates across countries, the PPP theory does predict exchange rates accurately.

Real Interest Rate
The inflation-adjusted interest rate.

Differences in Real Interest Rates. As was evident from the U.S. balance of payments, illustrated in Exhibit 21-1, more than goods flow between countries. There is financial capital, too, the flow of which is dependent on different countries' **real interest rates**—interest rates adjusted for inflation. Suppose we start at a position where the real interest rate is 3 percent in both the United States and in Great Britain. Then the real interest rate in the United States increases to 4.5 percent. What will happen? The British will increase the demand for dollars, and therefore supply more pounds to purchase financial assets in the United States that pay a higher real interest rate than financial assets in Great Britain. As the supply of pounds increases on the foreign exchange market, the exchange rate (dollar price per pound) will change;

COUNTRY	FOREIGN PRICE	U.S. EQUIVALENT	PPP THEORY PREDICTS FOREIGN CURRENCY WILL:
France	17.2 francs	$2.81	depreciate
Japan	370 yen	2.78	depreciate
Italy	3500 lire	2.60	depreciate
Spain	280 pesetas	2.30	depreciate
England	1.04 pounds	1.78	appreciate
Hong Kong	7.60 dollars	0.97	appreciate

You can explain it to a child, or to a prime minister.

—Georg Grimm, West German adviser to
Chancellor Helmut Kohl*

What Georg Grimm is talking about is the Big Mac Index. This is the price of a McDonald's Big Mac in different countries. The Big Mac Index is used to "test" the purchasing power parity (PPP) theory. According to the theory, the exchange rates between currencies will adjust so that one unit of a nation's currency (say, $1) will buy the same amount of a good everywhere in the world.

What does this have to do with a Big Mac? If the purchasing power parity theory holds up, we would expect the price of a Big Mac to be the same everywhere in the world. Is it? It wasn't on June 30, 1988. On that day in the United States a Big Mac was $2.19. The table above shows the price of a Big Mac in different countries.

*Cited in George Anders, "What Price Lunch?" *Wall Street Journal*, September 23, 1988. The data in this Theory in Practice are also from the Anders article.

To take one example, if the price of a Big Mac was $2.19 in the United States and 17.2 francs, or $2.81, in France, then $1 would have bought 46 percent of a Big Mac in the United States ($1.00 is 46 percent of $2.19) but only 36 percent of a Big Mac in France ($1.00 is 36 percent of $2.81). The purchasing power parity theory predicts that the franc would depreciate and the dollar appreciate so that $1 would buy the same fraction of a Big Mac in the United States as in France.

Did the franc depreciate? On June 30, 1988, the day the Big Mac prices were noted, $1 bought 6.12 francs, whereas on October 10, 1988, $1 bought 6.34 francs. Indeed, the franc did depreciate (but not by as much as the PPP theory predicted).

As to the other currencies, both the yen and lire depreciated (but not by as much as the PPP theory predicted), the peseta appreciated, the pound depreciated, and the Hong Kong dollar neither appreciated nor depreciated.

Lest anyone think that economists are serious when it comes to using the Big Mac Index to test the purchasing power parity theory, think again. Well, except maybe those economists at . . . yes, you guessed it . . . Hamburger U.

fewer dollars will be needed to buy pounds. In short, the dollar will appreciate and the pound will depreciate.

Combined Current and Capital Account Balances with Flexible Exchange Rates

Note that in the following discussion, the current and capital accounts have been lumped together into one account: the combined current and capital account.

Once again consider the exchange rate of $1.90 = £1 in Exhibit 36-4. As previously noted, at this exchange rate there is a surplus of pounds; more pounds are supplied than are demanded. But what does this mean in terms of the flow of goods, services, and funds between the two countries? Simply put, since the British are supplying more pounds than Americans are demanding, it implies that the British are demanding more dollars (since the demand for dollars is a reflection of the supply of pounds) than Americans are demanding pounds.

But what does this mean in terms of the U.S. combined current and capital account and Great Britain's combined current and capital account? In the United States it means that the sum total of the numbers that have a plus (+) in front of them in this combined account is greater than the sum total of the numbers that have a minus (−) in front of them.[4] In Great Britain it means that the sum total of numbers that have a minus (−) in front of them in this combined account is greater than the sum total of the numbers that have a plus (+) in front of them.[5] This is a roundabout way of saying that at the exchange rate $1.90 = £1, there is a surplus in the U.S. combined current and capital account (pluses outweigh minuses) and a deficit in the British combined capital and current account (minuses outweigh pluses).

This is a temporary state of affairs, though, because the combined current and capital account deficit in Great Britain and the combined current and capital account surplus in the United States are both the result of the above-equilibrium exchange rate, which is temporary. As soon as the exchange rate reaches its equilibrium level, the quantity demanded and supplied of pounds will be equal, as well as the quantity demanded and supplied of dollars (if the pound market is in equilibrium so is the dollar market). In short, the U.S. combined current and capital account and the British combined current and capital account will both be balanced.[6]

FIXED EXCHANGE RATES

Fixed Exchange Rate System
The system where a nation's currency is set at a fixed rate relative to all other currencies, and central banks intervene in the foreign exchange market to maintain the fixed rate.

The major alternative to the flexible exchange rate system is the **fixed exchange rate system.** This system works the way it sounds: Exchange rates are fixed or pegged, they are not allowed to fluctuate freely in response to the forces of supply and demand. The workings of the fixed exchange rate system are described in the next sections.

Fixed Exchange Rates and the Central Bank (The Fed)

Once again we deal with a two-country, two-currency world. Suppose this time that the United States and Great Britain agree to fix or peg their currencies; that is, instead of letting the dollar depreciate or appreciate relative to the pound, the two countries agree to set the price of one pound at $1.90. They agree to the exchange rate $1.90 = £1. Generally, we call this the fixed exchange rate or the *official price* of a pound.[7] Since we deal with more than one official price in our discussion, we refer to $1.90 = £1 as *official price 1* (see Exhibit 21-7).

If the dollar price of pounds is above its equilibrium level (which is the case at official price 1), the pound is said to be **overvalued.** It follows that if the pound is

Overvalued
A currency is overvalued if its price in terms of other currencies is above the equilibrium price.

---

[4]Recall that a plus (+) indicates a credit for the United States; it represents the demand for U.S. dollars. A minus (−), on the other hand, represents a debit for the United States; it represents the supply of dollars to the foreign exchange market, or the demand for a foreign currency. Since we have already said that the demand for dollars is greater than the demand for pounds, it follows that in the U.S. combined current and capital account, the sum total of the numbers that have a plus before them must be greater than the sum total of numbers that have a minus before them.

[5]In the British balance of payments a plus (+) represents a credit or the demand for pounds. A minus (−) represents a debit or the demand for foreign currency, which is the same as the supply of pounds. Once again, since we have already noted that the demand for dollars is greater than the demand for pounds, it follows that in the British combined capital and current account, the sum total of the numbers that have a minus in front of them is greater than the sum total of the numbers that have a plus in front of them.

[6]This assumes there is no government intervention in the foreign exchange market.

[7]If the price of one pound is $1.90, it follows that the price of one dollar is approximately 52 pence. Thus, setting the official price of a pound in terms of dollars and cents automatically sets the official price of a dollar in terms of pounds and pence.

■ **EXHIBIT 21-7**
A Fixed Exchange Rate System

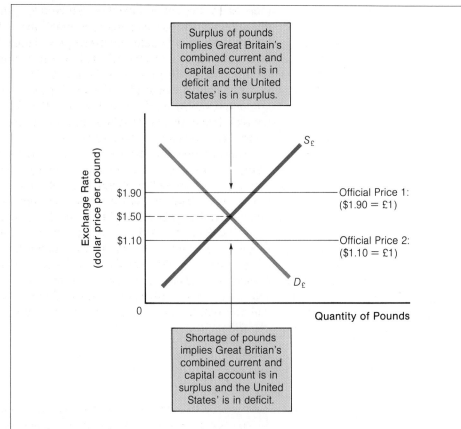

At official price 1, there is a surplus of pounds, which means that Great Britain's combined current and capital account is in deficit and the U.S. combined current and capital account is in surplus. To maintain the official price, the U.S. central bank, the Fed, could buy pounds. At official price 2, there is a shortage of pounds, which means Great Britain's combined current and capital account is in surplus and the U.S. combined current and capital account is in deficit. To maintain the official price, the Fed could sell pounds.

Undervalued

A currency is undervalued if its price in terms of other currencies is below the equilibrium price.

overvalued, the dollar is **undervalued.** Similarly, if the dollar price of pounds is below its equilibrium level (which is the case at official price 2 in Exhibit 21-7), the pound is undervalued. It follows that if the pound is undervalued, the dollar must be overvalued.

Notice that at the fixed exchange rate, or official price 1, a surplus of pounds exists. As we previously pointed out, this means the quantity supplied of pounds is greater than the quantity demanded of pounds. Great Britain's combined current and capital account is in deficit.

But what about the U.S. combined current and capital account? Is it in deficit or surplus? Since the quantity supplied of pounds is greater than the quantity demanded of pounds, it follows that the quantity demanded of dollars is greater than the quantity supplied of dollars. (For a review of the link between the pound market and the dollar market, see Exhibit 21-3.)

If the United States and Great Britain were operating under a flexible exchange rate system, the exchange rate would soon fall to $1.50 = £1, and the disequilibrium condition in each nation's combined current and capital account would disappear. But the two nations are not operating under a flexible exchange rate system. They are operating under a fixed exchange rate system. So what happens now?

To maintain the fixed exchange rate, the U.S. central bank, the Federal Reserve System (the Fed), could buy the surplus of pounds. This would show up in the official reserve account of the U.S. balance of payments as an increase in U.S. official reserve assets (see item 6 in Exhibit 21-1).

Alternatively, instead of the Fed buying pounds (to mop up the excess supply of pounds), the Bank of England could sell dollars (to eliminate the shortage of dollars, which is the other side of the coin of a surplus of pounds). Finally, there could be some combination of the two actions.

Suppose now that the exchange rate had been fixed at $1.10 = £1. This is *official price 2* in Exhibit 21-7. At this exchange rate there is a shortage of pounds; the quantity demanded of pounds is greater than the quantity supplied. This implies a surplus in Great Britain's combined current and capital account and a consequent deficit in the United States' combined current and capital account.

What happens? If the exchange rate is to be maintained, the Fed must now sell pounds to eliminate the shortage of pounds (alternatively, the Bank of England could buy dollars, or there could be some combination of the two actions). The United States will have to draw down the holdings of pounds that it might have acquired when the dollar price per pound was above the equilibrium level. Once again, this action will be recorded in the official reserve account of the U.S. balance of payments.

Question:

Why does the central bank, or the Fed, play a much larger role under a fixed exchange rate system than under a flexible exchange rate system?

Answer:

To support or maintain a fixed exchange rate, someone or something has to do the supporting or the maintaining. Central banks play this role. Under a flexible exchange rate system, there is no exchange rate to support or maintain; exchange rates simply respond to the forces of supply and demand.

Follow-up Question:

Suppose Great Britain and the United States agree to a fixed exchange rate, say, $1.90 = £1, and that at this exchange rate the U.S. combined current and capital account is in surplus and Great Britain's combined current and capital account is in deficit. Furthermore, suppose this condition continues indefinitely. Does the United States continue buying pounds indefinitely?

Answer:

A persistent deficit or surplus in a nation's combined current and capital account is usually dealt with in a way other than the nation continuing indefinitely to buy or sell the other nation's currency. We discuss this in the next section.

Options under a Fixed Exchange Rate System

A nation that persistently has a deficit or a surplus in its combined current and capital account has several options under a fixed exchange rate system. These include devaluation and revaluation, protectionist trade policies, and changes in macro-economic policies.

Devaluation and revaluation.   Suppose the United States and Great Britain have agreed to fix or peg the exchange rate at $1.90 = £1, which results in a *persistent* surplus in the U.S. combined current and capital account and a *persistent* deficit in Great Britain's combined current and capital account. At some point, the U.S. authorities tire of supporting the exchange rate by buying pounds, and/or the British authorities tire of supporting the exchange rate by selling dollars. The countries agree to reset the official price of the pound and the dollar. Suppose they reset it at its equilibrium level of $1.50 = £1. Afterward, economists say there has been a **devaluation** of the pound and a **revaluation** of the dollar. A devaluation occurs when the official price of a currency is lowered. A revaluation occurs when the official price of a currency is raised. If the official price of a pound is moved from $1.90 = £1 (or $1 = 52 pence) to $1.50 = £1 ($1 = 67 pence), it now takes fewer dollars and cents to buy a pound—so the pound has been devalued. It also takes more pence to buy a dollar—so the dollar has been revalued. The devaluation of the pound and revaluation of the dollar have the effect of eliminating the persistent disequilibrium situations in the two nation's combined current and capital accounts—at least for now.

The situation could arise where one nation would want to reset the official price of the currencies and another nation would not. Suppose the United States is experiencing a surplus in its merchandise trade balance (exports of goods > imports of goods) at the official price of $1.90 = £1 and doesn't want to give this up. It may be that U.S. export businesses are lobbying U.S. authorities not to revalue the dollar. In short, U.S. export interests feel they are benefiting from the undervalued dollar (and overvalued pound) and want to keep things this way.

Protectionist trade policy (quotas and tariffs).   A nation that has a merchandise trade deficit can erect quotas and tariffs to stem the tide of imports into the country. We saw in our last chapter how both tariffs and quotas meet this objective. Economists are quick to point out that merchandise trade problems are sometimes used as an excuse to promote trade restrictions—many of which simply benefit special interests.

Changes in monetary policy.   Sometimes monetary policy can be used by a nation to support the exchange rate or the official price of its currency. Suppose the United States is continually running a merchandise trade deficit; year after year, imports are outstripping exports. To remedy this, the United States might enact a tight monetary policy to retard inflation and drive up interest rates (at least in the short run). This action will make U.S. goods relatively cheaper than they were before (assuming other nations didn't also enact a tight monetary policy) and promote U.S. exports and discourage foreign imports, as well as generate a flow of investment funds into the United States in search of higher real interest rates.

Some economists argue against fixed exchange rates because they think it unwise for a nation to adopt a particular monetary policy simply to maintain an international exchange rate. Instead, they believe domestic monetary policies should be used to meet domestic economic goals—such as price stability, low unemployment, low and stable interest rates, and so forth. This naturally leads us into a discussion of the case for and against fixed exchange rates for promoting international trade.

Devaluation

An official governmental act that changes the exchange rate; specifically, it lowers the official price of a currency.

Revaluation

An official governmental act that changes the exchange rate; specifically, it raises the official price of a currency.

Promoting International Trade: Which Are Better, Fixed or Flexible Exchange Rates?

. . Paul Volcker replied that if you balance the world's greatest proponent of fixed rates and the world's greatest proponent of floating rates, you still won't know what to think.[8]

The Case for Fixed Exchange Rates. Proponents of a fixed exchange rate system often argue that fixed exchange rates promote international trade whereas flexible exchange rates stifle it. A major advantage of fixed exchange rates is certainty: Individuals in different countries know from day to day what their nation's currency will trade for. With flexible exchange rates, individuals in different countries will not be as likely to enter into international trade because of the added risk of not knowing from one day to the next how many dollars or francs or pounds they will have to give up to get, say, 100 yen. Certainty is a necessary ingredient in international trade; flexible exchange rates promote uncertainty, which hampers international trade. Economist Charles Kindleberger, a proponent of fixed exchange rates, believes that having fixed exchange rates is analogous to having 1 currency in the United States instead of having 1 currency for each of 50 states: 1 currency in the United States promotes trade and 50 different currencies would hamper it. In Kindleberger's view:

> The main case against flexible exchange rates is that they break up the world market. . . . Imagine trying to conduct interstate trade in the USA if there were fifty different state monies, none of which was dominant. This is akin to barter, the inefficiency of which is explained time and again by textbooks.[9]

The Case For Flexible Exchange Rates. Proponents of flexible exchange rates state that with fixed exchange rates there is too great a chance that the fixed exchange rate will diverge greatly from the equilibrium exchange rate, creating persistent balance of trade problems that lead deficit nations to impose trade restrictions (tariffs and quotas) that hinder international trade. As we have mentioned, advocates of flexible exchange rates also maintain that it is better for a nation to adopt the policies it wants to meet domestic economic goals than to sacrifice domestic economic goals to maintain an exchange rate.

The Gold Standard

Once nations have decided to adopt the gold standard they automatically fix their exchange rates. Suppose the United States defines a dollar as equal to 1/20 of an ounce of gold and Great Britain defines a pound as equal to ⅕ of an ounce of gold. This means that one ounce of gold could be bought with either $20 or £5. What then is the exchange rate between dollars and pounds? It is 4 dollars = 1 pound, or 1 dollar = ¼ pound. This then is the *fixed* exchange rate between dollars and pounds.

To have an international gold standard, countries must do the following: (1) Define their currencies in terms of gold (for example, $1 = 1/20 oz. of gold, £1 = ⅕ oz. of gold, and so on). (2) Stand ready and willing to convert gold into paper money and paper money into gold at the rate specified (for example, the United States

---

[8]Paul Volcker is a former Federal Reserve chairman. The quotation is from Robert Bartley, "Tracing an Idea: Monetary Policy Runs the Dollar," *Wall Street Journal*, January 6, 1988.

[9]Charles Kindleberger, *International Money* (London: Allen and Unwin, 1981), p. 174.

Theory in Practice

The Future Sometimes Looks Brighter with Futures: Or How To Lock in the Price of the Yen without Really Trying

Consider the case of (the fictional) Bill Whatley, the owner of a Toyota dealership in San Diego. It is currently May, and Bill is thinking about buying a shipment of Toyotas in August. He knows that he must buy the Toyotas from Japan with yen, but he has a problem. At the present time in May, the dollar price of yen is $.005. Bill wonders what will happen if the dollar price of yen rises in August when he plans to make his purchase. Suppose the dollar price of yen rises to $.006. If this happens, then instead of paying $15,000 for a Toyota priced at 3 million yen, he would have to pay $18,000.* This $3,000 difference may be enough to wipe out any profit on the sale of Toyotas.

What is Bill to do? He could purchase a *futures contract*

*If a yen equals $.005, then a Toyota with a price tag of 3 million yen actually costs $15,000 ($.005 × 3,000,000 = $15,000). If a yen equals $.006, then a Toyota with a price tag of 3 million yen actually costs $18,000 ($.006 × 3,000,000 = $18,000).

today for the needed quantity of yen in August. A futures contract is a contract in which the seller agrees to provide a particular good (in our example, a particular currency) to the buyer on a specified future date at an agreed-on price. In short, Bill can buy yen today at a specified dollar price and take delivery of the yen at a later date (in August).

But suppose the dollar price of yen falls to $.004 in August? If this happens, Bill would only have to pay $12,000 (instead of $15,000) for a Toyota priced at 3 million yen. Although this is true, Bill, like other car dealers, might not be interested in assuming the risk associated with changes in exchange rates. He may prefer to lock in a sure thing.

Who would sell yen to Bill? The answer is someone who is willing to assume the risk of changes in the value of currencies that Bill obviously is not—for example, Julie Jackson. Julie thinks to herself, "I think the dollar price of yen will go down between now and August. Therefore, I will enter into a contract with Bill saying that I will hand over to him 3 million yen in August for $15,000—the exchange rate specified in the contract being 1 yen = $.005. If I am right, and the *actual* exchange rate at the time is 1 yen = $.004, then I can purchase the 3 million yen for $12,000, and turn around and fulfill my contract with Bill by turning the yen over to him for $15,000. I walk away with $3,000 profit."

Many economists argue that futures contracts offer people a way of dealing with the risk associated with a flexible exchange rate system. If a person doesn't know what next month's exchange rate will be, and doesn't want to take the risk of waiting to see, then he or she can enter into a futures contract and effectively shift the risk to someone who voluntarily assumes it.

would buy and sell gold at $20 an ounce). (3) Link their money supplies to their holdings of gold. With this in mind, consider how a gold standard would work.

Once again assume there are two countries, Great Britain and the United States, and that the exchange rate 1 dollar = ¼ pound is the equilibrium exchange rate. Then, a change occurs: Inflation raises British prices by 100 percent. A British tea set that was priced at £20 before the inflation, is now priced at £40. At the fixed exchange rate, Americans find that they now have to give up $160 to buy the tea set whereas before the British inflation they only had to give up $80. Consequently, Americans buy fewer tea sets; Americans import less.

At the same time, however, the British import more. The reason is that American prices are now relatively lower than before the British inflation. Suppose an American pair of shoes was $80 before the inflation. In relative terms, the cost was 1 British tea set since the tea set cost £20 before the inflation and 1 dollar = ¼ pound. After the inflation, the American shoes are still $80 but the tea set is £40. This means the relative cost of American shoes has gone down to ½ British tea set (once again, since 1 dollar = ¼ pound). To the British, the inflation in their country has made American goods relatively cheaper. The British end up buying more American goods; they import more.

We see, then, that the British inflation has decreased American imports and increased American exports; at the same time it has decreased British exports and increased British imports. The U.S. merchandise trade balance moves into surplus; the British trade balance moves into deficit.

The British have to pay for the difference between their imports and exports with gold. Gold is therefore shipped to the United States. An increase in the supply of gold in the United States expands the U.S. money supply. A decrease in the supply of gold in Great Britain contracts the British money supply. Prices are affected in both countries. In the United States, prices begin to rise; in Great Britain, prices begin to fall. As U.S. prices go up, and British prices go down, the earlier situation begins to reverse itself. American goods look more expensive to the British, and they begin to buy less, whereas British goods look cheaper to Americans, and they begin to buy more. Consequently American imports begin to rise, and exports begin to fall; British imports begin to fall, and exports begin to rise. The gold standard, through changing domestic money supplies and price levels, begins to correct the initial trade balance disequilibrium.

The change in the money supply that the gold standard sometimes requires has prompted some economists to voice the same argument against the gold standard that is often heard against the fixed exchange rate system; that is, it subjects domestic monetary policy to international instead of domestic considerations. In fact, many economists cite this as part of the reason many nations abandoned the gold standard in the 1930s. At a time when unemployment was unusually high, many nations with trade deficits felt that matters would only get worse if they contracted their money supplies to live by the edicts of the gold standard. We explore this in greater detail in the next section.

WHERE WE'VE BEEN, WHERE WE ARE

Historians are quick to point out that we can only understand where we are if we first understand where we've been. With this in mind, we discuss a few key past and present events in U.S. international finance.

The Crack-Up of the Gold Standard

From the 1870s to the 1930s, many nations tied their currencies to gold. The United States, for example, stood ready to exchange an ounce of gold for $20.67. For most of this period—roughly from the 1870s to the end of World War I—many economists agree that the gold standard worked well. Critics of the gold standard say that of course it worked well during this time, but there were few problems for it to solve. For example, during this time no major trading country found itself with persistent "balance of payments" problems.

Then after World War I things began to change. Some countries (most notably the United States) began to break the rules of the gold standard by not contracting their money supplies to the extent called for by the outflow of gold. Under these circumstances, the gold standard could not restore balance of trade equilibrium.

In the 1920s Great Britain and France tried to restore the gold standard. They did so, however, by setting the "wrong" exchange rates: The pound was overvalued and the franc was undervalued. This action led to trade surpluses in France and high unemployment and trade deficits in Great Britain. To maintain the gold standard, both countries would have had to change their money supplies significantly (or revalue). The countries began to feel that it was not worth subjecting their domestic economies to such sharp changes in order to abide by the discipline of the gold standard.

As we noted earlier, the Great Depression was perhaps the straw that broke the back of the gold standard. In the face of widespread high unemployment, nations with trade deficits began to feel that abiding by the rules of the gold standard and contracting their money supplies to restore balance of trade equilibrium was too high a price to pay. So they went off the gold standard.

The Bretton Woods System

In 1944, once it appeared that the Allies were certain to win World War II, major negotiators from the Allied countries met in Bretton Woods, New Hampshire, to map out a new international monetary system. This system came to be known as the *Bretton Woods system*. It was based on fixed exchange rates and an international central bank called the **International Monetary Fund (IMF).**[10] Under the Bretton Woods system nations were expected to maintain fixed exchange rates (within a narrow range) by buying and selling their own currency for other currencies.[11] A nation experiencing a trade deficit could borrow international reserves from the IMF. It was expected that the nation that had borrowed reserves would, over time, generate a trade surplus with which it could pay off its loan. The IMF reserves were created by imposing a quota on each member nation—a fee based on the nation's trade and national income. Each member nation contributed 25 percent of its quota in gold or U.S. dollars and 75 percent in its own currency.

In the late 1960s the IMF created a new international money to add to its international reserves fund. This was the *special drawing right (SDR)*. In essence, SDRs are simply bookkeeping entries. However, once a country has an SDR account, it can use SDRs to settle a trade imbalance.

In the 1960s and early 1970s, the Bretton Woods system became strained at the seams. One of the major shortcomings of the system was that it encouraged speculative attacks on a currency. For example, suppose Great Britain is persistently running a trade deficit and West Germany is persistently running a trade surplus. Under these circumstances speculators know that sooner or later Great Britain will have to devalue its currency, although government officials in Great Britain will probably deny this. Speculators will likely respond by selling the weak British pound (before it is devalued and they are left holding a bag full of less valuable pounds) and buying the strong currency—in our example, the German mark. Obviously this speculative action will increase the supply of pounds on the foreign exchange market and cause the difference between the official price of pounds and the equilibrium price of pounds to increase. Thus, if the pound were overvalued before the speculative action, it is now even more overvalued; a bad situation has become worse.

International Monetary Fund (IMF)

An international organization that was created by the Bretton Woods system to oversee the international monetary system. Although the Bretton Woods system no longer exists, the IMF does. It does not control the world's money supply, but it does hold currency reserves for member nations and makes loans to central banks.

Special Drawing Right

An international money, created by the IMF, in the form of bookkeeping entries; like gold and currencies, they can be used by nations to settle international accounts.

[10]The IMF is sometimes confused with the World Bank (or International Bank for Reconstruction and Development) although it is something different altogether. The World Bank, which was also part of the Bretton Woods agreement, was set up to provide long-term loans to assist developing nations in building roads, dams, and other capital projects that it was felt would contribute to their economic development.

[11]Actually, the Bretton Woods system was not an absolutely rigid fixed exchange rate system. Because it was not, it is sometimes referred to as the *adjustable peg system*. Exchange rates were set, and then a narrow band around each exchange rate was specified within which the exchange rate could move without central bank intervention. In addition, the IMF allowed for periodic realignment in exchange rates.

This is in fact what happened to Great Britain in 1967. At the official price for a pound, the quantity supplied of pounds was greater than the quantity demanded of pounds. In short, the pound was overvalued, and Great Britain was faced with a combined current and capital account deficit. To maintain the official price (exchange rate), the Bank of England had to buy the excess supply of pounds. In doing this, though, it lost international reserves. By November 17, 1967, speculators began to suspect that despite IMF loans to Great Britain, the British pound would soon have to be devalued. They reasoned that Great Britain didn't have the reserves necessary to continue to maintain the official price of the pound. Speculators began to view a devaluation of the pound as (almost) certain and began to sell off pounds. This made the problem worse for the Bank of England because now with more pounds on the foreign exchange market, it was forced to buy up more pounds to maintain the official price of the pound. On one day alone the Bank of England had to buy $1 billion worth of pounds to keep the exchange rate from falling. Finally the Bank of England realized that it could not continue to defend the pound successfully at its present official price, and soon after devalued the pound by 14 percent. This meant that the speculators who had sold $1 billion worth of pounds to the Bank of England collectively earned $140 million. How did they manage this? The dollars they had bought by selling pounds to the Bank of England had appreciated in value 14 percent. If they sold $1 billion worth of pounds, then they realized $140 million in profits (since 14 percent of $1 billion = $140 million). The Bank of England had found that defending its currency against speculative attack was expensive. Critics of the Bretton Woods system began to point out that any fixed exchange rate system has this failing; it can prompt speculative attacks on currencies.

In 1971 speculators began to speculate on the dollar. Before we can understand this action fully, we need to point out that the U.S. dollar was convertible into gold (for foreign governments and central banks only) at $35 an ounce. In the 1960s the United States had witnessed an accelerating inflation that caused U.S. exports to become more expensive and U.S. imports to become less expensive. This difference in inflation rates between the United States and many other countries began to put pressure on exchange rates; more and more, it appeared that the dollar was overvalued at its official price. In short, there was a surplus of dollars. But this simply meant that some other currencies were undervalued and that there was an excess demand for them. According to the rules laid down under the Bretton Woods system, the countries whose currencies were in short supply had to buy up dollars and thus sell more of their currency to maintain exchange rates. For example, the German central bank, the Bundesbank, bought $2 billion of U.S. dollars between January and March 1971 to fulfill its obligation to keep the exchange rate fixed at 27 cents = 1 mark.

Now this meant that by buying dollars, the Bundesbank, and some other central banks, were increasing their holdings of dollars. But increasingly central banks became reluctant to hold dollars. U.S. monetary authorities became worried because they knew that if central banks did demand gold (for dollars), the U.S. gold stock would be severely diminished if the United States maintained a $35 price for gold. Add to this the screams from many American exporters of goods who complained that they were being severely hurt by the overvalued dollar, and you knew something would soon have to happen.

It did. On Sunday evening, August 15, 1971, President Nixon addressed the nation and announced that the United States would no longer honor its IMF obligation to sell gold at $35 an ounce. Soon after, the U.S. dollar began to fluctuate in the foreign exchange market. The overvalued dollar soon depreciated against other major currencies. By 1973 the Bretton Woods system was dead.

The Current International Monetary System

Today's international monetary system is best described as a *managed flexible exchange rate system*, sometimes referred to more casually as a *managed float*. In a way, this is a rough compromise between the fixed and flexible exchange rate systems. The current system operates under flexible exchange rates, but not completely. Nations now and then intervene to adjust their official reserve holdings to moderate major swings in exchange rates. For example, the United States intervened in foreign exchange markets in 1978 to moderate the depreciation of the dollar. Recent intervention has involved coordinated efforts on the part of major industrial nations. In September 1985 the finance ministers of five important industrial nations—France, Germany, Japan, Great Britain, and the United States—met at the Plaza Hotel in New York City and agreed to intervene in foreign exchange markets to achieve desired changes in exchange rates. At the time the meeting took place, the Group of Five (or G-5, as the countries came to be known) believed the dollar was overvalued and therefore agreed to achieve a depreciation of the dollar. At the Tokyo Summit Conference in May 1986, the Group of Five was joined by Canada and Italy and became known as the Group of Seven (G-7). The late 1980s saw central banks intervening in the foreign exchange market.

Proponents of the managed float system stress the following advantages:

1. **It allows nations to pursue independent monetary policies.** Under a (strictly) fixed exchange rate system, fixed either by agreement or by gold, a nation with a merchandise trade deficit might have to enact a tight monetary policy in order to retard inflation and promote its exports (refer back to our discussion of the fixed exchange rate system). This would not be the case with the emphasis on flexible exchange rates. Proponents of the current system argue that it is better to adjust one price—the exchange rate—than to adjust the price level to solve trade imbalances.

2. **It solves trade problems without trade restrictions.** As we stated earlier, with a fixed exchange rate system, nations sometimes impose tariffs and quotas to solve trade imbalances. For example, a deficit nation might impose import quotas so that exports and imports of goods will be more in line. With the current system, trade imbalances are usually solved through changes in exchange rates.

3. **It is flexible and therefore can easily adjust to shocks.** In 1973–74 the OPEC nations dramatically raised the price of oil, which resulted in many oil-importing nations running trade deficits. A fixed exchange rate system would have had a hard time accommodating such a major change in oil prices. The current system had little trouble, however. Exchange rates took much of the shock (there were large changes in exchange rates) and thus allowed most nations' economies to weather the storm with a minimum of difficulty for the most part.

Opponents of the current international monetary system stress the following disadvantages:

1. **It promotes exchange rate volatility and uncertainty and results in less international trade than would be the case under fixed exchange rates.** Under a flexible exchange rate system, exchange rates are volatile and therefore make it hard and risky for importers and exporters to conduct business; as a result, international trade is less than it would be under a fixed exchange rate system. Opponents of the current system often point to the sharp depreciation of the U.S. dollar in 1986. Proponents often retort that a futures market in currencies exists

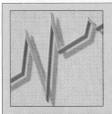

Theory in Practice

I'll Take Manhattan

At times during the late 1970s and the late 1980s, the U.S. dollar depreciated relative to the Japanese yen. For the Japanese, the lower-price dollar meant that many American assets became a lot cheaper. Predictably, the Japanese began to buy American hotels, businesses, land, apartment buildings, and so on. They made major purchases in cities such as New York (particularly Manhattan) and Honolulu. Many Americans began to complain that the Japanese were buying out Americans and taking over the United States. A debate over the seriousness of the issue ensued.

Some people said the following:

1. Foreign investment in the United States unfairly drives up real estate prices for the American buyer. The idea here is that with the Japanese bidding for real estate along with Americans, the price of real estate will rise. Americans will end up paying more to buy real estate than if the demand had been less. This is true enough; but the argument ignores the benefits to the sellers (perhaps American?) of American real estate. They benefit from the increased demand for real estate—whether it comes from other Americans, the Japanese, or someone else.

2. Foreign investment will result in foreign control of American businesses. The argument here is that if the Japanese, or other foreigners, buy American businesses, there will be a fundamental change in the nature of these businesses and ultimately Americans will be hurt. Looking at the opposite side of the coin, one may question whether foreigners will run American businesses differently than Americans run American businesses. Presumably, the Japanese buy American businesses to earn profits, which is the same reason Americans buy American businesses. The desire to earn profits limits one's behavior in a certain way, so that there will be little difference (if any) between a business in the United States owned by a foreigner and the same business owned by an American.

What are your thoughts on the subject?

that allows importers and exporters to shift the risk of fluctuations in exchange rates to others.

For example, if an American company wants to buy a certain quantity of a good from a Japanese company three months from today, it can contract today for the desired quantity of yen it will need, at a specified price; it will not have to worry about a change in the dollar price of yen over the next three months. There is, of course, a cost to this, but it is usually modest (see the Theory in Practice on p. 464).

2. **It promotes inflation.** As we have seen, the monetary policies of different nations are not independent of each other under a fixed exchange rate system. For example, a nation with a merchandise trade deficit is somewhat restrained from inflating because this will worsen the deficit problem—it will make its goods more expensive relative to foreign goods and promote the purchase of imports. In its attempt to maintain the exchange rate, a nation with a merchandise trade deficit would have to enact a tight monetary policy.

Under the current system, a nation with a merchandise trade deficit does not have to concern itself with maintaining exchange rates or trying to solve its deficit problem through changes in its money supply. Opponents of the current system argue that this frees nations to inflate. They predict more inflation will result than under a fixed exchange rate system.

3. **Changes in exchange rates alter trade balances in the desired direction only after a long time; in the short run, a depreciation in a currency can make the situation worse instead of better.** It is often argued that soon after a depreciation in a trade-deficit nation's currency, the trade deficit will increase (not decrease, as was hoped). The reason is that import demand is inelastic in the short run: imports are not very responsive to a change in price. For example, suppose Great Britain is running a trade deficit with the United States at the present exchange rate of $1.50 = £1. At this exchange rate the pound is overvalued, and Great Britain (we assume) buys 2,000 television sets each with a price tag of $500 from the United States. Great Britain therefore spends £666,666 on imports of American television sets. Now suppose the overvalued pound begins to depreciate, say, to $1.25 = £1. Furthermore, suppose in the short run, British customers only buy 100 fewer American television sets; that is, they import 1,900 television sets. At a price of $500 each, and at an exchange rate of $1.25 = £1, the British now spend £760,000 on imports of American television sets.

In the short run, then, a depreciation in the pound has widened the trade deficit because the percentage by which imports fall (5 percent) was less than the percentage by which the price of imports (in terms of pounds) increased (16.7 percent).[12] As time passes, imports will fall off more (it takes time for British buyers to shift from higher-priced American goods to lower-priced British goods), and the deficit will shrink. If we graph this phenomenon—namely, that a depreciation in a nation's currency widens the trade deficit in the short run and shrinks it in the long run—we obtain a **J-curve.** This is illustrated in Exhibit 21-8.

In the exhibit we have plotted time on the horizontal axis and British net exports on the vertical axis. Net exports = exports − imports; therefore negative net exports

J-curve

The curve that shows a short-run worsening in the trade deficit following a currency depreciation, followed later by an improvement.

---

[12]This is more succinctly put by saying that the demand for imports in the short-run is highly price inelastic. As time passes, the price elasticity of demand for imports increases, and the trade deficit problem begins to be solved.

◼ **EXHIBIT 21-8**
The J-Curve

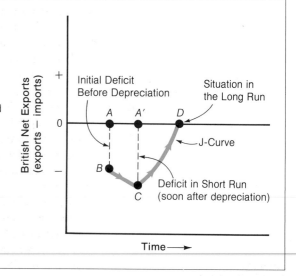

Great Britain starts out with a merchandise trade deficit equal to A–B. As the pound depreciates, the trade deficit initially widens to A'–C. With time, the trade deficit is eliminated. If we follow the course of the trade deficit, we map out a J. This is called the J-curve.

imply a trade deficit (imports > exports). As we can see, before the depreciation of the pound, Great Britain is experiencing a trade deficit equal to $A-B$. Next, the pound is depreciated and the trade deficit widens to $A'-C$. The movement from B to C is the first part of the J-curve. Next, as time passes, the trade deficit begins to shrink. The British are, with time, moving from American imports to domestic goods. At point D British net exports are zero (exports = imports). The movement from C to D is the second part of the J-curve. The J-curve is represented by the movement from B to C and from C to D.

Question:

Does the J-curve phenomenon mean that a system of flexible exchange rates is undesirable?

Answer:

Some economists would say that if there is a J-curve phenomenon, changes in exchange rates are a rather crude way of solving a trade imbalance because in the short run they make things worse.

■ CHAPTER SUMMARY

Balance of Payments

■ The balance of payments provides information about a nation's imports and exports, domestic residents' earnings on assets located abroad, foreign earnings on domestic assets, gifts to and from foreign countries, and official transactions by governments and central banks.

■ In a nation's balance of payments, any transaction that supplies the nation's currency in the foreign exchange market is recorded as a debit ($-$). Any transaction that supplies a foreign currency is recorded as a credit ($+$).

■ The three main accounts of the balance of payments are the current account, capital account, and official reserve account.

■ The current account includes all payments related to the purchase and sale of goods and services. The three major components of the account are exports of goods and services, imports of goods and services, and unilateral transfers.

■ The capital account includes all payments related to the purchase and sale of assets and to borrowing and lending activities. The major components are outflow of U.S. capital and inflow of foreign capital.

■ The official reserve account includes transactions by the central banks of various countries.

■ The merchandise trade balance is the difference between the value of merchandise exports and the value of merchandise imports. If exports are greater than imports, a nation has a trade surplus; if imports are greater than exports, a nation has a trade deficit. The balance of payments equals current account balance + capital account balance + official reserve balance + statistical discrepancy.

The Foreign Exchange Market and Flexible and Fixed Exchange Rates

■ The market in which currencies of different countries are exchanged is called the foreign exchange market. In this market, currencies are bought and sold for a price; an exchange rate exists.

■ If Americans demand British goods, they also demand British pounds and supply U.S. dollars. If the British demand American goods, they also demand U.S. dollars and supply British pounds. When the residents of a nation demand a foreign currency, they must supply their own currency.

■ Under flexible exchange rates, the foreign exchange market will equilibrate at the exchange rate where the quantity demanded of a currency equals the quantity supplied of a currency; for example, the quantity demanded of dollars equals the quantity supplied of dollars.

■ If the price of a nation's currency increases against a foreign currency, the nation's economy is said to have appreciated. For example, if the dollar price of a pound rises from $1.50 = £1 to $1.80 = £1, the pound has appreciated. If the price of a nation's currency decreases against a foreign currency, the nation's currency is said to have depreciated. For example, if the pound price of a dollar falls from 66 pence = $1 to 55 pence = $1, the dollar has depreciated.

■ Under a flexible exchange rate system, the equilibrium exchange rate is affected by a difference in income growth rates between countries, a difference in inflation rates between countries, and a difference in (real) interest rates between countries.

■ Under a fixed exchange rate system, countries agree to fix the price of their currencies. The central banks of the countries must then buy and sell currencies to maintain the agreed-on exchange rate. If a persistent deficit or surplus in a nation's combined current and capital account exists at a fixed exchange rate, the nation has a few options to deal with the problem: devalue or revalue its currency, enact protectionist trade policies (in the case of a deficit), or change its monetary policy.

The Gold Standard

■ To have an international gold standard, nations must do the following: (1) Define their currencies in terms of gold. (2) Stand ready and willing to convert gold into paper money and paper money into gold at a specified rate. (3) Link their money supplies to their holdings of gold. The change in the money supply that the gold standard sometimes requires has prompted some economists to voice the same argument against the gold standard that is often heard against the fixed exchange rate system: It subjects domestic monetary policy to international instead of domestic considerations.

The Current International Monetary System

■ Today's international monetary system is described as a managed flexible exchange rate system or managed float. For the most part, there is a flexible exchange rate system although nations do periodically intervene in the foreign exchange market to adjust exchange rates. Since it is a managed float system, it is difficult to tell if nations will emphasize the "float" part or the "managed" part in years to come.

■ Proponents of the managed flexible exchange rate system believe it offers several advantages: (1) It allows nations to pursure independent macroeconomic policies. (2) It solves trade problems without trade restrictions. (3) It is flexible and therefore can easily adjust to shocks. Opponents of the managed flexible exchange rate system believe it has several disadvantages: (1) It promotes exchange rate volatility and uncertainty, and thus results in less international trade than would be the case under fixed exchange rates. (2) It promotes inflation. (3) It corrects trade deficits only a long time after a depreciation in the currency; in the interim, it can make matters worse. Here we have the J-curve phenomenon.

■ QUESTIONS TO ANSWER AND DISCUSS

1. The following foreign exchange information appeared in a newspaper on Monday, October 10, 1988.

	U.S. $ EQUIVALENT		CURRENCY PER U.S. $	
	FRI.	THRS.	FRI.	THRS.
France (franc)	.1577	.1578	6.3410	6.3400
Japan (yen)	.007503	.007493	133.27	133.45
W. Germany (mark)	.5370	.5364	1.8563	1.8583

a. Between Thursday and Friday, did the dollar appreciate or depreciate against the French franc?
b. Between Thursday and Friday, did the dollar appreciate or depreciate against the Japanese yen?
c. Between Thursday and Friday, did the dollar appreciate or depreciate against the West German mark?

2. Suppose the United States and Greece are on a flexible exchange rate system. Explain whether each of the following events will lead to an appreciation or depreciation in the U.S. dollar and Greek drachma.
a. U.S. real interest rates rise above Greek real interest rates.
b. The Greek inflation rate rises relative to the U.S. inflation rate.
c. Greece puts a quota on imports of American radios.
d. Americans learn on the nightly news that terrorists at the Athens airport boarded a plane that they subsequently skyjacked with American citizens aboard. As a result, American tourism to Athens (Greece) drops off substantially.

3. Give an example that illustrates how a change in the exchange rate changes the relative price of domestic goods in terms of foreign goods.

4. Suppose the media report that the United States has a deficit in its current account. What does this imply about the U.S. capital account balance and official reserve account balance?

5. Suppose there are two countries, France and Great Britain. Great Britain has a merchandise trade deficit, and France has a merchandise trade surplus. Since the two countries are on a flexible exchange rate system, the franc appreciates and the pound depreciates. It is noticed, however, that soon after the depreciation of the pound, Great Britain's trade deficit grows instead of shrinks. Why might this be?

6. What are the strong points of the flexible exchange rate system? What are the weak points? What are the strong points of the fixed exchange rate system? What are the weak points?

7. Individuals do not keep a written account of their balance of trade with other individuals. For example, John doesn't keep an account of how much he sells Alice and how much he buys from Alice. Additionally, neither cities nor any of the 50 states calculate their balance of trade with all other cities and states. However, nations do calculate their merchandise trade balance with other nations. If nations do it, should individuals, cities, and states do it? Why?

8. Since every nation's balance of payments equals zero, does it follow that each nation is on an equal footing when it comes to international trade and finance with every other nation? Explain your answer.

9. Suppose your objective is to predict whether the British pound and the U.S. dollar will appreciate or depreciate on the foreign exchange market in the next two months. What information would you need to help you in making your prediction? Specifically, how would the information you mentioned help you in predicting the direction of the foreign exchange value of the pound and dollar? Next, explain how a person who could accurately predict exchange rates could become extremely rich in a short time.

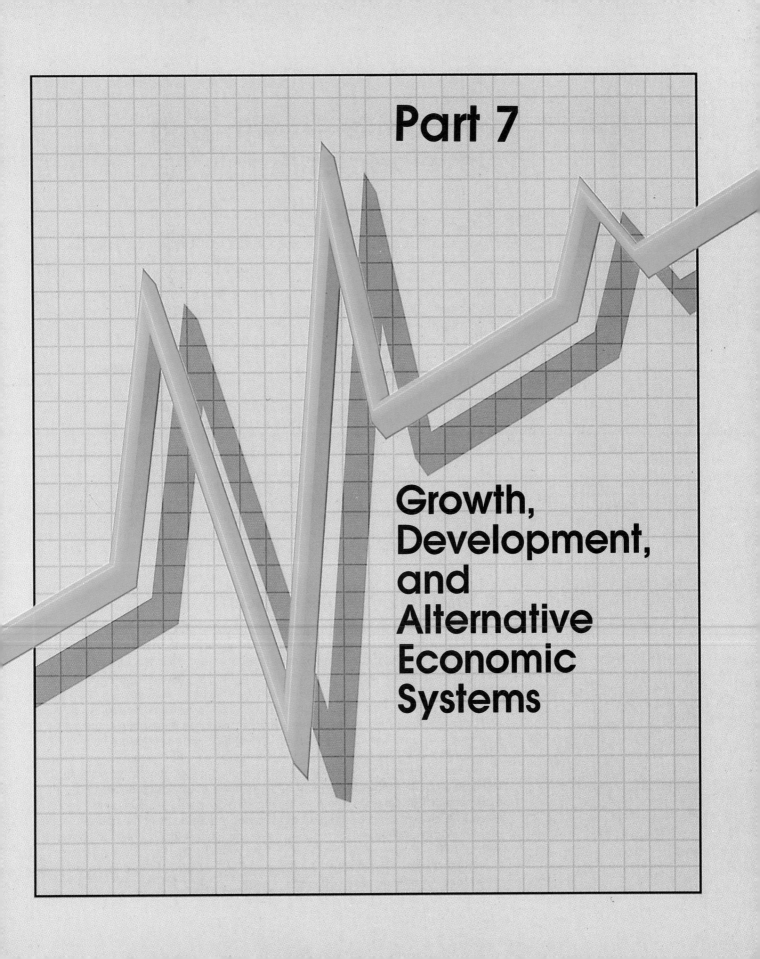

Part 7

Growth, Development, and Alternative Economic Systems

Chapter 22

Economic Growth and Development

■ INTRODUCTION

What would your life be like if you had been born in Ethiopia, India, or Tanzania instead of the United States? Most likely you wouldn't be driving a car because you wouldn't own one. You wouldn't have new clothes, a compact disc player, or a personal computer. You wouldn't go out to restaurants and movies regularly. You wouldn't be enrolled in a college or university studying economics!

You largely have what you have—things that Ethiopians, Indians, and Tanzanians do not have—because you were born to parents who live in a country that in this century experienced relatively more economic growth and development than most countries of the world. We examine the role economic growth and development play in our daily lives in the next few pages.

■ WHAT THIS CHAPTER IS ABOUT

This chapter discusses economic growth and economic development, which are two different concepts. Economic growth refers to increases in output or real GNP. It is essentially only a quantitative measurement. Economic development encompasses economic growth as well as production and institutional changes that imply an improvement in the overall (not just material) standard of living.

Consider a small country that at present only exports bananas. Its people are poor and can only barely meet the necessities of life. Certainly it is possible for the nation's economy to witness growth; it is possible to produce and export more bananas this year than last year. But even if it does this, the nation would still not be economically developed. Economic development implies more than economic growth. In this example, it implies the enhancement of the nation's ability to produce goods other than bananas. In general, it implies better ways to produce goods and services. Overall, it implies a higher standard of living for the residents of the nation—better transportation networks, better schools, more and higher-quality goods to consume, and so forth.

In the first part of the chapter, we discuss economic growth. In the second part, we examine economic development.

Key Questions to Keep in Mind as You Read

1. What is economic growth? What is economic development?
2. What factors affect economic growth?
3. What caused the U.S. productivity slowdown in the 1970s?
4. Why are some nations poor?
5. What is fungibility and what does it have to do with foreign aid and a basketball game?
6. What has caused the world debt crisis?

ECONOMIC GROWTH

Real Economic Growth

An increase from one period to the next in *real GNP*.

Per-Capita Real Economic Growth

An increase from one period to the next in *per-capita real GNP*, which is real GNP divided by population.

The term "economic growth" can be and is used to refer to either **real economic growth** or to **per-capita real economic growth.** Real economic growth is an increase from one period to the next in *real GNP*. Per-capita real economic growth is an increase from one period to the next in *per-capita real GNP*, which is real GNP divided by population.

Most economists think the per-capita measurement is more useful, since it, unlike absolute economic growth, tells us how much better or worse off the "average" person is in one period compared with another, assuming a given income distribution. For example, India has a higher real GNP than Norway. But it also has 171 times the population. It turns out that per-capita real GNP in Norway is approximately 50 times as high as per-capita real GNP in India.

Per-capita real economic growth is relatively new to the world. In the preindustrial world, real economic growth often encouraged the population to increase beyond the increase in real GNP, and consequently people's standard of living fell. It was only in sixteenth-century England and the Netherlands that per-capita real economic growth first appeared on a sustainable basis. This means that before this time, a son's standard of living was much like his father's, his grandfather's, and so on back a few more generations. To get an idea of the changes that have occurred, just think of how much higher your standard of living is than that of persons who lived in the United States only 50 years ago.

Question:

Suppose the real GNP of country X is $1 billion and the population is 1,000,000 persons. The per-capita real GNP is $1,000. In country Y the real GNP is $1 million and the population is 2,000 persons. The per-capita real GNP is $500. Does it necessarily follow that the average person in country X is better off than the average person in country Y (at least in material goods)?

Answer:

No, it does not. It could be that in country X one person has the entire real GNP, and in country Y the real GNP is spread evenly over the entire population. In short, per-capita real GNP does not tell us anything about the income distribution. This is not an argument against using the concept of per-capita real GNP, only against its misuse. For example, if for a given country and a given income distribution, the per-capita real GNP is higher in 1989 than in 1988, then it is accurate to say that the "average" person is better off in terms of material goods.

Growth in a Production Possibilities Frontier Framework

Growth can be seen in a production possibilities frontier (PPF) framework, as Exhibit 22-1 illustrates. On the horizontal axis we have placed agricultural goods, and on the vertical axis, manufactured goods. There are two production possibilities frontiers: PPF_{1989} and PPF_{1994}. The distance between the two frontiers represents the increased productive capabilities that can, but may not, be realized by the economy. If the economy actually realizes these increased capabilities (and moves from a point on PPF_{1989} to a point on PPF_{1994}), then growth has occurred between 1989 and 1994. If it does not, then growth has not been realized. The latter case would be analogous to discovering a new field of oil or inventing a new technology and doing nothing about it. Potential growth exists, but actual growth is not realized.

Question:

Suppose country A experiences a 3 percent growth rate in real GNP each year for five years, and country B experiences a 6 percent growth rate in real GNP each year for five years. Does it follow that the residents of country B are better off in terms of material goods than the residents of country A?

Answer:

No, it doesn't. Think about this in terms of the *PPF* and per-capita real economic growth. First, the *PPF* for country B might be much closer to the origin than the *PPF* for country A. If this is the case, then fewer goods are produced in country B, even though it has the higher growth rate. Second, we need to know something about the populations of the two countries. It might be that the per-capita real GNP growth rate of country A is greater than the per-capita real GNP growth rate of country B, even though country B has witnessed greater real economic growth.

The United States and Japan: Shifting *PPF*s

The United States and Japan each has a production possibilities frontier. Furthermore, each country has been experiencing economic growth, which means each

■ **EXHIBIT 22-1**
Economic Growth

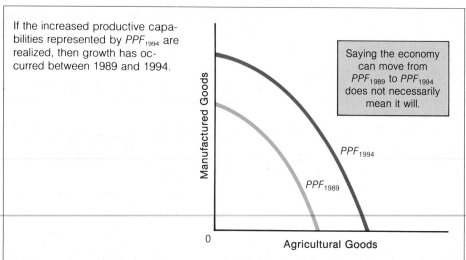

If the increased productive capabilities represented by PPF_{1994} are realized, then growth has occurred between 1989 and 1994.

Saying the economy can move from PPF_{1989} to PPF_{1994} does not necessarily mean it will.

country's *PPF* has been shifting outward. Exhibit 22-2 shows how much each country's *PPF* has shifted outward for different periods and years. In the exhibit, a positive growth rate represents an outward shift in the country's production possibilities frontier. For most periods and years cited in the exhibit, the growth rate in Japan was greater than the growth rate in the United States.

What Factors Affect Growth?

Why do some countries experience economic growth while others do not? Why do some countries experience fast economic growth while others experience slow economic growth? Is there a necessary factor for economic growth? For example, does a country need factor X before it can grow? Is there a sufficient factor for growth? If a country has factor Z is that enough (sufficient) to guarantee growth?

Unfortunately, economists do not have answers to all these questions. No one theory of economic growth is unanimously accepted. But you should not despair. Economists are agreed on a few factors that are linked to economic growth, although they disagree as to how heavily each of the factors should be weighted. The factors are natural resources, capital formation, technological advances, and property rights structure.

Natural Resources. People often think that countries that have a plentiful supply of natural resources experience economic growth whereas countries that are short on natural resources do not. In fact, some countries with an abundant supply of natural resources experience rapid growth (like the United States), and some experience no growth or only slow growth (like Bolivia, Ghana). Also, some countries that are short on natural resources, like Hong Kong, grow very fast. It appears that natural resources are neither a sufficient nor a necessary factor for growth: Nations rich in natural resources are not guaranteed economic growth, whereas nations poor in natural resources may grow. Having said all this, it is still easier and more likely for a nation rich in natural resources to experience growth, *ceteris paribus*. For example, if Hong Kong had been blessed with much fertile soil instead of only a little, and many raw materials instead of almost none, it might have experienced more economic growth than it has.

Capital Formation. Capital formation includes two types of capital: physical and human. Physical capital, such as a tractor or a machine, and human capital, such as knowledge and skills, increase the ability of an individual to produce (that is, there is a predictable relationship between capital formation and labor productivity). For example, modern American farmers produce much more than their grandfathers

■ **EXHIBIT 22-2**
U.S. and Japanese Growth Rates in Real GNP, 1961–87

A positive growth rate represents an outward shift in a country's production possibilities frontier (*PPF*). As the exhibit shows, for most periods and specific years Japan's *PPF* has been shifting outward by a greater percentage than the United State's *PPF*. Figures for 1987 are preliminary estimates.

	Growth Rates in Real GNP, 1961–87 (Percentage Change)										
COUNTRY	AVERAGE ANNUAL 1961–65	AVERAGE ANNUAL 1966–70	AVERAGE ANNUAL 1971–75	AVERAGE ANNUAL 1976–80	1981	1982	1983	1984	1985	1986	1987
JAPAN	12.4%	11.0%	4.3%	5.0%	3.7%	3.1%	3.2%	5.1%	4.7%	2.5%	3.6%
UNITED STATES	4.6	3.0	2.2	3.4	1.9	−2.5	3.6	6.8	3.0	2.9	2.9

SOURCE: Council of Economic Advisers, *Economic Report of the President, 1988* (Washington, D.C.: U.S. Government Printing Office, 1988).

largely because they have certain physical capital goods, such as tractors, that their grandfathers didn't have, and they know much more about the science of farming. In short, they possess more physical *and* human capital than their grandfathers.

Both physical and human capital formation do not come without cost. Tractors, computers, and factory machines do not fall from the sky. Education and knowledge are not obtained by snapping one's fingers. Sacrifices have to be made. To produce capital goods, which are not directly consumable, present consumption must be sacrificed. Robinson Crusoe, alone on an island fishing with a spear, must give up some of his present consumption of fish to weave a net (a physical capital good) with which he hopes to catch more fish.

If Crusoe gives up some of his present consumption, if he chooses not to consume now, he is in fact saving. There is a link between *non*consumption, or saving, and capital formation. As the savings rate increases, capital formation increases, and so does economic growth. Take the case of the United States and Japan. In the period 1960–85, Japan's per-capita real GNP growth rate was 7.1 percent; the United States's was 2.5 percent. Modern research indicates that Japan's higher per-capita real GNP growth rate is due to its higher savings rate, which is almost 75 percent higher than the U.S. savings rate.

Exhibit 22-3 makes this point. Suppose that in 1988 the production possibilities frontier was the same for both the United States and Japan. The United States decided to locate at point *A*, producing relatively more consumption goods and fewer investment goods than Japan, which decided to locate at point *B*. Because the two countries decided to produce a different investment-goods-to-consumption-goods ratio in 1988, they have different *PPF*s in 1994. Because Japan had a higher savings rate than the United States, which brought about greater investment in Japan than in the United States, it experienced greater growth than the United States.

Technological Advances. Technological advances make it possible to obtain more output from the same amount of resources. Contrast the amount of work that can

■ **EXHIBIT 22-3**
The Effect of Consumption/Investment Choices on Economic Growth

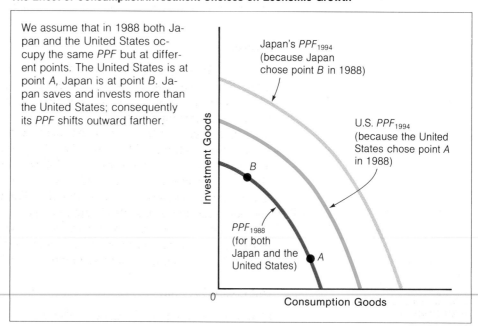

We assume that in 1988 both Japan and the United States occupy the same *PPF* but at different points. The United States is at point *A*, Japan is at point *B*. Japan saves and invests more than the United States; consequently its *PPF* shifts outward farther.

be done by a business that uses computers with the amount accomplished by a business that does not. The world has witnessed major technological advances in the past 100 to 200 years. Consider what your life would have been like if you had lived 200 years ago, around 1790. Most of the major technological achievements we take for granted today—the car, computer, telephone, electricity, mass production techniques—did not exist. It is sometimes said, and it is probably true, that a person living in the late 1700s had a living standard that was closer to the living standard of people living in the year 1 A.D. than of people living today.

Property Rights Structure. Some economists have argued that per-capita real economic growth first appeared in those areas where a system of institutions and property rights had evolved that encouraged individuals to direct their human capital and energy to effective economic projects. Here property rights refer to the range of laws, rules, and regulations that define rights over the use and transfer of resources.

Consider two property rights structures: one in which people are allowed to keep the full fruits of their labor and one in which people are allowed to keep only one-half of the fruits of their labor. Many economists would predict that the first property rights structure would stimulate more economic activity than the second, *ceteris paribus*. Individuals will invest more, take more risks, and work harder when the property rights structure allows them to keep more of the fruits of their investing, risk taking, and labor. Today there is some evidence that the governments of both the People's Republic of China and the Soviet Union believe that a move toward a more market-oriented, private property rights structure can and often does stimulate economic growth. We discuss this and related issues in our next chapter.

Question:

Do economic growth rates matter that much in the long run? For example, suppose one country has a growth rate of 4 percent per year for 20 years and another country has a growth rate of 3 percent per year for 20 years. Will the total growth be different in the two countries over a period of 20 years?

Answer:

There will be a sizable difference. For example, in 1989 in the United States a 1 percent higher annual growth rate represented approximately $50 billion worth of output. (This is based on a GNP of approximately $5 trillion.) As far as growth over the long run is concerned, the example of compound interest illustrates what happens. If you put $100 into a savings account at a 10 percent annual interest rate, in a year you will have $110. And then if you keep the $110 in the savings account at the same annual interest rate, the following year you have $121. It takes only about 7 years to double your $100 savings. And, of course, the higher the interest rate is, the quicker your savings doubles. For instance, at an interest rate of 12 percent, your money doubles in approximately 6 years. It works the same way with growth rates. At a 4 percent growth rate (per year), it will take 18 years to double in size. At a 3 percent growth rate (per year), it takes 24 years to double—or 6 years longer. Thus a 1 percent increase in the growth rate can mean a lot in the long run.

Follow-up Question:

How was the number of years calculated?

Answer:

We used the *Rule of 72*—a simple arithmetical rule for compound calculations. The Rule of 72, which is a rough rule of thumb, says that the time required for any variable to double is calculated by dividing its percentage growth rate into 72. For instance, an economy that experiences a 5 percent annual growth rate will take approximately 14.4 years (72/5 = 14.4) to double in size. The United States had an average annual growth rate in real GNP of 2.6 percent during the period 1981–86. If this annual growth rate were to continue, it would take 27.7 years (72/2.6 = 27.7) for the U.S. economy to double in size. During the same period, the Japanese average annual growth rate in real GNP was 3.7 percent. If this annual growth rate were to continue, it would take 19.4 years (72/3.7 = 19.4) for the Japanese economy to double in size.

The Composition of GNP, Economic Growth, and a Simple Equation

Economic growth is related to the *composition* of GNP. GNP is measured by summing consumption, investment, government expenditures, and net exports. In short,

$$GNP = C + I + G + (X - M)$$

Of the four spending components of GNP, most economists argue that investment (*I*) is the major component that creates capital goods and promotes economic growth. At this point, it is natural to ask how a country can stimulate investment and thus promote economic growth. Not all economists have answered this question the same way. More important, not all economies that have experienced growth have stimulated investment in the same way.

For example, the Soviet economy has grown largely because Soviet leadership has promoted investment and capital accumulation over consumption.[1] For the most part, there are few consumer goods in the Soviet Union (relative to Western nations, in particular); thus Soviet citizens have had little choice but to save, providing the pool from which investment and capital accumulation have come. Obviously the *opportunity cost* of this growth is measured in terms of the consumer goods that people have done without.

Some other countries have proceeded differently. For example, Singapore has sought to promote growth by, among other things, keeping taxes on corporate and personal income low, in the hope that this would stimulate saving and investment. During the period 1960–82, Singapore's average annual growth rate in per-capita real GNP was one of the highest in the world.

Some governments have sought to bring about growth by contracting with private suppliers to build industrial facilities, roadways, schools, and the like, and paying these contractors with newly printed money. In many cases the new money brought about inflation, which reduced the quantity of goods consumers could afford to buy. In short, the inflation was a "tax" on people's cash balances, causing them to consume less. Brazil proceeded this way during much of the 1960s and 1970s.

The Productivity Slowdown of the 1970s in the United States

In the early 1970s the United States began to experience a decline in real economic growth. This was noticed and recorded by many economists, in particular, by Edward

[1]There is some evidence that recently private consumption has been assigned a higher priority in the Soviet Union than in the past. But for the most part, since the 1917 revolution, investment has been given the top priority. See the next chapter for more on the Soviet Union.

Denison of the Brookings Institution. Denison calculated that the real national income growth rate was approximately twice as high for the United States in the period 1948–73 as it was in the period 1973–82.[2] This slowdown in economic growth appeared to be largely the result of a slowdown in labor productivity, as measured by output per hour of labor. But this then prompted individuals to ask what caused the slowdown in labor productivity. We note a few of the more frequently cited reasons here.

Decline in Capital per Hour Worked. We have discussed how labor, combined with capital goods, is more productive than labor alone. Recall that the farmer with a tractor is more productive than the farmer working alone. If we put capital goods on one hand and labor hours worked on the other, we can then look at one in terms of the other and speak of *capital per hour worked*. In the 1970s, the ratio of capital to labor hours worked began to decline. There were two reasons for this: (1) Growth of the capital stock slowed down. (2) Growth in labor hours worked speeded up. Thus both components of the ratio were affected. The growth in labor hours worked increased because a large number of women moved from home activity into the labor force during the seventies.

Why, however, did the growth of the capital stock decline? One economist, Martin Feldstein, argued that inflation and a tax system that did not adjust for inflation gains (but treated them instead as real gains) combined to overtax savings. As a result, saving, which is necessary for capital formation, was discouraged.

Decline in the Quality of the Labor Force. The early 1970s saw an increase in the number of women and young people who entered the labor force. As mentioned earlier, many of the women entering the labor force had come from home activity. The young people were largely the "baby boomers" who were coming of age and getting their first jobs. Some economists contend that because these two groups initially lacked work experience, they pulled down the average quality of labor during this time and prompted the slowdown in labor productivity. Denison's studies, however, suggest that this played only a minor part in the slowdown of labor productivity.

Major Oil Price Increases. It is occasionally argued that the substantial oil price increases of the 1970s caused the relative price of labor in terms of energy to decrease, prompting businesses to hire more labor and thus acquire less capital than they might ordinarily have acquired. Related to this, the sharp oil price increases caused much of the economy's capital stock to become obsolete. For example, many generators and gas-guzzling trucks had to be retired because high oil prices made them too costly to operate. Some say that this reduction in the capital stock reduced labor productivity substantially. Others, like economist Michael Darby, believe that the energy crises and high oil prices played no role in the slowdown in labor productivity. In fact Darby's work shows that there was no productivity slowdown. He notes that economists who use *output per hour of labor* as a measure of productivity fail to adjust for quality changes in labor and thus necessarily bias their results. In his work, Darby adjusted for quality changes in labor and concluded that hourly labor productivity has grown at a stable growth rate throughout the twentieth century.

Regulation. The 1970s witnessed an increase in the number of government safety, environmental, and health regulations that affected businesses. Some maintain that

[2]Edward Denison, *Trends in American Economic Growth, 1929–1982* (Washington, D.C.: Brookings Institution, 1985).

Theory in Practice

Do Special-Interest Groups Zap Productivity?

Economist Mancur Olson has put forth a theory that he and some others believe explains the productivity slowdown of the 1970s, among other things. Olson argues that when countries experience a long period of political stability, special-interest groups (or distributional coalitions, which want to redistribute income from others to themselves) have an opportunity to grow and achieve political power. For example, labor union special-interest groups will increasingly come to have the economic and political power to set wages and prevent employers from hiring nonunion labor, instituting robotics, and the like. Business-oriented special-interest groups will lobby government and receive favors in the form of tariffs and quotas.

Olson argues that the United States, having experienced a long period of political stability, currently has powerful special-interest groups that can often accomplish their goals. In comparison, Japan and Germany, having lost World War II, had their societies turned upside down, and in the process once powerful special-interest groups were dismantled; as yet these groups have not had the time to reestablish themselves and become as strong as their American counterparts. Olson implies that this gives the economic edge to Japan:

If the argument so far is correct, it follows that countries whose distributional coalitions have been emasculated or abolished by totalitarian government or foreign occupation should grow relatively quickly after a free and stable legal order is established. This can explain the postwar "economic miracles" in the nations that were defeated in World War II, particularly those in Japan and West Germany.*

In the Olson theory, powerful special-interest groups reduce the economy's flexibility and slow down its ability to adapt to changing circumstances and technologies (they suffer, in Olson's words, from *institutional sclerosis*). For example, if deflation occurs, business- and labor-oriented special-interest groups will react slowly; thus wages and prices are likely to stay fixed for some time, and unemployment will rise. Overall, the economy will not react smoothly and quickly to a new reality. Olson predicts that national output and labor productivity will suffer.

*Mancur Olson, *The Rise and Decline of Nations: Economic Growth, Stagflation, and Social Rigidities* (New Haven, Conn.: Yale University Press, 1982), p. 75.

since businesses were required to invest in equipment to meet these regulations, they could not invest as heavily in standard plant and equipment and this led to the slowdown in economic growth.

No Single Decisive Factor. Economist Lester Thurow has argued that no single factor was decisive for the productivity slowdown, but that many factors together—inflation, regulation, oil price increases—all played a part and that together they provide the explanation. Thurow has compared the many-factor explanation of the productivity slowdown to "death by a thousand cuts."

Two Worries over Future Economic Growth

It would not be unreasonable for someone who has read this far to conclude that growth is good and no growth is bad. If you have this impression, it is because we have not yet painted the full picture. Not everyone believes growth is better than no growth, or that faster growth is better than slower growth.

Two worries commonly crop up in discussions of economic growth. One concerns the *costs* of growth. Some individuals argue that more economic growth comes with more pollution, more factories (and thus fewer open spaces), more crowded cities, more emphasis on material goods and getting ahead, more rushing around, more psychological problems, more people using drugs, more suicides, and so on. They argue for less growth instead of more.

Others maintain there is no evidence that economic growth (or faster as opposed to slower economic growth) causes all or most of these problems. They argue that growth brings many positive things: more wealth, less poverty, a society that is better able to support art projects and museums, less worry in people's lives (not having enough is a huge worry), and so forth. As for pollution and the like, such "undesirables" would be diminished if the courts were to establish and strictly enforce property rights—for example, in the rivers and the air (which are often the first to become polluted).

As you can no doubt see, the debate between those who favor more growth and those who favor less is not a simple one. Economists have become engaged in it, as have psychologists, biologists, sociologists, and many others. The debate promises to continue for a long time.

Another debate surrounds the issue of economic growth and the future availability of resources. Some people believe that continued economic and population growth threatens the very survival of the human race, since such growth will simply shorten the time until the world runs out of resources; inevitably a time will come when there will be no more natural resources, no more food, no more clean air, no more pure water, no more land for people to live on comfortably. They urge social policies that will slow down growth and preserve what we have.

Critics of this position often charge that such "doomsday forecasts," as they have come to be called, are based on unrealistic assumptions, oversights, and flimsy evidence. For example, economist Julian Simon points out that, contrary to the doomsday forecasts, the quantity of arable land has increased in recent years owing to swamp drainage and land improvement, that there is not an inverse relationship between population growth and per-capita income growth, that the incidence of famine is decreasing, that we are not running out of natural resources, and that if and when scarcity of natural resources becomes a problem, rising relative prices of the resources will cause individuals to conserve them and stimulate economic activity to find substitutes.

Question:

It is easy to say that as oil reserves decline, for example, that the relative price of oil will rise, causing individuals to buy less oil and to search for a substitute for oil. But how can anyone be sure a good substitute will be found? Aren't the critics of the doomsday forecasts doing what they charge the doomsdayers with doing: simply making a claim instead of proving it?

Answer:

Probably some of them do this, and we need to watch out for it. But, then, the fact that someone can't come up with a substitute for X doesn't mean that a substitute won't one day be found. For example, it would have been hard for anyone living in eighteenth-century America to know that the car would one day be a substitute for the horse.

Economics in Our Times

Interview: Robert Solow

Robert Solow is the 1987 winner of the Nobel Prize in Economics. His major contributions have been in the field of economic growth theory. Solow is currently at the Massachusetts Institute of Technology. We interviewed Professor Solow on February 8, 1988.

Professor Solow, between 1961 and 1986 the U.S. growth rate in real GNP was approximately half of Japan's growth rate in real GNP. What do you think explains the higher growth rate in Japan?

I think there are two sources for the Japanese advantage in growth rates. One of them is that throughout most of this period Japan has been in the position of catching up with a level of technology that had already been established in the United States. So that whereas the rate of effective techno-

logical progress in the United States is limited mostly by the rate of innovation, Japan has the capacity to adopt known technologies at a faster rate.

Secondly, for as long as we have good data, at least going back to the late 1940s, Japan has been saving and investing a larger fraction of its national income than the United States. I think that this is especially advantageous to the Japanese while they are in this position of catching up with the American level of technology.

This situation is now changing because in much of industry Japan has caught up with, and in some cases even surpassed, the American level of technology.

Do you therefore expect that the difference between the growth rates in the United States and Japan will narrow in the future?

I think so, yes.

Looking at the U.S. economic scene today, what policies would you recommend to promote economic growth?

For long-run economic growth, if we want to make policy looking ahead over two to three decades, I think that our main effort ought to be to promote the creation of new technology and the adoption of new technology. This means both incentives for research and development and incentives for the investment that is needed to adopt new technology, and even on a longer time scale I think promoting education of industrial-minded engineers and scientists.

I think that in the shorter run we have to do a very delicate thing, which is to reduce the size of the budget deficit, which performs the malfunction of absorbing a good frac-

tion of our savings, but also to reduce the budget deficit without creating a recession because recessions are a bad time for the adoption of new technology and the investment that permits the adoption of new technology.

Do you have a preferred way to reduce the budget deficit?

My preferred way would be to combine a tax increase, preferably a consumption tax, with an easier monetary policy to promote the expenditures that a tax increase would reduce.

Do you see any role for the United States to play in the economic development of the less-developed countries? If so, what is it?

Yes I do, but this is a case where we have to get our own house in order first to permit ourselves to do good in the underdeveloped world. There are two or three things we can do to help poor countries.

One is to make capital available to them. That's where we have to get our own house in order first. We are now in the ridiculous position of being the richest country in the world and absorbing capital from the rest of the world, including absorbing capital from underdeveloped countries, some of which are trying to pay off debts they owe. We have to eliminate our current account deficit with the rest of the world, and increase our savings, so that we are in a position to export capital (and I hope on reasonable terms) to the underdeveloped world.

The second thing we can try to do is transfer technology to the underdeveloped world. Once we reestablish the productivity of American manufacturing, we will find that there are simpler kinds of manufacturing which are better done in lower-wage countries than in the United States, and we ought to be helping to transfer that technology there.

The third thing we ought to be doing is preserving an open trading economy in the world so that we and the rest of the advanced countries are prepared to absorb imports of under-developed countries.

What do you think will be our chances of preserving an open trading economy in the next few years?

Well, I have my hopes. Like most economists I am not a protectionist. I'm not naïve about free trade, but I think that on the whole an open trading system is better than one that is riddled with protection. I think that given the fact that American manufacturing seems to be on the upswing again—manufacturing output has been increasing quite rapidly in the United States in the past couple of years, probably because of the depreciation of the dollar—I hope we can fend off protectionist moves in the Congress. But I don't think that battle is won at all.

Professor Solow, you are the winner of the 1987 Nobel Prize in Economics. I think most people are interested in knowing how someone is notified that he has won the Nobel Prize, and how winning the prize changes his life. Would you talk about this?

I can only tell you how I was notified, I think it is the classic way. My telephone at home rang at about 6:15 or 6:30 in the morning and I was asleep. I got up with the absolutely routine parent's reaction, Oh-oh, something has happened to one of my children. And I call attention to the fact that my children are in their thirties. But this was still my first reaction. I got out of bed half asleep, picked up the phone, and I heard a Swedish-accent voice on the telephone, and the fog cleared and I knew what was happening.

It has changed my life in some ways for the better and in some ways for the worse. I get hundreds and hundreds of invitations to do things, and many of them are things that I would rather not do, and I'm trying desperately to find the strength to say no. On the good side I also get invitations to do things, which will not make me rich, but doors are open to speak to people (I'm doing it right now) which I would like to do, and I ought to do. Some of them are people with political roles, some of them are students, and it has given me the opportunity to get ideas across at length which I could not do otherwise, or fewer people anyhow would listen. The other nice thing that comes with this is that I hear from scores of former students, and I like that a lot.

By the way, I have learned, as a result of this, one bad lesson about American culture. Sometimes it seems there is a kind of hunger for authority, and sometimes it seems to me that there is nothing I can say that is so stupid that a magazine won't print it. And so I try desperately not to say anything about subjects I don't know anything about. Once in a while, all of a sudden I hear what's coming out of my mouth, and I'm horrified, and I stop immediately, but some of those words escape.

ECONOMIC DEVELOPMENT

In this section we discuss the less-developed countries (LDCs), sometimes referred to as developing nations or third-world countries. Mainly we shall be concerned with the question, Why are some nations poor?

The Problems of the Less-Developed Countries (LDCs): Why Some Nations Are Poor

Less Developed Country (LDC)
A country with a low per-capita GNP.

A **less developed country (LDC)** is a country with a low per-capita GNP. About three-quarters of the world's people live in LDCs.[3] Not all LDCs are alike; they differ as to economic and political systems, culture, and ethnicity, to mention a few important factors.

To get some idea what a "low" per-capita GNP figure is, consider a few nations with "high" per-capita GNP figures. In 1986, Switzerland had a per-capita GNP of

[3]When China and India have multiplied their per-capita incomes by about five times—to about where Greece is today—then three-quarters of the world's population will live in "rich" countries. Many experts in the field think this will happen in less than 100 years.

$17,680, the United States per-capita GNP was approximately $17,480, and Japan had a per-capita GNP of $12,840. Countries with low per-capita GNP figures include (to name only a few) Afghanistan, Bangladesh, Cambodia, China, Chad, Ethiopia, India, Nigeria, Pakistan, Somalia, Tanzania, Uganda, and Zambia. For example, in 1986 the per-capita GNP of India was $290, in China it was $300, and in Nigeria it was $640. The developed nations, as a group, accounted for approximately 80 percent of the world's GNP in 1986; the LDCs for 20 percent. Per-capita GNP in the developed nations is, on average, approximately 12 times that in the LDCs.

Why has economic growth and development largely bypassed the people of the LDCs? Why are some nations so poor? Here are a few of the obstacles that some economists believe stifle economic development in the LDCs.

Rapid Population Growth. It is commonly noticed that the population growth rate is higher in LDCs than in developed nations. For example, the population growth rate in developed nations has been around one-half of 1 percent to 1 percent, whereas it has been around 2 to 3 percent for LDCs. The population growth rate is equal to the birth rate minus the death rate. If in country X the birth rate is 3 percent in a given year, and the death rate is 2 percent, the population growth rate is 1 percent.[4]

What has caused the relatively fast population growth rate in the LDCs? First, the birth rate tends to be higher than in developed nations. In countries where pensions, Social Security, and the like do not exist, and where the economy revolves around agriculture, children are often seen as essential labor and as security for parents in their old age. In this setting people tend to have more children.

Second, in the past few decades in the LDCs the death rate has fallen, largely owing to medical advances. The combination of higher birth rates and declining death rates explains why the population grows more rapidly in LDCs than in developed nations.

But is this faster population growth rate an obstacle to economic development? In Exhibit 22-4 many of the countries with the fastest-growing populations are relatively poorer on a per-capita basis than those countries with the slowest-growing populations. But this is still not proof that rapid population growth causes poverty. For example, many of the developed nations today witnessed faster population growth rates when they were developing than the LDCs do today.

Also, when we check population density (instead of population growth), there are a number of examples where high-density populations are much richer than low-density populations. For example, Japan is more densely populated than India and has a higher per-capita income. The same is true for West Germany vis-à-vis East Germany and for Taiwan vis-à-vis China.

Nonetheless some still argue that rapid population growth, though not necessarily a deterrent to economic development, can stifle it. This is because in countries with fast-growing populations the **dependency ratio** rises. The dependency ratio is the number of children under a certain age plus the number of the elderly (age 65 and over) divided by the total population. For example, if the number of children and elderly equals 500 and the total population is 1,500, the dependency ratio is 33 percent. The high dependency ratio in LDCs like India, Bangladesh, and Egypt puts added burdens on the productive working-age population.

Low Savings Rate. Economic growth and development requires investment, among other things. Capital formation increases labor productivity and economic growth.

Dependency Ratio

The number of children under a certain age plus the number of the elderly (aged 65 and over) divided by the total population.

[4]In many cases the birth and death rates are not given in percentage terms but in births or deaths per thousand. For example, the birth rate of country X often is cited as "30 per thousand."

Some Countries with Fast- and Slow-Growing Populations

For the most part, countries with fast-growing populations tend to be poorer than countries with slow-growing populations. There are exceptions, though. (Population figures are estimates.)

Some Countries with Fast-Growing Populations			Some Countries with Slow-Growing Populations		
	POPULATION IN 1987 (MILLIONS)	AVERAGE ANNUAL GROWTH RATE 1980–87 (PERCENT)		POPULATION IN 1987 (MILLIONS)	AVERAGE ANNUAL GROWTH RATE 1980–87 (PERCENT)
Saudi Arabia	14.7	5.4%	West Germany	60.9	−0.1%
Qatar	0.3	4.5	Hungary	10.6	−0.1
Kuwait	1.8	4.4	United Kingdom	56.8	0.1
Kenya	20.3	4.2	Luxembourg	0.3	0.1
Bahrain	0.4	4.1	Italy	57.3	0.2
Equatorial Guinea	0.3	3.8	Bulgaria	8.9	0.2
Ivory Coast	10.7	3.8	Czechoslovakia	15.5	0.3
Zimbabwe	9.3	3.6	Norway	4.1	0.3
Iraq	16.9	3.6	Switzerland	6.4	0.4
Ghana	13.9	3.6	Greece	9.9	0.5
Syria	11.1	3.6	France	55.2	0.5
Zambia	7.2	3.6	Cuba	10.2	0.9
Rwanda	6.8	3.6	United States	243.8	1.0

SOURCE: U.S. Bureau of the Census *Statistical Abstract of the United States, 1988* (Washington, D.C.: U.S. Government Printing Office, 1988).

To accumulate capital, though, it is necessary to save: that is, to lower one's current consumption so that resources may be released for investment. It is generally argued that since living standards in the LDCs are barely above the subsistence level, and incomes must largely go for the necessities of life, there is little (if any) left over for saving. In short, LDCs are poor because they can't save and invest, but they can't save and invest because they are poor. Here we have what is usually referred to as the **vicious circle of poverty.**

Critics charge that low (or subsistence) incomes cannot possibly be a permanent barrier to development since high (or above-subsistence) incomes were not always a feature of today's developed nations.

Vicious Circle of Poverty

The idea that countries are poor because they do not save (and invest), and that they cannot save (and invest) because they are poor.

Cultural "Differences". Do some of the LDCs have cultures that retard economic growth and development? Some people think so. For example, some cultures are reluctant to deviate from the status quo. People may think that things ought to stay the way they always have been; they view change as dangerous and risky. In these countries it is not uncommon for a person's upward economic and social mobility to depend on who his parents were rather than on who he is or what he does. In some cultures the people are fatalistic—as measured by Western standards. They believe that a person's good or bad fortune in life is more dependent on fate or the spirits than on how hard one works, or how much he or she learns, or how hard he or she strives to succeed.

Political Instability and Government Expropriation of Private Property. Individuals in both developed nations and LDCs sometimes do not invest in businesses in the LDCs because they are afraid either that the current leaders of an LDC will be toppled and thrown out of office or that the government might expropriate private property. Both political instability and the risk of government expropriation of private property substantially increase an investor's risk and therefore reduce total investment in a

Theory in Practice

Fungibility: Say It Again

Fungibility is a key concept in economics. It comes from a Latin term that means "such that any unit is substitutable for another." In short, it simply means *substitutable*. For example, points in a basketball game are fungible. UNLV plays UC Santa Barbara in basketball and beats it by two points; the last two points are scored in the last second of the game by player Robinson, who is carried off the basketball court on the shoulders of his teammates. The headline in the newspaper the next day reads "Robinson Wins Game."

But what about player Petrie's two points in the first minute of the game? Had Petrie not gotten those two points, Robinson's two points would not have "won" the game. Why not then say that Petrie's two points were as important as Robinson's two points?

Well, that doesn't seem quite as exciting. But nevertheless it is true. Petrie's and Robinson's points are fungible: They are substitutable.

Money is fungible too. Suppose Jack's parents hand over $200 to him and tell him to buy his textbooks with the money. Will the $200 actually be used to buy textbooks? Possibly, it will; Jack may take the $200 and buy his books. But possibly it won't. The $200 Jack's parents gave him can be used to buy clothes, and the $200 he earned last week can now be used to pay for his books. In the latter case what did Jack's money really pay for—the books or the clothes? Since money is fungible, there is no sensible way to answer this question.

Now consider foreign aid. One government gives another government $100 million and makes the recipient government promise to use the money for project X. Is the money really used for project X? The answer is, not necessarily. Money, remember, is fungible. The $100 million might be used for project X, but then the recipient government has money it might have used for project X that it can now use on any project it wants.

Let's say country Z has $400 million to spend and the following list of projects if would like to complete:

1. Build factories for $200 million.
2. Build roads and schools for $100 million.
3. Upgrade agriculture for $100 million.
4. Build a lavish palace for the leader of the country for $100 million.

Currently, the country can only complete projects 1–3.

Now the United States, say, gives $100 million to country Z and specifies that the money must be used to build roads and schools. So country Z does as the United States says. But now it has $100 million that can be used to build a lavish palace for the leader of the country. Did the U.S. money go for schools and roads, or for a lavish palace? Once again, remember that money is fungible.

Question:

Is this an argument against the United States giving money to poor nations?

Answer:

No, it isn't. The point is simply that money given may not always be used for the purpose that the donor nation would prefer. However, the United States, or any other country for that matter, may decide that giving the money is preferable to not giving it even though some of the money may be spent for purposes the donor has not intended.

Fungibility

A term that is Latin in origin, meaning "such that any unit is substitutable for another." Fungibility means substitutable.

country. Probably the worst thing many governments of LDCs can do is to hint that they might nationalize industries. This usually scares off both domestic and foreign investors.

High Tax Rates. Some economists, like Alvin Rabushka of Stanford University, argue that high marginal tax rates (the *change* in a person's tax payment divided by the *change* in the person's taxable income) affect economic development. Rabushka undertook a study of the 1960–82 tax structures of 54 LDCs and categorized each LDC as a high-, low-, or medium-tax-rate nation. LDCs with top marginal tax rates

Economics in Our Times

A Problem of the 1980s: The World Debt Crisis

"Mexico was really sexy then."
—Angel Gurria, Mexican debt manager, talking about the time when Mexico was riding high on oil revenues and banks rushed to extend it loans.

Throughout the 1980s there was much talk about a world debt crisis. Some of the LDCs—Mexico, Argentina, Brazil, the Philippines, Chile, and Nigeria, for example—had huge outstanding loans they were scheduled to repay to (mostly) Western banks, many of them in the United States. At the time, some people thought that the LDCs would default on the loans and that one major U.S. bank after another would fail.

How did this situation develop? Is the crisis over? What will happen? To answer a few of these questions, we start at the beginning (as they say). Most economists believe that the debt crisis had its origin in the quadrupling of oil prices by OPEC in 1973. After the price increase, the oil-rich nations began to run huge current account surpluses. The OPEC nations in turn deposited much of their oil money in U.S. banks. At the same time, many of the LDC oil-importing nations began to run deficits in their current accounts. The U.S. banks began to *recycle* the oil money to the LDCs. Some of this money went for worth-

while investment projects, some did not. For example, in some countries the borrowed funds were used for consumption rather than for investment.

In the late 1970s some of the oil-exporting LDCs, such as Mexico, began to borrow huge sums from U.S. banks. Why did the U.S. banks extend them credit? Since oil prices were still rising, it looked as if Mexico and others would have no trouble paying off the loans. (If you are poor today, but your bank believes you will be rich tomorrow, then it will most likely be happy to extend you credit.) Then in 1981, the price of oil began to fall.

In August 1982 Mexico told Citibank of New York that it could not pay its loans on time. Other countries in a similar position began to follow suit. The list included both oil-importing LDCs, which had gotten into debt because of the rising price of oil in the 1970s, and oil-exporting LDCs, which had gotten into debt because

of the falling price of oil in the early-to-mid 1980s. Lending banks were largely forced into *restructuring* and *rescheduling* the debt—extending the payback period, reducing interest payments, and so on.

What the outcome will be largely depends on the state of the world economy (Will it grow enough so that debtor nations can export goods and earn the currency needed to meet their loan payments? Will it stagnate?) and the domestic economic policies that the LDCs with debt problems implement (Will they cut back on extravagant spending or not?).

The Baker Plan

In the fall of 1985, then Treasury Secretary James Baker announced a plan to deal with the debt crisis. The plan called for heavily indebted countries to restructure their economies in order to continue to receive loans from commercial banks and the World Bank. Specifically the countries were asked to reduce public-sector invest-

■ **EXHIBIT 22-5**

Ten Biggest U.S. Bank Lenders to Mexico

The outstanding loans to Mexico of the ten biggest U.S. bank lenders to that country totaled more than $15 billion in 1987. Late in December 1987 Mexico revealed a plan for dealing with its debt.

BANK	OUTSTANDING LOANS TO MEXICO AS OF SEPTEMBER 30, 1987 ($ BILLIONS)
Citicorp	$2.900
BankAmerica Corp.	2.407
Manufacturers Hanover Corp.	1.883
Chemical New York Corp.	1.733
Chase Manhattan Corp.	1.660
Bankers Trust New York Corp.	1.277
J. P. Morgan & Co., Inc.	1.137
First Chicago Corp.	0.898
First Interstate Bancorp.	0.689
Wells Fargo & Co.	0.587

SOURCE: Keefe, Bruyette & Woods Inc.

ment, freeze government workers' wages, and eliminate unproductive public-sector enterprises, among other things. As of this writing, some countries have abided by the plan and benefited (for example, the Ivory Coast), while others have been sidetracked (such as Brazil).

The Mexico Plan and More

On December 29, 1987, a rather ingenious plan to deal with the Mexican debt was revealed. Under the plan, Mexico would issue $10 billion of new 20-year bonds that it would swap on a voluntary, bank-by-bank basis for as much as $20 billion in existing bank loans. (The ten biggest U.S. bank lenders to Mexico shortly before the Mexico plan was announced are listed in Exhibit 22-5.)

Now why would some banks give up $20 billion in existing claims for $10 billion in bonds? The answer is simple enough; some banks thought the $20 billion in loans was not worth its face value. In short, the banks didn't think they could collect the $20 billion.

To make the swap more attractive, the $10 billion principal payment on the bonds, was collateralized (backed) by $2 billion worth of U.S. Treasury bonds which Mexico purchased.

The Mexico plan reduces Mexico's overall debt burden, allows the country to focus better on long-term economic growth, and probably does not result in any greater losses for banks than would have occurred anyway.

Other approaches are also being taken. Many large U.S. banks have traded foreign loans back to LDCs in exchange for business investments and other assets in those countries. These are referred to as debt-for-equity swaps.

of 50 percent or lower were classified as low-tax nations whereas LDCs with top marginal tax rates of 50 percent or more that applied to incomes less than $10,000 were categorized as high-tax nations. Rabushka found that the nation with the lowest marginal tax rate, Hong Kong, had the highest growth rate in per-capita income during the period under study, and that low-tax nations overall had an average growth rate in per-capita income of 3.7 percent whereas the high-tax nations had an average growth rate in per-capita income of 0.7 percent.

Question:

This approach to explaining why some nations are poor seems to be a "throw everything into the pot" approach—the poverty that some nations experience could be *because of a low saving rate, and* could be *because of high population growth, and* could be *because of this and that. Aren't there some explanations that apply to all LDCs?*

Answer:

This is one of the frustrations of research that we warned about earlier. Unfortunately, economists are not agreed on "the" reason why some nations are poor. It is not hard, however, to find *an* economist who will tell you what he or she thinks "the" reason is. Some economists might tell you that some nations are poor because they do not put free market practices into effect. Other economists will tell you that a very unequal wealth distribution retards economic development. With time and more and better research, we may be able to throw out a few of the things that are currently in the pot.

■ CHAPTER SUMMARY

Economic Growth

■ The term "economic growth" can be and is used to refer to either *real economic growth* or to *per-capita real economic growth*. Real economic growth is an increase from one period to the next in *real GNP*. Per-capita real economic growth is an increase from one period to the next in *per-capita real GNP*, which is real GNP divided by population.

■ Economists often argue that economic growth is dependent on a society's natural resources, rate of capital formation (physical and human), technological advances, and property rights structure. More natural resources, more and better capital goods and human capital, more and better technological advances, and a property rights structure that largely allows individuals to keep the fruits of their labor are thought to promote per-capita economic growth. However, it should not be inferred from this that a nation with, say, many natural resources will necessarily experience faster per-capita economic growth than a nation with a few natural resources. There could be offsetting factors.

■ When calculating how long it will take a nation's economy to double in size, economists use the Rule of 72: To calculate the time required for any variable to double, divide its percentage growth rate into 72.

The Productivity Slowdown of the 1970s

■ The decline in U.S. economic growth in the 1970s was largely caused by a slowdown in labor productivity which, it has been argued, was caused by one or more of the following: a decline in capital per hour worked, a decline in the quality of the labor force, major oil price increases, and regulation.

The Problems of the LDCs

■ Most economists cite one or more of the following problems as the reason(s) the LDCs are poor: rapid population growth rate (high dependency ratio), low savings rate, a culture that does not lend itself to economic growth, political instability and the threat of government expropriation of private property, and high tax rates.

■ QUESTIONS TO ANSWER AND DISCUSS

1. Suppose the population growth rate of country X is 3 percent and the population growth rate of country Y is 0.5 percent. How long will it take before the population of each country has doubled?

2. How do you explain that some countries with plentiful natural resources are developed whereas others are less developed (LDCs)? How do you explain that some countries with few natural resources are developed whereas some countries with plentiful natural resources are less developed?

3. What is one of the major failings of "doomsday" forecasts?

4. Would you expect the birth rate in LDCs to go up or down as a result of per-capita economic growth and economic development?

5. If, before you had read this chapter, someone had asked you why the LDCs were poor and what they should do to promote economic development, what would you have said?

What would you say now? Is there much difference between what you would have said before and after reading the chapter? What do you attribute the difference to?

6. Absolute economic growth is about increasing the size of the economic pie. Per-capita economic growth is about increasing the size of the economic pie faster than the population is growing, so not only is there more but also there is more per person. Explain how different property rights structures might help or hinder both absolute and per-capita economic growth.

7. Some people argue that the LDCs will not grow and develop without foreign aid from developed countries. Other people argue that foreign aid actually limits growth and development (they see it as a "handout" that distorts the incentive to produce) and propose in its place a heavy emphasis on foreign trade. In the real world, there is some of both. Do you think, however, that an increase in the aid-to-trade ratio (amount of foreign aid received divided by the amount of foreign trade) would decrease, increase, or leave unchanged the economic development of an LDC? What about a decrease? Explain your answers. How do they relate to the reasons cited for why some nations are poor (rapid population growth, low savings rate, cultural differences, political instability and government expropriation of private property, high tax rates)?

Chapter 23

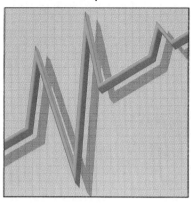

Alternatives to Mixed Capitalism

■ INTRODUCTION

How would an economics class in the Soviet Union, the People's Republic of China, or Yugoslavia be different from one in the United States?

Imagine that you're at the University of Moscow looking in on an economics class. Everything looks much the same as at your university. Forty students are sitting at desks, much like the one you sit at. The instructor is pacing back and forth in front of the blackboard with a piece of chalk in his hand.

But what would he say? Do you think he would discuss some of the same topics your instructor has discussed? Would he talk about supply and demand, prices, rationing devices, and opportunity cost? If someone brought up the topic of inflation, how might he respond? What would he say about economic planning? How would his discussion of how economic policy is made in the Soviet Union differ from a corresponding discussion in a U.S. university?

Think about these questions as you read this chapter. We think you'll have some of the answers at the end.

■ WHAT THIS CHAPTER IS ABOUT

The bulk of this book has described the workings of the economic system that is best known as *mixed capitalism*. It is the economic system that, to different degrees, exists in the United States, Canada, Australia, and Japan to name only a few countries. In this chapter we discuss a few of the alternatives to mixed capitalism. The list includes *pure capitalism, command-economy socialism,* and *decentralized socialism.*

Key Questions to Keep in Mind as You Read

1. What are mixed capitalism, pure capitalism, command-economy socialism, and decentralized socialism?
2. What are the economic realities that face all economic systems?

3. Does the law of demand hold for all economic systems?

4. What are some of the policy proposals that a pure capitalist would make?

5. How does economic planning work?

6. How does Gosplan, the central Soviet planning agency, work?

7. What are some of the new developments in the Soviet Union and in the People's Republic of China?

8. How does decentralized socialism work in Yugoslavia?

MIXED CAPITALISM AND ITS ALTERNATIVES

Mixed Capitalism

An economic system characterized by largely private ownership of the factors of production, market allocation of resources, and decentralized decision making; most economic activities take place in the private sector in this system, but government plays a substantial economic and regulatory role.

Pure Capitalism

An economic system characterized by private ownership of the factors of production, market allocation of resources, and decentralized decision making; most economic activities take place in the private sector, and government plays a small role or no role at all in the economy.

Command-Economy Socialism

An economic system characterized by government ownership of the nonlabor factors of production, government allocation of resources, and centralized decision making; most economic activities take place in the public sector, and government plays a very large role in the economy.

Decentralized Socialism

An economic system characterized by government ownership of the nonlabor factors of production, largely market allocation of resources, and decentralized decision making; most economic activities take place in the public sector, and government plays a major overseer role in the economy.

First we define mixed capitalism and its alternatives. Then, using these definitions as a base, we examine some of the similarities and differences of the various systems.

Mixed capitalism is an economic system characterized by largely private ownership of the factors of production, market allocation of resources, and decentralized decision making; most economic activities take place in the private sector, but government plays a substantial economic and regulatory role. The U.S. economic system is an example of mixed capitalism.

Pure capitalism is an economic system characterized by purely private ownership of the factors of production, market allocation of resources, and decentralized decision making; most economic activities take place in the private sector, and government plays a small role or no role at all in the economy. No nation in today's world operates under pure capitalism, although some economists note that Hong Kong, for example, is much closer to the pure capitalist ideal than is the United States.

Command-economy socialism is an economic system characterized by government ownership of the nonlabor factors of production, government allocation of resources, and centralized decision making; most economic activities take place in the public sector, and government plays a very large role in the economy. The Soviet economy is generally considered an example of command-economy socialism.

Decentralized socialism is an economic system characterized by government ownership of the nonlabor factors of production, largely market allocation of resources, and decentralized decision making; most economic activities take place in the public sector, and government plays a major overseer role in the economy. The Yugoslav economy is an example of decentralized socialism.

See Exhibit 23-1 for a review of the principal properties of the four economic systems outlined here.

Question:

Suppose seven countries are identified as mixed capitalist. Does it follow that the seven are mixed capitalist to the same degree?

Answer:

No, that is not exactly the case. An analogy is class grades. Suppose Rodriguez gets an 89 on a test and Trenton gets an 81. Both of them receive a B for a grade and thus both are B students. We can't really say which student is more of a B student, but we can say that Rodriguez, who is a B student, is a little closer to being an A student than Trenton, who is also a B student. Similarly, we might say that country X, with a mixed capitalist economic system, is closer to pure capitalism than country Y, or that country Y, with a mixed capitalist economic system, is closer to decentralized socialism than country X.

The Economic Realities Facing All Economic Systems

All economies share some features. We outline them in this section.

Scarcity. In Chapters 1 and 2 we introduced the concept of scarcity, which is the condition where wants outstrip the resources available to satisfy those wants. We already know that mixed capitalist economies must face up to the reality of scarcity. But what about pure capitalist, command-economy socialist, and decentralized socialist economies? Do they have to deal with scarcity? They certainly do. All economic systems must deal with scarcity. The people in the United States, the Soviet Union, the People's Republic of China, Japan, Venezuela, Saudi Arabia, and every other country in the world must grapple with it. What distinguishes economic systems is *not* that some economic systems have to deal with scarcity and others do not, but rather *how* different economic systems deal with scarcity.

Opportunity Cost, or No Free Lunch. We learned in earlier chapters that opportunity cost is a consequence of scarcity. It follows, therefore, that since all economic systems must deal with scarcity, all economic systems are faced with opportunity cost. In short, in all societies there is no such thing as a free lunch. This is the case in the United States, the Soviet Union, India, Chile, the People's Republic of China, and every other country.

Rationing Devices. Since all economic systems are faced with scarcity, all economic systems must ration goods. In the United States, for example, this is largely done through (dollar) price. Cars, houses, television sets, computers, toothbrushes, clocks, books, and much more are rationed by price. If, in some societies, money price is seen as a less than desirable rationing device, then some other rationing device must be put in its place. It may be first-come-first-served, political power, or something else, but in a world of scarcity societies must always decide on a rationing device or devices.

The Law of Demand. Does the law of demand only hold for mixed capitalist economies and not for command-economy socialist economies? It certainly does not. The law of demand holds for all economic systems. If the dollar price of television sets rises, Americans will buy fewer television sets, *ceteris paribus*. And if the ruble price of television sets rises, Russians will buy fewer television sets, *ceteris paribus*.

■ **Exhibit 23-1**
Four Economic Systems

The principal properties of four economic systems are summarized.

ECONOMIC SYSTEM	OWNERSHIP OF FACTORS OF PRODUCTION	ALLOCATION OF RESOURCES	DECISION MAKING	WHERE DO MOST ECONOMIC ACTIVITIES TAKE PLACE?	ROLE GOVERNMENT PLAYS IN THE ECONOMY
Mixed Capitalism	Largely private	Market allocation	Decentralized	Private sector	Plays a substantial economic and regulatory role
Pure Capitalism	Purely private	Market allocation	Decentralized	Private sector	Small or no role
Command-Economy Socialism	Government ownership of nonlabor factors of production	Government allocation	Centralized	Public sector	Very large role
Decentralized Socialism	Government ownership of nonlabor factors of production	Largely market allocation	Decentralized	Public sector	Major role

Rational Self-Interested Behavior. Rational self-interested behavior means to act in such a way as to maximize the difference between the benefits and costs as perceived by the individual. It is generally assumed that individuals all over the world, no matter what their economic system, exhibit this type of behavior.

What to Produce? How to Produce It? Who Produces It? For Whom Is It Produced? All economic systems must decide what goods are to be produced, how these goods will be produced, who will produce the goods, and for whom the goods will be produced.

For example, will the economy produce more books or more tape decks? Implicit here is the question who decides what the economy produces. Will it be the marketplace, composed of millions of buyers and sellers, or a central government committee?

Once this question is answered, the economic system must decide how the goods will be produced. Consider food staples that are produced in the United States and in the Soviet Union. In the United States these food staples are produced on private farms, and the individual farmer decides how the food staples will be produced. In the Soviet Union food staples are largely (but not exclusively) produced on large state-operated collective farms.

Next, who will do the producing? Two options are "anyone who wants to" and "a specific group of people." The implied question is how much personal freedom individuals have in deciding what they will do.

Finally, for whom are these goods produced? Are they produced for the people who pay the prices for them? Are they produced for whomever the government decides needs or should have them? Socialists often argue that capitalism produces houses for people who can pay the money prices for the houses, and that socialism produces houses for people who need houses. Some critics charge that socialism produces low-quality houses for people the government officials believe need houses, and that need usually is linked to political party loyalty.

Question:

Can the differences between economic systems be viewed in terms of the way they answer the four questions: What to produce? How to produce it? Who produces it? For whom is it produced?

Answer:

Yes, to a large degree, they can. The differences between economic systems become clearer if we make explicit what is implicit in the four questions. For example, the question How to produce it? implicitly asks who owns the resources that will be used to produce the goods, how the resources will be allocated, and what types of incentives will be used to get the goods produced. The question What to produce? implicitly refers to the level of decision making in an economic system. For example, is what is to be produced decided by a central committee or by individual consumers?

If we make explicit what is implicit in the four questions, we can narrow down the differences in economic systems to four categories: *the form of resource ownership* (who owns the resources—individuals or government?); *the form of resource allocation* (how are resources allocated—by the market or according to government plan?); *the type of incentives* (are goods produced by giving individuals monetary incentives to produce the goods or by issuing public-interest, "do-it-for-the-common-good" incentives or by threats?); and *the level of decision making* (is what is to be produced, where one is to work, and so forth to be decided by individuals or by government committees?). Exhibit 23-1 defines the economic systems of mixed capitalism, pure capitalism, command-economy socialism, and decentralized socialism with most of these categories in mind.

PURE CAPITALISM

Pure capitalism sometimes goes by the names *laissez-faire capitalism, anarcho-capitalism,* or *libertarianism.* Adherents to the pure capitalism position are usually referred to as *libertarians.* Libertarians either see a very limited role or no role at all for government. The former principally see government's role as protecting property rights and enforcing contracts. Some libertarians add the provision of national defense to this list. The latter argue that any government at all is too much government. They maintain that the free market is capable of providing roads, courts, police protection, and so forth. In this section we discuss the libertarians' case for pure capitalism.

The Nonaggression Axiom

Murray Rothbard, an economist and major libertarian thinker, has written: "The libertarian creed rests upon one central axiom: that no man or group of men may aggress against the person or property of anyone else. This may be called the 'non-aggression axiom.'"[1] Many libertarians arrive at this axiom through natural rights theory, which holds that each person has the right of self-ownership (you own yourself, no one else does), the right of ownership of previously unused and unowned resources that one has occupied and transformed, and the right of ownership of property conveyed through exchange or by gift. Libertarians often maintain that their policy positions on economic, political, and social matters are all derived from a consistent application of these natural rights. We present some libertarian policy positions in the next section.

Arguing the Pure Capitalism Case

For most libertarians, many public problems are caused by "too much government." As a solution to these problems, libertarians usually recommend "less government and greater reliance on the forces of the free market." Here are a few things libertarians say.

1. **Professional licensing.** Professional licensing reduces the supply of a service and increases its price. For example, because medical licensing makes it more difficult for individuals to become physicians and for nurses to compete directly with physicians, licensing increases the price of medical care. In a pure capitalist economy professional licensing would not exist; that it largely does exist today is because government, by licensing certain trades, serves as the cartel enforcer of a special-interest group.

2. **Minimum wage law.** Minimum wage laws are a restraint on free trade. Setting a minimum wage guarantees that individuals whose present skills are worth less than the minimum wage will go unemployed. Individuals have the (natural) right to work for whatever wage they voluntarily agree to and government, by passing a minimum wage law, prevents individuals from exercising this right in some instances. The minimum wage would not exist under pure capitalism.

[1]Murray Rothbard, *For a New Liberty* (New York: Collier Books, 1978), p. 23.

3. **The U.S. Postal Service.** Private companies can and should be allowed to deliver first-class mail. Under pure capitalism a number of competing mail services would deliver first-class mail, and such competition would drive prices down and quality up.

4. **Restraints on price.** All restraints on price, either price floors or price ceilings, reduce voluntary exchange to a level below that which would exist in a pure capitalist economy. Libertarians are against interest rate ceilings, minimum wages (as noted earlier), agricultural price supports, and rent controls.

5. **Discretionary fiscal and monetary policies.** Government intervention in the economy, via fiscal policy (taxing and spending policies) and monetary policy, often has negative effects—such as high interest rates, inflation, recession, and high unemployment. The free market is inherently stable and capable of equilibrating at full-employment output.

6. **The Federal Reserve.** The Federal Reserve System, the central bank of the United States, should be eliminated. It is an "engine of inflation," far too political, and the cause of unnecessary and harmful ups and downs in the economy. In monetary policy libertarians usually favor an automatic monetary mechanism as opposed to a discretionary one. This translates into a monetary rule or a gold standard.

7. **Antitrust policy.** Government antitrust policy too often stifles market competition and is used to attack firms for no other reason than that they are big. Pure capitalism, which maximizes competitive forces, is the best "antitrust" policy. Firms are much more afraid of successful competitors than they are of government antitrust policy. In a related argument, libertarians maintain that antitrust policy is sometimes used by firms to limit their competition. For example, firm X, in competition with firm Y, may argue before the antitrust authorities against the merger between firm Y and firm Z. Too often the authorities will accept the argument and a merger that possibly might increase productivity, reduce costs, and ultimately increase quality and lower price will not be permitted.

8. **Quotas and tariffs.** Quotas and tariffs increase prices and decrease exchange and only serve narrow special-interest groups. Neither would exist in a pure capitalist society.

9. **Social Security.** To libertarians, Social Security combines a compulsory savings program with a redistribution program—both of which they oppose. It is wrong to force people to save for old age (or anything else for that matter). How much one saves, or doesn't save should be up to the individual. As to the redistributory aspect of Social Security, it is tantamount to theft for the government to reach into one person's pocket, take out money, and redistribute that money to someone else.

10. **Welfare.** Welfare is a forced redistribution program. Additionally, in many instances welfare programs produce outcomes contrary to the designs and hopes of the persons who implemented the programs. For example, welfare often makes people more dependent on others and less likely to acquire work skills. Libertarians are in favor of voluntary charities.

A Critique of Libertarianism

The pure capitalism case, or libertarianism, has many critics. Here are some of the points the critics make:

1. **Libertarians do not see the merit of using government's taxing, subsidy, and regulatory powers to adjust for third-party effects.** In most exchanges, probably

Economics in Our Times

Interview: Murray Rothbard

Murray Rothbard is a leading member of the Austrian School of Economics and is widely considered to be the father of modern-day libertarianism. His work reaches beyond economics into the areas of history and political philosophy. Rothbard is currently at the University of Nevada, Las Vegas. We interviewed Professor Rothbard on October 9, 1988.

Professor Rothbard, what is libertarianism?

Libertarianism is the doctrine that nobody should be allowed to agress against or invade the person or property of anybody else. I think most people would agree with this doctrine. The difference between most people and libertarians, though, is that libertarians are consistent in applying it. Namely, we apply it to the government. Somehow the government is thought to be exempt from these moral rules that apply to everyone else. Libertarians are against exempting any institution, including government.

The critics of libertarianism argue that libertarians do not: (1) see the merit of using government's taxing, subsidy, and regulatory powers to adjust for third-party effects; (2) seriously consider complex exchanges; or (3) see the stabilizing effects of government monetary and fiscal policies. How would you respond to the critics on each of these points?

There are two types of third-party effects: positive and negative. A positive third-party effect would be my becoming more knowledgable and because of this my fellow men are benefitted without paying. I don't think that they should be taxed to subsidize me so that I may learn more. Fact is, there are always positive third-party effects of the type I have mentioned. I see no reason why government needs to enter the picture. If someone wants to compensate me to gain more knowledge, it should be up to his individual judgment.

Other kinds of third-party effects are invasions of property rights. The classic case is a locomotive in the 19th century pouring smoke into the air and harming the property of the farmers' orchards nearby. That's a third-party effect which is an invasion of a property right. I believe that should be stopped and that is what the courts are supposed to do. But unfortunately the courts stopped doing it and thereby allowed the polluting technology to proliferate. In conclusion, the only third-party effects I believe adjusting for are those that are an invasion of property rights.

The second point, concerning complex exchanges, is an interesting one. When I was entering the field of economics, simple exchange referred to barter and complex exchange referred to money exchange. Now I see that there has been a semantic twist here. I think what's happening is the deliberate use of a euphemism to call organized theft and coercion an exchange. An exchange means a voluntary trading of property titles. Coerced exchange is where someone holds you up at the point of a gun and says I want your money. I don't call that a true exchange, I call that coercion and theft.

Complex exchange sounds very much like the old British Tory concept of virtual representation. When the Americans were saying that they should be represented in Parliament, the British reply was that Americans were represented virtually although they were not allowed to vote. The Americans to their credit knew that this was nonsense and that they weren't being represented at all.

As to the effects of monetary and fiscal policies, I think these policies are usually destabilizing rather than stabilizing. For example, inflations are always caused by government money creation. Also, government creates business cycles by pumping money in through the banking system, keeping prices up, and therefore creating malinvestments in capital goods. In turn a recession is required to liquidate these malinvestments and return us to a free market economy. For example, consider the Great Depression. The Federal Reserve pumped up the money supply in the 1920s, which orthodox economists claim was not inflationary because the price level did not go up. But the point is that the price level would have fallen at this time because of increased productivity; thus, by preventing prices from falling, the Fed created business malinvestment that required liquidation in 1929, thereby generating a business cycle.

Then as soon as the Great Depression occurred, the government stepped in and started pushing up wage rates and prices and expanding credit, the result being that they prolonged the depression.

Most economists do not favor the completely free market world that you do. What is your criticism of most economists?

When I first entered economics very few economists were in favor of the market. Today that is not the case, so things have changed for the better. There has been a major increase in the appreciation of the workings of the market. Unfortunately, most economists haven't gone far enough. I don't know whether they don't have the courage, or vision, or whatever, to be consistent in free market principles.

Suppose on Tuesday morning everybody in the nation goes to the polls to vote on whether or not they want to live in a libertarian world. Tuesday night the results come in and we learn that 75 percent of the people do not want to live in a libertarian world. On Wednesday you mysteriously gain the power to bring about a completely libertarian world by simply snapping your fingers. Knowing the sentiments of the voters on Tuesday, would you snap your fingers?

Yes, I would snap my fingers because that is the only moral thing to do since I regard interventionism as organized crime and counterproductive economically. I would definitely snap my fingers. Of course, you may say that in the long run things aren't going to work out because the majority of the people want government and therefore they'll probably have it. But at least the world would have had a glorious holiday of liberty and prosperity. Of course maybe the

demonstration effect will convince more people that they ought not move back to government and give up all the things that liberty and the free market can do for them.

You have criticized almost everything that government does. What is the least objectionable thing that government does?

There are several candidates. One is receiving gifts for building monuments. This often happens in local government, whereby someone gives a monetary gift to be used to build a statue or something. Another candidate is to mint gold coins. Today the U.S. Treasury mints the American Eagle gold coin. This at least gives the idea of a gold coin standard to the public. It makes the public a little more accustomed to using gold coins as money. Also there is the issuing of special stamps or proof sets of coins to collectors. All these activities are fairly unobjectionable.

only two persons are affected—the person buying the good or service and the person selling the good or service. In some exchanges, however, there are *third-party effects,* whereby someone not involved in the exchange itself is nonetheless affected by it. Sometimes the third party is affected adversely by an exchange that others enter into: say, company X produces steel that it sells to customers; in the process it generates pollution that harms people that live near the steel factory. And sometimes the third party is affected positively: say, the university sells education to students; in the process it generates benefits for people who now reside in a community of well-educated individuals. Many economists argue that third-party effects should be taken into account, or adjusted for, and that government is the proper institution to do the adjusting—through regulation, taxes, subsidies, and so forth. For example, government might subsidize education so that the social benefits, not just the private benefits, are realized.

Libertarians do not want government to use its taxing, subsidy, and regulatory powers to adjust for these third-party effects. But, say the critics, sometimes the only way third-party effects *can be adjusted for* is through government—by way of regulations, taxes, and subsidies. Thus the critics see the choice as either letting government adjust or not adjusting at all.[2]

2. **Libertarians do not seriously consider complex exchanges.** A simple exchange might be one person trading an apple for $1. A complex exchange may be millions

[2]We discussed the whole issue of third-party effects (or externalities) in Chapter 18.

of voters choosing a political candidate who has promised, if elected, to increase government spending on defense, education, or public assistance programs. The critics of libertarianism argue that some goods and services simply cannot be obtained through the free market, and therefore people naturally turn to the political "market" to obtain them. They criticize libertarians for not seeing that exchange comes in different varieties; an exchange is not always as obvious as a person trading an apple for a $1. Many libertarians would maintain that a complex exchange is not really an exchange at all. What about the person who votes against the candidate who is elected and raises spending on defense? Libertarians might question whether this voter is benefiting from the so-called complex exchange. If not, then it is not clear an exchange has taken place.

The words of economist James Buchanan are relevant here:

> Politics is a structure of complex exchange among individuals, a structure within which persons seek to secure collectively their own privately defined objectives that cannot be efficiently secured through simple market exchanges . . . . In the market, individuals exchange apples for oranges; in politics, individuals exchange agreed-on shares in contributions toward the costs of that which is commonly desired, from the services of the local fire station to that of the judge.[3]

3. **Libertarians do not see the stabilizing effects of government monetary and fiscal policies.** Most libertarians will say that they do not see the stabilizing effects of government monetary and fiscal policies because there are no stabilizing effects to see. The critics argue otherwise, saying that since the economy does not always self-equilibrate at full-employment output, government management policies have a role to play.

KARL MARX

The latter part of this chapter deals with two varieties of socialism—namely, command-economy socialism and decentralized socialism. Karl Marx has played a major part in the development of socialist thought. Here we present a few of his major ideas.

The Basics of Marx's Thought

Few economists have had as much influence on the world as Karl Marx. In turn, Marx was influenced by the economist David Ricardo and the philosopher Georg Hegel, among others, in particular, by Ricardo's discussion of the **labor theory of value** and Hegel's **dialectic**.

Labor Theory of Value
Holds that the value of all commodities is equal to the value of the labor used in producing them.

Dialectic
The method of logic based on the principle that an idea or event (thesis) generates its opposite (antithesis) leading to a reconciliation of opposites (synthesis).

The Labor Theory of Value. The labor theory of value holds that all value in produced goods is derived from direct and indirect (or embodied) labor. A man or woman working on a factory line is an example of direct labor. A machine, made by a man or woman, is an example of indirect, or embodied, labor.

Marx argued that the value of a commodity is determined by the *socially necessary labor time* embodied in the commodity. This is the sum of the direct and indirect (or embodied) labor necessary to produce socially desired commodities. (By using the adjective "socially," Marx was able to differentiate between those goods that were genuinely desired by people—like shoes, coats, and houses—and those that were not—like sand castles on the beach.)

For example, if it takes 5 hours of socially necessary labor time to produce X, and 10 hours to produce Y, then Y will be twice as valuable as X. Marx realized that

[3]James Buchanan, "The Constitution of Economic Policy," *American Economic Review* 77 (June 1987): 244.

Theory in Practice

Can Pure Capitalism Conserve Natural Resources?

Can pure capitalism conserve natural resources? The critics say no; the proponents say yes. The critics maintain that the love of money is the motivating force behind capitalism, and that capitalists do not earn profits by conserving natural resources, they earn profits by selling them. The proponents of pure capitalism argue that the desire to earn profits is not inconsistent with conservation—money-hungry capitalists conserve natural resources every day. Here's one of their typical examples.

T. R. Hunter, a Texan, owns a piece of land under which lie 100,000 barrels of oil. At present prices it will cost $5 per barrel to extract the oil, and Hunter can sell each barrel for $15. His profit will be $1 million ($1.5 million in total revenues minus $500,000 in total costs). What does Hunter do? Does he drill for the oil and sell it to today's buyers, or does he conserve it and sell it later to future buyers? It depends on what Hunter expects the future price of oil will be. Suppose Hunter believes that oil will be in shorter supply next year and that the price will be $20 per barrel. Being a money-hungry oil man, he calculates his profits this year at $15 per barrel against his expected profits next year at $20 per barrel. Assuming oil extraction costs in the two years are the same ($5 per barrel), his expected profits next year are $1.5 million. In present value terms (what $1.5 million next year is worth today), he calculates that $1.5 million is

worth a little more than $1.363 million at a 10 percent rate of interest. (If invested at a 10 percent rate of interest, $1.363 million today will grow to $1.5 million next year.) He then compares the two dollar figures: $1 million and $1.363 million. Since $1.363 million is greater than $1 million, Hunter waits until next year to drill the oil. This year he conserves the oil.

But suppose Hunter has pressing cash needs and must have the money today to pay off bill collectors. Does he go ahead and drill for the oil now? He wouldn't necessarily do that. What he could do instead is to try to sell his oil land to someone for more than $1 million. For example, it could well be that Maggie Gemson, a Texas oil woman, believes that the price of oil next year will be $20 per barrel. Given this, she might be willing to buy Hunter's land from him for some price between $1 million (what Hunter can get today for selling his 100,000 barrels of oil) and $1.363 million (the present value of $1.5 million). Suppose Hunter and Gemson settle on a price of $1.10 million. Hunter is made better off because he has pressing cash needs, and he receives $100,000 more than he'd receive if he drilled for oil and sold it today. And Gemson is made better off because she buys for less than its present value the right to oil that (she hopes) will generate profits of $1.5 million next year.

But what has happened to oil conservation? This objective is met since once Gemson has bought Hunter's oil, she will conserve it. She will not drill for the oil now because if she does so at today's price, she will take a loss; instead, she will leave the oil in the ground until next year. She will save the oil for next year's oil buyers instead of selling it to today's oil buyers. The reason, say the proponents of pure capitalism, is that in a free market system resources are always allocated to their highest-valued uses and since next year's oil buyers are expected to value a barrel of oil more than today's oil buyers, oil will be conserved today and sold next year.

labor was not all of equal quality, but he believed that skilled labor could be calculated as some multiple of unskilled labor.

Marx maintained that the labor, or labor power, capitalists purchase is itself a commodity, and thus its value (like that of commodities) is determined by labor time. Additionally, the value of labor power tends toward a subsistence wage, in short the *labor time* necessary for the worker to earn the necessities consumed by the worker and his or her family.

To illustrate, consider an example from Marx's time. Suppose a worker needs 2 shillings a day to subsist. Furthermore, suppose it takes 4 labor hours to produce the gold that is in 2 shillings. This then means that the worker needs to work 4 hours to earn 2 shillings. Two shillings is the value of labor power—it is what workers would be paid for a day's work. But here is the sticking point: The workday is longer than 4 hours. It is 10 hours. In this case, the worker works a 10-hour day to earn 2 shillings (which is equal to 4 hours labor time), and the value produced by the worker in the 6 remaining hours is **surplus value** that the capitalist exploits from the worker.

Surplus Value
In Marxist terminology, the difference between the total value of production and the subsistence wages paid to workers.

Question:

Why couldn't the worker simply refuse to work more than 4 hours for 2 shillings? In short, why wouldn't the worker prevent the capitalist from exploiting him or her?

Answer:

Marx argued that capitalism creates a large *reserve army of the unemployed* and that this excess supply of labor keeps wages at the subsistence level. For Marx, it was a matter of the worker working on the capitalist's terms or not working at all.

Dialectic. According to Hegel, knowledge and progress occur through a process of opposing ideas or forces. An existing idea, or *thesis,* is at some point confronted with an opposing idea, *antithesis,* and there is a struggle of sorts. The outcome of the struggle is a *synthesis,* which in turn becomes the new thesis and the process starts again. Marx adapted Hegel's dialectic to explain the stages of economic development, which we turn to next.

Marx on Economic Development

Marx criticized many of his economic predecessors and contemporaries for not understanding that capitalism had emerged as a specific economic system, or mode of production, and through the dialectical process would eventually evolve into a different economic system. According to Marx there are six stages of economic development:

■ *Primitive communism.* In this stage of economic development there is common ownership of property, and people cooperate to earn a meager living from nature. People generally have to work all day simply to produce the bare necessities for survival. Under these conditions, there is no surplus value and thus no exploitation since both require workers to produce more than they need to consume for survival.
■ *Slavery.* At some point, the productive capabilities of people rise to such an extent that they are able to produce more than they need to consume for survival. Now slavery becomes a possibility; some people exploit others and garner the surplus value. Once this occurs, class conflict arises.
■ *Feudalism.* The economic actors in feudalism were lords and serfs, who, in Marx's view, had a relationship that was essentially the same as that between the slave-masters and slaves in the preceding stage of economic development. The serf was permitted to work a few days per week on the land allotted to him, but on other days he was required to till the lord's land.
■ *Capitalism.* Marx both disliked capitalism and marveled at its ability to greatly increase productivity and output. According to Marx, the means of production became more concentrated under capitalism. For him, the relationship between capitalist and worker was essentially the same as the relationship between slavemaster and slave and between lord and serf in earlier stages of economic development. The capitalist appeared to pay the worker for all the hours that he or she worked,

Biography
Karl Marx
(1818–1883)

Brief biography

Karl Marx was born on May 5, 1818, in Trier, Prussia, and died on March 14, 1883, in London, England. His studies at the University of Berlin covered many fields, but mostly focused on religion and philosophy. In 1842 he obtained a position as an editor at a Cologne newspaper, but emigrated to Paris after the newspaper was suppressed by the political authorities. It is certain that he became a communist, a proponent of the collective ownership of the means of production, in 1844 with the publication of his "Paris Manuscripts."

Marx returned to Cologne a few years later but was expelled in 1849 because of his political views. Thereupon he moved to England where he lived for the rest of his life. Much of his time was spent in the British Museum where he studied the writings of the major economists. In the summer of 1851, he was the European correspondent for the New York *Daily Tribune*.

Marx, his wife, and his seven children were often badly housed and fed, and lacked adequate medical care. Four of his seven children died in childhood. Marx's final years were marked by bad health. Marx did not live long after the death of his wife.

What Is History?

According to Marx, history is a dialectical process characterized by the struggle between social classes over the division of the social product.

Capitalism's Future

Marx believed that over time capitalist growth would lead to falling profits and severe economic depressions that would in turn cause the ruling economic class to exploit the workers further. Finally, the workers would revolt, ushering in a new stage of economic development.

A Revolutionary and Political Activist

Marx was torn between his life as an academic and his life as a political activist and revolutionary. He wanted more time for both. As a political activist, he was expelled from both Belgium and France (he was also a political activist in England, but England was more tolerant). He played a large part in the international workers' movement. Marx's daughters, Jenny, Laura, and Eleanor, also played active roles in the workers' movement.

No Eternal Economic Laws

Marx believed that there are no eternal economic laws that are valid at all times and in all stages of history. Instead, every general social framework has its own economic laws. Consequently Marx did not view economics as a distinct science separate from sociology, history, and anthropology.

A Personal Note

Although Marx wrote that "religion is the opium of the people" and his wife, Jenny, was an atheist, they still had a church wedding.

---

but in reality only paid for a few hours and appropriated the value produced in the remaining hours to himself. Marx predicted intense class struggles under capitalism between the capitalists, or *bourgeoisie,* and the workers, or *proletariat.* He believed that capitalists would increasingly exploit the workers in the search for higher profits.

■ *Dictatorship of the proletariat, or socialism.* According to Marx, the intense class struggles under capitalism will eventually result in the state being used as an instrument of oppression by the capitalists against the workers. The workers will rise in revolt and overthrow the bourgeois state and establish in its place the dictatorship of the proletariat in which the capital and land are owned by the proletarian government. Exploitation of the workers will cease.

■ *Pure communism.* The dictatorship of the proletariat eventually "withers away," only pure communism remains. In this stage of economic development, individuals produce according to their abilities and receive according to their needs. In pure communism, the highest stage of economic development, selfishness and greed are largely a thing of the past, and there is no need for a formal government apparatus.

The Critics of Marx

Here are some of the criticisms that have been levied against Marx's work:

1. **The labor theory of value is faulty.** Most contemporary economists agree that labor is not the sole source of value. They argue that land, capital, and entrepreneurship are independent factors of production and, like labor, are capable of creating value. Marxists sometimes retort that capital is ultimately created by labor, thus making it embodied labor. The critics agree that capital is *in part* past labor (and note that labor is paid its contribution to the production of capital), but they point out that capital is capable of creating value beyond the value of the labor employed to produce it.

2. **There is no large reserve army of the unemployed.** Marx argued that capitalism produced a large reserve army of the unemployed that capitalists could use to hold wages down to a subsistence level. Massive unemployment has occurred under capitalism, but this has been the exception rather than the rule.

3. **Most workers earn an above-subsistence wage.** Here the critics argue that the competition for workers among business firms puts upward pressure on wages and causes firms to improve working conditions, shorten working hours, provide fringe benefits, and so forth.

4. **Marxist revolutions have not appeared in the places Marx expected.** Marx expected worker revolutions to appear in advanced capitalist nations where capitalism has had the longest time to develop, and the class conflict between capitalists and workers has had the longest time to intensify. Thus, according to Marx, countries such as Great Britain and the United States were far more likely to experience revolutions than countries such as Russia and China.

COMMAND-ECONOMY SOCIALISM

Command-economy socialism, like pure capitalism, is an alternative to mixed capitalism. In this section we describe the workings of command-economy socialism by concentrating on the Soviet economy.[4]

The Public and Private Sectors in the Soviet Union

The private sector in the Soviet Union is very small; the public sector is very large. This is simply another way of saying that in the Soviet Union most of what there is to be owned is owned by the central government—the state. For example, the government owns and operates almost all the manufacturing, communication, trans-

[4]Many socialists prefer not to use the word "socialism" when discussing the Soviet Union. For example, in the textbook *Economics: An Introduction to Traditional and Radical Views,* 5th ed. (New York: Harper & Row, 1986), E. K. Hunt and Howard J. Sherman say "socialism means the democratic control of the economy by the entire working class." They go on to say that "the Soviet economy is run by the government, but the government is run by a small self-appointed group." It appears that for authors Hunt and Sherman, and for many socialists, the Soviet Union is not true to the principles of socialism. Hunt and Sherman call it an "undemocratic, dictatorial form of socialism." Most socialists argue that if the Soviet economy is to be termed "socialist," it is certainly one of the less attractive varieties of socialism and that socialism, as a whole, should not be judged exclusively by what goes on in the Soviet Union.

portation, and banking enterprises; wholesale and retail stores; and farms. A relatively few private farms (along with some garden plots), retail shops, and private personal services (such as psychiatry and carpentry) constitute the legal private sector. In addition to the legal private sector, there is the *black market* (or what some people call "the illegal private sector" or the "second economy"). Still, the black market and the legal private sector together represent only a small percentage of the total economic activity in the Soviet Union.

Gosplan

Gosplan

The Soviet central planning agency that has the responsibility of drafting the economic plan for the nation.

The central planning agency, or **Gosplan,** has the responsibility of drafting the economic plan for the Soviet economy. Gosplan does not, however, draft the economic plan without receiving input from the high Communist party officials in the Politburo. In addition, Gosplan is supervised by the Council of Ministers. It is thought that this group has considerable influence over what Gosplan does since the director of Gosplan is a vice-chairman of the Council of Ministers.

Gosplan has the responsibility of constructing two plans: a five-year (long-range) plan and a one-year (short-range) plan. The five-year plan allocates the nation's economic resources; it determines how much goes to investment, how much to the military, how much to consumption, and so forth. The one-year plans are much more detailed than the five-year plans; they outline what each of the more than 200,000 Soviet enterprises under Gosplan's supervision is to produce, the amounts of labor and raw materials each will be allocated, the amount and type of machinery that will be installed, and so on.

To get a sense of how the process works, let's translate it to the American scene. If there were an American Gosplan, it would probably be located in Washington, D.C. The American Gosplan would then issue orders to General Motors, IBM, USX, and other companies stating what each is to produce. For example, it might direct General Motors to produce 300,000 cars. In turn, Gosplan would direct the companies supplying General Motors to send so much steel, so much plastic, and so many tires to the company. It would also tell General Motors whether it could expect to have its factories updated, what type of new capital goods would be arriving, and other crucial information.

Allocating Resources: A Major Hurdle for Gosplan

Gosplan's task is monumental; it must take the inputs of the Soviet economy and direct them into outputs in a manner consistent with the objectives set forth by the government leadership. This requires a careful balancing between output goals and available resources.

To see this, suppose Gosplan sets as its annual goal the production of 100,000 units of X, 200,000 units of Y, and 300,000 units of Z. Next Gosplan must allocate resources in such a way that it meets its goals. Suppose input W is necessary to the production of goods X, Y, and Z. Gosplan must then allocate input W in such a way that 100,000 units of X, 200,000 units of Y, and 300,000 units of Z are produced. How will it know exactly how much input W to send to the enterprises producing goods X, Y, and Z, respectively? To know this Gosplan needs to know how many units of W are required to make 1X, 1Y, and 1Z.

Suppose Gosplan thinks that 5 units of W are needed to make 1X, 4 units of W are needed to make 1Y, and 6 units of W are needed to make 1Z. It follows that it will allocate 500,000 units of W to the enterprise producing good X (5W for each of the required 100,000X), 800,000 units of W to the enterprise producing good Y (4W for each of the required 200,000Y), and 1,800,000 units of W to the enterprise producing good Z (6W for each of the required 300,000Z). Although this sounds simple enough, several problems can easily arise.

First, Gosplan might incorrectly estimate the number of units of W that are required to make 1X, 1Y, and 1Z. It could, say, overestimate the number of units of W required to produce good X and underestimate the number of units of W required to produce good Z. If this happens, then too many units of W will be sent to one enterprise and too few units of W will be sent to another.

Second, the number of units of input W required to make 1X, 1Y, or 1Z is likely to change over time. The quality of input W might fall so that more units will be needed to make 1X. Will Gosplan know about this right away and adjust accordingly?

Third, the enterprise making W might require inputs from the enterprise that produces X before it can produce and ship W. Consider an enterprise that produces trucks. To produce trucks, the enterprise requires oil to generate the energy to run its plants. But, in turn, the enterprise producing oil needs trucks to move the oil to the truck factory. In such a situation, where one enterprise's production depends on another's, a failure by one enterprise to meet its production goals can make it impossible for other enterprises to meet their production goals, too.

Question:

First, if a U.S. enterprise fails to produce as expected, can't this make it impossible for other enterprises to meet their production goals, just as in the Soviet Union? After all, if firm X needs what firm Y produces and firm Y needs what firm Z produces, a slip-up by firm Z can prevent firms X and Y from producing as many units of their goods as they might want.

Second, suppose Gosplan finds out that there is not enough steel to meet every production goal. What does Gosplan do then?

Answer:

Certainly in the United States one firm might be dependent on receiving supplies from another firm, but if it doesn't receive its supplies, it is more likely than its Soviet counterpart to locate substitute inputs. In the Soviet Union if an enterprise doesn't receive the necessary inputs to make good X, the directors of the enterprise really have no incentive to locate substitute inputs. It is not the job of the directors of the enterprise to solve economic problems like this; it is the job of Gosplan. In the United States, however, the managers and owners of the business firm have an incentive to find substitute inputs because less output often means fewer dollars in their pockets.

As to the second question, if Gosplan learns that there is not enough steel to meet every production goal, it will prioritize its goals and allocate steel accordingly. For example, the Politburo may weight the production of missiles over the production of cars. If there is not enough steel to meet the production goals of both missiles and cars, fewer cars will be produced. In other words, Gosplan follows what is called a **priority principle:** industries most important to the Soviet leadership will be the last to take cuts in supplies.

Priority Principle

In the Soviet Union, a rule that is followed when there are too few resources to meet all the production goals of the economic plan. It specifies that those industries most important to the Soviet leadership will be the last to take cuts in supplies.

The Case Against Central Economic Planning

One of the major differences between individuals who favor pure capitalism and those who favor command-economy socialism is the issue of economic planning. Those who favor pure capitalism are against central economic planning, and those who favor socialism are for it.

Two major arguments are advanced against central economic planning. First, say its opponents, economic plans, made by economic planners, cannot take into account as much relevant information as a market does; therefore, economic plans cannot coordinate economic activity or satisfy consumer demand as well as market forces. Consider an economic planning board, composed of 30 to 40 persons, that must decide how many houses, apartment buildings, buses, cars, and pizza parlors should be built within the next year. Where would the planners start? Would they know about people's changing demands for houses, apartment buildings, and the rest? Critics of economic planning argue that they would not. At best, the planners would be making a guess as to what goods and services consumers would demand and how much they would buy at different prices. If they guess wrong, say the critics, resources will be wasted and demands will go unfulfilled. Private individuals, guided by rising and falling prices and by the desire to earn profits, are better at satisfying consumer demand. Economic planners risk little themselves when they draw up economic plans for others to follow (they don't put *their* money on the line), and therefore aren't as likely to avoid costly economic mistakes as are private entrepreneurs in a free market, who do put their money on the line.

Second, the critics of central economic planning say that economic planners mistakenly believe that the plans they construct will be followed by the members of society. Relevant here is Adam Smith's description of the economic planner or, as he called him, "the man of system":

> The man of system . . . seems to imagine that he can arrange the different members of a great society with as much ease as the hand arranges the different pieces upon a chess-board. He does not consider that the pieces upon the chess-board have no other principle of motion beside that which the hand impresses upon them; but that, in the great chess-board of human society, every single piece has a principle of motion of its own, altogether different from that which the legislature might choose to impress upon it. If those two principles coincide and act in the same direction, the game of human society will go on easily and harmoniously, and is very likely to be happy and successful. If they are the opposite or different, the game will go on miserably, and human society must be at all times in the highest degree of disorder.[5]

Question:

Everybody uses plans. A person makes plans for his or her life, which include going to college, getting a job, and so forth. A business might draw up a plan for the next five years. If individuals and firms plan, why not societies? What do the critics of central economic planning say to this?

Answer:

They say that there is a major difference between the plan an individual or business firm makes and an economic plan for all of society. First, if an individual or a firm makes a plan that fails, only the individual or the firm suffers. For the most part, the rest of society is unaffected. This is not the case if a central economic plan (for all of society) fails. One mistake here can have major consequences for many people.

Second, if one person makes a personal plan, this does not prohibit others from making and following their own plans. But an economic plan that encompasses all of society just might do that. For example, a young woman with computer skills living in one part of a command-economy nation may want to move to another part. But whether she can realize her plan depends on whether her plan is consistent with

[5]Adam Smith, *The Theory of Moral Sentiments* (Oxford: Oxford University Press, 1976), p. 234.

the economic plan set down by the central authorities. It may be that the economic plan calls for technological development in the area of the country where the young woman lives and that she will be required to continue to live and work there.

The Next Step: Supply and Demand

As we have seen, Gosplan determines the aggregate quantity of goods in the economy; that is, how many radios, television sets, cars, refrigerators, toasters, and so forth will be provided. This is the supply side of the market. As Chapter 3 explained, though, there is also a demand side to every market, and supply and demand together determine price.

Besides determining the supply of a particular good, the Soviet central planners also set its price. For example, they might decide that 11 million toasters will be produced this year and that each will sell for a price of 25 rubles. (Until recently, Gossnab, the state supply agency, fixed the prices for about 200,000 Soviet products.) Unless 25 rubles is the equilibrium price, though, there will be either a surplus or a shortage of toasters. Exhibit 23-2 illustrates what happens when the price for toasters is set below the equilibrium price. A shortage of toasters results. In a market system, the price of toasters would be bid up to the equilibrium price, and the quantity demanded of toasters would equal the quantity supplied. But in the Soviet Union it is illegal to bid up the ruble price of a good. So, instead, toasters are rationed by some combination of ruble price and waiting in line (that is, the rationing device, first-come-first-served).

Western travelers to the Soviet Union have observed long lines in front of some stores and no people at all in front of other stores. What accounts for this? Some prices are set below the equilibrium price, producing shortages and long lines of people, and some prices are set above the equilibrium price, producing surpluses and relatively empty stores. As long as price is centrally imposed, shortages or

■ **Exhibit 23-2**
Prices in the Soviet Union

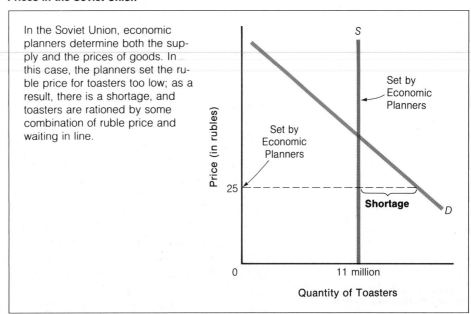

In the Soviet Union, economic planners determine both the supply and the prices of goods. In this case, the planners set the ruble price for toasters too low; as a result, there is a shortage, and toasters are rationed by some combination of ruble price and waiting in line.

surpluses are likely to result. It would be most unusual if the planners could correctly guess the equilibrium price.[6]

Question:

Although the Soviet planning authorities do not always set the prices of goods at the equilibrium level, don't they make certain that all Soviet citizens receive certain free goods and services, such as education and health care? If so, tax money must be used to finance these expenditures. What type of tax is used to raise the revenue?

Answer:

First, it is true that certain goods and services are provided "free"—but remember a fundamental economic lesson: there is no such thing as a free lunch. This is just as true in the Soviet Union as in the United States.

Critics of the Soviet system often argue that "free education and health care" are not really free because taxes have to be paid (by someone) to finance them, and that the so-called "free goods" come at the personal cost of living in a (largely) controlled society. The reply, by Soviet officials and some others inside and outside the Soviet Union, is that it is better to live in a somewhat less free society and have health care when one needs it than to live in a free society (as a poor person) and not receive necessary health care. But critics counter that the health care system in the Soviet Union is largely very poor.[7]

In any case, the tax used to finance many of these "free" or heavily subsidized goods (such as some housing) is the *turnover tax*. This is an excise tax, a tax on the sale of a particular good. In the Soviet Union the turnover tax is added to the retail price of a good. For example, if the retail price of one pair of shoes is 50 rubles, the retail price plus the turnover tax might be 60 rubles. The customer buying a pair of shoes would therefore have to pay 60 rubles. If individuals who receive the "free" health care and education buy goods in Soviet shops, they end up paying something toward their health care and education.

The Pricing of Labor

There is less mobility of labor in the Soviet Union than in many other countries. In the United States, for example, if Elaine Beck, living in Chicago, wants to try her luck at getting work in Los Angeles, no one will stop her. She is free to move where she pleases. In the Soviet Union, there are some restrictions on who can live and work in the major cities such as Moscow and Leningrad. Outside these two major cities, individuals may live and work where they choose. Many Soviet citizens and Western observers see this as a major improvement over past governmental policies. In the early years after the Bolshevik Revolution of 1917 and during World War II, the government told many people where they could live and work.

---

[6]For an interesting account of both the surplus and shortage problems in the Soviet Union from the point of view of an American journalist living in Moscow, see Hedrick Smith, *The Russians* (New York: New York Times Book Co., Inc., 1976).

[7]Yevgeny Chazov, minister of health in the Soviet Union, has said that 12 of the 33 maternity hospitals in Moscow do not meet sanitation standards. Furthermore, 35 percent of the rural hospitals do not have hot water, 27 percent do not have sewer systems, and 17 percent have no running water at all. Between the mid-1960s and 1980, male and female life expectancy declined. Between 1971 and 1985, infant mortality rose. The infant mortality rate in the Soviet Union is 2.5 times higher than the U.S. rate. For an interesting article that cites these and other statistics on the Soviet health system, see "Red Medicine" in the *Wall Street Journal*, August 18, 1987, p. 1.

Today, Soviet authorities, after determining the demand for labor in different industrial occupations, adjust wages so as to equate supply and demand. For example, work in the northern part of the Soviet Union where it is extremely cold and unpleasant pays higher wages than the same work in less cold, less unpleasant areas. Most Western economists agree that for labor, and in particular industrial labor, both the Soviet Union, a command-economy socialist nation, and the United States, a mixed capitalist nation allow supply and demand forces to operate. A relatively free labor market appears necessary to maintain worker incentives.

The Privatized Agricultural Sector

Advocates of the wealth-producing properties of the free market system are quick to point out that the state-owned and operated agricultural sector in the Soviet Union is a failure, but that the tiny privatized agricultural sector is a huge success. When one thinks of Soviet agriculture, one naturally thinks of the collective farm or *kolkhoz*. The workers on the collective farms are each assigned a small plot (usually one acre in size) for their private use. Products raised on these small plots may be consumed or sold. In total, the small private plots constitute approximately 1.5 percent of the total Soviet agricultural land under cultivation, yet they account for 25 percent of total agricultural output. If we look at the breakdown of some particular food staples, the disparity is even greater. For example, in 1980 the private plots produced 64 percent of the total potato output in the Soviet Union, 32 percent of the eggs, 31 percent of the meat and dairy products, and 58 percent of the fruit and berries output. Some analysts have predicted that the Soviet Union would be one of the world's major exporters of food instead of an importer of food if it would simply privatize a large percentage of its agricultural sector.

Economic Growth and the Distribution of Income

On a per-capita GNP basis, the Soviet Union is behind the United States, the nations of the European Economic Community (EEC)—composed of Belgium, Denmark, France, Greece, Ireland, Italy, Luxembourg, the Netherlands, Portugal, Spain, United Kingdom, and West Germany—and Japan, Canada, and Australia. For example, in 1987, the Soviet Union per-capita GNP was 46 percent of U.S. per-capita GNP, 70 percent of the EEC per-capita GNP, 66 percent of the Japanese per-capita GNP, 52 percent of the Canadian per-capita GNP, and 56 percent of the Australian per-capita GNP. Also, the United States, with a population that is 35 million fewer than the population of the Soviet Union, and with slightly less than one-half the land area of the Soviet Union, has a GNP roughly twice that of the Soviet Union.

During some periods, however, the growth record of the Soviet Union has been impressive. For example, during the 1950s the annual growth rate in real GNP was around 7 percent. A major reason for this was the heavy Soviet investment in plant and equipment. In the 1960s and 1970s the growth rate began to decline. In the 1980s, the real GNP growth rate in the Soviet Union has been relatively low. The average annual growth rate in real GNP in the Soviet Union during the period 1981–86 was 2.2 percent. The U.S. growth rate at 2.6 percent was only slightly higher, and the growth rates for France (1.6), Italy (1.7), the United Kingdom (1.9), and West Germany (1.4) were all lower. The Japanese growth rate was higher at 3.7 percent.[8] The growth rate in real GNP in China was 8.9 percent. See Exhibit 23-3.

[8]Both Lester Thurow and Robert Solow discuss aspects of Japanese economic growth in their interviews. See the interview with Thurow in Chapter 20 and the interview with Solow in Chapter 22.

■ **Exhibit 23-3**
Real GNP Growth Rates, Selected Countries

The average annual U.S. growth rate in real GNP (2.6 percent) in the period 1981–86 was slightly higher than the Soviet Union's growth rate (2.2 percent), but the growth rates of the EEC, France, West Germany, Italy, and United Kingdom were lower than the Soviet Union's during the same period. Japan's growth rate was 3.7 percent and China's was 8.9 percent.

COUNTRY	AVERAGE ANNUAL GROWTH RATE IN REAL GNP, 1981–86 (PERCENT)	GROWTH RATE IN REAL GNP, 1987 (PERCENT)P
West Germany	1.4%	1.7%
Eastern Europe	1.4	2.0
France	1.6	1.6
Italy	1.7	2.7
European Economic Community (EEC)*	1.7	2.3
United Kingdom	1.9	3.5
Soviet Union	2.2	1.0
United States	2.6	2.9
Canada	2.8	3.7
Japan	3.7	3.6
China	8.9	9.5

P = preliminary estimates for 1987.

*The EEC includes Belgium, Denmark, France, United Kingdom, Greece, Ireland, Italy, Luxembourg, the Netherlands, Portugal, Spain, and West Germany.

SOURCE: Council of Economic Advisers, *Economic Report of the President, 1988* (Washington, D.C.: U.S. Government Printing Office, 1988).

Some observers note that comparing the GNP growth rates of mixed capitalist nations with that of a nation such as the Soviet Union is somewhat like comparing apples and oranges. A comparison of, say, U.S. and Soviet GNPs does not take into account the qualitative aspects of the goods produced. They point out that U.S. goods are generally considered to be of higher quality than Soviet goods, and that the United States produces goods that consumers want to buy whereas in the Soviet Union this is not always the case.[9]

What about the income distribution in the Soviet Union? Does command-economy socialism lead to less income inequality? Yes, it does, if we compare the United States and the Soviet Union—*but the difference is not large.*

To illustrate, in the early 1970s economist Lowell Galloway estimated that the top 20 percent of households in the Soviet Union received 37.5 percent of the total Soviet income while the top 20 percent of households in the United States received 40.6 percent of the total U.S. income. The bottom 20 percent of households in the Soviet Union received 7.5 percent of the total Soviet income while the bottom 20 percent of households in the United States received 6.9 percent of the total U.S. income. Finally, the top 5 percent in the Soviet Union received 14.0 percent of the total Soviet income, while the top 5 percent in the United States received 15.9 percent of the total U.S. income. In short, it is true that in the Soviet Union the poor get a bigger slice and the rich get a smaller slice of the economic pie than they do in the United States—but not much bigger and not much smaller. See Exhibit 23-4.

[9]"Soviet industry doesn't make dishwashers. It doesn't even make soap for washing dishes. It allegedly makes hair dryers, but nobody knows where to buy one. The concept of a toaster is met with wonder." Barry Newman, "Gorbachev's Test," *Wall Street Journal,* June 17, 1988, p. 1.

■ **Exhibit 23-4**

Income Shares of the Poor and the Rich in the Soviet Union and the United States

The income share for the poor (lowest fifth) and the rich (highest fifth) is not much different in the United States and the Soviet Union. It is also important to note that the U.S. GNP is almost double the Soviet Union's GNP. Note: Galloway notes in the source article that "as nearly as possible, the income concept is an after-tax and transfer-payment one."

PERCENTAGE OF ALL FAMILIES	INCOME SHARE, SOVIET UNION (PERCENT)	INCOME SHARE, UNITED STATES (PERCENT)
Lowest fifth	7.5%	6.9%
Highest fifth	37.5	40.6
Top 5 percent	14.0	15.9

SOURCE: Lowell Galloway, "The Folklore of Unemployment and Poverty" in *Governmental Controls and the Free Market*, edited by Svetozar Pejovich (College Station, Texas, and London: Texas A&M University Press, 1976), pp. 41–69.

In addition, there are three points to consider. First, many economists note that some mixed capitalist nations, such as Japan and Great Britain, have approximately the same income distribution (the same degree of income inequality) as the Soviet Union.

Second, they point out that the degree of *income inequality* in a nation is not always an accurate measure of *economic inequality* overall. For example, in the Soviet Union the top government officials and members of favored groups, such as scientists, ballet stars, top athletes, and distinguished professors, are accorded special privileges not within the reach of other Soviet citizens. These persons may shop in special stores that are stocked with the finest goods, many of which are not available to the rest of the population. Members of this elite group do not have to wait in line to buy goods, and they are usually moved to the top of the waiting list when they want to buy a car or rent an apartment. It is generally argued that since the income statistics do not account for these special privileges, they underestimate the degree of economic inequality in the Soviet Union.

Third, it is important to remember that an individual's absolute standard of living can be higher in a nation where he or she receives a lower percentage of the total income than in a nation where he or she receives a higher percentage. Since the U.S. GNP is almost twice the Soviet Union's GNP, it follows that the poor in the Soviet Union receive a slightly bigger slice of a smaller economic pie, while the poor in the United States receive a slightly smaller slice of a bigger economic pie. In short, when it comes to international comparisons, less income inequality does not necessarily translate into the poor being better off.

RECENT ECONOMIC REFORMS IN THE SOVIET UNION AND THE PEOPLE'S REPUBLIC OF CHINA

Both the Soviet Union and the People's Republic of China have command-economy socialist economies, but in recent years both nations have been experimenting with free market practices on a limited scale. In this section we discuss these new developments, looking first at reforms in the Soviet Union and then at reforms in the People's Republic of China.

Economic Reform in the Soviet Union: Perestroika

Soon after Mikhail Gorbachev became general secretary of the Soviet Union in 1985, he began to institute *glasnost* and *perestroika*. Glasnost means greater openness in public discussions and the arts; perestroika means economic reform. As to the latter,

Gorbachev's stated goal was to shift the Soviet Union from "an overly centralized command system of management to a democratic system based mainly on economic methods." Most Western observers interpreted this statement to mean that the Soviet leader wanted his country to adopt some market practices.

Most Sovietologists thought this was a political gamble for Gorbachev. First, there are approximately 18 million bureaucrats in the Soviet Union who have a hand in managing the economy, and perhaps could not be expected to look favorably on perestroika. Second, the majority of the citizens in the Soviet Union are not accustomed to market practices. After all, except for some short periods under Lenin, the market system died in the Soviet Union with the Bolshevik Revolution of 1917. As of this writing, one cannot be sure how long-lived perestroika will be or how deep into Soviet society it will go. But this is how things looked at the beginning of 1989.

Planning and Peripheral Issues. Under perestroika, Gosplan's command over the economy has been reduced. On January 1, 1988, industrial managers were given greater control over the use of profits for reinvestment or workers' bonuses. Sales are increasingly important. (Before perestroika, production quotas were all-important.)

Worker Incentives. Currently the average Soviet worker earns $336 a month. Under perestroika, a worker can earn up to 40 percent more if he or she is in a team (of about 10 workers) that exceeds its output quota.

New Businesses. In May 1987 a law took effect that allowed individual and family businesses. As of early 1988, 200,000 Soviet citizens have gone into business for themselves. Common individual and family businesses include watch repair, clothing, and taxicabs. The law also permits cooperative businesses—businesses too large to be operated by an individual or family. A common cooperative business is a restaurant or store. Some commentators have noted that cooperative businesses have not taken off as many Soviet officials expected. For example, as of mid-1988, there were only 20,000 cooperatives employing about 150,000 people in a country with a population of 280 million.

International Trade. One of the goals of perestroika is to increase Soviet trade with the West and to increase Western investment in the Soviet Union. (Trade between the United States and the Soviet Union is small—about $2 billion in 1987. This largely consisted of U.S. grain sales.) At the summit meeting with President Reagan in Washington in December 1987, Gorbachev spent part of his time in discussions with U.S. business leaders. Current U.S.-Soviet ventures include the opening of two Pizza Huts in Moscow.

Subsidies and Prices. The issue of subsidies for, and prices of, basic goods and services is a sensitive one in the Soviet Union. For example, the Soviet Union spends approximately $110 billion annually to subsidize meat and milk consumption. Apartment rent is so heavily subsidized that a three-bedroom apartment in Moscow is said to rent for $24. As part of perestroika's reforms, there is talk of reducing subsidies and increasing prices. The Soviet leadership realizes that any attempts to lower subsidies and raise prices will require higher salaries for Soviet workers, or there is likely to be much discontent.

Farms. The *contract brigade* system in Soviet agriculture permits a group of farmers, or a single family, to manage a productive (agricultural) asset and keep a share of the profits. For example, a husband and wife might decide to raise some of the calves owned by a collective farm. The collective farm essentially contracts with the two-person contract brigade to raise so many calves to milking age and pays them according to the weight and general health of the cows. Such contracts have provided some Soviet citizens with a substantial increase in their monthly earnings. In some cases, monthly earnings have tripled or quadrupled.

Economic Reform in China: Bao Gan Dao Hu and More

It is better to eat communist weeds than capitalist grain.
—Jiang Qing, Mao Tse-tung's wife
It matters not whether the cat is black or white, but only whether it catches mice.
—Deng Xiaoping, Chinese leader and reformer

After the Communist (Maoist) takeover in 1949, the Chinese economy, using the Soviet economic system as a model, put command-economy socialism into effect, although Chinese economic planning was less centralized than Soviet planning.

In 1958, Mao Tse-tung instituted an economic plan known as the *Great Leap Forward,* which called for the development of heavy industry, a dramatic increase in output, and a more intensive use of labor. The plan was largely a failure. Goods were produced that no one wanted, large-scale projects (such as irrigation) were poorly planned, people were transferred from rural areas to the cities, and goods such as steel produced by unskilled workers in primitive work environments were of low quality. In Hunan province alone, 5,376 collectives were combined into 208 large people's communes with an average of 8,000 households in each. National income fell dramatically.[10]

The next major Maoist attempt to change Chinese society was the *Cultural Revolution,* which began in 1966. This movement aimed at remaking Chinese society in general and at eliminating all foreign influences from the country in particular. During the Cultural Revolution, teashops and private theaters were shut down; hand holding and kite flying were forbidden; the National Gallery of Fine Arts was closed, as were radio and television stations, newspapers, and magazines; and libraries were ransacked and books burned. (Mao disliked formal education. He once said, "The more books one reads, the stupider one becomes.") This was not an environment in which economic growth and development could flourish. National income fell once again during the Cultural Revolution. Mao's death on September 9, 1976, ended the Cultural Revolution and opened the way for change.

The economic changes in China today are generally attributed to China's leader, Deng Xiaoping, who came to power shortly after Mao's death. These changes are examined in the next sections.

Bao gan dao hu. *Bao gan dao hu* means "contracting all decisions to the household." It is the essence of China's economic reforms in rural areas. China's collective farms are currently operated by households under the following system: (1) The government gives collectives specific production quotas that they must meet. (2) The government buys the quota-procured output at a fixed price. (3) Although the state owns the farmland, it is divided into small plots that are farmed by the households; households are allowed to contract with the collective to produce a share of the quota. (4) Once the households have met their quota-procurement responsibilities

---

[10]Until this time China had received technical assistance from the Soviet Union. Soviet leader Khrushchev decided, however, that Soviet technical assistance was being wasted through Mao's Great Leap Forward, so he decided to end assistance in 1959. The Great Leap Forward came to an end on July 23, 1959. Mao said, "The chaos caused was on a grand scale, and I take responsibility." Later that year natural disasters combined with the poor condition of Chinese agriculture due to the Great Leap Forward caused large-scale famine.

they can produce and sell in the free market any output they want. These new agricultural reforms have led to a rise in agricultural output. For example, between 1978 and 1984 (a peak year) grain production increased 34 percent to 400 million tons. For a short while, China was a grain exporter instead of an importer.

A Shaky Free Market.   Saying that China in the 1980s has adopted some free market practices does not mean that a free market practice put into effect today will not be abandoned tomorrow. For example, Hong Kong buys many of its pigs from Guangdong, a province in China. A recent increase in the demand for pigs in Hong Kong raised the price of pigs in Guangdong. Farmers in Hunan, the province north of Guangdong, saw the higher prices for pigs in Guangdong and started to ship their pigs there. As a result, the supply of pigs in Hunan decreased, and the price of pigs in Hunan increased. The provincial government in Hunan responded to the higher prices by banning the export of pigs raised in Hunan. When the press criticized this policy, the provincial government repealed its ban on exports and imposed an export tax on pigs instead. This policy had basically the same effect as the ban. Such interventions by provincial governments are thought to hamper the efficiency of the Chinese agricultural sector.

Unleashing Industry.   In 1978, Zhao Ziyang, the first secretary of the Communist party in Sichuan province, ordered that six Sichuan enterprises be partly freed from the central planning system. These enterprises, like the agricultural collectives, were first obligated to meet a state procurement target after which they could produce according to the dictates of the marketplace. Since 1978, a few thousand enterprises have been allowed to operate under the same conditions as the original six Sichuan enterprises. In 1985, a truck-producing enterprise in China sold 55,000 of the 91,500 trucks it produced to the government and sold the remainder on the free market.

A Small Stock Exchange.   A small stock exchange opened in Shanghai in 1986. Many economists see this as a major move toward market practices.

Leasing Bankrupt State-Owned Enterprises.   A few state-owned enterprises that were on the brink of bankruptcy have been leased to private citizens. In many cases, these private citizens have turned the enterprises around and have been able to keep some of the profit for their efforts.

Evading the system.   In China, large, well-managed enterprises are often required to meet larger production quotas than small, inefficient firms. Some commentators have noted that such a system actually penalizes the large, well-managed firms since they have to allocate many of their resources to fulfill government plans and thus have little left over to produce goods that can be sold on the free market. To get around this, many large, well-managed firms have either tried to hide some of their productive capacity (to look smaller) or to disguise their relative efficiency in production by failing to meet some contracts. (The reasoning here is that if government believes the enterprise is small and inefficient, it will look elsewhere to meet its production quotas, leaving the enterprise to produce for the market.)

What Lies Ahead?   What type of economic system will China be operating under in five, ten, or twenty years? We can't answer that question. Some economists suggest that China will adopt farther-reaching market practices, as the rising standard of living that is bound to occur will stimulate more of the same. Other economists disagree. They believe that the provincial governments will continue to intervene in economic affairs, and that soon China will put a halt to its economic experiment with market practices.

Tamara, Vasily, Wang, Ju, and Li: Making it in the Soviet Union and in China

All the people you will read about here are real. Two of them, Tamara Alexandrovich and Vasily Pyatayev, live in the Soviet Union. Three of them, Wang Yongdi, Ju Youheng, and Li Jianhua, live in China. All five persons have done well under the new economic reforms in the two countries.

Tamara Alexandrovich has started producing winter caps and zippered jeans that she sells outside Moscow's Kiev railway station. Tamara, her mother, and her three children make the merchandise. She charges between $98 and $123 for the jeans. A hot item is a cap with an "Adidas" logo on it. It sells for $25, or two for $40.

Vasily Pyatayev used to be a truck driver earning $490 per month. Today he is part of a two-person contract brigade that raises calves. He and his wife earn about $1,800

per month and usually work 15 hours per day. Vasily says the work is hard but interesting. He and his wife are saving up to buy a car. In the Soviet Union there is one car for every 24 persons.

Wang Yongdi is a farmer in southeastern China who manages 1.64 acres on a collective farm. He regularly meets his quota-procurement responsibilities to the collective and then grows flowers to sell on the free market. Last year he earned approximately $28,000 from selling flowers.

Ju Youheng is a farmer who lives in the Sichuan province. He is 62 years old and has seen much change in China. He has lived through both the Great Leap Forward and the Cultural Revolution. Standing in the middle of his vegetable crop, he explains that last year he grew grain, but not this year. He says there is no money in grain. Some peasant farmers in his village raise this year's hot cash crop: chuanxiong, a leafy medicinal plant. Rising demand for the product has increased the price from $400 to $8,000 per ton.

Li Jianhua also lives in Sichuan. He used to be a farmer, but recently he has started a pipe-making factory that last year earned him $100,000 in revenues. Li has taken his money and opened eight stores, two restaurants, and two cafés. He has also built a 12-room mansion. He is a member of China's nouveau riche.

Source: "Beijing Finds a Folk Hero," Wall Street Journal, January 19, 1988.

DECENTRALIZED SOCIALISM

The major differences between command-economy socialism and decentralized socialism are that the latter is characterized by more decentralized decision making and a greater reliance on market allocation of resources and market-determined prices. In this section we describe the workings of one variety of decentralized socialism, that of worker-managed socialism in Yugoslavia. We focus mainly on the worker-managed Yugoslav business firm.

Worker-Managed Firms

Largely because of the sharp differences and antagonisms between the Soviet leader Stalin and the Yugoslav leader Tito (Tito once wrote a note to Stalin saying, "If you cannot help us, at least don't hinder us by useless advice."), Yugoslavia broke with the Soviet Union in 1948 and advocated independence for all socialist nations. Yugoslavs at this time began to argue that command or centrally directed economies might be useful in certain circumstances, but that generally a less centralized, more decentralized variety of socialism was preferable.

The socialist blueprint for Yugoslavia includes social ownership of capital (it is accessible to every member of society on equal terms), worker-managed firms, and use of the market mechanism. In practice, this means most of the production in the Yugoslav economy takes place in government-owned, worker-managed firms; the state owns the assets of the firm, and the workers manage the firm. This is different from the Soviet Union where most enterprises are managed by state-appointed managers who follow a central plan.

In Yugoslavia, the workers of a firm elect a *workers' council* that manages the firm. The council, not some central plan, decides (within limits) what to produce, the quality of the good to produce, how much to produce, the production techniques, the level of employment, and what price to charge for the finished good. Most importantly, when the firm earns profits, the workers' council decides how much to reinvest in the business firm and how much to divide up among the workers. The Yugoslav government argues that its economic system, and not the Soviet Union's, is closer to Marx's idea of the dictatorship of the proletariat.

The workers in a Yugoslav firm have been compared to the stockholders of an American firm largely because both are *residual claimants*—both Yugoslav workers and American stockholders receive the profits of the firm if there are any. From this, we might expect that Yugoslav firms would be run by Yugoslav workers in the same way that American stockholders run American firms. Both groups would be profit oriented and consumer oriented and would try to hire efficient management teams. But this appears not to be the case. A major reason is that although both Yugoslav workers and American stockholders are residual claimants, only American stockholders have an ownership right in the firm that they can *sell*, that is, shares in the company. Also, whereas the Yugoslav worker actually has to work for a firm to be a residual claimant, the American stockholder does not. In practice, when a Yugoslav worker is either fired, leaves his present job to look for another, or retires, he is no longer a residual claimant of the firm where he was once employed and is therefore no longer entitled to some of the profits of the firm. W. Brus says on the subject, "The workers' share in the enterprises' results is not based on any form of personal property rights, which they may carry with them, but exclusively on employment; upon termination of employment their stake disappears."[11] As we shall see, this policy has some predictable consequences.

Advantages and Disadvantages of Worker-Managed Firms

Economists who view worker-managed firms in favorable terms say that they decrease worker exploitation, maximize economic democracy, minimize (if not eliminate) the alienation a worker may feel in his or her work, and possibly stimulate worker incentives so as to increase productivity and output. With respect to increases in productivity and output, the Yugoslav economy did register impressive annual growth rates in real GNP during the period 1966–76. In recent years, though, Yugoslavia has been plagued with numerous economic problems. In particular, it has witnessed a high inflation rate, averaging 54 percent a year during the period 1981–86. In 1988, the inflation rate was 200 percent. It has also witnessed a decline in production in some industries, such as steel and petroleum, and rising unemployment. Over the five-year period 1980–84, its real GNP increased by a slight 1.28 percent, and during this same period its per-capita real GNP actually fell from $2,108 to $2,071 (many other countries had increases rather than decreases in per-capita real GNP during this time). Yugoslavia's per-capita real GNP is 13 percent of the comparable U.S. figure and 28 percent of the Soviet Union's. In 1988, Yugoslavia witnessed 800 strikes and real wages fell 8.4 percent.

The recent poor economic performance in Yugoslavia has prompted some economists to argue that its worker-managed firms, which lie at the heart of the Yugoslav

[11]W. Brus, "Market socialism" in *The New Palgrave: A Dictionary of Economics*, vol. 3 (London: The Macmillan Press, 1987), p. 339.

Economics in Our Times

Interview: Robert Lekachman

Robert Lekachman is a well-known and vocal critic of the free market system. Professor Lekachman is currently at the City University of New York. We interviewed Professor Lekachman on June 29, 1988.

Professor Lekachman, in the last paragraph of your book, *Greed Is Not Enough,* you say, "Sooner than the pessimists among us have thought possible, progress may resume toward the fuller democracy of libertarian socialism." How do you define libertarian socialism, how would it work in the real world, and what is it capable of accomplishing?

Basically it is the dispersion of economic power and control from the present concentration to cooperatives, community groups, worker managements, and so forth and a very considerable redistribution of wealth in the direction of equality (not complete equality, which would destroy incentives) but very, very diminished inequality. And, of course, it exists nowhere. The nearest approximations to this are the Scandinavian countries, the Netherlands, and, to some extent, Austria.

What good do you see arising from the sharp redistribution of wealth toward greater equality?

Partly it is a contrast to what we have now. Phillip Stern has written a book called *The Best Congress Money Can Buy,* and that's a pretty fair summary of the political situation in the United States. The fact of the matter is that the enormous concentration of wealth has translated into political power. Anyone who wants to get into Congress, or stay in Congress, has to basically court real estate developers, bankers, and corporate types. This is a fact of political life.

Now if income and wealth, particularly wealth, were more equitably distributed, a politician would have to depend upon small contributions from large numbers of people.

I might add one other thing as an economist, that the concentration of income and wealth radically affects the goods and services that are produced. For example, in a city like New York it is very difficult to find a reasonably priced restaurant where the food is edible. Spending $50 to $75 per person for dinner is not unusual. And this represents not only the concentration of income and wealth but also what happens to the market for the rest of the people. The restaurants are more expensive in New York because the concentration of wealth allows a relatively small percentage of the population to spend an inordinate amount of money.

How do you think the American economy will be structured in the year 2050 and how will it function?

It's up for grabs. If present trends continue, the American standard of living will fall beneath both the Japanese and the Germans and will tend to move toward the French, the Italians, and the English. Already it is observable that real wages are not keeping up with the inflation rate. Today's *Wall Street Journal,* for example, has an article which pointed to the corporate objective of keeping wage increases at or below 2 percent. Well, the inflation rate is running around 4–5 percent and rising. This suggests that if current trends continue this is going to be a much poorer country in 2050 than it is in 1988. Now it doesn't have to turn out that way, but for it to turn out differently a lot of things are going to have to happen. One is that there needs to be a transformation of American education. The numerous people who say the educational system is in trouble are right. I teach at the City University of New York where our student population is largely working class and the deficits in literacy and mathematical competence (by which I mean arithmetic) are simply enormous. If what we read is true, then what we are going to need are smart workers as well as smart technology. Under the current circumstances, we are very much in danger of retreating to third world status. So the education system needs to be transformed.

Now I have a modest proposal which I don't expect to be pursued tomorrow, but that is to throw out all the television sets. The fact of the matter is that students brought up in a television culture expect breaks at the end of every six or seven minutes for a commercial, and if you are trying to explain anything difficult—even moderately difficult, like the investment multiplier—for success you demand attention for at least half an hour.

Now I don't know exactly what can be done about this, and all the blather that comes from [former] Secretary of Education Bennett doesn't help the situation very much. But clearly it would help if we respected teachers more than we do and respect means that we increase their salaries to begin with.

Your critics might argue that if you do not want the American standard of living to decline to the level of the English, you ought not to propose the sharp redistribution in income and wealth that you favor because, if implemented, this would sharply dampen incentives to produce. What is your response?

We've had a more than seven-year experiment in cutting top marginal income tax rates. These are the rates the supply-siders emphasized. As a result, the savings rate has not gone up, in fact it has declined; much of the investment in factories is Japanese and German, or foreign in general; and the outburst in entrepreneurial spirit has not translated into very rapid productivity gains. I would say to the people who emphasize incentives to the already obscenely wealthy that we've tried it and it has failed.

In your book, *Economists at Bay*, you say, "When bright people say stupid things, the question inevitably arises, why is their perception of reality so blurred?" Our guess is that you believe free market economists have blurred vision when it comes to economic realities. If our guess is correct, do you have an explanation for this blurriness?

Well, yes. The fact is that the model around which economics is built, and much of the explanation of its success in the social sciences, has depended upon the free market. John Stuart Mill, in 1848 in his *Principles of Economics,* said that without the principle of competition, economics cannot be a science. So there is a very heavy intellectual investment on the part of economists in the free market model and the tendency to adjust reality to it rather than to modify the model. Because without the model where are you as an economist?

So, a young New York radical can go to the University of Chicago and get socialized (I won't use the unpleasant term "brainwashed") into the very astute free market economics of very bright people indeed at the University of Chicago. Gary Becker, who is my bet for the Nobel Prize this coming year (it's a conservative's turn) has extended the free market model into marriage and the family. People like Posner have extended it into the law and it's very powerful. It doesn't, though, by my criteria, describe significant portions of reality. But never underestimate the influence of a very strong intellectual idea which has enormous potential for detailed articulation and ramifications into other fields. The result is that economists as a group are an intensely conservative lot.

Most college students who take a principles of economics course learn neoclassical price theory and monetarist and Keynesian macroeconomics. They are not really exposed to Marxist economics. Are they missing much?

To begin with, Marxism is the official face of the majority of the world's population and students miss something (whether Marxism is good or bad economics) by missing what is enormously influential in much of the world. As to the usefulness of Marxist economics, it is not very helpful for the problems that occupy microeconomists. Nobody, even among the more enlightened Marxists, would try to use the labor theory of value to explain current market prices.

On the other hand, if you want something more than a set of techniques, which is what you tend to learn if you major in economics, and you want something of the view of human history, you really ought to study Marxism—even if you don't agree with the vision of history that the Marxists articulate. And above all, because the element that is missing in standard economics is prominent in Marxism. This is the issue of power. You can get a doctorate in economics, and still be innocent really of the influence of power of various kinds on the markets which we so sedulously analyze. I think there is a loss here in the failure to expose students to Marxism.

At one time or another, you have advocated price controls, an incomes policy, public works programs, a national health system, and economic planning. Your critics argue that you are naïve to believe government will do all the things you want it to do the way you want them to be done. In short, some of your critics argue that you mistakenly believe government can be made to work as a benevolent despot. What do you say to your critics?

Elements of what I advocate work perfectly well in societies at least as democratic as ours. You need to go no farther away than Canada, for example, to find a national health system which covers every resident and even visitors and takes 8.5 percent of the Canadian GNP versus the 11.2 percent of GNP in the United States where we have 37 million people totally uncovered and perhaps an equal number inadequately covered. So clearly as far as comprehensive health is concerned, it hasn't eroded

economy, are not without their problems. Here are some of the disadvantages of such firms that they have identified.

1. **Workers in worker-managed firms have an incentive to divide the profits among themselves rather than to reinvest them in the firm.** Brus notes that "in particular, older workers and those without prospects or willingness to stay on the job will have a low propensity to invest out of the enterprise's income."[12] Some economists say that such behavior is sensible from the point of view of the individual workers since they have no property rights in the firm that they can sell.

   To illustrate, contrast the situation with that for U.S. stockholders. Often U.S. stockholders vote to reinvest the profits of the firm instead of declaring stock dividends (effectively divying up the profits among themselves) because they know that the stock market views reinvestment of profits favorably, resulting in a higher price for their shares of stock, which they can sell if they choose. Since Yugoslav workers have no shares of stock to sell, they naturally do not weigh the reinvestment of profits as highly as the U.S. stockholder.

2. **The worker-managed firm often lacks internal funds for investment, causing it to borrow heavily.** Because workers have a tendency to allocate profits to themselves, the firm often lacks the funds necessary for investment. As a result, it borrows heavily. It is not uncommon for many Yugoslav firms to operate under constant indebtedness.

3. **In worker-managed firms, capital is often substituted for labor.** A Yugoslav worker knows that he or she receives a greater percentage of a given level of profits if there are only 100 workers in the firm rather than 200 workers. Because the worker is interested in *profits per worker,* the existing workers of a firm tend to favor more capital goods rather than more labor. For this reason, many Yugoslav firms employ relatively capital-intensive production techniques. This has caused many Yugoslav workers to emigrate to other countries to find work.

4. **Worker-managed firms are not likely to invest in new business enterprises.** In Yugoslavia, investing in a new business enterprise comes without management

[12]Brus, "Market socialism."

rights and without residual claimaint status. Both are reserved for the workers of the firm. As a result, few private individuals are willing to invest in new business enterprises. Most of the financing for new enterprises comes from the government. Critics of the Yugoslav economic system argue that private investors are much more likely to allocate scarce resources where they are most highly valued than are government authorities.

■ CHAPTER SUMMARY

Economic Realities and Economic Systems

■ The following hold for all economic systems: scarcity, opportunity cost (no free lunch), the need for a rationing device, the law of demand, and rational self-interested behavior. Additionally, all economic systems must answer the following questions: What to produce? How to produce it? Who produces it? For whom is it produced?

Pure Capitalism

■ Pure capitalism sometimes goes by the names laissez-faire capitalism, anarcho-capitalism, or libertarianism. Pure capitalism is an economic system characterized by private ownership of the factors of production, market allocation of resources, and decentralized decision making; most economic activities take place in the private sector, and government plays a small role or no role at all in the economy. The advocates of pure capitalism are often called libertarians.

■ Central to the case for pure capitalism is the belief that each person has the right of self-ownership, the right of ownership of previously unused and unowned resources that one has occupied or transformed, and the right of ownership of property conveyed through exchange or by gift. Libertarians argue that their policy positions on economic, political, philosophical, and social matters are derived from a consistent application of these rights.

■ Libertarians argue that in a pure capitalist economy, none of the following would exist: government-granted professional licenses, minimum wage laws, only one firm that delivers first-class mail, restraints on price, discretionary fiscal and monetary policies, the Federal Reserve, antitrust policy, quotas and tariffs, and compulsory saving or redistributory programs. Libertarians generally argue that whatever the government does, the private sector can do better, and that some things the government does shouldn't be done and wouldn't be done by the private sector.

■ The critics of libertarianism state that libertarians (1) do not see the merit of sometimes allowing government to adjust for third-party effects through taxes, subsidies, and regulations; (2) do not seriously consider complex exchanges; and (3) do not see the stabilizing effects of government monetary and fiscal policies.

Karl Marx

■ Two major intellectual strands in Marx's thinking are the labor theory of value and the dialectical process. Marx argued that the value of a commodity is determined by the *socially necessary labor time* embodied in it. Marx also argued that history could be interpreted in terms of the dialectic, in which two opposing forces or ideas (the thesis and antithesis) form a synthesis that becomes the new thesis, thereby starting the process all over.

■ Marx believed the stages of development are primitive communism, slavery, feudalism, capitalism, the dictatorship of the proletariat, and pure communism.

■ The critics of Marx argue that the labor theory of value is faulty, that there is no large reserve army of the unemployed as Marx predicted, that contrary to Marx most workers earn above-subsistence wages, and that Marxist revolutions have not appeared in the places Marx expected.

Command-Economy Socialism: The Case of the Soviet Union

■ The central planning agency in the Soviet Union, Gosplan, has the responsibility of drafting the economic plan for the Soviet Union. The priorities of the plan are greatly influenced by the Soviet leadership. Gosplan directs all major business tasks of Soviet enterprises; what goods to produce, how much of the goods to produce, when to produce the goods, and so forth. A major task of Gosplan is to allocate resources according to production objectives. Gosplan also follows a priority principle. Simply put, if there are not enough resources to produce all goods in the desired quantities, Gosplan will weight those goods that are most important to the Soviet leadership over other goods.

■ Gosplan determines both the supply of different goods produced in the economy and the price the goods will be sold at. Gosplan has very little control over the demand for most goods (especially consumer goods). Often Gosplan sets prices that are above or below the equilibrium price that would rule in a free market. Higher-than-equilibrium prices result in surpluses and empty shops; lower-than-equilibrium prices result in shortages, crowded shops, and waiting lines. Inflation in the Soviet Union largely (but not exclusively) takes the form of longer waits in line.

■ The turnover tax is used to finance many of the "free" and heavily subsidized goods in the Soviet Union.

■ The tiny privatized agricultural sector in the Soviet Union produces much more food per acre than the larger collectivized agricultural sector.

■ The Soviet distribution of income is more equal (less unequal) than the U.S. distribution of income, but not by much. Many analysts note, though, that the slightly greater income equality is not necessarily linked to a higher standard of living and that one's absolute standard of living may be higher in a country where one receives a lower percentage of a larger total income than in a country where one receives a higher percentage of a smaller total income.

Decentralized Socialism: The Case of Yugoslavia

■ The major differences between command-economy socialism and decentralized socialism are that the latter is characterized by more decentralized decision making and a greater reliance on market allocation of resources and on market-determined prices.

■ The worker-managed business firm is prominent in Yugoslavia. The workers of a firm elect a workers' council that manages the firm. The council (within limits) decides what to produce, the quality of the good to produce, how much to produce, the production techniques, the level of employment, what price to charge for the finished good, and how profits should be distributed.

■ The Yugoslav worker, unlike an American stockholder, has no shares in the company that he or she can sell. Also, whereas the Yugoslav worker actually has to work for a firm to be a residual claimant, the American stockholder does not. In practice, when a Yugoslav worker is fired, leaves his present job to look for another, or retires, he is no longer a residual claimant of the firm where he was once employed. In Yugoslavia, a person is only an ''owner'' of the firm (and therefore entitled to some of the profits of the firm) during the time he or she works for the firm.

■ Some economists point out that worker-managed firms tend to encounter certain problems: (1) Workers in worker-managed firms have an incentive to divide the profits among themselves rather than to reinvest them in the firm. (2) The worker-managed firm often lacks internal funds for investment, causing it to borrow heavily. (3) In worker-managed firms capital is often substituted for labor. (4) Worker-managed firms are not likely to invest in new business enterprises.

■ QUESTIONS TO ANSWER AND DISCUSS

1. Choose any of the fundamental economic realities that both the United States and the Soviet Union face, and explain the different ways in which the two economies would deal with it.

2. In theory, what group's objectives most influence a business manager's behavior in the United States, in the Soviet Union, and in Yugoslavia?

3. Socialists in the Soviet Union often remark that at least their economic plans maintain full employment whereas capitalism cannot. What is the likely libertarian response?

4. Some people argue that capitalism and socialism are usually evaluated on economic grounds where capitalism has a clear advantage. They argue that in order to evaluate the two economic systems even handedly, both should be evaluated on more than economic grounds. They propose that both systems be evaluated according to justice, fairness, the happiness of the people living under both systems, the crime rate, the standard of living of those at the bottom of the economic ladder, and much more. Do you think this is the proper way to proceed?

5. The *convergence hypothesis,* first proposed by a Soviet economist, suggests that over time the capitalist economies will become increasingly socialistic and that the socialist economies will become increasingly capitalistic. Do you believe the convergence hypothesis has merit? What real-world evidence can you cite to ''prove'' or ''disprove'' the hypothesis?

6. Predict how mixed capitalism, pure capitalism, and command-economy socialism would each deal with the problem of pollution.

Glossary

Absolute Advantage The situation where a country can produce more of a good than another country can produce with the same quantity of resources.

Absolute Price The price of a good in money terms.

Accounting Profit The difference between total revenue and explicit costs.

Antitrust Law Legislation passed for the stated purpose of controlling monopoly power and preserving and promoting competition.

Appreciation An increase in the value of one currency relative to other currencies.

Arbitrage Buying a good in a market where its price is low, and selling the good in another market where its price is higher.

Assets Anything of value to which the firm has a legal claim.

Average Fixed Cost Fixed cost divided by quantity of output: $AFC = FC/Q$.

Average Total Cost (Unit Cost) Total cost divided by quantity of output: $ATC = TC/Q$.

Average Variable Cost Variable cost divided by quantity of output: $AVC = VC/Q$.

Average-Marginal Rule When the marginal magnitude is above the average magnitude, the average magnitude rises; when the marginal magnitude is below the average magnitude, the average magnitude falls.

Bad Anything from which individuals receive disutility.

Balance of Payments A periodic statement (usually annual) of the money value of all transactions between residents of one country and residents of all other countries.

Balance Sheet An accounting of the assets, liabilities, and net worth of a business firm.

Bond An IOU statement that promises to pay a certain sum of money (the principal) at maturity and also to pay periodic fixed sums until that date.

Budget Constraint Graphic representation of the limit of all combinations or bundles of two goods a person can purchase given a certain money income and prices for the two goods.

Budget Deficit Occurs when government expenditures outstrip tax receipts.

Business Firm An entity that employs factors of production (resources) and produces goods and services to be sold to consumers, other firms, or government.

Capital Account Balance The summary statistic for the outflow of U.S. capital and the inflow of foreign capital. It is equal to the difference between the outflow of U.S. capital and the inflow of foreign capital.

Capital Account Includes all payments related to the purchase and sale of assets and to borrowing and lending activities. Components include outflow of U.S. capital and inflow of foreign capital.

Capital Consumption Allowance (Depreciation) The estimated amount of capital goods used up in production by depreciation, obsolescence, and accidental destruction.

Capital Capital consists of produced goods that can be used as inputs for further production, such things as machinery, tools, computers, trucks, buildings, and factories.

Capture Hypothesis Holds that no matter what the motive for the initial regulation and the establishment of the regulatory agency, eventually the agency will be "captured" (controlled) by the special interests of the industry that is being regulated.

Cartel Theory In this theory of oligopoly, firms act in a manner consistent with having only one firm in the industry.

Cartel An organization of firms that reduces output and increases price in an effort to increase joint profits.

Ceteris Paribus Latin phrase meaning "all other things held constant."

Choice The act of selecting among restricted alternatives.

Closed Shop An organization in which an employee must belong to the union before he or she can be hired.

Coase Theorem In the case of trivial or zero transaction costs, the property rights assignment does not matter to the resource allocative outcome.

Collective Bargaining The process whereby wage rates and other issues are determined by a union bargaining with management on behalf of all union members.

Command-Economy Socialism An economic system characterized by government ownership of the nonlabor factors of production, government allocation of resources, and centralized decision making; most economic activities take place in the public sector, and government plays a very large role in the economy.

Comparative Advantage   The situation where a country can produce a good at lower opportunity cost than another country.

Complements   Two goods that are used jointly in consumption. With complements, the demand for one rises as the price of the other falls (or the demand for one falls as the price of the other rises).

Concentration Ratio   The percentage of industry sales (or assets, output, labor force, or some other factor) accounted for by x-number of firms in the industry.

Constant Returns to Scale   Exist when inputs are increased by some percentage and output increases by an equal percentage, causing unit costs to remain constant.

Constant-Cost Industry   An industry in which average total costs do not change as (industry) output increases or decreases, as firms enter or exit the industry, respectively.

Consumer Equilibrium   Occurs when the consumer has spent all income and the marginal utilities per dollar spent on each good purchased are equal: $MU_A/P_A = MU_B/P_B = MU_C/P_C = \ldots = MU_Z/P_Z$, where the letters $A-Z$ represent all the goods a person buys.

Consumers' Surplus   The difference between the price buyers pay for a good and the maximum or highest price they would have paid for the good. It is a dollar measure of the benefit gained by being able to purchase a unit of a good for less than one is willing to pay for it.

Contestable Market   A market in which entry is easy and exit is costless.

Corporation   A legal entity that can conduct business in its own name the way an individual does; ownership of the corporation resides with stockholders who have limited liability in the debts of the corporation.

Coupon Rate   The percentage of the face value of the bond that is paid out regularly (usually quarterly or annually) to the holder of the bond.

Craft (Trade) Union   A union whose membership is made up of individuals who practice the same craft or trade.

Credit   In the balance of payments, any transaction that either supplies a foreign currency or creates a demand for the nation's currency in the foreign exchange market.

Cross Elasticity of Demand   Measures the responsiveness in quantity demanded of one good to changes in the price of another good.

Current Account Balance   The summary statistic for exports of goods and services, imports of goods and services, and net unilateral transfers.

Current Account   Includes all payments related to the purchase and sale of goods and services. Components of the account include exports, imports, and net unilateral transfers abroad.

Debit   In the balance of payments, any transaction that either supplies the nation's currency or creates a demand for foreign currency in the foreign exchange market.

Decentralized Socialism   An economic system characterized by government ownership of the nonlabor factors of production, largely market allocation of resources, and decentralized decision making; most economic activities take place in the public sector, and government plays a very large role in the economy.

Deciding at the Margin   Decision making characterized by weighing additional benefits of a change against the additional costs of a change with respect to current conditions.

Decreasing-Cost Industry   An industry in which average total costs decrease as (industry) output increases and increase as (industry) output decreases, as firms enter and exit the industry, respectively.

Demand Curve   The graphical representation of the law of demand.

Demand Schedule   The numerical tabulation of the quantity demanded of a good at different prices.

Dependency Ratio   The number of children under a certain age plus the number of the elderly (aged 65 and over) divided by the total population.

Depreciation   A decrease in the value of one currency relative to other currencies.

Derived Demand   Demand that is the result of some other demand. For example, factor demand is the result of the demand for the products that the factors go to produce.

Devaluation   An official governmental act that changes the exchange rate; specifically, it lowers the official price of a currency.

Dialectic   The method of logic based on the principle that an idea or event (thesis) generates its opposite (antithesis) leading to a reconciliation of opposites (synthesis).

Diamond-Water Paradox   The observation that those things that have the greatest value in use sometimes have little value in exchange and that those things that have little or no value in use sometimes have the greatest value in exchange.

Directly related   Two variables are directly related if they move in the same direction.

Diseconomies of Scale   Exist when inputs are increased by some percentage and output increases by a smaller percentage, causing unit costs to rise.

Disequilibrium Price   A price other than equilibrium price. A price at which quantity demanded does not equal quantity supplied.

Disequilibrium   A state of either surplus or shortage in a market.

Dividends   A share of profits distributed to stockholders.

Dumping   The sale of goods abroad at a price below their cost and below the price charged in the domestic markets.

Economics   The science that deals with the actions of individuals and societies directed toward meeting certain ends in a world where the means necessary to meet those ends have alternative uses.

Economic Profit   The difference between total revenue and total (opportunity) cost, including both its explicit and implicit components.

Economic Rent   A payment in excess of opportunity costs.

Economies of Scale   Exist when inputs are increased by some percentage and output increases by a greater percentage, causing unit costs to fall.

Efficiency   In terms of production, efficiency refers to the condition where the maximum output is produced with given resources and technology. Efficiency implies the impossibility of gains in one area without losses in another.

Elasticity of Demand for Labor   Percentage change in the quantity demanded of labor divided by the percentage change in the wage rate.

Elastic Demand   The percentage change in quantity demanded is greater than the percentage change in price. Quantity demanded changes proportionately more than price changes.

Employee Association   An organization whose members belong to a particular profession.

Entrepreneurship   The particular talent that some people have for organizing the resources of land, labor, and capital into the production of goods, and seeking new business opportunities and developing new ways of doing things.

Equilibrium Price (Market-Clearing Price)   The price at which quantity demanded of the good equals quantity supplied.

Equilibrium Quantity   The quantity that corresponds to equilibrium price. The quantity at which the amount of the good buyers are willing to buy equals the amount sellers are willing to sell, and both equal the amount actually bought and sold.

Equilibrium   Equilibrium means "at rest." Equilibrium is the price-quantity combination in a market from which there is no tendency for buyers or sellers to move away. Graphically, equilibrium is the intersection point of the supply and demand curves.

Excess Capacity Theory   States that a monopolistic competitor in equilibrium produces an output smaller than the one that would minimize its costs of production.

Exchange rate   The price of one currency in terms of another currency; e.g., 1 dollar = 2 marks.

Exchange   The process where one thing is traded for another.

Excludability   A good is excludable if it is possible, or not prohibitively costly, to exclude someone from receiving the benefits of the good once it has been produced.

Explicit Cost   A cost that is incurred when an actual (monetary) payment is made.

Exports   Total foreign spending on domestic goods.

Externality   A side effect of an action that affects the well-being of third parties.

Ex Ante Distribution of Income   The before-tax-and-transfer-payment distribution of income.

Ex Ante   Before, as in "before" the exchange.

Ex Post Distribution of Income   The after-tax-and-transfer-payment distribution of income.

Ex Post   After, as in "after" the exchange.

Face Value (Par Value)   Dollar amount specified on the bond.

Factor Markets   Markets where the factors of production are bought and sold.

Factor Price Searcher   A firm that drives up factor price if it buys an additional factor unit. It faces an upward-sloping supply curve of factors.

Factor Price Taker   A firm that can buy all of a factor it wants at the equilibrium price. It faces a horizontal (flat, perfectly elastic) supply curve of factors.

Fixed Costs   Costs that do not vary with output.

Fixed Exchange Rate System   The system where a nation's currency is set at a fixed rate relative to all other currencies, and central banks intervene in the foreign exchange market to maintain the fixed rate.

Fixed Input   An input whose quantity cannot be changed as output changes in the short run.

Flexible Exchange Rate System   The system whereby exchange rates are determined by the forces of supply and demand for a currency.

Foreign Exchange Market   The market in which currencies of different countries are exchanged.

Free Rider   Anyone who receives the benefits of a good without paying for it.

Fungibility   A term that is Latin in origin, meaning "such that any unit is substitutable for another." Fungibility means substitutable.

Game Theory   A mathematical technique used to analyze the behavior of decision makers who try to reach an optimal position for themselves through game playing or the use of strategic behavior, and who are fully aware of the interactive nature of the process at hand and anticipate the moves of other decision makers.

Gini Coefficient   A measurement of the degree of inequality in the income distribution.

Gold Standard   The monetary arrangement whereby a nation backs its paper money totally or partially with gold.

Good   Anything from which individuals receive utility or happiness.

Gosplan   The Soviet central planning agency that has the responsibility of drafting the economic plan for the nation.

Government Bureaucrat   An unelected person who works in a government bureau and is assigned a special task that relates to a law or program passed by the legislature.

Guaranteed Income Level   Income level below which people are not allowed to fall.

Herfindahl Index   Measures the degree of concentration in an industry. It is equal to the sum of the squares of the market shares of each firm in the industry.

Human Capital   Education, development of skills, and anything else that is particular to the individual and increases his or her productivity.

Implicit Cost   A cost that represents the value of resources used in production for which no actual (monetary) payment is made.

Implicit Marginal Tax Rate   The rate at which the negative income tax payment, or any cash grant or subsidy, is reduced as earned income rises.

Imports   Total domestic spending on foreign goods.

Income Effect   That portion of the change in the quantity demanded of a good that is attributable to a change in real income (brought about by a change in absolute price).

Income Elasticity of Demand   Measures the responsiveness of a change in quantity demanded to changes in income.

Income Elastic   The percentage change in quantity demanded of a good is greater than the percentage change in income.

Income Inelastic   The percentage change in quantity demanded of a good is less than the percentage change in income.

Income Unit Elastic   The percentage change in quantity demanded of a good is equal to the percentage change in income.

Increasing-Cost Industry   An industry in which average total costs increase as (industry) output increases and decrease as (industry) output decreases, as firms enter and exit the industry, respectively.

Independent   Two variables are independent if as one changes, the other does not.

Indifference Curve Map   Represents a number of indifference curves for a given individual.

Indifference Curve Represents an indifference set. A curve that shows all the bundles of two goods that give an individual equal total utility.

Indifference Set Group of bundles of two goods that give an individual equal total utility.

Industrial Union A union whose membership is made up of individuals who work in the same firm or industry but do not all practice the same craft or trade.

Inefficiency In terms of production, inefficiency refers to the condition where less than the maximum output is produced with given resources and technology. Inefficiency implies the possibility of gains in one area without losses in another.

Inelastic Demand The percentage change in quantity demanded is less than the percentage change in price. Quantity demanded changes proportionately less than price changes.

Inferior Good A good the demand for which falls (rises) as income rises (falls).

Inside Information Information that is not yet public; it is known only to a small group of people called insiders.

Internalizing Externalities An externality is *internalized* if the person(s) or group that generated the externality incorporate into their own private or *internal* cost-benefit calculations the external benefits (in the case of a positive externality) or the external costs (in the case of a negative externality) that third parties bear.

International Monetary Fund (IMF) An international organization that was created by the Bretton Woods system to oversee the international monetary system. Although the Bretton Woods system no longer exists, the IMF does. It does not control the world's money supply, but it does hold currency reserves for member nations and makes loans to central banks.

Interpersonal Utility Comparison Comparing the utility one person receives from a good, service, or activity with the utility another person receives from the same good, service, or activity.

Inversely related Two variables are inversely related if they move in opposite directions.

In-Kind Transfer Payment Transfer payments, such as food stamps, medical assistance, and subsidized housing, that are made in a specific good or service.

J-curve The curve that shows a short-run worsening in the trade deficit following a currency depreciation, followed later by an improvement in the trade deficit.

Kinked Demand Curve Theory A theory of oligopoly that assumes that if a single firm in the industry cuts price, other firms will do likewise, but if it raises price, other firms will not follow suit. The theory predicts price stickiness or rigidity.

Labor Theory of Value Holds that the value of all commodities is equal to the value of the labor used in producing them.

Law of Demand As the price of a good rises, the quantity demanded of the good falls, and as the price of a good falls, the quantity demanded of the good rises, ceteris paribus.

Law of Diminishing Marginal Returns As increasing amounts of a variable input are combined with fixed inputs, eventually the marginal physical product of the variable input will decline.

Law of Diminishing Marginal Utility Holds that the marginal utility gained by consuming equal successive units of a good will decline as the amount consumed increases.

Law of Supply As the price of a good rises, the quantity supplied

of the good rises, and as the price of a good falls, the quantity supplied of the good falls, *ceteris paribus*.

Least-Cost Rule Specifies the combination of factors that minimizes costs. This requires that the following condition be met: $MPP_1/P_1 = MPP_2/P_2 = \ldots = MPP_n/P_n$, where the numbers stand for the different factors.

Less Developed Country (LDC) A country with a low per-capita GNP.

Liabilities A debt of the business firm.

Limited Liability A legal term that signifies that the owners (stockholders) of a corporation cannot be sued for the corporation's failure to pay its debts.

Limited Partnership A form of business that is organized as a partnership, but which gives some of the partners the legal protection of limited liability.

Logrolling The exchange of votes to gain support for legislation.

Long Run A period of time in which all inputs can be varied (no inputs are fixed).

Long-Run Average Total Cost Curve A curve that shows the lowest (unit) cost at which the firm can produce any given level of output.

Long-Run Competitive Equilibrium The condition where $P = MC = SRATC = LRATC$. There are zero economic profits, firms are producing the quantity of output at which price is equal to marginal cost, and no firm has an incentive to change its plant size.

Long-Run Industry Supply Curve Graphic representation of the quantities of output that the industry is prepared to supply at different prices after the entry and exit of firms is completed.

Lorenz Curve A graph of the income distribution. It expresses the relationship between cumulative percent of families and cumulative percent of income.

Macroeconomics The branch of economics that deals with human behavior and choices as they relate to either highly aggregated markets or the entire economy.

Managerial Coordination The process in which managers direct employees to perform certain tasks.

Marginal Cost The change in total cost that results from a change in output: $MC = \Delta TC/\Delta Q = \Delta VC/\Delta Q$.

Marginal Factor Cost The additional cost incurred by employing an additional factor unit.

Marginal Physical Product The change in output that results from changing the variable input by one unit, holding all other inputs fixed.

Marginal Productivity Theory States that firms in competitive or perfect product and factor markets pay factors their marginal revenue products.

Marginal Rate of Substitution The amount of one good an individual is willing to give up to obtain an additional unit of another good and maintain equal total utility.

Marginal Revenue Product The additional revenue generated by employing an additional factor unit.

Marginal Revenue The change in total revenue that results from selling one additional unit of output.

Marginal Utility The additional utility a person receives from consuming an additional unit of a particular good.

Market Coordination The process in which individuals perform certain tasks, such as producing certain quantities of goods, based on changes in market forces such as supply, demand, and price.

Market Failure   A situation in which the market does not provide the ideal or optimal amount of a particular good.

Market Structure   The particular environment a firm finds itself in, the characteristics of which influence the firm's pricing and output decisions.

Market   Any arrangement by which people exchange goods and services.

Merchandise Trade Balance   The difference between the value of merchandise exports and the value of merchandise imports.

Merchandise Trade Deficit   The situation where the value of merchandise exports is less than the value of merchandise imports.

Merchandise Trade Surplus   The situation where the value of merchandise exports is greater than the value of merchandise imports.

Microeconomics   The branch of economics that deals with human behavior and choices as they relate to relatively small units—the individual, the firm, the industry, the single market.

Minimum Efficient Scale   The lowest output level at which average total costs are minimized.

Mixed Capitalism   An economic system characterized by largely private ownership of the factors of production, market allocation of resources, and decentralized decision making; most economic activities take place in the private sector in this system, but government plays a substantial economic and regulatory role.

Monitor   Person in a business firm who coordinates team production and reduces shirking.

Monopolistic Competition   A theory of market structure based on three assumptions: many sellers and buyers, firms producing and selling slightly differentiated products, and easy entry and exit.

Monopoly   A theory of market structure based on three assumptions: there is one seller, it sells a product for which no close substitutes exist, and there are extremely high barriers to entry.

Monopsony   A single buyer in a factor market.

Natural Monopoly   The condition where economies of scale are so pronounced in an industry that only one firm can survive; an industry in which it is not economical to have more than one firm providing a good.

Negative Externality   Exists when a person's or group's actions cause a cost (adverse side effect) to be felt by others.

Net Worth (Equity or Capital Stock)   Value of the business firm to its owners; it is determined by subtracting liabilities from assets.

Nominal Interest Rate   The interest rate determined by the forces of supply and demand in the loanable funds market; the interest rate in current dollars, unadjusted for expected inflation.

Nonexcludability   A good is nonexcludable if it is impossible, or prohibitively costly, to exclude someone from receiving the benefits of the good once it has been produced.

Nonprofit Firms   Firms in which there are no residual claimants; any revenues over costs must be plowed back into the operation of the firm so that "what comes in" equals "what goes out."

Nonrivalrous in Consumption   A good is nonrivalrous in consumption if its consumption by one person does not reduce its consumption by others.

Normal Good   A good the demand for which rises (falls) as income rises (falls).

Normal Profit   Zero economic profit. A firm that earns normal profit is earning revenues equal to its total opportunity costs. This is the level of profit necessary to keep resources employed in that particular firm.

Normative Economics   The study of "what should be" in economic matters.

Oligopoly   A theory of market structure based on three assumptions: few sellers and many buyers, firms producing either homogeneous or differentiated products, and significant barriers to entry.

Opportunity Cost   The most highly valued opportunity or alternative forfeited when a choice is made.

Overvalued   A currency is overvalued if its price in terms of other currencies is above the equilibrium price.

Own Price   The price of a good. For example, if the price of oranges is $1, this is (its) own price.

Parity Price Ratio   A ratio of an index of prices that farmers receive to an index of prices that farmers pay.

Partnership   A form of business that is owned by two or more co-owners (partners) who share any profits the business earns; each of the partners is legally responsible for all debts incurred by the firm.

Perfectly Elastic Demand   A small percentage change in price brings about an extremely large percentage change in quantity demanded (from buying all to buying nothing).

Perfectly Inelastic Demand   Quantity demanded does not change as price changes.

Perfect competition   A theory of market structure based on four assumptions: there are many sellers and buyers, sellers sell a homogeneous good, buyers and sellers have all relevant information, and there is easy entry into and exit from the market.

Perfect Price Discrimination   Occurs when the seller charges the highest price each consumer would be willing to pay for the product rather than go without it.

Per-Capita Real Economic Growth   An increase from one period to the next in *per-capita real GNP,* which is real GNP divided by population.

Positive Economics   The study of "what is" in economic matters.

Positive Externality   Exists when a person's or group's actions cause a benefit (beneficial side effect) to be felt by others.

Positive Rate of Time Preference   Preference for earlier availability of goods over later availability of goods. A person's "rate of time preference" equals the percentage increase in future consumption that the person needs to obtain before he or she will sacrifice some amount of present consumption.

Poverty Income Threshold (Poverty Line)   Income level below which people are considered to be living in poverty.

Present Value   The current worth of some future dollar amount of income or receipts.

Price Ceiling   A government-mandated maximum price above which legal trades cannot be made.

Price Discrimination   Occurs when the seller charges different prices for the product it sells, and the price differences do not reflect cost differences.

Price Elasticity of Demand   Measures the responsiveness of quantity demanded to changes in price.

Price Elasticity of Supply   Measures the responsiveness of quantity supplied to changes in price.

Price Floor A government-mandated minimum price below which legal trades cannot be made.

Price Leadership Theory In this theory of oligopoly the dominant firm in the industry determines price, and all other firms take their price as given.

Price Level The weighted average of the prices of all goods and services.

Price Searcher A seller that has the ability to control to some degree the price of the product it sells.

Price Support A government-mandated minimum price for agricultural products; an example of a price floor.

Price Taker A seller that does not have the ability to control the price of the product it sells; it "takes" the price determined in the market.

Priority Principle In the Soviet Union, a rule that is followed when there are too few resources to meet all the production goals of the economic plan. It specifies that those industries most important to the Soviet leadership will be the last to take cuts in supplies.

Producers' Surplus The difference between the price sellers receive for a good and the minimum or lowest price for which they would have sold the good. It is a dollar measure of the benefit gained by being able to sell a unit of output for more than one is willing to sell it.

Production Function Expresses the relationship between different combinations of inputs and the maximum output that each combination produces.

Production Possibilities Frontier Represents the possible combinations of two goods that an economy can produce in a certain period of time, given available resources and existing technology.

Product Price Searcher A firm that faces a downward-sloping demand curve for the product it sells. It sells fewer units at higher prices than lower prices.

Product Price Taker A firm that faces a horizontal demand curve for the product it sells. It can sell as many units of its good as it wants without affecting price.

Profit-maximization Rule Profit is maximized by producing the quantity of output at which $MR = MC$.

Proprietorship A form of business that is owned by one individual who makes all the business decisions, receives the entire profits, and is legally responsible for the debts of the firm.

Public Choice The branch of economics that deals with the application of economic principles and tools to public-sector decision making.

Public Employee Union A union whose membership is made up of individuals who work for the local, state, or federal government.

Public Franchise A right granted to a firm by government that permits the firm to provide a particular good or service and excludes all others from doing the same.

Public Good A good characterized by nonrivalry in consumption and nonexcludability.

Public Interest Theory of Regulation Holds that regulators are seeking to do and will do through regulation what is in the best interest of the public or society at large.

Purchasing Power Parity Theory States that exchange rates between any two currencies will adjust to reflect changes in the relative price levels of the two countries.

Pure Capitalism An economic system characterized by private ownership of the factors of production, market allocation of resources, and decentralized decision making; most economic activities take place in the private sector, and government plays a small role or no role at all in the economy.

Pure Economic Rent A category of economic rent where the payment is to a factor that is in fixed supply, implying that it has zero opportunity costs.

Quota A legal limit on the amount of a good that may be imported.

Rational Ignorance The state of not acquiring information because the costs of acquiring the information are greater than the benefits.

Rational Self-Interest When used to describe human behavior, it means to act to maximize the difference between benefits and costs.

Real Economic Growth An increase from one period to the next in *real GNP*.

Real Income Income adjusted for price changes. A person has more (less) real income as the price of a good falls (rises), *ceteris paribus*.

Real Interest Rate The nominal interest rate minus the expected inflation rate (this is the ex ante real interest rate); the nominal interest rate minus the actual rate of inflation, or the inflation-adjusted interest rate (this is the ex post real interest rate).

Regulatory Lag The period between the time when a natural monopoly's costs change and the time when the regulatory agency adjusts prices for the natural monopoly.

Relative Price The price of a good in terms of another good.

Rent Seeking Actions of individuals and groups who spend resources to influence public policy in the hope of redistributing (transferring) income to themselves from others.

Residual Claimant(s) Person(s) who share in the profits of a business firm.

Resource Allocative Efficiency The situation that exists when firms produce the quantity of output for which price equals marginal cost.

Revaluation An official governmental act that changes the exchange rate; specifically, it raises the official price of a currency.

Right-to-Work Laws Laws that make it illegal to require union membership for purposes of employment.

Rivalrous in Consumption A good is rivalrous in consumption if its consumption by one person reduces its consumption by others.

Roundabout Method of Production The production of capital goods that enhance productive capabilities and ultimately bring about increased consumption.

Satisficing Behavior Behavior directed to meeting some satisfactory (not maximum) profit target.

Scarcity The condition where our wants outstrip the limited resources available to satisfy those wants.

Screening The process used by employers to increase the probability of choosing "good" employees based on certain criteria.

Second-Degree Price Discrimination Occurs when the seller charges a uniform price per unit for one specific quantity, a lower price for an additional quantity, and so on.

Separation of Ownership from Control (or Management) Refers to the significant division between owners and managers that often occurs in large business firms; owners and managers are not the same people.

Shirking The behavior of a worker who is putting forth less than the agreed-to effort.

Shortage (Excess Demand) A condition in which quantity demanded is greater than quantity supplied. Shortages only occur at prices below equilibrium price.

Short Run A period of time in which some inputs are fixed.

Short-Run Industry (Market) Supply Curve The horizontal summation of all existing firms' short-run supply curves.

Short-Run (Firm) Supply Curve The portion of the firm's marginal cost curve that lies above the average variable cost curve.

Slope The ratio of the change in the variable on the vertical axis to the change in the variable on the horizontal axis.

Socially Optimal Output The output level at which all benefits (external as well as private) and all costs (external as well as private) have been taken into account and adjusted for.

Social Costs The sum of the private costs incurred by a decision-maker in carrying out an action and any cost (sometimes called external cost) imposed on a party not privy to the decision.

Special Drawing Right An international money, created by the IMF, in the form of bookkeeping entries; like gold and currencies, they can be used by nations to settle international accounts.

Special-Interest Groups Subsets of the general population that hold (usually) intense preferences for or against a particular government service, activity, or policy. Often special-interest groups gain from public policies that may not be in accord with the interests of the general public.

Strike The situation where union employees refuse to work at a certain wage or under certain conditions.

Substitutes Two goods that satisfy similar needs or desires. With substitutes, the demand for one rises as the price of the other rises (or the demand for one falls as the price of the other falls).

Substitution Effect That portion of the change in the quantity demanded of a good that is attributable to a change in its relative price.

Sunk Cost A cost incurred in the past that cannot be changed by current decisions and therefore cannot be recovered.

Supply Schedule The numerical tabulation of the quantity supplied of a good at different prices.

Surplus (Excess Supply) A condition in which quantity supplied is greater than quantity demanded. Surpluses only occur at prices above equilibrium price.

Surplus Value In Marxist terminology, the difference between the total value of production and the subsistence wages paid to workers.

Target Price A guaranteed price; if the market price is below the target price, the farmer receives a deficiency payment equal to the difference between the market price and the target price.

Tariff A tax on imports.

Technology Refers to the body of skills and knowledge concerning the use of inputs or resources in production. An advance in technology commonly refers to the ability to generate more output with a fixed amount of inputs, or the ability to generate the same output with fewer inputs.

Terms of Exchange Descriptive of how much of one thing is traded for how much of another.

Theory A simplified abstract representation of the real world used to better understand the real world.

Third-Degree Price Discrimination Occurs when the seller charges different prices in different markets, or charges a different price to different segments of the buying population.

Tie-in Sale A sale whereby one good can be purchased only if another good is also purchased.

Total Cost The sum of fixed and variable costs.

Total Revenue Price times quantity sold.

Total Utility Total satisfaction a person receives from consuming a particular quantity of a good.

Trade-off A situation in which the attainment of something desirable necessarily implies the loss of something else desirable.

Transaction Costs The costs associated with the time and effort needed to search out, negotiate, and consummate an exchange.

Transfer Payments Payments that are not made in return for goods and services currently supplied.

Transitivity The principle whereby if A is preferred to B, and B is preferred to C, then A is preferred to C.

Trend A long-run directional change in some economic variable.

Trust A combination of firms that come together to act as a monoplist.

Undervalued A currency is undervalued if its price in terms of other currencies is below the equilibrium price.

Union Shop An organization in which a worker is not required to be a member of the union to be hired but must become a member within a certain period of time after becoming employed.

Unit Elastic Demand The percentage change in quantity demanded is equal to the percentage change in price. Quantity demanded changes proportionately to price changes.

Unlimited Liability A legal term that signifies that the personal assets of the owner(s) of a firm may be used to pay off the debts of the firm.

Util An artificial construct used to ''measure'' utility.

Utility Maximizer One who strives to maximize utility or satisfaction.

Utility The satisfaction or happiness one receives from the consumption of a good.

Value Marginal Product The price of the good multiplied by the marginal physical product of the factor: $VMP = P \times MPP$. For a product price taker, $P = MR$, and thus $MRP = VMP$. For a product price searcher, $P > MR$, and $VMP > MRP$.

Variable Costs Costs that vary with output.

Variable Input An input whose quantity can be changed as output changes in the short run.

Veil of ignorance The imaginary veil or curtain behind which a person does not know his or her position in the income distribution.

Vicious Circle of Poverty The idea that countries are poor because they do not save (and invest), and that they cannot save (and invest) because they are poor.

Wage Discrimination The situation that exists when individuals of equal ability and productivity (as measured by their contribution to output) are paid different wage rates.

Wealth The value of all assets owned, both monetary and non-monetary, minus liabilities. (Sometimes wealth loosely refers to only the value of all assets owned.)

Welfare Cost Triangle   A diagrammatical representation of the welfare cost to society associated with monopoly.

Welfare Cost of Monopoly   The net value (value to buyers over and above costs to suppliers) of the difference between the monopoly quantity of output (where $P > MC$) and the competitive quantity of output (where $P = MC$).

X-Inefficiency   The increase in costs and organizational slack in a monopoly resulting from the lack of competitive pressure to push costs down to their lowest possible level.

(Shares of) Stock   A claim on the assets of a corporation that gives the purchaser a share of the ownership of the corporation.

(Upward-Sloping) Supply Curve   The graphical representation of the law of supply.

"Voluntary" Export Restraint   An agreement between two countries in which the exporting country "voluntarily" agrees to limit its exports to the importing country.

Index

World Bank, 466*n*. 10, 491
World debt crisis, 491–92

X-inefficiency, 221

Yugoslavia, 496, 519–20, 523–24, 525–26

Zero economic profit, 160, 367
    capitalization of profits and, 211–12
    and higher wages, 290–91

in long-run competitive equilibrium, 189,
    191–93, 200
in monopolistic competition, 229–30

Zhao Ziyang, 518